£9.10P

D0894137

THE LAW OF THE
EUROPEAN ECONOMIC COMMUNITY

The Law of the European Economic Community

K. LIPSTEIN, Ph.D.

of the Middle Temple, Barrister and Honorary Bencher,
Professor of Comparative Law in the University of Cambridge,
Fellow of Clare College

MIDDLEBURY COLLEGE LIBRARY

LONDON
BUTTERWORTHS
1974

5/1975
Pal Sci

ENGLAND: BUTTERWORTH & CO. (PUBLISHERS) LTD.
London: 88 Kingsway, WC2B 6AB

AUSTRALIA: BUTTERWORTHS PTY. LTD.
Sydney: 586 Pacific Highway, Chatswood, NSW 2067
Melbourne: 343 Little Collins Street, 3000
Brisbane: 240 Queen Street, 4000

CANADA: BUTTERWORTH & CO. (CANADA) LTD.
Toronto: 14 Curity Avenue, 374

NEW ZEALAND: BUTTERWORTHS OF NEW ZEALAND LTD.
Wellington: 26/28 Waring Taylor Street, 1

SOUTH AFRICA: BUTTERWORTH & CO. (SOUTH AFRICA) (PTY.) LTD.
Durban: 152/154 Gale Street

KJ
L5

©
Butterworth & Co. (Publishers) Ltd.
1974

ISBN 0 406 27200 x

MADE AND PRINTED IN GREAT BRITAIN BY
BUTLER AND TANNER LTD.
FROME AND LONDON

Preface

This book is not an introduction to the Constitution and organisation of the three European Communities or to that of any one of them. It assumes a basic knowledge of their structure and concentrates on the functions of one of them only, the European Economic Community, in all the spheres of economic and social activity assigned to it. Starting from the text of the EEC Treaty, the aim of the present work is to show how the individual articles of the Treaty, which frequently provide a general framework only, have been supplemented and filled in by Regulations, Directives, Decisions and other Measures of the Community organs, and how the entire body of rules has been interpreted and shaped by the Community Court. Thus the interpretation of the individual articles of the Treaty is followed, whenever possible, by a systematic exposition of the Community measures made thereunder. In form the hierarchical order of rules is stressed by a clear exposition of the means which are available in each instance to the Community organs for the execution of their tasks. By this method it is also possible to examine in each case whether a particular measure may have been made in excess of the powers conferred upon the Community organs or in disregard of any prescribed formalities.

While fifteen years ago it was necessary to set out the law of the EEC by attempting a speculative interpretation of the provisions of the Treaty, the completion of the transitional period and the promulgation of an immense body of implementing measures of a permanent character has changed the legal scene completely. Abstract principles have produced an abundance of concrete rules, and it may even be asked whether the time has not come to consolidate. Perhaps the years 1971 and 1972 have provided this occasion. Implementing legislation devised by the Executive often bears the mark of excessive haste, insufficient debate and of the knowledge that amending measures are readily available. Community legislation is not free from these blemishes, and ephemeral aspects tend to colour its permanent nature.

As far as possible, implementing measures of the Community organs and the decisions of the Community Court published up to 1 January 1973 are taken into account, but the quantity and speed of their production makes inaccuracies and omissions almost inevitable. The chapter on social security furnishes an example. A list of addenda and corrigenda is provided which seeks to cover the issues of the Official Journal for 1972 which were published up to April 1973, but not the decisions of the Court.

During the years of gestation, I have always had the whole-hearted support of my colleagues in the Faculty of Law and in Clare College, and I have enjoyed the invaluable help, always given cheerfully, by the staff of the Squire Law Library. To them, in particular the Assistant Librarian, Mr. G. Hughes, and to his assistants, Mr. A. Rawlings and Mr. P. Zawada, I offer my sincere thanks. Miss E. E. Jansen once again translated an illegible manuscript into a readable copy. I owe her a debt of gratitude which stretches over many years and can never be adequately repaid.

Mr. B. A. Hepple, Dr. P. O'Higgins and Mr. C. Turpin read portions of the book and generously gave me their advice. Much help came from my students who during the last decade discussed with me many of the problems which are now set out here. My wife patiently read the proofs and eliminated many formal errors. This work, like any other of mine, owes much to the encouragement given to me during a lifetime by two friends, Professor C. J. Hamson and Professor Clive Parry, *hac arte cum Castore Pollux*. My gratitude to them is only matched by that which I feel always towards the teacher, colleague and fatherly friend to whose memory this book is dedicated

Harold Cooke Gutteridge
one time Professor of Comparative Law and Fellow of Trinity Hall
in the University of Cambridge; One of Her Majesty's Counsel;
Bencher of the Hon. Society of the Middle Temple.

Clare College,   K. LIPSTEIN
Cambridge.
August 1973

Table of Contents

PART II—THE RANGE OF THE TREATY AND ITS IMPLEMENTATION

Table of Treaties

Table of Regulations and Rules

Table of Cases

Table of Abbreviations

A.J.C.L.	American Journal of Comparative Law
A.J.I.L.	American Journal of International Law
Ann. Inst. Dr. Int.	Annuaire de l'Institut de Droit International
Arch. V.R.	Archiv des Völkerrechts
Arch. Civ. Pr.	Archiv für die civilistische Praxis
BB AWD	Aussenwirtschaftsdienst des Betriebsberaters
BGBl.	Bundesgesetzblatt
BVerfGE	Entscheidungen des Bundesverfassungsgerichts
B.VerwGE	Entscheidungen des Bundesverwaltungsgerichts
B.Y.I.L. Brit. Yb. Int. L. }	British Yearbook of International Law
Cah. dr. eur.	Cahiers de droit européen
Calif. L.R.	California Law Review
Clunet	Journal du droit international
C.M.L.R.	Common Market Law Reports
C.M.L. Rev.	Common Market Law Review
C.L.R.	Commonwealth Law Reports (Australia)
Comm. e St.	Communicazioni e Studi
Cornell Int. L.J.	Cornell International Law Journal
D.J.	Recueil Dalloz, Jurisprudence
D. Chr.	Recueil Dalloz, Chronique
Dir. Fall.	Diritto fallimentare
EuR	Europarecht
Foro it.	Foro italiano
For. Pad.	Foro Padano
G.P.	Gazette du Palais
GRUR	Gewerblicher Rechtsschutz und Urheberrecht
HGB	Handelsgesetzbuch
Harv. L.R.	Harvard Law Review
Ill. Law Forum	Illinois Law Forum
I.C.L.Q.	International and Comparative Law Quarterly
I.I.C.	International Review of Industrial Property and Copyright Law
Int. L.R.	International Law Reports
Jahrb. öfftl. Recht	Jahrbuch des öffentlichen Rechts
J. Bus. L.	Journal of Business Law
J.C.M.St.	Journal of Common Market Studies
J.O.	Journal Officiel
J.T.	Journal des Tribunaux (Belgium)
J.W.T.L.	Journal of World Trade Law
J.C.P.	Juris-classeur périodique. La Semaine Juridique
Juriscl. dr. int.	Juris-classeur de droit international
J.Bl.	Juristische Blätter

J.Z.	Juristenzeitung
L.Q.R.	Law Quarterly Review
Mich. L.R.	Michigan Law Review
M.L.R.	Modern Law Review
Mon. Belge	Moniteur Belge
N.J.W.	Neue Juristische Wochenschrift
N.Y. Univ. J. Int. L. & Pol.	New York University Journal of International Law and Politics
Nw. U.L.R.	Northwestern University Law Review
OJ	Official Journal. This citation refers to the Journal Officiel (French version) of the Communities
Rabels Z.	Rabels Zeitschrift für ausländisches und international Privatrecht
Rec.	Recueil de la Jurisprudence de la Cour (Luxemburg)
Rec. Lebon	Recueil des décisions du Conseil d'État statuant aux Contentieux
Rev. belge dr. int.	Revue belge de droit international
Rev. crit. dr. int. priv.	Revue critique de droit international privé
Rev. dr. public sc. pol.	Revue de droit public et de la science politique
R.G.S.I.P.	Revue générale de droit international public
Rev. trim. dr. comm.	Revue trimestrielle de droit commercial
Rev. trim. dr. eur.	Revue trimestrielle de droit européen
Rev. M.C.	Revue du Marché Commun
Riv. dir. civ.	Rivista di diritto civile
Riv. dir. comm. obbl.	Rivista del diritto commerciale e del diritto generale delle obbligazioni
Riv. dir. eur.	Rivista di diritto europeo
Riv. dir. int. priv. proc. ⎫ Riv. dir. int. proc. ⎭	Rivista di diritto privato e processuale
Riv. soc.	Rivista delle società
Riv. trim. dir. proc. civ.	Rivista trimestriale di diritto e procedura civile
Sirey	Recueil général des lois et des arrêts fondé par J.-B. Sirey
U.N.T.S.	United Nations Treaty Series
U. Pa. L. Rev.	University of Pennsylvania Law Review
Z.H.R.	Zeitschrift für das gesamte Handels- und Wirtschaftsrecht

Bibliography

General

Bernini, Profili di diritto delle Communità europee, Naples, 1968
Campbell, Common Market Law, London, 1969, 1972
Cartou, Organisations Europénnes, 2nd Edn., Paris, 1967
Catalano, Manuel de droit des Communautés Europénnes, 2nd Edn., Paris, 1963
Commerce Clearing House, Common Market Reporter
Ganshof van der Meersch *et al.*, Le droit des Communautés Européennes, Brussels, 1969
Grisoli, Aspetti giuridici della integrazione europea, Padua, 1967
Juris-classeur de droit international, Vol. II, Fasc. 161 A–165, Paris
Ipsen, Europäisches Gemeinschaftsrecht, 1972
Kapteyn and Verlooren van Themaat, Inleiding tot het recht van de Europese Gemeenschappen, Deventer, Brussels, 1970
Lasok and Bridge, Introduction to the Law and Institutions of the European Communities, London, 1972
Mathijsen, A Guide to European Community Law, London, 1972
Megret, Louis Vignes and Waelbroeck, Le droit de la Communauté Economique Européenne, 4 vols., Brussels, 1970, 1971, 1972
Pinto, Les organisations européennes, Paris, 1963
Reuter, Organisations Européennes, Paris, 1965
Schrans, Inleiding tot het Europees Economisch Recht, 1969
Stein and Hay, Law and Institutions of the Atlantic Community, Indianapolis, 1967
Von der Groeben-Boeckh, Kommentar zum EWG Vertrag, Baden-Baden, Bonn, Frankfurt, 1963
Wortley (ed.), An Introduction to the Law of the European Economic Community, Manchester, 1972
Wohlfahrt–Everling–Glaesner–Sprung, Die Europäische Wirtschaftsgemeinschaft, Berlin and Frankfurt, 1960

The United Kingdom and the E.E.C.:
    Cmnd. 3269 (May 1967)
    Cmnd. 3301 (May 1967)
    Cmnd. 4715 (July 1971)
    Cmnd. 4862 I, II (January 1972)
    (1970) 8 Common Market Law Rev. 52, 232, 352
    Bathurst *et al.* (ed.), Legal Problems of the Enlarged European Community, London, 1972
    Chloros (1972) 36 Rabels Z. 601
    De Smith (1971) 34 Modern Law Rev. 597
    Gascoigne (1967) 111 Solicitors' Journal 244
    Gladwyn (1967) 111 Solicitors' Journal 265

March Hunnings (1968–69), 6 Common Market Law Rev. 50
Martin (1968–69) 6 Common Market Law Rev. 7
Mitchell (1967) 5 Common Market Law Rev. 112
     (1970) 6 Cahiers de droit européen 251
     (1971) 6 Europarecht 97
     (1972) 9 Common Market Law Rev. 134
Simmonds (1967) 111 Solicitors' Journal 644
     (1968–1969) 6 Common Market Law Rev. 156
     (1969–1970) 7 Common Market Law Rev. 455
     (1970–1971) 8 Common Market Law Rev. 325
Thompson and Marsh (1962) 11 International & Comparative Law Quarterly 73
Thompson (1964) 13 International & Comparative Law Quarterly 830
     (1967) 16 International & Comparative Law Quarterly 1
Wade (1972) 88 Law Quarterly Rev. 1

Journals

Aussenwirtschaftsdienst des Betriebsberaters
Cahiers de droit européen, 1965–
Common Market Law Review, 1963–
Europarecht, 1966–
Journal of Common Market Studies, 1962–
Revue du Marché Commun, 1962–
Revue trimestrielle de droit européen, 1965–
Rivista di diritto europeo, 1961–

Law Reports

Recueil de la Jurisprudence de la Cour, 1954–, 18 vols. so far
Common Market Law Reports, beginning with Vol. 7 (1961) of the Official Series
Répertoire de la Jurisprudence relative aux Traités instituant les Communautés Européennes (ed. Eversen and Sperl), 6 vols. covering 1953–67 (1965–68)
Valentine, The Court of Justice of the European Communities, II (1965) for an English translation of the cases in vols. 1–6 of the Official Series

Addenda and Corrigenda

P. 31 n. 3   Winter, [1972] C.M.L.R. 424; Conforti (1972) Riv. dir. int. proc. 225.

P. 50 n. 3   Yaounde Convention, amplified (national products): Council Reg. 2656/72, O.J., 1972, L 287/6. Turkey: add Protocol 23 November 1970, O.J., 1972, L 293/1, Cyprus Convention 19 December 1972, O.J., 1973, L 133/1.

P. 51 n. 4   For the Channel Islands and the Isle of Man see Council Reg. 706/73, O.J., 1973, L 86/1.

P. 94 n. 9   Amended by Council Reg. 2864/72, O.J., 1972, L 306/1, modifying arts. 1(s)a, 9(2), 18, 19(2), 27, 28(2), 28a, 31, 33, 37, 38, 45(1), 46(1)(2), 51–59, 64, 77(2), 78(2)(b)(ii), 79(2)(4), Annexes III B, V B.

P. 95 n. 1   Reg. 878/73, O.J., 1973, L 86/1. For forms see O.J., 1973, L 46/1.

P. 134 n. 13 See now Council Directive 73/148 of 21 May 1973, O.J., 1973, L 172/14.

P. 142 n. 1 Insert:
Line 6 after C 88/1; O.J., 1972, C 129/49.
Line 12 after para. 9476: the Fifth Draft Directive of 9 October 1972 concerning the guarantees for the benefit of shareholders and third parties in respect of the structure of companies and the powers and duties of their organs, O.J., 1972, C 131/49.
Line 15 after C 100/4/7: and the Draft Directive of 5 October 1972 concerning the control and the distribution of prospectuses of shares and bonds for admission to dealings on the stock exchange, O.J., 1972, C 131/61 and the Draft Recommendation, O.J., 1972, C 131/86.

P. 144 n. 1 *Banks:* Council Directive 73/183, 28 June 1973, O.J., 1973, L 194/1.

P. 152 n. 1 Opinion of the Economic and Social Committee, O.J., 1972, C 131/32.

P. 200 n. 1 Cerexhe, 1972 Cah. dr. eur. 272, at p. 280.

P. 205 n. 5 See also van Gerven in *Jus Privatum Gentium, Festschrift für Rheinstein,* II (1969) 505.

P. 206 n. 8 Such an improvement will only be decisive in exceptional cases. See *Cimbel,* Commission Decision, 22 December 1972, O.J., 1972, L 303/24, at pp. 36(19), 37(23).

P. 219 n. 2 Contrast *Cementregeling voor Nederland,* Commission Decision 18 December 1972, O.J., 1972, L 303/7.

P. 229 n. 2 See *Re European Sugar Industry,* Commission Decision, 2 January 1973, O.J., 1973, L 140/17, at p. 42(iii).

P. 233 n. 1 Jolliet, 1973 EuR. 97.

P. 234 n. 1 See now *Europemballage* v. *EEC Commission,* [1973] C.M.L.R.

199, at pp. 222, 224(25); *ZOJA/CSC-ICI*, Commission Decision, 14 December 1972, O.J., 1972, L 299/51.

P. 235 n. 7 But see the Community Court, above p. 234 n. 7.

P. 269 n. *Control of Animal Foodstuffs*, line 2 insert after 279/7:
amended Commission Directive, 5 December 1972, O.J., 1973, L 83/35; Third Commission Directive, 27 April 1972, O.J., 1972, L 123/6; Fourth Commission Directive, 5 December 1972, O.J., 1973, L 83/21; Council Decision, 20 July 1970, O.J., 1970, L 170/1 (Committee).
Additives in feeding-stuffs: Council Directive, 23 November 1970, O.J., 1970, L 270/1 amended by Council Directive, 28 April 1973, O.J., 1973, L 124/17.
Beet, forage plants, cereal, seed potatoes, oleaginous and fibrous plants, vegetable seed, catalogue of varieties of agricultural plants amended by Council Directive, 6 December 1972, O.J., 1972, L 287/22.
Vegetable seed: for new members Council Decisions, 26 March 1973, O.J., 1973, L 106/9–23.

P. 269 n. 1 *Hazardous substances . . . packing* amended by Council Directive, 21 May 1973, O.J., 1973, L 167/1.
Textiles: Council Directive, 26 February 1973, O.J., 1973, L 83/1.

n. 10 Council Directive, 19 February 1973, O.J., 1973, L 77/29 (electrical equipment for use within certain voltage limits).

P. 296 n. 1 Council Reg. 907/73, O.J., 1973, L 89/2 (European Monetary Co-operation Fund).

n. 4 Last Reg. 2843/73, O.J., 1973, L 294/1.

P. 298 n. 10 Council Decision, 19 December 1972, O.J., 1972, L 299/46.

P. 303 text
line 1 Add Norway, Convention, 14 May 1973, O.J., 1973, L 171/1.

n. 6 Council Decision, 14 May 1973, O.J., 1973, L 153/19.

n. 7 WHO, add: Council Decision, 26 September 1972, O.J., 1972, L 304/1; UNRWA, Convention, 18 December 1972, O.J., 1972, L 304/24.
Add after 66/25: (wheat and cereals). See also Convention, 23 March 1973, O.J., 1973, L 145/18 (World Food Aid Programme).

n. 9 Bangladesh (Yute) Council Decision, 12 December 1972, O.J., 1972, L 304/18.

P. 351 n. 8 For the delegation of signature, see Commission Decision, 73/2/ECSC/EEC/Euratom, 6 January 1973, O.J., 1973, L 7/2.

PART I

The Origins and Purpose
of the EEC

1

The European Coal and Steel Community[1]

I   THE PURPOSE OF THE ECSC

The creation of the EEC was the direct result of the failure of the European Defence Community to materialise and of the success of the European Coal and Steel Community (ECSC).[2] This had introduced an integrated supranational Common Market, a functional unity in the limited sphere of coal, iron and steel, including pig iron, for the benefit of all the members. The purpose was to eliminate intra-zone tariffs, to abolish quantitative restrictions and to harmonise external tariffs.[3] The related fields of labour, transport and commercial policy remained within the jurisdiction of member states, subject to the important restrictions which prohibit discrimination. The principal functions of the ECSC are thus: to supervise the formation of prices and to fix maximum or minimum prices, if necessary, to control investment and to stimulate it. For the latter purpose it disposes of capital funds, fed either by a levy of not more than one per cent upon all transactions touching the Community[4] or by the proceeds of loans floated at home or abroad, which may provide moneys for the purpose of re-adaptations, research and investment in the industry.

By granting each other a preferential status to the exclusion of third parties the Agreement violated *prima facie* GATT[5] and the agreement setting up OECD[6] which forbids any discrimination between members. At the same time it brought into operation the Most Favoured Nations clauses embodied in all the commercial treatises concluded with third states, thus conferring the benefit of the ECSC Treaty automatically upon all the other states, parties to such treaties. Only by way of international negotiations did it prove possible to obtain exemption from this obligation and to exclude states from benefiting unilaterally from the new functional

---

1   The literature is vast. See, *e.g.*, Mathijsen, *Le droit de la CECA* (1958); van Hecke, 1951 J.T. 277; Mosler, (1951) 14 Z.a.ö.R.V. 1; Ophüls, 1951 N.J.W., 289; *ibid.* 1963, 1967; Schlochauer, 1951 J.Z. 290; (1963) 11 Arch. V.R. 1; Bayer, (1952) 17 Rabels Z. 325; Mathies, 1954 J.Z. 305; Reuter, *La Communauté Européenne de Charbon et de l'Acier* (1953); Vignes in Juriscl. Dr. Int., Fasc. 162; Wellenstein, Suetens, Mertens de Wilmars in *Ganshof van der Meersch, Le Droit des Communautés Européennes* (1969, Brussels), pp. 485–550; Scheingold, *The Rule of Law in European Integration* (1965), pp. 54 ff.

2   Treaty of 18 April 1951, UNTS 261, 140 (1957) in force since July 1952.

3   ECSC art. 72, achieved on 10 February 1958.

4   ECSC art. 50(2).

5   GATT art. I, but see art. XXIV(5); UNTS 55, 187 as amended by the Protocol of 24 March 1948, UNTS 62, 56.

6   OECD art. 6; UK Treaty Series 59/49, Cmd. 7796.

federation without any corresponding duty to contribute to its proper working.[1]

II   REALISATION OF THE PURPOSE

The purpose of the organisation was to be achieved by nine different means.

(i) *Free and equal access of all users to the sources of production* (art. 4)—Free and equal access to the sources of production does not imply the exemption of these sources from the operation of national law, which continues to govern their operation and exploitation. Within the framework of the Treaty fair and equal access is identical with the abolition of all tariffs and quantitative restrictions between the members of the Community and with the establishment of the right to import and export without restrictions of that kind, provided that the origin of the goods or their introduction into the community by the proper customs procedure is verified by a *certificat de libre pratique*.[2] A rigid control of prices,[3] prohibition of national subsidies[4] and the suppression of cartels[5] served to ensure the observation of this general freedom.

(ii) *Co-operation and expansion* (art. 46(3))—The object of this specialised community is to increase its resources of productivity by rationalisation and expansion. This requires the formulation of general objectives and co-operation in their execution. In particular, the treaty requires an agreement on policy in all matters of energy (ECSC art. 46(3), see also art. 26).

(iii) *Investment—centralisation*—Since all pure national aids to the industry are prohibited as discriminatory, be it in the form of subventions, protection or discrimination (in the absence of tariffs and quantitative restrictions), the community itself must formulate a programme of investment and consider applications for aid and expansion.[6]

(iv) *Prices and quotations—control*[7]—The Community is not an organised market economy. Producers are free to fix their prices, provided that they do not discriminate against other members of the Community and as long as these prices are not distorted by aids or charges. The practice of the executive (formerly known as the High Authority) and of the Court show that this is probably the most active field of operation of the organs of the Community. Here the International Organisation comes into

---

1   GATT, 10 November 1952; OECD, 7 February 1953. See Juriscl. Dr. Int., Fasc. 163, Nos. 49, 60.
2   OJ of the ECSC, 4 May 1953.
3   ECSC art. 4(b), arts. 60–64.
4   ECSC art. 4(c), art. 67.
5   ECSC art. 4(d), arts. 65–66.
6   OJ of the ECSC 80/58, 5 July 1958; *Scheingold*, pp. 75 ff.; ECSC arts. 49–53. *Fedechar v. High Authority* (1956), 2 Rec. 199, at pp. 314, 315; *Soc. des Charbonnages de Beeringen* v. *High Authority* (1956), 2 Rec. 323, at p. 355; *Hamborner Bergbau AG* v. *High Authority* (1960), 6 Rec. 989, at p. 1014.
7   *Scheingold*, pp. 54 ff.

direct contact with individuals and with individual enterprises. It requests the publication of price lists, it can require detailed information about the formation of these prices[1] and it has the means of enforcing its measures.[2] Conversely, the individual can challenge these measures in the Court, subject to the conditions to be discussed later on.[3] Only in one respect can the Community, acting through its executive, interfere with the price mechanism. In case of over-production the executive can fix minimum prices; in case of shortage it can impose maximum prices (ECSC art. 61). Furthermore, in order to avoid a price formation on the basis of the highest cost to any of the producers (a situation which may arise in pursuance of the objectives defined in ECSC art. 3), the executive may allow compensatory payments to be made (ECSC arts. 62, 53). Of course, further distortions may result from the reduction of indirect domestic taxes and contributions. In so far as these are fiscal or social, nothing less than a harmonisation of laws will eliminate these discrepancies.[4]

(v) *Anti-trust—cartel legislation—control of monopolies*—The purpose of the Community would be defeated if the exclusion of interference by the member states in the production and distribution of the product of the industry opened the door to distortions of the markets through private combinations. Consequently, all agreements between enterprises, decisions of associations of enterprises and all concerted practices are illegal, if they exclude, restrain or falsify competition. This includes price fixing, restriction or control of production, the limitation of technical development and investment, the division of markets as regards clients, goods or raw materials (ECSC art. 65(1)) and mergers (ECSC art. 66).

This principle is, however, not without exceptions. Firstly, export cartels, which do not affect the countries of the Community, are permitted. Secondly, the following are not affected: buying and selling cartels, and cartels to facilitate specialisation if in the opinion of the executive the agreement improves substantially the production or distribution, is indispensable for this purpose, does not exceed it and is not apt to constitute a control of price, production or sale which extends to a significant part of the production in the Common Market or exempts these products in fact from competition by others (ECSC art. 65 (2)). Agreements contrary to art. 65 are void (ECSC art. 65(4)).

The executive proceeds by way of investigation, of declaration of nullity and fines (ECSC art. 65(4), (5)). Against these measures the appropriate remedy lies in the Court. But it is necessary at this stage to point out that the activity of the executive does not necessarily supersede that of the national authorities. Instead, they may operate hierarchically within the

---

1 ECSC art. 47; *France* v. *High Authority* (1954), 1 Rec. 7, at p. 20; *Italy* v. *High Authority* (1954), 1 Rec. 73, at p. 88; *Industrie Siderurgiche Associate (ISA)* v. *High Authority* (1955), 1 Rec. 177, at p. 195; *Assider* v. *High Authority* (1955), 1 Rec. 123, at p. 140. For flexible deviations from price lists see *Scheingold*, pp. 54 ff; for price lists see *Acciaierie Laminatoi Magliano Alpi* v. *High Authority* (1957), 3 Rec. 179, at p. 191.

2 ECSC art. 64.

3 ECSC art. 33 and see below.

4 See below, as regards the EEC.

national sphere of jurisdiction. If the executive, in the exercise of its exclusive powers, makes a preliminary decision (ECSC art. 65(4)),[1] this decision is binding upon the national courts unless reversed by the Court of the Community. Thus a conflict of laws of a special kind exists between a higher community order and an inferior order. Neither prevails over the other; instead the functions of the two legal systems are integrated into each other.

Vertical and horizontal concentrations of a monopolistic character require permission, which can only be given if the conditions of ECSC art. 66(2) are fulfilled.[2] Failing this, the executive declares the concentration to be void. If authorisation has been given and the combination becomes too strong, the executive can fix the prices and conditions of sale.

(vi) *Transport—control* (ECSC art. 70)[3]—The free access to the markets of the Community on equal terms may be frustrated, if the national carriers (who, in the case of railways, are state or state-owned enterprises) can offer discriminatory conditions. As a result, the Community exercises control, stimulates the creation of so-called international tariffs,[4] *i.e.* of tariffs which do not end at the frontier but are calculated as one, and promotes a general harmonisation of transport.

(vii) *Technical research*—Hand in hand with co-operation and expansion (above (ii)) and the control of investment (above (iii)) goes the encouragement of research, financed out of the resources of the Community (ECSC art. 55).

(viii) *Crisis measures*—Despite the control of investment, despite modernisation and rationalisation, over-production or shortages may make themselves felt in any one member state. In these circumstances the executive may act, in the case of over-production—

(a) generally by controlling the fixing of prices so as to avoid undercutting (ECSC art. 60(2)(b));
(b) by the application of internal financial mechanisms, such as the imposition of compensatory payments (ECSC art. 53(a));[5]
(c) by restricting imports (ECSC art. 74);

---

1 *Décision préliminaire, Vorabscheidung.*
2 *Geitling et al.* v. *High Authority* (1962), 8 Rec. 171, at p. 212.
3 ECSC art. 70; *Barbara Erzbergbau* v. *High Authority* (1960), 6 Rec. 367; *Germany* v. *High Authority* (1960), 6 Rec. 469.
4 Agreement of 21 March 1955—see Conseil d'Etat, 22 December 1961, [1961] Rec. Lebon 740, *SNCF.* Recommendation 1/61 of 1 March 1961, OJ, 1961, 469: duty to publish tariffs; and see *Netherlands* v. *High Authority* (1962), 8 Rec. 413.
5 ECSC art. 53(b): autonomous financial arrangements. *Mannesmann AG* v. *High Authority* (1960), 6 Rec. 241, at pp. 280–281; for compensation schemes: *Meroni* v. *High Authority* (1958), 4 Rec. 9, at pp. 42–44, 80–81; *Groupement des Hauts Fourneaux et Aciéries Belges* v. *High Authority* (1958), 4 Rec. 223, at p. 242; *Wirtschaftsvereinigung Eisen- und Stahlindustrie* (1958), 4 Rec. 261, at p. 287; *Soc. Duval* v. *High Authority* (1958), 4 Rec. 399, at p. 417, see also (1958), 4 Rec. 437, at pp. 453, 491; *Syndicat de la Sidérurgie du Centre-Midi* v. *High Authority* (1958), 4 Rec. 471; and see, as regards particular issues, *Soc. Nouvelle des Usines de Pontlieue (SNUPAT)* v. *High Authority* (1959), 5 Rec. 275–304; (1961), 7 Rec. 101, at p. 153; *Meroni* v. *High Authority* (1961), 7 Rec. 319, at p. 334; *Kloeckner et al.* v. *High Authority* (1962), 8 Rec. 615, at p. 645.

(d) by establishing minimum prices (ECSC art. 61, see above (iv));

and, in the case of shortages—

(e) by the imposition of maximum prices;[1]
(f) by the application of internal financial mechanisms, such as the imposition of compensatory payments (ECSC art. 53(a)); or
(g) by declaring a state of shortage coupled with the establishment of supply quotas.

(ix) *Labour—conditions, freedom of movement, salaries*—The competitive capacity of a country depends upon the cost of labour, its availability,[2] and the amount of social charges which burden the costs of the product. The European Coal and Steel Treaty does not provide any binding rules. It does envisage a communal effort to raise the standard of living and to improve the conditions of employment, to equalise salaries so as to avoid competition through depressed living standards and to provide social security.[3] The Treaty aims at a free labour market, so as to balance shortages of man-power and consequential increases in wages (ECSC arts. 67, 69), and the re-education of workers consequent upon rationalisation and modernisation (ECSC arts. 56, 86).[4] However, the Treaty and the institutions set up by it do not regulate wages (ECSC art. 68) unless they are abnormally low (ECSC art. 68(2)). In the latter case, special procedures enable the executive to try to remedy this situation.[5]

III   CONCLUSIONS

The European Coal and Steel Community is limited to particular industries. It is a technical institution which seeks to direct and to control output, supply, demand and markets. Being technical in character and restricted to the supervision of a limited, though important, branch of the industry within the Community it operates with direct effect upon enterprises and individuals and is thus truly part of the legal system which governs individuals and corporations, be it by way of incorporation or as a supranational order. For the reason that it affects individuals directly, the political element is pushed into the background and the technical element prevails. This means that a much greater function and importance can be, and has been, attributed to the executive (formerly the High Authority, now the Commission) and to the Court than to the more political organs,

---

1 *Cie. des Hauts Fourneaux de Chasse* v. *High Authority* (1958), 4 Rec. 155, at p. 187.
2 Juriscl. Dr. Int., Fasc. 162 G, Nos. 12 ff. (art. 69). For the earliest measures dealing with free circulation of labour see the decisions of 8 December 1954, OJ of the ECSC, 12 August 1957, 367, and of 16 May 1961, OJ, 15 June 1963, 1637.
3 Regs. 3 and 4, OJ, 1958, 561, 597, now Reg. 1408/71, OJ, 1971, L 149/2; Juriscl. Dr. Int., Fasc. 162 G, Nos. 26ff.; and see below, p. 93. See also the European Convention on Social Insurance of Migrant Workers, Rome, 9 December 1957. See *e.g.* the French Decree 61–558 of 31 May 1961, JO, 4 June 1961, p. 5072.
4 For details see Juriscl. Dr. Int., Fasc. 162 G, No. 22 with lit.
5 Juriscl. Dr. Int., Fasc. G, Nos. 4 ff.

the Council of Ministers and the European Parliamentary Assembly. The executive acts by means of either—

  (a) decisions (ECSC art. 14(2)) which are binding,[1] or
  (b) recommendations (ECSC art. 14(3)) which are binding as to their objective (ECSC art. 14(4)) but leave the choice of means to the addressee, or
  (c) opinions[2] (ECSC art. 14(4)) which are not binding.

When the executive can make a decision, it may substitute a recommendation for it (ECSC art. 14(5)).

The provisions of the treaty setting up the European Coal and Steel Community are not affected by the establishment of the European Economic Community (EEC art. 232). On the other hand, the overlap of functions, which is limited in its object in the European Coal and Steel Community and more or less unlimited in the European Economic Community, has led to the incorporation in the EEC Treaty of many of the topics which were first set out in the ECSC Treaty.

---

1   For the distinction between general and individual decisions see *Firma I. Nold KG* v. *High Authority* (1959), 5 Rec. 89, at pp. 112, 113.
2   Not justiciable: *Soc. des Usines à Tubes de la Sarre* v. *High Authority* (1957), 3 Rec. 201, at p. 223.

2

The EEC—Its Purpose and its Place in relation to Member States

I HISTORY

The success of the Coal and Steel Treaty and the desire to contribute to the economic development of Europe, after the creation of a common European Defence Community had proved impracticable, led the states concerned to consider a much broader field of integration. Faced with the fact that a general mutual concession abolishing all tariffs and quantitative restrictions among themselves would have caused insuperable difficulties in view of the obligations under the General Agreement on Tariffs and Trade (GATT) and individual treaties containing Most Favoured Nation (MFN) clauses,[1] the states concerned were forced to contemplate the formation of a complete customs union, an institution which was compatible with GATT (art. XXIV (5)) and with the maintenance of previous MFN clauses.

Upon the initiative of the Assembly of the ECSC in a resolution of 14 May 1955 and of the Benelux countries of 20 May 1955, the conference of foreign ministers of The Six, meeting in Messina, resolved on 3 June 1955 to call a conference and to start preliminary studies. Under the presidency of M. Spaak (Belgium) these were completed on 12 February 1956 and presented to the ministers in Venice on 29 May 1956. A conference working in two committees (EEC; Euratom) was set up on 26 June 1956. It transformed itself into a Conference of States on 19 February 1957, and after a very short period the Treaty was signed on 25 March 1957. A set of additional protocols was signed subsequently on 17 April 1957, and the Treaty came into force on 1 January 1958 (art. 247).[2]

---

1 For concessions to GATT see Council Decision of 24 November 1959; Hay (1962), 23 U. Pittsburgh L.R. 661; Schiavone, 1962 Riv. Dir. Eur. 33.

2 UNTS 298, 4, Cmnd. 4863 (1972) UNTS 294, 19 (French); *ibid.*, 295, 19 (German); *ibid.*, 296, 19 (Italian); *ibid.*, 297, 19 (Dutch). For its history and preliminary work see Ophüls, *Festgabe für A. Müller Armack* (1961) pp. 279, 288; Ophüls in *Festschrift für Riese* (1964) p. 1; Ophüls, "Recht im Wandel", 1965 Festgabe für Carl Heymann's Verlag 519, at p. 534; Comité Intergouvernemental de Messine, Rapports des Chefs de Délégation aux Ministres des Affaires Etrangères (Spaak Rep., Brussels 1956). S. Neri and H. Sperl, *Traité instituant la C. E. E., Travaux préparatoires*, Luxemburg, Cour de Justice des Communautés Européennes (1960, 440 pp. Annex 7 pp. mimeographed). *Europa, Dokumente zur Frage der Europäischen Einigung*, (2nd Edn., 1953) (German Foreign Office); *Comunità Economica Europea*, Servicio Informazioni, Pres. del Consiglio dei Ministri, Rome, 1958. For the importance of these reports as *travaux préparatoires* see *ASSIDER* v. *High Authority* (1955), 1 Rec. 122,

II   AMBIT

The Treaty operates among The Six and any associated countries or territories (Annex IV and arts. 131–136),[1] only the latter are subject to a somewhat modified regime which allows them, *inter alia*, to introduce new customs duties having regard for their need for development and industrialisation (art. 133(2)). European states can apply to join (art. 237), and any state, union of states or international organisation may enter into an association agreement (art. 238).

The purpose of the Treaty is economic;[2] it aims at creating one big market area. The means for achieving it are, primarily, the abolition of customs barriers and of quantitative restrictions; secondarily, the abolition of restrictions in those areas which either concern the exercise of trading itself, *i.e.* the free movement and establishment of members of the Community, the provision of services across the borders or through temporary presence in another country, or which facilitate trade, *i.e.*, the movement of capital, including currency restrictions, and transport. Incidentally, in order to eliminate distortions of trade, it includes means for the control of cartels and monopolies, of subsidies, and of transport rates, and for harmonising laws; and finally, in order to remedy any distortions arising from the establishment of the Common Market itself, a Social Fund and an Investment Bank are set up. In the last resort, the Treaty requires the co-ordination of policies in the field of agriculture, commerce, finance (both of capital investment and monetary policies), of taxation, social legislation, of patents and trade marks.

The new Community differs in character from its predecessor. While the running of the latter is largely entrusted to its executive and is, in the main, concerned with individual enterprises within the ECSC, the EEC embraces the economy of the member states in every field, even where it may be sensitive or vulnerable (*e.g.* agriculture). It affects not only individuals and corporations, but also public enterprises, and is primarily addressed to the member states themselves. For this reason the structure of the EEC is not fully hierarchical and only rarely reaches the individual directly in his relations with other private persons (arts. 85–90, 215). Instead, the EEC is a policy-making body entrusted with implementing the often very broad provisions of the Treaty, and it must rely on the co-operation of the member states within the broad obligations created by the

---

at pp. 158–172; *Netherlands* v. *High Authority* (1955), 1 Rec. 204, at p. 258; *Hauptzollamt Bremen-Freihafen* v. *Bremer Handels GmbH* (1970), 16 Rec. 451 at pp. 459(5), 460(8)–(9); [1970] C.M.L.R. 466; *Stauder* v. *City of Ulm* (1969), 15 Rec. 419, at p. 424(2); [1970] C.M.L.R. 112; Riese, Vom Deutschen zum Europäischen Recht II (1963), 507, at p. 515, n. 20.

1   Art. 227(4) which states that the Treaty applies to European territories for whose external relations a member state is responsible appears at first sight to extend to Monaco, San Marino and Andorra, but refers probably to the Saar only and is now obsolete. See the Franco-German Treaty of 27 October 1956, Vignes in Juriscl. Dr. Int., Fasc. 157 F, No. 56; Goldman, *Droit Commercial Européen* (1970), p. 125, n. 109.

2   See *e.g.* Pinto in *Ganshof van der Meersch, op. cit.*, pp. 625–644.

Treaty. Consequently the executive (called the Commission) has fewer powers than the political body, the Council, leaving aside the somewhat shadowy Assembly. It follows also that the measures at the disposal of the authorities (*i.e.* the Council and the Commission) are conceived somewhat differently from those entrusted to the executive and the Council of the ECSC. Co-ordination rather than control is the leading principle. The means of achieving this end are, in addition to the Treaty itself:

(i) *Regulations*—These are measures of general application binding upon states and, if they extend to them, also upon individuals as part of their own law (art. 189(2)).[1] Regulations are, therefore, legislative measures,[2] their position in relation to other domestic law will be considered below.

(ii) *Directives*—These may be individual measures or measures addressed to all. Like the recommendations in the ECSC Treaty, they are binding as regards their objective, but leave the choice of means to member states (art. 189(3)). However, if the choice of means is negligible, a measure which purports to be a directive or a decision may in fact operate directly with binding effects in the member states and must be characterised as a regulation or a decision.[3] The result is confusing since the EEC Treaty at times confers competence upon the organs to issue directives on decisions but denies them the power to make regulations.

(iii) *Decisions*—These are individual measures or measures addressed to all member states which are binding both as to their objective and as to the means which they prescribe (art. 189(4)).[4]

---

1 See *e.g.* Tosati, *I regolamenti delle Comunità Europee* (1965); Louis, *Les règlements de la Communauté Economique Européenne* (1969); Wohlfahrt and Schloh in *Ganshof van der Meersch, op. cit.*, pp. 409–426.

2 See *e.g.* Zweigert, (1964) 28 Rabels 601, at p. 613; Ipsen in *Festschrift für Ophüls*, (1965), pp. 67–84; Waelbroeck, (1967) 19 Stanford L.R. 1249, at p. 1250 and n. 7. And see below, pp. 39 ff. For the legislative procedure see *Einfuhr- und Vorratsstelle Getreide* v. *Köster* (1970), 16 Rec. 1161, at p. 1172(6); [1972] C.M.L.R. 255, at p. 288.

3 Waelbroeck, (1967) 19 Stanford L. R. 1249, at p. 1250 and n. 7.; Bebr, (1970) 19 I.C.L.Q. 257, at p. 294, and nn. 133, 136 and the lit. cited p. 295, n. 140; 1970 Cah. Dr. Eur. 3; *Ganshof van der Meersch*, 1970 Rev. Belge Dr. Int. 421, 425–427 and n. 69; Wagenbauer, 1970 B.B., A.W.D. 481; Grabitz, 1971 EuR, 1; De Ripainsel-Landy, 1971 Cah. Dr. Eur. 453, with lit. at p. 454, n. 4; Crétien, 1971 Rec. M.C. 231; Kellermann, 1969 Cah. Dr. Eur. 427; Confort, 1972 Riv. dir. int. fisc. 225; *Grad* v. *Finanzamt Traunstein* (1970), 16 Rec. 825, 838(5), 840(11); [1971] C.M.L.R. 1; *Transports Lesage & Cie.* v. *Hauptzollamt Freiburg* (1970), 16 Rec. 861, 875(5), 876(10); [1971] C.M.L.R. 1; *Haselhorst* v. *Finanzamt Düsseldorf-Altstadt* (1970), 16 Rec. 881, 894(5), 896(10); [1971] C.M.L.R. 1; *SACE* v. *Italian Ministry of Finance* (1970), 16 Rec. 1213, 1223(13)–(15); [1971] C.M.L.R. 123.

The material content of the act is determining: see *Soc. des Usines à Tubes de la Sarre* v. *High Authority* (1957), 3 Rec. 201, at pp. 221–222; Valentine II, 688; *Phoenix Rheinrohr AG* v. *High Authority* (1959), 5 Rec. 165, at p. 181; Valentine II, 602; *Felten & Guilleaume Carlswerke Eisen- und Stahl AG* v. *High Authority* (1959), 5 Rec. 213, at pp. 226–227; Valentine II, 608; *Confédération Nationale des Producteurs de Fruits et Légumes* v. *EEC Council* (1962), 8 Rec. 901, at 918; [1963] 1 C.M.L.R. 160; *Zuckerfabrik Watenstedt GmbH* v. *EEC Council* (1968), 14 Rec. 595, at pp. 604–605; [1969] C.M.L.R. 26. And see Bebr, (1970) 19 I.C.L.Q. 257, at p. 290, n. 118. See also below, p. 31, n. 3.

4 *Meroni* v. *High Authority* (1958), 4 Rec. 9, at pp. 29–31, 40–42; Valentine II, 457; *SA Cements-bedrijven* v. *EEC Commission* (1967), 13 Rec. 93, at pp. 116–117; [1967] C.M.L.R. 77.

(iv) *Recommendations or Opinions*—These are acts of the Community authorities which are purely advisory. They are not binding (art. 189(5)).

III   THE EEC AS A CUSTOMS UNION

The EEC is a full customs union, not limited to any one particular type of production, even if it makes temporary concessions in favour of national protective measures respecting particular industries. The fact that it is a customs union implies—

(a) directly: free circulation of goods (arts. 9, 12, 30 ff.), capital (art. 67), services (art. 59), traders and professional men (art. 52) and workers (art. 48), including the right of establishment;

(b) indirectly: the elimination of discrimination, both in the public and the private sectors of industry and trade (art. 7), the abolition of internal tariffs (arts. 9, 12) including quantitative restrictions (art. 30), the control of cartels and monopolies (arts. 85, 86), the suppression of subsidies (arts. 92, 54(3)(h)) and dumping (art. 91), the elimination of discriminatory tax legislation (art. 95) and, generally, the adaptation, co-ordination and harmonisation of all laws which have a direct bearing upon the creation and the operation of a common market (art. 100);[1]

(c) still more indirectly: the co-ordination of the economic policies and activities of the member states (arts. 6(i), 145). This includes the manipulation of rates of exchange (arts. 103–107), the movement of capital (arts. 70, 71(2)), and mutual assistance in case of any imbalance in the sphere of foreign exchanges (arts. 108 and 109), the creation of a uniform policy in foreign trade (arts. 110, 111, 113) culminating in the conduct of tariff and commercial negotiations with third states by the Commission (art. 113(3)),[2] and the development of common commercial policies on agriculture (art. 38), transport (art. 74) and social services (art. 118).[3]

All these aspects are closely interrelated, for the introduction of an unrealistic rate of exchange may falsify completely the so-called free exchange of goods and services between the member countries. The means by which such a distortion may occur are many: not only through a direct manipulation of currencies, but also through inflationary or deflationary budgeting and through the direction of investment.

---

1   Zweigert, (1964) 28 Rabels z. 601, at p. 613.

2   For the transitional period see art. 111(2).

3   The following committees have been established under arts. 103 or 105 or 145: on business cycle policy, 9 March 1960, OJ, 9 May 1960, 764; on commerce, co-operation, monetary policy, 8 May 1964, OJ, 1964, 1207; of Governors of central banks, OJ, 21 May 1964, 1206; on medium term economic policy, 15 April 1964, OJ, 22 April 1964, 1031; on budget policy, 8 May 1964, OJ, 1964, 1205, and on transport (art. 83), 15 September 1958, OJ, 27 November 1958, OJ, 27 November 1958, 509; see Mégret et al., *Le Droit de la Communauté Economique* (1970) Vol. I, p. 22; Lassalle, 1968 Cah. Dr. Eur. 395.

IV COMPETENCES

Although the EEC Treaty relies on procedural means for co-ordinating the activities, the policies and the legislation of member states, certain supranational features emerge—

(a) a number of competences are transferred to organs of the EEC;

(b) these organs have, in a limited number of cases, direct powers bearing upon individuals in the member states by the means enumerated above (II);

(c) these organs are *pro tanto* autonomous.

In the end, increasing co-ordination must lead to a fairly widespread integration which is not purely economic or legal, having regard to the many indirect factors of public life involved, which were mentioned above.

V SOURCES AND THEIR INTERPRETATION

The legal sources on which the Community relies are three:

(a) The Treaty itself; it is not supplemented by *travaux préparatoires*.[1]

(b) The law-making measures of the Community itself, namely regulations, directives and decisions (art. 189) as applied (art. 172) or controlled (art. 173) or interpreted (art. 177) by the Court. If these measures come up for decision in a national court, the latter can, if the matter is raised in an inferior court, be reserved for interpretation by the Court of the Community (art. 177(2)); if it is raised in a court of last resort the question must be reserved for the Community Court (art. 177(3)).[2]

(c) The general principles of the law common to the member states. Although this source is referred to only once (art. 215(2)), it

---

1 See, however, *Stauder* v. *City of Ulm* (1969), 15 Rec. 419; [1970] C.M.L.R. 112, and see above, p. 9, n. 2. For the problem of interpreting Community law see Zuleeg, 1969 EuR 97.

2 See below p. 32, for recent lit. As regards the binding force of decisions of the Community Court under art. 177 see Bebr, (1970) 19 I.C.L.Q. 256, at p. 266, n. 39 with cases. Precedent is not a source of Community law, but the Court will follow its own practice without questioning, unless distinguishing new facts can be shown or clarification is required: see *Da Costa en Schaake NV* v. *Nederlandse Belastingsadministratie* (1963), 9 Rec. 59; [1963] C.M.L.R. 224; *Albatros* v. *SOPECO* (1965), 11 Rec. 3, at p. 10; [1965] C.M.L.R. 159; *Dingemans* v. *Bestuur der Sociale Verzekeringsbank* (1964), 10 Rec. 1259, at pp. 1275–1276; [1965] C.M.L.R. 144; *Milch-, Fett- und Eierkontor GmbH* v. *Hauptzollamt Saarbrücken* (1969), 15 Rec. 165, at p. 180(3) [1969] C.M.L.R. 390; *Einfuhr- und Vorratsstelle für Getreide und Futtermittel* v. *Henck* (1970), 16 Rec. 1183, at p. 1192(2); [1972] C.M.L.R. 255, at p. 295; *Deutsche Tradax GmbH* v. *Einfuhr- und Vorratsstelle für Getreide und Futtermittel* (1971), 17 Rec. 145, at pp. 153(2)–(4); [1972] C.M.L.R. 213. However, modifying legislation applies, unless expressly provided otherwise, to all future effects of situations which occurred while the previous law was in force: *Bundesknappschaft Bochum* v. *Brock (Elisabeth)* (1970), 16 Rec. 171, at p. 178(6); [1971] C.M.L.R. 55. The effect of a decision by the European Court can never be the determination of the validity of domestic law of the member states in relation to Community Law. See below, p. 33, nn. 4 and 5, and see *Costa* v. *ENEL* (1964), 10 Rec. 1141, at p. 1158; [1964] C.M.L.R. 425, nor its annulment: cp. *Humblet* v. *Belgium* (1960), 6 Rec. 1125, at p. 1145(2); Valentine II, 817.

seems to express a general conviction that these principles are sources of the law of the community.[1]

It must not be overlooked that the Court to whom the control of the interpretation and application of the Treaty is entrusted (art. 164) is itself charged, as an institution of the Community, with rendering the tasks of the Community effective within its own jurisdiction (arts. 4, 164, see also ECSC art. 3). It differs, therefore, from that of an international tribunal proper, where the interpretation of agreements turns exclusively on the intention of the parties and is less functional.[2]

---

1 Lagrange, 1958 Rev. Dr. Pub. et Sc. Pol. 844, at pp. 850, 852; Mathijsen, *Le droit de la CECA* (1958) pp. 103 ff.; Grisoli, *Contributo alla Ricerca dei Principi Generali Comuni ai Diritti degli Stati della Comunità Europea in Materia di Responsibilità Extracontractuale* (1963), with lit. at p. 13, n. 19; Heldrich, *Die allgemeinen Rechtsgrundsätze der ausservertraglichen Schadenhaftung im Bereich der EWG* (1961); *id.*, 1960 J.Z. 861; Lorenz, 1962 J.Z. 269; (1964) 13 A.J.C.L. 1; (1965) 29 Rabels Z. 1; in *Festschrift für Nipperdey* II (1965) pp. 797–813; Reuter in *Mélanges Rolin* (1964), p. 263; Lagrange, (1965–66) C. M. L. Rev. 32; Zweigert in *Ganshof van der Meersch, op. cit.* pp. 441–445; Dumon, 1969 Cah. Dr. Eur. 37.

These principles include the fundamental provisions of the constitutions of the member states. See: *Stauder v. Ulm* (1969), 15 Rec. 419; at p. 420(7); [1970] C.M.L.R. 112; *Internationale Handelsgesellschaft* v. *Einfuhr- und Vorratsstelle für Getreide und Futtermittel* (1970), 16 Rec. 1125, at p. 1135(4); [1972] C.M.L.R. 255; *Einfuhr- und Vorratsstelle Getreide v. Köster* (1970), 16 Rec. 1161, at p. 1176(22); *Einfuhr- und Vorratsstelle Getreide v. Henck* (1971), 17 Rec. 1183, at p. 1192(2); *Deutsche Tradax GmbH v. Vorratsstelle Getreide*, (1971), 17 Rec. 145, at p. 153(2)-(4); [1972] C.M.L.R. 213, Conflict of laws in time: *Klomp* v. *Inspektie der Belastingen* (1969), 15 Rec. 43 at p. 50(13); *Henck* v. *Hauptzollamt Emmerich* (1971), 17 Rec. 743, at pp. 751(5), 774(5), 787(5).

See Mertens de Wilmars, 1970 Rev. Trim. Dr. Eur. 454, at p. 460, and see below, p. 26, n. 3, p. 27, nn. 1 and 2. It seems that a general doctrine of *ultra vires* was given effect to when it was held that the Council, enacting an implementing regulation, cannot go beyond the enabling terms of its basic regulation; see *Deutsche Tradax GmbH* v. *Vorratsstelle Getreide* (1971), 17 Rec. 145, at p. 155(10); [1972] C.M.L.R. 213.

Another general principle followed by the Court appears to be that the retroactive character of a decision is not necessarily contrary to the Treaty: see *Rewe-Zentrale des Lebensmittel-Gross-handels GmbH* v. *Hauptzollamt Emmerich* (1971), 17 Rec. 23 at pp. 36(13)–37(16); [1971] C.M.L.R. 238.

As regards torts see *Kampffmeyer* v. *EEC Commission* (1967), 13 Rec. 317; *Sayag v. Leduc* (1968), 15 Rec. 329, at p. 336(5), [1969] C.M.L.R. 12; for unjustifiable enrichment: *Danvin v. EEC Commission* (1968), 14 Rec. 463, at p. 473, and see Lorenz in *Festschrift für Nipperdey* (above) at p. 811; for *force majeure: Schwarzwaldmilch GmbH* v. *Einfuhr- und Vorratsstelle für Fette* (1968), 14 Rec. 549, at p. 562; [1969] C.M.L.R. 406. See also below, p. 135, for a reference to general principles of law in the Draft Statute of a European Company submitted by the Commission (art. 7); see below, pp. 151 ff.

For the absence of a duty to take into consideration penalties imposed in criminal proceedings abroad see Boehringer, Commission Decision 25 November 1971, OJ, 1971, L 282/46, at p. 49, para. 12.

See also, as regards the ECSC Treaty: *ASSIDER v. High Authority* (1955), 1 Rec. 123, at pp. 169–175, see also pp. 149–169 (*détournement de pouvoir*), and Valentine II, 45; *Groupement des Industries Sidérurgiques Luxembourgeoises v. High Authority* (1956), 2 Rec. 53, at p. 91; Valentine II, 131; *Fédéchar v. High Authority* (1956) 2 Rec. 199, at pp. 225 and 253–259, *per* Adv. Gen. Lagrange; Valentine II, 95; *Algera v. European Assembly* (1957), 3 Rec. 81, at p. 115 (nullity of administrative acts); *Groupement des Hauts Fourneaux et Aciéries Belges v. High Authority* (1958), 4 Rec. 223, at pp. 242, 243; Valentine II, 511; *Humblet v. Belgium* (1960), 6 Rec. 1125, at p. 1149(2); Valentine II, 817; *De Geus* v. *Robert Bosch GmbH* (1962), 8 Rec. 89, at p. 104.

2 Lagrange, 1958 Rev. Dr. Pub. et Sc. Pol. 844, at p. 847 with reference to decisions of the Community Court applying the ECSC Treaty: (1958) 4 Rec. 223, at p. 233; 261, at p. 273; 363, at p. 383; 399, at p. 423; 435, at p. 461; 471, at p. 499; 53, at p. 151; Monaco in *Mélanges Rolin* (1964) p. 217; Chevallier, (1964), 2 C.M.L.Rev. 21; Scheingold, *The Rule of Law in European Integration* (1965), pp. 51 ff; Green, *Political Integration in Jurisprudence* (1969); Degan, 1966 Rev. Trim. Dr. Eur. 189, with lit. n. l.

Quite generally, interpretation must not be literal, but must seek out the common intention or *ratio legis: Humblet* v. *Belgium* (1960), 6 Rec. 1125 at pp. 1155 and 1169, 1182, 1194 (Adv. Gen. Lagrange); Valentine II, 817. For this purpose, the general provisions expressing the policy of the Treaty are important: *German Federal Republic* v. *EEC Commission* (1963), 9 Rec. 129, at p. 142; [1963] C.M.L.R. 347; *German Federal Republic* v. *EEC Commission* (1963), 9 Rec. 269, at p. 296; [1963] C.M.L.R. 369; *EEC Commission* v. *EEC Council* (*ERTA* case) (1971), 17 Rec. 263, at p. 274(12); [1971] C.M.L.R. 335; *Deutsche Grammophon GmbH* v. *Metro-SB-Grossmärkte GmbH* (1971), 17 Rec. 487, at pp. 498(5), 499(8); [1971] C.M.L.R. 631. This functional interpretation has manifested itself in the reliance on the following aids— implied powers: *Fédéchar* v. *High Authority* (1956), 2 Rec. 199, at p. 305; Valentine II, 163, 110; *Netherlands Government* v. *High Authority* (1960), 6 Rec. 723, at pp. 757–758; Valentine II, 309; *Max Neumann* v. *Hauptzollamt Hof/Saale* (1967), 13 Rec. 571, at p. 588; Louis, 1971 Cah. Dr. Eur. 479; Gori, (1971) 11 Riv. Dir. Eur. 155. Contrast *France* v. *High Authority* (1954), 1 Rec. 7, at p. 30; Valentine II, 18; Adv. Gen. Dutheillet de Lamothe in *EEC Commission* v. *EEC Council* (1971), 17 Rec. 263, at p. 294, see also Costonis, (1967–68) 5 C.M.L.Rev. 431; restrictive interpretation in favour of state sovereignty: *Niederrheinische Bergwerks AG* v. *High Authority* (1961), 7 Rec. 261, at pp. 286, 288; Schüle, (1962) 22 Z.a.ö.R.V. 461, at p. 469; retention of incidental sovereign competence: *Soc. Comm. A. Vloeberghs SA* v. *High Authority* (1961), 7 Rec. 391, at pp. 435, 468–469; (1962) 56 A.J.I.L. 1083; balancing rights and duties of the executive: *Cie. des Hauts Fourneaux de Chasse* v. *High Authority* (1958), 4 Rec. 155, at p. 190; Valentine II, 485; in favour of community officials: *Humblet* v. *Belgium* (1960), 6 Rec. 1125, at pp. 1189, 1217; Valentine II, 817.

Differences in the formulation of the Treaty in the four languages may either

(a) provide a means of ascertaining the intention of the parties: *e.g.* Barème (ECSC art. 60): *France* v. *High Authority* (1955), 1 Rec. 7, at p. 26; Valentine II, 18 (ECSC art. 33(2)); *"Les décisions individuelles—individuell betreffende Entscheidungen* (ECSC art. 33): *Groupements des Industries Sidérurgiques Luxembourgeoises* v. *High Authority* (1956), 2 Rec. 53, at pp. 86, 87, and see Adv. Gen. Roemer at p. 120, n.l, and pp. 123–125; Valentine II, 131; *"tendraient à empécher," "abzielen", "kunnen leiden"* (ECSC art. 65(1)): *Worms* v. *High Authority* (1962), 8 Rec. 377, at p. 409, *per* Adv. Gen. Lagrange; [1963] C.M.L.R. 1; *fixer, déterminer* (ECSC art. 65(2)): *Geitling* v. *High Authority* (1962), 8 Rec. 165, at pp. 200, 201 and 237–242, *per* Adv. Gen. Roemer; [1962] C.M.L.R. 113; *"d'affecter", "zu beeinträchtigen," "pregiudicare", "ongunstig kunnen beinvloeten"* (EEC art. 85(1)): *De Geus* v. *Robert Bosch GmbH* (1962), 8 Rec. 89, at pp. 106 and 139, *per* Adv. Gen. Lagrange; [1962] C.M.L.R. 1; *"prestations de maladie", "Leistungen bei Krankheiten"* (Reg. 3, arts. 2(a), 22): *Dekker* v. *Bundesversicherungsanstalt für Angestellte* (1965), 11 Rec. 1111, at p. 1116; [1966] C.M.L.R. 503; *institutions et autorités* (Reg. 3 art. 45(3)): *Guerra* v. *Inst. Nat. d'Assurances Maladie-Invalidité* (1967), 13 Rec. 283, at p. 289; *"een ... bedrijf ... waarby zij gewoonlijk werkzaam zijn," "un établissement ... dont il relève normalement"; "occupation," "tewerkstelling"* (Reg. 3, art. 13(a), old version): *Bestuur der Soziale Verzekeringsbank* v. *Van der Vecht* (1967), 13 Rec. 445, at pp. 456, 458; [1968] C.M.L.R. 151; *intituire* (Reg. 24, art. 1(1)): *EEC Commission* v. *Italy* (1970), 16 Rec. 93, at pp. 100, 101(5); [1971] C.M.L.R. 466. *"Dans les cas où les dispositions du ... Traité prévoient" ... "soweit der Vertrag vorsieht"* (EEC art. 228): *EEC Commission* v. *EEC Council* (1971), 17 Rec. 263, at pp. 281(75), 290, 294; [1971] C.M.L.R. 335; *per* Adv. Gen. Dutheillet de Lamothe. *"Difficulte", "Streit"* (Statute of the Court, art. 37): *ASSIDER* v. *High Authority* (1955), 1 Rec. 263, at pp. 279–280, 290, *per* Adv. Gen. Lagrange. *"Privilèges", "Vorrechte"* (Protocol on Immunities): *Humblet* v. *Belgium* (1960), 6 Rec. 1125, at p. 1149. *"Bon mentionant leur nom", "bon individualisé"* (EEC Commission Decision 69/71 of 12 February 1969, art. 4, second sentence): *Stauder* v. *City of Ulm* (1969), 15 Rec. 419 at p. 424(2); [1970] C.M.L.R. 112. *"Taux moyen"* (art. 97): *Milch, Fett- und Eierkontor GmbH* v. *Hauptzollamt Saarbrücken* (1969), 15 Rec. 165, at p. 180(5); [1969] C.M.L.R. 390;

Footnote continued on next page

VI SPHERE OF APPLICATION

The Treaty applies to all branches of the economy with the following exceptions: it leaves the ECSC unaffected (art. 232); it does not extend to transport by sea or air, at least for the time being (art. 84(22); it leaves a wide exemption in favour of security (art. 223) and envisages a clash with national action for reasons of grave external troubles affecting public order, war or serious international tensions or the observation of international obligations to maintain peace and international security (art.

---

or (b) lead to a construction unaffected by domestic legal connotations: *détournement de pouvoir, Ermessensmisbrauch*: *ASSIDER* v. *High Authority* (1955), 1 Rec. 123, at pp. 149 ff., *per* Adv. Gen. Lagrange; Valentine II, 45; *Fédéchar* v. *High Authority* (1956), 2 Rec. 199, at pp. 253, 259, *per* Adv. Gen. Lagrange; Valentine II, 95; (1956) 2 Rec. 291, 302, 312, 316; Valentine II, 103; *Wirtschaftsvereinigung Eisen- und Stahlindustrie* v. *High Authority* (1958), 4 Rec. 261, at pp. 292, 294; Valentine II, 582; Stein and Hay, (1960) 9 A.J.C.L. 375, at pp. 420–422 (cp. above, p. 14, n. 1); Lorenz, in *Festschrift für Nipperdey* II (1965), p. 807, and n. 28 with lit.

"*Force majeure*" (Reg. 102/64, art. 8; Reg. 136/64, art. 612): *Schwarzwaldmilch GmbH* v. *Einfuhr- und Vorratsstelle für Fette* (1968), 14 Rec. 549, at pp. 562–563; [1969] C.M.L.R. 406; *Einfuhr- und Vorratsstelle Getreide* v. *Köster* (1970), 16 Rec. 1161, at p. 1179, (37)–(40); *Internationale Handelsgesellschaft* v. *Einfuhr- und Vorratsstelle Getreide* (1970), 16 Rec. 1125, at p. 1139(23)–(25); [1972] C.M.L.R. 255. "*Eau de vie*" (Reg. 7 (b), OJ, 1961, 71): *EEC Commission* v. *Italy* (1969), 15 Rec. 377; cp. *EEC Commission* v. *Luxemburg and Belgium* (1964), 10 Rec. 1217, at pp. 1231–1232; [1965] C.M.L.R. 58; *Germany* v. *EEC Commission* (1966), 12 Rec. 227, at p. 245; [1967] C.M.L.R. 22; offer: *Hagen* v. *Einfuhr- und Vorratsstelle Getreide* (1972), 18 Rec. 23, at pp. 35(6), (8), 36(10), (11); *Wünsche* v. *Einfuhr- und Vorratsstelle Getreide* (1972), 18 Rec. 53, at pp. 53, 65(6), 66(8), (11); [1973] C.M.L.R. 35;

or (c) result in a construction according to the technical notions of the legal system in the language of which the term is expressed, as the following,

"*Faute de service*", "*Dienstfehler*": *FERAM* v. *High Authority* (1959), 5 Rec. 501, at pp. 516–518, 543, *per* Adv. Gen. Lagrange; Valentine II, 654; see also *Fives Lille Cail* v. *High Authority* (1961), 7 Rec. 559, at p. 593; [1962] C.M.L.R. 251.

"Wage earner or assimilated worker" (Reg. 3, art. 19): *Unger* v. *Bestuur der Bedrijfsvereniging voor Detailhandel* (1964), 10 Rec. 347, at p. 363; [1964] C.M.L.R. 319; "*Schokoladenmasse*": *Lütticke* v. *Hauptzollamt Passau* (1971), 17 Rec. 121, at p. 128(6); [1971] C.M.L.R. 752.

Regulations must be interpreted uniformly, and member states are not free to determine by themselves their own interpretation: *Hauptzollamt Hamburg-Oberelbe* v. *Bollmann* (1970), 16 Rec. 47, at p. 80(4), (5); [1970] C.M.L.R. 141; (Reg. 22/62, art. 14; Reg. 950/68 art. 5); *EEC Commission* v. *EEC Council* (1971), 17 Rec. 263, at pp. 281(77), 282(84), [1971] C.M.L.R. 335; (art. 75 and Reg. 543/69); *Hagen* v. *Einfuhr- und Vorratsstelle* (above), at p. 35(6),(9); *Wünsche* v. *Einfuhr- und Vorratsstelle* (above) at pp. 65(6), 66(10), [1973] C.M.L.R 35.

For the purposes of interpretation reference is made also to the "general principles of community law". See, *e.g.*, *Wilhelm* (*Walt*) v. *Bundeskartellamt* (1969), 15 Rec. 1, at pp. 13(2), 16(11); [1969] C.M.L.R. 100 and of international law: *EEC Commission* v. *Italian Government* (1962), 8 Rec. 1, at p. 22; [1962] C.M.L.R. 187. But see below, p. 44, n. 3. For the problem of linguistic differences in interpreting the Community Treaties see Dölle in *20th Century Comparative and Conflicts Law* (1961), pp. 277–292; *id.* in (1961) 26 Rabels Z. 4–39; Riese, in Vom Deutschen zum Europäischen Recht II 1963, 507–524, at pp. 514, 517 ff; Makarov in *Mélanges Guggenheim* (1968), p. 403; Akehurst in Wortley (ed.), *Introduction to the Law of the EEC* (1972), pp. 20–31 with lit., nn. 1, 7; Hardy, (1961) 37 B.Y.I.L. 72–155 and, as regards Community law in particular, Stevens (1967) 32 Nw.U.L.R. 701; Zuleeg, 1969 EuR 97. *Stauder* v. *City of Ulm* (1969), 15 Rec. 419, at p. 424(2); [1970] C.M.L.R. 112; *Schwarze* v. *Einfuhr- und Vorratsstelle für Getreide* (1965), 11 Rec. 1081, at p. 1097; [1966] C.M.L.R. 172. A good synopsis of the Treaty in the four languages of the Community is to be found in [1957] II BGBl 753.

224). Distortion of trade is another ground (art. 115). The provisions (art. 226), that a member state may ask for authorisation to take protective measures if a sector of the economy or a region experiences serious difficulties, have ceased to operate with the ending of the transitional period.[1] Particular escape clauses concern import, export and transit of goods affecting public morality, safety, life or health (art. 36), capital movements (art. 73), balance of payment difficulties (arts. 104, 108, 109), changes in the rate of exchange (art. 107), deflection of trade (arts. 115, 134) and defence against state trading monopolies (art. 37(3), 2nd para.).[2]

The Benelux union is left untouched in so far as its objects are not fulfilled by the EEC Treaty (art. 223), and previous treaties are not affected, but member states must take steps to eliminate any incompatibility between such obligations towards third countries and the provisions of the EEC Treaty (art. 234).

The duration of the Treaty is unlimited (art. 240).[3] It has been argued, therefore, that states are either bound in perpetuity or precluded from denouncing it except by a unanimous decision or, possibly, only if they can rely on the *clausula rebus sic stantibus*, self-preservation or fundamental breach. The absence of any mention of these eventualities may be due to the consideration that it is psychologically inadvisable in treaties of this kind to provide for their termination,[4] even if the intention to allow withdrawal is implied. Naturally, the possibility of revision is foreseen (art. 236).[5] Where gaps emerge because the Treaty has established a purpose, but has not provided the means for realising it and a present need exists, a simplified procedure of supplementing the Treaty is provided (art. 235).[6]

---

1 For a recent instance (30 September 1969) see *Germany v. EEC Commission.* (1969) 15 Rec. 449; [1971] C.M.L.R. 724; *EEC Commission v. Italy* (1970), 16 Rec. 47, at p. 55(3); [1970] C.M.L.R. 77; see also *Italy v. EEC Commission* (1963), 9 Rec. 335, at pp. 357–360; [1963] C.M.L.R. 289.

2 *EEC Commission v. Italian Government* (1961), 7 Rec. 633, at p. 656; [1962] C.M.L.R. 39; *Salgoil v. Italy* (1968), 14 Rec. 661, at p. 667; [1969] C.M.L.R. 181; *Germany v. EEC Commision* (above, n. 1). Their existence seems to exclude a general right of the member states to deviate from the Treaty, *e.g.*, if other member states do not comply with it: *EEC Commission v. France* (1969), 15 Rec. 523, at pp. 523, 540(17), 542(29), 543(41); [1970] C.M.L.R. 43; *EEC Commission v. Luxemburg and Belgium* (1964), 10 Rec. 1217, at pp. 1231–1232; [1965] C.M.L.R. 58, and see below, p. 18, n. 2.

3 Contrast ECSC art. 97: 50 years. For the problems arising therefrom see Dagtoglou in *Festschrift für Ernst Forsthoff*, pp. 77–102.

4 Bindschedler, *Rechtsfragen der Europäischen Einigung* (1954), p. 42. According to the Official Commentary of the Federal German Government presented to the Federal German Parliament, the "constitutional character" of the Treaty excludes any express or implied acknowledgment of termination. See von der Groeben-Boeckh, *ad* art. 240, n. 1; Wohlfahrt-Everling, *ad* art. 240. For the desuetude of individual provisions see *EEC Commission v. France* (1971), 17 Rec. 3, at p. 1018(18)–(20); [1971] C.M.L.R. 453.

5 Catalano 100; Bindschedler, *loc. cit.* p. 40 with reference to the practice of the UNO, WHO and UNESCO; but see Wagner, *Grundbegriffe des Beschlussrechts der Europäischen Gemeinschaften* (1965), pp. 112 ff, especially p. 113, n. 60 with lit. Compare ECSC art. 95(3)(4); and see (1961), 7 Rec. 481.

6 Cp. *Fédéchar v. High Authority* (2nd Opinion) (1956), 2 Rec. 294, at p. 305; Valentine II, 103, at p. 110 (implied powers), above, p. 15, n. 2, and see *EEC Commission v. Italy* (1970), 16 Rec. 47, at p. 57(10); [1970] C.M.L.R. 77. See also *Mégret*, Vol. I, p. 10; and *e.g.* Council Reg. 542/69, OJ, 1969, No. L77.

Thus the Council acting unanimously upon a proposal of the Commission and after consulting the Assembly can add to its power (*Kompetenz-Kompetenz*) within these limits.[1] A slightly simpler power enables the Council to amend scales of contributions due by the member states (art. 200(3)). Unlike in other treaties, failure of a party to it, or of an organ created by it, to perform its duties does not justify a refusal by another party to fulfill its own obligations.[2]

VII METHODS OF REALISATION

The general objects of the Treaty are to be achieved by way of non-discrimination[3] and co-ordination,[4] a harmonious development of the economy, a constant and balanced expansion, greater stability, an accelerated rise of living standards and a closer relationship between states (art. 2). The field of activity is outlined in art. 3 (see above III). The duties are outlined in general terms in art. 5.[5] Some of them[6] must be carried out by the member states without any further action on the part of the Community, and amongst these a fair number create corresponding rights in favour of individuals.[7] Others, such as the provisions concerning adaptation or approximation (*Rapprochement; Angleichung*, arts. 3(h), 27,[8] 100(1), 117(2)), co-ordination (arts. 6(1), 40(2)(b), 54(3)(g), 56(2), 57(2) and (3), 66, 70(1), 105(1), 111(1)) and harmonisation (arts. 99, 112(1), 117)[9] which affect national laws in the broadest sense, are subject to a process in two stages, since the Community can only act here by means of directives. Still others require prior consultation (art. 101(1)). In one instance, at least, states are under a duty to amend their law (art. 95(3)).

---

1 Similar provisions limited to a particular field ceased to operate at the end of the transitional period: arts. 14(7), 33(8).

2 *EEC Commission* v. *Luxemburg and Belgium* (1964), 10 Rec. 1221, at pp. 1231–1232; [1965] C.M.L.R. 58, and above, p. 17, n. 1; (1969), 15 Rec. at pp. 540(17), 542(29), 543(41).

3 Arts. 7, 33(1)(i), 36, 37(1); 40(3)(2); 44(1), 45(1) (2), 48(2), 52(2), 53, 57(3), 60(3), 65, 67(1), 68(2), 79(1), but see 75(3), 95, 111(5), 119(1)(1); 132(4)(5), 133(5). For a discussion of this notion see *Italy* v. *EEC Commission* (1963), 9 Rec. 335, at pp. 360–362; [1963] C.M.L.R. 289; *Barbara Erzbergbau* v. *High Authority* (1960), 6 Rec. 367, at p. 405(3); Valentine II, 325. The fact that situations incapable of comparison are treated differently from each other does not necessarily constitute discrimination. Discrimination in form may not be discrimination in substance.

4 See below, text after n. 8; it is implied in art. 51; see Lyon-Caen, *Droit Social Européen* (1969), p. 289, n. 145.

5 For the importance of art. 5 in interpreting the Treaty see above, p. 14, n. 2.

6 *E.g.* arts. 12, 30.

7 See below.

8 Cp. *e.g.* Council Reg. 827/68, art. 8, OJ, 1968, L 151: agriculture, plants.

9 The distinctions between these three types of Community action are blurred but see below, p. 268. For the present achievement see below, pp. 267 ff. Seidl-Hohenveldern, 1962 J. Bus. L. 247, at p. 363; Everling, *Right of Establishment*, p. 107. For the various measures see van Ommeslaghe, 1969, Cah. Dr. Eur. 495, at pp. 513–520 with lit., nn. 38, 39, for pharmaceuticals see Seidel, (1967–68) 6 C.M.L.Rev. 309.

VIII BENEFICIARIES

The prohibition of discrimination (art. 7)[1] on grounds of nationality benefits nationals of the member states only.[2] Although art. 7 does not prescribe this interpretation, other articles dealing with individual prohibitions of discrimination (arts. 37(1), 40(3)—residents—but see arts. 45(1), 48(2), 52, 132(4) and (5), 221, but see art. 95—products of— member states) and the purpose of the Treaty impose this conclusion. Express extension to others is provided exceptionally (art. 59(2)), but there are circumstances where the Treaty provision must necessarily extend to other nationals as well, e.g. that requiring equal pay for men and women (art. 119). At the same time it must be remembered that separate and different treatment of situations which are dissimilar from others is not discrimination.[3]

The question as to how to determine the nationality of companies has given rise to some difficulties in international and in domestic law. According to most continental legal systems it is determined by the location of the seat of the company, except perhaps in the Netherlands. The English solution, which relies on the place of incorporation, is different. The question will be discussed below in connection with the treatment of the right of establishment and the recognition of foreign companies (arts. 58, 220(4), 221).

IX TRANSITORY PERIOD[4]

A Treaty embodying arrangements of such far-reaching character and scope both in substance and in time cannot be put into operation at once

---

1 Including resident nationals of the member states itself to which the provision of the Treaty or of the regulation is addressed; see *Caisse de Maladie des CFL* v. *Cie. Belge d'Assurances* (1969), 15 Rec. 405, at p. 410; [1970] C.M.L.R. 243 (Reg. 3, arts. 4, 52); cp. *Unger* v. *Bestuur der Bedrijfsvereniging etc.* (1964), 10 Rec. 347, at p. 362; [1964] C.M.L.R. 319; *Gemeenschappelijke Verzekeringskas "de Sociale Voorzorg"* v. *Bertholet* (1965), 11 Rec. 111, at p. 118; [1966] C.M.L.R. 191; *Betriebskrankenkasse der Heseper Torfwerke GmbH* v. *Van Dijk* (1965), 11 Rec. 131, at p. 140, [1966] C.M.L.R. 191. This seems to apply in particular to art. 119 of the Treaty.

2 See above, p. 12, 3(b). Now that certain provisions of the Treaty and regulations are held to be directly applicable, the question arises whether, as part of domestic law, they also apply to individuals who are not nationals of Community countries and are not resident there. Probably the answer is that domestic courts may, but need not, apply such provisions to outsiders. For an incipient discussion of this problem see *Wilhelm (Walt)* v. *Bundeskartellamt* (1969), 15 Rec. 1, at p. 16(13); [1969] C.M.L.R. 100; *Sociaal Fonds voor de Diamantarbeiders* v. *Brachfeld* (1969), 15 Rec 211, at p. 223(26); [1969] C.M.L.R. 335.

3 *Italy* v. *EEC Commission* (1963), 9 Rec. 335, at pp. 360–362; [1963] C.M.L.R. 289; see above, p. 18, n. 3.

4 Arts. 8, 10(2), 13, 14, 15, 16, 17(1), (2), 20, 21, 22, 23, 24, 27, 28, 32(2), 33, 34(2), 35, 37(1), (3), (6), 38(3), 40(1), 43(1), (2), 44(1), (3), (4), (5), (6), 45(1)2(iii) (v), 48(1), 52(1), 54(1), (2), 56(2), 57(1),(2), 59, 63, 67, 69, 75(1), 79(3), 87(1), 88, 91(1), 95(3), 108(2) last para.; 111, 112, 115(2), 116(2), 119, 136, 212(2), 221, 223(2), 226, 227(2), *i.e.* altogether 51 articles. For the effect of the expiry of the transitional period upon the direct applicability of a provision see Bebr, (1970) 19 I.C.L.Q. 257, at pp. 281–283. And see generally *Mégret*, Vol. I, pp 28–33.

in all the spheres which it covers. Instead, a running-in period is required in practically every branch of activity which the Treaty embraces, and the Treaty itself takes this into account.[1] Much of its content is made up of transitional provisions which regulate either the regime applicable during the transitional period or part of it, or with the procedures which determine progress during such a period. In addition, given the short time in which the Treaty was drawn up, the magnitude of its range and the complexity of the details to be worked out, the Treaty itself is limited in many of its aspects either to provisions of a general character (blanket norms) which require supplementation by detailed arrangements, or to general expressions of policy which require not only to be developed in detail, but which need, first of all, to be implemented by decisions as to the methods or means by which the particular policy can be put into practice.

The running-in or transitional period was fixed at twelve years divided into three stages of four years each (art. 8(1)) with certain safeguards (art. 8(3) and (5)), culminating in the power of postponement up to three years in all (art. 8(6)). In fact the Treaty came fully into force on 31 December 1969.[2]

The need to supplement the provisions of the Treaty and the gradual introduction of its provisions are reflected in detailed arrangements of substance and procedure setting out the stage at which the individual aims of the Treaty were to be achieved (art. 8(2)). Now that the transitional period has come to an end, these provisions, which make up nearly one-fifth of the Treaty, need not be examined any longer, and it is possible to concentrate the discussion on the substance of the Treaty and its implementation. The latter aspect must be stressed at once, for the implementation of the Treaty either by procedural means operating on the member states, and, frequently, on their nationals directly, or by the creation of supplementary rules, again operating on the member states or on individuals, gives the EEC its special character. It differs from an ordinary Treaty, whether law-making or not, because it creates autonomous legislative organs affecting The Six and its members alike.[3] It differs from any other international organisation because its functions overlap with those normally regarded as falling within the ambit of domestic jurisdiction. Consequently, it is necessary to examine the relationship of Community law and domestic law; incidentally it will be indispensable to consider the repercussion of the Treaty and of the implementing measures upon the constitutional law of the member states and of the constitutional law of the member states upon the operation of the Treaty.

---

1   For a detailed survey of the development of the EEC at the end of the period see Sattler, (1970) 19 Jahrb. öfftl. Recht (N.F.) 1–128.
2   See Puissochet, 1969 Rev. M.C., 403; Rambow, (1967–68) 6 C.M.L.Rev. 434.
3   *Hauptzollamt Hamburg-Oberelbe* v. *Bollmann* (1970), 16 Rec. 67, at p. 80(4); [1970] C.M.L.R. 141, to the effect that the member states have delegated powers to the Community, and that member states have abandoned the power to modify or supplement regulations. See also *Hauptzollamt Bremen-Freihafen* v. *Krohn* (1970), 16 Rec. 451, at p. 459(4),(5); [1970] C.M.L.R. 466 and the cases cited below.

X COMMUNITY LAW AND DOMESTIC LAW

It is a trite observation that in the relations between themselves the Treaty, as an international obligation, determines the duties of the member states and not their domestic law. The Treaty follows this pattern when it envisages the failure of states to act in accordance with its provisions (arts. 169, 170, 171) and in so far as it confers the right upon individuals to challenge acts of a legislative character laid down by the EEC (arts. 173(2), 175(3), 184), but not measures of national law. However, the Treaty affects many spheres of domestic law and, at times, confers rights on individuals of a substantive character which can only be enforced in the courts of the member states. At this moment the question of the relationship between the Treaty and domestic law arises and the problem of monism or dualism presents itself, divided into a number of separate aspects.[1]

(a) In the first place, it may have to be examined whether the incorporation of the Treaty and of the implementing measures violates the constitution of the member state in the courts of which an individual asserts a right under the Treaty or the implementing measures.

(b) In the second place, it must be examined whether the Treaty or the implementing measure confers an individual right upon the claimant individual.

(c) In the third place, the relationship between the Treaty and any implementing measures on the one hand, and any previous or subsequent domestic legislation conflicting with it on the other hand, poses the problem of priority. At this stage a distinction must be noted.

(i) The problem may arise in a court of the member state. In this case the question is primarily one of domestic constitutional law.
(ii) The problem may arise simultaneously in the Court of the Community, seeing that domestic courts of the member states must refer questions involving the interpretation of the Treaty and the validity and interpretation of acts of the institutions of the Community to the court in Luxemburg for a preliminary ruling (art. 177). In this case the question is primarily one of Community law.

All three questions involve fundamental principles in the legal systems of the member states, but the third involving the relationship between Community law and subsequent law to the contrary is the most controversial in theory, even if in practice a balance appears to have been struck.[2]

---

1 For the need to distinguish these aspects clearly see Constantinesco, EuR (1968), p. 319.

2 Among the copious literature see Chevallier, (1962) 78 Rev. Dr. Public et Sc. Pol. 646; Schlochauer, (1963) 11 Arch. V.R. 1; Carsten, in *Festschrift für Riese* (1964) pp. 65 ff.; Ipsen, 1964 N.J.W. 342; (1964) 2 C.M.L.Rev. 379; Zweigert, (1964) 28 Rabels Z. 600, especially

A. INCORPORATION OF THE TREATY AND IMPLEMENTING MEASURES
INTO DOMESTIC LAW—THE CONSTITUTIONS OF THE MEMBER
STATES

According to the constitutional laws of the member states, treaties become part of the municipal law by way of incorporation, whether by implementing legislation or automatically.[1] While those techniques suffice generally to forge a link between international conventions and municipal law, the special features of the EEC Treaty have created a number of new problems. The first is whether the Treaty itself contravenes the constitution of a member state in form or in substance. While this problem does not arise as such in Belgium, France,[2] Luxemburg or the Netherlands,[3] it does arise in Germany[4] and in Italy,[5] where a procedure of constitutional

pp. 623–643; Bülow, "Das Verhältnis des Rechts der Europäischen Gemeinschaften zum nationalen Recht, Abhandlungen aus dem gesamten bürgerlichen Recht, Handelsrecht & Wirtschaftsrecht", (1965) Heft 39; Munch, "Droit Communautaire et Droit International". Semaine de Bruges, 1965); id. in Le Juge National et le Droit Communautaire (Leyden, 1966); Ophüls in Festschrift für Riese (1964); p. 26; id., Recht im Wandel, Festschrift für Carl Heymanns Verlag (1965), pp. 519, 565; Donner, Chevalier, Waelbroeck et al., Le Juge National et le Droit Communautaire (1966); Erades, (1966) 15 I.C.L.Q. 117; Ganshof van der Meersch, 1966 Rev. Int. Dr. Comp. 707; Pappalardo, (1966) 4 C.M.L.Rev. 84; Tallon and Gaudemet-Tallon, 1971 Cah. Dr. Eur. 360; Tallon and Kovar, (1966) 4 C.M.L.Rev. 64, (1967) 5 C.M.L.Rev. 488, at p. 501, (1968) 6 C.M.L.Rev. 419, at p. 491; Hay, Federalism and Supra-national Organisations (1966), especially pp. 42 ff; Sasse, (1966) 75 Yale L.J. 695; Constant-inides-Mégret, Le Droit de la CEE et l'Ordre Juridique des Etats Membres (1967); Ebb (1967) 115 U. Pa. L. Rev. 855; Monaco, Diritto delle Comunità Europee e diritto interno (1967); Waelbroeck, (1967) 19 Stanford L.R. 1249, especially pp. 1158–1265 and lit. cited at p. 1248, n.2; March Hunnings (1968–69) 5 C.M.L.Rev. 50; Möller, (1969) 18 Jahrb, öfftl. Recht (N.F.) 1; Ridian, Juridictions Internationales et Contrôle du Respect des Troités Constitutifs des Organisation Internationales (1969); Waelbroeck, Traités Internationaux et Juridictions internes dans le Pays du Marché Commun (1969); Campbell, Common Market Law (London, 1969, 1972) s.1.78- s. 1.109, pp. 36–57; Mertens de Wilmars, (1970) 6 Rev. Trim. Dr. Eur. 454; Pescatore, (1970) 7 C.M.L.Rev. 167 (3); 1970 Cah. Dr. Eur. 501; 1971 ibid. 564; 1970 EuR 56; 1969 Rev. Trim. Dr. Eur. 697 with lit.; 1970, ibid. 296; Bebr, (1971) 34 M.L.R. 481.

1 Belgium, constitution of 1831, art. 68, as amended; Federal German Republic, constitution of 1949, art. 59; France, constitution of 1958, arts. 53–55; Italy, constitution of 1947, arts. 80, 87; Luxemburg, constitution of 1868, art. 37; Netherlands, constitution of 1815 as amended (1956, 1963), arts. 60–66; for the United Kingdom see Blackburn v. A.-G., [1971] 1 W.L.R. 1037; [1971] 2 All E.R. 1380; 1971 EuR 267; for Denmark see Grønborg v. Prime Minister of Denmark, [1972] C.M.L.R. 516.

2 In France it may arise, however, before the treaty is signed: Conseil Constitutionnel, 16 June 1970, [1971] C.M.L.R. 70; 1971 EuR 60.

3 See Zweigert, (1964) 28 Rabels Z. 600, at pp. 631,634,635. For doubts in respect of Belgium see Hayoit de Termicourt, 1963 J.T. 481; Ganshof van der Meersch, 1968 J.T. 485, 1969 Rev. Belge Dr. Int. 1; Waelbroeck, 1965 Rev. Belge Dr. Int. 348, at p. 353; (1967) 19 Stanford L.R. 1248, and n. 6; but see now the lit. cited below, p. 43, n. 3; for the Netherlands see van Dijk, (1968–69) C.M.L. Rev. 283; Constantinescu, 1969 R.G.D.I.P. 378; for Luxemburg see Chambre des Métiers-Pagani v. Ministère Public, 14 July 1954, (1954–1956) 16 Pas. Lux 150; 1955 Rev. Crit. Dr. Int. Priv. 293; Brinkhorst & Schermers, Judicial Remedies in the European Communities (1969), p. 171.

4 Constitution, art. 100; Zweigert, loc. cit.; Waelbroeck, (1967) 19 Stanford L.R. ss, at p. 1260, n. 59; Stein, (1965) 63 Mich. L.R. 491, at p. 508; Bleckmann, (1969) 4 EuR 109; Constantinesco, 1969 Rev. Belge Dr. Int. 425.

5 Constitution, art. 134.

review is available.[1] By German law a treaty becomes part of German law in consequence of incorporation by legislation if it falls within the ambit of art. 59 of the German constitution, and in all other circumstances automatically upon its signature by the constitutionally appointed organ of the executive. The EEC Treaty was so transformed into German law.[2] However, art. 189 of the Treaty confers also upon subsequent regulations and decisions, and in certain circumstances upon measures posing as directives[3] or decisions, the same force of Community law as if they were part of the Treaty itself.[4] Thus the incorporation of the Treaty, of which art. 189 is a part, into German law includes the incorporation of subsequent Community measures of a general character adopted by the organs of the Community. According to the German constitution (arts. 20, 80, 129(3)) the German Parliament cannot divest itself of the power to legislate in favour of the executive, except in strictly limited circumstances. Thus the question arose whether the formal delegation of powers to the Council and the Commission of the EEC as a result of the ratification and incorporation of the Treaty, including art. 189, into German law, to make binding regulations and decisions exceeded the powers of the German Parliament.

Upon a reference to the German Constitutional Court[5] the latter held on 5 July 1967[6] that the question before the court was not one involving a regulation (*i.e.* Reg. 19) made by the Council by virtue of a provision of the Treaty and which might therefore contravene the prohibition of art. 129(3) of the German constitution to delegate legislative powers, but involved a provision of the Treaty itself (art. 95).[7] Thus the crucial question was evaded, but the Court added *obiter* that, if art. 189 of the Treaty were contrary to the German constitution, only this provision (and thus all regulations made on the strength of it) and not the Treaty as a whole would be unconstitutional.[8]

On 18 October 1967, the German Constitutional Court went further[9] and refused to entertain a constitutional complaint against Council and Commission and regulations in general, but it must be remembered that

---

1   For further literature see Stein & Hay, *Law and Institutions in the Atlantic Area* (1967), p. 133, n. 8.
2   [1957] II BGB1 753.
3   First discussed by Carsten in *Festschrift für Riese* (1964), pp. 65 ff.; and by Ophüls, *Recht im Wandel* cited above, p. 22, at pp. 550–551 and n. 102; Waelbroeck (1967) 19 Stanford L.R. 1253 and n. 7.
4   See above, p. 11, n. 3 with cases and lit. and below, p. 31, n. 4.
5   From the *Finanzgericht Rheinland-Pfalz*, 14 November 1963, 1964 N.J.W. 376; 1964 B.B.A.W.D. 26; [1964] C.M.L.R. 130; (1963–64) 1 C.M.L.Rev. 463; Brinkhorst and Schermers, *Judicial Remedies in the European Communities* (1969), p. 144.
6   22 BVerfGE 134; 1967 N.J.W. 1707; 1967 B.B.A.W.D. 364; 1967 EuR 351; [1967] C.M.L.R. 481; Brinkhorst and Schermers, p. 149.
7   Referring to the decision of the Community Court, *Lütticke* v. *Hauptzollamt Sarrelouis* (1966), 12 Rec. 293; [1971] C.M.L.R. 674.
8   See also Rupp, 1970 N.J.W. 353.
9   22 BVerfGE 293, 295; 1967 N.J.W. 1707; 1968 J.Z. 99; 1967 B.B.A.W.D. 477; 1968 EuR 134; [1970] C.M.L.R. 295; Frowein, (1968) 5 C.M.L.Rev. 483; Immenga, 1968 N.J.W. 1036; Brinkhorst and Schermers, p. 152.

the petition challenged the constitutionality as such of Council and Commission regulations. The problem was, therefore, a limited one, restricted to a declaration and not concerned with the application of the regulations in a German court in a particular case.[1] Nor was the compatibility in substance of particular regulations with the principles of the German constitution in issue here.[2] Within this limited framework the Court said:

"(c) The Regulations of the Council and the Commission are acts of a special 'supra-national' public authority created by the Treaty and clearly distinguishable from the member states. The institutions of the E.E.C. exercise sovereign rights of which the members have divested themselves in favour of the Community set up by them. The Community itself is neither a state nor a federal state. It is a gradually integrating community of a special nature, 'an inter-state institution' in the sense of art. 24(1) of the Basic Law (*Grundgesetz*) to which the Federal Republic of Germany has transferred certain sovereign rights. A new public authority was thus created which is autonomous and independent with regard to the state authority of the separate member states; its acts do not require ratification by the latter nor can they be annulled by them. The E.E.C. Treaty is as it were the Constitution of the Community.[3]

The legal provisions issued by the Community institutions within the sphere of competence conferred upon them by the Treaty (the 'secondary' Community law) form a special legal order whose rules are neither international law nor national law of the member state. The Community law and the national law of the member states are 'two independent legal orders different from each other'; the law created by the E.E.C. Treaty comes from an 'autonomous legal source'.[4]

Within this legal system there exists a special system of legal protection. . . .

(d) It results from the legal nature of the Community that the sovereign acts issued by institutions within their competence, to which the Regulations belong according to art. 189(2) of the Treaty, do not constitute acts of German public authority in the sense of *Bundesverfassungsgerichtsgesetz* para. 90. A Constitutional Complaint lodged directly against such acts is therefore not allowed.

3. The appellants contend that the regulatory measures which emanate from a supra-national body should also be considered to be acts of German public authority, when this body bases its legislative powers for the Federal Republic of Germany on art. 24(1) of the *Basic Law* (*Grundgesetz*). This [argument] cannot be accepted. Only the formal qualifications of the body having issued the act is dispute is decisive for the competence of the Constitutional Court . . . a body outside the structure of the German

---

1   Bundesverfassungsgerichtsgesetz, para. 90.   2   See below, p. 25.
3   Art. 24(1) of the German constitution provides: "The Federation may by legislation transfer sovereign powers to international institutions." See also Italian constitution, art. 11; Netherlands constitution, art. 67; Luxemburg constitution, art. 49 *bis*; Belgian constitutional amendment, 20 July 1970, Mon. Belge. 8421 of 18 August 1970, 1971 EuR 263; 1970 Rev. M.C. 410.

Art. 24 of the German constitution by itself formed the basis of a decision of the *Bundesfinanzhof* of 25 April 1967 (*Neumann* case), 1967 EuR 239; 1967 B.B.A.W.D. 227; (1967–68) C.M.L.Rev. 211; Brinkhorst and Schermers, p. 147. See also Verw. Ger. Frankfurt, 18 March 1970, [1970] C.M.L.R. 294 and the answer given by the Community Court in *Internationale Handelsgesellschaft mbH* v. *Einfuhr- und Vorratsstelle Getreide* (1970), 16 Rec. 1125, at p. 1135; [1972] C.M.L.R. 255. See below.
4   *De Geus* v. *Robert Bosch GmbH* (1962), 8 Rec. 89, at p. 101; [1962] C.M.L.R. 1; *Humblet* v. *Belgium* (1960), 6 Rec. 1125, at p. 1145; Valentine II, 817; *Costa* v. *ENEL* (1964), 10 Rec. 1141, at p. 1159.

state organisation does not exercise any German public authority. It is here of no importance that the public authority of the E.E.C. could only come into being by the co-operation of the German state authority."

It has been observed above that the decision is restricted to formal applications for declarations of unconstitutionality by a special procedure, but in substance the Court shirked the issue once again. By stressing the separation of legal orders (Community and national) the Court relied on the *Bosch* case; by stressing the autonomous character of community law it repeated the words in the *Van Gend en Loos* v. *Nederlandse Administratie der Belastingen* and *Costa* v. *ENEL* cases; by passing over the Community Courts' claim to the supremacy of Community law and the parties' contention that art. 24(1) of the German basic law did not include the delegation of legislative powers, the German Constitutional Court preferred a formal argument, *i.e.* that the complaint concerned a different body of law, namely Community legislation, and neglected the corresponding argument based on German law that such delegated legislation cannot form part of German law because any delegation was invalid.

In effect the decision implies that the formal validity of Community law, both of the treaty and of the measures taken by virtue of the Treaty, cannot be challenged in *form* in a German court by a constitutional complaint. But the German Constitutional Court made it clear at the same time that the question of substance whether Community law which conflicts with the German constitution can be challenged in an individual case, when Community law fails to be applied, was still open. In short, the question remained whether under art. 24(1) of the constitution the German Federal Republic can delegate powers to the Community which the German legislature cannot delegate to its own executives without violating the constitution and, correspondingly, whether the EEC must respect the constitutional restrictions upon legislation in the member states of the Community.[1]

On 9 June 1971 the German Constitutional Court went further[2] upon another application for a declaration of unconstitutionality.

The Court admitted that the power granted by art. 24(1) of the constitution to delegate sovereign rights to an international institution included the power to confer upon that institution the competence to exercise acts of sovereignty. These include the competence to make regulations. Thus the Court was able to counter the argument drawn from art. 129(3) which prevents the German Parliament from delegating its legislative powers by another argument which, once again, side-stepped the question whether, as a result, EEC regulations were part of German law. At the same time the Court affirmed the right of all German courts to examine whether a rule of German law is incompatible with directly applicable

---

1 For an extensive and functional interpretation of art. 24(1) of the German constitution in relation to art. 189 of the EEC Treaty see the decision of the German *Bundesfinanzhof* of 25 April 1967, above, p. 24, n. 3.

2 Application in the matter of *Re Lütticke GmbH*, 31 BVerfGE 145, at p. 173; 1972 EuR 51; 1972 B.B.A.W.D. 418–420; cp. *Lütticke* v. *Hauptzollamt Sarrelouis* (1966), 12 Rec. 293, above, p. 23, n. 7; *Lütticke* v. *EEC Commission* (1971), 17 Rec. 325.

Community law and, while acknowledging the existence of the rule of German law to the contrary, not to apply German law to that extent in the individual case. The Court referred to art. 100 of the German constitution, according to which the compatibility of German law with the constitution or with public international law is reserved for the determination of the constitutional law which may declare such laws invalid. Thus the first question left open by the decision of the Constitutional Court in its decision of 18 October 1967 has been answered, but the second is still open, namely whether the German Constitutional Court can declare a law-making measure of a Community organ to be contrary to the substantive provisions of the German constitution and *pro tanto* inapplicable.[1]

The problem has thus shifted. It is no longer whether the formal power to make regulations offends against the monopoly of the German legislature to make laws. It is now whether Community law which is incompatible with substantive guaranties enshrined in the German constitution is *pro tanto* ineffective in Germany. The relationship between Community law and German law to the contrary is left to the ordinary courts since, in the opinion of the German constitutional law, it does not involve any problem of formal or substantive constitutional law, but only one of reconciling two sets of legal rules, one higher and one lower.[2]

A lower court in Germany has since held that, in Germany at least, the entrenched provisions of the constitution must prevail.[3]

The decision of the German Constitutional Court of 18 October 1967 was matched in Italy by two judgments of the Italian Constitutional Court, dated 12 July 1965[4] and 27 December 1965.[5] The latter, faced with a request to enforce a decision of the Community Court and an objection that the Community Court was not a regular court within the meaning of art. 102 of the Italian constitution of 1947, held that the Community legal order was separate and distinct from the municipal legal system and not subject to constitutional review. Thus while the Treaty

---

1 See below, p. 40, n. 4 and Ipsen, 1972 EuR 57, at p. 58, who believes that the increasing regard paid by the Community Court to the constitutional law of the member states (below, p. 27, n. 6) has induced the German Constitutional Court to abandon its role as a protector of the German constitution when directly applicable constitutional law is concerned.

2 See below C, p. 31. For an instructive parallel in Australia see *Carter* v. *Egg and Egg Pulp Marketing Board (Vict.)*, [1962] 66 C.L.R. 557, at p. 573.

3 Verw. Ger. Frankfurt, 24 November 1971, [1972] C.M.L.R. 177, as a sequel to *Internationale Handelsgesellschaft mbH* v. *Einfuhr- und Vorratsstelle Getreide* (1970), 16 Rec. 1125, at p. 1135; [1972] C.M.L.R. 255, upon a previous request by the Verw. Ger. Frankfurt, 18 March 1970, [1970] C.M.L.R. 294. See Kropholler, 1969 EuR 128; Zuleeg, (1971) 8 C.M.L.Rev. 346; Schwaiger, 1972 A.W.D. 265; Hessischer Verw. Ger. Hof, [1972] C.M.L.R. 871 at p. 845(9).

4 *Costa* v. *ENEL*, [1965] I, 1 Giur. It. 1377; re-stating Cass. 7 March 1964; [1964] I, 1 Giur. It. 516 (below, p. 40, n. 6).

5 *Acciaierie San Michele* v. *High Authority*, [1966] I, 1 Giur. It. 193; [1965] I Foro It. 8; 1966 EuR 146; [1967] C.M.L.R. 160; Brinkhorst and Schermers, p. 165, on a reference by C. A. Turin, 11 December 1964 (1964–65) 2 C.M.L. Rev. 450; for the same case previously in the Community Court see (1963), 9 Rec. 661; [1964] C.M.L.R. 146 and numerous decisions of lower courts in Italy collected by Green, *Political Integration by Jurisprudence* (1969), p. 645; March Hunnings, (1968–69) 6 C.M.L.Rev. 50, at p. 55; Panico, (1969) 9 Riv. Dir. Eur. 123, at p. 217 with lit.

represents both the law of the Comunity and also the law within the member states, this identity in substance appears to conceal a difference in nature, and a dualist system of identical law administered either by a supranational court or by national courts appears to emerge. Nevertheless, Italian courts enforce decisions given by the European Court.

Conversely, the fundamental provisions of the constitutions of the member states are part of Community law.[1] However, any provisions of the constitution (*in casu* Belgian and Italian impeding the implementation of the Treaty) can be disregarded by the European Court.[2] Nevertheless, in the particular circumstances of the Belgian case concerned, it is difficult to reconcile this conclusion with an express provision of the Treaty itself (art. 201).

B.   DIRECT APPLICATION TO INDIVIDUALS OF THE TREATY AND OF IMPLEMENTING MEASURES[3]

Over a long period of time public international law has distinguished between executory and executed treaties. While the former require implementing legislation on the part of the member states, the latter enter into operation immediately. This distinction does not fit the character and the needs of the EEC since the Treaty itself consists to a great extent of framework provisions only, which are to be filled in by the Community, and since a provision which is complete may either purport to apply to the member states or to individuals who are nationals of these states.[4] In these circumstances the consideration whether the Treaty requires implementation or is applicable between member states is not the only one, and it is supplemented by another which is whether the particular provision is "directly applicable" to individuals in the sense that it confers rights (and possibly duties)[5] upon them.[6]

As understood by the European Court, a provision to be directly applicable to individuals must have direct effects and give rise to in-

1   *Stauder* v. *City of Ulm* (1969) 15 Rec. 419; [1970] C.M.L.R. 112; *Einfuhr- und Vorratsstelle Getreide* v. *Köster* (1970), 16 Rec. 1161, at p. 1176(22); [1972] C.M.L.R. 206; *Internationale Handelsgesellschaft mbH* v. *Einfuhr- und Vorratsstelle Getreide* (1970) 16 Rec. 1125, at p. 1125; *Deutsche Tradax GmbH* v. *Vorratsstelle Getreide* (1971), 17 Rec. 145, at p. 153(2)–(4); [1972] C.M.L.R. 213; see also Mertens de Wilmars, 1970 Rev. Trim. Dr. Eur. 454, at p. 560; Zuleeg, (1971) 8 C.M.L.Rev. 446; von der Groeben, in *Festschrift für Hallstein* (1966), p. 226.

2   *EEC Commission* v. *Belgium* (1970), 16 Rec. 237, at p. 244; *EEC Commission* v. *Italy*, [1972] C.M.L.R. 699 at p. 708(5)–(8). For the earlier practice under the ECSC Treaty see Jeantet and Kovar in Juriscl. Dr. Int., Fasc. 1616, Pt. 2(2), No. 3.

3   For the following see the detailed studies by Bebr, (1970) 19 I.C.L.Q. 257; *id.* 1970 Cah. Dr. Eur. 3; Dumon, 1968 *ibid.* 369; Daig, 1970 EuR 1. Constantinesco, *L'Applicabilité directe dans le Droit de la C.E.E.* (1970).

4   See above, pp. 10–11.

5   See below, n. 6, at pp. 23, 226 respectively.

6   *Van Gend en Loos* v. *Nederlandse Administratie der Belastingen* (1963), 9 Rec. 1, at p. 23; [1963] C.M.L.R. 105; *Molkerei Zentrale Westfalen-Lippe GmbH* v. *Hauptzollamt Paderborn* (1968), 14 Rec. 211, at p. 226; [1968] C.M.L.R. 187. For a similar practice under the ECSC treaty see *Groupement des Hauts Fourneaux et Aciéries Belges* (1958), 4 Rec. 223, at p. 242, third para; *Netherlands* v. *High Authority* (1960), 6 Rec. 723 at p. 756 (A).

dividual rights which the national courts must respect;[1] it must be by its nature conducive to the creation of direct effect between the member states and individuals subject to their legal order.[2] It is directly applicable if it is "complete and legally perfect".[3] It is sufficient for this purpose if the provision purports expressly to apply to member states,[4] but does not *a priori* exclude direct application to individuals.[5] Any interpretation must be guided by the spirit, structure and wording of the provision in question.[6] The provision must be clear in describing the kind of measure which it embodies[7] and must not express a general principle only[8] or be sufficiently uncertain as to preclude its general application.[9] Thus the provision must be unconditional[10] and leave no room for the exercise of discretion.[11] While there is authority for stating that no further measure must be required,[12] it seems equally accepted that the requirement of a positive act does not deprive a provision of its character as one which is directly applicable.[13] The reason for reconciling the latter with the former

---

1   "... *produit des effets immédiats et engendre des droits individuels que les juridictions internes doivent sauvegarder*", see *Van Gend en Loos* v. *Nederlandse Administratie der Belastingen* (1963), 9 Rec. 1, at p. 25; [1963] C.M.L.R. 105; *Lütticke* v. *Hauptzollamt Sarrelouis* (1966), 12 Rec. 293, at p. 304; [1971] C.M.L.R. 674; *Molkerei Zentrale Westfalen-Lippe* v. *Hauptzollamt Paderborn* (1968), 14 Rec. 211, at p. 232; [1968] C.M.L.R. 187.

2   See *Molkerei Zentrale Westfalen-Lippe* v. *Hauptzollamt Paderborn* (1968), 14 Rec. 211, at p. 226; [1968] C.M.L.R. 187.

3   *Lütticke* v. *Hauptzollamt Sarrelouis* (1966), 12 Rec. 293, at p. 302; [1971] C.M.L.R. 674.

4   *Van Gend en Loos* v. *Nederlandse Administratie der Belastingen* (1963), 9 Rec. 1, at p. 24 (above, n. 1); *Costa* v. *ENEL* (1964), 10 Rec. 1141, at pp. 1162, 1164; [1964] C.M.L.R. 425; *Lütticke* v. *Hauptzollamt Sarrelouis* (1966), 12 Rec. 293, at p. 302 (above, n. 3) *Fink Frucht GmbH* v. *Hauptzollamt München-Landsbergerstrasse* (1968), 14 Rec. 327, at pp. 341–342; [1968] C.M.L.R. 228; *Salgoil* v. *Foreign Trade Ministry of the Italian Republic* (1968), 14 Rec. 661, at p. 673; [1969] C.M.L.R. 181.

5   *Van Gend en Loos* v. *Nederlandse Administratie der Belastingen* (1963), 9 Rec. 1, at p. 24; *Lütticke* v. *Hauptzollamt Sarrelouis* (1966), 12 Rec. 293, at p. 302; *Molkerei Zentrale Westfalen-Lippe* v. *Hauptzollamt Paderborn* (1968), 14 Rec. 211, at p. 226.

6   *Van Gend en Loos* v. *Nederlandse Administratie der Belastingen* (1963), 9 Rec. 1, at pp. 22, 25; *Molkerei Zentrale Westfalen-Lippe* v. *Hauptzollamt Paderborn* (1968), 14 Rec. 211, at p. 226.

7   *Lütticke* v. *Hauptzollamt Sarrelouis* (1966), 12 Rec. 293, at pp. 302, 303.

8   *Albatros* v. *SOPECO* (1965), 11–3 Rec. 1, at p. 9; [1965] C.M.L.R. 159.

9   *Wilhelm (Walt)* v. *Bundeskartellamt* (1969), 15 Rec. 1, at p. 28, *per* Adv. Gen. Roemer arguendo; [1969] C.M.L.R. 100.

10 Bebr, (1970) 19 I.C.L.Q. 257, at p. 272; *Lütticke* v. *Hauptzollamt Sarrelouis* (1966), 12 Rec. 293 at p. 302.

11 *Molkerei Zentrale Westfalen-Lippe* v. *Hauptzollamt Paderborn* (1968), 14 Rec. 211, at p. 226; [1968] C.M.L.R. 187, at pp. 219, 220; *Salgoil* v. *Foreign Trade Ministry of the Italian Republic*, (1968), 14 Rec. 661, at p. 674. For the problem where a marginal discretion exists, see *Lütticke* v. *Hauptzollamt Sarrelouis* (1966), 12 Rec. 293, at p. 302 (above, n. 1).

12 Either by the Community organs or by member states: *Van Gend en Loos* v. *Nederlandse Administratie der Belastingen* (1963), 9 Rec. 1, at p. 24, (above, n. 1); *Costa* v. *ENEL* (1964), 10 Rec. 1141, at p. 1162 (above, n. 1); *Lütticke* v. *Hauptzollamt Sarrelouis* (1966), 12 Rec. 293, at p. 302 (above, n. 2); *Molkerei Zentrale Westfalen-Lippe* v. *Hauptzollamt Paderborn* (1968), 14 Rec. 211, at p. 226 (above, n. 1); *Fink Frucht GmbH* v. *Hauptzollamt München-Landsberger-strasse* (1968), 14 Rec. 327, at pp. 341–342; *Salgoil* v. *Foreign Trade Ministry of the Italian Republic* (1968), 14 Rec. 661, at p. 673 (above, n. 4).

13 *Molkerei Zentrale Westfalen-Lippe* v. *Hauptzollamt Paderborn* (1968), 14 Rec. 211, at p. 228;

is drawn from art. 95 of the Treaty and appears to be as follows: a stand-still provision (such as art. 12) does not differ in essence from a provision requring the modification of national law (such as art. 95), since in the absence of modification the national law is automatically inapplicable.[1]

The practice of the European Court shows at present that only a limited number of provisions of the Treaty are applicable to individuals. They include art. 9 (free movement of goods),[2] art. 12 (standstill on customs duties),[3] art. 13 (gradual abolition of customs duties),[4] art. 16 (prohibition of export duties),[5] arts. 31 and 32(1) (standstill on quantita-tive restrictions),[6] art. 37(2) (standstill on measures concerning state monopolies),[7] art. 53 (prohibition of new restrictions on establishment),[8] arts. 85 and 86 (cartels and monopolies),[9] art 95(1) and (3) (abolition or amendment of internal charges on imports in excess of those applied to domestic products),[10] as well as art. 95(2) (prohibition of indirect protec-tion of different goods by internal charges on other products)[11] and art. 119 (equality of sexes).[12]

It is still an open question whether they include art. 7 (non-discrimin-ation generally),[13] art. 30 (prohibition of quantitative import and export

---

Gebrüder Lück v. Hauptzollamt Köln-Rheinau (1968), 14 Rec. 359, at pp. 363, 370; Ipsen, 1966 EuR 352, at p. 358; *Lütticke v. Hauptzollamt Sarrelouis* (1966), 12 Rec. 293, at p. 302. But see J. V. Louis, 1972 Cah. Dr. Eur. 330, at p. 345 and n. 48; *Norddeutscher Vieh- und Fleischkontor v. Hauptzollamt Hamburg* (1971), 17 Rec. 49, at p. 58(4).

1 Bebr, (1970) 19 I.C.L.Q. 257, at p. 275; cp. *EEC Commission v. Italy*, [1972] C.M.L.R. 699, at p. 708(5)–(8).

2 *SACE v. Italian Ministry of Finance* (1970), 16 Rec. 1213, at p. 1223(10); [1971] C.M.L.R. 123; *SAS Eunomia di Porro v. Italian Minister of Public Education* (1971), 17 Rec. 811, at p. 816(6); [1972] C.M.L.R. 4, at p. 10(6).

3 *Van Gend en Loos v. Nederlandse Administratie der Belastingen* (1963), 9 Rec. 1; *Da Costa en Schaake NV v. Nederlandse Belastingsadministratie* (1963), 9 Rec. 59; [1963] C.M.L.R. 224; *Sociaal Fonds voor de Diamantarbeiders v. Brachfeld* (1969), 15 Rec. 211, at p. 223(22), (23); [1969] C.M.L.R. 335.

4 *SACE v. Italian Ministry of Finance* (1970), 16 Rec. 1213, at p. 1223(10).

5 *Eunomia di Porro v. Italian Minister of Public Education* (1971), 17 Rec. 811; [1972] C.M.L.R. 4; *EEC Commission v. Italy*, [1972] C.M.L.R. 699(4), (5).

6 *Salgoil v. Foreign Trade Ministry of the Italian Republic* (1968), 14 Rec. 661, at pp. 673, 675; see also *EEC Commission v. Italian Government* (1961), 7 Rec. 633, at pp. 655–657; [1962] C.M.L.R. 39 (the obligation arising under art. 31 is absolute) and the earlier practice of the Italian Council of State, 7 November 1962, [1963] III Foro. It. 144. And see Robert 1963, Sirey-Chr. 29; Hamann, 1963 B.B.A.W.D. 683.

7 *Costa v. ENEL* (1964), 10 Rec. 1141, at pp. 1162, 1164; see also *Cinzano v. Hauptzollamt Saarbrücken* (1970), 16 Rec. 1089, at pp. 1096–1097.

8 *Costa v. ENEL* (1964), 10 Rec. 1141, at p. 1162.

9 *De Geus v. Robert Bosch GmbH* (1962), 8 Rec. 89, at p. 103; [1962] C.M.L.R. 1.

10 *Lütticke v. Hauptzollamt Sarrelouis* (1966), 12 Rec. 293, at p. 302; *Molkerei Zentrale Westfalen-Lippe v. Hauptzollamt Paderborn* (1968), 14 Rec. 211, at p. 228; Waelbroeck, (1967) 19 Stanford L.R. 1248, at p. 1269 and n. 122; Hostert, (1968–69) 43 B.Y.I.L. 147.

11 *Fink Frucht GmbH v. Hauptzollamt München-Landsbergerstrasse* (1968), 14 Rec. 327, at pp. 341, 342; *August Stier v. Hauptzollamt Hamburg-Ericus* (1968), 14 Rec. 347, at p. 356; [1968]. C.M.L.R. 222; *Lück v. Hauptzollamt Köln-Rheinau* (1968), 14 Rec. 359, at p. 360.

12 *Sabbatini v. European Parliament*; *Chollet v. EEC Commission* (1972), 18 Rec. 345, at p. 363; [1972] C.M.L.R. 945, and distinguish *Defrenne v. Belgium* (1972), 17 Rec. 445.

13 In view of the detailed provisions of the Treaty this seems doubtful. But see Adv. Gen.

restrictions),[1] art. 32(2), first sentence (abolition of quantitative restrictions), art. 37(1) (adjusting state monopolies),[2] art. 48 (freedom of movement of workers), arts. 52 and 59 (abolition of restrictions on establishment and services across frontiers), art. 62 (standstill on new restrictions on exchange of services), art. 68 (non-discrimination in applying rules on capital markets or credits)[3], arts. 76 and 78 (prohibition of new measures discriminating against foreign transport undertakings), arts. 90(1), 96 and 98 (prohibition of discriminatory taxes or drawbacks on imports and exports).[4]

Doubts have been expressed as to whether art. 36 (quantitative restrictions, public order), art. 52 (abolition of restrictions on establishment), art. 58 (same—companies)and art. 92(1)[5] apply to anybody except member states.[6] On the other hand it has been established that art. 5 (general duty to co-operate in the execution of the Treaty),[7] art. 32(2), last sentence (abolition of quantitative restrictions) and art. 33 (conversion of bilateral quotas),[8] art. 34 (export—quantitative restrictions),[9] art. 90(2) (public enterprises, competition),[10] art. 93 (aids),[11] art. 97(1) (aggregate turnover equalisation tax)[12] and art. 102 (countering distortions)[13] do not.

Directly applicable rules are to be found not only in the Treaty itself but also in Council and Commission regulations (art. 189), and most regulations bear this character.[14] It must be stressed once more, however,

---

Roemer in *Wilhelm (Walt)* v. *Bundeskartellamt* (1969), 15 Rec. 1, at p. 29; [1969] C.M.L.R. 100.

1 *Mégret*, Vol. I, p. 104, ca. Adv. Gen. Gand in *Salgoil* v. *Foreign Trade Ministry of the Italian Republic* (1968), 14 Rec. 661, at p. 682, but see the Court at pp. 672, 673.

2 *Mégret*, Vol. I, p. 134(16); Catalano in *Festschrift für Riese* (1964), pp. 133, 147.

3 *Mégret* Vol. III, p. 185(2).

4 For these questions see Deuxième Colloque International de Droit Européen (1966), pp. 9, 49, 115, 137, 203, 235; Waelbroeck, (1967) 19 Stanford L.R. 1248, at p. 1249, n. 3; *Sociaal Fonds voor de Diamantarbeiders* v. *Brachfeld*, (1969), 15 Rec. 211, at p. 223 [1969] C.M.L.R. 335.

5 Case 77/72, *Capolongo* v. *MAYA*, OJ, 1973, C 3/8.

6 Bebr, (1970) 19 I.C.L.Q. 253, at p. 283; *Campbell*, Vol. I, s. 1. 84 for further details and see below, n. 12.

7 *Albatros* v. *SOPECO* (1965), 11 Rec. 3, at p. 23; [1965] C.M.L.R. 159.

8 *Salgoil* v. *Foreign Trade Ministry of the Italian Republic* (1968), 14 Rec. 661, at p. 674; *SACE* v. *Italy* (1970), 16 Rec. 1213, at p. 1222(9); [1971] C.M.L.R. 123.

9 *Van Gend en Loos* v. *Nederlandse Administratie der Belastingen* (1963), 9 Rec. 1; [1963] C.M.L.R. 105 applied analogously; see *Mégret*, Vol. I, 113(4).

10 *Ministère Public of Luxemburg* v. *Müller* (1971), 17 Rec. 723, at p. 730 (12)–(16).

11 *Costa* v. *ENEL* (1964), 10 Rec. 1141 at p. 1162; [1964] C.M.L.R. 425.

12 *Molkerei Zentrale Westfalen-Lippe* v. *Hauptzollamt Paderborn* (1968), 14 Rec. 211, at p. 230; 1968] C.M.L.R. 187; *Kurt Becher* v. *Hauptzollamt München-Landsbergerstrasse* (1968), 14 Rec. 275, at p. 288; [1968] C.M.L.R. 232; *Milch-, Fett- und Eierkontor* v. *Hauptzollamt Saarbrücken* (1968), 14 Rec. 305, at p. 321; [1968] C.M.L.R. 225; *Lück* v. *Hauptzollamt Köln-Rheinau* (1968), 14 Rec. 359, at p. 369. And see now *Algemene Transport- en Expeditie Onderneming Van Gend en Loos* v. *Inspecteur der Invoerrechten en Accijnzen Venlo (Tariefcommissie, Netherlands)* [1970] C.M.L.R. 1. See also *Lütticke* v. *Hauptzollamt Sarrelouis* (1966), 12 Rec. 293, at p. 303; [1971] C.M.L.R. 674.

13 *Costa* v. *ENEL* (1964), 10 Rec. 1141, at p. 1161; [1964] C.M.L.R. 425.

14 *Max Neumann* v. *Hauptzollamt Hof/Saale*, (1967), 13 Rec. 571, at p. 589; [1969] C.M.L.R. 284; *Hauptzollamt Hamburg-Oberelbe* v. *Bollmann* (1970), 16 Rec. 69, at p. 80(4); [1970]

that the material and not the formal character of the measure determines whether it is in reality a regulation in the meaning of art. 189[1] and has immediate legal effects with regard to the persons designated.[2] Thus the regulation must not require further implementation by additional measures. In view of the recent pronouncements of the European Court attributing to directives the character equivalent to regulations if they leave no room for discretionary action by member states, the latter also may be directly applicable.[3] Decisions, too, in particular if they bind one or several member states to follow a certain behaviour may be directly applicable.[4]

C. DIRECTLY APPLICABLE COMMUNITY RULES IN THE DOMESTIC LAW OF THE MEMBER STATES—SUPREMACY[5]

1 The Practice of the Community Court

The provisions of the Treaty which are directly applicable and any other measures bearing this character are part of the law of the Community which is applied by the European Court and are also part of the law of the member states as a result of the incorporation of the Treaty and of its implementing measures into the law of the member states.[6] But, as

C.M.L.R. 141; *Hauptzollamt Bremen-Freihafen* v. *Bremer Handelsgesellschaft mbH.* (1970), 16 Rec. 427, at p. 434(9); [1970] C.M.L.R. 466; *Hauptzollamt Bremen-Freihafen* v. *Waren-Import-Gesellschaft Krohn & Co.* (1970), 16 Rec. 451, at p. 459(4); [1970] C.M.L.R. 486: Reg. 19/62; *Caisse de Maladie des C.F.L.* v. *Cie Belge d'Assurances Générales* (1969) 15 Rec. 405, at p. 411(18); [1970] C.M.L.R. 243: Reg. 3, art. 52(a), (b); *Unger* v. *Bestuur der Bedrijfsvereniging voor Detailhandel* (1964), 10 Rec. 347, at pp. 361–363; [1964] C.M.L.R. 319: Reg. 3; *Politi* v. *Ministry of Finance of the Italian Republic* (1971), 17 Rec. 1059, at p. 1049(8), (9); [1973] C.M.L.R. 60; *Marimex* v. *Italy* (1972), 18 Rec. 89, at p. 96(5); *Leonesio* v. *Italian Minister of Agriculture* (1972), 18 Rec. 287, at pp. 294(5), 297(22); *Brasserie de Haecht* v. *Wilkin-Janssen*, [1973] C.M.L.R. 287; Gitter, 1965 N.J.W. 1108, at p. 1111; J. V. Louis, 1972 Cah. Dr. Eur. 330, at p. 334. Treaties may bear this character: see Reg. 2387/71, OJ, 1971, L 249/18, art. 4.

See also, as regards duties of individuals, *e.g.* Council Reg. 1018/68 of 19 July 1968, arts. 1, 5, OJ, 1968, L 175/3; Commission Recommendation 69/191 of 9 June 1969, OJ, 1969, L 165/7; Reg. 1617/69, OJ, 1969, L 212.

1 *Confédération Nationale des Producteurs de Fruits et Légumes* v. *EEC Council* (1962), 8 Rec. 901, at pp. 918–920; [1963] C.M.L.R. 160; *Zuckerfabrik Watenstedt GmbH* v. *EEC Council* (1968), 14 Rec. 595, at p. 604; [1969] C.M.L.R. 26.

2 *Gemeenschappelijke Verzekeringskas "de Sociale Voorzorg"* v. *Bertholet* (1965), 11 Rec. 111, at p. 118; [1966] C.M.L.R. 191.

3 See above, p. 11, n. 3 with lit. But see the distinction between "direct effects" conferring rights upon individuals and "direct applicability" which may depend upon national implementing measures in J. V. Louis, 1972 Cah. Dr. Eur. 330, at p. 341. *Grad* v. *Finanzamt Traunstein* (1970), 16 Rec. 825, at p. 838(5), (10); [1971] C.M.R.L.1.

4 *Haselhorst* v. *Finanzamt Düsseldorf-Altstadt* (1970), 16 Rec. 881, at p. 893(5), 894(6); [1971] C.M.L.R. 1; *SACE* v. *Italian Minister of Finance* (1970), 16 Rec. 1213, at p. 1224(15); [1971] C.M.L.R. 123. But see Bebr, *loc. cit.* p. 297 and see Grabitz, 1971 EuR 1.

5 For recent literature see Bebr, (1970) 19 I.C.L.Q.253, at p. 283; Stein, (1965) 63 Mich. L. R. 491; Sasse, (1966) 75 Yale L. J. 695; Hay, (1968) 16 A.J.C.L. 524 and see notes in (1965) 1 Texas Int. Law Forum 101; (1969) *ibid.*, 184, at pp. 314, 320; (1967) 18 Syracuse L.R. 548.

6 It is irrelevant for the purpose of the present discussion whether the incorporation is automatic following an act of the executive or dependent upon incorporating legislation. See above, p. 22, n. 1 for the provisions of the constitutions of the member states. See also

will be shown below,[1] the European Court acts as a trial court involving private individuals in a limited number of instances only (arts. 172, 178), and individuals have only a restricted standing in annulment proceedings, where their direct concern is defined specifically in procedural terms (art. 173(2)). Instead, the European Court is seized of cases involving directly applicable rules of Community law upon a reference for a preliminary ruling, submitted by a court in one of the member states where the action was begun, requesting the interpretation of a provision of the Treaty or of acts of institutions of the Community (art. 177).[2] The purpose of this provision is to ensure a uniform *interpretation* of Community law throughout the member states. The details of the procedure will be set out below,[3] but it is necessary to indicate certain of its features at this stage.

The European Court, acting on a reference from a national court under art. 177, is restricted to an abstract interpretation of the Treaty provision to which it is referred,[4] cannot consider the facts of the case[5] or any aspects

---

Valentine, 1962 J.C.M.St.; Zweigert, 1964 Rabels Z. 600, at pp. 631, 634, 635; Waelbroeck, (1967) 19 Stanford L.R. at p. 1259, n. 58, 1260, n. 59.

1　See p. 321.

2　The jurisdiction of the Community Court under art 177 to rule on the validity of the acts of institutions of the Community upon a request by a court in a country of the member states need not be taken into account here. In this case, too, the court can only pronounce on the compatibility of the act with the Treaty or with regulations made thereunder, but it cannot annul the act. See below, p. 33; Daig, 1968 EuR, 258, at p. 371; *Schwarze* v. *Einfuhr- und Vorratsstelle für Getreide und Futtermittel* (1965), 11 Rec. 1081, at p. 1094; [1966] C.M.L.R. 172.

3　Page 327.

4　In order to ensure uniformity of application in domestic courts: *Molkerei Zentrale Westfalen-Lippe* v. *Hauptzollamt Paderborn* (1968), 14 Rec. 211, at p. 228; [1968] C.M.L.R. 187, at p. 219. For this purpose the Court singles out the problems involving the interpretation of the Treaty: *Costa* v. *ENEL* (1964), 10 Rec. 1141, at p. 1158; [1964] C.M.L.R. 456; see also *De Geus* v. *Robert Bosch GmbH* (1962), 8 Rec. 89, at p. 102; *Deutsche Grammophon Gesellschaft mbH* v. *Metro-SB-Grossmärkte GmbH* (1971), 17 Rec. 487, at p. 498(3); [1971] C.M.L.R. 631; *Pubblico Ministero* v. *Soc. Agricola Industria Latte* (1972), 18 Rec. 119, at p. 136(3); [1972] C.M.L.R. 723, at p. 740(3).

　　For the question whether a request by one of the parties suffices and for the effect of previous decisions of the Community Court involving the same provisions of the Treaty see Waelbroeck, (1967) 19 Stanford L.R. 1248, at p. 1256 and n. 41; van Kleffens in *Festschrift für Riese* (1964), 45, at p. 57; Ganshof van der Meersch, 1970 Rev. Belge Dr. Int. 409, at pp. 439 ff. *Costa* v. *ENEL* (1964), 10 Rec. 1141, at pp. 1181–1182, *per* Adv. Gen. Lagrange; *Da Costa en Schaake NV* v. *Nederlandse Administratie der Belastingen* (1963), 9 Rec. 59, at pp. 75, 76; [1963] C.M.L.R. 224; *Dingemans* v. *Sociale Verzekeringsbank* (1964), 10 Rec. 1259, at pp. 1275, 1276; [1965] C.M.L.R. 144; *Kurt Becher* v. *Hauptzollamt München-Landsbergerstrasse* (1968), 14 Rec. 275, at p. 287; *Molkerei Zentrale Westfalen-Lippe* v. *Hauptzollamt Paderborn* (1968), 14 Rec. 212, at p. 225; [1968] C.M.L.R. 187; *Milch-, Fett- und Eierkontor GmbH* v. *Hauptzollamt Saarbrücken* (1968), 14 Rec. 305, at p. 321; [1968] C.M.L.R. 225; *Lück* v. *Hauptzollamt Köln-Rheinau* (1968), 14 Rec. 359, at p. 369; *Politi* v. *Ministry of Finance of the Italian Republic* (1971), 17 Rec. 1039, at p. 1048(7); [1973] C.M.L.R. 60.

　　It is for the national court, and not for the parties, to define the issue; see *Hessische Knappschaft* v. *Singer* (1965), 11 Rec. 1192, at p. 1198; *Rheinmühlen Düsseldorf* v. *Einfuhr- und Vorratsstelle für Getreide* (1971), 17 Rec. 719, at p. 720(1), (2). It may concern any branch of domestic law: *Ministère Public of Italy* v. *SAIL* (1972), 18 Rec. 119, at p. 136(5), (below, p. 33, n. 5).

5　*Costa* v. *ENEL* (1964), 10 Rec. 1141, at p. 1158; [1964] C.M.L.R. 425; *Witt* v. *Hauptzollamt Lüneburg*, (1970), 16 Rec. 1021, at p. 1026(2); [1971] C.M.L.R. 163, except for the purpose of elucidating the content of the abstract question presented to it.

or characteristics of domestic law[1] and cannot render a decision on the merits.[2] Nor can it determine whether the question put to it is relevant in the circumstances of the particular case which led to the reference by the national court.[3] It cannot determine the validity of national law in relation to EEC law[4] or annul it[5] and cannot interpret national law.[6] Only within these narrow limits can the decision bind national courts.[7] Acting within this framework, the European Court has acknowledged that Community law and the domestic law of the member states constitute independent legal orders.[8] When called upon to determine the ambit of

1 *De Cicco* v. *Landesversicherungsanstalt Schwaben* (1968), 14 Rec. 689, at p. 698; [1969] C.M.L.R. 67; *Haselhorst* v. *Finanzamt Düsseldorf-Altstadt* (1970), 16 Rec. 881, at p. 897(18); [1971] C.M.L.R. 1 and see below, p. 330.
2 *Costa* v. *ENEL* (1964), 10 Rec. 1141, at p. 1158; [1964] C.M.L.R. 425; *Albatros* v. *SOPECO* (1965), 11–3 Rec. 1, at p. 8; [1965] C.M.L.R. 159; *Van der Veen* v. *Bestuur der Sociale Verzekeringsbank* (1964), 10 Rec. 1105, at p. 1121; [1964] C.M.L.R. 548; *Dingemans* v. *Bestuur der Sociale Verzerkeringsbank* (1964), 10 Rec. 1259; at p. 1273; [1965] C.M.L.R. 144; *Vaassen-Göbbels* v. *Beambtenfonds* (1966), 12 Rec. 377, at pp. 396, 397; [1966] C.M.L.R. 508; *De Moor* v. *Caisse de Pension des Employés* (1967, 13 Rec. 255, at p. 267; [1967] C.M.L.R. 223; *Milch-, Fett- und Eierkontor GmbH* v. *Hauptzollamt Saarbrücken* (1968), 14 Rec. 305, at p. 323; [1968] C.M.L.R. 225, at p. 227; *Salgoil* v. *Foreign Trade Ministry of the Italian Republic* (1968), 14 Rec. 661, at p. 672; [1969] C.M.L.R. 181; *De Cicco* v. *Landesversicherungsanstalt Schwaben* (1968), 14 Rec. 689 at pp. 697–698; *Portelange* v. *Smith Corona* (1969), 15 Rec. 309, at p. 315(5)–(6); *Völk* v. *Vervaecke* (1969) 15 Rec. 295, at p. 302(2) [1969] C.M.L.R. 273; *Witt* v. *Hauptzollamt Lüneburg* (1970), 16 Rec. 1021, at p. 1026(2); [1971] C.M.L.R. 163.
3 *Van Gend en Loos* v. *Nederlandse Administratie der Belastingen* (1963), 9 Rec. 1, at p. 22; [1963] C.M.L.R. 105; *Schwarze* v. *Einfuhr- und Vorratsstelle für Getreide und Futtermittel* (1965), 11 Rec. 1081, at p. 1094; [1966] C.M.L.R. 172; *Caisse Régionale de Sécurité Sociale du Nord de la France* v. *Torrekens* (1969), 15 Rec. 125, at p. 134(7); [1969] C.M.L.R. 377.
4 *Costa* v. *ENEL* (1964), 10 Rec. 1141, at p. 1158; [1964] C.M.L.R. 425; *Albatros* v. *SOPECO* (1965), 11–3 Rec. 1, at p. 8; *Caisse Régionale de Sécurité Sociale du Nord de la France* v. *Torrekens* (1969) 15 Rec. 125, at p. 134(6); *Otto Scheer* v. *Einfuhrstelle für Getreide* (1970), 16 Rec. 1197, at p. 1206(4); *Ministère Public of Luxemburg* v. *Müller* (1971, 17 Rec. 723, at p. 729(7); *Ministère Public of Italy* v. *SAIL* (1972), 18 Rec. 119, at p. 136(3).
5 *Humblet* v. *Belgium* (1960), 6 Rec. 1125, at p. 1145; Valentine II, 817. The same applies to acts of Community institutions in domestic courts: *Schwarze* v. *Einfuhr- und Vorratsstelle für Getreide und Futtermittel* (1965), 11 Rec. 1081 at pp. 1094–1095. But see *EEC Commission* v. *Italy*, [1972] C.M.L.R. 699, at p. 708(5), (6); (1973), *Times*, 19 February, where effects not unlike annulment are envisaged.
6 *Unger* v. *Bestuur der Bedrijfsvereniging voor Detailhandel* (1964), 10 Rec. 347, at p. 365; [1964] C.M.L.R. 319; *Dingemans* v. *Sociale Verzekeringsbank* (above, n. 2); *Dekker* v. *Bundesversicherungsanstalt für Angestellte* (1965), 11 Rec. 1111, at p. 1116; [1966] C.M.L.R. 503; *Deutsche Grammophon Gesellschaft mbH* v. *Metro-SB-Grossmärkte GmbH* (1971) 17 Rec. 487, at p. 498(3); [1971] C.M.L.R. 631; *Merluzzi* v. *Caisse Maladie Paris* (1972), 18 Rec. 175, at pp. 179(3), 180(10), (12); [1972] C.M.L.R. 377.
7 Bebr, (1970) 19 I.C.L.Q. 257, at p. 266, n. 39; *Albatros* v. *SOPECO* (1965), 11–3 Rec. 1, at p. 10; [1965] C.M.L.R. 159; *Milch-, Fett- und Eierkontor GmbH* v. *Hauptzollamt Saarbrücken* (1969), 15 Rec. 165, at p. 180(3); [1969] C.M.L.R. 390.
8 *Van Gend en Loos* v. *Nederlandse Administratie der Belastingen* (1963), 9 Rec. 1, at p. 23; [1963] C.M.L.R. 105; *Costa* v. *ENEL* (1964), 10 Rec. 1141, at pp. 1158–1159; [1964] C.M.L.R. 425; but see *Molkerei Zentrale Westfalen-Lippe* v. *Hauptzollamt Paderborn* (1968), 14 Rec. 211 at p. 226; [1968] C.M.L.R. 187; *Wilhelm (Walt)* v. *Bundeskartellamt* (1969), 15 Rec. 1, at p. 15(6) (7); [1969] C.M.L.R. 100.
    See also *Humblet* v. *Belgium* (1960), 6 Rec. 1125, at p. 1145 (above, n. 5); *De Geus* v., *Robert Bosch GmbH* (1962), 8 Rec. 89, at p. 101; [1962] C.M.L.R. 1.

certain provisions of Community law, and more specifically whether they purport to apply directly in the sphere of domestic law because they confer rights on individuals, the court developed its attitude progressively in a series of decisions.

In *Van Gend en Loos* v. *Nederlandse Administratie der Belastingen*[1] the Court said in connection with the interpretation of art. 12:

> "The purpose of the E.E.C. Treaty . . . implies that this Treaty is more than an agreement creating only mutual obligations between the contracting parties . . . the Community constitutes a new legal order in international law, for the benefit of which states have restricted their sovereign rights, albeit in limited areas, and the subjects of which are not only the member states but also their nationals. Thus Community law, independent of the legislation of the member states, not only imposes duties upon individuals but can also create rights which become part of their property. Such rights arise not only when they are explicitly created by the Treaty, but also through duties which the Treaty imposes in a clearly defined manner not only upon individuals but also upon member states and Community institutions."

Read in isolation, the Court's assertion of the existence of a new legal order and of a corresponding curtailment of the sovereign powers of the member states could be regarded as an affirmation that a truly supranational legal order had been created. Read in the light of general international law, the statement could be understood to reiterate in somewhat high-flown terms the general learning on the place of treaties in international law.

However, when the European Court gave its decision in *Costa* v. *ENEL*,[2] it drew some much more far-reaching conclusions from the principles which it had first formulated in *Van Gend en Loos* v. *Nederlandse Administratie der Belastingen*[3] when it said:

> "Differently from ordinary national treaties the Treaty instituting the E.E.C. has created its own legal system *which was integrated into the legal systems of the member states when the Treaty came into force* [italics mine], and as such it is binding upon them . . . the member states, albeit within a limited area, have restricted their sovereign rights and have created a body of law applicable both to their nationals and to themselves. The integration into the laws of each member state of provisions having their source in the Community, and more generally the spirit and the terms of the Treaty, *have as a consequence the impossibility for the member states to make prevail a subsequent unilateral measure* [italics mine] over a legal order which they have accepted on a basis of reciprocity . . . the realisation of the

And see generally Mashaw, (1970) 7 C.M.L.Rev. 258, 423 and the lit. cited by Ganshof von der Meersch, 1970 Rev. Belge Dr. Int. at p. 439, n. 128.

1 Above, p. 33, n. 8, see also *Da Costa en Schaake NV* v. *Nederlandse Administratie der Belastingen* (1963), 9 Rec. 59; [1963] C.M.L.R. 224; *EEC Commission* v. *Luxemburg and Belgium* (1964), 10 Rec. 1219, at p. 1232, [1965] C.M.L.R. 58; *Molkerei Zentrale Westfalen-Lippe* v. *Hauptzollamt Paderborn* (1968), 14 Rec. 211, at p. 226, [1968] C.M.L.R. 187.

2 Above, p. 33, n. 8, at pp. 1158–1160. For the terms of the questions put by the *Giudice Conciliatore* in Milan see [1964] I Foro It. 460; for the position of the *Giudice Conciliatore* in Italian law see *Codice di Procedura Civile*, art. 7 as amended by the Law of 18 July 1956, n. 761; Cappelletti and Perillo, *Civil Procedure in Italy* (1965), pp. 69–70.

3 Above, p. 33, n. 8.

objectives of the Treaty would be endangered, and the prohibition of discrimination . . . would be violated if Community law were to have different force from one state to another as a result of subsequent inconsistent national legislation . . ."[1]

Acting upon a reference by the *Giudice Conciliatore* in Milan for an interpretation of arts. 37(2), 53, 93 and 102, the Community Court was primarily concerned with the problem whether any or all of these provisions were directly applicable in domestic courts[2] with the result that according to the Treaty any individual concerned was entitled to rely on the Treaty.[3] The Court could have rested here, or it could have pointed to the remedy accorded by the Treaty to the Commission (art. 169) or to member states (art. 170) to summon the Italian government for having failed to comply with the Treaty. However, the European Court rejected these alternatives on the ground that a reference under art. 177 by a national court was sufficient to justify the application and enforcement by domestic courts of those provisions which enure directly for the benefit of individuals.[4] It has since been held that in declaring a provision of the law of a member state to be incompatible with the Treaty (art. 171) the decision of the Community Court does not operate directly upon national law and that, for this reason, a direct action by the individual is the only means of effecting a change of municipal law.[5] According to this view, a reference under art. 177 is not only sufficient but necessary to set aside conflicting domestic law. Yet it must not be overlooked that the Community Court recognises the existence of separate national legal systems[6]

---

1   At pp. 1158–1160. See also *Molkerei Zentrale Westfalen-Lippe* v. *Hauptzollamt Paderborn* (1968) 14 Rec. 211, at p. 226 (above, p. 34, n. 1), where direct effect was attributed not only to an express provision to this effect, but was also derived from obligations of a specific nature imposed upon individuals, States or Community institutions; *Wilhelm (Walt)* v. *Bundeskartellamt* (1969), 15 Rec. 1, at p. 14(4); [1969] C.M.L.R. 100.

2   For the answer see above, p. 29.

3   Otherwise the provisions operate between the member states only.

4   (1964), 10 Rec. 1141, at p. 1160; *Van Gend en Loos* v. *Nederlandse Administratie der Belastingen* (1963), 9 Rec. 1, at p. 24; *Molkerei Zentrale Westfalen-Lippe* v. *Hauptzollamt Paderborn* (1968), 14 Rec. 211, at p. 227 (above, p. 34, n. 1).

    Conversely, the fact that a regulation is directly applicable and can be enforced in the courts of the member states by individuals having an interest is no ground for a refusal by the Community Court to assume jurisdiction in proceedings by the Commission against a member state for failure to act (art. 169). See *EEC Commission* v. *Italy* (1970), 16 Rec. 25, at p. 33(9); [1970] C.M.L.R. 175.

    For examples where the Commission or the member states invoked arts. 169 and 170 in order to expose a breach of obligations under the Treaty by another member of the Community see *EEC Commission* v. *Luxemburg and Belgium* (1964), 10 Rec. 1217; [1965] C.M.L.R. 58; *EEC Commission* v. *Italy* (1965), 11 Rec. 1057; [1966] C.M.L.R. 97. And see Waelbroeck, (1967) 19 Stanford L.R. 1248, at p. 1266 and n. 100; Stein, (1965) 63 Mich. L.R. 490, at p. 498, n. 28.

5   *Molkerei Zentrale Westfalen-Lippe* v. *Hauptzollamt Paderborn* (1968), 14 Rec. 211 at p. 228 (above p. 34, n. 1). For this problem see Stein, (1965) 63 Mich. L.R. 491, at p. 510, n. 53.

6   See above, p. 34, and see *Molkerei Zentrale Westfalen-Lippe* v. *Hauptzollamt Paderborn* (1968), 14 Rec. 211, at p. 226 [1968] C.M.L.R. 197, at p. 217; *Wilhelm (Walt)* v. *Bundeskartellamt* (1969), 15 Rec. 1, at p. 13(3) (above, n. 1); *Norddeutsches Vieh- und Fleischkontor GmbH* v. *Hauptzollamt Hamburg-St. Annen* (1971), 17 Rec. 49, at p. 58(4); [1971] C.M.L.R. 281.

and, acting on a reference under article 177, does not determine a dispute[1] or set aside domestic law.[2] Called upon to determine whether a particular provision of the Treaty created individual rights in the sphere of domestic law, the Court decided also whether such rights could be abridged by domestic legislation. At first sight, it might be thought that the Community Court confused a question of interpretation with one of enforcement in order to render its interpretation effective. In fact the Court regarded the conclusion as unacceptable that, despite its incorporation into the domestic law of the member states, the Treaty could be defeated by subsequent legislation inconsistent with it, which rendered individuals unable to assert their direct rights under the Treaty. Yet, since the Community Court cannot set aside domestic law and can only offer an abstract interpretation of a provision of the Treaty, it is possible to argue that the bold assertions made by the Community Court amount to no more than this: in interpreting provisions of the Treaty to be directly applicable, the Community Court must disregard subsequent domestic legislation. However, such a trite conclusion would not have demanded a monist assertion of a hierarchy between Community law and the domestic law of the member states. The aim of the Community Court was more far-reaching. It was based on three grounds, i.e.,

(a) that by entering into the Treaty and by incorporating it into their domestic law the member states had limited their sovereign power in a defined area;

(b) that the spirit and terms of the Treaty demanded its supremacy over the domestic law of the member states;[3]

(c) that the wording of art. 189(2) would be meaningless, unless regulations were superior to domestic law.

The first ground resolves itself into two, which are that the member states have in effect renounced their sovereign powers to a limited extent, and secondly that they could so renounce them. The latter aspect may be irrelevant from the point of view of the court called upon to apply nothing but the Treaty, but it raises a question of domestic constitutional law in the domestic courts of the member states which will be discussed below, when the attitude of the domestic courts of the member states in a conflict between Community law and domestic law will be considered.[4]

The second ground is obvious for a court called upon to apply nothing else than its own law.

The third ground, relying on the binding effect of regulations, could be

---

1 See above, p. 32, text to n. 4.

2 See above, p. 33, text to nn. 2 and 5.

3 Cp. *EEC Commission* v. *France* (1969) 15 Rec. 523, at p. 540(15)–(17); [1970] C.M.L.R. 43; *Hauptzollamt Hamburg* v. *Bollmann* (1970), 16 Rec. 69, at p. 80(5) —Reg. 22/62, 950/68; [1970] C.M.L.R. 141; *Syndicat National des Céréales* v. *Office National Interprofessionnel etc.* (1970), 16 Rec. 1233, at p. 1241(10)—Reg. 1028/68; *Norddeutsches Vieh- und Fleischkontor* v. *Hauptzollamt Hamburg-St. Annen* (1971), 17 Rec. 49, at pp. 58(4), 59(6); [1971] C.M.L.R. 281— Council Regs. 805/68, 888/68, Commission Reg. 1082/68.

4 Below, pp. 39–44.

regarded as no more than an affirmation that regulations, being in a sense delegated legislation, do not require separate incorporating legislation as and when they emanate from the competent community organ. However, the Court has since indicated that the supremacy of the Treaty provisions attaches equally to regulations,[1] basing its arguments once again on the alleged delegation of powers to the EEC.[2]

Shortly after it had given its advice in *Costa* v. *ENEL* the Community Court went even further and held that the Treaty (art. 95(3)) was directly applicable to individuals and prevailed over a German statute, although art. 95(3) was neither framed in terms which constituted a concrete rule capable of being applied in an individual case nor imposed a mere standstill obligation.[3] Instead, art. 95(3) enjoins member states to abrogate or to amend legislation which imposes internal charges on imports from other member states in excess of those applied directly or indirectly to similar domestic products. In effect the domestic (German) court was required to undertake a legislative task by adjusting of its own motion the German law concerned, seeing that the German legislature had failed to carry out the obligation imposed by art. 95(3). The overriding effect attributed to art. 95(3) by the Community Court raises a difficult question of policy, for by enjoining the German court to apply the general and uncertain precept of art. 95(3) in preference to a clear provision of German law, the German court was placed in a serious predicament. In order to comply with the interpretation given to art. 95(3) by the Community Court, the German court could either reduce the charge on imported goods or increase the charge on German products; thus the German court was asked to disregard the German law in force and to act as a legislature in the absence of a clear cut rule expressed in art. 95(3). Upon an invitation by several German courts to review this position, the Community Court maintained it, leaving it to the German courts to determine the manner of carrying out their difficult task of adjusting German law to the requirement of art. 95(1).[4] The Court said:

> "The Treaty's objective of establishing a Common Market, the functioning
> of which affects the subjects of member states, entails that the Treaty is

---

1 See *e.g. Max Neumann* v. *Hauptzollamt Hof/Saale* (1967), 13 Rec. 571, at p. 589; [1969] C.M.L.R. 284 (Council Reg. 22, art. 6(3), (4); Commission Regs. 109/62, 135/62); *Hauptzollamt Hamburg* v. *Bollmann* (1970), 16 Rec. 69, at p. 80; [1970] C.M.L.R. 141 (Reg. 22/62, art. 14, Reg. 950/68 art. 5); *Schwarzwaldmilch GmbH* v. *Einfuhr- und Vorratsstelle für Fette* (1968), 14 Rec. 549 (Commission Reg. 136/64, art. 6(2): *force majeure*); [1969] C.M.L.R. 406; *EEC Commission* v. *Italy* (1969), 15 Rec. 376, at p. 383(6) and see above, p. 36, n. 3.
  For directives see above, p. 11, n. 3.
  For decisions see *Stauder* v. *City of Ulm* (1969), 15 Rec. 419; [1970] C.M.L.R. 112 (Commission Decision 69/71 of 12 February 1969). And see Tosato, *I regolamenti delle Comunità Europee* (1965), pp. 283 ff.
2 *Hauptzollamt Bremen-Freihafen* v. *Waren-Import-Ges. Krohn & Co.* (1970), 16 Rec. 451, at pp. 459(4), (5), 460(8)–(10); [1970] C.M.L.R. 466.
3 *Lütticke GmbH* v. *Hauptzollamt Sarrelouis* (1966), 12 Rec. 293; [1971] C.M.L.R. 674; Waelbroeck, (1967) 19 Stanford L.R. 1269 and n. 122.
4 *Molkerei Zentrale Westfalen-Lippe* v. *Hauptzollamt Paderborn* (1968), 14 Rec. 211, at pp. 226–228; [1968] C.M.L.R. 187, at p. 217; *Milch-, Fett- und Eierkontor GmbH* v. *Hauptzollamt*

something more than an agreement creating obligations between the state-parties alone. The Community is a new legal system, in support of which the member states have limited their sovereign rights in a certain number of fields, and the subjects of the new legal system are not only the member states but their own nationals as well. *Community law is therefore quite independent of the legislation passed by the member states* [italics mine] and creates both obligations and rights for individual persons.[1] Those rights and obligations are created not only when the text of the Treaty expressly provides for them but also by reason of the definite imposition by the Treaty of duties on nationals of member states, or on the states themselves or on the institutions of the Community. It is a necessary and sufficient condition for that purpose that the provision of the Treaty in question is capable by itself of producing immediate effects on the legal relations between a member state and its subjects.[2] . . . None of the above arguments, based on the provisions of internal law as they are, can invalidate the rules established by the E.E.C. Treaty. It follows from the basic principle of E.E.C. Treaty law, as well as from the nature of the Treaty's objectives, that the rules are incorporated into the internal judicial systems of member states without the need for any intervention on their part, insofar as the character of those rules permits such incorporation. Difficulties arising within a member state cannot change the legal character of an immediately effective rule of Community law, especially as the rule must apply with equal force to all member states . . . the prohibition contained in article 95 would lose the effectiveness ensured for it by the Treaty if its validity depended on the member states taking measures to implement it which are not provided for in the Treaty but are necessary for it to take effect."[3]

The argument pursued by the Community Court in the circumstances described above,[4] *i.e.* where directly applicable Community rules require the equalisation of import charges with domestic charges, but do not introduce any scale of charges themselves to take the place of the domestic rules regulating charges on imports and domestic production, seems to be as follows: the effectiveness of the Treaty requires its direct application, even if the Treaty does not express a clear rule applicable to the parties and has to be implemented by the states concerned. On this argument most provisions of the Treaty would have to be regarded as supreme and therefore as directly applicable, in disregard of the criteria developed previously by the Court itself.[5]

Recently, when faced with a potential conflict between Community law (art. 85) and the domestic law of one of the member states (German

---

Saarbrücken (1968), 14 Rec. 305; [1968] C.M.L.R. 225; *Fink Frucht GmbH* v. *Hauptzollamt München* (1968), 14 Rec. 327; [1968] C.M.L.R. 228; *August Stier* v. *Hauptzollamt Hamburg* (1968), 14 Rec. 347; [1968] C.M.L.R. 222; *Gebrüder Lück* v. *Hauptzollamt Köln-Rheinau* (1968), 14 Rec. 359, at pp. 363, 373. And see Meier, 1968 B.B.A.W.D. 168.

For the problems of reconsidering or reviewing an earlier decision of the Community Court see *Milch-, Fett- und Eierkontor* v. *Hauptzollamt Saarbrücken* (above).

1 *Quaere* in what court these rights and duties are to be enforced.
2 *Molkerei Zentrale Westfalen-Lippe* v. *Hauptzollamt Paderborn* (1968), 14 Rec. 211, at p. 228.
3 *Ibid.*, p. 228, para. 8; [1968] C.M.L.R. 197, 219. See also *EEC Commission* v. *Italy*, [1972] C.M.L.R. 699, at p. 708(5)–(7).
4 Above, pp. 37–38.
5 Above, pp. 27–30.

UWG), in so far as the sphere of operation of domestic law might overlap to a certain extent with the Treaty, while in other respects domestic law would operate in wholly domestic circumstances outside the sphere of the EEC Treaty, the European Court said:[1]

> "Community law and domestic law in matters of cartels treat the latter from two different points of view; . . . while art. 85 considers cartels in view of the effect which may result therefrom upon the commerce between member states, domestic legislation inspired by considerations proper to each country concerned deals with cartels within the domestic sphere only . . . the same cartel can be the object of two concurrent proceedings, one before the authorities of the Community by virtue of art. 85 of the E.E.C. Treaty, the other before the authorities of a member state based on domestic law[2] . . . however, having regard to the general purpose of the Treaty the concurrent application of domestic law can only be allowed to the extent that it does not affect adversely the uniform application of Community rules on cartels in the entire Common Market and the direct effect of the measures taken thereunder.[3] . . . The E.E.C. Treaty has created a legal order of its own which is integrated with the domestic law of the member states and which is superior to their own jurisdiction. It would be contrary to the nature of such a system to permit that the member state can take or maintain in force any measures which might endanger the practical effect of the Treaty. The binding force of the Treaty and of the measures taken in order to put it into effect cannot differ from state to state in consequence of domestic measures, if the operation of the Community system is not to be interfered with and the realisation of the purposes of the Treaty is not to be endangered . . . conflicts between a Community rule and domestic legislation in matters of cartels must be resolved by the application of the principle of the primacy of Community law. . . . If domestic decisions concerning cartels should turn out to be incompatible with a decision adopted by the Commission in proceedings instituted by the latter, the authorities of the member states must respect the effects of the latter . . ."[4]

Thus the primacy of Community Law has become restricted to areas which are completely pre-empted by provisions of the Treaty which are directly applicable. In all other spheres domestic law must so be applied by domestic courts as not to disturb the uniform interpretation and application of Community law.[5]

2   The Practice of the Courts of the Member States

(a) Effect upon Previous Domestic Law

Whatever view the European Court may have expressed about the supremacy of Community law when it was called upon to interpret the

---

1   *Wilhelm (Walt)* v. *Bundeskartellamt* (1969), 15 Rec. 1, at pp. 13(3) ff.; [1969] C.M.L.R. 100.
2   *Ibid.*, at pp. 13(3)–14(3).
3   *Ibid.*, at p. 14(4).
4   *Ibid.*, at p. 15(6); for the application of this principle to subsequent domestic legislation see *Marimex* v. *Italy* (1972), 18 Rec. 89, at p. 96(5); *Ministère Public of Italy* v. *SAIL* (1972), 18 Rec. 119, at p. 139(15).
5   *EEC Commission* v. *Italy* (1972), 18 Rec. 8; [1972] C.M.L.R. 699, at pp. 708(5)–(8); *Leonesio* v. *Italian Ministry of Agriculture* (1972), 18 Rec. 287, at pp. 294(5), (6), 297(22) with a note by J. V. Louis, 1972 Cah. Dr. Eur. 325, at p. 330; [1973] C.M.L.R. 343.

Treaty, the overriding effect of Community law within the domestic law of the member states must be found in their constitutions. If Community law is only incorporated into domestic law and ranks as part of domestic law, it supersedes previous domestic law to the contrary and must itself give way to subsequent legislation with which it is incompatible.

(b) Effect upon Subsequent Domestic Law

In Germany and Italy treaties normally occupy this position and the supremacy of treaties incorporated into German[1] and Italian[2] law respectively by the proper constitutional processes appears to be beyond question. On the other hand, dealing with treaties in general, the German Constitutional Court in the *Concordat* case affirmed that a treaty concluded by the German Federal Republic and incorporated into German law does not bind the legislature to the law contained in it.[3] It has been contended that the EEC Treaty has such a binding effect, seeing that according to art. 24 of the German constitution "the Federation may by legislation transfer sovereign powers to inter-governmental institutions"[4] and that it has done so. This conclusion was adopted by the German Constitutional Court on 28 April 1971, but the effect upon German law to the contrary appears to be restricted to the individual case where the offending German rule is disregarded and does not appear to invalidate as such the rule of German law to the contrary.[5] In Italy, however, the Constitutional Court in *Costa* v. *ENEL*, decided on 7 March 1964, came out emphatically in favour of the supremacy of the Italian legislature on the ground that the EEC Treaty had been transformed into Italian law by legislation which can be abrogated by subsequent legislation to the contrary, notwithstanding art. 11 of the Italian constitution which provides "Italy . . . agrees, on conditions of equality with other states, to the limitations of her sovereignty necessary for an order which is to assure peace and justice among nations . . ."[6] This rigid attitude is not affected (contrary to the beliefs of

---

1   German constitution, art. 59.

2   Italian constitution, arts. 80, 87.

3   *German Federal Republic* v. *Niedersachsen*, 26 March 1957, 6 BVerfGE 309; 1957 Int. L.R. 592.

4   See above, p. 25; Carsten in *Festschrift für Riese* (1964), p. 75, and see Holch, 1967 EuR 217; Schumann, 1965 Z.f. ZP. 77; Ehle, 1964 N.J.W. 321; Wohlfahrt, *Europäische und deutsche Rechtsordnung* (1965). See also the German decisions cited by Bebr, (1970) 19 I.C.L.Q. 257, at p. 266, n. 39, p. 289 n. 115; and for Italy see March Hunnings, (1968–69) 6 C.M.L. Rev. 50, at p. 55.

   Treaties, as distinct from the generally accepted principles of public international law (art. 25 of the German constitution) do not enjoy an entrenched position.

5   See above, pp. 25 ff.; 31 BVerfGE 145, at p. 173.

6   [1964],I Foro It. 466; [1964] I, 1 Giur. It. 516; [1964] IV For. Pad. 9; [1964] C.M.L.R. 454, at p. 456; 1964 B.B.A.W.D. 219; 1964 N.J.W. 2338; 1966 EuR 146; on a reference from the *Giudice Conciliatore* of Milan, dated 10 September 1963, [1963] I Foro It. 2368 concerning the compatibility of the Law concerning the Nationalization of the Generation and Distribution of Electric Power of 6 December 1962, No. 1643. And see also *Costa* v. *ENEL* decided by the Constitutional Court on 4 April 1963, [1963] I Foro It. 859. And see the comments in [1964] V Foro It. 1, at p. 10 (Rodière, Hayot de Termicourt), Catalano, [1963] IV Foro It. 69, at p. 153; Maziotti, (1965) 169 Arch. Giur. Serafini 17; Sacerdoti, *L'Efficacia del*

some) by the decision of 27 December 1965[1] to the effect that the ECSC Treaty has created a separate legal order within the Community which is exempt from the control of the Italian Constitutional Court and yet must be enforced, at least in respect of fines and penalties imposed by the executive of the ECSC.

Finally, the attitude of the *Giudice Conciliatore* in response to the opinion of the European Court upon a reference by the *Giudice Conciliatore* himself deserves attention. Although the European Court had held that art. 102 of the EEC Treaty was not directly applicable in the courts of the member states, the *Giudice Conciliatore* felt entitled to give art. 102 a broader interpretation.[2] It must remain an open question whether an interpretation of the Treaty *in favorem actoris* by a domestic court in the member states is admissible after the European Court has given what it regards as a binding interpretation.[3] The *Giudice Conciliatore* apparently felt bound when the interpretation was unfavourable to the supremacy of the Italian legislature and not so bound when it was favourable.[4]

A long established practice in France has avoided clashes between treaties and domestic law which, at first sight, conflicted with them by interpreting the treaties[5] and domestic law restrictively so as not to conflict with each other.[6] If this is impossible, the latter law is applied on the strength of the maxim *lex posterior derogat legi priori*.[7] The French constitution of 1958, art. 55, reproducing in substance a provision of the constitution of 1946,[8] provides:

> "Treaties or agreements duly ratified or approved shall, upon their publication, have an authority superior to that of laws subject, for each agreement or treaty, to its application by the other party."

Dealing with specific provisions of the EEC Treaty, both the ordinary courts[9] and the *Conseil d'Etat*[10] have applied the Treaty when the occasion

---

diritto della C.E. nell' ordinamento Giuridico Italiano (1966); Panico, (1969) 9 Riv. Dir. Eur. 122, at pp. 141, 144, 146, n. 63 (lit.).

1 See above, p. 26, nn. 4 and 5, with references.
2 *Costa* v. *ENEL*, 4 May 1966, [1966] I Foro It. 938. For the subsequent constitutional history of this case see Cass. 12 July 1965, [1965] I Foro It. 1372.
3 See above, p. 33, n. 7.
4 Cp. Zuleeg, 1969 EuR 262, at p. 266 and n. 17.
5 Bial, (1955) 49 A.J.I.L. 347; Chevallier, *Rev. Dr. Pub. Sc. Pol.* 1962, 646; Lardy, *La Force Obligatoire du Droit International en Droit Interne* (1966); Conseil d'Etat, 7 April 1965, *Sieur Hurni*, [1965] Rec. Lebon 225; Kovar, 1968 Rev. Crit. Dr. Int. Priv. 527, at p. 530 with references.
6 Conseil d'Etat, 18 June 1958, *Sieur Girard*, [1958] Rec. Lebon 360.
7 *Caisse prim. sécur. soc. de la région parisienne* v. *Dame Klaiss*, Cass. civ. 28 March 1962, 1963, D.J. 518 and the cases cited in *Stein and Hay*, p. 36, n. 28.
8 Arts. 26, 28.
9 C. A. Paris, 26 January 1963, *Consten* v. *UNEF*, [1963] D.J. 189 with a note by J. Robert, 1963 Clunet 728; [1963] C.M.L.R. 176; C. A. Paris, 7 July 1965, *L.T.M.* v. *M.B.U.*, [1966] II J.C.P., 14578 (Case 4) with a note by Jeantet [1966] I J.C.P. 1987; Colmar, 1 June 1965, *Hessische Knappschaft* v. *Singer*, [1966] III J.C.P. 14578 (Case 2); Cass. 27 April 1967, *R.C.S.S. Nord-Est* v. *Goffart*, 1967 Rev. Trim. Dr. Eur. 701; 1968 R.G.D.I.P. 242 with a note by Rousseau; Colmar, 15 November 1967, [1968] G.P. CEE 6; Cass. 24 October 1968, *Caisse Régionale de Sécurité Sociale* v. *Torrekens*, 1969 Rev. Trim. Dr. Eur. 138; 1969 R.G.D.I.P.

[footnotes continued on next page

arose. At the same time, they have retained much of their freedom by insisting on their exclusive right to interpret the Treaty if in the opinion of the Court (as distinct from that of the parties) the interpretation of the provision in dispute leaves no room for doubts (*acte clair*).[1] Quite recently both the Court of Cassation and the *Conseil d'Etat* have had occasion to deal with the novel situation that the EEC Treaty conflicted with subsequent French domestic legislation.

The *Conseil d'Etat* in the *Semolina* case,[2] decided on 1 March 1968, was faced with a French Decree, dated 28 July 1962, incorporating Reg. 19 of the EEC Council and a French Ministerial Decision to the contrary based on a French Ordinance of 19 September 1962, transformed into a statute by a law of 15 January 1963. In lapidary language the *Conseil d'Etat* held that the French law of 15 January 1963, being the *lex posterior*, must prevail. The *Conseil d'Etat* refused to be drawn into an examination of the supremacy of Community law as such or by virtue of art. 55 of the French constitution of 1958. In what appears to be similar circumstances, the criminal cham-

---

215, see also Cass. 1 December 1965, [1966] D. 373; [1966] II J.C.P. 14578 (Case 1); Cass. crim. 5 January 1967, *Lapeyre* v. *Administration des Douanes*, [1967] D. 465, [1967] J.C.P. 15249.

10 22 December 1961, *SNC* v. *Ministère des Travaux Publics* [1961] Rec. Lebon 738, at p. 739; 15 February 1967, *Comité National de la Meunerie d'Exportation*, [1967] Rec. Lebon 73; [1967] II J.C.P. 15283; 23 May 1969, *Jammes* v. *Fédération des Ass. Viticoles de France*, [1969] Rec. Lebon 266; [1969] II J.C.P. 16020 with a note by Ruzié. And see now 10 July 1970, *Syndicat National du Commerce Extérieur des Céréales* (*Synacomex*), [1970] Rec. Lebon 477; [1971] II J.C.P. 16701 with a detailed note by Ruzié, 1972 Rev. Trim. Dr. Eur. 503; Lassalle, (1971) 11 Riv. Dir. Eur. 194; for the ensuing result see (1971), 16 Rec. 1233 and Conseil d'Etat, 27 January 1971, [1971] Rec. Lebon 69; [1971] II J.C.P. 16703; [1971] D. 645.

1 Conseil d'Etat, 19 June 1964, *Re Soc. des Pétroles Shell-Berre*, [1964] Rec. Lebon 344; [1964] Clunet 794; 1964 N.J.W. 2338; [1964] C.M.L.R. 462 (art. 37); C.A. Amiens, 9 May 1963, *Soc. Photo-Radio Club* v. *Nicholas Brandt*, [1963] D. 556 with a note by Hémard, [1963] II J.C.P. 13222; [1963] I G.P. 426; [1964] Clunet 93; [1963] C.M.L.R. 239 (art. 85); Cass. crim. 22 October 1964, *Etat Français* v. *Nicholas and Soc. Brandt*, [1964] D. 753; [1964] II G.P. 386; [1965] Clunet 90; [1965] C.M.L.R. 36; Cass. crim., 19 February 1964, *Riff* v. *Soc. Grande Limonaderie Alsacienne*, [1964] II G.P. 42; [1965] Clunet 85; [1965] C.M.L.R. 29 (arts. 77, 80); Conseil d'Etat, 25 January 1967, *Syndicat National des Importateurs des Produits Laitiers and Dekker & Co.*, [1967] Rec. Lebon 41, 1967 Rev. Trim. Dr. Eur. 398; 1967 Rev. Dr. Pub. 185 (arts. 30, 31, 34); Conseil d'Etat, 10 February 1967, *SA des Etablissements Petitjean*, [1967] Rec. Lebon 63; 1967 Rev. Trim. Dr. Eur. 681 (arts. 91, 93).

And see the literature cited 1968 EuR 317, at p. 326, n. 19, especially Chevallier, (1965–1966) 3 C.M.L.Rev. 100; see also Lagrange, 1969 Rev. Trim. Dr. Eur. 240, at p. 247; *id.*, (1971) 8 C.M.L.Rev. 313; Bonnefoy, [1971] Clunet 501; Ganshof van der Meersch, 1970 Rev. Belge Dr. Int. 446–448.

For Germany see now similarly in reliance on the argument of "*acte clair*" Bundesverwaltungsgericht 14 February 1969, 31 BVerwGE 279, at p. 284; Bundessozialgericht 22 January 1970; [1971] C.M.L.R. 530, at p. 534(9); for the Netherlands see Hoge Raad, 22 December 1965; [1971] C.M.L.R. 462, at p. 465.

2 *Syndicat Général de Fabricants de Semoules de France* v. *Minister of Agriculture*, [1968] Rec. Lebon 149; [1968] D. 285 with note by M. L(agrange), 1968 Rev. Trim. Dr. Eur. 388 with a note by Constantinidès-Mégret; 1968 EuR 317 with a note by Constantinesco; 1968 Rev. Crit. Dr. Int. Priv. 516 with a note by Kovar; 1968 R.G.D.I.P. 1128; [1970] C.M.L.R. 395. And see the reply of the Commission to a question by Deringer, OJ, 17 July 1968; OJ, 1968, C. 71; 1968 Rev. Crit. Dr. Int. Priv. 785.

ber of the French Court of Cassation, in a decision of 22 October 1970 took a different view when faced with subsequent conflicting domestic legislation, involving Council Reg. 24, incorporated into French law by a decree of 4 June 1963, and general legislation, namely the General Revenue Code, the Wine Code and a French Decree of 4 October 1963. Taking into account art. 55 of the constitution and Council Reg. 24, the Court said:

> "According to article 55 of the Constitution of 4 October 1958 treaties and agreements which have been duly ratified or approved have with effect from their publication an authority superior to that of laws . . . On the other hand, according to the combined effect of articles 520 ff of the General Revenue Code and article 2 of the Decree 1001 of 4 October 1963 imported alcohol, wines, cider . . . are subject to all the provisions of domestic law and must therefore comply with the requirements of French law. In view of these provisions the Court of Appeal has correctly applied article 55 of the Constitution by holding that the provisions of article 4 of the Wine Code cannot be applied to the wines [which have been imported and that the accused] is not subject to the penalties provided by art. 3 of the Law of 5 August 1905 and of articles 443, 444 and 445 of the General Revenue Code . . . the principle of the territoriality of Revenue Law cannot defeat the international rule, the force of which is obligatory in virtue of the Constitution . . ."[1]

If the Court of Cassation had been dealing with previous French legislation contrary to the EEC or regulations, the pronouncement in support of the Treaty or regulations would not be surprising.[2] But if subsequent French legislation was involved, the Court of Cassation has broken new grounds. If the latter conclusion is correct, it must be noted, however, that subsequent French domestic law is merely denied application in so far as it conflicts with the EEC Treaty and regulations. In all other situations the relevant rules of French law retain their binding force, which must be respected by the courts. This is also the conclusion reached by the Belgian Court of Cassation in a decision of 27 May 1971.[3]

The principle developed in the cases discussed above has found concrete

---

1   *Administration des Contributions Indirectes et Comité Interprofessional etc.* v. *P. Ramel*, [1971] D. 221 with a note by Rideau; 1970 Rev. Trim. Dr. Eur. 750; 1971 Cah. Dr. Eur. 356 with a note by Tallon and H. Gaudemet-Tallon; [1971] C.M.L.R. 315.

2   See the cases cited above, p. 41, n. 9.

3   *SA Fromagerie Franco-Suisse "le Ski"* v. *Ministère des Affaires Economiques*, 1971 J.T. 471, No. 4750 with a detailed discussion by Salmon, 1971 J.T. 509–520, No. 4752 of 18 September 1971 with lit.; 1971 J.T. 529, at p. 535, No. 4753; 1971 Rev. Trim. Dr. Eur. 494, at p. 423 (Concl. Ganshof van der Meersch); 1971 EuR 261 with a note by Bebr; [1972] C.M.L.R. 330, on appeal from C.A. Brussels, 4 March 1970, 1970, J.T., No. 4137; 1970 Rev. Trim. Dr. Eur. 369; [1970] C.M.L.R. 219; 1970 EuR 345.

  And see Hayoit de Termicourt, 1963 J.T. 481; Ganshof van der Meersch, 1968 J.T. 481, at p. 486; 1969 J.T. 537, at p. 540; 1970 Rev. Belge Dr. Int. 421; Walbroeck, *Traités*, pp. 247 ff. See also Juge de Paix, Antwerp, 24 December 1968, *Fonds Social* v. *Chougal Diamond Co. et al.*, 1969 Cah. Dr. Eur. 683, with a note by Verhoeven with references to Belgian lit. and the cases cited by Salmon, 1971 J.T. 509, at pp. 518–520; P. de Visscher, *Mélanges Guggenheim* (1968), p. 605.

  For Luxemburg see Cour Sup. de Justice, 14 July 1954, 1955 Rev. Crit. Dr. Int. Priv. 293.

expression in the constitution of the Netherlands (art. 66) which was enacted with a view to the problem for examination here, namely the effect of directly applicable Community rules upon previous *and* subsequent domestic legislation. It provides:

> "Legislation enforced within the kingdom shall not apply, if this application would be incompatible with provisions of agreements which are binding upon anyone and which have been entered into force before or after the enactment of such legislation."[1]

It is obvious that as a result of this constitutional amendment the problem has not been eliminated but only been removed one stage further back. It reappears as the problem whether the constitutional amendments can be abrogated.

CONCLUSIONS

The attitude of the Community Court towards the nature of Community law has vacillated a little in the course of the last ten years. Treated first as a separate legal order, it was then accorded overriding character when directly applicable, only to be given precedence in cases of concrete conflicts. The relationship between Community law and the domestic law of the member states is not the same as that between an ordinary treaty and domestic law[2] nor is it exclusively determined by public international law.[3] It is derived from the intention of the member states, parties to the Treaty, as interpreted by the Community Court.

While this is the attitude of the Community Court and of the executives of the member states, the situation is not necessarily the same for the domestic courts of the member states. The procedure to enforce the Treaty (arts. 169, 170) is directed to the member states concerned, and any failure of the member state concerned to adjust its law is not visited by any direct enforcement. The courts of the member states, acting after a reference to the European Court (art. 177), are only bound by the abstract interpretation of the relevant provision of the Treaty or regulation.[4] Since the Com-

---

1 See van Panhuys, (1964) 58 A.J.I.L. 88, at pp. 107–108; van Dyk, (1969) 6 C.M.L.Rev. 283; Constantinesco, 1969 R.G.D.I.P. 378.

2 See also Hayoit de Termicourt, 1963 J.T. 481, at p. 486: *"Certes, si un texte constitutionnel prescrivait aux tribunaux d'appliquer les lois internes, même dans la mesure où elles contredisent un traité antérieurement approuvé et publié, encore en vigueur, ou si une loi, soit par une disposition générale, soit par une disposition concernant une matière déterminée, énonçait formellement pareille obligation, les tribunaux seraient contraints de se conformer à cette prescription, s'agit-il de traités ayant les caractères spécifiques des traités instituant les Communautés européennes. Mais que, en l'absence de pareil texte, la jurisprudence crée cette obligation ne saurait . . . être justifié."* Cited by Salmon 1971 J.T., at p. 518 who shows, at pp. 532 ff. that this argument found favour with the C.A. Brussels but not with the Belgian Court of Cassation. But see above, p. 39, text to notes 1–4.

3 *EEC Commission* v. *Belgium and Luxemburg* (1964), 10 Rec. 1217, at pp. 1231–1232; [1965] C.M.L.R. 58, according to which the ordinary rule of international law does not apply which permits a party to a treaty to refuse performance, if the other party fails to carry out its obligations. See also *Germany* v. *EEC Commission* (1966), 12 Rec. 227; [1967] C.M.L.R. 22. And see above, p. 18.

4 Above, pp. 32, 33; *Molkerei Zentrale Westfalen-Lippe* v. *Hauptzollamt Paderborn* (1968), 14 Rec. 211, at p. 228, [1968] C.M.L.R. 187.

munity Court does not even consider municipal law,[1] the domestic courts of the member states must determine themselves whether their domestic law is contrary to the Treaty and whether they must disregard it at least to this extent. The terms and the spirit of the Treaty provide a pointer to the intention of the parties, but the question whether a member state can relinquish or delegate its power to enact subsequent legislation contrary to the Treaty[2] and as to how the domestic courts of the member states must supplement domestic law, when it fails to measure up to the particular requirements of the Treaty,[3] is a matter for the Constitutions of the member states.[4]

Various attempts have been made to explain the peculiar phenomenon represented by the EEC Treaty, which does not fit into any regular pattern of international law or federal law.[5] At present it may be necessary to conclude that, like the German Empire in the 17th and 18th centuries, it is a *"mirabile quidam monstrum"*.

---

1 See above, p. 33, nn. 1, 4, 5, 6. And see *Ministère Public of Italy* v. *SAIL* (1972), 18 Rec. 119, at p. 136(3); [1972] C.M.L.R. 723, at p. 740(3).

2 See above, p. 25.

3 *E.g.* art. 95(3), and see above, p. 37; see also Hayoit de Termicourt, above, p. 44, n. 2.

4 These general considerations must also prevail over the specific provisions of the Treaty permitting the member states to deviate only in clearly defined circumstances unilaterally either without (arts. 15, 93(3), 223–225), or after (arts. 8(4), 17(4), 25, 26, 73, 93(2), 226), consulting the Community organs. See, however, *Costa* v. *ENEL* (1964), 10 Rec. 1141, at p. 1159; [1964] C.M.L.R. 425; *Unger* v. *Bestuur der Bedrijfsvereniging voor Detailhandel* (1964), 10 Rec. 347, at p. 365; [1964] C.M.L.R. 319; *Nonnenmacher* v. *Bestuur der Sociale Verzekerings-bank* (1964), 10 Rec. 557, at p. 573; [1965] C.M.L.R. 338; *Hauptzollamt Hamburg-Oberelbe* v. *Bollmann* (1970), 16 Rec. 69, at p. 80(4); [1970] C.M.L.R. 141; Ophüls in *Recht im Wandel, Festschrift für Carl Heymanns Verlag* (1965) 519, at p. 552 and n. 107, but see p. 546 and n. 88.

   Support for the latter view can be based on art. 11 of the EEC Treaty which binds the member states to adapt their constitutional law and procedure so as to enable the governments to regulate customs tariffs by way of delegated legislation. See also Reg. 23, art. 16, OJ, 1962, 965; *EEC Commission* v. *France* (1969), 15 Rec. 523, at pp. 540(17), 541(21); [1970] C.M.L.R. 43.

5 See *e.g. Humblet* v. *Belgium* (1960), 6 Rec. 1125, at p. 1145; Valentine II, 817; *Costa* v. *ENEL* (1964), 10 Rec. 1141, at p. 1158; [1964] C.M.L.R. 425.

PART II

*The Range of the Treaty
and its Implementation*

3

Customs and Duties and Quantitative Restrictions[1]

I FREE EXCHANGE OF GOODS

The free exchange of goods[2] is the corner-stone of the Treaty (arts. 9–11). It includes their import and export and any tariffs or equivalent charges burdening them (arts. 12–17) as well as any quantitative restrictions (arts. 30–37) existing between them. The place of origin of the goods is irrelevant if they are in free circulation (*en libre pratique, im freien Verkehr*) in one of the member countries (art. 9(2)).[3] This condition is enjoyed by all goods, even if they originate in a non-treaty country, provided that full customs duties have been paid (art. 10(1)). Difficulties arise either where goods have been made in one member state with some products of a third country which are not in free circulation or where a drawback has been allowed (art. 2(2)).

Measures: Commission—directives for goods in free circulation (art. 10(2), 1st para.);[4] Commission—decisions for products of member states which incorporate goods from third countries (art. 10(2), 2nd para.).[5]

---

1 Van der Mensbrugh in *Ganshof van der Meersch, op. cit,* pp. 659–675; Le Roy in 1967 Juriscl. Dr. Int., Fasc. 164 D; *Mégret,* Vol. I.

2 Merchandise in the meaning of art. 9 are all "products capable of being valued in terms of money and, as such, of forming the object of commercial transactions", see *EEC Commission v. Italy* (1968), 14 Rec. 617, at p. 626; [1969] C.M.L.R. 1.

3 See Council Reg. 802/68, OJ, 1968, L 148 amended as to art. 2 by Reg. 1318/71, OJ, 1971, L 139/6; Commission Reg. 518/72, OJ, 1972, L 67/25. For the treatment of exceptional customs contingents see *Mégret,* Vol. I, p. 44.

4 Commission Directive 4 December 1958, OJ, 1958, 688, superseded by Commission Directive 5 December 1960, OJ, 1961, 29, 32 (form of certificate): *Mégret,* Vol. I, p. 5*. For the exceptional treatment of goods imported from the German Democratic Republic see Juriscl. Dr. Int., Fasc. 164 B, No. 5; Protocol OJ, 1958, 694, but see OJ 1964, 2413; *Mégret,* Vol. I, p. 46, implemented as regards *produits originaires* in the meaning of Council Decision 64/349, OJ, 1964, 1472 by Council Decision 66/303, OJ, 1966, 1445, modified 20 February 1968, OJ. 1968, L 55/19 and 70/533, OJ, 1970, L 284.

5 Commission Decisions, 28 January 1960, OJ, 1960, 933 (special levy), replacing Decision of 16 December 1958, OJ, 1958, 694; 14 July 1962, OJ, 1962, 2140; 14 October 1963, OJ, 1963, 2782, modified (art. 9) by a Decision of 23 March 1967, OJ, 1967, 1294, abrogated with exceptions by Decision 68/284, OT, 1968, L 167, *Mégret,* Vol. I, p. 95. See also Decisions 66/682, OJ, 1966, 3745; 66/683, OJ, 1966, 3748.

[footnote continued on next page

Article 11 imposes the curious duty upon member states to adapt their constitutional law so as to enable the governments to regulate customs tariffs by way of delegated legislation.[1] The reason is to be found in the need for the speedy concerted application of common customs regulations.[2]

An exception was provided originally (arts. 132(2), 133, 134, Annex IV, art. 227(2)) for the benefit of certain overseas territories of the member states, but these provisions are now obsolete to a great extent, and the convention mentioned in the Treaty (art. 136 and Annex IV) lapsed on 31 December 1962.[3] Today only the following non-European areas enjoy Community status as part of the Community, while some of the remaining countries enjoy the benefit of a conventional status equal to that of association: Guadeloupe, Martinique, French Guyana and Réunion as part of France.

Among the others mentioned in Annex IV which have retained their connection with the mother country, St. Pierre et Miquelon, French Somaliland, New Hebrides, Comoros Islands, French Southern and Arctic Territories, Netherlands Antilles, are covered by special Conventions.[4] These territories must be distinguished from "associated countries".

For products of fisheries see Commission Decisions 64/503, OJ, 1964, 2293; modified by Decision 64/718, OJ, 1964, 3622, *Mégret*, Vol. I, p. 162.

For goods imported from association countries see Yaoundé Association Convention, 20 July 1963, Protocol No. 3, OJ, 1964, 1449.

For countries and territories retaining their former status see Council Decision 25 February 1964, OJ, 1964, 1484; 5 May 1966, OJ, 1966, 1495.

1   For an enumeration of domestic legislation see *Mégret*, Vol. I, p. 50.

2   See *Mégret, loc. cit.*

3   Replaced by a Brussels Convention of 20 December 1962, 1963, Rev. M.C. 22, culminating in the Yaoundé Convention of 20 July 1963, OJ, 1964, 1429—see Olivier, 1963, Rev. M.C. 480, Juriscl. Dr. Int., Fasc. 164 C—implemented by Council Decision 64/349, OJ, 1964, 1430, 1473, renewed by the Yaoundé Agreement of 29 July 1969, Council Decision 70/539 of 29 September 1970, OJ, 1970, L 282/1; see also 70/540, OJ, 1970, L 282/2, 71/353, OJ, 1971, L 243/27 concluded with the eighteen African states set out in the Preamble to which Mauritius must be added: Convention 12 May 1972, OJ, 1972, L 156/2. For Kenya, Tanzania and Uganda see the Arousha Convention of 24 September 1969, Council Decision 70/545, OJ, 1970, L 282/54/55. The Convention of 16 July 1966 with Nigeria is not in force; see 1966 J.C.M.St. 200; Tromm, (1967) C.M.L.Rev. 30.

Further association agreements were concluded with Greece, Convention of 9 July 1961, OJ, 1963, 293, 294; with Turkey, Convention of 13 September 1963, OJ, 1964, 3685; Agreement of 5 June 1971, OJ, 1971 L 1301; Protocol 23 November 1970, OJ, 1972, L 293/1; Malta, Agreement of 5 December 1970, OJ, 1971, L 61/2; L 70/20; Morocco, Convention of 31 March 1969, OJ, 1969, L 197/3; 1971 L 53/1, L 70/20; Tunisia, Convention of 28 March 1969, OJ, 1969, L 198/1, 198/3, 1970, L 218.

Commercial conventions, short of creating association status were concluded with Iran, Convention of 14 October 1963, OJ, 1963, 2554, prolonged OJ, 1966, 3742; OJ, 1967, L 309/6; OJ, 1969, L 302/15; Israel, Convention of 4 June 1964, OJ, 1964, 1517, prolonged; Spain, 29 June 1970, OJ, 1970, L 182/2; Austria, Interim Agreement, 25 September 1972, OJ, 1972, L 223/1; Convention 22 July 1972, OJ, 1972, L 300/1; Sweden, 22 July 1972, OJ, 1972, L 300/96; Switzerland and Liechtenstein, 22 July 1972, OJ, 1972, L 300/188/281; Iceland, 22 July 1972, OJ, 1972, L 301/1; Portugal, OJ, 1972, L 301/164. For a complete survey see below p. 302, nn. 14–19, p. 303, nn. 1–9.

4   For the French overseas territories see Council Decision 64/350 of 25 February 1964, OJ, 1964, 1484.

Monaco, San Marino (art. 227(4)), Jungholz and Mittelberg are treated as part of France, Italy and Germany respectively.[1]

II ABOLITION OF CUSTOMS DUTIES (arts. 12–17)

The aim of the convention was to abolish all customs duties and taxes of an equivalent effect[2] between member states within twelve years. This was to be achieved by 31 December 1969 and was in fact achieved on 30 July 1968. It is therefore sufficient to give a brief outline only of the provisions of the Treaty which served this purpose. Since it appeared impossible to abolish all internal customs barriers immediately and since even a gradual proportional reduction might have affected certain valuable systems of production, if applied indiscriminately, the system of a so-called linear reduction was combined with a system of selective reductions, at least during the later stages when the accumulated reductions were expected to make themselves felt more radically.

As a first step a standstill was imposed for customs tariffs affecting imports and exports and in respect of any charges of a like character (art. 12).[3] A time-table, which was divided into three stages which were themselves divided into three successive stages, laid down minimum rates of reduction for each stage but provided some flexibility (arts. 13(1), 14, 15). Early on, the member states agreed on its acceleration.[4] The rate of reductions grew so fast that the last phase of the second stage, due to be completed on 31 January 1965, was reached by 1 July 1963. As a result the remaining

---

For St. Pierre etc. see Council Decision 64/349 of 15 February 1964, OJ, 1964, 1472, 1484 and Annex VII taking the place of an implementing convention in virtue of art. 236. See Everling, *Establishment* (1965), p. 34, n. 24.

For the Netherlands Antilles see Council Decision 64/532, OJ, 1964, 2413 giving effect to the Convention of 13 November 1962, OJ, 1964, 2414–2419; 70/551, OJ, 1970, L 284/57. For their position in relation to the EEC as a whole see Council Decision 70/549 29 September 1970, OJ, 1970, L 282/83.

None of the territories enumerated above are, however, within the uniform customs area. This includes Belgium, France, including the four overseas departments set out in the text and Monaco, Germany, excluding Heligoland and Büsingen but including the Austrian territory of Jungholz and Mittelberg—see Karner, 1969, B.B.A.W.D. 185—Italy, except the Communes of Livigno and Campione d'Italia, but including San Marino; Luxemburg and the Netherlands; Denmark, except the Faroe Islands, United Kingdom including the Channel Islands and the Isle of Man. See Council Reg. 1496/68, OJ, 1968, L 238, art. 1, but see art. 2 and the Annex and see *Mégret*, Vol. I, p. 3*; amended by the Accession Treaty, Annex I, I(4), Cmnd. 4862 II, p. 5, OJ, 1972, L 73/1.

1   Council Reg. 1496/68, OJ, 1968, L 238/1, art. 2 and Annex as amended by the Accession Treaty, Pt. II, Annex I, I(4), Cmnd. 4862 II, p. 5, OJ, 1972, L 73/1.

2   *EEC Commission* v. *Luxemburg and Belgium* (1962), 8 Rec. 813, at pp. 826–829; [1963] C.M.L.R. 199. It includes all those measures which, under a different name or under a different procedural slant would have the same discriminatory or protective effects as customs duties.

3   It included agriculture: *EEC Commission* v. *Luxemburg and Belgium* (1964), 10 Rec. 1217; [1965] C.M.L.R. 58.

4   Agreements of 12 May 1960, OJ, 1960, 1217; of 15 May 1962, OJ, 1962, 1284; 22 May 1963, OJ, 1963, 1561.

stages were advanced to 1 January 1965 (70 per cent) and 1 July 1967,[1] and the final reduction took place on 1 July 1968. At this moment all internal customs duties ceased to exist.

> *Measures:* Council upon advice of the Commission—
> Directives (art. 14(2)(c));
> Member states by agreement upon
> recommendations of the Commission for
> acceleration (art. 15(2)).

If the reductions had required further implementation, because the Commission had perceived the danger that the purpose could not be achieved in time, the Treaty would have provided an additional

> *Measure:* Commission—Recommendation (art. 14(6)).

The duty to refrain from creating new or from increasing existing duties (art. 12) is not only a duty imposed upon the member states in relation to each other. It confers actionable rights upon individual members of the Community[2] to complain of any violation of art. 12 in any proceedings in the domestic courts of member states on the ground that it is directly applicable.[3] The prohibition against introducing new or increasing existing customs duties must be construed strictly[4] and does not permit exceptions.[5] It covers any duties which are effectively applied and cannot be evaded by a form of reclassification of the goods so as to fall under another category of objects in the tariff which attracts a higher duty,[6] Safeguarding measures (art. 226) were, however, permitted during the transitional period.[7]

---

1   Council Decision 66/532 CEE, OJ, 1966, 2971; for its nature see *EEC Commission* v. *Italy* (1970), 16 Rec. 47, at pp. 57(10)(11).

2   See above, p. 29. *Quaere* whether residence or nationality of one of the member states is a prerequisite for bringing an action. Clearly a national of a country outside the Community and residing abroad cannot benefit from this privilege. See above, p. 19, n. 1.

3   *Van Gend en Loos* v. *Nederlandse Administratie der Belastingen* (1963), 9 Rec. 1, at pp. 23–24; [1963] C.M.L.R. 105; *Da Costa en Schaake* v. *Nederlandse Administratie der Belastingen* (1963), 9 Rec. 59; [1963] C.M.L.R. 224; *Sociaal Fonds voor de Diamantarbeiders* v. *Brachfeld* (1969), 15 Rec. 211, at p. 223(22); [1969] C.M.L.R. 335.

4   See above, n. 3.

5   *EEC Commission* v. *Luxemburg and Belgium* (1962), 8 Rec. 813, at p. 827; [1963] C.M.L.R. 199; see also *EEC Commission* v. *Italian Government* (1961), 7 Rec. 633, at pp. 656, 657; [1963] C.M.L.R. 39, including such exceptions as might be read into arts. 39–46 relating to agricultural products: *EEC Commission* v. *Luxemburg and Belgium*, (1964), 10 Rec. 1217, at p. 1225; [1965] C.M.L.R. 58; cp. and contrast: *EEC Commission* v. *Italy* (1968), 14 Rec. 617, at p. 628; [1969] C.M.L.R. 1.

6   See above, n. 3, and *EEC Commission* v. *Italian Government* (1962), 8 Rec. 1, at p. 21; [1962] C.M.L.R. 187.

7   *N.V. Internationale Crediet- en Handelsvereniging "Rotterdam"* v. *Minister van Landbouw en Visserij;* (1964), 10 Rec. 1, at p. 26; [1964] C.M.L.R. 198; cp. *Italian Government* v. *EEC Commission*

Concurrently with, but independently of, the abolition of import duties and levies goes the abolition of export duties and levies and of equivalent charges (art. 16).[1]

Although customs duties of a fiscal nature (*i.e.* impositions for purposes other than protectionism) are included in the customs duties which had to be abolished (art. 17(1)), subject to exemptions to be granted by the Commission (art. 17(4)),[2] member states retain the right to substitute for such duties equalising taxes in order to counter distortions (arts. 17(3), 95).[3]

III ABOLITION OF OTHER CHARGES EQUIVALENT TO CUSTOMS DUTIES[4]

Charges equivalent to customs duties must also be abolished (art. 13(2)).[5] Such charges include all impositions, however small, on imports and exports irrespective of their purpose and the destination of the moneys received thereby,[6] but do not include charges on goods for internal consumption and except services requested by a party.[7] Such charges differ greatly in character and their number is considerable.[8]

The rhythm follows that prescribed by the Treaty for customs duties (arts. 13(2), 14(2) and (3)) and by the directives authorised by art. 14(2) (c)).

Measure: Commission—Directives (art. 13(2)).[9]

(1961), 7 Rec. 633, at p. 656; (1963), 9 Rec. 335, at p. 358; [1963] C.M.L.R. 289; (1964), 10 Rec. 473, at p. 485; (1967) C.M.L.R. 207.

They may be applied also in the sphere of agriculture: *Rewe-Zentrale des Lebensmittel-Grosshandels GmbH* v. *Hauptzollamt Emmerich* (1971), 17 Rec. 23, at p. 34(3), referring to EEC art. 38(2); [1971] C.M.L.R. 238.

1 For the notion of equivalent charges see below.

2 For the effect of such exemptions on the application of the common customs tariff by that member see EEC art. 23(2).

3 For duties of a fiscal nature see Council Decision of 20 July 1960, OJ, 1960, 1873. For a list of such duties in the Community see *Mégret*, Vol. I, pp. 63–64.

4 *EEC Commission* v. *Luxemburg and Belgium* (1962), 8 Rec. 813, at p. 827; [1963] C.M.L.R. 199; *Germany* v. *EEC Commission* (1966), 12 Rec. 227, at p. 243; [1967] C.M.L.R. 22; *EEC Commission* v. *Italy* (1968), 14 Rec. 617, at p. 627; [1969] C.M.L.R. 1; *EEC Commission* v. *Italy* (1969), 15 Rec. 193, at pp. 200(7), 201(9), 203(18); [1971] C.M.L.R. 611; the notion is the same in the Treaty and in the regulations; *EEC Commission* v. *Italy* (1970), 16 Rec. 961, at p. 966(4)–(6); *Politi* v. *Ministry of Finance of the Italian Republic* (1971), 17 Rec. 1039, at p. 1048(7); *Marimex* v. *Italy* (1972), 18 Rec. 87, at p. 95(2)–96(3). And see Seidel, 1967 N.J.W. 2081.

5 For the abolition of such charges in the field of agriculture see the list in *Mégret*, Vol. I, p. 56.

6 *EEC Commission* v. *Italy* (1969), 15 Rec. 193, at p. 200(7); [1971] C.M.L.R. 611; *EEC Commission* v. *Italy* (1968), 14 Rec. 617, at p. 627; [1969] C.M.L.R. 1.

7 *EEC Commission* v. *Italy* (1968), 14 Rec. 617, at p. 627; [1969] C.M.L.R. 1; *Milch-, Fett- und Eierkontor GmbH* v. *Hauptzollamt Saarbrücken* (1968), 14 Rec. 305, at p. 324; [1968] C.M.L.R. 225; *EEC Commission* v. *Italy* (1969), 15 Rec. 193, at pp. 201(11), 202(15), but see p. 203(16); [1971] C.M.L.R. 611.

8 *Mégret*, Vol. I, pp. 54–55.

9 First Directive, 11 April 1967, OJ, 1967, 1301; Second Directive, 11 April 1967, OJ, 1967, 1303; Third Directive, 9 December 1969, OJ, 1969, L 320/34; Fourth Directive, 20 December 1971, OJ, 1971, L 293/14; Fifth Directive, 4 July 1972, OJ, 1972, L 162/19.

It must be noted, however, that charges levied upon imports as an equalisation for the imposition of a local tax are not prohibited.[1] Consequently charges intended to equalise the turnover tax in Germany, Belgium and the Netherlands, the tax on increased value in France and the production tax in Italy or any excise or excise equalisation payments for oil, tobacco or spirits exacted in some countries, for coffee, tea, sugar, matches or salt in others were not caught by the prohibition (arts. 95(1), 97, 98). A standstill was declared in 1960 on turnover equalisation taxes[2] and subsequently a uniform added value tax was introduced in all countries of the member states with a view to replacing the various equalisation taxes (art. 99).[3]

The practice, at one time employed by France and by the United Kingdom (1964) under the heading 'surcharge', which consists of imposing a financial levy upon all payments to foreign countries when economic reasons so demand, is really a measure of devaluation. The sum in local currency (French francs, pounds sterling) due by the importer and representing the seller's invoice price in foreign currency is increased by the surcharge, but the seller's price remains the same and he does not receive the excess. More francs or pounds sterling must be paid for the same amount of foreign currency. As a form of devaluation it may therefore be caught by the provisions on the manipulation of currencies (arts. 103–107).[4]

As stated above a member state may, however, make good any financial loss arising from the abolition of customs duties of a fiscal nature by a general tax on all goods of a particular nature, whether imported or not, provided that the tax operates without discrimination (art. 95(1) and (3)) and does not operate so as to raise the cost of imported goods in favour of a related (but not the same) type of goods produced locally (art. 95(2)).[5] For this purpose a fiscal charge differs, therefore, from charges of a different economic complexion.[6] But administrative fees payable for import licences for agricultural products from member states are no longer permissible, since they do not burden similar domestic products (art. 95).[7]

---

1   *EEC Commission* v. *Italy* (1969), 15 Rec. 193, at p. 201(11) (above, p. 53, n. 7).

2   Thompson & Campbell, *Common Market Law* (1962), para. 202, p. 30.

3   For this measure see above, p. 53, n. 9. It was introduced in January 1970, but compliance with it was postponed until January 1972; see Third Directive, 9 December 1969, OJ, 1969, L 320/34.

4   See above, p. 12, (c), and below, ch. 17.

5   Arts. 12 and 95 do not overlap. See *Lütticke* v. *Hauptzollamt Sarrelouis* (1966), 12 Rec. 293, at p. 303; [1971] C.M.L.R. 674. For the place of art. 95 see also *EEC Commission* v. *Luxemburg and Belgium* (1962), 8 Rec. 813, at pp. 826–829; [1963] C.M.L.R. 199. And see p. 53, nn. 4 and 6.

6   *Lütticke* v. *Hauptzollamt Sarrelouis* (above, n. 5), at p. 303 and see *EEC Commission* v. *Luxemburg and Belgium* (above, n. 5), at pp. 827, 829.

7   *EEC Commission* v. *Italy* (1969), 15 Rec. 193, at p. 201(9); [1971] C.M.L.R. 611; (1970), 16 Rec. 961, at p. 966(1); *Deutschmann* v. *Aussenhandelsstelle für Erzeugnisse der Ernährung und Landwirtschaft* (1965), 11 Rec. 601, at pp. 607–608; [1965] C.M.L.R. 259, at p. 266; *EEC Commission* v. *Italy* (1965), 11 Rec. 1057; [1966] C.M.L.R. 97. See also *Germany* v. *EEC Commission* (1966), 12 Rec. 227; [1967] C.M.L.R. 22; for drawbacks see *EEC Commission* v. *Italy* (1965), 11 Rec. 1057. And cp. Commission Directive 68/31, OJ, 1968, L 12/8.

Similarly, before the harmonisation of turnover and added value taxes in the countries of the member states, a turnover equalisation tax could not be charged when no turnover tax was payable on domestic products.[1] The former requirement of a fee for a licence or a similar document which is granted automatically and serves *e.g.* statistical purposes is also prohibited within the Community, but not in relation to third countries.[2]

> *Measures:* Automatic duty to eliminate local provisions to
> the contrary (art. 95(3));
> Council on proposal of Commission grants
> exemptions (art. 98).

IV QUANTITATIVE RESTRICTIONS (arts. 30–37, see also art. 111(5))[3]

Following the endeavours of GATT (XI)[4] and of OEEC, transformed into OECD,[5] and in accordance with the strict obligations imposed by ECSC art. 4(a), the Treaty prohibits quantitative restrictions on imports (art. 30). For this purpose a standstill was declared (art. 31) on the basis of the decisions of the Council of OECD,[6] which had already achieved a considerable degree of liberalisation of trade. This standstill was extended (art. 32(1)) to goods which had not been the object of liberalisation by OECD.[7] All such quotas were to be increased according to a scheme (art. 33) and were to be abrogated at the end of the transitory period (art. 32(2). As in the case of customs duties, states were given the possibility of accelerating this process.

> *Measure:* Agreement between member states upon
> recommendation of the Commission (art. 35).

Such an agreement was reached together with that accelerating the reduction of customs duties,[8] and quantitative restrictions were eliminated

---

1 See *Lütticke* v. *Hauptzollamt Sarrelouis* (1966), 12 Rec. 293; [1971] C.M.L.R. 674.

2 *Mégret,* Vol. I, p. 103. In favour of their admission see Cass. crim. 29 June 1966, [1966] D. J. 595; (1966–67) 4 C.M.L.Rev. 338, and, by implication, the Commission in their recommendation 67/68 of 5 October 1966, OJ, 1967, 260. See now *Politi* v. *Ministry of Finance of the Italian Republic* (1971), 17 Rec. 1039, at p. 1048(6), (7); *International Fruit Co.* v. *Produktschap voor Groenten* (1971), 17 Rec. 1107, at p. 1116(6)–(9), and above, p. 53, n. 4.

3 (1971) 4 N.Y. Univ. J. Int. L. & Pol. 134. Council Reg. 2513/69, OJ, 1969, L 318/6 permits the imposition of customs duties and quantitative restrictions in respect of certain horticultural products during the first months of the year. See also Council Reg. 1229/69, art. 2, OJ, 1969, L 159/5; Council Reg. 2514/69, OJ, 1969, L 318/8.

4 But see GATT XII, XIX.

5 14 December 1960.

6 14 January 1955, revised 30 October 1956; art. 31 is absolutely binding upon member states. See *EEC Commission* v. *Italian Government* (1961), 7 Rec. 633, at p. 656; [1962] C.M.L.R. 39, and is directly applicable: *Salgoil* v. *Foreign Trade Ministry of Italian Republic* (1968), 14 Rec. 661, at p. 673; [1969] C.M.L.R. 181.

7 Art. 32(1) is equally directly applicable; see *Salgoil* v. *Foreign Trade Ministry of Italian Republic* (above, n. 6), but not art. 32(2).

8 12 May 1960, OJ, 1960, 1270.

on 31 December 1961. Consequently the elaborate system devised to guide by the following

> *Measures:* Commission—Decision (art. 32(2) and (4));
> Commission—Directive (art. 33(7));
> Commission—Approval (art. 33(6));
> Council—Decision or proposal of Commission (art. 33(5) and (8))

the process of reduction and abolition has become obsolete among the member states.[1]

The abolition of quantitative restrictions also includes measures having an effect equivalent to quotas (art. 33(7)).[2] These have been defined as "any measures impeding imports or exports which would take place in their absence, including those which render imports or exports more burdensome or more difficult with a view to the sale of domestic production in the domestic market".[3] They include impediments in granting licences and in making foreign currency available. It is disputed whether the prohibition as such, or its substance or effects, renders it illegal[4] but it seems that the latter test is more in accordance with the practice. The Commission issued two directives[5] prohibiting measures which

(a) subordinate the import of goods in free circulation in virtue of arts. 9 and 10 to the export or purchase of domestic products of the same or similar kind; or

(b) impose any restrictions on the use *in toto* or in part of imported goods or require the use *in toto* or in part of domestic products or tie the benefit other than subventions in virtue of art. 92 to the use *in toto* or in part of domestic products;[6]

(c) impose conditions on import which are discriminatory.[7]

Thus the purpose of the Treaty in abolishing quantitative restrictions can-

---

1 *Mégret*, Vol. I, p. 110(3); for the operation of these provisions see *Albatros* v. *SOPECO* (1965), 11–3 Rec. 1; [1965] C.M.L.R. 159.

2 For public supply contracts see Commission Directives 66/683 of 7 November 1966, OJ 1966, 3748, especially art. 4(b); 70/32 of 17 December 1969, OJ, 1970, L 13/1. For the procedure see Commission proposal 15 March 1971, OJ, 1971, C 50/15.

3 Commission Answer 30 June 1967, OJ, 1967, 169/12; Fagnart, 1968 Cah. Dr. Eur 560, at p. 571, nn. 45, 46.

4 *Mégret*, Vol. I, p. 102 and the lit. cited there, especially Ehle, 1967 B.B.A.W.D. 453; Béraud, 1968, Rev. Trim. Dr. Eur. 293; Fagnart (above, n. 3); Anon., 1966 Rev. M.C. 572; Commission Answer 14 March 1967, OJ, 1967, 901; *Mégret*, Vol. I, p. 184.

5 66/682, 66/683 of 7 November 1966, OJ, 1966, 3745, 3748, modified by Directive 70/50 of 17 December 1969, OJ, 1970, L 13/29 made by virtue of art. 33. See also the Programme of 28 May 1969, OJ, 1969, C 76; Proposal of a Directive, 15 March 1971, OJ, 1971, C 50/15.

6 Subject to exceptions arising under art. 37(1) for agriculture, also for German wines and tobacco. As regards the import of potatoes to Germany see the Commission Directive 64/486 of 28 July 1964, OJ, 1964, 2253.

7 Directive 70/50 of 22 December 1969, OJ, 1970, L 13/29 with the exception of measures under art. 37 of the Treaty, and of agricultural organisations not yet subject to a Community organisation.

not be circumvented by the imposition of unjustified conditions or obstacles. The prohibition is absolute.[1]

At the same time the system of quotas agreed with third countries is not affected by these provisions since, unlike customs duties, they are not replaced by the common customs tariffs (arts. 18–29). Instead they fall within the ambit of a common commercial policy (art. 113).[2]

Hand in hand with the relaxation of import quotas goes that of export quotas and of equivalent measures, such as licensing subject to unjustified restrictions. They were abrogated at the end of the first stage (art. 34) and could be abolished more speedily (art. 35).

Measure: Member states by agreement upon
recommendation of the Commission (art. 35).[3]

Nevertheless, the elimination of quantitative restrictions was hedged around with certain safeguards based on *bona fide* considerations of public morals, public policy and safety, human, animal and plant health[4] or for the preservation of articles of historic, artistic or archaeological value of national importance or for the protection of industrial property, such as trade marks and the exclusion of false indications of origin (art. 36).[5] This provision is based on non-economic considerations, as distinct from the now obsolete art. 226, and is specific in character.[6] Only its interpretation is left to the *lex fori*.[7] It does not extend to the sphere covered by art. 85.[8] The safeguards envisaged by art. 36 may be achieved through prohibitions and restrictions, but not by the use of pecuniary impositions.[9] Neither the Council nor the Commission are given any powers to control or to coordinate or to harmonise the divergent national provisions in the countries of the member states which interrupt the flow of goods on any of the

1 *EEC Commission* v. *Italian Government* (1961), 7 Rec. 633, at p. 656; [1962] C.M.L.R. 39; see, however, for the vacillating practice of domestic courts: Cass. crim. 29 June 1966, [1966] D.J. 595, 1966 Rev. Trim Dr. Eur, 729; Conseil d'Etat, 27 January 1967, *Syndicat Nationale des Importateurs des Produits Laitiers and Dekker* [1967] Rec. Lebon 41; 1967 Rev. Trim. Dr. Eur. 398, Brussels, 9 June 1966, 1968 Cah. Dr. Eur. 551; *Mégret*, Vol. I, p. 102.
2 *International Fruit Co. N.V.* v. *Produktschap voor Groenten* (1971), 17 Rec. 1107. at pp. 1116(7)–1117(10).
3 For an account of the relevant measures of acceleration see *Mégret*, Vol. I, p. 114.
4 Cp. arts. 48(3), 56, 66, 68(2).
5 See also GATT, XX. For the interpretation of the term "industrial and commercial property" see *Mégret*, Vol. I, pp. 116(3)–117(4). As regards the relationship between art. 36 and patents see *Parke, Davis & Co.* v. *Probel* (1968), 14 Rec. 81, at p. 109; [1968] C.M.L.R. 47; Gotzen, 1958 Rev. Trim. Dr. Comm. 261; for trademarks see *Sirena v. Eda*, (1971), 17 Rec. 69; [1971] C.M.L.R. 260. For copyrights: *Deutsche Grammophon GmbH* v. *Metro-SB-Grossmärkte GmbH* (1971), 17 Rec. 487, at p. 499(9)(11); [1971] C.M.L.R. 631.
6 *EEC Commission* v. *Italian Government* (1961), 7 Rec. 633, at p. 657; [1962] C.M.L.R. 39. It must be interpreted restrictively: *Salgoil* v. *Foreign Trade Ministry of Italian Republic* (1968), 14 Rec. 661, at p. 676; [1969] C.M.L.R. 181.
7 *Mégret*, Vol. I, p. 115(3). Cp. Oppermann, 1969 EuR 231.
8 *Consten and Grundig GmbH* v. *EEC Commission* (1966), 12 Rec. 429, at p. 500; [1966] C.M.L.R. 418: *Deutsche Grammophon GmbH* v. *Metro-SB-Grossmärkte GmbH* (1971), 17 Rec. 487, at p. 500(12), (13); [1971] C.M.L.R. 631.
9 *EEC Commission* v. *Italy* (1968), 14 Rec. 618; [1969] C.M.L.R. 1.

grounds enumerated in art. 36. Consequently, the Commission has sought, by way of recommendation, to enjoin states not to violate the purpose of the Treaty by measures which regulate the quality, composition, condition and control of particular products and to inform the Commission of any new measures of this kind before they come into force.[1]

The provision on quotas and limitation of exports apply also to state trading monopolies (art. 37(1)),[2] which are defined (art. 37(1)) as organisations (German: *Einrichtungen*) through which a member state controls, directs or influences significantly, in law or in fact, directly or indirectly, the import or export of goods.[3] It is not necessary that the organisation should be expressly charged with international transactions, provided that the transactions involved can concern competition or the exchange of goods and are effectively of this character[4] within the member states.[5] It appears to be irrelevant whether or not within the state the objects are available in open sale.[6] State trading monopolies must gradually "adjust themselves"[7] so as to eliminate discrimination, and member states must abstain from introducing new discriminatory measures or measures which limit the scope of the undertaking to abolish customs duties and quanti-

---

1   Commission Recommendation 65/428 of 20 September 1965, OJ, 1965, 2611; Programme adopted by the Council on 28 May 1969, OJ, 1969, C 76; *Mégret*, Vol. I, 119–120.

2   Van Hecke, (1965–66) 3 C.M.L.Rev. 450. Franceschelli, 1968 Rev. M.C. 855; Ginkel; 1970 *ibid* 248; Deringer 1971 EuR 193; Kaiser 1967 *ibid* 1; in *Miscellanea Ganshof van der Meersch*, Vol. II (1972), p. 173. They include public utilities, such as postal, telephonic and telegraphic services, railways, the control of central banks and aviation, electricity and gas undertakings in some countries as well as coal mining. In addition, they include, in Germany, schnapps, matches and saccharine; in France explosives, tobacco, phosphorus, potash, newsprint, matches, minerals and oil products; in Italy, sulphur (sale), gold (import), bananas, cigarette paper (sale), quinine, cinefilm (import), saccharine, salt, tobacco, matches, lighters, flints; in the Netherlands, natural gas (export). See *Mégret*, Vol. I, p. 124. For the fiscal aspects see below, p. 240.
    See the symposium on state trading in (1967) 20 Vanderbilt L.R. 253 ff., especially Schmitthoff, 355; for the EEC, Mestmaecker, *ibid.*, 321; Deringer in *Les Monopoles dans le Marché Commun*, p. 91. Colliard, [1964] D. Chr. 263. It is disputed whether they cover production monopolies (see Ginkel, Franceschelli 862). For the question whether Community law or national law provides the criticism see de Vergottini, (1967) 21 Rev. Trim. Dir. Proc. Civ. 550.

3   The monopoly must be commercial in character: *Costa* v. *ENEL*, (1964), 10 Rec. 1141; at p. 1164; [1964] C.M.L.R. 425; *i.e.*, it must have as its object transactions concerning a commercial product capable of competition and exchanges between member states; and it must play an effective part in such exchanges. This seems to exclude state service monopolies. But see the lit. to the contrary cited by *Mégret*, Vol. I, pp. 125, 127(8). On the other hand it seems to include any body which fulfils such trading functions, even if it is not formally an organisation forming part of the government: *Mégret*, Vol. I, p. 126.

4   *Costa* v. *ENEL* (1964), 10 Rec. 1141, at p. 1165; [1964] C.M.L.R. 425.

5   Ca. with regard to third countries: *Mégret*, Vol. I, p. 132.

6   Such as ammunition, *Mégret*, Vol. I, p. 128(11).

7   The French text says: "*aménager*" (in the other languages: "*formen um*"; "*procedono a un . . . riordinamento*"; "*passen . . . aan*") as distinct from "*progressivement supprimés*" (arts. 13, 16, 44, 52, 59, 67). For the difference see Colliard, [1964] D. 263, at p. 264; van Hecke, (1966) 3 C.M.L.Rev. 450, at p. 459; Mestmaecker, (1967) 20 Vanderbilt L.R. 321; Franceschelli, 1968 Rev. M.C. 870. See also art. 37(3) which requires the time table to be "adapted" to the abolition of quantitative restrictions.

tative restrictions.[1] It is disputed whether adjustment implies abolition,[2] but in conjunction with art. 90 it is unlikely that total abolition is required.

Measure: Commission—Recommendation (art. 37(6)).[3]

By these general recommendations the Commission requires, firstly, that imports must not be limited in relation to potential sales in the national market; secondly, that monopolies must not determine imports in their discretion; thirdly, that potential sales must be determined without discrimination[4] in profit margins and, fourthly, that no discrimination must occur in retail sales.

If a product is subject to a state trading monopoly in one or several member states, but not in all, other member states may be permitted to take protective measures while the adjustment of the state trading monopolies takes place as required by art. 37(1).

Measure: Commission—authorisation (art. 37(3)).

It has been held by the Community Court that the duty to abstain from new discriminatory measures contrary to art. 37(1) or from measures which detract from the obligation to abolish customs duties and quantitative restrictions (art. 37(2))[5] constitutes a rule which is directly applicable.[6]

---

1   This provision incorporating the so-called "double standstill rule" does not require the immediate abrogation of existing restrictions. See *Albatros* v. *SOPECO* (1965), 11–3 Rec. 1, at p. 9; [1965] C.M.L.R. 159. It includes goods which are not themselves the object of a monopoly, but parts of which do: *Cinzano* v. *Hauptzollamt Saarbrücken* (1970), 16 Rec. 1089; [1971] C.M.L.R. 374.

2   *Mégret*, Vol. I, p. 130(3) with lit.

3   2 February 1962, OJ, 1962, 342 (Italy, bananas);
6 April 1962, OJ, 1962, 1500 (France, tobacco);
11 April 1962, OJ, 1962, 1502, 1505 (Italy, France, matches);
12 April 1962, OJ, 1962, 1506 (France, potash);
4 July 1963, OJ, 1963, 2150 (Italy, bananas);
24 July 1963, OJ, 1963, 2271 (France, mineral oil);
26 November 1963, OJ, 1963, 2857 (Germany, alcohol);
26 November 1963, OJ, 1963, 2858 (France, alcohol);
29 July 1966, OJ, 1966, 2819 (Italy, salt, cigarette paper);
29 July 1966, OJ, 1966, 2820 (France, powder, explosives);
25 November 1969, OJ, 1970, L 6/13 (France, potash).
25 November 1969, OJ, 1970, L 6/16 (Italy, lighters);
9 February 1970, OJ, 1970, L 31/1–26 (France, Germany, Italy, various items);
Commission Reply, 24 July 1964, 28 January 1965, OJ, 1965, 390. And see *Mégret*, Vol. I, p. 155(36).

4   For the notion of discrimination in art 37 see *Mégret*, Vol. I, pp. 129–130 with lit.; Mestmaecker in *Festschrift für Böhm* (1965), p. 345.

5   *Quaere* whether it is permitted to introduce new state trading monopolies within the framework of art. 37, if its provisions are observed. See *Costa* v. *ENEL* (1964), 10 Rec. 1141; [1964] C.M.L.R. 425, and *Mégret*, Vol. I, p. 131. For the criteria determining the prohibition in art. 37(2) see *Cinzano* v. *Hauptzollamt Saarbrücken* (1970) 16 Rec. 1089 at pp. 1096(4)–(9); 1097(10)–(11); [1971] C.M.L.R. 374.

6   *Costa* v. *ENEL* (above, n. 5), at p. 1164.

The question whether a particular instance of import control through licensing of, and the imposition of conditions on, trade outlets which affect foreign traders (such as oil producers) constitutes a government monopoly is not easily determined.[1]

The duty of state trading monopolies to abolish quantitative restrictions is modified where the distribution or marketing of agricultural products is concerned (art. 37(4)). In deference to the international obligation incumbent upon Germany which precludes the latter country from introducing any change in the German state monopoly of matches until the debt arising under the Kreuger Loan Agreement[2] has been repaid, an exemption couched in general terms releases member states bound by international agreement from complying *pro tanto* with the requirements of this article (art. 37(5)). This provision forms an exception to the duty of member states to re-negotiate international agreements conflicting with the duties arising under the Treaty (art. 234).

It must be noted that, in addition to the provision on state trading monopolies in the section dealing with quantitative restrictions (art. 37), another article in the section on the control of monopolies (art. 90) deals with public enterprises and enterprises to which the state has granted special or exclusive rights. They must observe the Treaty, but if such an enterprise manages services of general economic interest or has the character of a fiscal monopoly, it is only subject to the provisions of the Treaty in so far as the latter do not impair, in fact or in law, the discharge of the functions entrusted to the enterprise.

The relationship between the two articles (37, 90) is not quite clear. Both deal with state monopolies, though art. 90 is not limited to them. For the purpose of art. 37 the state monopoly organisation, no matter whether it is expressly charged with the conduct of international transactions, must be concerned with an exchange of goods which can involve competition across the frontiers. Discrimination and quantitative restrictions must disappear.[3] For the purposes of art. 90(1), which concerns cartels and monopolies as such, all state monopolies are included. They must observe the Treaty in full, but for the purposes of art. 90(2), *i.e.* of public utilities and fiscal monopolies, this duty exists in an attenuated form.

The two provisions differ, therefore, in the functional character of the

---

1   The Community Court avoided this question in *Albatros* v. *SOPECO* (1965), 11–3 Rec. 1, at p. 9; [1965] C.M.L.R. 159, following a holding of the Commission based on the Recommendation of 24 July 1964 (above, p. 59, n. 3 and OJ, 1965, 392(7)). According to the Conseil d'Etat the system in question (petrol) constitutes the exercise of a state trading monopoly as envisaged in art. 37, though in the circumstances (distribution) it did not attract the operation of art. 37(2): 19 June 1964, *Re Soc. des Pétroles Shell-Berre*, [1964] Rec. Lebon 344; [1964] C.M.L.R. 462 (above, p. 42, n. 1).

2   Treaty of 26 August 1926 with Sweden and the *Svenska Tändsticksaktiebolaget*, which prohibits any change in the German state monopoly of matches until the loan is repaid.

3   New measures are prohibited. See *Albatros* v. *SOPECO* (1965), 11–3 Rec. 1, at p. 10; [1965] C.M.L.R. 159; *Cinzano* v. *Hauptzollamt Saarbrücken* (1970), 16 Rec. 1089, at pp. 1096(7) and 1103(2), Concl. Dutheillet de Lamothe; [1971] C.M.L.R. 374.

entity to which the rule is addressed. The monopolies envisaged by art. 37 have specific commercial functions, while those mentioned in art. 90 are of a general character. Accordingly the duties imposed on the various entities are different. According to art. 37 only discrimination and import and export restrictions of any kind must disappear; according to art. 90(1) all the provisions of the Treaty apply, while according to art. 90(2) states are given a wide discretion as to how to apply the Treaty. It has been held that art. 37(2) is directly applicable[1] and it would appear that art. 90(2) is not. As regards art. 90(1) the answer would appear to be that, within the framework of directly applicable rules laid down by the Treaty, the provisions of art. 90(1) are of the latter character.

The effect of the provisions on quantitative restrictions upon restrictions imposed by the individual member states on imports from third countries was left undetermined.[2] The introduction of the common tariff has modified the problem. Where quotas have since been allowed by the Commission, they were concessions to the importing state waiving the Community tariff under art. 25(1) (3) or Protocols VII and XI to List G, arts. 28, 111 and in one case a specific regulation (Reg. 14/64 art. 4).[3]

V   COMMON CUSTOMS TARIFF (arts. 18–25)[4]

The formation of a customs union, as distinct from a free trade area, requires the formation of a common tariff. Exceeding the obligations under GATT (art. I, XXIV (5)(a)) which obliges a customs union to reduce its tariffs to a level equal to the average of previously existing tariffs, the common customs tariff was to be established at a level below that of the general incidence of tariffs (art. 18). In principle the common tariff was to be calculated on the basis of the arithmetical mean of the tariffs of the member states existing on 1 January 1957 (arts. 19(1), 21).[5] Detailed agreements are annexed (Annexes A–G) which deal respectively with the basis of calculation for certain French tariffs (List A), the maximum customs duties to be imposed on certain goods (Lists B–E), agreed customs tariffs (List F) and with items for which the tariffs were to be agreed upon later (List G) (arts. 19(2), (3), (4), 20, 23(1) (d)).[6] This process was chosen as an interim solution since the elaboration of an entirely

---

1   *Costa* v. *ENEL* (1964), 10 Rec. 1141; [1964] C.M.L.R. 425, (above, p. 59, n. 5).

2   See the explicit reference to member states in arts. 30, 31, 32, 33, 34, 35, 36 (last line), 37.

3   OJ, 1964, 564, *Contingents tarifaires à droit réduit ou nul* (see below, p. 62, n. 4, and p. 64, n. 3). See *e.g.* the Reply of the Commission dated 31 May 1967, OJ, 1967, 2187; *Mégret*, Vol. I, 179–184.

4   Mennens (1967) 1 J. World Trade L. 73.

5   For the method of accelerating the adjustment of the effective duties see *EEC Commission* v. *Italian Government* (1962), 8 Rec. 1; [1962] C.M.L.R. 187.

6   The list of articles was dealt with by an Agreement of 2 March 1960, OJ, 1960, 1825 and by later agreements, except for petroleum products, tobacco and newsprint. See OJ, 1960, 1973. The measures envisaged in art. 20 of the EEC Treaty were not called in aid. But see Commission, 10 April 1961, OJ, 1961, 742–747; see also decisions of 8 May 1964, OJ, 1964, 1209 and of 11 June 1964, OJ, 1964, 1488 (petroleum products, tobacco, newsprint). And see *EEC Commission* v. *Italy* (1970), 16 Rec. 47 (see above, p. 52, n. 1).

new tariff based on a uniform nomenclature presented many difficulties. Instead, the Brussels Convention of 15 December 1950, in force since 28 July 1953,[1] establishing a Customs Co-operation Council, as amended on 1 July 1955, was adopted as a basis of calculation and incorporated into the law of member states.[2] The Treaty itself (art. 27) requires the member states to *approximate*[3] their customs legislation and regulations during the first stage.[4] Although the elaboration of the common tariff lay thus with the member states acting together and not with the organs of the EEC, the possibility of technical difficulties was to be met by the following

> *Measures:* Council—Directives within the first two years (art. 21(1));
> Council—upon recommendation of Commission at the end of the first stage—decides as to adjustments of internal law (art. 21(2)).[5]

In so far as it was necessary to determine to what extent customs duties are to be regarded as fiscal duties (art. 17(2)) for the purpose of including or excluding them in ascertaining the arithmetical mean (art. 19(1)), the Commission was to state within the first two years the relative proportion of the duties to be included, because they were of a protectionist rather than of a fiscal nature (art. 22(1)). The Commission did so on 20 July 1960.[6] In so far as they are of a fiscal nature the Treaty requires their abrogation (arts. 17(1), 22(1)), subject to the rights to replace them by an internal tax (arts. 17(3), 95).

The gradual introduction of a common tariff was regulated in detail (art. 23), beginning in certain cases (art. 23(1)) on 1 January 1962. The common tariff was to come into full operation at the end of the transitory period, *i.e.* on 31 December 1969 (art. 23(3)), but the member states used

---

1　UNTS 157, 131 (No. 2052) ratified by the United Kingdom on 23 September 1952. See also the Convention on the Valuation of Goods for Customs Purposes of 15 December 1950, UNTS 171, 306 ratified by the United Kingdom on 27 September 1952. Cp. Council Reg. 1445/72. OJ, 1972, L 161/1 for the nomenclature of goods for the purpose of foreign trade statistics (NIMEXE), modified OJ, 1972, L 305/1/89.

2　Germany (1 January 1958), France (1 January 1957), Italy (1 January 1959), Benelux (1 March 1960); United Kingdom TS 29/1960, Cmnd. 1070 am. TS 83/1965, Cmnd. 2786, and see TS 49/1965 Cmnd. 2681; Council Decision 71/227, OJ, 1971, L 137/10; 72/1, OJ, 1972, L 1/383; General Report 5 (1972) 77—below, n. 3.

3　Art. 100; EEC Commission Report, IV (1961), 29; V (1962) 33; VI (1963) 29; VII (1964) 25; VIII (1965) 31; IX (1966) 41; X (1967) 62; 1 (1968) 32; 2 (1968) 22; 3 (1969) 44; 4 (1971) 2; 5 (1972) 76.

4　The following types appeared, though not uniformly, in the Community: seasonal duties, mixed duties (where the assessment is based on the value of the goods coupled with maximum and minimum dues), optional duties (where the importer can choose, *e.g.* between an assessment based on weight or value, in Benelux and France) and preferential duties up to a certain quantity (*contingents tarifaires à droit réduit ou nul*), see art. 25(2).

5　Recommendations have been made concerning the tariff treatment of goods re-imported after temporary processing or repair; see OJ, 1962, 79, 1545, 2767.

6　OJ, 1960, 1873.

their liberty to adjust their tariffs earlier (art. 24)[1] and agreed on 11 May 1966[2] to bring it into full effect on 1 July 1968.[3] In relation to certain countries (associated states and Israel) the common tariff was put into operation immediately, at least for agricultural products.[4] It was first published by a Council regulation of 28 June 1968.[5] However, a great many obstacles remain to be overcome and the need for the harmonisation of customs legislation is foremost. The member states gave a lead by concluding a Convention on Customs Co-operation on 7 September 1967 in Rome.[6] The application of a uniform nomenclature was required,[7] the classification of certain goods had to be revised[8] and the area of the customs tariff had to be defined.[9] The same was necessary for the notion of origin of goods,[10] the certificate of origin,[11] the valuation for customs purposes[12] and goods in transit.[13] The process of harmonisation of laws, regulations and administrative practices in the field of customs was initiated by a series of directives.[14] The administrative co-operation is assured by a long series

---

1 Accelerated by Agreements of the Governments of 13 February 1960, OJ, 1960, 1217, followed by Council Decision of 12 May 1960, OJ, 1960, 1537; subsequent acceleration by the Second Resolution of 15 May 1962, OJ, 1962, 1284 and the Third Resolution of 22 May 1963, OJ, 1963, 1561.

2 Council Decision 66/532, OJ, 1966, 2971; *Mégret*, Vol. I, p. 17*; Directive 67/364, OJ, 1967, 2158: except for cereals, for which the common tariff was to operate one year earlier. See Juriscl. Dr. Int., Fasc. 164 D, No. 57.

3 The Commission was given powers to postpone the process of adaptation in individual cases, if a member encountered special difficulties (art. 26).

4 Resolution of Governments, 26 February 1964, OJ, 1964, 1472 (Associated States); Resolution of Government, 29 May 1964, OJ, 1964, 1525 (Israel).

5 950/68, OJ, 1968, L 172; *Mégret*, Vol. I, p. 19* republished in amended form by Council Reg. 1/73, OJ, 1973, L 1. For previous republication see Council Reg. 2451/69 of 8 December 1969, OJ, 1969, L 31; 1/72, OJ, 1972, L 1. For its interpretation see *Interfood* v. *Hauptzollamt Hamburg-Ericus*, (1972), 18 Rec. 231, at pp. 243(5)–244(6).

6 1967 EEC Bull. No. 11, p. 13.

7 Council Reg. 97/69, OJ, 1969, L 14; (Common Customs Tariff Nomenclature Committee); see General Report on the Activities of the Communities, 4 (1971) 2, n. 3; 5 (1972) 77; Commission Reg. 679/72, OJ, 1972, L 81/1.

8 Council Reg. 955/69, OJ, 1969, L 124; Council Directive 69/184, OJ, 1969, L 159.

9 Council Reg. 1496/68, OJ, 1968, L 238; *Mégret*, Vol. I, p. 3* (in virtue of art. 235).

10 Council Reg. 802/68 of 27 June 1968, OJ, 1968, L 148/1; *Mégret*, Vol. I, p. 25*.

11 Generally: Commission Decisions, 4 December 1958, OJ, 1958, 688; 5 December 1960, OJ, 1961, 29 and see now Commission Reg. 582/69, OJ, 1969, L 79; 641/69, OJ, 1969, L 83/15; Commission Decision 19 December 1969, OJ, 1970, L 13/13; 7 December 1970, OJ, 1971, L 6/35.
    For travellers' personal luggage see Council Reg. 1544/69, OJ, 1969, L 191/1; Proposed Council Reg. 30 July 1971, OJ, 1971, C 106/16.

12 Council Reg. 803/68, OJ, 1968, L 148; *Mégret*, Vol. I, p. 30*; for their declaration: Commission Reg. 375/69, OJ, 1969, L 52; for the inclusion of air freight in the value: Commission Reg. 1769/68, OJ, 1968, L 285, in virtue of arts. 111, 113, 155, 227, 235.

13 Council Reg. 542/69, OJ, 1969, L 77.

14 Council Directives 68/132, OJ, 1968, L 194, *Mégret*, Vol. I, p. 37*: customs clearance and temporary warehousing; 69/73, OJ, 1969, L 58/1, *Mégret*, Vol. I, p. 41*: processing traffic; 69/74, OJ, 1969, L 58, *Mégret*, Vol. I, p. 47*: bonded stores; 69/75, OJ, 1969, L 58, *Mégret*, Vol. I, p. 54*: deferment of payment of customs duties (all made in virtue of art. 100) and 69/73 (also under art. 155).

of Council and Commission regulations and decision.[1] Within certain limits the common tariff can be and has been modified on numerous occasions (art. 28).[2]

Where goods enumerated in Lists B, C and D are involved, which are normally imported from third countries by one of the member states and which cannot be supplied by the other member states, that member state suffering from the introduction of the common tariff (which, in its new tariff position, imposes a higher tariff or a tariff where none existed before) can be allowed tariff quotas at a reduced rate or duty-free (art. 25(1)).[3]

---

1   *Generally*: certificates inside the Community, Commission Decision 19 December 1969, OJ, 1970, L 13/13; certificates inside the Community in respect of goods containing materials from third countries, not yet subjected to tax, Commission Decision of 28 June 1968, OJ, 1968, L 167/10.

   Co-operation—inter-community levies; Commission Decision, 17 July 1962, OJ, 1962, 2140; Commission Decision 67/642 of 17 October 1967, OJ, 1967, No. 258/15.

   Inter-community levies—fisheries; Commission Decision 64/503 of 30 July 1964, OJ, 1964, 2293, modified by Decision 64/718 of 4 December 1964, OJ, 1964, 3622;

   Conditions for issuing certificates for packed goods: Commission Decision 65/8 of 8 January 1965, OJ, 1965, 49, extended to regime of egg albumen (Council Reg. 48/67 of 7 March 1967, OJ, 1967, 646) by Commission Decision of 28 April 1967, OJ, 1967, 1778;

   Extended to regime of processed goods (Council Reg. 160/66 of 27 October 1966, OJ, 1966, 3361) by Commission Decision 67/336 of 19 May 1967, OJ, 1967, 1985;

   Extended to new regimes of cereals, pork meat, eggs, poultry meat, by Commission Decision 67/434 of 30 June 1967, OJ, 1967, No. 150/9;

   Extended to the regime of certain types of grain (Council Reg. 136/66, OJ, 1966, 3025) by Commission Decision 67/504 of 3 July 1967, OJ, 1967, No. 180/12;

   Extended to the regime of rice, Commission Decision 67/615 of 20 September 1967, OJ, 1967, No. 248/3;

   Extended to the regimes of sugar, milk and milk products, beef, by Commission Decision 68/330 of 13 August 1968, OJ, 1968, L 206/19. For beef see also Commission Decision 64/200 of 28 October 1964, OJ, 1964, 2763;

   Certificate for sugar rendered non-commercial: Council Reg. 1076/69 of 10 June 1969, OJ, 1969, L. 139/11;

   As modified by Commission Decision 70/41 of 19 December 1969, OJ, 1970, L 13/13.

   Distortion of Trade

   Cereals: Commission Reg. 86 of 25 July 1962, OJ, 1962, 1894.

   Rice: Commission Reg. 83/64 of 6 July 1964, OJ, 1964, 1793.

   Frozen Beef: Commission Reg. 207/66 of 12 December 1966, OJ, 1966, 3878, amended by Commission Reg. 40/67 of 28 February 1967, OJ, 1967, 570; see also Commission Reg. 160/64 of 29 October 1964, OJ, 1964, 2737.

   Milk and Milk Products: Commission Reg. 12/65 of 2 February 1965, OJ, 1965, 252.

   Powdered Milk for Animal Consumption: Council Reg. 190/66 of 24 November 1966, OJ, 1966, 3715.

   For co-ooeration with associated countries see, as regards Greece: the Convention OJ, 1963, 355 and the Council Decision 63/115 of 25 September 1962, OJ, 1963, 354.

2   See *e.g.*, OJ, 1960, 1873; 1961, 992, 1038, 1039, 1040; 1962, 47, 49, 50, 2001, 2885; 1963, 1258, 2019, 2288, 3077, 3079, 3089; 1964, 1033, 1208, 1209, 1211, 1485, 1525, Council Reg. 2093/68, OJ, 1968, L 308/1; Reg. 2094/68, OJ, 1968, L 308/7; Reg. 2095/68, L 308/11; Reg. 1159/69, OJ, 1969, L 157/8.

3   For *contingents tarifaires à droit réduit ou nul* see above, p. 61, n. 3, and p. 62, n. 4. The grant of quotas is subject to art. 39: *Germany* v. *EEC Commission* (1963), 9 Rec. 269; [1963] C.M.L.R. 369. For quotas in trade with agricultural products see Reg. 3/63, OJ, 1963, 153, amended by Reg. 107/64, OJ, 1964, 2137; Reg. 173/65, OJ, 1965, 3270; Reg. 1026/67, OJ, 1967, L 313/1. See now Council Reg. 1023/70, OJ, 1970, L 124/1, below, p. 300.

The same measures can be applied for goods in Lists E and G, if a change of sources of supply or a shortage of supplies within the Community has harmful effects upon the processing industries of the member states concerned (art. 25(2)).

> *Measures:* Council decision upon report of the
> Commission for goods in Lists B, C and D
> (art. 25(1)).
> Commission decision for goods in Lists E and G
> (art. 25(2)).[1]

Similarly, a member state may be empowered to reduce or waive its customs duties for certain agricultural products set out in Annex II or may be allotted quotas of the kind mentioned above.

> *Measure:* Commission, decision (art. 25(3)).[2]

Further, such quotas have been granted under art. 111 during its operation within the transitional period, in order to comply with Treaty obligations and, once, by virtue of a Council regulation.[3]

It would seem that only a member state and not an individual can challenge a Commission or Council decision refusing an exception.[4]

---

1   For List G see Agreement of 2 March 1960, OJ, 1960, 1825; as regards the remainder (oil etc.) see Council Decision of 8 May 1964, OJ, 1964, 1209.

2   For an enumeration of such quotas granted to member states see Commission Reply, 31 May 1967, OJ, 1967, 2187. *Mégret*, Vol. I, p. 179; for the practice see *Germany* v. *EEC Commission*, (1963), 9 Rec. 129; [1963] C.M.L.R. 347, and *Germany* v. *EEC Commission*, above, p. 64, n. 3.

3   Reg. 14/64, art. 4, OJ, 1964, 562; Commission Reply 31 May 1967, OJ, 1967, 2187; *Mégret*, Vol. I, p. 179.

4   *Plaumann* v. *EEC Commission* (1963), 9 Rec. 197; [1964] C.M.L.R. 29.

4

Agriculture

(Articles 38–47)[1]

I GENERAL

Agriculture enjoys a special position in most countries, and the countries of the member states form no exception. No country has been able or willing to expose its agriculture to the free play of economic forces and all have in some manner or another, afforded special protection to this industry and have devised measures to safeguard national producers against the effects of cheaper imports. These measures have not been confined to the manipulation of customs duties but have included devices such as minimum price fixing, at which point imports are cut off, or in the case of exporting countries by limiting exports to restore the balance. Quantitative restrictions have also been employed.

The English system of support or deficiency payments to agricultural producers avoids the need, in principle at least, to use methods which exclude imports or which raise the price of agricultural imports. It combines thus cheap imports with a sufficient return to agricultural producers at home, while the technique of graduated deficiency payments prevents the accumulation of subsidised local surpluses which must be siphoned off in order to maintain the level of prices.

The drafters of the EEC Treaty were faced with the question whether

---

1 Mégret in Juriscl. Dr. Int., Fasc. 164, I; Olmi in Ganshof van der Meersch, *La Droit des Communautés Européennes* (1969), pp. 677–728; Mégret, Louis Vignes and Walbroeck, *Le droit de la Communauté Economique Européenne*, (1970), Vol. II. Agriculture cited: *Mégret*, Vol. II. Olmi, (1963) 1 C.M.L.Rev. 118; 1963 Rev. M.C. 420; (1967–68) 5 C.M.L.Rev. 359; Campbell, Vol. I, s. 2.1–2.53; Mayoux, 1962 Rev. M.C. 7; Jänicke, (1963) 23 Z.a.ö.R.V. 485; Heller, (1963) 5 Harv. Int. L. Cl. G. 45; Teitgen, 1964 Droit social 705; Allen Harris, (1965) 1 (Pt. ii) Texas Int. Law Forum 89; Riesenfeld, (1965) Ill. Law Forum 658; Ehlermann, 1966 Rev. M.C. 179, 574; Dam, (1967) 67 Col. L.R. 1; Melchior, 1967 Cah. Dr. Eur. 247; 1970 Cah. Dr. Eur. 127; Gueben and Keller-Noêllet, 1969 Rev. Trim. Dr. Eur. 293; Ventura, *Principes de Droit Agraire Communautaire* (1967); Götz, 1968 N.J.W. 1545; Teucei, (1968) 8 Riv. Dir. Eur. 221; Comment, (1968) 1 Cornell Int. L.J. 36; Mégret, 1971 Rev. Trim. Dr. Eur. 457. For the practice of the Community Court see Brändel, 1972 B.B.A.W.D. 545.

As regards the relationship with the United Kingdom see Norton, (1967) 6 Texas Int. Law Forum 221; *The Common Agricultural Policy of the E.E.C.*, Cmnd. 3274, (1967). Maes in *Bathurst et al, "Legal Problems of an Enlarged Community"*, (1972), p. 295

On management committees see Bertram, (1967–68) 5 C.M.L.Rev. 246; Schindler, (1971) 8 C.M.L.Rev. 184. And see as to the legitimacy of their function in co-operation with the Commission, *Einfuhr- und Vorratsstelle Getreide* v. *Köster*, (1970), 16 Rec. 1161, at pp. 1173(8), 1181; [1972] C.M.L.R. 255.

to include agriculture in the general scheme or to provide a special solution. They preferred the former (art. 38(1)),[1] subject to a number of far-reaching exceptions and safeguards which have taken the place of the rule itself (art. 38(2)).[2]

The Common Market includes agriculture and the trade with agricultural products (art. 38(1)). In principle these include all products of the soil, of animal husbandry and fisheries, and their first stage of preparation. They do not include products of forestry. Special regimes (arts. 39–46) are provided for the goods enumerated in Annex II of the Treaty (art. 32(2), (3)) which include most important agricultural products, but also fats other than animal fats, tinned meat and vegetables. Further items could be added within the first two years.

Measure: Council upon the proposal of the Commission—
Decision (art. 38(3)).[3]

The inclusion of agriculture in the Common Market, subject to special considerations for the protection of producers, conflicts with the general purpose of a Common Market, which is the free circulation of goods in competition with those produced in the other territories of the Common Market. If special protection is accepted for the producers in the individual territories, this protection must not be stultified by other states outside the Common Market or, during the transitional period, within the Common Market. It follows that the member states must establish a common agricultural policy (arts. 38(4), 39, 40(1)),[4] and a common organisation to carry it out (art. 40(2)–(4)). It must operate without discrimination (art. 40 (3), 2nd para.) although the general rules of competition established by the Treaty itself are only applicable subject to suitable modifications (art. 42, 1st para., supplemented by Council Reg. 26, of 4 April 1962)[5] and although the free exchange of goods is restricted by a new marketing organisation. In view of the foregoing the organisation of the market in agricultural products cannot be limited in its activity to the agricultural market inside the Community. Together with the creation of a common tariff and the abolition of quantitative restrictions goes the need to control imports from and exports to third states

---

1 For the relationship between art. 12 (standstill on customs duties) and the provisions on agriculture (38–47) see *EEC Commission* v. *Luxemburg and Belgium* (1964), 10 Rec. 1217; [1965] C.M.L.R. 58; for quotas see above, p. 64, n. 2; for quantitative restrictions see above, p. 55.

2 *Neumann* v. *Hauptzollamt Hof/Saale* (1967), 13 Rec. 571, at p. 588; [1964] C.M.L.R. 178; Reg. 22/62.

3 Reg. 7a of 18 December 1960, OJ, 1961, 71: coloured sugar, processed alcohol, vinegar.

4 For its execution see *Neumann* v. *Hauptzollamt Hof/Saale* (above, n. 2), at p. 589.

5 OJ, 1962, 993 amended by Reg. 49, OJ, 1962, 1571, but see Reg. 67/67. The reasons for the suspension of the application of the rules of competition including state aids and dumping pending the establishment of a common policy under a common organisation are discussed by Olmi in Ganshof van der Meersch, *Droit des Communautés Européennes*, pp. 692–694, Nos. 1783, 1784. And see below, p. 229.

(art. 40(3), 1st para., end).[1] In so far as the special character of the Common Market in agricultural products entails the modification of, or the derogation from, some of the guiding principles of the Treaty, the special provisions, being exceptions, must be interpreted restrictively.[2] In contrast to the attitude taken elsewhere in the Treaty, the transitional period was not accompanied by a complete standstill (see art. 44),[3] and the regime of quantitative restrictions was not curtailed as such where local marketing organisations existed, but was to be converted into one of long-term contracts, subject to non-discrimination (art. 45).

II   COMMON POLICY

The common policy must be determined by economic considerations common to the member states (arts. 38(4), 40(1), 43(1)), even if its formulation is entrusted to the Commission (art. 43(1)) and is put into practice by the Council (art. 43(2)). Such a formulation much exceeds that of co-ordinating the domestic legislation of the member states. In fact, three possible courses were open to the Commission and to the Council and were recognised as such by the Treaty itself (art. 40(2)(a)–(c)), namely either a free market subject to common rules of competition or the co-ordination of national marketing organisations or the creation of European market organisations. In the meantime, during the period of transition, the member states were allowed to exercise certain independent powers of market control (arts. 44, 45(1), 46) concerning the maintenance of minimum prices at their frontiers[4] in addition to the power, discussed above, to substitute long term contracts for quotas where a national marketing scheme existed[5] and to maintain compensatory taxes in certain circumstances.[6] In fact, these exceptional powers granted to member states during the transitional period were little used since the Community adopted as early as 1962[7] as its common policy the third alternative set out

---

1   Common machinery to stabilise imports and exports. See also the EEC Treaty, Annex I, List F, n. 2 to tariff position 07.01 (vegetables).

2   See *EEC Commission* v. *Luxemburg and Belgium* (1962), 8 Rec. 813, at p. 827; [1963] C.M.L.R. 199; (1964), 10 Rec. 1221, at p. 1235; [1965] C.M.L.R. 58.

3   Arts. 12, 31 and 32(1) apply however. See *EEC Commission* v. *Luxemburg and Belgium* (1964), 10 Rec. 1221; [1964] C.M.L.R. 58.

4   Council Decision 4 April 1962, arts. 3, 4 and 6, OJ, 1962, 995, modified by Reg. 49 of 29 June 1962, OJ, 1962, 1571 and prolonged successively until 31 December 1973 by a Decision of 19 December 1972 made by virtue of art. 44(3), 1st para., which fixes the criteria for the administration of minimum prices according to the regime defined in art. 44(1), dispensing with any prior authorisation by the Commission but requiring notice (44(4)). See now OJ, 1972, L 291/152.

5   For the definition of the term "national marketing organisation" (art. 40(2)(c), 45(1)) see Commission, OJ, 1960, 1531 criticised by Olmi (above, p. 66, n. 1) in Ganshof van der Meersch, *Droit des Communautés Européennes*, p. 690, No. 1782.

6   See *e.g.* Council Decision 4 April 1962, OJ, 1962, 999, terminated by Reg. 160/66 of 27 October 1966, OJ, 1966, 3361; cp. GATT art. VI 2 ff.

7   14 January 1962: Regs. 19–23: grain, pork, meat, eggs, poultry meat, fruit and vegetables, wine; Regs. 13/64, 14/64, 16/64: rice, milk, dairy products; Regs. 136/66, 159/66: fats and oil, processed fruit.

in art. 40(2) and introduced common market organisations to be developed as such during the transitional period, having regard to the considerable advantages offered by the means and the procedure available for this purpose (arts. 40(1), 39(2)(b)). As a result the regime of minimum prices and long term contracts came in principle to a premature end, and it is unnecessary to examine its characteristics and its limitations.[1]

III   FORMULATION OF THE COMMON POLICY

The development leading up to the creation of a European marketing organisation may be summed up thus: when the Commission, acting in accordance with the procedure laid down by art. 43(1), called a conference of the member states,[2] the member states set out their position in a resolution.[3] Thereupon the Commission, acting in virtue of art. 43(2) produced proposals for a common agricultural policy and common organisations, known as the *Mansholt* plan (December 1959), a revised version of which appeared in June 1960, after the Economic and Social Committee had been consulted (art. 43(2)).[4] Finally, the Council was called upon to put these proposals into practice by regulations, directives and decisions (art. 43(3)) and was able to embark upon the programme after an understanding was reached on 14 January 1962. These measures were inspired by the ensuing considerations expressed in the Treaty.

The common agricultural policy must aim at increasing production through technical developments and rationalisation, raising the standards of living of the agricultural community by raising the individual earnings of persons engaged in agriculture; establishing markets; guaranteeing supplies and ensuring reasonable prices for the consumers (art. 39(1)).[5] At the same time certain social aspects are to be taken into account (art. 39(2)); subsidies are not excluded (art. 42(a), (b)); education and research are also to be encouraged (art. 41(a)).[6]

In order to facilitate the co-ordination of agriculture within the member states, the Council could select between any one of the three systems set out in the Treaty (art. 40(2)). It could either apply an unregulated system of free competition as elsewhere in the Treaty dealing with the exchange of goods (art. 40(2)(a)) or co-ordinate the national markets

---

1   Such as that minimum prices must be based on objective criteria (art. 44(3), 1st para.) (see above, p. 68, n. 4), the prohibition of discrimination (art. 44(1)) and the incompatibility of quantitative restrictions with minimum prices (art. 44(1)); the criteria underlying art. 45, *i.e.* guaranteed market *and* price, and the question whether art. 45 applies to an exporting country. See Olmi, *loc. cit.*, p. 688, No. 1779.

2   Stressa, 3–11 July 1958. See *Recueil des documents de la Conférence Agricole des Etats Membres de la C.E.E.* (1959).

3   OJ, 1958, 281.

4   Doc. VI Com. (60) 105; it envisaged a development in two stages, supplemented by the creation of a European Agricultural Fund to make up deficiency payments and to assist in measures of rationalisation.

5   See also arts. 40, 41, 42, 43(2); for the relation between art. 39 and arts. 25, 29, see *Germany v. EEC Commission* (1963), 9 Rec. 269; [1963] C.M.L.R. 369.

6   See Council Decision of 4 December 1962, OJ, 1962, 2892.

organisations (art. 40(2)(b))[1] or create a European market organisation.[2] In fact the Commission chose different forms for different areas of production, but also adopted general rules for common purposes, such as finance[3] and created organisations in which national and common organisations are combined. Even where full freedom of production and marketing is adopted, as it is for the marketing in fruit and vegetables, this freedom is no longer complete since the protection, if required, against imports from third countries is necessarily entrusted henceforth to Community organs.

Both as regards the various branches of agriculture and as regards the methods of market control the programme was realised in stages. Individual types of agricultural products were brought into the common organisation in successive waves. The most important were in 1962 (grain, pork meat, eggs, poultry meat, fruit and vegetables and wine), 1963 (rice, milk and dairy products, beef and veal), 1966 (fats and oils, sugar). In 1964 it proved possible to vary the technique of marketing after an agreement had been reached on a common fixing of prices within the Community as a whole, while until then local pricing conflicted with a controlled market in agricultural products and required complicated intra-state measures of adjustment. After 1964 the older regulations dealing with grain, pork meat, eggs, poultry meat, fruit and vegetables and wine, rice, milk and dairy products, beef and veal had to be revised, and new areas of common marketing organisations were opened up (tobacco, flax and hemp, fisheries products, plants and horticultural products, hops, seed corn and certain goods enumerated in Annex II of the Treaty).[4]

---

1   National marketing organisations existed in the Community for grain, sugar and milk products; for wine in France; for rice in Italy.

2   See also art. 54(4).

3   Reg. 25 of 25 April 1962, OJ, 1962, 991; Council Regs. 17/64 of 5 February 1964, OJ, 1964, 586; 130/66 of 26 July 1966, OJ, 1966, 2965; 741/67 of 24 October 1967, OJ, 1967, No. 258/3; 729/70, OJ, 1970, L 94/19; 2/71, OJ, 1971 L 3/1.

4   The various areas of production covered by the Common Agricultural Policy are contained in the following Council regulations:

   (i) *Cereals:* Reg. 19 of 4 April 1962, OJ, 1062, 933 *replaced* by Reg. 120/67, OJ, 1967, 2269, based on the Council Resolution of 15 December 1964; amended by Regs. 359/67 of 25 July 1967, art. 32, OJ, 1967, No. 741/1 (Annex A), 643/68, OJ, 1968, L 122 (art. 23); 830/68, OJ, 1968, L 151 (art. 1 and Annex A), 969/68, OJ, 1968, L 166 (art. 16); 289/69, OJ, 1969, L 41 (art. 22 A); 831/69, OJ, 1969, L 107 (arts. 9, 12, 22A, 24); 1393/69, OJ, 1969, L 179 (art. 32(3)); 1398/69, OJ, 1969, L 179; 2463/69, OJ, 1969, L 312 (art. 12(1)); 1253/70, OJ, 1970, L 143/1 (art. 12(1)); 2434/70, OJ, 1970, L 262 (art. 15(2)); 2727/71, OJ, 1971, L 282/8; 796/72, OJ, 1972, L 94/7 (arts. 2(1), 4, 23).

   For target, basic intervention, threshold and guaranteed prices, refunds, levies, sale by intervention agencies, denaturation, special intervention measures, compensation, import and export certificates, see the regulations enumerated in *Mégret*, Vol. II, pp. 230–234 and 42*–79* covering the period up to 26 June 1969. For detailed comment see *Mégret*, Vol. II, pp. 87–97.

   (ii) *Rice:* Reg. 16/64 of 5 February 1964, OJ, 1964, 574, *replaced* by Reg. 359/67 of 25 July 1967, OJ, 1967, No. 174/1, amended by Reg. 830/68, OJ, 1968, L 151 (art. 1, para 1(c)), 1398/69, OJ, 1969, L 179; 2463/69, OJ, 1969, L 312 (art. 10(1)); 1253/70, OJ, 1970, L 143/1 (art. 10); 1553/71, OJ, 1971, L 164/5; (art. 17(5)); 2726/71, OJ, 1971, L 282/6.

   For target, intervention prices, quality standards, levies, refunds, derived intervention,

The differing features, in substance or in form, of the various types of marketing practice chosen could only be demonstrated by a tabular survey. For the most important products the Council adopted the technique of a common organisation of the Community, which operates in conjunction with national marketing organisations and controls both the

sale by intervention agencies, import and export certificates, special intervention measures, see the regulations enumerated in *Mégret*, Vol. II, pp. 235–237, and pp. 80*–100* covering the period up to 17 April 1969. For detailed comment see *Mégret*, Vol. II, pp. 97–105.

(*iii*) *Milk and Dairy Products:* Reg. 13/64 of 27 February 1964, OJ, 1964, 549 *replaced* by Reg. 804/68 of 27 June 1968, OJ, 1968, L 1483, amended by Reg. 876/68, OJ, 1968, L 155/1, 1380/69, OJ, 1969, L 178 (art. 35); 1398/69, OJ, 1969, L 179; 2463/69, OJ, 1969, L 312 (art. 13(2)); 2622/69, OJ, 1969, L 328 (arts. 14, 15, 22); 1253/70, OJ, 1970, L 143/1; 1261/71, OJ, 1971, L 132/1 (art. 22a); 1410/71, OJ, 1971, L 148/3 (arts. 14, 15); 1411/71, OJ, 1971, L 148/4; 2180/71, OJ, 1971, L 231/1; 2732/71, OJ, 1971, L 282/21; 2864/71, OJ, 1971, L 288/2; 646/72, OJ, 1972, L 79/1; 650/72, OJ, 1972, L 79/6.

For target, intervention and threshold prices, levies, storage, qualitative restrictions, refunds, aids, import certificates and export sales, sale of butter by intervention agencies, see the regulations enumerated in *Mégret*, Vol. II, pp. 241–246 and pp. 132*–164* for the period up to 28 June 1969. For detailed comment see *Mégret*, Vol. II, 119–131.

(*iv*) *Sugar:* Reg. 1009/67, OJ, 1967, No. 308/1 *replacing* Reg. 44/67, OJ, 1967, 597, amended by Reg. 2100/68, OJ, 1968, L 309 (arts. 8(1), 27, 32(2), Annex); 1393/69, OJ, 1969, L 179 (arts. 8(1), 10(1), 25(1) (3), Annex); 2463/69, OJ, 1969, L 312 (art. 11(2)); 2485/69, OJ, 1969, L 314 (arts. 1(1), 5, 9(3)(4), 11, 14(1), 27(4)–(7), 28, 30(2)); 853/70, OJ, 1970, L 103 (art. 14(1)); 1253/70, OJ, 1970, L 142 (arts. 11(1), 14(1), 15(5)(6)); 1060/71, OJ, 1971, L 115/16 (arts. 26(2), 34(2)); 2863/71, OJ, 1971, L 288/1.

For target, intervention, derived intervention, threshold and guaranteed minimum prices, aids, levies and refunds, basic quotas, standard contracts, denaturation, compensation, import and export certificates, see the regulations enumerated in *Mégret*, Vol. II, 237–240 and 100*–131* covering the period up to 24 July 1969. For detailed comment see *Mégret*, Vol. II, pp. 105–119.

(*v*) *Pork Meat:* Reg. 20, OJ, 1962, 945 *replaced* by Reg. 121/67, OJ, 1967, 2283, amended by Reg. 830/68, OJ, 1968, L 151 (art. 1(1)(c)); 1398/69, OJ, 1969, L 179; 2463/69, OJ, 1969, L 312 (art. 14); 1253/70, OJ, 1970, L 143/1 (art. 14); 771/71, OJ, 1971, L 85/30 (art. 4(2)); 1261/71, OJ, 1971, L 132/1 (art. 20); 2727/71, OJ, 1971, L 282/8; 224/72, OJ, 1972, L 28/1.

For target, intervention and sluice gate prices, levies, the definition of "pilot and derived products", refunds, classification, safeguard measures and storage aids see the regulations enumerated by *Mégret*, Vol. II, pp. 246–248 and 165*, 175*, 191**–212*, 220*–221* covering the period up to 20 May 1969. For detailed comment see *Mégret*, Vol. II, pp. 131–142.

(*vi*) *Eggs:* Reg. 21, OJ, 1962, 953, *replaced* by Reg. 122/67, OJ, 1967, 2293, amended by Reg. 830/68, OJ, 1968, L 151 (art. 1(1)) 1261/71, OJ, 1971, L 132/1 (art. 13 *bis*).

For sluice gate prices, levies, refunds and standardisation, see *Mégret*, Vol. II, pp. 246–248 and 175*–182*, 212*–219* covering the period up to 20 May 1969. For detailed comment see *Mégret*, Vol. II, pp. 131–142.

(*vii*) *Albumen:* Reg. 170/67, OJ, 1967, 2596, *replacing* Reg. 48/67, OJ, 1967, 646.

(*viii*) *Poultry Meat:* Reg. 22, OJ, 1962, 959 *replaced* by Council Reg. 123/67, OJ, 1967, 2301.

For sluice gate prices, levies and refunds see *Mégret*, Vol. II, pp. 246–248 and 183*–190* covering the period up to 20 May 1969. For detailed comment see *Mégret*, Vol. II, pp. 131–142.

(*ix*) *Fats and Oil:* Reg. 136/66, OJ, 1966, 3025, amended by Reg. 2146/68, OJ, 1968, L 314 (arts. 4, 16, 18, 22(1), 28, 35, 42A); Reg. 1253/70, OJ, 1970, L 143 (art. 17(1)), 2554/70, OJ, 1970, L 275/5; 2730/71, OJ, 1971, L 282/18; 1547/72, OJ, 1972, L 165/1.

For intervention and world prices, levies, intervention centres, classification, import and

maintenance of a stable price level within the member states and any disturbances of this level by permanent or fluctuating cheap imports from abroad.

The primary bulk products (grain, rice, dairy products and sugar) are regulated by a comprehensive scheme, some of the characteristics of

---

export certificates, customs duties, aids, refunds, purchase by intervention agencies, denaturation, and storage contracts see *Mégret*, Vol. II, pp. 249–253 and 222*–263* for the period up to 24 June 1969. For detailed comment see *Mégret*, Vol. II, pp. 142–154.

(x) *Beef and Veal*: Reg. 14/64, OJ, 1964, 562, *replaced* by Reg. 805/68, OJ, 1968, L 148, amended by Reg. 1398/69, OJ, 1969, No. 179; Reg. 2463/69, OJ, 1969, L 312 (art. 15(1)); Reg. 1253/70, OJ, 1970, L 143; 1261/71, OJ, 1971, L 132/1 (art. 23); 2838/71, OJ, 1971, L 286/1 art. 12(5) (12 *bis*); 1109/72, OJ, 1972, L 126/1 (art. 27).

For guide price, intervention measures, levies, refunds, storage aids and import certificates, see *Mégret*, Vol. II, pp. 253–255 and 264*–285* for the period up to 24 June 1969. For detailed comment see *Mégret*, Vol. II, pp. 155–163.

(xi) *Fruit and Vegetables*: Reg. 23, OJ, 1962, 965 (quality only) amended by Reg. 46/64, OJ, 1964, 1141; 65/65, OJ, 1965, 1458; 158/66, OJ, 1966, 3282; 159/66, OJ, 1966, 3286 (organisation); 1229/69, OJ, 1969, L 159; 2513/69, OJ, 1969, L 318/6; 2423/70, OJ, 1970, L 261, now *replaced* by Council Reg. 1035/72, OJ, 1972, L 118/1. And see *International Fruit Co.* v. *Produktschap voor Groenten* (1971), 17 Rec. 1107, at p. 1117(15).

See *Mégret*, Vol. II, pp. 255–258 and 286*–306* for the period up to 26 June 1969. For detailed comment see *Mégret*, Vol. II, pp. 164–168.

(xii) *Fruit Products*: Reg. 865/68, OJ, 1968, L 153/8, amended by 1604/68, OJ, 1968, L 253; 455/69, OJ, 1969, L 64; Reg. 1398/69, OJ, 1969, L 179; 1837/69, OJ, 1969, L 236 (arts. 3, 9); 1906/69, OJ, 1969, L 274; 2463/69, OJ, 1969, L 312 (art. 6(1)); 1253/70, OJ, 1970, L 143; 2275/70, OJ, 1970, L 246/4; 1425/71, OJ, 1971, L 151/1.

See *Mégret*, Vol. II, pp. 258–259 and 307*–314*, 322*–333* for the period up to 11 March 1969. For detailed comments see *Mégret*, Vol. II, pp. 175–181. For common safeguard measures see Regs. 1427/71; 1428/71, OJ, 1971, L 151/5/7; *Schroeder* v. *German Federal Republic* (1973), *Times*, 19 February.

(xiii) *Cereal and Rice Products*: Reg. 1052/68, OJ, 1968, L 179/8 *replacing* Reg. 360/67, OJ, 1967, No. 174/13, and modified by Reg. 302/69, OJ, 1969, L 43; Reg. 968/68, OJ, 1968, L 166 (animal food), *replacing* Reg. 194/67, OJ, 1967, 2813.

See *Mégret*, Vol. II, pp. 258–259 and 315*–331* for the period up to 18 February 1969. For detailed comment see *Mégret*, Vol. II, pp. 181–184.

(xiv) *Wine*: Reg. 24, OJ, 1962, 989, amended by Reg. 92/63, OJ, 1963, 2239; Reg. 816/70, OJ, 1970, L 99, amended by Reg. 1253/70, OJ, 1970, L 143/1, Reg. 2612/70, OJ, 1970, L 281; 817/70, OJ, 1970, L 99, 2312/71, OJ, 1971, L 244/9; 2504/71, OJ, 1971, L 261/1 (arts. 3, 5), 1972, L 57/15; 1769/72, OJ, 1972, L 191/1.

For the regulations before 1969 see *Mégret*, Vol. II, pp. 259 and 337*–339*. For a more detailed but incomplete discussion see *Mégret*, Vol. II, pp. 185–186.

(xv) *Tobacco*: Reg. 727/70, OJ, 1970, L 94/1; 1574/71, OJ, 1971, L 167/1; 2279/71; OJ, 1971, L 282/17.

(xvi) *Flax and Hemp*: Reg. 1308/70, OJ, 1970, L 146; 1054/72, OJ, 1972, L 120/1.

(xvii) *Fishing Industry*: Reg. 2141/70, OJ, 1970, L 236/1; 2142/70, OJ, 1970, L. 236/5, amended OJ, 1971, L 9/7.

(xviii) *Plants*: Reg. 234/68, OJ, 1968, L55/1.

(xix) *Products in Annex II*: Reg. 827/68, OJ, 1968, L 151/16. For mutton see Vignes, 1972 Rev. M.C. 185.

(xx) *Products outside the Common Policy*: Reg. 1059/69, OJ, 1969, L 141/1, amended by Reg. 2520/69, OJ, 1969, L 317 (art. 8) *replacing* Reg. 160/66, but not Reg. 127/67, OJ, 1967, 2341 as amended by Reg. 988/69, OJ, 1969, L 130—see Reg. 1059/69 art. 16.

(xxi) *Export of Agricultural Products not falling within Annex II*: Reg. 204/69, OJ, 1969, L 29/1 (cereals, eggs, rice, sugar, milk); 1537/71, OJ, 1971, L 163/1; 2066/71, OJ, 1971, L 219/1.

which are adopted by the schemes for other products in various forms and combinations. In its comprehensive form the scheme shows two principal characteristics. Firstly, it attempts to maintain stable prices within the Community. Secondly, it seeks to control imports so as not to disturb the level of prices within the Community.

The maintenance of stable prices within the Community is achieved by the following scheme.

(i) *Target Price, Base Price*—Firstly a *target price* is chosen.[1] This is the market price (*prix indicatif*) which is established annually. For cereals and rice it is set at the point within the Community where the greatest scarcity exists (Duisburg);[2] for milk it is based on an average price intended to be assured for all the milk sold by producers during the marketing year according to the sales possibilities by the markets inside and outside the Community,[3] while that for sugar is fixed in respect of manufactured white sugar in the Community area having the greatest surplus.[4]

For agricultural products based on grain consumption (pork meat, eggs, albumen, poultry meat) different considerations apply according as the Community is a surplus or a deficiency area. No *target price* is provided for pork meat; instead a *base price* is set which is derived from the controlled price at the frontier (*sluice-gate* price and levy—see below).[5] The result is that no internal price forms the initial yardstick but intervention measures (aids, purchases—see below) can be taken exceptionally by the Management Committee and the Commission or by the Council if there is a substantial drop in prices.[6] No target price or base price exists for eggs, albumen and poultry meat. The market is free and can only enjoy external protection through *sluice-gate* prices.[7] Its characteristic is that it is set on a two-tier level, namely the world market price of the quantity of feed grain needed in third countries to produce one kilogram of slaughtered poultry of each type and a flat rate representing production and marketing costs including other feed costs. Fats and oils again present a different picture. The Community is a serious deficit area for fats and is not entirely self-sufficient in olive oil; in addition, the market in olive oil is concentrated on the finished product and not on that of the highly perishable fruits. Consequently, the *target price* is here the production *target price*,[8] which is to secure the producers of olive oil (as distinct from the growers of olives) a fair level of return, having regard to the need to

---

(xxii) *Hops:* Reg. 1696/71, OJ, 1971, L 175/1; 1037/72, OJ, 1972, L 118/19; 1350/72, OJ, 1972, L 148/11; 1351/72, OJ, 1972, L 148/13.

(xxiii) *Seed-Corn:* Reg. 2358/71, OJ, 1971, L 246/1, amended 1674/71, OJ, 1972, L 177/1. No organisation exists as yet for potatoes; see OJ, 1972, C 23/9.

1 Cereals: art. 2(3); monthly increase: art. 6; rice: art. 2(3); monthly increase: art. 7.

2 Cereals, art. 4(1).

3 Milk, art. 3.

4 Sugar, art. 2(1).

5 Pork meat: art. 4(1).

6 Pork meat: arts 3, 5(1).

7 Eggs: art. 7; albumen: art. 5; poultry meat: art. 7.

8 Fats and oils: art. 5.

maintain the necessary volume of production in the Community; there is also a *market target price*[1] which serves here the dual purpose of preparing a minimum (*intervention*) price for the producers[2] of olive oil if the *production target price* is higher than the *market target price*.[3] All other vegetable oils and oil seeds produced in the Community enjoy the protection of a *uniform target price*, although the Community is a deficit area.[4] It is to assure the producers of a fair level of return;[5] being a deficit area, this goal can be achieved better, at times, by making deficiency payments (aids) to the producers than by raising the protective wall against necessary imports, and the regulations make provision for this.[6] Similar considerations apply to beef and veal, in which the Community is also deficient. A *guide price* is set which, since this production is geared to that of milk and dairy products market, is based in part on the situation in that market.[7] Fruit and vegetable products do not enjoy the benefits of a regulated price system. They are open to the play of free competition within the Community. Fruit and vegetables occupy an intermediate position. A *base price* is established annually. It is equal to the arithmetical average of prices determined on the representative market or markets of the Community located in the surplus areas where prices are lowest during the last preceding three years. The areas selected must represent between 20 and 30 per cent of the production in the Community during the relevant period.[8] Here again the *base price* does not serve to ensure a certain price for the producer, but only as a criterion for the operation of special *intervention* measures and the formation of import prices (see below). An annual *guide price* is established for wine.[9] It is set on the basis of the *average* of the price determined for the type of wine concerned in the last two preceding wine marketing years and on the basis of the price trend in the current wine marketing year.[10] The *average* price for each type of wine is determined weekly.[11] The *guide* price serves to fix the *reference* price which controls imports (see below).[12] The organisation of the market for the fisheries products follows the same pattern. A *guide* price is set for the most important types of catches[13] as well as for frozen fish.[14] It does not serve to ensure a certain income except for fresh or refrigerated sardines,[15]

---

1 Fats and oils: art. 6.
2 Fats and oils: art. 7.
3 Fats and oils: art. 10.
4 Fats and oils: art. 22(1), 23.
5 Fats and oils: art. 23.
6 Fats and oils: art. 27.
7 Beef and veal: art. 3(2).
8 Fruit and vegetables: Reg. 159/66, art. 4; cp. Reg. 23, art. 11(2), for a similar criterion to determine the *reference* price underlying the import price (art. 11(2), para. 8).
9 Wine: Reg. 816/70, art. 2(1).
10 Wine: Reg. 816/70, art. 2(2).
11 Wine: Reg. 816/70, art. 4.
12 Wine: Reg. 816/70, art. 9.
13 Fisheries products: Reg. 2142/70 art. 8(1) and (2) and Annexes IA and C.
14 Fisheries products: Reg. 2142/70, art. 13.
15 Fisheries products: Reg. 2142/70, arts. 8(1) and (3), 11.

but forms the basis of the control of imports through a *reference* price.[1] Tobacco is in short supply for the Community. Consequently the aim of the market organisation must be here to ensure the survival of the local industry in face of necessary foreign competition. For this purpose a *goal* price is set which is based on the *goal* price applied for the previous crop and is fixed at an amount which will reflect the need to promote specialisation, which takes into account the economic structure and natural conditions of production in the Community and, on the basis of rational management and of the economic viability of enterprises, helps to improve quality and ensures a fair income to producers.[2] The *goal* price serves to establish the *intervention* price which ensures a certain income for the producers,[3] but it is not matched by a controlled import price. While the Community is self-sufficient in flax, it is an importer of hemp. The policy is therefore to rely on the unimpeded and largely uncontrolled operation of imports.[4] Similar considerations apply to plants where only a *minimum export* price is foreseen[5] and to certain products in Annex II of the Treaty[6] which include livestock, offal, innards and sausages, dried vegetables and artichokes, dates, mangoes etc., tea, plants for medical and similar use, cocoa, apple cider, animal fats and other cereal products[7] as well as to the products not falling within the common agricultural policy which are enumerated in a special Regulation.[8]

In a limited number of instances only, a *guaranteed minimum* price takes the place of the target (guide, goal) price which sets the mechanism for the *intervention* price or intervention measures. Such is the case for durum wheat,[9] sugar beet,[10] and, through the use of *premiums* to purchasers, for tobacco,[11] or of *aids* to growers for flax and hemp and seed corn.[12]

(ii) *Intervention Price*—Secondly, the determination of a *target* or *base price* is balanced by an *intervention price* or by special intervention measures. These operate if, inside the Common Market, the price of the commodity in the areas of production has fallen because a surplus has occurred due either to seasonal or qualitative factors or because transport costs make it unprofitable to sell the commodity in other parts of the Common Market. In these circumstances, the national marketing organisation must purchase the existing surplus, if the price of the commodity has fallen to the extent of a certain percentage below the *target price*. Such is the solution

---

1   Fisheries products: Reg. 2142/70, art. 18.; seed-corn: art. 6.
2   Tobacco: art. 2(2).
3   Tobacco: art. 2(2).
4   Flax and Hemp: arts. 4, 5.
5   Plants: art. 7.
6   Reg. 827/68 art. 3, OJ, 1968, L 151/16: safeguard measures only.
7   Processed products based on cereals and rice: cp. Regulations 1052/68, OJ, 1968, L 179/8, 302/69, OJ, 1969, L 43/1, 968/68, OJ, 1968, L 166.
8   Reg. 1059/69, OJ, 1969, L 141/1; Reg. 160/66, OJ, 1966, 3361.
9   Cereals: art. 2(1), (3); see also art. 10.
10 Sugar: arts. 4, 5, 7.
11 Tobacco: arts, 3, 4.
12 Flax and hemp: art. 4; seed-corn: art. 3.

for grain,[1] rice,[2] dairy products,[3] white sugar,[4] pork meat,[5] olive oil,[6] vegetable oil and oil seeds,[7] poultry meat,[8] fruit and vegetables, though on a very low level of prices,[9] wine (called here a *trigger price*),[10] tobacco,[11] and, among fisheries products, for fresh or refrigerated sardines and anchovies.[12]

For some products *derived intervention prices* exist side by side with a *base intervention price*. By this method *intervention prices* are fixed for market centres in the Community other than that where the greatest scarcity (Duisburg for grain) or the greatest surplus (Arles, Vercelli for rice) exists[13] and, in the case of tobacco, for baled tobacco. Such differing prices presuppose that several areas of production exist.

In addition, special measures of intervention are available for different types of products. They include: a premium to purchasers,[14] a denaturation premium,[15] compensation for seasonal surplus stocks,[16] aids,[17] aids for private storage[18] or distillation,[19] refunds on production,[20] withdrawal prices,[21] special intervention measures sanctioned by the Council upon the proposal of the Commission (art. 43(2)),[22] the establishment of regulating stocks,[23] compensatory indemnities[24] and minimum prices for exports.[25]

---

1 Cereals: basic intervention price: art. 2(1).

2 Rice: arts. 4, 5.

3 Dairy Products: arts. 5, 6 (butter), art. 7 (skimmed powdered milk), art. 8 (cheese).

4 Sugar: arts. 3, 9.

5 Pork meat: art. 5(1); purchase price not more than 92 per cent and not less than 85 per cent of base price for slaughtered hogs.

6 Fats and oils: arts. 7, 11; equal to market target price minus an amount sufficient to permit olive oil to move from production area to consumption area.

7 Fats and oils: arts. 22(1), 24, 26.

8 Poultry meat: art. 6(1)(a); optional if lower than 98 per cent, obligatory if lower than 93 per cent of the guide price.

9 Fruit and vegetables: Reg. 159/66, arts. 4(1)(3), 7: buying in price equal to 40 and 45 per cent of the base price for cauliflower and tomatoes; between 50 and 55 per cent for apples and pears; between 60 and 70 per cent for all other fruit covered by Reg. 159/66, Annex I.

10 Wine: Reg. 816/70, art. 3.

11 Tobacco: arts. 2(1), (2), 5; 90 per cent of the goal price.

12 Fisheries products: arts. 8(1), (3); between 35 and 45 per cent below the guide price.

13 Cereals: art. 4(1), (3), except corn: art. 4(2); monthly increase: art. 6; rice: art. 4(3), (4), monthly increase: art. 7; Sugar: art. 3(2)(6); tobacco: art. 6.

14 Tobacco: arts. 3, 4.

15 Cereals: art. 7(3); sugar: art. 9(2).

16 Cereals: art. 9; rice: art. 8.

17 Dairy products: art. 11 (casein from skimmed milk); cereals: art. 10; fats and oils: art. 11 (olive oil), art. 27 (vegetable oil and oilseeds), art. 30 (grapeseed), art. 31 (linseed), art. 32 (aids); flax and hemp: art. 4; seed-corn: art. 3.

18 Dairy products: art. 9 (cheese); sugar: art 8; pork meat: arts. 3, 7; beef and veal: arts. 5(1)(b), 8; flax and hemp: art. 5; fisheries products: art. 14.

19 Wine: Reg. 816/70, art. 6.

20 Cereals: art. 11; sugar: art. 9(6); wine: Reg. 816/70, arts. 5, 6; rice: art. 9.

21 Fruit and vegetables: Reg. 159/66, arts. 3, 7B; fisheries products: art. 7.

22 Cereals: art. 8; rice: art. 6; dairy products: art. 12 (surplus butter-fat); eggs: art. 6; poultry meat: art. 6; beef and veal: art. 6; wine: Reg. 816/70, art. 33; fisheries products: art. 25.

23 Fats and Oils: art. 12 (olive oil).

24 Fisheries products: arts. 10(1), (3), 15(1), (4).

25 Plants: art. 7.

(iii) *Threshold Price*—Thirdly, the *target price* with slight modifications upwards constitutes the *threshold* or *sluice-gate* or *reference price*. These different terms denote different methods of prices. In the case of cereals the *threshold price* serves to ensure that the sales price of the imported products at the place for which the *target price* is set[1] is equal to the *target price*. This equality is achieved by taking the price of the product of identical quality at a single port of entry, namely at Rotterdam, and by adding to it the cost of transport to the place where the *target price* is set. Where the price is seasonally determined, periodic (monthly) increases are foreseen.[2] For sugar a slightly different method is applied, inasmuch as the *threshold price* is calculated in relation to the *target price* in the area having the greatest surplus, increased by the cost of transport to the most distant deficit area in the Community.[3] For dairy products the *threshold price* is set for certain products described as 'pilot products' so as to reach the level of the *target price* reached for milk, having regard also to the need to protect the processing industry.[4] Thus the *threshold price* for one type of product is related to the *target price* for another. The latter method is followed uniformly for grain conversion products where the *target price* is replaced by a *sluice-gate price* which is set with reference to the value on the world market of a quantity of feed grain equivalent to the quantity of fodder needed in third countries to produce one kilogram of pork meat, eggs, albumen or poultry meat, coupled with a flat rate representing other feed costs and, except in the case of eggs, the general production and marketing costs.[5] The difference between the *threshold price* for sugar and the average c.i.f. price for white sugar is the basis of an *import levy*, unaccompanied by any determination of a *sluice-gate price* in the case of fruit base or vegetable base products.[6] For olive oil the *threshold price* is related to the *market target price for this product* (see above), so that the sale price of the imported products at the frontier is equal to the *market target price*,[7] while the shortage of vegetable oils and oil seeds excludes the need for such a protection at the frontier for products of the latter type. For beef and veal, as well as for live bovine cattle, an *import price* is established which is determined on the basis of the quotations on the most representative third-country markets or a special *import price* in certain other circumstances.[8] The considerations which excluded a *threshold price* for vegetable oils and oil seeds apply also to tobacco, flax and hemp, plants, products enumerated in Annex II and cereal products and products outside the common agricultural policy listed in Council Reg. 1059/69. On the other hand, for fruit and vegetables a notional *import price*, which is geared to the *reference price*, attracts in

---

1 Cereals: art 5; monthly increase: art. 6; rice: arts, 14, 15.
2 Cereals: art. 6; rice: art. 7.
3 Sugar: art. 12.
4 Dairy products: arts. 4; 1(a)(2) and (b)–(g).
5 Pork meat: art. 12, but see art. 12(3); eggs: art. 7; albumen: art. 5; poultry meat: art. 7.
6 Fruit products: art. 2.
7 Fats and oils: art. 8.
8 Beef and veal: art, 10(1), (3), (4).

certain circumstances the operation of a *compensatory tax*,[1] comparable to, but not identical with, a levy in the case of other agricultural products (see below). For wine a *reference price* is set which is geared to the *guide price* (see above), augmented by the cost of bringing Community wine to the same marketing stage as imported wines. If the free to frontier *offering price* of foreign wine, plus the customs duties, is lower than the *reference price* for this wine, a *compensatory tax* equal to a levy in the case of other agricultural products applies subject to certain qualifications.[2] Fisheries products are protected by a *reference price* which is related to the *guide price* as regards certain products, while as regards others it is calculated on the basis of the weighted average of the quotations determined on the most representative import markets in the preceding three years, reduced by customs charges and transport costs to the Community border point.[3] The *reference price* is, in turn, related to an *entry price*.[4] Where this is not reached, suspension or restrictions of imports or a compensatory charge may be imposed,[5] subject to certain qualifications.[6]

(iv) *Levies, Compensatory Taxes, Refunds, Safeguard Measures*—While within the Community the *target* or *base price* can be maintained through the operation of the *intervention price* and of other measures of intervention, the *threshold price* alone cannot prevent disturbances in the Community, if the world price as quoted at the frontier falls below the amount represented by the *threshold price* combined with the regular customs duties (if any). In these circumstances a *variable levy* fulfils the function of levelling up the world price to that fixed inside the Community.[7] In the case of vegetables and wine the levy is replaced by a *compensatory charge*[8] or by an *import charge*[9] for cereals products. Special measures may be taken if the c.i.f. price of any one product is substantially above the *threshold price* and is likely to remain so, thus creating a serious disturbance within the Community.[10] In addition, a special procedure enables the Commission and the member

---

1   Fruit and vegetables: Reg. 23 art. 11; seed-corn: art. 6(1), (3).
2   Wine: art. 9.
3   Fisheries products: art. 18(1)(2).
4   Fisheries products: art. 18(3).
5   Fisheries products: art. 18(4).
6   Fisheries products: art. 18(5).
7   Cereals: arts. 13–15; rice: arts. 11–13; dairy products other than milk: art. 14; sugar: arts. 14, 15; for the exceptional case of export levies and import subsidies see art. 16; pork meat: arts. 8, 9, 10, quarterly: art. 8, supplementary levy: arts. 13, 28; eggs: arts. 3, 4, 5, quarterly: art. 3; supplementary levy: arts. 8, 21; albumen: arts. 2, 5(3), supplementary levy: art. 5(3); poultry meat: arts. 3, 4, 5; quarterly: art. 3; supplementary levy: arts. 8, 21; fats and oils (olive oil): arts. 13, 14, 15; beef and veal: arts. 10, 11, 13, 14 (exception); fruit products: arts. 2, 5, 6.

   For the method of fixing these prices see *Schwarze* v. *Einfuhr- und Vorratsstelle für Getreide and Futtermittel* (1965), 11 Rec. 1081; [1966] C.M.L.R. 172; Ehlermann, 1966 Rev. M.C. 574; 1966 B.B.A.W.D. 67.

8   Fruit and vegetables: Reg. 23, art. 11; wine: Reg. 816/70, art. 9(3); fisheries products: art. 18(4)(b).
9   Cereals products: arts. 5, 6, 7, 8; quarterly: art. 6(1).
10   Cereals: art. 19; rice: art. 21; dairy products: art. 20; sugar: art. 16 (import subsidy, export levy). No such measure is provided for any other product.

states to apply suitable *safeguard measures* in trade with third countries, if the Community market for any one product is threatened as a result of imports or exports with serious disturbances likely to jeopardise the objectives of the Treaty (art. 39).[1]

Conversely, in order to make it possible to export agricultural products (whether untreated or processed) which are protected or supported by a special regime within the Community, the difference between the price in the Community and on the world market may be recovered by the exporter from an export fund.[2]

(v) *Conclusions*—Thus, although the world price may have fallen below the target price of the commodity within the Community, the product from abroad will be kept out, and local surpluses will have to be taken up at the intervention price. The foreign commodity can only compete if the world price, as levelled up to the threshold price, is still below the price inside the Community, *i.e.* if the target price has been exceeded inside the Community. This will only happen if a scarcity has developed which can thus be remedied.

The basic scheme is therefore simple. In the first place, a common target price is established. This is determined by the price either at the place of the greatest scarcity or of the greatest surplus within the Community. In the second place, an intervention price must be fixed, if the commodity is in surplus within the Community; it is fixed at a certain percentage of the target price. If the commodity is permanently in short supply, measures not unlike those taken in the United Kingdom ensure that the producers within the Community receive a sufficient return; such are the various types of aids and special intervention measures.[3] In the third place, the target price with slight modifications upwards constitutes the threshold price against which the price c.i.f. at the port of Rotterdam must be measured and by reference to which the variable levy operates.[4]

IV Technical Execution

The operation of the common agricultural policy as laid down in the various schemes for individual agricultural products requires frequent

---

1 Cereals: art. 20; rice: art. 22; dairy products: art. 21; sugar: art. 21; pork meat: art. 18; eggs: art. 12; albumen: arts. 4, 6; poultry meat: art. 12; fats and oils (olive oil): art. 20; beef and veal: art. 21; fruit and vegetable products: Reg. 865/68, art. 11; wine: Reg. 816/70, art. 14; tobacco: art. 10; flax and hemp: art. 8; fisheries products: art. 20; plants: art. 3.

    During the transitional period art. 226 applied as well. See above, p. 52, n. 7. And see generally Ehlermann, 1966 EuR 305.

2 Cereals: art. 16; rice: art. 17; dairy products: art. 17; sugar: art. 17; pork meat: art. 15; eggs: art. 9; poultry meat: art. 9; fats and oils (olive oil): arts. 18, 19; (vegetable oil): art. 28; beef and veal: art. 18; fruit and vegetable products: Reg. 865/68, arts. 3, 4, 5; wine: Reg. 816/70, art. 10; tobacco: art. 9; fisheries products: art. 21; cereal products: Reg. 1052/68, arts. 6, 7, 8; products outside agricultural policy: Reg. 1059/69, art. 9. No such aid is allowed for albumen.

3 See above, pp. 75–76.

4 See above, pp. 77–78.

action by the Council (art. 43(2)) to implement the schemes and by the Commission in setting prices and levies. For this purpose each scheme envisages the creation of a Management Committee to act together with the Commission in the determination of technical matters delegated to the latter by the regulations. The compatibility of this procedure with the Treaty and the general principles underlying it have since been confirmed by the Community Court.[1] The regulation of prices for imports and of refunds for exports requires a strict system of licensing which is provided by the existing regulations. The need for commerce to engage in forward transactions requires a measure of calculation which a variable levy precludes altogether. Consequently, the licence in such transactions determines the rate of the levy in advance; as a corollary, the licence is limited in kind and requires the holder to execute the transaction within the period set, subject to certain exceptions arising from Acts of God,[2] and to give security as a guarantee of its execution.[3]

V Transitional Provisions

Before the present scheme of uniform target prices was agreed upon, and while different prices existed within the Community, coupled with different intervention prices, the relationship between target and intervention prices was not one of percentages only. The difference in transport costs from one part of the Community to another required intervention prices at a level which made it profitable to sell in the area of greater scarcity, even if the target price could be obtained there. This meant that the intervention price at the place of surplus together with the transport costs to an area of scarcity had to be somewhat below the target price at the place of scarcity. Otherwise the national marketing organisation at the place of surplus would have been called upon to intervene, and the market of greater scarcity would have been supplied by imports. Thus regional intervention prices had to be introduced which became known as derived intervention prices.[4]

At the same time the danger existed before 1 July 1967, when the common target price replaced national or regional target prices, that as a result of price fluctuations within the Community the producers in one

---

1 *Einfuhr- und Vorratsstelle Getreide* v. *Köster* (1970), 16 Rec. 1161, at p. 1171(3)–1173(8); [1972] C.M.L.R. 255; see also above, p. 66, n. 1. *Deutsche Tradax GmbH* v. *Einfuhr- und Vorratsstelle Getreide* (1971) 17 Rec. 145, at p. 153(2); [1972] C.M.L.R. 213, below, n. 3.

2 See above, p. 16, n.

3 The legality of this measure has been confirmed by the Community Court. See *Einfuhr- und Vorratsstelle Getreide* v. *Köster* (1970), 16 Rec. 1161, at p. 1176, (above, n, 1); *Internationale Handelsgesellschaft mbH* v. *Einfuhr- und Vorratsstelle Getreide* (1970), 16 Rec. 1125, at pp. 1135(3)–1138(20); [1972] C.M.L.R. 255; *Deutsche Tradax GmbH* v. *Einfuhr- und Vorratsstelle für Getreide und Futtermittel* (1971), 17 Rec. 145, at p. 153(2)–(4); [1972] C.M.L.R. 213. For this purpose the levy is fixed in advance with reference to the month of import specified in the application for an import licence: see *Cie. Continentale* v. *Hoofproduktschap voor Ackerbouwproduktion etc.* (1971), 17 Rec. 163; *Deutsche Tradax GmbH* v. *Einfuhr- und Vorratsstelle für Getreide und Futtermittel*, at p. 155(12).

4 For derived intervention prices in the present system see above, p. 76.

country of the Community might swamp the other countries with a cheaper commodity than the others could produce, unless some protection was permitted in place of customs duties and quantitative restrictions, now abrogated. In these circumstances the threatened countries were allowed to impose a variable levy by virtue of a provision of the Treaty (art. 44(1)) which allowed member states during the transitional period to fix minimum prices in order to counter the effect of the abolition of customs duties among the member states.[1] These were variable owing to the daily fluctuations of the commodity price in the different parts of the Community, and its administration has given rise to some notable decisions.[2] Now that a uniform price is fixed on an annual scale by the Community organs for each regulated commodity, the variable levy no longer operates inside the Community.

VI FINANCIAL PROVISIONS

The Treaty itself makes only a fleeting reference (art. 40(4)) to the financial problems which arise from the common agricultural policy described above when it authorises the creation of "one or more agricultural orientation and guarantee funds". In fact, the beginnings of a common policy in 1962 were marked by the enactment of a regulation concerning the financing of the common agriculture policy.[3] Two separate considerations required this. On the one hand, the contemplated advent of a single market and a unified price system required the central administration of interventions, refunds on exports and of the measures designed to adapt and ameliorate the conditions of agricultural production, to adapt and orientate the production itself and to improve the marketing of agriculture products (art. 39(1)(a)).[4] On the other hand, the revenues from the levies and possibly those arising from the common customs tariff or from the member states assessed by the common budgetary process (arts. 200, 201) were to form a fund called the European Agricultural Guidance and Guarantee Fund (EAGGF) which could meet the obligations.[5] Regulation 25 envisaged such a regime at the end of the transitional period. During the latter, a complex system existed, composed of increasing contributions from the fund in respect of intervention and refunds (Guarantee Fund)[6] and of contributions with a fixed ceiling as a

---

1   See Council Decision of 4 April 1962, OJ, 1962, 995 restricted to products not covered by the common agricultural policy. And see Ehlermann, 1966 Rev. M.C. 574. For variable levies in the present system see above, pp. 78–79.

2   *Toepfer* v. *EEC Commission* (1965), 11 Rec. 525; [1966] C.M.L.R. 111; *Kampffmeyer* v. *EEC Commission* (1967), 13 Rec. 317; *Kurt Becher* v. *EEC Commission* (1967), 13 Rec. 369; [1968] C.M.L.R. 169.

3   Reg. 25 of 4 April 1962, OJ, 1962, 991; *Mégret*, Vol. II, p. 369*, amended by Reg. 49, OJ, 1962, 1571 (art. 8); Reg. 130/66, OJ, 1966, 2695, *Mégret*, Vol. II, p. 383*; 741/67, OJ, 1967, No. 258/2 (art. 3(1)(a)), *Mégret*, Vol. II, p. 388*; 728/70, OJ, 1970, L 94 (art. 5(2)).

4   Reg. 25, arts, 2(2), 3; Reg. 17/64, art. 11, OJ, 1964, 586.

5   Reg. 25, art. 2(1).

6   Reg. 25, art. 7; see also Reg. 17/64, especially arts. 2–10, OJ, 1964, 586 amended by Reg.

[*Footnote continued on next page*

maximum for restructuring and orientation (Guidance Fund).[1] The remainder was borne by the member states who retained the levies and customs duties. This solution applied between 1962 and 1965.[2] In the course of the accelerated introduction of the final phase in 1965, the French government pressed for the implementation of the basic principle of Reg. 25,[3] *i.e.* for the complete assumption of liability by the Community. The Commission, in turn, postulated the concentration in their hands of the revenues from levies and from other sources envisaged by the Treaty in accordance with the same Reg. 25.[4] The compromise solution[5] embraced contributions by the member states only according to a fixed proportion for the period between 1965 and 1967[6] and then to the end of the transitional period.[7] The income from levies and the like remained with the member states.

With the end of the transitional period a further interim arrangement[8] preceded Reg. 729/70[9] which reaffirmed that the expenditure arising from the common agricultural policy is to be based on the concept of financing through the European Agricultural Guidance and Guarantee Fund as part of the budget of the Communities and that a new system is to be defined whereby funds are no longer to be advanced by the member states but by the Community.

The Ministerial Agreement of 15, 16, 19, 20 and 21 December 1969 culminating in the decision of 21 April 1970[10] provided the effective financial basis for the operation of the Fund as defined by Regs. 25 and 729/70.[11] From 1975 onwards the financial basis is entirely provided out of the revenues of the Community, which will be made up of the levies, the customs duties and a proportion of the added value tax.[12] A further interim solution up to that date combines some direct income with contributions from the member states.[13]

741/67, OJ, 1967, No. 258/2 and repealed by Reg. 729/70, art. 16(1), below, n. 9. For an account see *Mégret*, Vol. II, p. 206, No. 346 ff., p. 216, No. 365 (expenses); p. 219, No. 368–p. 221, No. 370 (revenues).

1   Reg. 25, art. 1 (above, p. 81, n. 6); Reg. 17/64, arts. 11–22 (above, p. 81, n. 6).
2   Reg. 25, art. 5(1).
3   Reg. 25, art. 2(1), 2nd para.
4   Reg. 25, art. 2(2).
5   Reg. 130/66, OJ, 1966, 2695; *Mégret*, Vol. II, p. 219, No. 368 ff., especially p. 221, No. 371.
6   Reg. 130/66, art. 3.
7   Reg. 130/66, art. 11.
8   Reg. 728/70, OJ, 1970, L 94/9.
9   Reg. 729/70 of 21 April 1970, OJ, 1970, L 94/13, amended by Reg. 1566/72, OJ, 1972, L 167/15.
10 70/243/CEE/CECA/EURATOM, OJ, 28 April 1970, L 94/19.
11 Reg. 729/70, OJ, 1970, L 94/13, art. 16(1), 3(3), 6(4), repealing Reg. 17/64. OJ, 1964, 586, except arts. 5 and 6 and Pt. II (excluding arts. 14(1)(a) and (16), and Council Reg. 728/70, art. 14, OJ, 1970, L 94/9; cp. Council Reg. 1600/68, OJ, 1968, L 253.
12 Council Decision 70/243/CEE/CECA/EURATOM of 21 April 1970, OJ, 1970, L 94/19, arts. 1, 2, 4. For details concerning the execution of this measure see Council Reg. 2/71, OJ, 1971, L 3/1.
13 *Ibid.*, art. 3.

VII Unit of Account

A uniform system of prices, both target, intervention, threshold and refund, to mention only the most representative, requires a common unit of account. Given the variety of currencies within the Community which are, however, geared to each other by a standard of parities accepted by the International Monetary Fund, the Community selected 0·88867088 grams of fine gold as the common units.[1] In practice this may mean that amounts shown in one currency must be expressed in another, both of which are geared to the same standard of parity. If fluctuations occur within the permissible band of parity[2] or outside it,[3] the measures outlined in Reg. 129 may be taken. In the case of the French devaluation on 11 August 1969 and of the revaluation of the German mark on 27 October 1969, the Council took special measures[4] in order to enable the country concerned to benefit from its action rather than to eliminate its effects immediately. The result was the admission of countervailing measures inside the Community in respect of imports from France and the sanctioning of aids for exports to France. In the case of German revaluation the opposite effects had to be reached.[5] Imports from Germany were accorded an aid; exports to Germany were met with a countervailing duty.

---

1 Reg. 129 of 23 October 1962, art. 1, OJ, 1962, 2553, amended by Reg. 653/68, OJ, 1968, L 123/4; see in general *Mégret*, Vol. II, p. 200. No. 337–p. 203, No. 342. For the new members see Reg. 222/73, OJ, 1973, L 27/4. For fluctuations in margins see Reg. 974/71, OJ, 1971, L 106/1 amended by Reg. 509/73, OJ, 1973, L 50/1.

2 Reg. 129, art. 2.

3 Reg. 129, art. 3.

4 Reg. 1586/69 of 11 August 1969, OJ, 1969, L 202.

5 Reg 2111/69, of 28 October 1969, OJ, 1969, L 270; Commission Decision 69/375 of 30 October 1969, OJ, 1969, L 273/35; 69/410 of 17 November 1969, OJ, 1969, L 290/21.

5

Freedom of Movement—
Workers, Free Circulation

(Articles 48–51)[1]

The rules of the Treaty on freedom of movement deal with three aspects of life in the Community which all serve to make the Community more mobile and to put its manpower, trading and professional skills and its financial resources to more rational use for the benefit of the Community as a whole. These three aspects concern the free circulation of workers, freedom of establishment for self-employed persons and the unimpeded flow of capital.

I In General

States have the right under international law to control the entry of aliens, and they exercise this right with special rigour when the entering aliens intend to become part of the national labour market. This attitude, created by the fear of unemployment and of undercutting, has no place in a Community aiming at full employment and a stable market throughout. In these circumstances it is necessary to utilise the common labour force where it is most needed. This aim was given concrete expression for the first time by OECD,[2] subject to certain safeguards, then by the Council of Europe,[3] and unconditionally by the ECSC Treaty (art. 69). This tendency was followed by the EEC Treaty, the relevant portions of which must be interpreted in favour of the beneficiaries and must be regarded as minimum requirements, if the decision of the Community Court concerning Council Reg. 3 (now superseded by Reg. 1408/71) on social security implementing art. 51 is typical of the Court's approach to this chapter on the movement of workers as a whole (arts. 48–51).[4]

The free circulation of workers was treated as one of the most pressing needs and was achieved before the end of the first stage in advance of the provision of the Treaty (art. 48(1)). The meaning of the expression

---

1 Vignes, (1965) II Juriscl. Dr. Int., Fasc. 164 F; Troclet in *Ganshof van der Meersch*, pp. 729–737; van Gerven, *ibid.*, pp. 739–753; Mégret, Louis, Vignes et al. in *Mégret*, Vol. III, (1971), pp. 1–86, 3*–51*; Everling, *The Right of Establishment* (1964); Platz, *EWG Niederlassungsrecht und individuelle Rechtspositionen* (1966); Simmonds in (1972) 21 I.C.L.Q. 307.
2 OEEC Council Decision 30 October 1953, as amended 5 March 1954, 27 January 1956, 7 December 1956; OEEC Resolution of 20 December 1956.
3 European Convention on Establishment of 13 December 1955, European T.S. No. 19.
4 *Nonnenmacher* v. *Bestuur der Sociale Verzekeringsbank* (1964), 10 Rec. 557; [1964] C.M.L.R. 338.

"worker" is not defined by the Treaty and requires clarification. According to German law, for instance, it includes not only manual operatives but also white collar staff, including leading employees, apprentices and persons engaged in cottage industries. It also appears to include persons who have immigrated in another capacity and who subsequently wish to take up employment. The earlier regulations made by virtue of art. 49 of the Treaty[1] did not provide any guidance, but the regulation at present in force,[2] by establishing the "right to accept and to exercise a *wage-earning* occupation . . . in accordance with the . . . provisions applicable of that state" appears to combine the criterion of remuneration by a wage with any further criterion enforced in the state concerned. On the other hand, Reg. 3 on social security benefits made by virtue of art. 51 (now replaced by Reg. 1408/71) spoke of "wage earners and assimilated persons".[3] This was interpreted by the Community Court to include artisans, if by the law of their place of permanent residence they are treated as being persons equivalent to workers.[4] It may be that this interpretation is not limited to its own sphere of operation in the law relating to social security and finds confirmation in Council Reg. 1612/68, art. 1(1) set out above. At the same time, the Community Court has held that Reg. 3 (now superseded) must be interpreted as a rule of Community law irrespective of the notion of worker as laid down by the domestic law of the countries of the Community.[5] The new Reg. 1408/71[6] on social security defines a worker by reference to the test whether the person concerned is insured by means of an insurance against any one or several risks relating to salaried workers or covered by the Regulation itself.[7] No final conclusion is thus possible at the present stage but it may be that special considerations apply to the uniform administration of social security which do not apply to the right to take employment.

Although the German text of art. 48(2) of the Treaty, which requires the abolition of discrimination between workers on the ground of nationality, leaves certain doubts as to whether only workers who are nationals of the member states can benefit from this provision,[8] the French text[9] seems to support the restrictive interpretation (see also art. 227),[10] and

---

1 Reg. 15, OJ, 1961, 1073.
2 Reg. 1612/68, art. 1(1), OJ, 1968, L 257/2, formerly Reg. 38/64, art. 1, OJ, 1964, 965, see also art. 60.
3 Reg. 3, art. 4(2), OJ, 1962, 581; but see now Reg. 1408/71, art. 1(a), OJ, 1971, L 149/2.
4 *De Cicco* v. *Landesversicherungsanstalt Schwaben* (1968), 14 Rec. 689; [1969] C.M.L.R. 67.
5 *Unger* v. *Bestuur der Bedrijfsvereniging voor Detailhandel en Ambachten at Utrecht* (1964), 10 Rec. 347; [1964] C.M.L.R. 319.
6 OJ, 1971, L 149/2, art. 1(a).
7 *Ibid.*, art. 1(a)(i)–(iii). See below, p. 103.
8 It speaks of "*Arbeitnehmer der Mitgliedstaaten*".
9 It speaks of "*travailleurs des Etats Membres*".
10 In general see von der Groeben in *Festschrift für Hallstein* (1966), p. 226, at p. 238; Directives of 23 November 1959, OJ, 1960, 147, art. 1 (French overseas territories and departments; now as regards French overseas departments only: Council Decision 68/359, OJ, 1968, L 257/1). And see *Württembergische Milchverwertung-Südmilch-AG* v. *Ugliola* (1969), 15 Rec. 363, at pp. 369(3)(4), 370(7); [1970] C.M.L.R. 194. However, Council Directive 68/360

Council Reg. 1612/68 is explicitly confined to nationals only. Once again, Council Reg. 1408/71, formerly Reg. 3, takes a broader view inasmuch as stateless persons and refugees who reside permanently in one of the member states are based on an equal footing with nationals for the purpose of social security.[1] Once again the rules on social security attached to the provisions on the free movement of workers are conceived in terms of a policy which is not restricted to what appears to be the express goal of the present chapter and which embraces not only persons other than salaried workers, not only nationals of the Community but persons residing permanently in a country of the Community and (as will be shown below)[2] not only situations involving a change of a place of employment.

The principle of non-discrimination in the employment of workers assures equal opportunities without differentiation in the recruitment of workers by allowing the acceptance of specific offers (art. 48(3)(a)),[3] except where the special nature of the position to be filled is inextricably linked with certain linguistic requirements.[4] It also includes the right to move freely in the countries of the Community of workers who have been so recruited (art. 48(3)(b)), to reside in any such country in order to carry out duties under the contract of employment (art. 48(3)(c)) and, most important, to remain there at the end of the term of employment subject, in the latter case, to conditions to be laid down (art. 48(3)(d)) by the following

Measure: Commission, Regulation.[5]

The entire subject matter was first made the subject of a regulation by the Council in the exercise of the powers granted by art. 49 (and not by the Commission which approached this aspect only later on[6]) in 1961[7] which tied the right to seek new employment to a stay of three or four years, revised in 1964[8] so as to require one year's residence, and now freed of all restrictions based on a fixed period of residence.[9]

The duty to liberalise the rules on the employment of alien workers does not extend to employment in the public administration (art. 38(4)). As

---

of 15 October 1968, art. 4(4), OJ, 1968, L 257/13 envisages the possibility that a member of the family does not possess the nationality of a member state. For refugees see the Resolution 64/305 of the governments of the Six of 25 March 1964, OJ, 1964, 1225 recommending favourable treatment.

1   Reg. 1408/71, art. 1(d), (e); Reg. 3, art. 4.
2   See below, p. 128.
3   Reg. 1612/68, arts. 1–6; formerly Reg. 38/64, arts. 8, 9–13. It follows by implication that the right to seek employment is not unlimited. For various interpretations see *Mégret*, Vol. III, p. 4.
4   Reg. 1612/68, art. 3(1).
5   Note the Protocol concerning Luxembourg attached to the EEC Treaty, art. 2.
6   See below, p. 92, comment to art. 49(c) and see Commission Reg. 1251/70 of 29 June 1970, OJ, 1970, L 142.
7   Reg. 15 of 16 August 1961, OJ, 1961, 1073 and Reg. 18 of 28 February 1962, OJ, 1962, 722.
8   Reg. 38/64, arts. 6, 7, OJ, 1964, 965 and Council Directive of 25 March 1964, OJ, 1964, 981.
9   Reg. 1612/68, art. 1, amended by Reg. 1251/70, OJ, 1970, L 142/24.

is usual, the national regulation on public order,[1] security and health must be observed. The framework of their exercise is determined by the Council Directive of 25 February 1964[2] which applies also to the Directive on Establishment of Self-Employed Persons and to Services across the Frontiers and will be discussed below.[3] Thus the general provisions of the domestic legislation in the member states concerning aliens which require registration and sanitary control and which provide for refusal of admission and expulsion for reasons of public safety remain untouched (art. 48(3)).[4] In administering any such aliens' legislation it must be kept in mind that the provisions of the Treaty on the free movement of workers envisage only such persons who "accept and . . . exercise a wage earning occupation"[5] and do not accord a similar right to potential wage earners who are in fact lay-abouts who live by their wits.[6]

In order to establish effectively the free circulation of workers a number of procedures are foreseen by the Treaty—

> *Measures:* Council upon recommendation by the Commission after consulting the Economic and Social Council—Regulations and Directives (art. 49).

The regulations envisaged here (art. 49) were passed during successive stages of the transitional period. On 16 August 1961 the Council passed Reg. 15,[7] followed by Reg. 18.[8] Regulation 15 was replaced by Reg. 38/64[9] but was not superseded in substance,[10] and Reg. 18 was retained *pro tanto*.[11] The final solution upon the end of the transitional period was provided by Reg. 1612/68 whereby Reg. 38/64 was repealed.[12] It has since been supplemented by a Commission regulation.[13] Unlike the earlier Reg. 15, Reg. 1612/68 covers all wage earners, including frontier and

---

1 For the meaning of this term see Verw. Ger. Hof Baden-Württemberg, 23 December 1965, [1971] C.M.L.R. 541, 543. It is construed in the wide sense which is attributed to it generally in continental law. For the implementation of Council Directive 64/221 (below, n. 2, in Germany see *ibid.*, p. 544, n. 11. And see Lyon-Caen, 1966 Rev. Trim. Dr. Eur. 690.

2 Council Directive 64/221 of 25 February 1964, OJ, 1964, 850; extended to cover residence under Commission Reg. 1251/70 (below, p. 90, and n. 12) by Council Directive 72/194, 18 May 1972, OJ, 1972, L 121/32.

3 Council Directives 64/240 of 25 March 1964, OJ, 1964, 981; 64/220 of 25 February 1964, OJ, 1964, 845. See below, p. 133.

4 LG Göttingen, 23 December 1963, 1964 N.J.W. 987; [1965] C.M.L.R. 285.

5 Reg. 1612/68, art. 1(1).

6 *City of Wiesbaden* v. *Barulli* decided by the LG Wiesbaden on 14 November 1966; [1968] C.M.L.R. 239, 246 with further references, provided always that the worker has entered lawfully.

7 OJ, 1961, 1073.

8 OJ, 1962, 722.

9 OJ, 1964, 965.

10 Reg. 38/64, art. 59.

11 Reg. 38/64, art. 4(2).

12 Reg. 1612/68, art. 48.

13 Commission Reg. 1251/70, OJ, 1970, L 142/4.

seasonal workers,[1] the worker's spouse and children under 21 years of age or who are dependent upon him, if they pursue a wage earning activity,[2] under equal conditions of employment.[3] National workers no longer enjoy any priority, subject to certain important safeguards.[4] While formerly foreign workers were permitted to introduce their family if adequate housing was provided,[5] a foreign worker who is in employment in a member state other than his national state is entitled to national treatment concerning housing.[6] He may acquire ownership of a house and is entitled to be placed on the waiting list for houses,[7] not only for himself but also for his family.[8] Equal access must be given to vocational training,[9] schooling for his children[10] and in setting up family enterprises by his dependents.[11] Workers from member states are entitled to unrestricted membership in Trade Unions and have the right to vote.[12] Formerly after three years and now from the beginning of their employment, they can hold office in the Union, except when it is combined with governmental functions.[13] All individual or collective contracts of employment which discriminate in their terms against Community workers in so far as access to employment, employment itself, wages or other conditions of work or discharge are concerned are void by operation of law.[14]

II PARTICULAR AIMS

In accordance with the principles set out in the Treaty (arts. 48, 49) Reg. 1612/68 seeks to foster the following in particular:

(a) A close collaboration between the national authorities dealing with labour (art. 49(a)). For this purpose the co-operation between member states and the Commission is envisaged through special agencies in the member states in undertaking joint studies, where necessary, dealing with employment and unemployment, in matching job offers and applications and in the resulting placement of workers,[15] and a detailed matching procedure is laid down.[16] It provides for the submission of offers of available manpower in one country for employment in another within a

---

1 Reg. 1612/68, Preamble, 5th para.; see also art. 16(3)(b) and (c); see for the previous law Reg. 38/64, arts. 1(2), 9(2), but see art. 3(1), 14.
2 Reg. 1612/68, art. 11.
3 Reg. 1612/68, art. 7.
4 Reg. 1612/68, art. 20; see below, p. 92.
5 Reg. 38/64, arts. 17 ff., 21.
6 Reg. 1612/68, art. 9(1). And see Commission Recommendations of 23 July 1962, OJ, 1962, 2118 (social services) and of 7 July 1965, OJ, 1965, 2293 (housing).
7 Reg. 1612/68, art. 9(1), (2).
8 Reg. 1612/68, art. 10(3).
9 Reg. 1612/68, art. 7(3), formerly Reg. 38/64, art. 12.
10 Reg. 1612/68, art. 12; formerly Reg. 38/64, art. 21.
11 Reg. 1612/68, art, 11: ". . . or independent activity".
12 Reg. 1612/68, art. 8(1), formerly Reg. 38/64, art. 9.
13 Reg. 1612/68, art. 8(1).
14 Reg. 1612/68, art. 7(4).
15 Reg. 1612/68, arts. 13, 14, 19, 20.
16 Reg. 1612/68, arts. 15–18. See OJ, 1969, C 83/1.

given period of time, and for certain priorities in favour of nationals of member states as against those of non-member states, subject to special exceptions.[1] The participation of individual employers and of the regional employment offices is not excluded, especially where offers of employment to named individuals are concerned.[2] In addition, a European Co-ordination Bureau for Matching Job Offers and Applications, which is established within the Commission, serves to co-ordinate the efforts of the agencies in the member states.[3] It is assisted by an advisory committee[4] and a technical committee.[5]

(b) The planned gradual abolition of administrative procedures and practices (art. 49(b)) which put the foreign worker at a disadvantage in obtaining employment and, in particular, the abolition of waiting periods based on national legislation and international agreements between member states impeding free movement of workers and the immediate access of alien workers to local employment. This purpose is realised generally by Reg. 1612/68 which abolished the remaining restrictions affecting seasonal workers,[6] and by the Council Directive of 15 October 1968.[7]

The reference to international agreements envisages the Resolution of the Council of OECD of 17 April 1957 which allows member states to postpone the issue of a labour permit until it has been ascertained that the job cannot be filled by nationals. Other international conventions are also included, whether they are multi-lateral[8] or bi-lateral.[9]

While it was provided during the transitional period that three weeks must have lapsed since the vacancy was declared before it could be advertised abroad,[10] no such restriction exists today, although the wording of the regulations now in force seems to require that the vacancy cannot, or is not likely to, be filled by the manpower available on the national labour market.[11]

The systematic and gradual abolition of the administrative procedures and practices required by the Treaty (art. 49(b)) was taken one step further by the Council Directive 68/360 of 15 October 1968 on the Re-

---

1 Reg. 1612/68, art. 16; for the exceptions see art. 16(3).

2 Reg. 1612/68, arts. 6(2), 17.

3 Reg. 1612/68, arts. 21–23.

4 Reg. 1612/68, arts. 24–31, appointed by the Council (art. 27) and consisting of groups of six representatives for each member state, two of which represent, respectively, the government, the trade unions and the employers' associations (art. 26(1).

5 Reg. 1612/68, arts. 32–37, appointed by the governments of the member states from their representatives on the Advisory Committee.

6 For the solutions during the transitional period see Reg. 2/64, OJ, 1964, 49; Reg. 38/64, arts. 13, 14.

7 OJ, 1968, L 257, replacing the directive added to Reg. 38/64, OJ, 1964, 981, superseding the Council Directive of 16 August 1961, OJ, 1961, 1513.

8 *E.g.*, ILO Convention No. 97 of 1 September 1949.

9 *E.g.*, Franco-German Treaty of Commerce and Navigation of 27 October 1957, art. V(1), [1957] II BGBl 1662; German-Italian Treaty of 21 November 1957, art. 9, [1959] II BGBl 949.

10 Reg. 16/62 and Directive of 16 August 1961, OJ, 1961, 1513, replaced by Reg. 38/64, arts. 1(1), 2(3) and the Council Directive 64/240 of 25 March 1964, OJ, 1964, 981.

11 Reg. 1612/68, arts. 15(1)(a), 16(1), (2).

moval of Restrictions on Travel and Residence for Workers of the Member States and their Families within the Community.[1] In the circumstances in which Reg. 1612/68 applies, it requires the removal of restrictions on travel and residence of the workers concerned and of members of their families[2] and, in particular, of restrictions of emigration,[3] of entry[4] and of residence on the strength of a residence permit to be issued as a matter of course if certain documents are produced, including a certificate of employment or a declaration by the employer stating that the worker has been engaged.[5] The residence permit is to be valid in the entire territory of the issuing member state for a period of at least five years and is to be automatically renewable.[6] The Directive deals also with the relationship between the requirement of a residence permit and the contract of employment.[7]

The validity of the residence permit is not affected by an absence abroad up to six months or due to the performance of military service.[8] Nor does loss of employment as a result of illness, accident or involuntary redundancy affect it.[9] Temporary residence permits are issued to seasonal workers and to workers whose employment is restricted to a period of between three and twelve months.[10] If the worker has been involuntarily unemployed in the host state for more than twelve consecutive months, the residence permit may be limited to a period of not less than twelve months at the time of the first renewal.[11] Commission Reg. 1251/70 of 29 June 1970,[12] issued in virtue of art. 48(3) of the Treaty[13] and not of Council Reg. 1612/68, purports to supplement the latter[14] by filling a gap. While Reg. 1612/68 covers the case where a Community worker has taken up employment in another member state and wishes to remain, either when out of work due to accident, illness or involuntary unemployment or in order to take up another employment, the Regulation fails to make provision for the case where the worker desires to continue his

---

1 OJ, 1968, L 257/13 intended to replace Council Directive 64/240 of 25 March 1964, OJ 1964, 981. See Directive of 15 October 1968, art. 13.

2 Directive 68/360 (above, n. 1), art. 1 replacing Directive 64/240 (above, n. 1), art. 1.

3 Directive 68/360, art. 2; 64/240, art. 2.

4 Directive 68/360, art. 3; 64/240, art. 3.

5 Directive 68/360, art. 4 exceeding the scope of 64/240, art. 4.

6 Directive 68/360, art. 61 exceeding the scope of 64/240, art. 5.

7 Directive 68/360, art. 5; cp. p. 88, n. 14.

8 Directive 68/360, art. 6(2) and cp. *Württembergische Milchverwertung-Südmilch-AG* v. *Ugliola* (1969), 15 Rec. 363, at pp. 369(4)–370(7); [1970] C.M.L.R. 194.

9 Directive 68/360, arts. 6(2), 7(1).

10 Directive 68/360, art. 6(3) amending the wording of Directive 64/240, art. 6. No residence permit is required if the migrant or seasonal worker enters for a period of less than three months: Directive 68/360 art. 8, except for workers benefiting from Council Directive 64/220 of 25 March 1964 (above, p. 87, n. 2).

11 Directive 68/360, art. 7.

12 OJ, 1970, L 142/24. And see below, p. 133, n. 4 for the extension of Council Directive 64/221 of 25 February 1964 to this situation by Council Directive 72/194, 18 May 1972, OJ, 1972, L 121/32.

13 See above, p. 86.

14 In respect of same range of persons as those envisaged by Council Reg. 1612/68, art. 1.

residence in the member state after his retirement on reaching the age limit, after premature retirement owing to an accident in the course of his employment or an occupational disease, or if he takes up employment in an adjacent member state. Nor does it regulate the position of the surviving spouse and of the members of the family residing with the worker. As a result of Commission Reg. 1251/70[1] such a worker may continue to reside in the member state—

(a) if, before his ordinary retirement he had been employed there within the last twelve months and has resided there continuously for three years[2] *or*

(b) if, when he retired prematurely owing to an occupational disease or industrial accident, he had been resident there continuously for two years; this residential requirement is waived if the accident or disease qualifies the worker for a pension or rent locally,[3] *or*

(c) if he takes up employment in another member state while retaining his previous residence, provided that he has resided and worked in employment in the latter continuously for three years.

The computation of periods of employment under (a) and (b) does not apply in the case envisaged under (c).[4]

The requirements of qualifying periods of residence and employment under (a) or of residence under (b) are waived, if the spouse is a local national. The same privilege is granted to members of the worker's family who resided with him before he died while employed in the state concerned,[5] provided that the deceased resided there continuously for two years, or if his death was due to an industrial accident or occupational disease or if the surviving spouse is a national of the state of residence or was such a national before losing the nationality upon marriage.[6] Continuous residence, for this purpose, is not affected by an annual absence of up to three months, and periods of employment include periods of involuntary unemployment or absence from such work through illness.[7]

The Regulation is less than perfect inasmuch as it fails to state whether the residence or employment must have been continuous immediately before the retirement, assumption of work abroad or death. Moreover, it remains an arguable point whether the Commission Reg. 1251/70 is *ultra vires* art. 48(3). Certain it is that it has no basis in Council Reg. 1612/68. For this reason the Commission appears to have relied on the Treaty itself (art. 48(3)). The question remains as to whether provisions for the continuation of residence in the host country for purposes of retirement or taking up employment elsewhere serve the objects of art. 48,

---

1   Commission Reg. 1251/70, art. 2 (above, p. 90, n. 12).
2   *Ibid.*, art. 2(1)(a).
3   *Ibid.*, art. 2(1)(b).
4   *Ibid.*, art. 2(1)(c).
5   *Ibid.*, art. 3(1).
6   *Ibid.*, art. 3(2).
7   *Ibid.*, art. 4.

which is to facilitate the free movement of workers. Perhaps it can be argued that it does so indirectly. Exceptions are permitted for reasons of public policy, national security or public health in accordance with art. 48(3) of the Treaty discussed above,[1] where it was pointed out that the details of the permitted deviation are contained in the Council Directive of 25 February 1964,[2] which will be discussed more conveniently in the chapter on the right of establishment of self-employed persons,[3] for the implementation of which it is primarily intended.

(c) The abolition of all discriminatory qualifying periods and restrictions which impede the immediate free choice of a place of employment of alien workers, whether contained in national legislation or in international agreements made between member states, is envisaged (art. 49(c)).[4] The meaning of this paragraph is not entirely clear. It seems to implement the general principles set out in art. 48(b)–(d), which are already covered, as regards initial waiting periods, by art. 49(d). It would seem, therefore, that art. 49(c) seeks to enable workers who have been admitted to work in a member state to change their place of employment. In this case, the procedure of implementation laid down by the Council upon recommendation of the Commission must overlap with that envisaged in art. 48(3)(d) entrusted to the Commission acting alone.[5] Council Reg. 1612/68, replacing Council Reg. 36/64[6] in combination with Commission Reg. 1251/70 appears to have filled the gap.[7]

(d) To balance the supply of and the demand for labour on the basis of conditions which exclude a serious danger to the standard of living and to employment in the different industries (art. 49(d)). This provision appears to empower the Council to take temporary or long term, single or general measures. Council Reg. 1612/68 implemented it by an appropriate procedure. Whenever a state suffers, or foresees, a disturbance of its labour market which is capable of seriously threatening the standard of living or employment in a region or occupation, the member states and the Commission, upon being advised by the member state concerned, shall take measures to inform workers of other Community countries and to discourage them from seeking employment in that region or occupation. Further, the Commission upon the application of the member state concerned may decide to suspend the matching procedure in part or completely.[8]

At the same time the member states have bound themselves to work out a programme for the exchange of young workers (art. 50) and, more generally, to abolish all discrimination between male and female workers.[9]

---

1 See above, p. 87, text to n. 2.
2 OJ, 1964, 850.
3 Below, p. 133.
4 Cp. art. 54(3)(d).
5 See above, p. 86, text to nn. 6 and 7.
6 Arts. 1(1), 5.
7 Council Reg. 1612/68, art. 20; Commission Reg. 1251/70, OJ, 1970, L 142/4.
8 Reg. 1612/68, art. 20.
9 See Regs. 14, OJ, 1962, 1054 and 28, OJ, 1962, 1277, abrogated in 1964. See now Council

III SOCIAL SECURITY[1]

1 The Problem to be Solved

The mobility of labour is not assured, unless a worker can be certain that the benefits of social security which he has acquired or to which he can look forward in the future in the first member state accompany him to the second member state into which he moves, and that while he is in the second member state his benefits and expectations will continue to run and to be maintained. At the same time provision must be made that such a worker is not subject to social security charges in more than one country, for such a double imposition itself might act as a deterrent against migration.[2] Without some co-ordination these aims cannot be easily realised since two principles seem to dominate the allocation and administration of social security which are apt to defeat any such aims.

In the first place, social security legislation touches only persons and events inside its own geographical sphere of operation and may thus be described as territorial. In the second place, even when it applies, it refuses to acknowledge claims by dependent persons, such as widows and children who reside permanently outside its territorial sphere.

Finally, the types of social security benefits which are available in the countries of the Community differ considerably in their nature and their conditions of application.[3] They may be contributory or non-contributory, compulsory or voluntary or facultative, and even if their conditions of application should appear to be identical, external factors such as the fictitious imputation of periods of contribution or the suspension of benefits while the interested party continues to work may distort their character so as to render comparison and integration more difficult.

With these considerations in mind the Treaty provides (art. 51) that in the field of social security the free movement of workers is to be buttressed by the introduction of a system which ensures to migrant workers and their dependents that—

(a) all periods recognised by the domestic law of the countries concerned as qualifying periods for acquiring and retaining rights to benefits and for calculating these benefits are to be added together (aggregation), and

(b) any such benefits will be paid even if the beneficiaries are resident in another country of the Community.

Decision 64/307 incorporating a Resolution of Ministers of 21 April 1964, OJ, 1964, 1226 setting out a Programme. See also Commission Reply No. 265/72, 29 November 1972, OJ, 1972, C 134/7; 138/74.

1 Lyon-Caen, *Droit Social Européen* (1969), p. 288, No. 414 ff. and in 1968 Rev. Trim. Dr. Eur. 148; Seché, 1968 Rev. Trim. Dr. Eur. 475 with lit., (1969) 6 C.M.L.Rev. 170; Tantaroudas, 1972 Rev. Trim. Dr. Eur. 36.

2 See *Bestuur der Sociale Verzekeringsbank* v. *Van der Vecht* (1967), 13 Rec. 445, at p. 457; [1968] C.M.L.R. 151.

3 Cp. CECA, Etude Comparative des Sources du Droit de Travail dans les Pays de la CECA: "Les Systèmes de Sécurité Sociale . . ." (1957).

Measure: Council, unanimously upon a proposal by the Commission (art. 51).

As a result Reg. 3 concerning Social Security of Migrant Workers,[1] supplemented in certain technical details by Reg. 4[2] came into being soon after the Treaty had been concluded. Special regulations dealt with seamen,[3] frontier workers[4] and seasonal workers.[5] The principal Regulation was to be replaced and consolidated with those dealing with specialised types of workers,[6] and this final consolidation has now taken place.

The regulations on social security owe much to the collaboration of the International Labour Office which had previously lent its expertise to the ECSC. Nevertheless, the principal Reg. 3 left many problems open and gave rise to a considerable body of litigation in the Community Court.[7] It was replaced after much preliminary work[8] by Council Reg. 1408/71 of 14 June 1971[9] and supplemented in its technical details by Council

---

1 Council Reg. 3 of 25 September 1958, OJ, 1958, 561, amended 35/63, OJ, 1963, 1313; 36/63, OJ, 1963, 1314 (frontier workers); 73/63, OJ, 1963, 2011; 130/63, OJ, 1963, 2998; 1/64, OJ, 1964, 1; 24/64, OJ, 1964, 746; 80/65, OJ, 1965, 1889; 109/65, OJ, 1965, 2124; 47/67, OJ, 1967, 641 (seamen); 419/68, OJ, 1968, L 87. As regards Annex B of Reg. 3 see for Luxembourg, OJ, 1970, L 123/14.

2 Council Reg. 4 of 3 December 1958, OJ, 1958, 597 amended OJ, 1961, 831, 993–998, OJ, 1962, 157; 8/63, OJ, 1963, 383; 35/63, OJ, 1963, 1313; 36/63, OJ, 1963, 1314; 73/63, OJ, 1963, 2011; 1/64, OJ, 1964, 1; 2/64, OJ, 1964, 49; 24/64, OJ, 1964, 746; 108/64, OJ, 1964, 2138; 80/65, OJ, 1965, 1889; 109/65, OJ, 1965, 2124; 47/67, OJ, 1967, 641.

3 Reg. 47/67, OJ, 1967, 641.

4 Reg. 36/63, OJ, 1963, 1314, amended OJ, 1972, L 159/24.

5 Reg. 73/63, OJ, 1963, 2011; Reg. 2/64, OJ, 1964, 49.

6 Reg. 38/64, art. 60, OJ, 1964, 965 and see the Report of the European Parliament, Doc. 158 of 30 December 1967, Commission Proposal 29/1966 of 28 October 1966, OJ, 1966, 3333.

7 *Unger* (1964), 10 Rec. 347; [1964] C.M.L.R. 319; *Nonnenmacher* (1964), 10 Rec. 557; [1964] C.M.L.R. 338; *Van der Veen*, (1964), 10 Rec. 1105; [1964] C.M.L.R. 548; *Dingemans* (1964), 10 Rec. 1259; [1965] C.M.L.R. 144; *Bertholet* (1965), 11 Rec. 111; [1966] C.M.L.R. 191; *Van Dijk* (1965), 11 Rec. 131; [1966] C.M.L.R. 191; *Dekker* (1965), 11 Rec. 1111; [1966] C.M.L.R. 503; *Singer* (1965), 11 Rec. 1191; [1966] C.M.L.R. 82; *Vaassen-Göbbels* (1966), 12 Rec. 377; [1966] C.M.L.R. 508; *Hagenbeek* (1966), 12 Rec. 618; *Ciechelski* (1967), 13 Rec. 235; [1967] C.M.L.R. 192; *De Moor* (1967), 13 Rec. 255; [1967] C.M.L.R. 223; *Guerra* (1967), 13 Rec. 283; *Colditz* (1967), 13 Rec. 297; *Cossuta* (1967), 13 Rec. 399; [1968] C.M.L.R. 5; *Goffart* (1967), 13 Rec. 413; [1967] C.M.L.R. 343; *Welchner* (1967), 13 Rec. 427; *van der Vecht* (1967), 13 Rec. 445; [1968] C.M.L.R. 151; *Couture* (1967), 13 Rec. 487; [1968] C.M.L.R. 14; *Guissart* (1967), 13 Rec. 551; *De Cicco* (1968), 14 Rec. 689; [1969] C.M.L.R. 67; *Torrekens* (1969), 15 Rec. 125; [1969] C.M.L.R. 377; *Entr'aide Médicale* (1969), 15 Rec. 405; [1970] C.M.L.R. 243; *Duffy (Jeanne)*, (1969), 15 Rec. 597; [1971] C.M.L.R. 391; *Brock (Elisabeth)* (1970), 16 Rec. 171; [1971] C.M.L.R. 55; *Di Bella* (1970), 16 Rec. 415; [1970] C.M.L.R. 232; *La Marca* (1970), 16 Rec. 987; *Manpower SARL* (1970), 16 Rec. 1251; [1971] C.M.L.R. 222; *Janssen (Michel)* (1971), 17 Rec. 359; *Gross*, (1971), 17 Rec. 871; *Keller* (1971), 17 Rec. 885; *Höhn* (1971), 17 Rec. 893.

8 Reg. 38/64, art. 60, OJ, 1964, 965; Commission Proposal 66/614, OJ, 1966, 3333 (on which Reg. 1408/71 is closely modelled); OJ, 1968, C 95, p. 18; Opinion of the Assembly, OJ, 1968, C 10, p. 30; C 135, p. 4 and of the Economic and Social Council, OJ, 1967, 1009, OJ, 1969, C 21, p. 18.

9 OJ, 1971, L 149/2, amended by the Accession Treaty, 22 January 1972, Cmnd. 4862 Pt. II, Annex I. Art. 51 and Reg. 1408/71 were extended to the French overseas departments by Council Decision 71/238, OJ, 1971, L 149/1.

Reg. 574/72 of 21 March 1972.[1] Since the new Regulation is not merely a consolidating measure restricted to technical improvements, but has introduced drastic changes of principle which are opposed to the previous practice of the Community Court, it is necessary to set out both the previous rules as well as those introduced with effect from 1 October 1972.[2] Only thus the existing case law of the Community Court can be properly appreciated. Moreover, doubts as to whether Reg. 1408/71 may be *ultra vires* invite a comparison.[3]

2 Art. 51 of the Treaty and the Regulations on Social Security—Purpose and Limits

The Community Court, in determining a spate of cases has stressed throughout that the basis of Reg. 3 must be found in arts. 48–51 of the Treaty.[4] Thus the Court has held that ". . . the Treaty has . . . imposed the duty upon the Council to draw up regulations which will prevent that, as a result of the absence of legislation applicable to them, interested parties remain without any protection of social security measures . . . or that [they] are placed . . . in an unfavourable position".[5] "Articles 48–51 . . . which form the basis of the framework of Regulation 3 do not give the power to prevent a state from granting to its population as a whole, including those of its nationals who work abroad, an additional measure of social protection."[6] "Its purpose is, instead, to abolish the territorial limits of application of the various social security schemes."[7] "Art. 51 . . . envisages essentially the situation where the law of a state does not admit, on its own, a claim to benefits by an interested party for the reason that the number of qualifying periods according to that law have not been completed . . . *pro-rata-ing* presupposes aggregation."[8] "It permits the

---

1 OJ, 1972, L 74, amended (arts. 26, 50, German version) by Reg. 2059/72, OJ, 1972, L 222/18. For the necessary forms see Decision 71/376 of the Administrative Commission, OJ, 1972, L 261/2.

2 Reg. 574/72, art. 122.

3 Tantaroudas, 1972 Rev. Trim. Dr. Eur. 36, at pp. 54–56. The latter author's doubts as to whether any effective remedy will be available, having regard to the limited range of art. 173 *ratione temporis* and *ratione personae*, can be met by a reference to art. 177(b) of the Treaty.

4 It is interesting to note that in its Preamble, Reg. 3 relies on arts. 51 and 227(2) of the Treaty, while the new Regulation 1408/71 refers to arts, 2, 7 and 51.

5 *Nonnenmacher* v. *Bestuur der Sociale Verzekeringsbank* (1964), 10 Rec. 557, at p. 572; [1964] C.M.L.R. 338; see also *Caisse d'Assurance de Vieillesse des Travailleurs Salariés de Paris* v. *Duffy (Jeanne)* (1969), 15 Rec. 597, at p. 604(6) and (7); [1971] C.M.L.R. 391; *De Cicco* v. *Landesversicherungsanstalt Schwaben* (1968), 14 Rec. 689, at p. 699; [1969] C.M.L.R. 67; *Bundesknappschaft Bochum* v. *Brock (Elisabeth)* (1970), 16 Rec. 171, at p. 179(13); (14); [1971] C.M.L.R. 55.

6 *Nonnenmacher* v. *Bestuur der Sociale Verzekeringsbank* (1964), 10 Rec. 557, at p. 584.

7 *Hessische Knappschaft* v. *Singer* (1965), 11 Rec. 1191, at p. 1199; [1966] C.M.L.R. 82; *Vaassen-Göbbels* v. *Beambtenfonds voor het Mijnbedrijf* (1966), 12 Rec. 377, at p. 400; [1966] C.M.L.R. 508; *De Moor* v. *Caisse de Pensions des Employés Privés* (1967) 13 Rec. 255, at p. 268; [1967] C.M.L.R. 223. But see Reg. 3, art. 10 and Annex E.

8 *Caisse Régionale de Sécurité Sociale du Nord-Est* v. *Goffart* (1967), 13 Rec. 413, at p. 421; [1967] C.M.L.R. 343; *Guissart* v. *Etat Belge* (1967), 13 Rec. 552, at p. 562.

migrant worker to obtain admission of his right to benefits for all working periods without discrimination."[1] "Art. 51 . . . does not serve to equalise the benefits but to exclude loss of benefits by aggregation; aggregation and *pro-rata-ing* are linked, but the Treaty does not require *pro-rata-ing* as such."[2]

In the opinion of the Community Court Reg. 3 sought at the same time to avoid unnecessary cumulation resulting from the successive or alternative operation of several legal systems.[3] Yet, since arts. 48–51 serve to ensure the free movement of workers by conferring upon them certain rights, it would be contrary to the purpose and the framework of these provisions if such workers were to suffer a reduction of their right as a result of their migration, except when the regulations offer equivalent advantages[4] or eliminate double impositions of contributions.[5] In the absence of such compensating advantages any curtailment of rights acquired under the law of one of the member states would in the opinion of the Court have the effect of placing the worker in a less favourable position than that which he would have enjoyed under the domestic law of one state alone.[6] This result was not to be countenanced in the opinion of the Community Court unless the qualifying periods overlap.[7]

The pronouncements of the Community Court explaining the principles which inspire arts. 48–51 of the Treaty and Reg. 3 make it clear that neither the Treaty nor the Regulation seek to create an overriding system of social security.[8] The aim is to co-ordinate the operation of the systems of social security of the member states in order to preserve for the

---

1   *Hagenbeek* v. *Raad van Arbeid* (1966), 12 Rec. 617, at p. 625; *Caisse Régionale de Sécurité Sociale du Nord* v. *Torrekens* (1969), 15 Rec. 125, at p. 135(11), (12); [1969] C.M.L.R. 377.

2   *De Moor* v. *Caisse de Pension des Employés Privés* (1967), 12 Rec. 256, at p. 268 (above, p. 94, n. 7); see also *Ciechelski* v. *Caisse Régionale de Sécurité Sociale du Centre, Orléans* (1967), 13 Rec. 235, at pp. 244–245; [1967] C.M.L.R. 192; *Colditz* v. *Caisse d'Assurance Vieillesse des Travailleurs Salariés de Paris* (1967), 13 Rec. 297, at p. 304; *Office National des Pensions pour Ouvriers* v. *Couture* (1967), 13 Rec. 487, at p. 500; [1968] C.M.L.R. 14.

3   *Sociale Verzekeringsbank* v. *van der Vecht* (1967), 13 Rec. 445, at pp. 456, 457; [1968] C.M.L.R. 151. For the problem of cumulation see *Nonnenmacher* v. *Bestuur der Sociale Verzekeringsbank* (1964), 10 Rec. 557, at pp. 573, 574; [1964] C.M.L.R. 559; *De Moor* v. *Caisse de Pension des Employés Privés* (1967), 13 Rec. 255, at p. 268; [1967] C.M.L.R. 223.

4   *Caisse d'Assurance Vieillesse des Travailleurs Salariés de Paris* v. *Duffy (Jeanne)* (1969), 15 Rec. 597, at p. 604(7); [1971] C.M.L.R. 391; *Michel Janssen* v. *Alliance Nationale* (1971), 17 Rec. 359, at p. 365(13). And see Reg. 1408/71, arts. 9(1), 10(1).

5   *Nonnenmacher* v. *Bestuur der Sociale Verzekeringsbank* (1964), 10 Rec. 557, at p. 574; [1964] C.M.L.R. 338; Seché, 1968 Rev. Trim. Dr. Eur. 475, at p. 489; for double impositions burdening employers see *Sociale Verzekeringsbank* v. *Van der Vecht* (1967), 13 Rec. 445, at pp. 457, 459; [1968] C.M.L.R. 151.

6   *Caisse d'Assurance Vieillesse des Travailleurs Salariés de Paris* v. *Duffy (Jeanne)* (1969), 15 Rec. 597, at p. 604(8), (9) (above, n. 4); *Caisse Régionale de Sécurité Sociale du Nord-Est* v. *Goffart* (1967), 13 Rec. 413, at p. 421; [1967] C.M.L.R. 343.

7   *De Moor* v. *Caisse de Pensions des Employés Privés* (1967), 13 Rec. 255, at pp. 268, 269; [1967] C.M.L.R. 223; *Caisse Régionale de Sécurité Sociale du Nord-Est* v. *Goffart* (1967), 13 Rec. 413, at p. 421; [1967] C.M.L.R. 223.

8   *De Moor* v. *Caisse de Pension etc.* (1967), 13 Rec. 255, at p. 268 (above, n. 7), *Colditz* v. *Caisse d'Assurance Vieillesse des Travailleurs Salariés de Paris* (1967), 13 Rec. 298, at p. 304.

worker rights which he has acquired before migration[1] and to carry over into the country of immigration any expectations and qualifying periods which have accrued in the country of his previous residence,[2] if there should be any need to aggregate periods or benefits. Neither the Treaty nor Reg. 3 seeks to curtail rights fully and unconditionally acquired under any one system of laws and to replace them by the system of co-ordination in time.[3] Moreover, even if cumulation of benefits is not the purpose of the Treaty and of the Regulation[4] the Court held that they do not prohibit the simultaneous enjoyment of several benefits of a similar nature, if each is acquired on a different ground.[5] Finally, the aggregation of two separate periods spent in two countries, neither of which alone qualifies for a benefit, is admitted, even if *pro-rata-ing* is excluded.[6]

However, if the failure to qualify arises from the technical provisions of the law of a state which counts qualifications in terms of years beginning at the first day of the year and another state's law which counts it in months, the authorities in the former must break down their annual qualification into one of months. If the periods served amount to twelve completed months, the qualification is acquired, even if the initial date for qualifying does not coincide with the first day of the year.[7]

The newly formulated art. 13(1) of Reg. 1408/71[8] seems to reverse the principle crystallised by the Community Court stated above[9] that even if the cumulation of benefits is not the purpose of the Treaty, such cumulation is allowed, because it is not expressly prohibited.[10] The new Reg. 1408/71, treating the principle of non-discrimination[11] as identical with that of equality,[12] states that workers to whom the Regulation applies are subject to the laws of one state only.[13] For this purpose Reg. 1408/71, in terms which are more or less identical with those provided by Reg. 3,[14] determines the law governing the obligatory systems by a series of choice

---

1 Reg. 3, art. 10(1); Reg. 1408/71, art. 10(1).
2 Reg. 3, art. 9; Reg. 1408/71, art. 9(2).
3 *Nonnenmacher* v. *Bestuur der Sociale Verzekeringsbank* (1964), 10 Rec. 557, at pp. 573, 574; *Office National des Pensions* v. *Couture* (1967), 13 Rec. 487, at p. 500; *Guissart* v. *Etat Belge* (1967), 13 Rec. 551, at pp. 562, 563.
4 See Reg. 3, art. 21; but see Reg. 1408/71, art. 21.
5 *Caisse d'Assurance Vieillesse des Travailleurs Salariés de Paris* v. *Duffy* (*Jeanne*) (1969), 15 Rec. 597, at p. 604(9); [1971] C.M.L.R. 391: wife's old age pension in Belgium in respect of work there coupled with widow's pension in France where the husband had worked, notwithstanding that under French law the pension cannot be granted to a widow if she receives a pension in her own right.
6 *Union Nationale des Mutualités Socialistes* v. *La Marca* (1970), 16 Rec. 987, at p. 994(13); cp. Seché, 1968 Rev. Trim. Dr. Eur. 475, at p. 497.
7 *Cossutta* v. *Office National des Pensions pour Ouvriers* (1967), 13 Rec. 399; [1968] C.M.L.R. 5.
8 Otherwise identical with Reg. 3, art. 12.
9 But see Reg. 3, art. 21.
10 Above, nn. 2–4.
11 See above, p. 18 and n. 3; p. 19, n. 1.
12 Reg. 1408/71, art. 3 and Heading, formerly Reg. 3, art. 8.
13 Reg. 1408/71, art. 13(1).
14 Reg. 3, arts. 12–14a.

of law rules.[1] It adds that a cumulation of benefits arising from two compulsory insurance schemes relating to the same period of insurance cannot be claimed, except for invalidity, death, and old age benefits or arising from occupational diseases.[2] If the cumulation arises out of a conflict of laws in time and involves a system of compulsory insurance and one which is voluntary or facultative and continuous, the beneficiary is thrown by operation of law upon that which is compulsory.[3] If, however, the cumulation of laws and benefits involves voluntary or facultative continuous systems of insurance only, the beneficiary must opt.[4] Once again in the case of invalidity and old age benefits and death pensions, a cumulation is admitted, but in these circumstances only if the state where the voluntary or facultative scheme operates allows the cumulation.[5]

In so far as Reg. 3 provided an unqualified threefold option to employees of the European Communities,[6] Reg. 1408/71 reaffirms it.[7] Service personnel employed in diplomatic missions, if nationals of the receiving state, have an option between the system of insurance in the sending and the receiving state,[8] but in this case the option appears to affect alternative systems of compulsory insurance.

The conclusion to be drawn from the statement of principle formulated in Reg. 1408/71, art. 13(1), from the prohibition of cumulating compulsory systems of insurance by art. 12 and from the options conceded in case of cumulation of a compulsory and one or more continuous voluntary or facultative systems of insurance[9] appears to be the following.

The new Reg. 1408/71 has set its face against any cumulation of benefits from several systems of compulsory insurance relating to the same period of insurance and from a combination of compulsory and voluntary or facultative continuous insurance. The question remains whether this prohibition applies also to benefits under compulsory insurance schemes which have been acquired successively. Must the state where the benefit was first acquired reduce or suspend its performance because the laws and insurance regime of another state have subsequently become applicable and because in the latter a similar benefit has been acquired fully or in part? Regulation 3 gave a neutral answer except for old age, death and invalidity pensions[10] where aggregating is compulsory, even if domestic law would not allow it. Regulation 1408/71,[11] by a change of wording in the proviso seems to have modified the meaning of the exception as pre-

---

1 Reg. 1408/71, arts. 13(2)–16. These rules do not apply to continuous voluntary or facultative systems of insurance: Reg. 1408/71, art. 15(1).
2 Reg. 1408/71, art. 12(1), (2), and distinguish aggregation: arts. 18, 38, 45, 64, 67.
3 Reg. 1408/71, art. 15(2), seeing that the legislative competence of the state allowing voluntary or facultative schemes is not curtailed.
4 Reg. 1408/71, art. 15(2).
5 Reg. 1408/71, art. 15(2); for a special case see art. 15(3), 2nd para.
6 Reg. 3, art. 14a.
7 Reg. 1408/71, art. 16(3).
8 Reg. 1408/71, art. 16(1) and (2).
9 Reg. 1408/71, arts. 15, 16.
10 Reg. 3, art. 11(2).
11 Reg. 1408/71, art. 12(2), reproducing Reg. 3, art. 11(2).

viously interpreted by restricting the operation of such domestic law to the process of aggregation.[1]

If this interpretation is correct the case law in this matter to the contrary[2] is disregarded by Reg. 1408/71 and it remains a matter for debate whether the change will be upheld by the Community Court or not. If the practice of the Court was primarily influenced by the restrictive wording of Reg. 3 and not by the letter and the spirit of art. 51 of the Treaty, the new principle of equality, non-cumulation and option may prevail.[3] But if in the opinion of the Court art. 51 of the Treaty only seeks to co-ordinate rights acquired under domestic law, but not to adjust and to curtail them, not even reliance on the more general provision of art. 7 of the Treaty can support the new principle. Directly or indirectly it interferes with and modifies domestic systems of social security.[4] Non-discrimination and equality of treatment are not the same as egalitarianism and do not exclude dual benefits regularly acquired in accordance with the general law.[5]

The solution of the difficulties which may arise is rendered more complex by the variety of circumstances which may affect the individual situation. Not only are a number of different social security benefits involved; their nature varies also from country to country. Not only the interests of migrant workers must be considered. A change of residence following the termination of employment and sojourn abroad otherwise than for the purpose of work may call for attention according to the nature of the benefit claimed (transfer of pensions, accident abroad). Thus no single rule can serve to solve the many types of claims brought by persons in a variety of circumstances for diverse benefits. Much depends upon whether *e.g.* the claim is for an old age widow's or invalidity pension on the one hand, which are likely to be founded on contributions (whether voluntary, facultative or compulsory) over a period of time, or for sickness, accident, maternity or unemployment benefits, which may be due on the strength of residence only.

---

1 See also Reg. 1408/71, art. 14(3) which seems to represent an attempt to eliminate any such contingency from the outset. Cumulation is still possible under Reg. 1408/71, arts. 21, 54, 66.

2 *Nonnenmacher* v. *Bestuur der Sociale Verzekeringsbank* (1964), 10 Rec. 557, at pp. 573, 574; [1964] C.M.L.R. 338; *De Moor* v. *Caisse de Pension des Employés Privés* (1967), 13 Rec. 255, at p. 268 [1967] C.M.L.R. 223; *Sociale Verzekeringsbank* v. *Van der Vecht* (1967), 13 Rec. 445, at p. 457; [1968] C.M.L.R. 151; and see *Caisse d'Assurance Vieillesse des Travailleurs Salariés de Paris* v. *Duffy (Jeanne)* (1969), 15 Rec. 597, at p. 604(7), (8), (9); [1971] C.M.L.R. 391; *Caisse Régionale de Sécurité Sociale du Nord-Est* v. *Goffart* (1967), 13 Rec. 413, at p. 421; [1967] C.M.L.R. 343.

3 But see *Keller* v. *Caisse d'Assurance Vieillesse de Strasbourg* (1971), 17 Rec. 885, at p. 891(13): ". . . *avantager un travailleur migrant . . . découlerait non de l'interprétation du droit communautaire, mais du système actuellement en vigueur qui, faute d'un régime commun de securité sociale repose sur une simple coordination de législations nationales non-harmonisées*".

4 See, *e.g.*, Reg. 1408/71, arts. 3(3), 12, especially 12(4).

5 According to Tantaroudas, 1972 Rev. Trim. Dr. Eur. 36, at p. 57 cumulation remains possible, if the benefits are derived on two separate grounds—one on the strength of the position of the beneficiary as a worker, the other as a member of the public in general.

3 Jurisdiction *ratione loci*

Any system of co-ordination must proceed from a fixed place in space.[1] For the purpose of co-ordinating the laws of social security this is the place where the worker is employed (*lex laboris*), even if he is permanently resident in the territory of another member state or if the employer resides or the registered office of the enterprise by which he is employed is situated in the territory of another member state.[2] The law of the flag is the *lex laboris* for seamen,[3] while officials are subject to the law of their administration.[4] The *lex laboris* is not changed by a call up for military service in the home country.[5] While the previous Reg. 3 was in force, it was held that this rule must be observed where the worker is employed (which must accord him all benefits due under its own law),[6] but that it did not preclude the country of his permanent residence from according him benefits, especially if the *lex laboris* withheld them.[7] As stated above, such a cumulation may no longer be permissible after Reg. 1408/71 has come into operation. However, the general principle establishing the pre-eminence of the *lex laboris* and of the authorities where the employment is carried out[8] is subject to a number of far reaching exceptions.

In the first place, and most important, a worker whose permanent residence is in country A but who is sent to country B by an undertaking which has an establishment in country A, to which the worker is normally attached, in order to carry out some work on behalf of that enterprise, remains subject to the laws of country A as if he continued to work there, provided that the likely duration of the work to be carried out in country B does not exceed twelve months and that the worker has not been sent as a replacement of another who has come to the end of his stay abroad on behalf of this enterprise.[9] If for unforeseen reasons the stay exceeds

---

1 *Nonnenmacher* v. *Bestuur der Sociale Verzekeringsbank* (1964), 10 Rec. 559, at p. 573; [1964] C.M.L.R. 338.

2 Reg. 1408/71, arts. 13(2), 14, formerly Reg. 3, art. 12(1).

3 Reg. 1408/71, art. 13(2)(b), formerly Reg. 3, art. 12(2) inserted by Reg. 47/67, art. 2.

4 Reg. 1408/71, art. 13(2)(c).

5 Reg. 1408/71, art. 12(d) reproducing the decision of the Community Court in *Württem-bergische Milchverwertung-Südmilch-AG* v. *Ugliola* (1969), 15 Rec. 363; [1970] C.M.L.R. 194.

6 Reg. 3, art. 10, now Reg. 1408/71, art. 10(1).

7 *Nonnenmacher* v. *Bestuur der Sociale Verzekeringsbank* (1964), 10 Rec. 557, at p. 565; [1964] C.M.L.R. 338; Seché, 1968 Rev. Trim. Dr. Eur. 475, at p. 488, and n. 2 with lit.

8 Reg. 1408/71, arts. 13(2), 14, formerly Reg. 3, art. 12. While Reg. 3 was in force the question arose whether social security includes those provisions which apply as public law or also those which are contractual arising from wage agreements concluded in certain industries and binding on the industry as a whole, see below, p. 108, and n. 1) and whether such private law agreements are open to the operation of the ordinary rules of private international law, or whether Reg. 3 excluded the application of any law other than the *lex laboris*. See the German *Bundesarbeitsgericht* in *Zusatzversorgungskasse des Baugewerbes VVaG* v. *Van Hamond*, [1971] C.M.L.R. 585, at p. 588, Seché, 1968 Rev. Trim. Dr. Eur. 475, at p. 489. Reg. 1408/71 art. 1(j) now solves the question by excluding them generally, but allows states to bring them within the scheme covered by Reg. 1408/71.

9 Reg. 1408/71, art. 14(1)(a)(i); formerly Reg. 3, art. 13(1)(a), 1st para. as amended by Reg. 24/64, art. 1 and by Reg. 47/67, art. 2; Seché 1968 Rev. Trim. Dr. Eur. 475, at pp. 490–491.

twelve months, the law of the country A continues to apply until the job is completed, provided that the competent authority[1] of country B or anybody designated by it has given its consent before the initial period of twelve months has expired.[2] In line with the general purpose of Reg. 1408/71, art. 14(1)(a), formerly Reg. 3, art. 13(a), seeks to overcome obstacles impeding the free circulation of workers and to avoid administrative complications. If this provision did not exist workers would have to cease being members of one social security system, if only for a short period, and become attached to another.[3]

It has been held by the Community Court that art. 13(a) of Reg. 3 in its old version (which for this purpose does not differ from the new version and is now expressed in Reg. 1408/71, art. 14(1)(a)) applies, and not art. 12, even if the employee has been engaged for a short period only and for the exclusive purpose of carrying out a job abroad. It is not necessary that the execution of the work abroad is merely incidental to an engagement of a longer duration in the country of the worker's permanent residence established there where the worker carries out his functions normally.[4] Article 13(a) (old version), now Reg. 1408/71, art. 14(1)(a), applies equally if the worker is engaged in the country of his permanent residence by an enterprise established there which supplies enterprises abroad with qualified workers who are needed for a short period to execute particular tasks. The test is not whether during his stay abroad the worker is subject to instruction by the enterprise situated there but whether he remains subordinate to the enterprise which engaged him and whether the latter continues to be his employer, pays his wages and can dismiss him.[5]

In the second place, employees of an international transport undertaking with a registered office in one member state of the Community who are employed as travelling personnel in another or several member states are subject to the laws of the member state where the registered office is situated, no matter whether the enterprise acts as an agent or on its own account. If the employee is engaged by a branch of the enterprise in one member state while the registered office is in another, the laws of the state where the branch is situated apply; on the other hand if he is exclusively employed in the member state of his permanent residence which is neither the country where the enterprise has its registered office nor a branch, the employee is subject to the laws of the country of his permanent residence.[6]

---

1 For the meaning of this term see Reg. 1408/71, art. 1(l); formerly Reg. 3, art. 1(d).
2 Reg. 1408/71, art. 14(1)(a)(ii); formerly Reg. 3, art. 13(1)(a), 2nd para, as amended by Reg. 24/64, art. 1 and Reg. 47/67, art. 2.
3 *Manpower SARL* v. *Caisse Primaire d'Assurance Maladie de Strasbourg* (1970), 16 Rec. 1251, at p. 1257(9)–(13); [1971] C.M.L.R. 222.
4 *Sociale Verzekeringsbank* v. *Van der Vecht* (1967), 13 Rec. 445, at pp. 456, 457, [1968] C.M.L.R. 151. Seché, 1968 Rev. Trim. Dr. Eur. 475, at p. 488, n. 3 with lit.
5 *Manpower SARL* v. *Caisse Primaire d'Assurance Maladie de Strasbourg*, (1970), 16 Rec. 1251, at p. 1257(14)–(18); [1971] C.M.L.R. 222.
6 Reg. 1408/71, art. 14(b); formerly Reg. 3, art. 13(1)(b).

In the third place, a worker other than an employee of an international transport undertaking envisaged in Reg. 1408/71, art. 14(b), formerly Reg. 3, art. 13(1)(b) discussed previously, who normally performs his tasks in several member states is subject to the laws of the country of his residence.[1] If the worker does not reside in any of them, he is subject to the laws of the country where the employer is established or where the enterprise which employs him has its seat.[2]

If the worker is employed in one member state by an enterprise having its seat in another member state, and the two member states have a common frontier, the law of the state applies where the enterprise has its seat.[3]

Special solutions apply to workers who are either normally employed by an enterprise in one member state or on board vessels flying the flag of a member state and who are sent on board a vessel flying the flag of another member state in order to carry out work there,[4] to workers who, without being habitually employed on the high seas, are sent to work in the territorial waters or in a port of a member state on board a vessel flying the flag of another member state[5] and to workers who are employed on board a vessel flying the flag of one member state but have their residence in another member state and receive their wages from an employer in the latter member state.[6] A further provision deals with service personnel employed at diplomatic or consular posts or in the personal service of officials of such posts.[7] In principle the *lex laboris* applies,[8] but workers who are nationals of the sending or the receiving member state may exercise an option in favour of the law of their country of origin,[9] and a similar option, both a little broader and a little narrower, is open to *subordinate personnel* employed by the European Community.[10]

4 Jurisdiction *ratione personae*

The original Reg. 3 applied to wage earners or assimilated workers who are or have been subject to the legislation[11] of one or more of the member

---

1 Reg. 1408/71, art. 14(c)(1), formerly Reg. 3, art. 13(1)(c), 1st para., as amended by Reg. 24/64, art. 1.

2 Reg. 1408/71, art. 14(c)(ii), formerly Reg. 3, art. 13(1)(c), 2nd para., first sentence.

3 Reg. 1408/71, art. 14(1)(d), formerly Reg. 3, art. 13(1)(d).

4 Reg. 1408/71, art. 14(2)(a), formerly Reg. 3, art. 13(2)(a), added by Reg. 47/67, art. 2.

5 Reg. 1408/71, art. 14(2)(b), formerly Reg. 3, art. 13(2)(b), added by Reg. 47/67, art. 2.

6 Reg. 1408/71, art. 14(2)(c), formerly Reg. 3, art. 13 (2) (c).

7 Reg. 1408/71, art. 16(1), (2), formerly Reg. 3, art. 14.

8 Reg. 1408/71, art. 16(1), formerly Reg. 3, art. 14(1).

9 Reg. 1408/71, art. 16(2), formerly Reg. 3, art. 14(2).

10 Reg. 1408/71, art. 16(3), formerly Reg. 3, art. 14a, added by Reg. 80/65, art. 1.

11 For the meaning of "legislation" in this context see Reg. 1408/71, art. 1 (j) as amended by the Treaty of Accession, Pt. II, Annex I, IX, 1; Reg. 3, art. 1(b); *Vaassen-Göbbels* v. *Beambten-fonds voor het Mijnbedrijf* (1966), 12 Rec. 377, at p. 396; [1966] C.M.L.R. 508.

The term "subject to the legislation" ("*soumis à la législation*") has been held to mean, negatively, in relation to Reg. 3, art. 42(b) in the version of Reg. 1/64, art. 1, that legislation

states and are nationals of a member state or are stateless persons or refugees permanently resident in the territory of a member state, including members of their families and their survivors.[1] The meaning and extent of the term "wage earners or assimilated workers" gave rise to litigation in the course of which it was held that this provision was based on the notion that a broad range of beneficiaries was to be included. According to the Community Court, art. 4 of the relevant Reg. 3 was inspired by a general tendency of the social legislation in the countries of the Community to extend its benefits to new categories of persons who are exposed to the same risks and dangers.[2] However, the Regulation itself did not enumerate the circle of beneficiaries and left the specification to the law of the member states.[3] Thus, while it was the task of the courts of the member states to determine in each case whether a claimant was qualified to receive social security benefits, because he possessed all the attributes of a worker and whether his qualification had been maintained because he was likely to resume this activity,[4] the notion of a "wage earner or assimilated worker" was one of Community law, the uniform interpretation of which could not be modified by the law of the member states.[5] According to Community law a wage earner or assimilated worker could include an individual in a member state who has continued to be affiliated to a national social security scheme covering the same risks on a voluntary basis because he was likely to resume a wage earning or assimilated activity.[6] In cases involving the aggregation of contributions (*e.g.* invalidity pensions) more than one national system of laws is involved. In these circumstances the Community Court appears to have relied on the law of the last permanent residence, which was also the national law of the deceased.[7]

The difficulties and uncertainties created by the definition of workers in Reg. 3 have led to its reformulation in Reg. 1408/71.[8] Once again the Regulation extends to nationals of the member states; it also extends to

---

under which no benefit is conferred is to be disregarded as being legislation to which the person concerned is *not* subject: *Caisse de Compensation etc. de Mons* v. *Di Bella* (1970), 16 Rec. 415, at p. 421(10)–(15); [1970] C.M.L.R. 232. The same meaning probably attaches to art. 4.

For the meaning of the term "who have been subject . . ." see *Janssen* v. *Alliance Nationale* (1971), 17 Rec. 859, at p. 865(12).

1   Reg. 1408/71, art. 2 (1), (2), formerly Reg. 3, art. 4(1), (2). Seché, 1968 Rev. Trim. Dr. Eur. 475 at pp. 483–486.

2   *De Cicco* v. *Landesversicherungsanstalt Schwaben* (1968), 14 Rec. 689, at p. 700; [1969] C.M.L.R. 67.

3   *Ibid.*, p. 700; *Janssen* v. *Alliance Nationale* (1971), 17 Rec. 859, at p. 864(2), (above, n. 11).

4   *Unger* v. *Bestuur der Bedrijfsvereniging voor Detailhandel* (1964), 10 Rec. 347, at p. 363; [1964] C.M.L.R. 319 and the lit. cited by Seché, 1968 Rev. Trim. Dr. Eur. 475, at p. 483, n. 2.

5   *Ibid.*, at pp. 363–364, 367; *Janssen* v. *Alliance Nationale* (1971), 17 Rec. 859, at p. 864(6), (8), (9), (above, n. 11).

6   *Janssen* v. *Alliance Nationale* (1971), 17 Rec. 859, at p. 864 (11) (above, n. 11).

7   According to Italian law artisans were placed on the same footing with wage-earners (see above, n. 2; for the position in other EEC countries; see Seché, 485 n. 1.

8   Reg. 1408/71, art. 2(1).

stateless persons[1] and refugees[2] who reside in one of the member states.[3] The notion of worker itself has now been given as objective a content as possible and comprises persons who qualify under one of three headings. The basic test is whether the person concerned is—

(a) covered by an obligatory or facultative insurance against one or several risks enumerated in social security schemes through a scheme which is applicable to salaried workers, *or*

(b) covered by an obligatory insurance against one or several risks enumerated in Reg. 1408/71 through a general system of social insurance for all residents or persons of working age, *or*

(c) covered by a voluntary insurance against one or several risks enumerated in Reg. 1408/71, by a scheme applicable either to salaried workers, or to all residents or to certain categories of residents.[4]

In case (a) no further conditions are attached.

In case (b) the manner of administering or of financing the scheme must make it possible to classify the insured as a worker or, if this should be impossible, a continuous obligatory or facultative insurance must cover certain risks set out in Annex V as part of a scheme for salaried workers.

In case (c) a previous obligatory insurance against the same risks must have been in existence as part of a scheme for salaried workers in the same state.

As in the old Reg. 3,[5] the new Regulation applies to workers who are or were subject to the law of one or more of the member states.[6] The term subject (*soumis*) clearly relates to the solution, *ratione loci*, of the choice of law set out above and does not attract the meaning given to it by the Community Court in relation to Reg. 3, art. 42(6).[7] Frontier[8] and seasonal workers[9] are included.

For the more limited purpose of allowing a social security institution to recover from a third party the equivalent of social security payments made to a beneficiary in connection with an accident abroad caused by the third party,[10] the Community Court has relied on the general provision of Reg. 3, art. 4, now Reg. 1408/71, art. 2(1), and has held that the worker concerned need not have been a migrant worker.[11] ". . . The

---

1 For the definition see Reg. 1408/71, art. 1(e).
2 For the definition see Reg. 1408/71, art. 1(d).
3 Reg. 1408/71, art. 2(1).
4 Reg. 1408/71, art. 1(a).
5 Reg. 3, art. 4.
6 Reg. 1408/71, art. 2(1).
7 See above, p. 102, n. 11; *Caisse de Compensation etc. de Mons* v. *Di Bella* (1970), 16 Rec. 415, at p. 422(14); [1970] C.M.L.R. 232. For the term "legislation" see below, p. 108, n. 1.
8 Reg. 1408/71, arts. 1(b), 20.
9 Reg. 1408/71, art. 1(c).
10 Reg. 1408/71, art. 93, formerly Reg. 3, art. 52.
11 *Hessische Knappschaft* v. *Singer* (1965), 11 Rec. 1192, at p. 1199; [1966] C.M.L.R. 82; *Caisse de Maladie des CFL* v. *Cie. Belge d'Assurances Générales* (1969), 15 Rec. 405, at p. 410(3), (4), (5); [1970] C.M.L.R. 243.

application of the Regulation is not restricted either to workers who have been employed in several states or to workers who are employed in one state while residing or having resided in another."[1] The purpose of the specific provisions permitting the social security institution to recover expenses from a third party *tortfeasor* is not to benefit migrant workers, who are entitled to accident payments in some jurisdiction, irrespective of concurrent or successive employment abroad. In the particular circumstances considered here (Reg. 3, art. 52, Reg. 1408, art. 93) the definition of a wage earner or assimilated worker in general terms fitting the purpose of Reg. 3 and Reg. 1408/71 as a whole is irrelevant. What matters here is that a social security payment has been made and that recovery abroad is to be facilitated. To this end the territorial limits of the application of different social security regimes are to be suppressed and an action of recourse or reimbursement (which arises out of a social security payment but does not as such constitute a claim to social security benefits) is created. Consequently the extension of the range of persons to whom Reg. 3, art. 52 and Reg. 1408/71, art. 93 refer should have no bearing upon the interpretation of the term "wage earners or assimilated workers" in art. 4(1) of Reg. 3[2] and now of the term "workers" as defined in Reg. 1408/71, art. 1(a).

The Regulation applies also to the families of such wage earners and their survivors.[3] Under Reg. 3 the term "members of the family" was to be construed according to the law of the country of their permanent residence.[4] Thus the strange situation could arise that the wage earner was subject to the laws of member state A according to which the claimant was not regarded as a member of his family, while according to the laws of member state B the claimant enjoyed the status of being a member of the beneficiary's family and was to be treated as such by the authorities in member state A.

Regulation 1408/71, art. 1(f) now provides that the qualification of being a member of the family is to be determined by the law under which the benefits accrue. It must be assumed that this is the law which applies to the benefits of the worker himself.[5] However, Reg. 1408/71 once again

---

1 *Gemeenschappelijke Verzekeringskas "De Sociale Voorzorg"* v. *Bertholet* (1965), 11 Rec. 111, at p. 119; [1966] C.M.L.R. 191; *Betriebskrankenkasse der Heseper Torfwerk GmbH* v. *Van Dijk* (1965), 11 Rec. 131, at p. 141; [1966] C.M.L.R. 191.

2 The wording of Reg. 1408/71, art. 93, formerly Reg. 3, art. 52 read by itself leads to the same conclusion. It refers simply to "a person [who] is in receipt of benefit under the legislation of one member state . . ."; *Gemeenschappelijke Verzekeringskas "De Sociale Voorzorg"* v. *Bertholet* (1965), 11 Rec. 111, at p. 119; [1968] C.M.L.R. 191; *Betriebskrankenkasse der Heseper Torfwerk* v. *Van Dijk* (1965), 11 Rec. 131, at p. 141; [1966] C.M.L.R. 191; *Caisse de Maladie des CFL* v. *Cie. Belge d'Assurances Générales* (1969), 15 Rec. 405, at p. 410(3)–(5); Seché, 1968 Rev. Trim. Dr. Eur. 475, at p. 485 with lit. n. 6, and p. 486, n. 1; cp. *Unger* v. *Bestuur der Bedrijfsvereniging voor Detailhandel* (1964), 10 Rec. 347, at p. 364; [1964] C.M.L.R. 319, Reg. 3, art. 19.

3 Reg. 3, art. 4(a), Reg. 1408/71, art. 2(1). For exceptions see Reg. 3, art. 17(1), Reg. 1408/71, art. 19.

4 Reg. 3, art 1(n). They must be permanently resident in a member state: see Reg. 3, art. 4(1); Reg. 1408/71, art. 1(f).

5 *I.e.* Reg. 1408/71, arts. 13–16.

relies on the law of the place of residence of the dependant in two cases. The first concerns benefits in kind for illness or confinement during a temporary stay[1] (*sojourn*) abroad;[2] the second, in connection with invalidity pensions, applies if the worker is subject exclusively to regimes according to which the amount of invalidity benefits is independent of the periods of insurance.[3] Going still further, Reg. 1408/71, art. 1(f), formerly Reg. 3, art. 1(n), does not only provide a choice of law rule, but supplies an overriding rule of Community law as well. If, according to the laws of the member states where the benefits accrue or where in the two cases set out above a claimant who alleges that he is a member of the family resides permanently, only those persons living under the same roof as the worker are regarded as members of the family, such persons are deemed for the purposes of the Regulation to be members of the household, if they are primarily dependent on the workers concerned.[4]

The notion of "survivors", on the other hand, is interpreted somewhat differently. Under the old Reg. 3 it was determined according to the legislation applicable,[5] which probably meant that which applied according to Reg. 3, arts. 12 and 13[6] to the insured himself. Thus a conflict between the law applicable to the insured and the claimant was eliminated. The new Reg. 1408/71[7] replaces the reference to the law applicable by one to the law on the strength of which the benefits are provided, thus giving the rule governing survivors the same range as that dealing with members of the family, except that the reference to arts. 22(1)(a) and 39 is omitted since the latter are inapplicable in the circumstances. In substance Reg. 1408/71 has not changed the beneficial solution first provided by Reg. 3.[8] It must be noted that the same overriding rule of Community Law as in the case of a "member of the family" (Reg. 1408/71, art. 1(f)) is provided here as well. If according to the law applicable only those persons who were living under the same roof as the deceased worker are regarded as survivors such persons are deemed to be survivors if they were primarily dependent upon the deceased.[9] Such survivors enjoy an additional advantage. If the wage earner was subject to the legislation of one or more member states but was not a national of a member state (as the Regulation requires in principle),[10] his survivors as defined here[11] are entitled to the benefit of the Regulation if they themselves are nationals of a member state, or stateless persons or refugees permanently resident in the territory of a member state.[12]

---

1   Defined in Reg. 1408/71, art. 1(i).
2   Reg. 1408/71, art. 22(1)(a).
3   Reg. 1408/71, art. 39(4).
4   Reg. 1408/71, art. 1(f), formerly Reg. 3, art. 1 (n).
5   Reg. 3, art. 1(o).
6   See above, pp. 100–102.
7   Reg. 1408/71, art. 1(g).
8   Reg. 3, art. 1(o).
9   Reg. 1408/71, art. 1(g), formerly Reg. 3, art. 1(o).
10 Reg. 1408/71, art. 2(1), formerly Reg. 3, art. 4(1), art. 1(a) and Annex A.
11 Reg. 1408/71, art. 1(g), formerly Reg. 3, art. 1(o).
12 Reg. 1408/71, art. 2(2), formerly Reg. 3, art. 4(2).

Regulation 3 stated expressly that it did not apply to established members of the diplomatic and consular services or to persons who form part of the staff of an administrative branch of government of a member state who are sent into the territory of another member state.[1] In a somewhat obscurely worded provision, Reg. 1408/71 appears to have reversed this rule in so far as officials of a member state are concerned and may, possibly, include diplomats as well.[2]

5 Jurisdiction *ratione materiae*

In substance Reg. 3 as well as the new Reg. 1408/71[3] applies to all legislation[4] which deals with social security benefits of the following types: sickness and maternity, invalidity[5] including grants for the purpose of maintaining or improving earning capacity,[6] old age, survivors' pension,[7] industrial accidents or occupational diseases, death, unemployment and family allowances.[8] The sphere of operation of the Regulation does not extend to social and medical assistance, war pensions and to special schemes for officials.[9]

By enumerating the types of legislation concerning social security benefits to which the Regulation applies Reg. 3, art. 2(1), now Reg. 1408/71, art. 4(1), serves to attach to each type of benefit the occurrence of concrete loss and stresses that the benefit is a concomitant of the loss, at least in the German version of the text, or a consequence of it.[10] The list does not include ancillary benefits outside this range which are intended *e.g.* to assist the holder of a pension covered by the Regulation in financing the conclusion and maintenance of a subsequent sickness insurance for the future.[11]

Legislation concerning social security in the meaning of Reg. 1408/71, art. 4(1), formerly Reg. 3, art. 2(1), includes all laws, regulations and

---

1 Reg. 3, art. 4(5).

2 Reg. 1408/71, art. 2(3).

3 Reg. 1408/71, art. 4(1), formerly Reg. 3, art. 2(1).

4 Reg. 1408/71, art. 5, formerly Reg. 3, art. 3: to be enumerated by member states.

5 Cp. *Dingemans* v. *Bestuur der Sociale Verzekeringsbank* (1964), 10 Rec. 1259, at p. 1273; [1965] C.M.L.R. 144.

6 Reg. 1408/71, art. 2(1)(b) omits the exception of the latter arising from industrial accidents or occupational diseases, as expressed formerly by Reg. 3, art. 2(1)(b).

7 Once again Reg. 1408/71, art. 4(1)(d) omits to mention the exception, expressed formerly in Reg. 3, art. 2(1)(d), of benefits arising from an industrial accident or an occupational disease. During the operation of Reg. 3 it included widows' pensions under Dutch law which are granted irrespective of the deceased worker's period of insurance: *Van der Veen* v. *Bestuur der Sociale Verzekeringsbank* (1964), 10 Rec. 1105, at p. 1125; [1964] C.M.L.R. 548; Reg. 130/63, art. 7 and see Reg. 3, art. 2(2). It would seem that in the particular circumstances the decision of the Community Court has been replaced by Reg. 1408/71, art. 12(4).

8 See above, nn. 3 and 4.

9 Reg. 1408/71, art. 4(4), formerly Reg. 3, art. 2(3). Seché, 1968 Rev. Trim. Dr. Eur. 475, at pp. 481–483.

10 *Leistungen bei Krankheiten,* but see *prestations de maladies: Dekker* v. *Bundesversicherungsanstalt für Angestellte* (1965), 11 Rec. 1111, at pp. 1116, 1117; [1966] C.M.L.R. 503.

11 *Ibid.,* p. 1117.

other *dispositions statutaires*[1] present and future relating to the social
security schemes and branches of social security set out in the Regulation.[2] The Community Court, applying Reg. 3, held that in the meaning
of the term used in the Regulation, *dispositions statutaires* included schemes
laid down by institutions other than public authorities who exercise
delegated powers.[3] Regulation 1408/71, art. 1(j) proviso now provides
that in the future such schemes are only included after the state concerned
has made a declaration to this effect. Agreements, past or future, even if
they have been rendered obligatory by a decision of a public authority,
are excluded, unless they can be brought within the framework of a
statute or of delegated powers.

The Regulation applies to all general and special security schemes,
whether contributory or non-contributory.[4] The social security legislation in each member state at the time of the adoption of Reg. 3 was set
out in Annex B of the Regulation, which was amended.[5] Given the need
to keep the information on domestic social security legislation constantly
under review, Reg. 1408/71 envisages periodical publication by the
member states.[6] The requirement of notice of all consequential amendments to Annex B of Reg. 3 as a result of the adoption of new domestic
legislation[7] has given rise to disputes, since it has been contended, in some
cases, that certain types of subsequent domestic legislation were inapplicable in the absence of notification. In the cases before the Community
Court these arguments did not succeed on the grounds—

(a) that notification was only required according to Reg. 3, art. 3(2)
     if any consequential amendments to Annex B were involved and
     that it was not necessary when the subsequent legislation intro-
     duced new types of social security, and
(b) that the term "legislation" according to the definition section
     covered all present and future laws.[8]

Thus the Community Court was able to hold that Reg. 3 applied with
effect from 1 January 1959, and any amendments to it, including Annex

---

1 Reg. 1408/71, art. 1(j) equates legislation with *"dispositions statutaires et toutes autres mesures
   d'application"*. The latter may be translated as "enforceable provisions"; cp. above, p. 100,
   n. 8, and contrast Reg. 3, art. 1(b).
2 Reg. 1408/71, art. 1(j) referring to art. 4(1) and (2), formerly Reg. 3, art. 1(b) referring to
   art. 2(1), (2).
3 *Vaassen-Göbbels* v. *Beambtenfonds voor het Mijnbedrijf* (1966), 12 Rec. 378; [1966] C.M.L.R. 508.
4 Reg. 1408/71, art. 4(2), formerly Reg. 3, art. 2(2): *Caisse Régionale de Sécurité Sociale du Nord*
   v. *Torrekens* (1969), 15 Rec. 125, at p. 135(12), (13), [1969] C.M.L.R. 377: *allocations aux
   vieux travailleurs salariés; Vaassen-Göbbels* v. *Beambtenfonds voor het Mijnbedrijf* (1966), 12 Rec.
   378; [1966] C.M.L.R. 508: widow's right to be a member of the Sickness Fund. Reg. 1408/71,
   art. 1(r), formerly Reg. 3, art. 1(p) does not exclude non-contributory schemes.
5 Reg. 3, art. 3(1); Reg. 130/63, OJ, 1963, 2996; further amended OJ, 1970, L 123/14.
6 Reg. 1408/71, arts. 5, 96. See *e.g.* OJ, 1973, C 90/1.
7 Reg. 3, art. 1(b): *Van der Veen* v. *Bestuur der Sociale Verzekeringsbank* (1964), 10 Rec. 1105, at
   pp. 1122, 1125; [1964] C.M.L.R. 548; *Dingemans* v. *Bestuur der Sociale Verzekeringsbank* (1964),
   10 Rec. 1259, at pp. 1273–1275; [1965] C.M.L.R. 144.
8 *Hessische Knappschaft* v. *Singer* (1965), 11 Rec. 1191, at p. 1200; [1966] C.M.L.R. 82.

B, could apply retroactively to this date.[1] Yet the facts which give rise to a claim under it may have occurred before 1959 and previously acquired rights are not affected.[2]

It must remain an open question whether in its new version the corresponding provision of Reg. 1408/71[3] supports the interpretation given to its predecessor in Reg. 3. Given that, unlike in Reg. 3,[4] the new Regulation does not contain in one Annex a compendious survey of the social security legislation in force at the time when the Regulation came into operation, it would seem that the restrictive interpretation given previously by the Community Court is inappropriate in the changed circumstances. Thus all legislation (in the broad sense of the Regulation as set out above) and not only that which amends previous law must now be notified.

6 Relationship between Regs. 3 and 1408/71 and any other Treaties Covering the Same Subject Matter

Generally speaking Reg. 3 superseded any social security conventions concluded between two or more member states as the exclusive parties[5] as well as all multilateral social security conventions which bound *inter alia* two or more member states, but in the latter circumstance no scheme or institution of a non-member state must have been involved.[6] A number of multilateral conventions were exempted,[7] and the member states remained bound by the bilateral conventions concluded between themselves which were set out in Reg. 3, Annex D.[8] These bilateral conventions must only give way to Reg. 3 (now Reg. 1408/71) if they are incompatible with it.[9] Where Reg. 3 envisaged the implementation of any of its provisions by bilateral agreements, the operation of the particular provision of the Regulation is not suspended while no bilateral agreement has been concluded.[10]

---

1 *Bundesknappschaft Bochum* v. *Brock* (1970), 16 Rec. 171, at p. 178(6); [1971] C.M.L.R. 55; Seché, 1968 Rev. Trim. Dr. Eur. 475, at pp. 486–488; Reg. 3, art. 53.
2 *Van der Veen* v. *Bestuur der Sociale Verzekeringsbank* (1964), 10 Rec. 1105, at pp. 1125 (above, p. 108, n. 7).
3 Reg. 1408/71, art. 5 in conjunction with art. 96.
4 Reg. 3, art. 3(1).
5 Reg. 3, art. 5(1).
6 Reg. 3, art. 5(1), (2); Reg. 1408/71, art. 5(a), (b) replacing "scheme" by "institution".
7 Reg. 3, art. 6 and Annex D; Reg. 1408/71, art. 7(2)(c) and Annex II.
8 Reg. 3, art. 6(2), (e); now Reg. 1408/71, art. 7(2)(c). The list could be amended subject to the procedure laid down in Reg. 3, art. 6(3); Reg. 1408/71 does not contain a corresponding provision. However, new conventions may be added in accordance with Reg. 1408/71, art. 8 (formerly Reg. 3, art. 7), and it may be that the right to enter into new conventions was regarded as including the right to amend existing conventions.
9 *Caisse Régionale de Sécurité Sociale du Nord* v. *Torrekens* (1969), 15 Rec. 125, at pp. 136(19)–(21); [1969] C.M.L.R. 377.
10 See, with reference to Reg. 3, art. 52 (now Reg. 1408/71, art. 93): *Gemeenschappelijke Verzekeringskas "De Sociale Voorzorg"* v. *Bertholet* (1965), 11 Rec. 111, at p. 118(1); [1966] C.M.L.R. 191; *Betriebskrankenkasse der Heseper Torfwerk* v. *Van Dijk* (1965), 11 Rec. 131, at p. 139; [1966] C.M.L.R. 191; *Caisse de Maladie des CFL* v. *Cie. Belge d'Assurances Générales* (1969), 15 Rec. 405, at p. 410(19); [1970] C.M.L.R. 243. See also Reg. 3, arts. 15, 25; Reg. 1408/71, art. 17.

These provisions, with some slight modifications in substance and in form were taken over by Reg. 1408/71.[1] However, Reg. 1408 confers the benefit of existing and future bilateral conventions between member states to all the beneficiaries of the new convention, whether they be nationals of other member states, stateless or refugees.[2]

IV GENERAL CONCLUSIONS

The provisions of Reg. 3 and the practice of the Community Court based on it as well as the text of the Treaty (arts. 48–51) bear out the following conclusions:

(a) the principle of territoriality of social security legislation is left untouched;[3]

(b) the operation of the various systems is co-ordinated so as to prevent the loss to any worker of social security benefits as a result of migration;[4]

(c) the separate interests of dependents and survivors resident in one member state in respect of social security benefits arising out of the employment of a worker in another member state are given protection where previously they were disregarded;

(d) rights accrued under one system of social security which exceed those obtainable under the system of co-ordination are not curtailed and replaced by the latter system;[5]

(e) although the cumulation of benefits is not the purpose of their co-ordination, simultaneous enjoyment of pecuniary benefits, each of which has been acquired on a different ground, is not prohibited; but in principle at least, and subject to far-reaching exceptions, simultaneous enjoyment of several benefits of the same type in respect of the same period of compulsory insurance is excluded.[6]

With these fundamental aims in mind Reg. 3 and now Reg. 1408/71 proclaims:

(i) The principle of equality of treatment or non-discrimination in favour of persons to whom the Regulation applies, in so far as rights and duties under the social security legislation of the state of residence are involved;[7]

(ii) the principle of aggregation (if necessary) of insurance and assimilated periods completed under the legislation of other member states for the purposes of admission to compulsory,

---

1 For exceptions see above, p. 109, nn. 5–10.
2 Reg. 1408/71, art. 3(3).
3 Ca. Seché, 1968 Rev. Trim. Dr. Eur. 475, at p. 480.
4 Seché, 1968 Rev. Trim. Dr. Eur. 475, at pp. 480–481.
5 Cp. Reg. 3, art. 17(4).
6 See now Reg. 1408/71, art. 12, and cp. art. 15 as to the cumulation of compulsory and voluntary insurances.
7 Reg. 1408/71, art. 3, formerly Reg. 3, art. 8, Seché, 1968 Rev. Trim. Dr. Eur. 475, at pp. 479–80.

voluntary or optional[1] continued insurance in the member state where the person has taken up permanent residence;[2]

(iii) the principle of the respect of acquired rights when pensions and death benefits have accrued in one member state in favour of a person who is resident in another member state,[3] subject to specific exceptions under Reg. 3, but not under Reg. 1408/71;[4]

(iv) the principle of non-cumulation of benefits of the same type in respect of the same period of compulsory insurance without aggregation.[5]

V INDIVIDUAL BENEFITS

1 Sickness—Maternity

Migrant workers enjoy the privilege that the insurance periods and assimilated periods completed under the legislation of each member state are aggregated, in so far as these periods do not overlap.[6] After providing for aggregating periods of sickness or maternity insurance in respect of periods of employment elsewhere,[7] Reg. 1408, in contrast to Reg. 3,[8] envisages the case that a worker employed in one state resides in another.[9] Such a worker is entitled to benefits in kind in the country of his residence, in accordance with the law of the latter at the expense of the authority which is competent *ratione loci*.[10] Unless the authorities concerned have made an agreement to the contrary, benefits in money are provided by the latter authority,[11] The same rights accrue to members of his family,

---

1 Reg. 1408/71, art. 9(2), formerly Reg. 3, art. 9(1); *Vaassen-Göbbels* v. *Beambtenfonds voor het Mijnbedrijf* (1966), 12 Rec. 377, at p. 399; [1966] C.M.L.R. 508.

2 Reg. 1408/71, art. 10(1), formerly Reg. 3, art 10(1); for individual instances see Reg. 1408/71, art. 18 in the wording of the Treaty of Accession, Pt. II, Annex I, IX 1, Reg. 3, art. 16 (sickness, maternity), Reg. 1408/71, art. 38 as amended by the Treaty of Accession II, *loc. cit.*, Reg. 3, art. 26 (invalidity), Reg. 1408/71, art. 45 as amended by the Treaty of Accession II, *loc. cit.*, Reg. 3, art. 27 (old age and death pensions), Reg. 1408/71, art. 64, Reg. 3, art. 32 (death benefits), Reg. 1408/71, art. 67, Reg. 3, art. 33 (unemployment); Reg. 1408/71, art. 72 as amended by the Treaty of Accession II, *loc. cit.*, Reg. 3, art. 39 (family allowances). Thus aggregation is not required in respect of accidents or occupational diseases. Seché, 1968 Rev. Trim. Dr. Eur. 475, at p. 480.

3 Reg. 1408/71, art. 10(1); Reg. 3, art. 10(1), Seché, 1968 Rev. Trim. Dr. Eur. 475, at p. 479.

4 Reg. 3, art. 10(2) and Annex E.

5 Reg. 1408/71, art. 12(1), (2), formerly Reg. 3, art. 11.

6 Reg. 1408/71, art. 18 (as amended); formerly Reg. 3, art. 16. For the notion of workers in the meaning of the chapter dealing with sickness benefits in Reg. 3 see above, p. 102; *Unger* v. *Bestuur der Bedrijfsvereniging voor Detailhandel*, (1964), 10 Rec. 347, at p. 363; [1964] C.M.L.R. 319. For the same notion in Reg. 1408/71 see art. 1(c); for the present purpose it includes seasonal workers subject to certain conditions: Reg. 1408/71, art. 18(2).

7 Reg. 1408/71, art. 18 (as amended).

8 Reg. 3, art. 17(1), (2), 19(1), (2).

9 Reg. 1408/71, art. 19(1). For frontier workers see Reg. 1408/71, art. 20 as restated in the Treaty of Accession, Pt. II, p. 91; Reg. 3, art. 17(1), last para., 20(6) in the version of Reg. 73/63, art. 2; Reg. 80/65, art. 1 envisages the converse case.

10 Reg. 1408/71, art. 19(1)(a), formerly Reg. 3, art. 17(3). For the competent authority see above, p. 100, and Reg. 1408/71, art. 1(o).

11 Reg. 1408/71, art. 19(1)(b); for their calculation see art. 23.

unless the law of the place of residence entitles them to benefits.[1] If such a worker and the members of his family reside temporarily in the country which is competent *ratione loci* or take up permanent residence there, they are entitled there to both types of benefits, even if they may have received some such benefits in the country of their residence and a cumulation may occur.[2] If a worker who is entitled to benefits *ratione loci*, if necessary after a process of aggregation, happens to be temporarily abroad and requires sickness or maternity benefits,[3] or is in receipt of them in the country which is competent *ratione loci* and has been authorized to resume or to establish his residence abroad[4] or in order to recuperate,[5] he is treated on the same footing as the worker who resides elsewhere,[6] but members of his family, if they displace themselves in the same circumstances, are only entitled to benefits in kind in the country of their sojourn or of their new residence.[7]

The same principles apply to unemployed workers who either reside in a country other than that which is competent *ratione loci* or who displace themselves in search of work,[8] and to members of their family no matter where they reside or are sojourning.[9] Provision is made for the case that a worker or member of his family or surviving member ceases to be entitled to benefits in kind according to the applicable law while seeking to obtain a pension or periodical payment[10] or where they are entitled to several pensions or periodical payments and in addition to benefits in kind in the country of their residence[11] or not so entitled to the latter benefits.[12] Similarly provision is made for the case that the worker is entitled to a pension or to periodical payments according to the law of one or several member states, and the members of his family requiring sickness or maternity benefits reside in a country other than that where the worker resides or, having so resided, join the worker in the country of his residence,[13] or if either the worker or members of his family sojourn in another country.[14]

As stated above, Reg. 1408/71 starts from the situation that a worker

---

1 Reg. 1408/71, art. 18(2); the exception formed the rule in Reg. 3, art. 20(1) and (5).
2 Reg. 1408/71, art. 21 and contrast Reg. 3, art. 21. This provision does not apply to frontier workers. Cp. Reg. 3, art. 17(1), 19(1).
3 Reg. 1408/71, art. 22(1)(a), formerly Reg. 3, art.19(1).
4 Reg. 1408/71, art. 22(1)(b), formerly Reg. 3, art. 19(3). For the authorisation see Reg. 1408/71, art. 22(3), as amended by the Treaty of Accession, *loc. cit.*
5 Reg. 1408/71, art. 22(1)(c), formerly Reg. 3, art. 19(3).
6 See above Reg. 1408/71, art. 19(1)(a)(b); for benefits of a substantial nature see Reg. 1408/71, arts. 24, 31 (as amended by the Treaty of Accession, *loc. cit.*), formerly Reg. 3, art. 19(4).
7 Reg. 1408/71, art. 22(3); for benefits of a substantial nature see above, n. 6.
8 Reg. 1408/71, art. 25(1); frontier workers are treated differently: *ibid.*, art. 25(2).
9 Reg. 1408/71, art. 25(3) as amended by the Treaty of Accession, Pt. II *loc. cit.*
10 Reg. 1408/71, art. 26.
11 Reg. 1408/71, art. 27 as amended by the Treaty of Accession, *loc. cit*; for frontier workers see art. 32. Cp. Reg. 3, art. 22.
12 Reg. 1408/71, art. 28 as amended by the Treaty of Accession, *loc. cit.*
13 Reg. 1408/71, art. 9; for benefits of a substantial nature see arts. 30, 24.
14 Reg. 1408/71, art. 31; for frontier workers see art. 32.

is employed in one state and resides in another. It develops this case by considering variants such as a transfer of residence or a temporary sojourn abroad. Unlike Reg. 3[1] it does not start from the situation of a migrant worker, whose mobility is to be encouraged. It must be remembered, however, that sickness and maternity benefits accrue normally directly upon the entry into employment in the state of entry and that, while aggregating may be necessary,[2] *pro-rata-ing* is hardly ever required,[3] since one authority in one member state is finally responsible.[4] The situation requiring serious attention appears to be that where the worker moves to another country after having given up his previous employment elsewhere and before taking up employment in the country of his new residence,[5] and this seems to have prompted the thorough revision of the relevant provisions of Reg. 3.

2   Industrial Accidents and Occupational Diseases

Like sickness and maternity benefits, those arising from industrial accidents are partly rendered in kind and partly in money.[6] Consequently the rules dealing with the latter follow the former closely. However, since the grounds for providing the benefit arise from the employment itself, no aggregation of periods of insurance is required in order to preserve any expectations or rights arising out of industrial accidents,[7] but for the purpose of benefits arising from occupational diseases periods of similar employment in another country are taken into account[8] as well as for the grant of death benefits.[9] Regulation 1408[10] envisages primarily the case that a worker employed in one state residing in another state sustains an injury or contracts a disease in the state of his residence. He is entitled to benefits in kind in the country of his residence in accordance with the law of the latter at the expense of the authority which is competent *ratione loci*.[11] Benefits in money are provided by the latter authority, unless the states concerned have made an agreement to the contrary.[12] The worker who is temporarily resident in the state which is competent *ratione loci*, or who takes up residence there, is equally entitled to the benefits under the law of the latter, even if he has already received benefits in the country of his previous residence.[13] If the worker sojourns in a

---

1   Reg. 3, arts, 16–23.
2   Reg. 1408/71, art. 18 as amended; formerly Reg. 3, art. 16.
3   But see Reg. 1408/71, art. 32.
4   See Reg. 1408/71, art. 19(1).
5   Reg. 3, art. 19(2).
6   Reg. 1408/71, art. 52(2); Reg. 3, art. 29(1), (7).
7   For this purpose an accident in transit is treated as an accident arising in the country which is competent *ratione loci*: Reg. 1408/71, art 56.
8   Reg. 1408/71, art. 57(3)(b).
9   Reg. 1408/71, art. 64.
10   It does not differ from the scheme followed in Reg. 3.
11   Reg. 1408/71, arts. 52(1)(a), 63. Frontier workers have the same rights in the state which is competent *ratione loci*: *ibid.* art. 53; see formerly Reg. 3, art. 29(1), 1st para., as amended by Reg. 73/63, art. 3. For details see Reg. 1408/71, art. 62.
12   Reg. 1408/71, art. 52(b).
13   Reg. 1408/71, art. 54; a frontier worker is not entitled to any such cumulation.

state other than that which is competent *ratione loci* or, having established his entitlement in the latter state, has received permission by the latter to return to his residence abroad, or to take up residence in a member state,[1] or to go abroad in order to recuperate there,[2] benefits in kind are provided by the country of residence or sojourn in accordance with its own law at the expense of the authority which is competent *ratione loci*, but the duration of the benefit is determined by the law of the latter.[3] Benefits in money are provided by the authority which is competent *ratione loci* unless the states concerned have made an agreement to the contrary.[4]

Special provision is made for extending the rules concerning the cost of transport of a victim of such an accident or disease to his home or to an hospital in the country of his residence[5] or of his body for interment.[6]

If the occupational disease was possibly contracted during a previous employment in another state, the allocation of benefits remains subject to the law of the last state of employment.[7] If the law of the latter requires that the illness must have been diagnosed medically for the first time within the jurisdiction, it is sufficient if this diagnosis was first made in another member state.[8] Special provisions apply in the case of sclerogenic pneumoconiosis.[9] If a worker who has worked in several member states suffers an aggravation of an occupational disease in one of them which calls for a redistribution of the charges, provision is made as to which member state concerned must bear the additional burden.[10]

In the absence of an insurance scheme for industrial accidents and occupational diseases in the state where the worker resides, or if it does not provide benefits in kind, the institutions in that state which administer benefits in the event of illness must supply the benefits.[11] If the law of a member state ties the issue free of charge of benefits in kind to the utilisation of the medical service organised by the employer, any benefits in kind supplied by an institution in another member state are deemed to have been supplied by the employer's medical service.[12] If according to the law of the state which is competent *ratione loci* the accident or injury is not covered by compulsory insurance, the duty to provide the benefits

---

1   Having previously resided in the state which is competent *ratione loci*, it must be assumed; formerly Reg. 3, art. 29(1), 2nd para., as amended by Reg. 73/63, art. 3. For the authorisation see Reg. 1408/71, art. 55(2).
2   Reg. 1408/71, art. 55(1)(a)–(c).
3   Reg. 1408/71, art. 55(1)(i), art. 63; the difference between this provision and that applicable to sickness and maternity benefits (art. 19(1)(i)) is explained by the difference in the nature of the services.
4   Reg. 1408/71, art. 55(1)(ii).
5   Reg. 1408/71, art. 59(1), formerly Reg. 3, art. 29(8), (9).
6   Reg. 1408/71, art. 59(2).
7   Reg. 1408/71, art. 57(1); Reg. 3, art. 31(1).
8   Reg. 1408/71, art. 57(2), Reg. 3, art. 31(2).
9   Reg. 1408/71, art. 57(3); they can be extended to other illnesses: art. 57(4).
10 Reg. 1408/71, art. 60, Reg. 3, art. 31a added by Reg. 8/63, art. 2, OJ, 1963, 383.
11 Reg. 1408/71, art. 61(1), formerly Reg. 3, art. 29(3).
12 Reg. 1408/71, art. 61(2), (3), formerly Reg. 3, art. 29(4).

falls directly upon the employer or his insurer.[1] If in assessing the degree
of incapacity, previous industrial accidents and occupational diseases are
to be taken into account; those suffered or contracted previously in
another member state are treated as if they had occurred locally.[2]

Death benefits are granted on the basis of the same principles,[3] including
that which charges the state of residence with their immediate service,
subject to reimbursement from the state which is competent *ratione loci*.[4]

3   Unemployment

If the law of the state which is competent *ratione loci* requires the completion of a certain period of insurance, insurance periods completed in
several countries are aggregated for the purpose of determining the
acquisition, maintenance or recovery as well as duration of unemployment benefits, provided that they would qualify as such in the state which
is competent *ratione loci*.[5] Similarly, if the law of the state which requires
the completion of certain periods of *employment*, periods of employment
in another member state are taken into account.[6] Where the law of
the state which is competent *ratione loci* makes such a condition, the worker
must have been last insured or employed in that state.[7] An exception
exists if the person concerned last resided in that state as an unemployed
person. If the unemployed worker was last employed in a country other
than that of his residence, a distinction must be drawn between frontier
workers and others. A frontier worker who is partly or casually unemployed in the enterprise which he serves is treated as if he were resident
in the country of his employment.[8] If he is completely unemployed, he is
subject to the law of the state of his residence which must bear the burden
without reimbursement.[9] Other workers are treated in accordance with
the same principle,[10] except that a worker who is completely unemployed
and who now seeks employment in the country of his residence is treated
as an unemployed worker who seeks work in another state,[11] and cannot
during this period claim unemployment benefit under the law of his place
of residence while the authorities of his former place of employment are
liable to provide the benefits.[12] In all other cases, too, enjoyment of
benefits in the state of employment excludes the enjoyment of benefits in
the country of residence.[13]

---

1 Reg. 1408/71, art. 61(4).
2 Reg. 1408/71, art. 61(5).
3 Reg. 1408/71, art. 65.
4 Reg. 1408/71, art. 66.
5 Reg. 1408/71, art. 67(1), (4) and contrast Reg. 3, art. 33(1).
6 Reg. 1408/71, art. 67(2).
7 Reg. 1408/71, art. 67(3).
8 Reg. 1408/71, art. 71(1)(a)(i).
9 Reg. 1408/71, art. 71(1)(a)(ii).
10 Reg. 1408/71, art. 71(1)(b)(i) and (ii).
11 Reg. 1408/71, art. 69; see below.
12 Reg. 1408/71, art. 71(1)(b)(ii), Proviso.
13 Reg. 1408/71, art. 71(2).

Regulation 1408/71 introduced a new element by extending its operation to unemployed workers who leave the state which is competent *ratione loci* to provide benefits in order to seek employment in another member state. Such a worker retains his rights to unemployment benefits in the former state, provided that he was registered there, and had been available for employment for at least four weeks, unless authorized to depart earlier.[1] In addition he must have registered in the state of his new residence within seven days after ceasing to be available in the state of his previous employment.[2] In those circumstances unemployment benefits are granted for three months at most or for any shorter period to which he is entitled under the law of the state of his previous employment.[3] Upon his return to the latter state before the expiry of the period for which unemployment benefits are granted, he retains his rights which he enjoys under the latter's law, but not if he returns later.[4] A worker can avail himself of his right only once between two periods of employment.[5] During his stay in another state in search of employment, the benefits are provided by the state where he happens to be, which can claim reimbursement from the state where the worker was last employed.[6]

4   Family Benefits and Allowances

If the acquisition of the right to a family allowance is dependent upon the completion of periods of employment, all periods completed in the various member states may be aggregated.[7]

Family allowances are divided into "family benefits"[8] and "family allowances".[9] If family *benefits* are due under the law of the state which is competent *ratione loci*, the members of the worker's family[10] who reside in another member state other than France are included in the family *benefits* due to the worker under the law of the former state.[11] If the worker is subject *ratione loci* to the law of France, he is entitled to family *allowances* for the members of his family who reside abroad under the conditions laid down by French law, if and to the extent that the law of the place of their residence grants them.[12] The same principles apply to unemployed

---

1   Reg. 1408/71, art. 69(1)(a).

2   Reg. 1408/71, art. 69(1)(b).

3   Reg. 1408/71, art. 69(1)(c).

4   Reg. 1408/71, art. 69(2).

5   Reg. 1408/71, art. 69(3).

6   Reg. 1408/71, art. 70(1); for details see art. 70(2), (3).

7   Reg. 1408/71, art. 72 as replaced by the Treaty of Accession Pt. II (above, p. 111, n. 2), formerly Reg. 3, art. 39.

8   *Prestations familiales:* Reg. 1408/71, art. 1(u)(i), which include all benefits in kind or in money intended to compensate for changes arising from family life, other than maternity benefits; and distinguish arts. 77(1), 78(1).

9   *Allocations familiales:* Reg. 1408/71, art. 1(u)(ii) which embrace periodical payments based exclusively on the number and age of the members of the family.

10   For this term see above, p. 105; Reg. 1408/71, art. 1(f). The more detailed definition, restricted to family allowances, in Reg. 3, art. 40(3) is now obsolete.

11   Reg. 1408/71, art. 73(1).

12   Reg. 1408/71, art. 73(2); subject to an exception concerning family benefits, if he works

workers subject to the same distinction between those subject to French law or not,[1] with the difference that in the case of unemployed workers subject to French law with members of their family residing in another country, family *allowances* are payable only if the law of the state where the members of the family reside makes provision for them.[2]

Detailed provisions regulate which state is ultimately liable for these benefits and allowances.[3] In principle they are payable by the authorities of the state which is competent *ratione loci* in respect of the worker himself, irrespective of whether the beneficiaries reside in that state or not.[4] If necessary they are paid not to the worker himself but to the person or institution having charge of these members of the family, even if they are in another member state.[5] Conversely in a number of specific situations, payment may be made through or by the authorities of the state where the members of the family reside, subject to reimbursement.[6] Cumulation is expressly prohibited if, as a result of some professional activity of the worker concerned, further family benefits or allowances are due under the law of their residence.[7] The incidence of children's benefits[8] due to beneficiaries of pensions or of periodical payments of specified types are regulated in some detail[9] as are those payable in respect of orphans.[10]

5   Death Benefits

The acquisition, maintenance and recovery of death benefits, including those connected with industrial accidents or occupational diseases,[11] is determined by aggregating the periods of insurance provided that they do not overlap.[12] If the worker, beneficiary of a pension or of periodical payments or a member of his family,[13] dies in a member state other than that which is competent *ratione loci* death abroad is deemed to have occurred in the country which is competent *ratione loci*.[14] The fact that the beneficiary is in the territory of another member state is irrelevant[15] and once

---

temporarily abroad and the members of the family accompany him: see Reg. 1408/71. arts. 73(3), 74(2), 75(2).

1   Reg. 1408/71, art. 74.
2   Reg. 1408/71, art. 74(2).
3   Reg. 1408/71, art. 75.
4   Reg. 1408/71, art. 75(1)(a).
5   Reg. 1408/71, art. 75(1)(b); cp. Reg. 3, art. 40a added by Reg. 109/65 art. 1, OJ, 1965, 2124.
6   Reg. 1408/71, art. 75(1)(c), (2).
7   Reg. 1408/71, art. 76; see also art. 79(3) as amended by the Treaty of Accession, Pt. II, *loc. cit.*; formerly Reg. 3, art. 40(8) added by Reg. 73/63, art. 5, OJ, 1963, 2011.
8   For the meaning of this term for the limited purpose of this provision see Reg. 1408/71, arts. 77(1), 78(1).
9   Reg. 1408/71, arts. 77, 79 (as amended by the Treaty of Accession, Pt. II, *loc. cit.*).
10 Reg. 1408/71, arts 78, 79 (as amended by the Treaty of Accession, Pt. II, *loc. cit.*).
11 Reg. 1408/71, art. 65(3); formerly Reg. 3, art. 32 excluded for this purpose death benefits arising from industrial accidents and occupational diseases, but it is believed that no change was intended in so far as aggregation is concerned.
12 Reg. 1408/71, art. 64; formerly Reg. 3, art. 31(1).
13 Reg. 1408/71, art. 65(1).
14 Reg. 1408/71, art. 65(1), formerly Reg. 3, art. 32(2).
15 Reg. 1408/71, art. 65(2), formerly Reg. 3, art. 32(3).

again the territorial operation of social security legislation is made to extend to occurrences elsewhere. For these purposes it also makes no difference whether the death benefit is connected with an industrial accident or an occupational disease or not.[1]

6   Invalidity Pensions and Allowances—Old Age and Death Pensions[2]

The acquisition, maintenance and recovery of invalidity pensions and allowances is closely geared to that of old age and death pensions, especially if the benefits are dependent upon the duration of periods of insurance[3] (see below), and subject to a small number of detailed variations they must be treated together.

a   Invalidity Pensions

These are to be granted according as the insured person has completed the necessary requirements under legislation according to which invalidity benefits are calculated as a rule, either

   (a) without reference to the duration of completed periods (known formerly as Type A legislation when Reg. 3, art. 24(1)(a) was in force); *or*
   (b) with reference to the duration of completed periods (known formerly as Type B legislation when Reg. 3 was in force);[4] *or*
   (c) with reference to both types of legislation.[5]

The type of legislation in the various member states which accords invalidity benefits independently of the duration of periods of insurance is now set out in Annex III.[6] If the laws to which the worker has been subject *ratione loci*, either successively or alternatively, all provide invalidity benefits which are assessed independently of the periods of insurance,[7] he receives his benefits from the institution of that member state where he was insured when the incapacity to work, followed by invalidity, occurred.[8] For this purpose the conditions for the entitlement and the extent of the benefits are governed by the law of the state mentioned above.[9] If the latter law requires the completion of certain periods of

---

1   Reg. 1408/71, art. 65(3), formerly Reg. 3, art. 32(4).
2   Reg. 1408/71, arts. 37–43, 44–51, as amended by the Treaty of Accession, Pt. II, *loc. cit.*, formerly Reg. 3, arts. 24–26; 27–28; Seché, 1968 Rev. Trim. Dr. Eur. 475, at pp. 494–508.
3   Reg. 1408/71, art. 40(1), formerly Reg. 3, art. 26(1) including aggregation of periods for invalidity benefits: *Union Nationale des Mutualités Socialistes* v. *La Marca* (1970), 16 Rec. 987, at p. 992(o).
4   For an example see *Dingemans* v. *Sociale Verzekeringsbank* (1964), 10 Rec. 1259 at p. 1274; [1965] C.M.L.R. 144.
5   Reg. 1408/71, art. 40(1); Reg. 3, art. 24(1).
6   Reg. 1408/71, art. 37(2), formerly Reg. 3, art. 24(2) and Annex F.
7   Reg. 1408/71, art. 37(1) as amended by the Treaty of Accession, Pt. II, *loc. cit.*
8   Reg. 1408/71, art. 39(1).
9   Reg. 1408/71, art. 39(1), (2).

assurance for the acquisition, retention or recovery of benefits any such periods served elsewhere are to be taken into account.[1] If according to the law of the state where the benefits must be claimed, these periods of insurance must have been completed in connection with membership of a profession which is subject to a special regime or in a particular type of employment, periods served in other member states which do not correspond to these requirements can be disregarded.[2] Nevertheless, these periods completed abroad are taken into account in granting invalidity benefits as they are accorded to the public in general, or to workers or employees, as the case may be.[3] If no benefits accrue, even after aggregation, the benefits are assessed according to the law of the former state of insurance, if any benefits remain according to that law.[4] If invalidity benefits accrue either according to the law of the state where the incapacitating event occurred or according to the law of the former state of insurance, any provision of the respective law applicable that members of the family other than children who reside in another member state are qualified to claim must be applied in either case as if they were locally resident.[5]

If the worker has been subject *ratione loci* either successively or alternatively to the laws of two or more member states, one of which requires the completion of certain periods of insurance before benefits accrue, the principles relating to old age insurance, namely aggregation and *pro-rata-ing*, apply.[6]

If the accident arising from employment which underlies the claim for invalidity benefits occurred while the worker was subject *ratione loci* to a system of insurance which does not require the completion of certain periods of insurance, he qualifies for benefits, even if he did not so qualify under the law to which he was subject previously, subject to two conditions, namely—

(a) that he qualifies under the system which applied when he suffered the incapacity or under a similar system, but not one which requires the completion of periods of insurance;

(b) that he does not qualify under a system which does require the completion of periods of insurance.[7]

---

1 Reg. 1408/71, arts. 37(1), 38(1) as amended by the Treaty of Accession, Pt. II, *loc. cit.*; cp. art. 40(1). The relationship between arts. 38(1) and 40(1) is a little obscure. Article 38(1) in conjunction with art. 39 appears to sanction aggregation by a system which requires the completion of certain periods when the completion of periods of insurance is not foreseen by the law of the other states concerned where the beneficiary has worked and is difficult to assess. Art. 40 provides similarly for aggregation coupled, however, with *pro-rata-ing*.

2 Reg. 1408/71, art. 38(2).

3 Reg. 1408/71, art. 38(2).

4 Reg. 1408/71, art. 39(3).

5 Reg. 1408/71, art. 39(4).

6 Reg. 1408/71, art. 40(1). For this purpose a finding of invalidity in one member state must be recognised in another, if their notion of invalidity is identical, as evidenced in Annex IV of Reg. 1408/71; art. 40(3).

7 Reg. 1408/71, art. 40(2).

By these means Reg. 1408/71 seeks to achieve one of its aims, which is to prevent a cumulation of benefits. Detailed provisions determine the distribution of final liability if the invalidity is aggravated while the beneficiary remains subject to the same law *ratione loci* or has become subject successively of one or more other member states,[1] if the service of benefits is restored after a suspension[2] or is freshly accorded after it had lapsed.[3]

Invalidity benefits are converted into old age benefits in accordance with the law or laws which regulate the original invalidity pension.[4] Until such old age benefits accrue under the law which determines the old age pension, the institution of the state under the law of which the invalidity pension accrued must continue to provide invalidity benefits,[5] subject to an exception if the paying institution became responsible as a result of the fact that the accident giving rise to the incapacity occurred in the country of that institution. In this case, the paying institution may convert the benefit into an old-age benefit in accordance with its own provisions.[6]

b   Old Age and Death Pensions[7]

According to Reg. 3, in force until 1 October 1972, the guiding principle was here, even more importantly than anywhere else, that of aggregation[8] of insurance and assimilated periods,[9] since the benefit may be made up of component parts based upon rights acquired in several jurisdictions. The term "assimilated periods" bore the meaning attributed to it in the definition section[10] which referred in turn to the domestic law under which they were alleged to have been completed. The latter legislation was therefore called upon to determine the extent to which any periods other than periods normally qualifying for old age benefits were regarded as their equivalent, and Reg. 3 did not attempt to modify or to supplement the domestic law of the Community.[11] The principle of aggregation applied also to non-contributory schemes,[12] and to legislation, such as the Dutch *Algemene Weduwen en Wezenwet* which does not make the amount of the

---

1   Reg. 1408/71, art. 41.
2   Reg. 1408/71, art. 42(1), formerly Reg. 3, art. 26(3): the institution which was liable to pay the benefits must resume payments.
3   Reg. 1408/71, art. 42(2); cp. Reg. 3, art. 26(3), last sentence.
4   Reg. 1408/71, art. 43(1), subject to the provisions on old age pensions laid down in arts. 44–57; cp. Reg. 3, art. 26(5).
5   Reg. 1408/71, art. 43(2).
6   Reg. 1408/71, art. 43(3).
7   For the implementation of Reg. 3, arts. 26–28, see Reg. 4, arts. 28–47; for Reg. 1408/71, arts. 44–51, see Reg. 574/72, arts. 35–59, OJ, 1972, L 74/1.
8   Reg. 3, art. 27(1).
9   For the basic aims of Reg. 3, arts. 27, 28 see *Hagenbeek* v. *Raad van Arbeid* (1966), 12 Rec. 618, at p. 625.
10   Reg. 3, art. 1(r); this definition has now been dropped; see Reg. 1408/71, art. 1(a).
11   *Landesversicherungsanstalt Rheinland-Schwaben* v. *Welchner* (1967), 13 Rec. 427, at p. 436; see also Reg. 3, art. 1(r): "... in so far as they are regarded by the said legislation as being equivalent to insurance periods or periods of employment".
12   Reg. 3, Introduction, 4th para., art. 2(2) and Annex B.

benefit depend upon the duration of the insurance.[1] If in a member state the grant of certain benefits depended upon the completion of insurance periods in an occupation covered by a special scheme, only periods completed in other member states under corresponding schemes or in the same occupation under other schemes were to be aggregated.[2] If, however, the periods so aggregated did not satisfy the conditions on which the right to this type of benefit depended, these periods were to be aggregated for the purpose of admission to benefits under the general scheme of the member states concerned.[3] Aggregation in the particular circumstances of invalidity, old age, and death (widow's) pensions was accompanied by the principle of *pro-rata-ing* (Reg. 3, art. 28) which determined the manner of payment. The institution of each member state determined in accordance with its own legislation after aggregation (Reg. 3, art. 27) whether the person concerned satisfied the conditions for entitlement to the benefits set out by that legislation.[4] The same institution then determined for accounting purposes the amount of benefit due, as if all the aggregated periods of insurance had been completed exclusively under its own law; it then proceeded to determine the amount due pro rata with the length of the periods completed under its own law before the risk materialised, as against the total length of the combined periods under the laws of the member states concerned. The proportion of the total ascertained by the institution of the member state concerned was the charge payable by that institution.[5]

It must be noted at the outset that the procedure of *pro-rata-ing* envisaged by Reg. 28(1), beginning, and (b) applied only if a procedure of aggregation had taken place previously[6] because without it the person concerned would have suffered a reduction of benefits. If, therefore, aggregation was not called for, because the person concerned had fulfilled all the conditions of entitlement in one member state only, it was irrelevant whether any additional periods had been completed under the laws of another member state. The interested party applied to the institution of the first state, relying exclusively on the qualifying periods there. If, however, the person concerned had qualified unconditionally under the law of one of the member states involved for the payment of a qualitatively inferior benefit,[7] while aggregation of periods completed in another member state would lead to the grant of a qualitatively superior benefit,[8] the process of aggregation was not excluded by the acquisition

---

1 *Hagenbeek* v. *Raad van Arbeid* (1966), 12 Rec. 618, at p. 624; Reg. 3, Annex G, Pt. III, Netherlands-Belgium as amended by Reg. 130/63 art. 7; *Van der Veen* v. *Bestuur der Sociale Verzekeringsbank* (1964), 10 Rec. 1105, at p. 1125; [1964] C.M.L.R. 548.
2 Reg. 3, art. 27(2), first sentence.
3 Reg. 3, art. 27(2), second sentence.
4 Reg. 3, art. 28(1)(a).
5 Reg. 3, art. 28(1)(b).
6 *Van der Veen* v. *Bestuur der Sociale Verzekeringsbank* (1964), 10 Rec. 1109, at p. 1124 (above, n. 1).
7 France: *rente de vieillesse* in accordance with the *Code de la Sécurité Sociale*, art. L.336.
8 France: *pension de vieillesse* in accordance with *Code de la Sécurité Sociale*, art. L. 331.

of an unconditional benefit in the first member state.[1] When no aggregation was necessary because the benefits accrued under the law of the one member state alone constituted an acquired right, the procedure of *pro-rata-ing* was excluded.[2] According to the Community Court *pro-rata-ing* must not result in the reduction of benefits acquired under the law of a member state,[3] just as it must not lead to a cumulation of payments in respect of the same periods of work.[4] If, however, the qualifying periods do not overlap, a full entitlement according to the domestic law of one country could be combined with a benefit in another country according to the domestic law of the member states concerned without offending against the provisions of the Treaty (art. 51) and of Reg. 3 (art. 11(1)).[5]

In other words, Reg. 3, arts. 27 and 28 applied only in well-defined circumstances represented by objective conditions and did not apply where the effect sought by the Treaty (art. 51) was achieved on the strength of one system of domestic law alone which has conferred a fully accrued right.[6] In such a case the person concerned was neither entitled nor obliged to exercise an option[7] nor under a duty to apply at the same time for the simultaneous liquidation of his benefits.[8] However, as the Community Court pointed out in *Guissart* v. *Etat Belge*,[9] the complexity of

---

1   *Gross* v. *Caisse d'Assurance Vieillesse de Strasbourg* (1971), 17 Rec. 871, at p. 877(9), (10), (12); *Höhn* v. *Caisse d'Assurance Vieillesse de Strasbourg* (1971), 17 Rec. 893.

2   *Ciechelski* v. *Caisse Régionale de Sécurité Sociale du Centre, Orléans* (1967), 13 Rec. 235, at pp. 243–245; [1967] C.M.L.R. 192; *De Moor* v. *Caisse de Pension des Employés Privés* (1967), 13 Rec. 255, at p. 267; [1967] C.M.L.R. 223.

3   *Office National des Pensions* v. *Couture* (1967), 13 Rec. 487, at p. 501; [1968] C.M.L.R. 14; *Guissart* v. *Etat Belge* (1967), 13 Rec. 552, at p. 562.

4   *De Moor* v. *Caisse de Pensions des Employés Privés* (1967), 13 Rec. 255) at pp. 268, 269 (above, n. 2); *Caisse Régionale de Sécurité Sociale du Nord-Est* v. *Goffart* (1967), 13 Rec. 413, at p. 421; [1967] C.M.L.R. 343.

5   *Ciechelski* v. *Caisse Régionale de Sécurité Sociale du Centre, Orléans* (1967), 13 Rec. 235, at p. 245, (above, n. 2) *De Moor* v. *Caisse de Pension des Employés Privés* (1967), 13 Rec. 255, at pp. 268, 269 [1967] C.M.L.R. 223; *Caisse Régionale de Sécurité Sociale du Nord-Est* v. *Goffart* (1967), 13 Rec. 413, at p. 421; *Caisse d'Assurance Vieillesse des Travailleurs Salariés de Paris* v. *Duffy* (*Jeanne*) (1969), 15 Rec. 597, at pp. 602(2)–604(9); [1971] C.M.L.R. 391; Seché, 1968 Rev. Trim. Dr. Int. 475, at pp. 502, 505, 506, 507.

6   *Office National des Pensions* v. *Couture* (1969), 13 Rec. 487, at p. 500; [1968] C.M.L.R. 14; Seché, Rev. Trim. Dr. Eur. 475, at p. 506.

7   See above, n. 6, *Guissart* v. *Etat Belge* (1967), 13 Rec. 552, at p. 562; *Keller* v. *Caisse d'Assurance Vieillesse de Strasbourg* (1971), 17 Rec. 885, at p. 891(12), (13); Seché, 1968 Rev. Trim. Dr. Eur. 475, at pp. 495, 501 ff.; cp. Reg. 3, art. 28(4).

8   *Office National des Pensions* v. *Couture* (1967) 13 Rec. 487, at p. 500; [1968] C.M.L.R. 14; *Colditz* v. *Caisse d'Assurance Vieillesse des Travailleurs Salariés de Paris* (1967), 13 Rec. 297, at p. 305. But see Reg. 3, art. 28(e) and (f) in cases where aggregation is called for and the Treaty applies.

9   Above, n. 7, at p. 563. In the particular circumstances of this case, full benefits based on a period of 216 months equal to 18 years completed in Luxemburg were sought to be cumulated with a pro-rata benefit in Belgium base on a period of 145 months equal to 12 years. The Belgian authorities, in aggregating the periods and in *pro-rating* the quotas disregarded a portion counted in Luxemburg even though not based on actual periods of employment, and disregarded equally certain periods allowed in Belgium on the basis of a fiction. The Community Court upheld the computation made by the Belgian authorities. See Seché, Rev. Trim. Dr. Eur. 475, at p. 503.

the problem which is posed by the attempt to co-ordinate domestic social security legislation makes it impossible to attribute absolute validity to the interpretation set out here, seeing that in certain circumstances it may lead to the grant of unjustified benefits. Such is the case where actual qualifying periods in one member state overlap with fictitious periods in another. In these circumstances the actual periods served abroad may be discounted in favour of the local fictitious periods.[1]

As stated before, the process of aggregation seeks to preserve for an interested person the expectations, rights and benefits which were acquired in a member state before migration and which would be lost if the principle of the territoriality were applied in accordance with the general practice of states.

While Reg. 3 was in force, the Community Court held that, if the process of aggregation would assist an interested person claiming invalidity benefits in the jurisdiction to which he is subject but for a rule of domestic law of Type A (see Reg. 3, r. 24(1), now Reg. 1408/71, Annex III) requiring a minimum qualifying period of six months, and if in the jurisdiction of his previous residence that person has not qualified because in the law of the latter country the benefits are calculated in relation to the duration of complete periods, the periods spent in the latter must be aggregated with the former in accordance with Reg. 3, arts. 26–28. The procedural and administrative provision contained in the Implementing Reg. 4 (art. 28(2)) was to be disregarded in the circumstances. Otherwise the latter provision would assume the character of an overriding rule of Community law, thereby depriving a migrant worker of potential benefits.[2] Technically, aggregation followed by *pro-rata-ing* may create difficulties, if the qualifying periods in the various member states which must be taken into account are expressed in different quantities of time. In these circumstances, a system of common numerators and denominators is to be calculated.[3] On the other hand, if, after aggregation, it appeared that the person concerned only satisfied the conditions of one or more but not of all the laws applicable to him in respect of the various periods underlying the aggregation, the process of *pro-rata-ing* (Reg. 3, art. 28(1)(b), discussed above) was to be applied nevertheless; and if the person concerned was thereby entitled under no less than two laws any qualifying period under the law of yet another member state was to be disregarded.[4] All the more, if the person concerned satisfied the conditions of the law of one member state only, but not of the other member states involved, the process of aggregation benefits the person in question, but in this case no *pro-rata-ing* is called for.[5] A procedure of review was envisaged in

---

1   *Ibid.*, p. 563; this is, however, a matter of domestic and not of Community law.
2   *Union Nationale des Mutualités Socialistes* v. *La Marca* (1970), 16 Rec. 987, at p. 992(13).
3   *Cossutta* v. *Office National des Pensions pour Ouvriers* (1967), 13 Rec. 399, at p. 405; [1968] C.M.L.R. 5.
4   Reg. 3, art. 28(1)(e).
5   Reg. 3, art. 28(1)(f). It must be noted that the situation envisaged here differs from that which underlies the decisions of the Community Court in *Office National* v. *Couture* (1967), 13 Rec. 487, at p. 501; [1968] C.M.L.R. 14, and *Guissart* v. *Etat Belge* (1967), 13 Rec. 552,

order to preserve for the interested party all the advantages which may subsequently accrue to him under the law of a member state which could not be taken into account previously, because the necessary condition had not yet been satisfied.[1]

Regulation 3, art. 28(3) dealt in the form of a statutory provision with the problem of cumulation and stated that if as the result of aggregating the relevant qualifying periods in accordance with art. 27 the interested person received smaller benefits than if he had lodged a claim independently of the procedure of aggregating by relying on the domestic law of one member state only, such a person was entitled to receive from the institution in that member state a supplementary benefit equal to the difference. In the end the cost of it was to be apportioned among the institutions of a member state.[2]

At first sight it seems difficult to reconcile this provision with the practice of the Community Court set out above.[3] According to the latter, the procedure of aggregating and *pro-rata-ing* applied in the specific conditions laid down by Reg. 3. In all other circumstances domestic law applied, and if the qualifying periods do not overlap, a full entitlement according to the domestic law of one member state may be combined with another in a second member state. Moreover, according to the Community Court, the interested person was not compelled to liquidate his claims simultaneously and was not given the option between reliance on the old Reg. 3 or on domestic law unaffected by Reg. 3.

It will have been noted that, if the interested party could delay the presentation of his claim so as to present it in the member state which confers greater benefits not subject to aggregation in another member state only after the expiration of a full qualifying period in that member state, the claim was no longer caught by arts. 27 and 28 of Reg. 3 and displayed all the features of the cases outside Reg. 3 which were discussed above.[4] This alternative was, however, open only to those who could wait before they lodged their claim, since Reg. 3, art. 28(4) provided expressly that "persons who may claim under the provisions of this Chapter shall not be entitled to claim a pension under the legislation of one member state only". Such an interpretation of art. 28(4) assumed that the reference to "persons who may claim" was restricted to those who require aggregation in order to maintain their full rights and have lodged a claim. Such persons fulfilled the objective conditions for the application of Reg. 3, arts. 27 and 28[5] and could not evade its operation. On this interpretation art. 28(4) did not cover persons who required aggregation when they could claim first but preferred to wait until their claim matured fully under the domestic law of the member states concerned.

---

at p. 562, where no aggregation was necessary and domestic law rather than the Treaty and Reg. 3 applied.

1   Reg. 3, art. 28(2).
2   Reg. 3, art. 28(3); the procedure was to be laid down by another regulation.
3   P. 120 ff.
4   Pp. 121–123.
5   See p. 122.

Regulation 1408/71 seems to have made a break with the system as it was evolved by the Community Court in the course of applying Reg. 3. The new principle appears to be expressed in the general provision[1] that, where a claim for an old age or death pension is introduced, all payments due under the laws which applied at one time or another must be liquidated simultaneously and be brought into hotchpotch.[2] Upon the express demand of the interested party the realisation of payments due under the laws of other member states may be postponed, provided that the periods completed under the laws of other member states are not aggregated in other member states.[3]

Thus *pro-rata-ing* appears to be the principle; if excluded, aggregation is also not permitted. The question remains whether it is now forbidden to cumulate claims in respect of separate periods of insurance which include fictitious periods, actually completed under another law.[4]

Aggregation is allowed if the law of a member state requires the completion of certain periods of insurance.[5] If these periods must have been completed in a trade subject to a special scheme or in a particular type of employment, periods served in other member states in circumstances which are not comparable are not to be taken into account, but they may be counted as qualifying periods for payments under the general scheme of insurance or that for workers or employees as a whole.[6] If the worker was formerly subject *ratione loci* to a law which did not require the completion of periods of insurance in order to qualify, and the law which applies *ratione loci* at the time when the event occurred does demand it,[7] the former scheme is deemed to continue for the purpose of claiming benefits in another member state which applies to him at the time when the event occurred.[8]

If no aggregation is required in order to qualify, the competent institution in each member state, the law of which has applied to the worker at some time and by which the necessary conditions have been fulfilled in order to qualify for invalidity benefits, calculates the amount of the benefits to which he is entitled by reference to its own law, taking into

---

1   Reg. 1408/71, art. 44(2).

2   Thus overruling *Caisse Régionale de Sécurité Sociale Nord-Est* v. *Goffart* (1967), 13 Rec. 413, at p. 421, [1967] C.M.L.R. 343; *Guissart* v. *Etat Belge* (1967), 13 Rec. 551; *Ciechelski* v. *Caisse Régionale de Sécurité Sociale du Centre, Orléans* (1967), 13 Rec. 235, at p. 245; [1967] C.M.L.R. 192; *Caisse d'Assurance Vieillesse des Travailleurs Salariés de Paris* v. *Duffy* (1969), 15 Rec. 597, at p. 603(7)–(10); [1971] C.M.L.R. 391.

3   Nevertheless any possibility of cumulating benefits by virtue of this option is excluded by the overriding provisions of arts. 46(1) and (2), 49(2); see below, p. 126. Cp. *Ciechelski* v. *Caisse Régionale de Sécurité Sociale du Centre, Orléans* (1967) 13 Rec. 235, at p. 245(3) (above. n. 2): no cumulation of overlapping periods.

4   Cp. *Guissart* v. *Etat Belge* (1967), 13 Rec. 551, at p. 563. It is possible that Reg. 1408/71, art. 46(2) as amended by the Treaty of Accession, Pt. II, *loc. cit.* alludes to this eventuality.

5   Reg. 1408/71, art. 45(1) as amended by the Treaty of Accession, Pt. II, *loc. cit.* and by art. 45(4) added thereby.

6   Reg. 1408/71, art. 45(2).

7   And, it must be assumed, does not treat him as qualified in the absence of the necessary periods of insurance completed under its own law.

8   Reg. 1408/71, art. 45(3).

account all those periods of insurance which that law required to be counted.[1] By a second operation the same competent institution proceeds to a process of aggregation and *pro-rata-ing* as it is prescribed in the case where the law applicable requires the completion of certain periods of insurance.[2] The higher figure reached by either of these processes represents the benefit due by the institution of the member state concerned.[3]

Thus, by compelling the authorities in each member state to take into consideration the periods served in all other member states, even where no aggregation is necessary either because the necessary period of insurance has been completed or because no such completion is required, and by establishing a maximum entitlement, which is then *pro-rated*, the Regulation has created a general scheme which excludes any serious cumulation of alternative or successive benefits. As shown above,[4] it must remain an open question whether this new device is *ultra vires* the Treaty, because it goes beyond co-ordination.

Naturally the same process of *pro-rata-ing* is prescribed where aggregation is necessary.[5] Naturally the competent institution must calculate the benefits by reference to all completed periods in other member states,[6] *pro-rate* them according to the periods completed in all the member states concerned,[7] and if the aggregate of the periods under the laws of all the member states concerned exceeds the maximum required in one member state for a complete service of benefits, the maximum so found is decisive in lieu of the total periods.[8] The sum so found is due to the claimant by the various competent institutions respectively.[9]

If the claimant does not fulfil the conditions which would qualify him for benefits under all the laws to which he has been subject *ratione loci* at one time or another, irrespective of aggregation or not, but does qualify under the laws of some of these member states, the system of aggregation and *pro-rata-ing* applies to those states where the conditions for qualifying have been fulfilled.[10] If the claimant is fully qualified under the laws of at least two legal systems without any need to have recourse to aggregation, all other periods can be disregarded for the purpose of the final calculation.[11] The same applies if the qualifying conditions of only one

1   Reg. 1408/71, art. 46(1), 1st para. as amended by the Treaty of Accession, Pt. II, *loc. cit.*
2   Reg. 1408/71, art. 46(1), 2nd para. as amended (see above, n. 1).
3   Reg. 1408/71, art. 46(1), 2nd para., last sentence as amended (see above, n. 1).
4   Above, p. 99.
5   Reg. 1408/71, art. 46(2) as amended (above, n. 1).
6   Reg. 1408/71, art. 46(2)(a) as amended (above, n. 1), art. 47 as amended (above, n. 1).
7   Reg. 1408/71, art. 46(2)(b) as amended (above, n. 1).
8   Reg. 1407/71, art. 46(2)(c), (d) as amended (above, n. 1).
9   Reg. 1408/71, art. 46(d) as amended; art. 47 as amended (above, n. 1) concerning the basis of calculations and the relevance of members of the family other than children; as regards the treatment of periods of insurance lasting less than one year which do not serve as a qualification in a member state within the general scheme of art. 46(2), see art. 48 as amended by the Treaty of Accession, Pt. II, *loc. cit.* and art. 51 inserted by the Treaty, *loc. cit.* For revalorisation see art. 51.
10 Reg. 1408/71, art. 49(1)(a).
11 Reg. 1408/71, art. 49(1)(b)(i) as amended by the Treaty of Accession, Pt. II, *loc. cit.*

law have been complied with,[1] but the calculation of the respective benefits is re-opened as and when the qualifying period is completed under the law of another member state.[2] Thus an eventual cumulation is excluded once again.[3]

At the same time a beneficiary of an old age or death pension who receives a benefit in the country of his residence cannot receive an amount which is smaller than that which is allowed by the law of that state in respect of a period of insurance equal to the total period after aggregation.[4]

VI   ADMINISTRATIVE COMMISSION—CONSULTATIVE COMMITTEE

An Administrative Commission[5] is to settle all questions concerning the administration and interpretation of the Regulation as well as of any subsequent instruments or arrangements, to carry out all translations of documents relating to the implementation of the Regulation, to foster co-operation in matters of social security, especially of effecting payments, to establish methods of claiming refunds between the competent institutions of the member states, to exercise implied powers given by Regulations and to submit proposals for the revision of relevant regulations.[6]

It is provided expressly that the right of the authorities, institutions and persons concerned to have recourse to the procedures and legal remedies prescribed by the laws of member states, or in the Treaty or by the Regulation itself are not affected.[7] For this purpose claims may be submitted in the official language of another member state to the authorities and institutions of other member states.[8]

Regulation 1408/71 has added a Consultative Committee of six established on a tripartite basis, which includes representatives of the governments, of trade unions and of employers' federations, and which is chaired by a member or representative of the Commission.[9] Its task is very general and includes the consideration of all questions arising from the application of regulations made under art. 51 of the Treaty, the submission of advice and the formulation of proposals for the revision of the regulations.[10]

---

1 Reg. 1408/71, art. 49(1)(b)(ii) as amended by the Treaty of Accession, Pt. II, *loc. cit.*
2 Reg. 1408/71, art. 49(2); the same applies if liability to provide such benefits ceases under the law of one of the member states.
3 Cp. above, p. 125, n. 1.
4 Reg. 1408/71, art. 50 as amended by the Treaty of Accession, Pt. II, *loc. cit.*; the difference is made up by the state where the beneficiary resides. See also Reg. 3, art. 28(3).
5 For its composition see Reg. 1408/71, art. 80(1), formerly Reg. 3, art. 44.
6 Reg. 1408/71, art. 81, formerly Reg. 3, art. 43(a)–(f).
7 Reg. 1408/71, art. 81(a), formerly Reg. 3, art. 43(a). See also *Sociale Verzekeringsbank* v, *Van der Vecht* (1967), 13 Rec. 446, at pp. 457 ff.; [1968] C.M.L.R. 151.
8 Reg. 1408/71, art. 84(4), formerly Reg. 3, art. 45(4). The Belgian Conseil d'Etat falls within the ambit of this provision which extends to an authority charged with the judicial control of the application of social security. See *Guerra* v. *Institut National d'Assurances Maladie-Invalidité* (1967), 13 Rec. 283, at p. 289.
9 Reg. 1408/71, art. 82.
10 Reg. 1408/71, art. 83.

VII   SUBROGATION

Claims by an individual who has sustained an injury in the territory of another member state and who has a claim for damages for that injury from a third party who is in the latter state, pass to the institution which is liable to pay benefits to the injured party and which has paid such benefits, if according to the law governing the institution the latter steps into the shoes of the injured party by way of subrogation or is given a direct action against the third party.[1] When Reg. 3 applied, the relevant art. 52 was operative, even in the absence of implementation by bilateral conventions as envisaged in its last sentence.[2] The new Regulation 1408/71 omits any reference to eventual bilateral agreements.

This choice of law rule, which relies on the law of the insurer and not only the law governing the tort itself to determine subrogation to a claim in tort is unusual, but it has its modern counterparts.[3]

The desire to afford the greatest possible assistance to the authorities charged with administering social security in the member states to recover their expenses justifies this solution which is not concerned with safeguarding social security benefits for migrant workers but to reach as many tortfeasors as possible. If a member state is compelled to grant benefits to the victim of a tort abroad, the Regulation applies, if he is entitled to benefits in the former state, no matter whether he is a migrant worker or not. Not the protection of migrant workers but that of social security institutions in the Community is the purpose of art. 93 of Reg. 1408/71.[4] It adds that the law of the insuring institution must also determine whether the employer or fellow workmen are exempt from liability.[5] This principle is novel and open to objections since it exceeds the aim of facilitating recourse against the tortfeasor and purports to supersede the application of the *lex loci delicti* in favour of another legal system, the possible application of which may not be foreseeable by the tortfeasor who is vicariously responsible.

---

1   Reg. 1408/71, art. 93; Reg. 3, art. 52; Gitter, 1965 N.J.W., 1108; Seché, Rev. Trim. Dr. Int. 475, at pp. 508–509.

2   *Gemeenschappelijke Verzekeringskas "De Sociale Voorzorg"* v. *Bertholet* (1965), 11 Rec. 111, at p. 118; [1966] C.M.L.R. 191; *Betriebskrankenkasse der Heseper Torfwerk GmbH* v. *Van Dijk* (1965), 11 Rec. 131, at p. 139; [1966] C.M.L.R. 191. The requirement of the conclusion of bilateral treaties appears to have been included by an oversight and to be derived from an additional Draft Protocol.

3   Hague Convention on the Law applicable to Traffic Accidents, 1968, art. 9, 3rd para.; Lyon-Caen, 1965 Rev. Trim. Dr. Eur. 425; 1968 *ibid.* 151.

4   These considerations explain the broad approach towards art. 52 of Reg. 3, now art. 93 of Reg. 1408/71 taken by the Community Court. See *Gemeenschappelijke Verzekeringskas "De Sociale Voorzorg"* v. *Bertholet* (1965), 11 Rec. 111, at p. 119; *Hessische Knappschaft* v. *Singer* (1965), 11 Rec. 1191, at p. 1199; [1966] C.M.L.R. 82; *Caisse de Maladie des CFL etc.* v. *Cie. Belge d'Assurances Générales* (1969), 15 Rec. 405, at p. 410(3), (4), (5); [1970] C.M.L.R. 243.

5   Reg. 1408/71, art. 93(2).

6

Freedom of Movement—
Establishment

(Articles 52–58)[1]

The free movement of persons within the EEC is not limited to workers (arts. 48–51). It extends also to self-employed persons engaged in trading, professional, agricultural, productive or creative economic activities, to mention only a few (arts. 52–58). The problems raised by this extension of the freedom of movement are of a different nature and are more complex than those created by the admission of foreign manual and white collar workers. They differ, moreover, according as self-employed persons wish to establish themselves permanently in a member country or to render services across the border. For this reason separate provisions of the Treaty serve to regulate the establishment and the services across the frontiers by persons in one country of the EEC who do not take up permanent residence in another state of the EEC (arts. 59–66). In so far as the establishment of self-employed persons involves members of the professions and traders it touches upon the legislation of each member state which requires certain qualifications. Short of harmonising or unifying these provisions, which is a technique envisaged only to a limited extent through the co-ordination of certain rules of company law (art. 54(3)(g))[2] and of the conditions for the exercise of the medical, para-medical and pharmaceutical professions (art. 57(3)), the Treaty can seek only to eliminate any discrimination based upon foreign nationality. Moreover, since the unconditional reception of members of professional and trading communities affects not so much the labour market (which operates through the mechanism of supply and demand) as the society of a country as a whole, a complete liberalisation by the Treaty itself was excluded for the time being. Nevertheless, the Treaty envisages freedom of establishment within the Community (art. 52, 1st para.), but the subtle difference must be noted between the article dealing with the free movement of workers (art. 48: "The free movement of workers shall be

---

1 See the literature cited above, p. 84, n. 1; *Mégret*, Vol. III, pp. 87–172, 55*–*126 and van der Geeven in *Ganshof van der Meersch*, pp. 739–753, Nos. 1855–1870; Odette Loy, [1968] Clunet 673; Loussouarn, (1965) Rev. Trim. Dr. Eur. 169; 1967 *ibid.* 62, 859; Goldman, *Droit Commercial Européen* (1969), pp. 121–207.

2 Namely those concerning guarantees demanded from companies in the meaning of art. 58(2) for the purpose of protecting the interests both of the members of such companies and of third parties. See below, pp. 142, n. 1, 146.

secured . . .") and that dealing with the right of establishment of self-employed persons (art. 52: "Within the framework of the provisions . . . below, restrictions on the freedom of establishment . . . shall be gradually abolished . . .").

1   BENEFICIARIES—INDIVIDUALS

Nationals of the member states (but not necessarily refugees and stateless persons domiciled in a member state[1] or nationals of third countries) are to be admitted freely to establish themselves in another member state (art. 52, 1st para.) for the purpose of any gainful activity (art. 52, 2nd para.) not covered by the provisions on employment (arts. 48–51). Existing restrictions must be abolished (arts. 52, 54(2)), and new restrictions must not be introduced (art. 53).[2]

Measures: Council—upon proposal of the Commission:
Programme (54(1));[3] Directives (54(2)).[4]

Gainful activities include not only the supply of particular services, especially of a professional kind, but all aspects of trading, including banking and insurance, gas, water and electricity supplies and sanitation,[5] as well as the creation of new enterprises and their direction.[6] Nationals of member states may also establish agencies, branches or subsidiaries of enterprises, but in this case the national concerned must have his residence in one of the member states (though not necessarily in the state of which he is a national (art. 52, 1st para., end). A national of an EEC country may also establish himself in his capacity of manager of an association of a member state created and established in another country of the Community in accordance with the provision on the operation of companies in the Community (art. 52, 2nd para., art. 58, 2nd para.).

While any national of the EEC may invest in the capital of associations or companies established in the Community (arts. 221, 58) the right to set up and to manage such associations or companies in a particular member state of the Community appears to benefit only those nationals

---

1   See however above, p. 85 and n. 10; but see the Declaration of the Member States dated 25 March 1964, OJ, 1964, 1225; for the position of the German Democratic Republic see Goldman, *Droit Commercial Européen*, pp. 123–124, No. 108; for the French overseas departments see Council Decision 68/359, OJ, 1968, L 257/1.

2   Art. 53 applies directly to individuals: *Costa* v. *ENEL* (1964), 10 Rec. 1141; [1964] C.M.L.R. 425.

3   See the detailed enumeration in the Programme on Establishment of 18 December 1961, OJ, 1962, 36, Annex; *Mégret*, Vol. III, p. 55*.

4   See Council Directives below, p. 144, n. 1.

5   See the Programme of 18 December 1961, OJ, 1962, 36, Annex.

6   The question must be considered whether art. 52, 2nd para. purports to enable individuals, nationals of EEC countries, to set up new companies and associations in the host country or only to manage such companies as are covered by art. 50. The narrow view is supported by art. 54(2)(f), but the use of the term "setting up" in art. 52, 2nd para., accompanied by the illustrative reference "in particular" seems to support the broader interpretation.

of the Community who are established in that state unless the law of the local member state concedes the same right to non-residents.[1]

1   Restrictions—Qualifications—Diplomas—Languages—Public Functions

Throughout, the right of a national of a member state to establish himself and to carry on a trade or occupation is subject to the general law of the state where the establishment is set up. Consequently, general rules such as those relating to banking and insurance must be observed, as well as those controlling professional qualifications.[2] The purpose of the rules on establishment is to ensure equality of treatment, but not to confer privileges on nationals of the other member states which are not available to the nationals of the local state. It would seem that even the imposition of certain conditions may be permissible, although at first sight they may appear to be discriminatory, such as the passing of a language test where the exercise of a profession, such as medicine, involves necessarily a close contact with the local population. It must be noted, for the purpose of this argument, that the chapter on establishment, unlike that on services (art. 65) and elsewhere (arts. 33(1), 44(1)), does not contain an absolute prohibition against discrimination, and it seems that any requirements touching upon qualifications which may incidentally place the national of another state of the Community at a disadvantage, is not discriminatory in law.

> *Measure:* Council upon proposal of the Commission after consulting the Economic and Social Council—Programme (art. 54(1)).

The mutual recognition of certificates, diplomas and other evidence of qualifications, such as professional examinations is to be determined by the Council.

> *Measure:* Council upon proposal of the Commission—after consulting the Assembly: by a qualified majority—Directives (art. 57(1)).[3]

Similarly, the legislative and administrative provisions of the member states concerning access to, and the exercise of, non-wage-earning activities are to be co-ordinated by the Council.

> *Measure:* Council upon proposal of the Commission—after consulting the Assembly—Directives (art. 57(2), first sentence).

---

1   The argument is drawn from art. 52, 2nd para., end, in conjunction with art. 54(3)(f).

2   On the co-ordination of such provisions see art. 57(2); below, pp. 131–132.

3   Including school leaving certificates. See European Convention of 11 December 1953 (European Treaty Series No. 15). And see the General Programme on the Abolition of Restrictions on Freedom of Establishment of 18 December 1961, OJ, 1962, 36, Title V issued by virtue of art. 54(1), below, p. 142.

If the topic is regulated by legislation in *at least one* country of the Community or concerns any matter which, in the words of the Treaty, affects "la protection de l'épargne",[1] "Schutz des Sparwesens", *i.e.* establishment of banks and savings institutions, the medical, para-medical and pharmaceutical professions, including, it would seem, dentists, veterinary surgeons, midwives and osteopaths, the far reaching social and economic repercussions of the measures justify the requirement of a unanimous directive (art. 57(2), second sentence).[2] Since the mutual right of establishment of doctors and persons of similar qualifications can only be achieved in practice if a certain degree of uniformity in the legislation exists, in so far as it affects the conditions of their admission to practise (art. 57(2)), the co-ordination of the education for, and the control of the exercise of, these professions is envisaged as well.

Measure: Directive (art. 57(3)).[3]

The mutual obligation to admit self-employed persons is not, however, without limits. If such activities are connected in the host state with the exercise of public functions, be they permanent or temporary, no right to establishment exists (art. 55, 1st para.).[4] Thus in France, Belgium and Luxemburg the exercise of the profession of lawyer may be excepted, since any such person may be called upon temporarily to exercise the function of public prosecutor or judge.[5] It has been argued, however, that the wording of art. 55 (which excepts certain activities) permits the exercise of the profession limited to those functions which are not public.[6] No such claim can perhaps be made by the *Länder* in Germany, and it has therefore been asked whether French lawyers will be permitted to practise in Germany, while German lawyers cannot do so in France.[7] In Germany and in France, on the other hand, the exercise of the profession of notary public (who is entrusted with the task of issuing and receiving

---

1   A term derived from French law; it includes all measures regulating the market of capital, banks, stock- and commodity-exchanges; cp. Ripert, Traité élémentaire de Droit Commercial (4th Edn., 1959) I, No. 891, 908, 980, 1524.

2   During the transitional period, when according to art. 57(2) the subject matter was to have been determined. Upon the analogy of art. 57(1) it may be argued that after the end of the transitional period a qualified majority is required in respect of outstanding measures. For the directives and proposals of Council directives see below, p. 144.

3   The co-ordination is not confined to the right of establishment but extends also to services across frontiers (art. 66).

4   Everling, cited above, p. 84, n. 1, at p. 86.

5   See Schneider (1971), 8 C.M.L.Rev. 44, especially p. 46; Degan, 1966 Rev. Trim. Dr. Eur. 242; Terré, [1967] Clunet, 265; Jacob 1970 Cah. Dr. Eur. 663. Proposed Directive of 17 April 1969, OJ, 1969, C78/1, OJ, 1972, C103/19 concerning advocates and the comments by de Crayencour, 1970 Rev. M.C. 158 and see the survey in 1970 Rev. Trim Dr. Eur. 433 and 607.

6   *Mégret*, Vol. III, p. 98 referring to Council Directive 64/224, OJ, 1964, 871, art. 4(2); see also de Crayencour 1970 Rev. M.C. 158 at pp. 163, 165.

7   For an authoritative answer in respect of the profession of commercial agents see Council Directive 64/224 of 25 February 1964, OJ, 1964, 871, art. 4(2). And compare *e.g.* Directive 66/162 of 28 February 1966, OJ, 1966, 584, 586, art. 3.

public documents) and in Germany of district chimney sweep (who exercises certain functions involving public safety), are excepted. Certain other activities which preclude the participation of aliens may be added to the list (art. 55, 2nd para.), but none seem to have been added.

> *Measure:* Council by a qualified majority—upon proposal
> of the Commission (art. 55).

The Community Court has held by implication that if in a particular country an industry, trade or profession is a state monopoly of a non-commercial character or, being of a commercial character, does not play an important part in the exchange of goods across frontiers, aliens can be excluded, and thus also members of the countries of the Community,[1] as are nationals of the country concerned.

2   Public Order—Public Safety—Public Health[2]

In addition, the member states retain the powers under their national legislation which discriminate against aliens on grounds of public order, public safety and public health (art. 56(1)). Nevertheless, these legislative or administrative provisions are to be co-ordinated.[3]

> *Measure:* Council—upon proposal of the Commission and
> after having consulted the Assembly—Directive
> (art. 56(2)).

The Council issued on 25 February 1964 the directive required by art. 56(2).[4] It covers self-employed persons who are established in another country of the Community or render services across the frontiers as well as wage earners, and applies therefore also in the situation to which arts. 48(3) and 49 refer (namely workers in employment).[5] The range of persons affected includes also wives and members of the family of those immediately concerned under the regulations and directives.[6] In substance it affects local laws concerning entry, residence permits and removal

---

1   *Costa* v. *ENEL* (1964), 10 Rec. 1141, at p. 1165; [1964] C.M.L.R. 425.
2   See Lyon-Caen, 1966, Rev. Trim. Dr. Eur. 693.
3   Art. 56 requiring co-ordination is *lex specialis* in relation to art. 100 empowering the Council to issue directives concerning the approximation of laws.
4   Directive 64/221 of 25 February 1964, OJ, 1964, 850; *Mégret,* Vol. III, p. 76*. The Directive applies also to services across the frontiers (art. 66) and was extended by Council Directive 72/194, 18 May 1972, OJ, 1972, L 121/32 to workers staying on after the termination of their employment by virtue of Commission Reg. 1251/70, OJ, 1970, L 142/24 (above, p. 90, n. 12) and by Council Directive 73/148, OJ, 1973, L 172/14 to self-employed persons. It has been asked whether art. 56(2), unlike art. 57(2), permits co-ordination if only one member state has legislative and administrative provisions touching upon the subject matter regulated by art. 56. In fact, all countries of the Six have laws and regulations of the kind envisaged by art. 56. See von der Groeben-Boeckh, Kommentar ad. art. 56, n. 8.
5   Directive 64/221 (above, n. 4) art. 1(1).
6   *Ibid.,* art. 1(2).

in so far as such laws are determined by considerations of public order, public safety or health.[1] Any measures based on these considerations must be occasioned exclusively by the personal conduct of the individual concerned,[2] must not operate automatically on conviction in criminal proceedings[3] and must not be motivated by economic reasons.[4] The fact that a travel document has expired which permitted entry and the delivery of a residence permit is insufficient to justify any such measures.[5] As a corollary the state which issued the travel document must receive back any person whose travel document has expired, even if nationality of the holder is disputed.[6] A list of illnesses which alone permit measures of refusal to admit or to issue the first residence permit is drawn up,[7] and subsequent illnesses or infirmities do not justify a refusal to renew a residence permit or the removal of the holder.[8] The procedure of admission is regulated.[9] All remedies at the disposal of nationals against administrative acts are to be available in those circumstances to nationals of the other member states.[10] If such remedies are only admissible on points of law or if none are available at all, a party who has been refused the renewal of his residence permit or who is to be removed, must be given an opportunity to be heard personally or through a representative.[11] The authority to which representations are to be made must differ from that which has refused the renewal of the residence permit or has ordered the removal.[12] Upon analysis this somewhat obscure provision appears to impose a duty upon those countries of the Community where the admission and expulsion of aliens is entrusted to the executive and where either no systems of administrative courts exist or where the control of the courts is restricted to points of law, to create new procedures or new remedies which permit a review of the facts by a body other than that which took the original decision.

At the same time another Council Directive of 25 February 1964 on the Abolition of Restrictions on Travel and Residence of Nationals of the Member States inside the Community in respect of Establishment and the Free Exchange of Services came into force.[13] Like its counterpart dealing

---

1 Directive 64/221 (above, p. 133, n. 4), art. 2(1).
2 *Ibid.*, art. 3(1).
3 *Ibid.*, art. 3(2).
4 *Ibid.*, art. 2(2).
5 *Ibid.*, art. 3(3).
6 *Ibid.*, art. 3(4).
7 *Ibid.*, art. 4(1) and Annex.
8 *Ibid.*, art. 4(2).
9 *Ibid.*, arts. 5–7.
10 *Ibid.*, art. 8.
11 *Ibid.*, art. 9(1); it will be noted that this provision does not extend to the refusal to grant admission or to issue the first residence permit; see *ibid.*, art. 9(2).
12 *Ibid.*, art. 9(1), 2nd para.
13 64/220, OJ, 1964, 845; *Mégret*, Vol. III, p. 73* to be replaced; see Commission proposal 14 July 1971, OJ, 1971, C91/19; OJ, 1972, C67/4 and to be supplemented by a directive not unlike the Commission Reg. 1251/70 (above, p. 90, n. 12). See Commission Proposal 29 June 1972, OJ, 1972, C94/7.

with Travel and Residence of Workers,[1] it requires the removal of restrictions on travel and residence of nationals of the member states who wish to settle in another member state in a non-wage earning capacity,[2] their wives and children under twenty-one, as well as any ascendants and descendants of each of the spouses, irrespective of their nationality.[3] In particular entry is to be granted upon the production of an identity paper or passport,[4] but visas may be required for spouses, children and ascendants or descendants who are not nationals of a member state.[5] If the restrictions on the exercise of a particular non-wage earning activity have been lifted, a residence permit must be issued to a person wishing to settle for the purpose of exercising that profession.[6] The permit is to be valid for at least five years and automatically renewable.[7] The same applies to residence permits issued on the strength of domestic law.[8] The residence permit must cover the entire territory of the issuing member state.[9] The provisions of the Directive can only be disregarded on grounds of public order, public security and public health.[10]

II BENEFICIARIES—ASSOCIATIONS AND COMPANIES (art. 58)[11]

Article 58 states that foreign "associations"[12] or "Gesellschaften"[13] are to enjoy the same privileges as those accorded to individuals (arts. 52–57). The terms "associations" or "Gesellschaften" are defined in some detail (art. 58(2)). They are broader than the notion of companies in English law. *Ratione personae* they embrace associations formed under civil or commercial law and include, therefore, not only companies limited by share, whether public or private,[14] but also partnerships, provided that they enjoy legal personality in the country of their origin.[15] The reference

---

1 Council Directive 64/240 of 25 March 1964, OJ. 1964, 981 to be *replaced* by Council Directive 68/360 of 15 October 1968, OJ, 1968, L 257/13 (above, p. 89).
2 Council Directive 64/220, (above, n. 1) art. 1(1)(a).
3 *Ibid.*, art. 1(1)(c), (d).
4 *Ibid.*, art. 2(1).
5 *Ibid.*, art. 2(2).
6 *Ibid.*, art. 3(1).
7 *Ibid.*, art. 3(1), 2nd para.
8 *Ibid.*, art. 3(1), 3rd para.
9 *Ibid.*, art. 4.
10 *Ibid.*, art. 8.
11 Stein, (1970) 68 Mich. L.R. 1327; Goldman, (1968–69) 6 C.M.L. Rev. 104; Dieu, (1968) 4 Cah. Dr. Eur. 532; Cerexhe, 1968 Rev. M.C. 578; (1968) 13 Riv. Soc. 817; Loussouarn, 1971 Rev. M.C. 59, and see below, p. 148, n. 3.
12 French version.
13 German version.
14 *Sociétés anonymes, sociétés en responsabilité limitée, Aktiengesellschaft, Gesellschaft mit beschränkter Haftung; Società anonima, società a responsabilità limitata; Grote Naamlooze Vennootschap, Besloten Namlooze Vennootschap met beperkte aansprakelijkheid.*
15 *E.g.* the German *Offene Handelsgesellschaft* and the Dutch *Vennootschap onder firma*; see Cerexhe, 1968 Rev. M.C. 578, at p. 583. And see the Treaty of 29 February 1968 (below, p. 148, n. 3), art. 1: *"les sociétés . . . constituées en conformité de la loi d'un Etat contractant qui leur accorde la capacité d'être titulaires de droits et d'obligations".*

to their creation under civil or commercial law takes account of the distinction, in continental law, between commercial law, which applies to merchants and to legal entities devoted to trading, and civil law, which governs all activities of a gainful nature except those of a merchant. The Treaty expressly includes co-operatives and all other legal entities, but excludes [non-profit making] associations which do not pursue a "but lucratif", "Erwerbszweck". This term, which is derived from French law[1] concentrates not on the profit motive but on the economic character of the activity, which is the object of the Treaty. Thus foundations and unincorporated associations may be within the ambit of art. 58, the former because they can be profit-making (if they have an economic purpose), the latter because they may enjoy some independent standing although they are not legal entities.[2]

Since associations, treated as a broad category, have no nationality, even if public international law may seek to attribute to them artificially the nationality of some country for the purpose of determining the nationality of claims and the right to protect particular associations, the requirement that the beneficiaries must possess the nationality of one of the member states, stipulated for individuals (art. 52, 1st para.), does not figure here.[3]

Ratione loci the associations concerned must have been created or incorporated in accordance with the law of one of the member states, and they must have either their statutory seat (registered office) or their centre of management or their principal place of business within one of the countries of the Community (art. 58(1)). The reference to law of the place where the corporation was formed as the first condition for conferring the status of a Community association is strange within the setting of the Community. With the exception of Dutch[4] and, to a minor extent, of Italian law,[5] continental legal systems, unlike English law, rely on the law of the real seat of an association to determine whether it has validly come into existence and attach no importance to incorporation in a country as such. However, this seeming change of attitude is counterbalanced by a second requirement that the association must have its statutory seat or its central management or its principal place of business within the countries of the Community. This provision is not surprising, given the approach of con-

---

1   Cp. Cass. réun. 11 March 1914, D. 1914. I.257; Cerexhe, *loc. cit.*, at p. 584; Goldman, *Droit Commercial Européen*, No. 120, p. 134; Santa Maria in (1969) XIII Comm. e St. 293, at p. 306, n. 17 with lit.

2   It is a matter for discussion whether art. 58(2) must be interpreted restrictively so as to exclude unincorporated associations, but the answer is probably that given above. For the whole problem see Everling, p. 67 ff.; for an enumeration see *ibid.*, p. 70, nn. 35, 36.

3   But see the General Programme on the Suppression of Restrictions of the Freedom of Establishment of 18 December 1961, OJ, 1962, 36, Tit. I, para. 6 which added the requirement of an effective link for associations which qualify for the privileges of establishment by virtue of their statutory seat in the Community. See below.

   And see Goldman, *Travaux du Comité Français de Droit International Privé, 1966–69*, pp. 215–243.

4   Wetboek van Koophandel art. 36 e; Cerexhe, 1968 Rev. M.C. 578, at p. 580; Stein, (1970) 68 Mich. L.R. 1327, at p. 1330; Grossfeld, (1967) 31 Rabels Z, 1–16.

5   Codice civile, art. 2390.

tinental law set out above. According to the latter, an association must have complied with the requirements of the law of its seat in order to come into existence at the place of its seat and in order to be recognised elsewhere. If it has not complied with these requirements, it does not exist at all. However, art. 58 introduces as an alternative a new criterion, namely, the statutory seat. The statutory seat, as distinct from that where the centre of control and management or the principal place of business is located, has not, so far, fulfilled any function in the domestic law of the Community.[1] The result is that a corporation formed in France, having its statutory seat in France or in Belgium (if this should be possible), can establish itself in Germany, in order to carry on business there. The fact that its links with France and Belgium are tenuous is set off by the fact that it carries on business in Germany. An effective link with the Community is formed by the activities in the latter country.[2] However, another situation must not be overlooked. An association in the meaning of art. 58, *i.e.* one which is formed in accordance with the law of a member state and which has its registered office within the Community but is not otherwise connected with the Community by a centre of management or principal place of business, can avail itself of the right accorded by art. 52, 1st para., and set up an agency, branch or subsidiary in a state of the Community and claim that it is established in the territory of a member state (art. 52, 1st para.). In the latter case the danger exists that an association which can show no more than a formal connection with the Community can obtain a foothold as if it were a national of the Community. The General Programme on the Suppression of Restrictions on the Freedom of Establishment of 18 December 1961[3] and that on the Suppression of Restrictions on the Free Supply of Services of the same date[4] have tried to close this loophole.[5] Following literally the provision of art. 58 the General Programme envisages the establishment for non-wage earning purposes within a member state of associations created in accordance with the laws of a member state or of an overseas country or territory[6] which have their statutory seat, their central administration or their principal establishment within the Community or an overseas country or territory.[7] But if the establishment of an agency, branch or subsidiary is sought within a member state, an association as defined by art. 58 which has only a statutory seat within the Community or in an overseas country

1 See, however, the Hague Convention of 1 June 1956 concerning the Recognition of the Legal Personality of Companies etc., art. 1 which has not come into force hitherto; Institut de Droit International, Warsaw 1965, 1965 II, Ann. Inst. Dr. Int. 263, at p. 272.

2 See, however, the General Programme on the Suppression of Restrictions of the Freedom of Establishment of 18 December 1961, OJ, 1962, 36, Tit. I, para. 3, below, p. 142.

3 OJ, 1962, 36, Tit. I, para. 6.

4 OJ, 1962, 32, Tit. I, para. 3.

5 For an early discussion of this problem see Von der Groeben-Boeckh, *Kommentar zum EWG Vertrag*, Baden-Baden, Bonn, Frankfurt, (1963), *ad* art. 58, n. 5; Wohlfahrt-Everling-Glaesner-Sprung, *Die Europäische Wirtschaftsgemeinschaft*, *ad* art. 58, nn. 1 and 3.

6 For the meaning of this term see above, p. 50.

7 General Programme on the Suppression of Restrictions of the Freedom of Establishment, Tit. I, para. 3.

or territory, and not its central administration or its principal establishment, must show in addition that its activity establishes an effective and continuous link with the Community or an overseas country or territory. For this purpose it is insufficient that the partners, directors, members of the supervisory board, or persons controlling the assets, possess the nationality of a member state of the Community.[1]

The requirement of an effective link in terms identical with those laid down in the General Programme on Establishment in respect of associations which have no more than a statutory seat in a country of the Community is repeated generally by the General Programme on the Suppression of Restrictions on the Free Supply of Services.[2]

It is evident that the provision of the Treaty (art. 58, 1st para.) has been modified in an important aspect by the terms of the Programmes set out above. Where the Treaty envisages as minimum requirements two formal acts in order that an association may qualify as a Community association, namely, formation in accordance with the law of a member state and the adoption of a statutory seat within the Community (art. 58, 1st para.), the Programme, while reiterating these conditions, adds the material requirement of an effective link other than that of the nationality of the persons involved, if the company or association wishes to establish agencies, branches or subsidiaries in another country of the Community.

It may be that the Programme, by adding the requirement of an effective link to the other requirements of Community nationality as laid down by art. 58, 1st para., wished to do no more than to reflect, in the sphere of activities by companies and associations, the provision of art. 54, 1st para. As stated above, this provision states that a national of a member state who wishes to establish an agency, branch or subsidiary in another member state must be established in a member state.

Unless this interpretation is accepted, it is difficult to explain how the Council upon the proposal of the Commission can use its power to issue a Programme (art. 54(1))[3] in order to amend the Treaty itself. It may be debated, therefore, what force is to be attributed to the additional requirement that in certain circumstances an effective link must exist.[4] However, since Programmes are addressed to the member states with the aim of influencing their legislation, a provision of a Programme which asks member states to concede a lesser freedom of establishment than the Treaty itself seems to postulate is unlikely to create a wave of discontent throughout the Community, and it may be safe to assume that an effective link must be shown where there is only a statutory seat in the Community.

---

1   General Programme on the Suppression of Restrictions of the Freedom of Establishment, Tit. I, para. 6.

2   OJ, 1962, 32, Tit. I, para. 3; see below, p. 163. Thus a company formed in a member state and having only a registered office there but which operates in effect in Sweden does not qualify as a Community company for this purpose.

3   For a similar charge in respect of Company Law Directives see: Rodière, 1965 Rev. Trim. Dr. Eur. 336; Van Ommeslaghe, 1969 Cah. Dr. Eur. 495, at p. 503. For other details see below, p. 146.

4   See Goldman, *Droit Commercial Européen* (1969), No. 123, p. 137.

The purpose of art. 58 and of Title I of the Programme issued by virtue of art. 54(1) is to facilitate the free movement of companies and associations within the Community without opening the door to intruders who are really alien to the Community. In the absence of an acceptable test such as nationality or residence which apply to individuals to determine the Community character of companies and associations, the Treaty has resorted to tests taken from private international law, namely, place of incorporation, statutory seat, centre of administration and principal place of business. While these tests may serve the static purpose of defining companies and associations as aliens or Community nationals where admission to establishment is concerned, they are ill-suited for the dynamic purpose of the Treaty which is to encourage the movement of workers, employers and capital, if organised in the form of a company or association. Judged by the latter standard, the tests adopted by art. 58 are deficient. In the first place, with the exception of Dutch[1] and to a minor extent, of Italian law,[2] continental legal systems, unlike English law, rely on the law of the real seat of an association in order to determine whether it has validly come into existence, and attach no importance to incorporation in any one country as such.[3]

In the second place, in the absence of a valid formation according to the law of the real seat, the company or association does not exist.

In the third place, the adoption of a statutory seat as distinct from the existence of the centre of control and management or of the principal place of business has not, so far, been attributed the function of attracting the operation of the law of that country in order to determine the formation of the company or association.

Thus a company or association must be formed in accordance with the law of the place where its actual seat, its centre of management, of control, or of its principal place of business is, and it will not be recognised by any other of these countries unless this condition has been fulfilled.[4] Further, if a company or association transfers its seat, it must be liquidated in the country of its former seat and must be recreated in the country of its new seat. Thus a migration of companies and associations in the same sense as it is assumed for individual members of the EEC (arts. 52–57) is impracticable according to the law, including the rules of private international law of the majority of the countries of the Community.[5] Nothing more than the establishment of agencies, branches or subsidiaries (art. 52) is possible under the Treaty, since the Treaty itself does not regulate the domestic private international law of the member states.[6] The admission

---

1 Above, p. 136, n. 4 and see the Hague Convention of 1 June 1956, art. 1, above, p. 137, n. 1, English text in (1952) 1 A.J.C.L. 277; Doelle, 1952 Rabels Z. 185, at p. 270.
2 Above, p. 136, n. 5.
3 And see the Hague Convention of 1 June 1956 (above, n. 1), art. 2.
4 See also Kohler, (1969) 43 Tulane L.R. 58, at p. 88; Cerexhe, 1968 Rev. M.C. 568, at p. 570.
5 Stein, (1970) 68 Mich. L.R. 1327, at p. 1330 and nn. 14–16; Scholten, (1967) 4 C.M.L. Rev. 377, at p. 384, but see Mann, (1970) 19 I.C.L.Q. 468.
6 See Drobnig, (1967) 15 A.J.C.L. 204; 1970 Cah. Dr. Eur. 526, at p. 531. But see, as regards labour relations, the Draft Regulation submitted on 23 March 1972 by virtue of art. 49,

[footnote continued on next page]

of companies formed in other member states to trade is thus primarily a matter concerning the admission of aliens.[1]

This conclusion is supported by art. 220(3) which enjoins the member states to enter into negotiations with each other for the purpose of ensuring (a) "the mutual recognition of associations within the meaning of article 58(2), (b) the retention of their legal personality in case of a transfer of their seat from one country to another, and (c) the possibility of mergers of associations formed according to different legal systems".[2] It is also borne out by the attempts, which have remained at a stage of development hitherto, to evolve detailed rules for a so-called European company.[3] These attempts and the convention in response to art. 220(3), signed by the member states on 29 February 1968,[4] will be discussed below.[5]

III   IMPLEMENTATION OF THE RIGHT OF ESTABLISHMENT

1   In General

For the purpose of liberalising the rights of members to establish themselves in the EEC a standstill was declared of all restrictions on immigration and establishment (art. 53).[6] It must be noted that the standstill does not rule out the creation or modification of domestic law concerning professions, provided that no new discriminations are introduced. During the first stage a programme for the abolition of restrictions on establishment, covering each type of activities (art. 54(1), 2nd para.) was to be introduced.

> *Measure:* Council, unanimously on the proposal of the
> Commission after consulting the Social and
> Economic Council and the Assembly—
> Programme (art. 54(1)).

The Council complied with this provision on 18 December 1961 when it issued the General Programme on the Suppression of Restrictions on the

---

OJ, 1972, C 49/26, 142/5, 1973, C 4/14. The requirement of art. 52, 1st para., that nationals of the member states must be established in a member state is met as regards companies by the requirement of an effective link set out in the Programme of 18 December 1961.

1   Cp. Santa Maria in (1969) XIII Comm. e St. 293, at pp. 296 ff. and nn. 6, 7.

2   See above, p. 139; below, p. 148.

3   See *e.g.* Bärmann, (1961) 160 Arch. Ziv. Pr. 97; Duden, (1962) 27 Rabels Z. 89; Fikentscher and Grossfeld, (1964) 2 C.M.L.Rev. 259; Beitzke, (1964) 127 Z.H.R. 1; Vasseur, 1964 J. Bus. L. 358; (1965) *ibid.* 73; Houin, 1966 Rev. Trim. Dr. Eur. 307; Scholten, (1967) 4 C.M.L. Rev. 377 with lit.; van der Groeben, 1967 Rev. Trim Dr. Eur. 224; Lacan, *ibid.* 319; D.V. in 1967 Rev. M.C. 344; Chartier, *ibid.* 310; Grossfeld, (1967) 31 Rabels Z. 2, at p. 16; Mann, (1970) 19 I.C.L.Q. 468; Stein, (1970) 68 Mich. L.R. 1327, Schmitthoff in *Legal Problems of an Enlarged EEC* (1972), p. 211; and the lit. cited below, p. 152, nn. 1, 2.

4   (1969) EEC Bull., Suppl. No. 2, (1968) 4 Rev. Trim Dr. Eur. 400; 2 C.C.H. Common Market Reporter, para. 6083; see below, p. 148.

5   And see below, p. 148, n. 3.

6   Art. 53 is directly applicable: *Costa* v. *ENEL* (1964), 10 Rec. 1141; [1964] C.M.L.R. 429.

Freedom of Establishment.[1] The Programme was to be implemented for specific activities by directives.

> *Measures:* Council by a qualified majority upon a
> proposal of the Commission after consulting the
> Social and Economic Council and the Assembly
> —Directives (art. 54(2)).

The Council assumed this task and has since issued a number of directives, and many more are in the stage of preparation.[2]

For the purpose of carrying out these duties, the Council and the Commission are guided by a number of principles, some of which are self-evident (art. 54(3)).

The competent administrative organs of the member states are to be co-ordinated (art. 54(3)(b))[3] and procedures and practices based on municipal law or on treaties inhibiting freedom of establishment are to be eliminated (art. 54(3)(c));[4] foreign salaried workers are to be assured the right to leave their employment and instead of taking up other employment (art. 48(d)) to establish themselves of their own, if they meet the conditions for establishment (art. 54(3)(d)).[5] The acquisition and exploitation of land is to be permitted,[6] subject to special considerations applicable to agriculture (art. 54(3)(e)).[7] The place of this general principle in the chapter dealing with establishment suggests that the concession is limited to resident aliens, nationals of the other member states, who are already established there. However, this guarantee must be read in connection with art. 54(1), which requires the abolition of restrictions on establishment and may thus include the right to acquire land for the purpose of creating an establishment. Article 220 must also be taken into account, which envisages, if only in principle, the equal protection of all property rights of all persons, nationals of the EEC, whether resident or not, but does not guarantee the right to *acquire* property of any kind for investment only.[8]

The establishment of agencies, branches and subsidiaries is to be facilitated, and the entry of staff from the main office abroad for the purpose of running or controlling the former is to be made possible (art. 54(3)(f)).[9] As far as necessary the company laws of the member states are to be co-

---

1   OJ, 1962, 36.
2   See below, p. 144.
3   EEC Treaty, art. 49(a).
4   Cp. art. 49(b); see General Programme, Tits. II A, III A for details of offending practices; according to Tit. III B the same holds good for procedures and practices which apply generally without regard to nationality but which affect exclusively or primarily the admission to, and the exercise of, lucrative activities by aliens.
5   See General Programme, Tit. II B.
6   See General Programme, Tit. III A, second section (d).
7   See General Programme, Tit. III A, second section (a), Tit. IV F.
8   Cp. art. 222: the domestic law of the member states remains expressly outside the Treaty.
9   General Programme, Tit. I, last para.

ordinated so as to bring the provisions on third parties' and shareholders' protection into line (art. 54(3)(g)). This was achieved in part by the First Council Directive 68/151 of 9 March 1968[1] which will be discussed below.[2]

2   The Programme of 18 December 1961[3]

The notion of beneficiaries of the right of establishment is developed in Title I of the Programme; it is restricted to individuals who are nationals of the member states; in the particular circumstances defined by art. 54, 1st para., they must be resident in a member state; in these circumstances companies and associations who qualify for Community status (art. 58, 1st para.) must show an effective link with a Community state. This requirement was examined above.[4] In accordance with art. 54(c) all legislation, delegated legislation and administrative regulations which are

---

1   OJ, 1968, L 65/8 reproducing with few amendments the Commission Proposals for 3 October 1964, OJ, 1964, 3241; *Mégret*, Vol. III, p. 80. Other directives proposed by the Commission under art. 54(3)(g) have remained abortive so far. See the Second Draft Directive of 9 March 1970 concerning the co-ordination of guarantees for the benefit of shareholders and third parties in respect of the creation of companies and the maintenance or modification of their capital, OJ, 1970, C48/8/16; OJ, 1971, C88/1; the Third Draft Directive of 16 June 1970 concerning the co-ordination of guarantees for the benefit of shareholders and third parties in respect of mergers of companies, OJ, 1970, C 89/20; OJ, 1971, C 88/18; see also (1968) 13 Riv. Soc. 737 and Santa Maria, (1968) 13 *ibid*. 58 with lit.; the Fourth Draft Directive of 16 December 1971 concerning the co-ordination of the national laws on the form and content of annual financial statements, valuation and publicity, OJ, 1972, C 7/11, C 28/15; C.C.H. Common Market Reporter, para. 9476. See also the Draft Directive of 16 January 1969 prepared by the Commission dealing with the taxation of mergers between companies in different member states, OJ, 1969, C 39/1 and mother and daughter companies: *ibid*. C 39/7; C 100/4/7. Incidentally, under the provisions on the necessary approximation of laws in general and of the harmonisation of certain taxes and duties (arts. 100, 99) two Draft Directives were published, namely, of 16 January 1969 on the Approximation of the Tax Systems for Mergers, Split-ups and Transfers of Assets involving Companies of different member states, OJ, 1969, C 39/1; of 16 January 1969 on the Approximation of the Common Tax Systems for Parent Companies and Subsidiaries of different member states, OJ, 1969, C 39/7; and Council Directive 69/335 of 17 July 1969 on the Approximation of Indirect Taxes on Accumulations of Capital was promulgated, OJ, 1969, L 249/25 rectified OJ, 1969, L 269/12 (as to art. 7(2)); implementing measure Council Directives 73/79, 73/80, OJ, 1973, L 103/13/15. As regards the latter see the Treaty of Accession, Pt. II Annex VII, V(2), p. 149 (Cmnd. 4862). For the preparatory work see OJ, 1965, 2227. Acting under art. 220(3) the member governments have engaged in the preparation of two conventions dealing respectively with International Mergers between Joint-stock Companies, OJ, 1971, C 50/10 and the Maintenance of Legal Personality on the Transfer of a Company's Seat from one Member State to Another (5th General Report on the Activities of the Communities 1971, p. 117, No. 163). They concluded on 29 February 1968 a Convention on the Mutual Recognition of Companies and Legal Persons; see below, p. 148.

See generally van Ommeslaghe, 1969 Cah. Dr. Eur. 495, at p. 501, Conard, (1966) 14 A.J.C.L. 573; Commission Memorandum on Concentrations, 1966 Riv. Soc. 1182; Hauschild, 1968 Rev. M.C. 317, at p. 330. On 17 September 1971 the Commission submitted a proposal of a regulation concerning the special creation of common enterprises in the field of the Treaty: OJ, 1971, C 107/15; 1972, C 131/15.

2   P. 146.

3   OJ, 1962, 36; Oppermann, 1964 Rev. M.C. 544.

4   P. 138; and see Vignes, Juriscl. Dr. Int., Fasc. 164 F, Nos. 19, 37, 69.

likely to impede the freedom of establishment for lucrative non-wage earning activities and are not based on grounds of public order, public safety and public health[1] must be abrogated.[2]

Subject to arts. 55 and 56, all restrictions on the various types of activities are lifted in accordance with a time-table (Tit. IV), and the type of restrictions affected are set out (Tit. III). The professions and activities which must be admitted are enumerated in Annexes. The priorities in time follow art. 54(3); the effect of the failure to observe this time-table following the failure to issue the necessary directives as required (art. 54(2)) will be discussed below.[3]

The freedom of establishment extends to the right to conclude contracts, including leases,[4] to participate in concessions by the state and by public bodies,[5] to tender for public works[6] subject to exceptions,[7] to acquire movable, immovable and other property,[8] access to credit and aids,[9] to sue and be sued,[10] and to join professional organisations.[11]

In accordance with art. 54(2) and in pursuance of the aims set out by the Programme,[12] the Council issued on 25 February 1964 a Directive which deals with the Abolition of Restrictions upon the Movement and Residence of Individuals, nationals of the member states, who wish to establish themselves or to provide services across the frontiers.[13] Subject to the safeguards in the interest of public order, public safety and public health,[14] all restrictions must be lifted in favour of nationals of members of the Community, who are established or wish to establish themselves in another member state. This benefit extends to their spouses, their children under 21 years of age, whatever their nationality and to the ascendants and descendants of such spouses equally irrespective of their nationality.[15] The admission of other members of such families is also to be considered favourably.[16] A document of identity or passport is sufficient in order to obtain admission, except where the beneficiary is not a national of a member state.[17] Permanent residence and the right to exercise a non-wage earning activity is to be accorded, once all restrictions of exercising the particular activity have been suppressed.[18] The Directive enumerates in

---

1 See above, p. 133; Council Directive 64/221 of 25 February 1964, OJ, 1964, 850.
2 Tit. II.
3 See p. 145.
4 Programme Tit. III A (a).
5 *Ibid.*, Tit. III A (b).
6 *Ibid.*, Tit. III A (c).
7 *Ibid.*, Tit. IV B.
8 *Ibid.*, Tit. III (d)–(e).
9 *Ibid.*, Tit. III (f), (g).
10 *Ibid.*, Tit. III (h).
11 *Ibid.*, Tit. III (i).
12 *Ibid.*, Tit. II, III.
13 64/220 of 25 February 1964, OJ, 1964, 845.
14 Directive 64/221 of February 1964, OJ, 1964, 850, above, p. 133.
15 Directive 64/220, art. 1(a)–(d).
16 *Ibid.*, art. 1(2).
17 *Ibid.*, art. 2.
18 *Ibid.*, art. 3(1).

detail the accompanying formalities, such as the delivery of a document called residence permit, the duration of its validity and its renewal.

The Council has issued a series of directives implementing the Programme in so far as it envisages the liberalisation of individual activities, and the Commission has drawn up and submitted an additional number, which have not been adopted by the Council as yet.[1] After the transi-

---

1 See generally, *Droit d'Etablissement et Services* published by the Commission (see OJ, 1972, C 85/13); *Mégret* Vol. III, pp. 166–169; 55*–125*, Lando, (1971) 8 C.M.L. Rev. 343. Directives in force are printed in italics.

Self-employed generally—Council Directive 64/220, OJ, 1964, 845.

    Accountants—Commission Proposal 6 July 1970, OJ, 1970, C 115/1/5, 1971, C 38/15, C 45/14.

Agriculture

    abandoned uncultivated land—Council Directive 63/262, OJ, 1963, 1326;

    ancillary activities—Council Directive 71/18, OJ, 1971, L 8/24;

    if previously farm labourer—Council Directive 63/261, OJ, 1963, 1323;

    change of farming activities—Council Directive 67/530, OJ, 1967, No. 190/1;

    co-operatives, access to—Council Directive 67/532, OJ, 1967, No. 190/5;

    assistance, aids—Council Directive 68/415, OJ, 1968, L 368/17; rectified 1969, L 4/6;

    credit, access to—Council Directive 68/192, OJ, 1968 L 93/13;

    farm leases—Council Directive 67/531, OJ, 1967 No. 190/3;

    general trades—Council Directive 65/1, OJ, 1965, 1; see also 1969 C 53/4.

Architects—Commission Proposal 16 May 1967, OJ, 1967, No. 239/5.

Artisans, small industry—Council Directive 64/429, OJ, 1964, 1880;

    transitional—Council Directive 64/427, OJ, 1964, 1863.

Attorneys—Commission Proposal 17 April 1969, OJ, 1969, C 78/1, 1972 C 103/19.

Banks—Commission Proposal 30 July 1965, OJ, 1965, 2576; Commission Proposal 9 June 1970, Fifth Gen. Rep. 114.

Brokers etc., Agents—Council Directive 64/224, OJ, 1964, 869, 871.

Coal Wholesalers—Council Directive 70/522, OJ, 1970, L 267/14;

    transitional—Council Directive 70/523, OJ, 1970, L 267/18.

Doctors, Dentists—Commission Proposal 3 March 1969, OJ, 1969, C 54/8/20, 1970, C 101/13.

Drug Industry—Commission Proposal 10 March 1969, OJ, 1969, C 54/32;

Drug Industry, Wholesale, Depositories—Commission Proposal 10 March 1969, OJ, 1969, C 54/38.

Electricity, Gas, Water, Sanitation—Council Directive 66/162, OJ, 1966, 584.

Engineers, Technicians (see Technical Consultants).

Extractive Industries (Mining etc.)—Council Directive 64/428, OJ, 1964, 1871.

Fisheries (see Various Trades).

Films

    foreign (restrictions)—Council Directive 63/607, OJ, 1963, 2661;

    distribution—Council Directive 68/369, OJ, 1968, L 260/22;

    distributors—Commission Proposal 9 August 1970, OJ, 1971, C 106/25; 1972, C 36/39;

    production—Council Directive 70/451, OJ, 1970, L 218/37;

    display, foreign—Council Directive 65/264, OJ, 1965, 1437.

Food and Beverage Processing—Council Directive 68/365, OJ, 1968, L 260/9;

    transitional—Council Directive 68/366, OJ, 1968 L 260/12.

Forestry—Council Directive 67/654, OJ, 1967, No. 263/6 also 1969, C 53/4.

Hairdresser—Commission Proposal 29 July 1971, OJ, 1971, C 106/6; 1972, C 89/9, 103/14.

Insurance

    Agents, Brokers—Commission Proposal 4 December 1970, OJ, 1971, C 14/1; C 78/14;

    Agents, transitional—Commission Proposal 4 December 1970, OJ, 1971, C 14/4; C 78/16;

    Agents, (except life etc.)—Commission Proposal 2 February 1967, OJ, 1967, 955;

    (see also Commission Proposal 17 June 1966, OJ, 1966, 3056.)

tional period has come to an end the question must be raised whether a complete liberalisation of lucrative non-wage earning establishment has occurred, seeing that the Treaty and the Programme clearly envisaged that such liberalisation would have taken place by that time. Nevertheless, the answer must probably be in the negative, because the Treaty itself (art. 52, 1st para.) provides that the freedom of establishment is only to take place "within the framework of the provisions set out below", which include the requirement of specific directives (art. 54(2)).[1]

Insurance–Reinsurance—Council Directive 64/225, OJ, 1964, 878.

Itinerant Trades and Services—Commission Proposal 4 June 1970, OJ, 1970, C 89/12.

Midwives—Commission Proposal 12 December 1969, OJ, 1970, C 18/1–8, 146/17.

Nurses—Commission Proposal 14 October 1969, OJ, 1969, C 156/13.

Oil, Gas Extraction—Council Directive 69/82, OJ, 1969, L 68/4.

Opticians—Commission Proposal 10 November 1969, OJ, 1969, C 155/2–16, 1971, C 36/22, 78/19.

Pharmacists—Commission Proposal 10 March 1969, OJ, 1969, C 54/32.

Poisonous Substances—Commission Proposal 21 December 1968, OJ, 1969, C 12/6, 63/21.

Press—Commission Proposal 6 July 1964, OJ, 1965, 493, 1971, C 113/1.

Processing
    (*general*)—Council Directive 64/429, OJ, 1964, 1880;
    transitional—Council Directive 64/427, OJ, 1964, 1863;
    modified—Council Directive 69/77, OJ, 1969 L 59/8.

Public Works (Contracts) — Council Directive 71/304, OJ, 1971, L 185/1; see 71/305, OJ, 1971, L 185/5 (public tenders of work); Directive 72/277, OJ, 1972, L 176/12 (co-ordination of procedures); Council Decision 26 July 1971, OJ, 1971, L 185/15 (Consultative Committee). And see Turpin, (1972) C.M.L.Rev. 411. Elke Schmitz, *Das Recht der öffentlichen Aufträge im Gemeinsamen Markt* (1972).

Professions requiring aptitude tests—Commission Proposal 30 November 1970, OJ, 1970, C 6/17.

Real Estate Business—Council Directive 67/43, OJ, 1967, 140.
(agents, valuers, administration)

Restaurant Business—Council Directive 68/367, OJ, 1968, L 260/16 (Lodging houses, camping);
    transitional—Council Directive 68/368, OJ, 1968, L 260/19.

Retail Trade—Council Directive 68/363, OJ, 1968, L 260/1;
    transitional—Council Directive 68/364, OJ, 1968, L 260/6.

Tax Consultants—Commission Proposal 11 August 1971, OJ, 1971, C 107/8, 1972, C 36/34, 67/8.

Technical Consultants (Engineers)—Commission Proposal 8 May 1969, OJ, 1969, C 99/1/5, 1970, C 51/18, 108/2.

Transport Industry—Commission Proposal 20 Dec. 1965, OJ, 1966, 1095, 1099; OJ, 1967, 283;
    (goods)—Commission Proposal 31 March 1970, OJ, 1970, C 72/10;
    (persons)—Commission Proposal 31 March 1970, OJ, 1970, C 72/12;
    (persons and goods by waterways—Commission Proposal 31 March 1970, OJ, 1970, C 72/15.

Various Services (Agencies)—Council Directive 67/43 art. 3, OJ, 1967, 140, 142.

Various Trades (Tobacco, Transport, Fisheries, Personal) — Commission Proposal 23 December 1969, OJ, 1970, C 21/1, 101/12, 146/19.

Veterinary Surgeons—Commission Proposal 1 June 1970, OJ, 1970, C 92/18.

Wholesale Trade—Council Directive 64/223, OJ, 1964, 863;
    transitional—Council Directive 64/222, OJ, 1964, 857.

[1] See Goldman, *Droit Commercial Européen*, p. 164, No. 150, p. 205, no. 195; see also art. 59; but see *Mégret*, Vol. III, p. 90 to the contrary.

3 Company Publicity (Art. 54(3)(g))—Council Directive 68/151 of 9 March 1968[1]

The co-ordination, as far as necessary and in order to render them equivalent, of the rules embodying *guarantees* (publication in a central or local or company register and in an official journal) demanded by the municipal law of the member states for the protection of companies in the meaning of art. 58 (art. 54(3)(g)), of shareholders etc. and company creditors was attempted by the First Council Directive 68/151 of 9 March 1968.[2] It affects only companies in the sense of English law and their equivalent in continental law.[3] Certain uniform rules of publicity are envisaged.[4] They concern the memorandum of association and the articles,[5] amendments, the names of the persons entitled to represent the company in relation to third parties and to manage its affairs internally and whether they can act alone or only together with others, an annual disclosure of the subscribed capital,[6] the annual publication of the balance sheet and of the profit and loss account, the names of the auditors[7] (except for Dutch closed corporations, and any *Gesellschaft mit beschränkter Haftung, société à responsabilité limitée* in the other Five), notice of any transfer of the registered office, notice of winding-up, the appointment of liquidators and their powers other than statutory powers, the termination of the winding-up and dissolution and of a decree declaring the foundation of the company to be void (art. 2). The form in which the information is to be made available at the Commercial Register (art. 3), its effect in relation to publication in an official journal (art. 3),[8] on the letterhead (art. 4) and to persons *having knowledge*[9] of the real situation (art. 8) is set out in detail. The Directive provides for the appointment of persons charged with these duties of publication (art. 5) and states the sanctions (art. 3(7), 7).[10]

---

1   OJ, 1968, L 65/8; see above, p. 142, and n. 1. For literature see van Ommeslaghe, (1969) 5 Cah. Dr. Eur. 495–563 with lit. at pp. 500, 619–665; Renault, (1967) 3 *ibid.* 611 with lit. at pp. 611–613; Fikentscher and Grossfeld, (1964–65) 2 C.M.L.Rev. 259; Houin, 1965 Rev. Trim Dr. Eur. 11; 1966 *ibid.* 307; Lutter, 1966 N.J.W. 273; Valenti, 1965 Riv. Dir. Eur. 204. Capotorti, (1966) 11 Riv. Soc. 969; Uniken Venema, (1966) 11 *ibid.* 944; Ubertazzi, (1970) 15 *ibid.* 526; Collin and Sealy, [1973] C.L.J. 1.

2   OJ, 1968, L 65/8; see now European Communities Act 1972, s. 9 (1). Rodière, 1965 Rev. Trim Dr. Eur. 336, at p. 346 underlines the strictly limited function of this measure as related to establishment. It is also limited to guarantees; see van Ommeslaghe, (1969) 5 Cah. Dr. Eur. 495, at p. 518. And see the Italian critique in (1970) 15 Riv. Soc. 786.

3   Art 1.

4   Art. 2(1)(a)–(k).

5   If such a distinction exists in the legal system concerned; see van Ommeslaghe, (1969) 5 Cah. Dr. Eur. 495, at p. 553.

6   For authorised capital see van Ommeslaghe, (1969) 5 Cah. Dr. Eur. 495, at p. 535.

7   If according to the domestic law concerned they form an organ of the company; van Ommeslaghe (1969) 5 Cah. Dr. Eur. 495, at p. 555.

8   Especially arts. 3(5), (6), 2nd para., (7). For the origin of art. 3(5) see German HGB, para. 15(2).

9   It is debated whether this includes constructive notice; see van Ommeslaghe, (1969) 5 Cah. Dr. Eur. 495, at p. 551; the wording "in good faith" was intentionally omitted on the ground that it is uncertain (*ibid.*, p. 552), but the term used by the Directive may include this notion. Cp. arts. 3(5), 8 with art. 9(1).

10 Nullity for lack of publicity according to domestic law.

A number of the provisions of the Directive are substantive in character. The liability for dealings carried out on behalf of the company before it came into being is incumbent upon the persons who carried out the dealings, if the company does not ratify the acts (art. 7).[1] If the name of a person figures on the register as having the power to bind the company, the latter is estopped from relying on the invalidity of the appointment, unless the third party had knowledge of the defect (art. 8). The doctrine of *ultra vires* as it appears in *Ashbury Ry Carriage & Iron Co.* v. *Riche*[2] is to be disregarded except in so far as the activities exceeded the powers given by law[3] (art. 9(1), 1st para.), where the organs of a company, as distinct from other representatives are concerned, but member states retain the right to relieve the company of any liability for acts *ultra vires* if the third party knew or ought to have known that the act concerned went beyond the powers of the company. However, the fact that the constitution of the company had been properly published is insufficient to impute knowledge on the part of the third party (art. 9(1), 2nd para.). A principle not unlike but broader than the rule in *Turquand's* case[4] is given official sanction (art. 9(2)), coupled with what may be termed the same rule in reverse. When the law governing the company permits the attribution of powers by the constitution of the company and such powers have in fact been delegated to a single person or to several persons, that legal system may provide that this delegation may be pleaded in dealings with third parties. This part of the Directive is not entirely clear since it may mean that the company may rely on this provision in its constitution in proceedings against a third party or that the third party may rely on it in proceedings against the company or both.[5]

A series of provisions (arts. 10–12) concerns the certification of the instrument setting up the company (art. 10) as valid and the grounds on which alone the formation of a company may be held void, and the effects of a decree declaring a company to be invalidly created (arts. 11, 12).[6] Thus, to a certain degree, the procedure comes near to the English system of registration either as such or by way of retrospective certification. In certain respects the provisions of the Directive are a powerful instrument in the development of domestic law in the Community.[7]

---

1 Following French, German and Italian law. See van Ommeslaghe, (1969) 5 Cah. Dr. Eur. 495, at p. 638.

2 (1875), 7 L.R.H.L. 653.

3 This is the German solution, now also embodied in French law. See van Ommeslaghe, (1969) 5 Cah. Dr. Eur. 495, at pp. 620 ff.

4 *Royal British Bank* v. *Turquand* (1856), 6 E. & B. 327; if, however, the other party knew that the power was being abused or himself acted collusively, the general law applies. See van Ommeslaghe, (1969) 5 Cah. Dr. Eur. 495, at p. 632; the invalidity of the appointment is irrelevant: van Ommeslaghe, *loc. cit.*, at pp. 632–633.

5 Van Ommeslaghe, *loc. cit.*, at p. 631 sheds no light on this question.

6 The grounds enumerated in art. 11 of the Directive are comprehensive and exhaustive. They do not, it is believed, go beyond those admitted by English law.

7 Especially arts. 1, 7, 8, 9, 11. The Directive does not itself provide at what stage the company comes into existence; see van Ommeslaghe, (1969) 5 Cah. Dr. Eur. 495, at p. 550.

4   Mutual Recognition of Associations within the Meaning of Art. 58(2)—Art. 220, 3rd para., first sentence

As was shown above, the present rules of private international law relating to associations in the Community (except the Netherlands), which determine the creation, existence and extinction of those entities by reference to the law of their seat, prevent the realization of the principle established by art. 58 to the effect that the freedom of movement and establishment is to extend to companies and associations as well. Nothing less than either the mutual recognition of such companies and the maintenance of their corporate character, even if their seat is transferred from one country of the Community to another, or the adoption of a uniform system of company law can achieve the principal goal which is freedom of movement.

The Treaty (art. 220, 3rd para.) envisages mutual recognition and freedom to transfer the seat by means of an agreement to be reached by the member states. After careful preparation[1] an agreement was reached by the member states "meeting within the forum of the Council" and not by the Council acting within the framework of the Treaty itself (art. 220)[2] and was signed on 29 February 1968.[3] *Functionally* the agreement supplemented the Treaty (art. 58 (1), 220, 3rd para.), but the admission and recognition of "companies formed in accordance with the law of a member state"[4] must necessarily depend upon a prior determination whether the companies concerned have been validly formed in accordance with the law of a particular member state. This raises a question of private international law, namely as to what law governs a company, whether it is the law of the place of incorporation or of the seat (statutory or real) and as to what is the effect of a change of such a seat.

Technically it raised the problem as to whether individuals are to be free to select the law which is to govern a company or association or whether a company or association can, by its nature, only be governed by one

---

1   Beitzke, Report, (1964) 1 Z.H.R. 127.

2   For this technique see Stein, (1970) 68 Mich. L.R. 1327, at p. 1338 and n. 45 with references. The result is that states joining the EEC or wishing to be associated with it may have to accede expressly to this Treaty.

3   *Convention sur la Reconnaissance Mutuelle des Sociétés et Personnes Morales* (1969), 12 Bull EEC, Suppl. No. 2; Campbell Suppl., Ch. 9; (1968) Rev. Trim. Dr. Eur. 400; (1968) 3 Riv. Soc. 706; (1969) XIII Comm. e St. 623; with a report by Goldman, *ibid.*, 405–423, 712–736 respectively. Among the copious literature see Renaud, *Droit Européen des Sociétés* (1969), 2.28–2.35, 2.65–2.66, 6.04–07; Goldman, (1968–69) 6 C.M.L.Rev. 104; Goldman, (1967) 31 Rabels Z. 201; Dieu, (1968) 4 Cah. Dr. Eur. 532, at p. 534; Cerexhe, 1968 Rev. M.C. 578; Houin, (1968) 4 Rev. Trim. Dr. Eur. 131; Beitzke, (1968) 14 B.B.A.W.D. 91, at p. 99; Drobnig, (1966–67) 15 A.J.C.L. 204, at pp. 207–210; (1969) 129 Z.H.R. 93; Gessler, 1967 D.B. 324; Grossfeld, (1967) 31 Rabels Z. 1; Capotorti, (1966) 11 Riv. Soc. 969; Caruso, *Le Società nella CEE* (1969), p. 217; Santa Maria in (1969) XIII Comm. e St. 293; van Hecke in *Europees Vennootschapsrecht*, "Le Régime Juridique des Sociétés dans la C.E.E." (1968), p. 149; van Ryn, 1971 Rev. Trim. Dr. Eur. 563; Morse, 1972 J. Bus. L. 195. For earlier literature see Goldman in *Mélanges Juliot de la Morandière* (1964), p. 175, at pp. 176–178; Grossfeld, (1964–65) 2 C.M.L. Rev. 259; Scholten, (1966–67) 4 C.M.L. Rev. 377.

4   EEC Treaty art. 58(1).

legal system which is peculiar to it owing to its nature. The latter contention leads necessarily to the application of the law of the seat for the time being, the former permits registration in the country of a company which is to operate in another.[1] The task was therefore to harmonise, if not to unify, the domestic rules of private international law of the Community relating to companies.

All companies according to private or commercial law, including cooperatives, within the Community are recognized if they are established (*constitués*) in accordance with the law of one of the member states and have their registered seat (*siège statutaire*) in one of the territories to which the Convention applies (art. 1). For the purposes of recognition it suffices if the company is capable of having rights and duties, even if it is not granted the status of a legal entity by the law of the place of incorporation (art. 8). The latter provision covers, e.g. the German commercial partnership (*Offene Handelsgesellschaft*) and creates a situation where, for the purposes of recognition, the character of a private or commercial combination of persons or resources as a separate legal entity is irrelevant within the EEC, provided that the law of the place of incorporation permits the combination of persons or resources not only to operate formally in the name of the combination—which is a purely procedural device—but to hold assets and to incur obligations in its name. Thus a joint tenancy or a tenancy in common suffices for the purposes of the Convention. In addition to the companies, associations and combinations mentioned above (art. 1), the Convention applies to legal entities of a private or public law character which fulfil the conditions set out in art. 1 and which, in law or in fact, exercise an economic activity which is normally carried out for remuneration (art. 2).[2] If they do so *de facto* only, the activity must not contravene the law of the place of incorporation (art. 2).

The Convention relies, for the purpose of recognising the companies etc. enumerated there, upon the place of incorporation and the statutory seat within the EEC, though not necessarily in the same country of the EEC. The statutory seat may not coincide with the real seat, which is the place where the centre of control and management is situated (art. 5). In these circumstances three situations must be envisaged; two of these are treated by the Convention (arts. 3, 4).

Firstly, if the real seat is in a third country outside the EEC, any con-

---

1 Cp. Beitzke, Report, (1964) 1 Z.H.R. 127, at p. 15; van Hecke, (1961) 8 N.T.I.R. 223, at p. 227. In favour of the law of the place of incorporation see the Hague Convention concerning the Recognition of the Legal Personality of Companies etc. of 1 June 1956, art. 1; (1965) 51 II Institut de Droit International, arts. 1–4; Drucker, (1968) 17 I.C.L.Q. 28.

2 Contrast art. 58(2) of the EEC Treaty which excludes from its operation associations which are non-profit making companies. If this test is factual only, no difference exists between that article and the Convention. The former excludes non-profit making associations, the latter admits them but only if they can engage, or do in fact lawfully engage, in profit-making activities. If the test is juridical, the wording of the Convention covers a broader range of associations than art. 58(2) of the EEC Treaty. See Stein, (1970) 68 Mich. L.R. 1327, at p. 1340, n. 55 for examples taken from German, Italian and Dutch law.

For the difference between the term "for remuneration" as against the term "for gainful purpose" adopted by the EEC Treaty see Stein, *loc. cit.*, p. 1341.

tracting party may declare that it refuses to apply the Convention to the association concerned, if no effective link (the Convention says "serious link")[1] exists between the company and the economy of one of the territories of the Community.   In short, the fact alone that the real seat is in a country outside the Community does not automatically exclude the operation of the Convention (art. 3).

Secondly, if the company fulfils the requirements of arts. 1 and 2, but its real seat is situated in another country of the Community, the country where the real seat is located may, following a general declaration, apply the mandatory provisions (*lois impératives*) of its own law to such a company (art. 4(1)).[2] Thus, within the country of the real seat, the rules of private international law of the latter may apply to a certain extent, if they refer to the law of the seat, but only in respect of questions other than those concerning legal personality itself. The directory provisions (*lois supplétives*) apply only if the articles of the company do not deviate from them either in specific matters or generally by referring to the law of the place of incorporation (art. 4(2)(i)), or unless the company proves that it has exercised its activities for a reasonable time in the member state where it was incorporated (art. 4(2)(ii)).

Finally, the convention does not deal with the third situation, namely, when the company is incorporated and has its statutory seat in one or two countries of the Community, its real seat in a third and requires recognition in a fourth country of the EEC.   In these circumstances the fact that the real seat does not coincide with the country of incorporation or with that of the statutory seat appears to be irrelevant.[3]

The recognition of the companies and associations established according to the criteria laid down in arts. 1–4 is assured by arts. 6–8. In principle such companies are accorded the status and capacities conferred upon them by the law of the place of incorporation, subject to the limitations laid down by arts. 3 and 4 which either deny the application of the law of the place of incorporation (art. 3) or require a cumulation of the latter with the law of the real seat (art. 4).

By a somewhat tortuously worded provision (art. 7) the Convention seems to ensure that, while Convention companies retain the capacity to have rights and duties, such as to enter into contracts, to sue and to be sued, which they acquired under the law of the place of incorporation, they cannot claim rights which are not accorded to corresponding types of companies in the country where recognition is sought.   It would seem that this restriction envisages disabilities of a public law character, such as the prohibition to engage in the business of banking or insurance, but it may be that it concerns also the distribution of powers between the organs, the internal and external management.[4]   If the latter interpre-

---

1   See the General Programme on Establishment, above, p. 138; Loussouarn and Bredin, *Droit du Commerce International* (1969), p. 505, no. 422.
2   For the reasons underlying this provision see Stein. *loc. cit.*, p. 1343.
3   For the difficulties which may arise nevertheless see Stein, *loc. cit.*, pp. 1344–1345.
4   See Goldman, (1967) 31 Rabels Z. 201, at p. 209, Goldman, (1968–69) 6 C.M.L. Rev. 104,

tation should be correct, art. 7 would constitute an extension of art. 4. It must be noted, however, that this restriction cannot be pleaded by the foreign company (art. 7(3)), which is thus estopped from raising its own incapacity to this extent.

As in most treaties on private international law an escape clause based on local public policy is provided (arts. 9, 10). However, in this treaty concluded between the member states the range of this escape clause is limited, for recognition can only be refused if the company's objects set out in its constitution, its purpose or its activities which are effectively carried out, offend against local public policy (art. 9(1)). It is expressly provided that a one-man company does not offend public policy (art. 9(2)),[1] which is defined, perhaps unnecessarily, in order to distinguish it from domestic public policy, as public policy in the meaning employed in private international law (art. 9(2)).[2]

In particular, any principles or rules of domestic law which contravene the Treaty setting up the EEC are not to be regarded as rules of public policy. Although the meaning is clear *i.e.* that community law is to prevail over local law claiming to bear the character of public policy—the wording is unfortunate. It seems to imply that particular principles and rules of domestic law may have overriding effect, and thus to revive the discarded notion of *ordre public interne* and of the mandatory application of rules of domestic law.[3] It would have been preferable if art. 10 had stated positively that, in applying its notions of public policy in refusing to recognize the companies and associations established in accordance with the law laid down in art. 1, the member states must give due regard to the principles and rules embodied in the EEC Treaty.

5 Formation—Capital—European Company

Proposals of directives concerning the formation of companies and the maintenance and alteration of their capital, of 9 March 1970[4] concerning mergers within the same country, of 16 June 1970,[5] of 16 November 1971 on annual financial statements,[6] and on various tax aspects[7] were submitted by the Commission to the competent authorities.

---

at p. 110; Cerexhe, 1968 Rev. M.C. 578 at p. 588; Dieu (1968) 4 Cah. Dr. Eur. 532, at p. 543; ca. Santa Maria in (1969), XIII Comm. e St. 293, at p. 300, n. 9, p. 303 and n. 13.

1 For one-man companies in the EEC see Stein, *loc. cit.*, p. 1349, n. 95 with references; van Ommeslaghe, (1969) Cah. Dr. Eur. 658–659; and see generally Grisoli, *Le Società con un solo Socio* (1971).

2 It might have been better if the Convention had adopted the technique followed by the Hague Conferences on Private International Law, where the term "manifestly against public policy" is employed.

3 Cp. Santa Maria, (1969) XIII Comm. e St. 293, at pp. 316 ff.

4 OJ, 1970, C 48/8 of 24 April 1970; 1970 Rev. Trim. Dr. Eur. 559; Beitzke, 1967 Rev. Crit. Dr. Int. Priv. 1; above, p. 142, n. 1.

5 OJ, 1970, C 89/70 of 16 June 1970; 1970 Rev. Trim Dr. Eur. 568; 1970 EEC Bull, Suppl. No. 5.

6 OJ, 1972, C 7/11, above, p. 142, n. 1.

7 See above, p. 142, n. 1.

Finally, on 30 June 1970[1] the Commission, acting by virtue of art. 235 of the Treaty, presented a proposal for a European company. Whatever the aims of previous preparatory drafts,[2] the type of company which is the object of the Commission proposal is not designed to replace the various forms of companies which exist in the member states or to offer uniform rules for adoption by the domestic law of the Community. Instead it is a type of company which is wholly removed from the realm of domestic law. It meets, therefore, the requirements discussed above which enable it to survive according to continental notions, even if it transfers its seat, or if it desires to establish a second seat.[3] In addition it enables two or more companies, established according to the laws of different member states, to merge across frontiers into a European company. Hitherto mergers between companies governed by different laws could only be brought about either by the formation of a joint holding company which itself had to be subject to the law of a particular country, or by the merger of a company governed by the law of one country with a company governed by another system of laws. In either case the emergence of a new and powerful company bearing the national character of one member state was bound to affect adversely the national susceptibilities of the other member state who witnessed the liquidation of a domestic company and the entry of a foreign corporation.

---

1   OJ, 1970, C 124/1 of 10 October 1970; 1970 Bull. EEC, Suppl. No. 8; (1970) 15 Riv. Soc. 1261 and see the commentaries by Sanders, (1971) 8 C.M.L. Rev. 29; and by Loussouarn, 1971 Rev. Crit. Dr. Int. Priv. 383 with lit. n. 1; 1971 Rev. M.C. 59. See also the Report of the Intergovernmental Working Party of 26 April 1967, (1967) 12 Riv. Soc. 669; for the prior draft of December 1965 proposed by the Commission see 1966 Rev. Trim. Dr. Eur. 409 with the Berkhouwer Report at p. 434; (1966) 11 Riv. Soc. 1096; (1968) 13 ibid. 737; Santa Maria (1968) 13 ibid., 581 and the lit. cited at p. 582, n. 6; Sanders, ibid. p. 232; Sanders, Société Anonyme Européenne, "Projet d'un Statut d'une Société Anonyme Européenne", issued by the Commission (December 1966) with lit. pp. XXXI–XXXIII (English translation: European Stock Corporation, C.C.H. Chicago 1969); Storm, (1967–68) 5 C.M.L. Rev. 265; Thompson, (1968) 17 I.C.L.Q. 183; Mann, (1970) 19 ibid. 468; Bayer, (1971) 35 Rabels Z. 201; van Ryn, 1971 Rev. Trim Dr. Eur. 563; Saint Esteben 1971 ibid. 62; Ficker, 1971 J. Bus. L. 167.

2   See above, n. 1 and cp. Sanders, 1959 Riv. Soc. 1163; (1968) 13 Riv. Soc. 237; Thompson, (1961) 10 I.C.L.Q. 851; Vasseur, 1964 J. Bus. L. 353; 1965 ibid. 73; Lanza, (1965) 10 Riv. Soc. 960.
     For general surveys see: (1970) 15 Riv. Soc. 1248; Bramonte, (1967) 12 ibid. 725; von Caemmerer, Festschrift für Kronstein (1967), pp. 171–202; (1968) II Gesammelte Schriften 159 with lit. (up to 1967) at p. 163, n. 6; Drobnig, (1967) 129 Z.H.R. 193; Lacan, (1967) 3 Rev. Trim. Dr. Eur. 319; Houin, (1968) 4 ibid. 131; Leleux, (1968) 83 J.T. 109–112; Ficker, 1967 N.J.W. 1160; Hauschild, 1968 Rev. M.C. 317, at p. 321; Rabels, (1967) 2 EuR 258, at p. 261; note (1967) 12 Riv. Soc. 689–698; Minervini, (1966) 11 ibid. 984; Ruta, (1969) 14 ibid. 426; Franceschelli, (1968) 14 II Riv. Dir. civ. 285; Goldman, Travaux du Comité Français de Droit Internationale Privé 1966–69, p. 215, at p. 232; (1968) 13 Riv. Soc. 1005, at p. 1025; Guarino, (1967) 651 Riv. Dir. Comm. Obbl. 268; Von der Groeben, (1967) 3 Rev. Trim. Dr. Eur. 224; Kastner, (1969) 91 JBl 127; van Ommeslaghe, Cah. Dr. Eur. 495, at p. 504, n. 18. Cp. Kahn, (1969) 3 J.W.T.L. 493.

3   This need should have been much reduced by the Treaty of 29 February 1968; above, p. 148; for the plan to introduce national mergers across frontiers see Commission Reply No. 8/71 of 8 May 1971, OJ, 1971, C 50/10.

The proposals made by the Commission seek to avoid these disadvantages by creating a company of a supranational type which takes it out of the orbit of any system of domestic law by submitting it more or less exclusively[1] to Community law and jurisdiction. In the course of this endeavour, the goal of harmonising European company law in general had to give way to the overriding aim to facilitate mergers across the frontiers within the area of the EEC.[2]

The fact that the European company serves exclusively the purpose of facilitating mergers determines the principal feature of the European company. It cannot be formed *de novo* by individuals, but only by companies[3] established according to the laws of at least two member states[4] or by European companies acting together with each other or with companies established according to domestic law.[5] In form it has the characteristics of a public company as it is known in most Western legal systems.[6] In substance it is either the result of a merger, or of the creation of a holding company or of the creation of a common branch.[7] It possesses legal personality and must be treated in all the member states as if it were a company formed in accordance with domestic law,[8] but it is not governed or controlled by domestic law and by domestic authorities but by the Statute on European Companies, by the general principles underlying the Statute, and the general principles common to the Laws of the member states. Only topics which are not regulated by the Statute are determined by domestic law. None of these sources is easily applied.[9] The general principles underlying the Statute are to be found by way of analogous reasoning and in the last resort through a comparative analysis of the company law of the EEC, particularly those of France and Germany on which the Statute is based.[10] It will be difficult to determine the limits of the Statute, at which stage domestic law retains its influence.[11]

The company must be registered in the European Commercial Register which is to be kept in Luxemburg under the control of the court;[12] it must

---

1 But see the Statute art. 7(2).

2 Loussouarn, 1971 Rev. Crit. Dr. Int. Priv. 383, at p. 385.

3 Not by private companies (GmbH; S.a.r.l.; BNV); Loussouarn, 1971 *ibid.* 383, at p. 389; but see art. 238 of the Statute, below, p. 160, n. 10.

4 Art. 2; no company established according to the law of a non-member state can participate. See Loussouarn 1971 *ibid.* 383, at pp. 399 ff. who doubts whether this restriction is sufficient to keep out outsiders in the absence of the requirement of an effective link within the Community. See above, p. 138. This may, however, be in reality a problem affecting the ownership of the shares; see Loussouarn 1971 *ibid.* 383, at p. 403.

5 Art. 3.

6 Art. 1.

7 Arts. 2, 3.

8 Art. 1(4).

9 Cp. the Hague Convention of 1 July 1964 on a Uniform Law of Sale of Movable Objects, art. 17.

10 Cp. EEC Treaty art. 215; Loussouarn, 1971 Rev. Crit. Dr. Int. Priv. 383, at pp. 411, 412 and see above, p. 13, V(c).

11 Restrictions on the capacity to hold land or to raise floating charges come to mind; see Loussouarn, 1971 *ibid.* 383, at p. 412.

12 Art. 8(1) (2).

also register in the country of its seat in a special register kept there.[1] The formation of the company is regulated in detail,[2] subject to the control of the Community Court.[3] It acquires legal personality on the day when the registration is published in the Official Journal of the Communities.[4] Before that date the founders and those acting on behalf of the company are personally liable.[5] They remain liable for three years from that date for all omissions or misrepresentations unless they did not then know of them and could not reasonably have known them.[6] The constitution of a European company is preceded either by merger proceedings[7] or by the creation of a holding company[8] or by the creation of a common branch.[9]

A European branch may also be created by a European company.[10] The provisions on the creation, increase and reduction of capital[11] cover familiar ground, except that the sanction of the court for a reduction of capital is not required unless objecting creditors apply to the court of the country where the company has its seat.[12] The company must not acquire its own shares or receive them as a security.[13] Nor can there be any reciprocal shareholding if one of the companies is a European company,[14] and a daughter company of a European company cannot hold any shares in the latter.[15] Shares,[16] which can be bearer shares or registered shares,[17] may be of different denominations[18] and may carry different benefits in the division of profits and capital;[19] non-voting shares are admissible subject to certain conditions[20] but multiple voting shares are prohibited,[21] and each class of shareholders forms a special body for voting purposes when their rights are adversely affected.[22] Bonds may be issued,[23] but if they are convertible,

---

1   Art. 8(3). In case of discrepancy the entries in the register in Luxemburg prevail.
2   Arts 7–20.
3   Art. 17(1).
4   Art. 19(1).
5   Art. 19(2).
6   Art. 20(1).
7   Arts. 21–28; for the protection of creditors see art. 27. With the registration of the European company the constituent companies governed by domestic law are automatically dissolved: art. 28(2). For the importance of this rule in determining the fairly high minimum capital see Loussouarn, 1971 Rev. Crit. Dr. Int. Priv. 383, at p. 394.
8   Arts. 29–35.
9   Arts. 35–37.
10   Arts. 38–39.
11   Arts. 40–47.
12   Art. 45.
13   Art. 46(1).
14   Art. 47.
15   Art. 46(2).
16   Arts. 48–53.
17   Art. 50(1); see also arts. 52, 53.
18   Art. 48(2).
19   Art. 49(1).
20   Art. 49(2)
21   Art. 49(3).
22   Art. 49(4), (5).
23   Arts. 54–60.

a special procedure is prescribed.[1] The bondholders form a group endowed with specific rights;[2] the company must in the first instance, and the bondholders may subsequently, appoint a representative of the bondholders, in accordance with a well established continental practice, whose powers are not unlike those of an English trustee for bondholders.[3] The organs of the company are three. Of these the *directors* represent the company in its dealings[4] but they are subject to the control of the Supervisory Board[5] which also appoints and dismisses them and may designate one to be president.[6] Only physical persons, and if there are no more than one or two directors, only nationals of member states can be directors;[7] in all other circumstances at least the majority of the directors must be Community nationals.[8] In their dealings with third parties the directors can bind the company even if their acts are *ultra vires*, provided that they do not exceed their powers under the Statute on European Companies. It is irrelevant that they have exceeded their powers under the constitution of the company[9] unless these are attributed to other organs by the Statute on European Companies.[10] The internal distribution of competences among several directors has no effect in relation to dealings with outsiders.[11] These and the following provisions recall the identical solution adopted by the Council in its Directive 68/151 of 9 March 1968.[12] Any changes in the board of directors and any appointment or revocation of managers who may represent the company singly or jointly[13] must be entered in the European Commercial Register.[14] Until registration, the company cannot rely on them in relations with third parties, unless the latter had knowledge, but third parties are not so precluded.[15] However, any such registration precludes the company from pleading that the appointment of a director or manager was irregular, unless the third party knew.[16] The directors must present annually a balance sheet and a statement of profit and losses in a report to the Supervisory Board[17] as well as interim reports every three months[18] and special reports where the importance of the subject matter warrants it.[19] The duties of the directors and their liability towards the

---

1   Art. 60.
2   Arts. 56, 58, 59.
3   Art. 57; cp. Lipstein, (1969) III *Studi Ascarelli* 1.
4   Arts. 62–71.
5   Art. 62 and see arts. 73–81.
6   Art. 63(1), (6), (7).
7   Art. 63(2), (3).
8   Art. 63(3).
9   Art. 67.
10 Art. 64(1); in certain cases the Statute (art. 66) subordinates their powers to previous authorisation by the Supervisory Board, but this restriction does not affect third parties.
11 Arts. 64(2), 65(1). See, however, as regards statutory powers art. 67.
12 Above, p. 146.
13 *Fondés de pouvoirs, Prokuristen.*
14 Art. 65(3).
15 Art. 65(4).
16 Art. 65(5).
17 Art. 68(1).
18 Arts. 68(2), 72(i), (ii).   19 Art. 68(3).

company are set out in detail.[1] In particular the right of shareholders to bring a derivative action is enshrined, subject to certain conditions.[2]

The Supervisory Board exercises an important indirect control of the management of the company.[3] Its position had been firmly established in German law, and the provisions of the Statute on European Companies reflect this experience. The Board is appointed by the General Assembly[4] and, as stated above, itself appoints and dismisses the directors[5] who must report to them every three months.[6] The Supervisory Board may offer advice to the directors,[7] but it cannot itself conduct the business of the company.[8] It represents the company in actions against, and in dealings of the company with the directors.[9] Casual vacancies among the directors can be filled temporarily by a member of the Supervisory Board.[10] The members of the Board are jointly and severally liable to the company for breaches of the Statute on European Companies or of the constitution of the company, subject to certain defences.[11] The action against them can be brought by the general meeting or by the shareholders in a derivative action.[12]

Directors, members of the Supervisory Board, the persons appointed auditors who acquire shares for themselves, their wives or minor children, in the company, must hold them as registered shares or deposit them in a bank.[13] The same applies to holders of more than 10 per cent of the company's capital[14] and to any company, whether European or national, which holds such a proportion of the share capital.[15] Any such person or company must notify the European Commercial Register of the number, nominal value and the name of the owner together with the evidence from the shareholders' register or from the depository,[16] and must report any subsequent fluctuations in his holdings.[17] Profits resulting from sales or purchases of shares within six months of their acquisition or disposal respectively enure to the benefit of the company.[18]

The general meeting[19] has the powers set out by the Statute of the Euro-

---

1 Arts. 69–72.
2 Art. 72(2)–(4).
3 Arts. 73–81, especially arts. 73(1), 78; for its composition and operation see arts. 74–77, 79, 80.
4 Art. 83(c).
5 Art. 63(1), (6), (7).
6 Art. 73(1), 2nd para.
7 Art. 73(2).
8 Art. 73(3).
9 Art. 73(3), 2nd sentence.
10 Art. 73(4).
11 Art. 81.
12 Arts. 81(5), 72(2)–(4).
13 Art. 82(1), 1st para.
14 Art. 82(1), 2nd para.
15 Arts. 82(1), 2nd para., 47(5).
16 Art. 82(2).
17 Art. 82(3), (4).
18 Art. 82(5).
19 Arts. 83–99.

pean Company, which include decisions on the size of the capital, the floating of bonds, the appointment of the Supervisory Board and of the auditors, the distribution of annual profits, any modifications of the constitution of the company,[1] the winding-up of the company and the appointment of liquidators,[2] any change in the form of the company, merger or disposal of all or an "important"[3] part of the assets and any agreements to pool the whole or part of its income with another enterprise, to let the enterprise or otherwise place it at the latter's disposal or to administer it for the account of another.[4] The general meeting is convoked by the directors and must meet at least once annually, namely during the second part of the financial year.[5] Failing the directors, the Supervisory Board may call a general meeting.[6] The same right is given to shareholders holding at least five per cent of the capital or 100,000 units of account.[7] If the directors do not comply, the domestic courts at the place of the company's seat may authorise the applicant shareholders to call such a meeting;[8] the court may also order certain items to be put on the agenda.[9] The procedure for holding the general meeting is regulated in detail,[10] including voting[11] as well as the procedure for annulling decisions of the general meeting.[12] A special procedure of investigation, not unlike that by inspectors of the Board of Trade may be ordered by the court of the seat or which has been specially designated by domestic law on application by a qualified minority of shareholders, the bondholders' representative or the European Enterprise Committee (see below).[13]

An interesting feature of the Statute is the creation of European Enterprise Committees.[14] These are derived from comparable bodies composed of workers' representatives in all countries of the Community[15] and draw their name from the *Comités d'entreprise* of French law.[16] In the individual establishments of the European company situated in the member states the domestic law of the respective states concerned continues to determine the form of workers' representation.[17] The European Enterprise Committee of a European company consists of representatives of the workers'

---

1 For the procedure see arts. 241–246.
2 For the procedure of voluntary and compulsory winding-up see arts. 247–263.
3 See art. 83; as regards the disposal of an important part of the assets see art. 83(j) and for the meaning of the adjective "important" see the comment to the Commission proposal.
4 Art. 83(a)–(k).
5 Art. 84(1), (2).
6 Art. 84(3).
7 Art. 85(1).
8 Art. 85(2).
9 Art. 85(3).
10 Arts. 86–90, 94.
11 Arts. 91–93; for a provision which may seem strange to an English lawyer see art. 92 (usufruct; naked owner = remainderman).
12 Art. 95: by the court where the company has its seat; and see art. 96.
13 Arts. 97–99.
14 Arts. 100–147.
15 See art. 102.
16 Ordinance of 22 February 1945.
17 Art. 101, but see the possibility of a European Collective Agreement envisaged in art. 127.

committees set up in the establishments of the company in the various member states[1] and elected in accordance with the rules of domestic law.[2] The number of its members,[3] their tenure[4] and method of election[5] and their duties[6] and procedure[7] are set out. They cannot be dismissed during their appointment or for three years thereafter except on grounds recognised by domestic law.[8] They must be given the necessary leave and remuneration.[9] Their function is to represent the interests of workers in the European company,[10] but is restricted to the concerns of the latter as a whole,[11] and not concerned with collective bargaining which is done by the individual enterprises in the various member states, but may be conducted on a European level.[12] The relations between the committee and the directors, including the holding of regular meetings, the presentation of reports by the directors on the situation of the European company in all its aspects,[13] including any information given to the shareholders as well as the annual accounts and progress report[14] are determined by the Statute. The European Enterprise Committee may request information and summon any director.[15] The directors, on the other hand, must seek the agreement of the European Enterprise Committee in matters of employment which are strictly enumerated;[16] failure to obtain such consent results in the nullity of the measure taken by the directors[17] but this consent may be replaced by the consent of the arbitration committee set up in accordance with the Statute.[18] The advice of the European Enterprise Committee is required for the evaluation of jobs and the establishment of piece rates and failure to obtain this advice results in, once again, the nullity of the relevant measures[19] unless the advice is not forthcoming within a reasonable time.[20] Such advice is also required where important decisions concerning the stopping or transfer of the enterprise or far-reaching restrictions or modifications are involved,[21] but in these cir-

---

1   Art. 103.
2   Art. 104.
3   Art. 105.
4   Arts. 107, 108.
5   Arts. 109, 110.
6   Arts. 114, 119(3).
7   Arts. 116–118.
8   Arts. 111, 112.
9   Art. 113.
10 Art. 119(1).
11 Art. 119(2).
12 Art. 119(2), 2nd sentence; arts. 146–147; see also art. 127.
13 Art. 120.
14 Art. 121.
15 Art. 122.
16 Art. 123(1), they do not include collective bargaining on a strictly national level; see arts. 123(4), 119(2), above, text to n. 12, or if the Group Enterprise Committee is competent (art. 135(1)).
17 Art. 123(2).
18 Arts. 123(3), 128, 129.
19 Art. 124(2).
20 Art. 124(3).
21 Art. 125(1).

cumstances the absence of the advice does not appear to affect the validity of the measures.[1]

A special system of workers' representation, differing from that described above,[2] is envisaged for any European company which is the dominant enterprise of a group of enterprises with establishments in several countries or whose dependent enterprises have establishments in various countries. Here a Group Enterprise Committee is to be set up[3] or a similar body.[4] In substance these consist either of representatives of European Enterprise Committees (if the group consists of European companies) or of representatives of workers' councils according to domestic law (if the group consists of companies established according to national law).[5] The Statute provides for the numerical composition of the Committees. Within this framework, its powers and duties correspond to those of the European Enterprise Committee.[6]

Finally, the workers employed by a European Company are represented on the Supervisory Board,[7] unless they decide by a majority of two-thirds not to be represented during the current period of office of the Supervisory Board.[8] The representatives act *propria persona*.[9]

In pursuance of the requirement of art. 54(3)(g) of the Treaty that the guarantees demanded in member states for the purpose of protecting the interests of the shareholders and of third parties are to be co-ordinated to the extent that is necessary, the Statute on European Companies draws[10] on the preparatory work for the co-ordination of balance sheets,[11] profit and loss accounts,[12] and methods of valuation,[13] and of auditing[14] in the law of the member states.[15] Nevertheless, the report of the Commission suggests that the rules for the European company are both stricter and more detailed, leaving room for choice. The accounting rules do not apply to banking and insurance institutions, which remain subject to the domestic law for this purpose.[16] A number of fairly general provisions apply to group accounts.[17] The procedure to be followed by the directors and the Supervisory Board in submitting the accounts is set out,[18] as well

---

1   Arts. 125, 126.
2   P. 157; arts. 101, 103, 104.
3   Art. 130(1); for the regulation of this type of grouping see arts. 223–240.
4   Art. 130(2).
5   Art. 131.
6   Arts. 133–136, referring to arts. 111–118, 123–127.
7   Art. 137; arts. 139–145.
8   Art. 138.
9   Art. 139(1).
10 Arts. 148–222.
11 Arts. 152–166.
12 Arts. 167–178.
13 Arts. 179–189.
14 Arts. 203–210; 220.
15 Art. 203(2) and see the introductory comment to Tit. VI.
16 Art. 149.
17 Arts. 196–202.
18 Arts. 211–215.

as that to be observed by the general meeting.[1] Violations of the provisions of the Statute on European Companies concerning the accounts or the annual report can be the object of special proceedings brought by shareholders holding at least five per cent of the nominal capital or 100,000 units of account or by the bondholders' representative.[2] These provisions touch upon domestic law so as to require slight modifications in the English law of procedure.

Separate rules apply to a grouping of enterprises where either the controlling or a daughter company is a company of the European type.[3] In the first place, the fact that all the shares in the daughter company created in accordance with domestic law are concentrated in the hands of a European company does not deprive the daughter of its corporate status, even if the domestic law concerned prohibits one-man companies.[4]

Secondly, the particular rules of arts. 228–240 of the Statute on European Companies apply to the daughter companies although the latter are governed by domestic law, provided that the mother company is a European company[5] and, in the converse case, that the daughter company, but not the mother company, is a company of the European type.[6] The question whether a company forms part of a group governed by these articles of the Statute on European Companies is to be determined by the Community Court.[7]

Thirdly, any European company which becomes part of a grouping must enter this information in the European register of companies.[8]

Fourthly, a European company which forms part of a group, whether in a dominant or a dependent capacity, must prepare its accounts in accordance with arts. 196–202, i.e. the accounts must be consolidated for the whole or the dependent part of the group.[9]

The primary purpose of these provisions is to protect the shareholders[10] and creditors[11] or daughter companies.

Shareholders of the dependent company[12] can require the dominant company, whether it be a European company or a company created according to domestic law, to buy them out[13] or, in the case of a European company, to exchange their shares in the dependent company for shares in the controlling European company[14] and vice versa.[15] A further con-

---

1 Arts. 216–219.
2 Arts. 220–222.
3 Arts. 223–240.
4 See instead of all others: Grisoli, *La Società con un solo socio* (1971).
5 Art. 224 (1).
6 Art. 224(2).
7 Art. 225.
8 Art. 226.
9 Art. 227.
10 Arts. 228–238.
11 Art. 239.
12 For the purpose of the ensuing measures a dependant company includes what is the equivalent of an English private company (GmbH, S.a.r.l. etc.). See art. 238.
13 Art. 229; for the procedure of valuation see arts. 232–237.
14 Art. 230(1).
15 Art. 230(2).

tingency is also envisaged which arises if the controlling company is it-self controlled by another.[1] In addition, a controlling company which has its seat[2] inside or outside the Community may offer the independent shareholders of the dependent company with a seat inside the Community to pay them "compensatory annuities" related to the nominal value of the shares.[3] This appears to amount to a conversion of the shares into what are, in English law, preference shares with a preferential dividend.

Creditors of a dependent company are given the right to claim against the controlling company, if they fail to obtain payment from their original debtor.[4]

Among the provisions on voluntary and compulsory winding-up,[5] the most notable establishes the automatic liquidation of the company if the general meeting has failed to assemble or has been unable to decide validly during a period of two years on a necessary voluntary liquidation or reduction of capital following losses amounting to more than half of the capital.[6] In addition, the compulsory winding-up (described by the Statute on European Companies in terms of continental law as a bank-ruptcy of the company) is to be subject to the provisions of a convention on the jurisdiction in matters of bankruptcy and, incidentally, on the recognition of foreign bankruptcy orders and proceedings. It is, therefore, clear that compulsory winding-up is entrusted to the courts of the member states. A Draft Convention on Jurisdiction in Bankruptcy has been pre-pared at the instance of the Commission by a group of experts which reported on 16 February 1970.[7]

A number of isolated points deserve additional attention. In the first place, after a certain time, a European company may determine to be-come a company governed by the law of a member state.[8] According to the Statute this can only be the law of the place where the European company has its real seat,[9] which is the country with which the company has an effective link.

In the second place, a European company can merge with another

---

1   Art. 230(3).
2   The reliance on the seat and not on the place of incorporation and the statutory seat as laid down in art. 58 of the EEC Treaty (above, p. 136) by the Programme of 18 December 1961 (above, p. 137) and by the Treaty of 29 February 1968 (above, p. 148) is to be noted. See also art. 262 where for the purpose of bankruptcy proceedings the statutory seat is identical with the centre of business and management.
3   Art. 231.
4   Art. 239.
5   Arts. 247–263.
6   Art. 249 (4).
7   Commission Doc. 3/327/XIV/70–I; (1970) 6 Riv. Dir. Int. Proc. 693 made by virtue of art. 220 of the EEC Treaty. See Nadelmann, *Conflict of Laws: International and Interstate* (1972), p. 340 with lit. at p. 348, n. 45; *ibid.*, (1970) 6 Riv. Dir. Int. Proc. 501 and the lit. at p. 510, n. 5; Colesanti, (1970) 6 *ibid.* 522; Noel and Lemontey, 1968 Rev. Trim. Dr. Eur. 705, at p. 714; Houin in *Ganshof van der Meersch*, p. 1017; Ganshof, 1971, Cah. Dr. Eur. 127; Jahr, (1972) 36 Rabels Z. 620; see below, p. 284.
8   Art. 264 (1); for the procedure see arts. 265, 266, 268.
9   Art. 264(3), 267.

European company either by creating a new company of European character or by transferring its assets without having to be wound up.[1]

In the third place, a European company, without going through a process of winding-up, can merge with a company governed by the domestic law of a member state either by creating a new European company or by the acquisition of the assets of the company according to domestic law.[2]

In the fourth place, the Statute purports to affect the tax laws of the member states when it declares that the exchange of shares in a European company for shares in companies governed by domestic law is not to attract taxation, except in certain circumstances.[3]

In the fifth place, the Statute fixes jurisdiction to tax a European company at the centre of its business management,[4] and any conflict of jurisdictions claiming power to tax is to be resolved by the Community Court.[5] The situation where the European company has additional centres of business or branches[6] in other member states or owns at least 50 per cent of the capital of a company in another member state[7] is regulated expressly.

In the sixth place, the member states will have to introduce legislation containing penalties for the offences defined in the Annex to the Statute, which are to take the place of the domestic law in so far as violations of the Statute of the European Company are concerned.[8]

---

1   Art. 269(1); for the procedure see arts. 270, 271.
2   Art. 272; for the procedure see arts. 273, 274; 11–28.
3   Art. 275.
4   Art. 276(1); for the case where the seat is transferred to another country see art. 277.
5   Art. 276(4).
6   Arts. 278–280.
7   Art. 281.
8   Art. 282.

7

Freedom of Movement—
Services across the Frontiers

(Articles 59–66)

At first sight it might appear as if special provisions for ensuring the free exchange of services were not required, given the general provisions on the free circulation of workers (arts. 48–51) and on establishment (arts. 52–58). Nevertheless, different economic considerations make it necessary to regulate this topic separately, since services aross the frontiers may either involve temporary residence in another country of the EEC or the transfer of funds. These aspects are not taken into account in the other chapters of the Treaty dealing with the conditions for taking up residence or employment.[1]

The meaning of the term "services" is defined (art. 60). This definition makes it clear that services across the frontiers are meant to include all those activities by independent persons, including associations (arts. 66, 58), based upon a contract of employment or services and the like involving by way of non-exhaustive enumeration a broad range of industrial, commercial, artisan or professional activities which are normally, but not necessarily, rendered for remuneration and which are not covered by the preceding sections on the circulation of workers and on establishment, or by those on the circulation of goods or capital (art. 60, 1st and 2nd paras). It is thus an omnibus clause capable of expansion, if new techniques or services should emerge. As in the case of the provisions on establishment, and differently from those on the free circulation of workers, restrictions on the free supply of services within the Community are to be abolished gradually during the transitional period "within the framework of the provisions set out below" (art. 59, 1st para.).[2]

For this purpose, member states must admit nationals of other member states who fulfil certain conditions (art. 59, 1st para.) to temporary residence and must allow them to exercise their activities on the same footing as a citizen (art. 59, 1st para.). Thus discrimination is excluded once

---

1 As regards currency restrictions see art. 106. Where the transfer of payments is the only obstacle to the free exchange of services across frontiers, art. 106(2) links the abolition of existing restrictions to those dealing with services across frontiers (arts. 63–65), quantitative restrictions (arts. 31–35) and the free movement of capital (arts. 67–71): see Everling, *Right of Establishment* (1964), pp. 114 ff. For the practical application of this principle see Council Directive 63/340, OJ, 1963, 1609; *Mégret*, Vol. III, p. 71*.

2 See above, pp. 144–145, and p. 145, n. 1; and see arts. 48, 52.

again,[1] limited to specific, if broad, sets of circumstances (art. 60, 1st and 2nd paras); in addition the benefit of non-discrimination is conferred upon nationals of member states who are not resident in the host state[2] and it may be extended to nationals of non-member states who are resident in a member state.[3]

> *Measure:* Council, unanimously, upon proposal by the
> Commission—Regulation (art. 59, 2nd para.).

Meanwhile a standstill of the existing restrictions was declared (art. 62) and discrimination between nationals and residents of the different member states was prohibited (art. 65).[4]

In practice, services across the frontiers are most likely to be important in the commercial sector and will include the activities of foreign banks and insurance companies. However, any activities by these institutions which are concerned with the movement of capital are regulated by the chapter on capital (arts. 61(2), 67–73), and inter-state transport is subject to special rules (arts. 74–84). The admission of foreign banking and insurance businesses to trade within the countries of the Community, even if no local establishment or agency or subsidiary is contemplated, involves complicated problems as to the extent to which the local regulations for the control of such institutions and for safeguarding the public must be observed by these enterprises which operate abroad. Another problem is whether this chapter covers activities by employees of an enterprise in another member state who are sent on temporary errands elsewhere within the Community. It is possible that this aspect of services must be considered in the light of the chapters on the employment of workers.[5]

Ratione personae the liberalisation applies to nationals of the EEC resident in a country of the EEC other than that in which the service is rendered (art. 59, 1st para.). It does not apply, therefore, for reasons which are apparent, to nationals of EEC countries resident in countries outside the EEC. In limiting the liberalisation to *resident* nationals this provision differs from those on the free exchange of goods (art. 12), and by adding the requirement that the beneficiary must be a national of a member country it differs from that on the movement of capital (art. 67). It agrees, however, in the latter respect, with the notion of beneficiaries of the liberalisation of the movement of workers (art. 48) and the right of establishment (art. 52). It must be noted, however, that for the purpose of

---

1   See also arts. 48(1), 52, 1st para. and generally above, p. 18.
2   Art. 59, 1st para. Cp. arts. 12, 31, 76, 106(3), and contrast arts, 48(2), 53.
3   Art. 59, 2nd para.; see below, p. 165.
4   The process of liberalisation could be accelerated (art. 64). See also the Programme for the Abolition of Restrictions on the Free Exchange of Services across Frontiers of 18 December 1961 Tit. IV, OJ, 1962, 32; see below, p. 166.
5   Cp. the Programme of 18 December 1961 (above, n. 4) Tit. I, para. 4; see below, pp. 166–167.

services across the frontiers the *recipient* of the services, if resident in a member state, need not be a national of a member state.

The requirement that the supplier of the services must be a national of a member state may be waived in favour of nationals of other countries who reside in a member state.[1]

Measure: Council, upon a proposal of the Commission: Regulation (art. 59, 2nd para.).[2]

The usual safeguards allowing restrictions for the protection of the Community as a whole apply in respect of the free admission of services as they do in respect of the duty of member states to permit the freedom of establishment (art. 66). Thus the liberalisation of services across the frontiers does not apply to those services which involve the exercise of governmental functions (art. 55)[3] and does not rule out the exclusion of aliens on grounds of public order, public safety and public health (arts. 66, 56)[4]. The rules on the mutual recognition of professional examinations, diplomas and qualifications and on the co-ordination of conditions of admission to these professions or occupations apply here as well (arts. 66, 57).[5] Similarly, the provisions on the establishment of EEC companies and associations apply (arts. 66, 58), but it would seem *mutatis mutandis* only.[6] Thus the rule that the provision of services across the frontiers may be extended to nationals of third states, resident within one of the countries of the EEC (art. 59, 2nd para.), causes some difficulties in the light of art. 58, 1st para. which defines the companies benefiting from the Treaty. For the purpose of art. 58 a company which is a national of a third state would have to be incorporated and have its registered office, central administration or principal place of business in a third country and be established in a member state. In so far as companies are concerned, the requirement that the alien must be established in a member state (art. 59, 1st para.) leaves it open whether the company must have its seat there, or whether a branch or a particular enterprise is sufficient. If it must have its seat there, the rules of private international law of the EEC, excluding the Netherlands, will require the company to form a company according to the domestic law of these countries, in order to be recognised at all as a company.[7] The Convention of 29 February 1968 on the recognition of companies formed in accordance with the law of a member state cannot apply.[8]

---

1   See above, p. 164.
2   No such measure has been promulgated so far.
3   See above, pp. 132 ff.
4   The Directive 64/221 of 25 February 1964, OJ. 1964, 850 applies. For a detailed account see above, p. 133 and n. 4.
5   See above, pp. 135–140.
6   Cp. *von der Groeben-Boeckh*, *ad* art. 66, n. 4.
7   See above, p. 136.
8   See above, pp. 148–151.

During the first stage a Programme for the abolition of restrictions on the free supply of services was to be drawn up in respect of each type of services.

> *Measures:* Council—on proposal of the Commission after consulting the Economic and Social Committee and the Assembly—Programme (art. 63(1)).

The Programme was to be implemented by the following.

> *Measure:* Council—upon a proposal of the Commission after consulting the Social and Economic Council—Directives (art. 63(2)).

The method of implementing the liberalisation of services across the frontiers is identical with that presented for the liberalisation of the right of establishment (art. 54).[1] For the purpose of carrying out both these tasks, the Council and the Commission were guided by a single principle of priorities (art. 63(3)) as distinct from the detailed set of principles to be observed in drawing up the Programme on Establishment.[2] The Programme was published on 18 December 1961 together with that on Establishment[3] and has much in common with the latter.[4] The beneficiaries are only[5] nationals of the member states who must reside within the Community[6] and companies and associations formed in accordance with the law of a member state which have a registered office, central administration or principal place of business within the Community. In addition, if the company or association has only its registered office within the Community, it must show an effective and continuous economic link with a member state. For this purpose it is insufficient that the partners, directors, members of the supervisory board, or persons controlling the assets possess the nationality of a member state.[7] However, while this requirement was restricted in the Programme on Establishment to the situation where a company belonging to one member state wishes to set up agencies, branches or subsidiaries in another member state (art. 52, 1st para.),[8] it is of general application in the Programme on the Abolition of Restrictions of the Free Exchange of Services having regard to the generality of the requirement (art. 59, 1st para.) that the national of the member state who offers such services must be established in a state of the Community.

---

1   See above, pp. 144–145.
2   Art. 54(3), but see art. 54(3)(a).
3   OJ, 1962, 32 (services).
4   OJ, 1962, 36 (establishment); see above, pp. 142 ff.
5   See above, p. 164.
6   Programme, Tit. I, para. 2.
7   *Ibid.*, para. 3; see above, p. 138.
8   Art. 52, 2nd para. requires that the principal must be "established in the territory of a member state".

Like the Programme on Establishment, that on Services deals with the abolition of the restrictions due to economic considerations imposed by the law and administrative practice of the member states upon the entry, departure and sojourn of nationals of the member states entitled to render services across the frontiers, as well as specialist or confidential personnel who accompany them or who carry out a task on their behalf.[1] Exceptions are permitted on grounds of public policy, public safety and public health,[2] because the exercise of public authority,[3] or the regulation of transport,[4] or the free circulation of goods, capital, persons and the fiscal system is involved. Subject to these exceptions all restrictions set out in detail in the Programme[5] must be removed together with all limitations indirectly connected with the exercise of work by aliens. A time-table contains special provisions for the abolition of restrictions on services connected with direct insurance, banks, the motion picture industry, agriculture and horticulture and public works contracts,[6] but leaves the mutual recognition of diplomas open.[7]

The Programme was implemented by directives,[8] but it does not appear that all necessary directives had been passed when the transitional period came to an end. Thus the question arises here, as it did in connection with freedom of establishment,[9] as to whether all services across frontiers may now be supplied freely. As in the case of the freedom of establishment the answer must probably be in the negative because the Treaty itself (art. 63, 1st para.; cp. art. 52, 1st para.) provides that the free exchange of services is only to take place "within the framework of the provisions set out below". Thus specific directives are required.

Technically, the Programme was implemented by the Council Directive of 25 February 1964 on the Abolition of Restrictions on Travel and Residence of Nationals of the Member States inside the Community in respect of Establishment and the Free Exchange of Services.[10] The provisions on entry and residence of nationals of member states who wish to establish themselves, which were set out above,[11] apply also *mutatis mutandis* to nationals of member states desirous of providing a free exchange of services across the frontiers.

---

1 Programme Services Tit. II; Council Directive 63/340, OJ, 1963, 1609 (currency restrictions); Council Directive 64/220 of 25 February 1964, OJ, 1964, 845; see above, p. 134 and n. 13.
2 *Ibid.*, Tit. III.
3 *Ibid.*, Tit. III.
4 *Ibid.*, Tit. III.
5 *Ibid.*, Tit. III A–D.
6 *Ibid.*, Tit. V.
7 *Ibid.*, Tit. VI.
8 See above, p. 144, n. 1.
9 Above, p. 145, and the literature cited there.
10 64/220, OJ, 1964, 845.
11 Above, p. 134.

8

Movement of Capital

(Articles 67–73)[1]

The Treaty envisages, together with the liberalisation of the right of establishment and of services across the frontiers the liberalisation of capital movements as well (art. 3 (c)). In principle this entails the right of persons and associations (art. 58) within the Community freely to acquire, use and transfer capital, to receive without restriction payment of profits and repayments arising out of investments, credits and loans; to turn investments into money by sale and liquidation and to transfer the balance; and that no discrimination should be allowed in the administration of laws and regulations concerning these topics, even if this legislation aims at purposes other than exchange control. Thus the liberalisation of capital movements must include the acquisition of stocks and shares, the investment in existing local companies and associations and the formation of new enterprises, the acquisition of land and the transfer of money and goods.[2]

A first step towards liberalisation was made by the Bretton Woods Agreement of 1 and 22 July 1944,[3] but its effects were limited. The OEEC (now OECD) concentrated in its Code of Liberalisation in the wording of 12 December 1961 on the liberalisation of invisible transactions[4], but made the first approach to the problem of direct investment.[5] The Six, in concluding the Treaty, restated their obligation, entered into previously (arts. 67, 68, 106 and Annex III). Generally speaking, these include all current transactions and repayments of loans as well as the transfer of successions and dowries (art. 67 (2), Annex III); they also include the import and export of long-term capital (art. 67 (1)), the transfer of the product of the sale of such capital investments and the free use of blocked accounts.[6]

The provisions of the Treaty on the freedom of capital movements are imprecise and fragmentary owing to the reluctance of the member states to undertake commitments which might strain their resources excessively. The member states assume a general obligation to liberalise movements of capital only to the extent that the proper functioning of the Common

---

1 *Mégret*, Vol. III, pp. 173–259; 129*–155*; Clavière in Juriscl. Dr. Int., Fasc. 164 E (1969); Heenen in *Ganshof van der Meersch*, pp. 755–772, nos. 1872–1919.
2 This seems to follow from arts. 52, 2nd para. 54(2), especially (e) and (f), 106(1), (2), 221.
3 UNTS 2, p. 39.
4 *European Yearbook* (1962), p. 331.
5 *Ibid.*, pp. 437 ff.
6 See *von der Groeben-Boeckh*, Introductory Note 3 *ad* art. 67.

Market requires it (art. 67 (1)). The meaning of this proviso leaves room for much flexibility. Clearly a completely free movement of capital is most likely to lead to higher productivity by stimulating the division of labour and by inducing capital to flow where investment will be most lucrative. However, a completely free movement might denude the capital market of one country and inflate that of another. Conversely, it may create a disequilibrium in the balance of payments. These considerations are relevant in determining the proper function of capital movements in the Common Market.

The obligation to liberalise capital movements, which is thus circumscribed, is subject to further limitations, of which that of spreading it over the transitional period (art. 67 (1) and (2)) can now be disregarded. Restrictions, all of which must disappear, probably comprise primarily exchange control regulation (art. 67 (1) in conjunction with art. 71 (1)).[1] They must be abolished in favour of beneficiaries resident in member states (art. 67 (1)) only. Any discrimination based on the nationality or residence of the parties concerned or on the place of investment (art. 67 (1)) is forbidden. Read in conjunction with the obligation, stated above, to abolish restrictions on the movement of capital in favour of residents within the Community this latter provision requires an explanation. The persons resident in the Community appear to benefit irrespective of their nationality, seeing that the test of nationality is omitted in the previous sentence.[2] Consequently, the reiteration that nationality and residence as well as the place of investment are irrelevant appears to concern the duty of non-discrimination towards members of the EEC, their nationals and nationals of other states, resident in the member state, as against those resident in another, and regardless of where the capital may be invested. The duty of non-discrimination seems to apply to the administration of existing restrictions pending their abolition.[3]

It has been suggested, however, that the wording of art. 67 (1) indicates concern for nationals of EEC resident outside the EEC. However, this conclusion would do violence to the final part of art. 67 (1); moreover, the liberalisation would operate outside the economic sphere of the EEC.[4] Whichever be the correct interpretation of art. 67 (1), the undertaking is less precise in terms and timing than that concerning current payments (art. 67 (2)) in respect of which complete liberalisation had been achieved under the auspices of OECD.[5]

---

1 For particular aspects of liberalising capital movements which require the relaxation of exchange controls see arts. 68(1), 106(1)–(3); for their relationship see *Mégret*, Vol. III, p. 176, no. 6.

2 For the notion of residence and the problem of corporations see *Mégret*, Vol. III, pp. 178(10), 216–218.

3 *Wohlfahrt-Everling-Glaesner-Sprung, ad* art. 67, n. 6, but see art. 70(1) which envisages common policies of the member states towards third countries.

4 *Von der Groeben-Boeck*, Introductory Note 6 *ad* art. 67.

5 Current payments include those arising out of imports and exports, services across frontiers, short term banking transactions, including credits, interest on loans, net income from investments, amortisation of loans or representing the written-off value of investments and

[*footnote continued on next page*

Measures: Council, upon proposal of the Commission,
after consulting the Monetary Committee
(art. 105 (2))[1]—Directives (art. 69).

As a result the First and Second Directives of 11 May 1960[2] and of 18 December 1962,[3] a Directive of 31 May 1963 on Payment for Services,[4] a Directive of 30 July 1963 on Invisible Transactions not covered otherwise[5] and a Draft Third Directive of 7 February 1967[6] were issued.[7] In the meantime licences for the benefit of capital and current payments were to be granted as generously as possible (art. 68 (1)). The existing legislation of the member states regulating the capital market and the provision of credit must be applied without discrimination to the liberalised movement of capital (art. 68 (2)). Thus the laws on the functioning of stock exchanges, the issuing of shares and bonds to the public at large, on convertible bonds, on credit etc. remain untouched,[8] even if they affect not only the domestic market, but the movement of capital in the Community.

One clear exception to the general plea of liberalisation exists. Loans intended to finance directly or indirectly a member state of the EEC or one of its subordinate territorial organs[9] may only be floated in any other member state with the consent of the latter (art. 68 (3)). The purpose of this provision is to avoid a local shortage of credit through a process of siphoning off the available local capital to satisfy the needs of another member state. It is a matter for discussion whether this provision operates directly in the domestic law of the member states and affects private rights. Since the duties imposed by art. 68 (3) fall upon the member state wishing to float a loan in another state of the Community, and since the latter is under a duty to act or to refrain from acting, it cannot be said that its domestic law is directly affected or that any individual can derive any rights therefrom.

The term "subordinate territorial organs" appears to include governmental entities having a territorial character, such as provinces, districts or cities, but may not include public corporations which have an economic rather than a territorial character,[10] or private corporations which are wholly or partly owned by a state or local governmental agency, unless the loan is floated on behalf of these agencies. The activities of the European

---

maintenance of members of the family. See Bretton Woods Agreement (above, p. 168) art. XIX(i); OECD Code (above, p. 168) Annex A.

1   Cp. arts. 71, 3rd para., 73(1), (2).
2   OJ, 1960, 921; Delvaux, 1960 Rev. M.C. 338.
3   OJ, 1963, 62.
4   OJ, 1963, 1609.
5   OJ, 1963, 2240.
6   C.C.H., Common Market Reporter, para. 1671 based on an earlier Draft of 14 April 1964. No other reference to this document could be found; *Mégret*, Vol. III, p. 187, *ad* art. 69.
7   See below, p. 174.
8   *Von der Groeben-Boeckh, ad art. 68, n. 8; Wohlfahrt-Everling-Glaesner-Sprung, ad art. 68, n. 4.*
9   *Collectivités publiques territoriales, Gebietskörperschaften, uno Stato membro o i suoi enti locali, van een Lid-Staat of van zijn territoriale publiekrechteliijke lichamen.*
10 *Von der Groeben-Boeckh, ad art. 68, n. 8; Wohlfahrt-Everling-Glaesner-Sprung, ad* art. 68, n. 4.

Investment Bank are expressly exempted from the disabilities laid down in art. 68 (3).

Pending the implementation of the outlines of liberalisation of capital (arts. 67, 69), the Treaty envisaged a period of standstill (art. 71 (1)). Unlike the other standstill duties proclaimed in other parts of the Treaty[1] that provided for restrictions of movements of capital and payments on current account is purely programmatical and not directly applicable (art. 71 (1)).[2] This policy is opposed not only to the creation of new restrictions, but also to the tightening-up of existing restrictions (art. 71(1)).

As elsewhere in the Treaty[3] an accelerated procedure was made possible.

> *Measure:* Commission, after consulting the Monetary Committee—recommendations 71 (3) concerning the implementation of articles 71(1) and (2).

As in the case of the abolition of customs barriers between the member states, where a corresponding common tariff towards third states had to take its place if a distortion of trade was to be avoided, so in the case of a liberalisation of movements of capital a common policy towards measures of exchange control was required as they affect payments to and from third countries. The reason is that a more lenient exchange control legislation in one country of the EEC, coupled with the abolition of exchange controls between the member states, would enable capital to flow freely to that member state from which it can be transferred to third countries with the least restriction. Consequently, the exchange policies of the member states in respect of the movement of capital between the countries of EEC and third countries are to be *co-ordinated* (art. 70 (1)).[4]

> *Measure:* Council, upon proposal by the Commission— Directives (art. 70(1)).

If a danger of practices such as those outlined above should develop in spite of the efforts of the Council to co-ordinate the measures of exchange control, the member state whose balance of payments is thereby put under pressure is empowered to take unilaterally the necessary

---

1 Arts. 12, 31, 62; cp. however arts. 76, 106 (3).

2 The French text states: "... *s'efforceront de n'introduire aucune nouvelle restriction*"; the German text says: "... *werden bestrebt sein weder neue devisenrechtliche Beschränkungen ... einzuführen*"; see also the Dutch version: "... *streven ernaar geen nieuwe deviezen beperkingen ... in te voeren ...*" and compare the Italian version: "... *procurano di non introdurre ...*"; see also the First Directive of 11 May 1960, art. 6 (above, p. 170, n. 2). For the effective removal of restrictions on invisible transactions and current payments by OECD and by virtue of art. 106(3) of the Treaty and Annex III see above, p. 169, n. 5.

3 Arts. 15(2), 35, 64, 106(1), (4).

4 On the basis of arts. 105(1), 113, it must be assumed. It is a matter for debate whether the co-ordination is restricted to matters of exchange in a narrow sense; see *Mégret*, Vol. III, p. 188. See the proposed Directive of 4 November 1965, OJ, 1966, 969.

> *Measures:* Member state after consulting the other member
> states and the Commission (art. 70(2)).[1]

Such measures are only permissible in relation to the efflux of capital to third states. If, in the opinion of the Council, the protective measures taken by a state by virtue of the power given under art. 70(2) are excessive:

> *Measure:* Council, by a qualified majority, upon proposal
> of the Commission—Decision that the state con-
> cerned must amend or abrogate the protective
> measure in issue (art. 70(3)).

In order to enable the Commission to co-ordinate the exchange policies of the member states (art. 70 (1)) and to control any unilateral measures by member states (art. 70(2)), member states must inform the Commission of movements of capital to and from third countries, in so far as they have obtained the relevant information (which need not, therefore, be collected *ad hoc*) (art. 72).

> *Measure:* Commission—Opinion (art. 72).

Given the delicate nature of the capital market, the Treaty provides a safety valve for the protection of the market within the countries of the EEC (art. 73). If the proper functioning of the capital market has been disturbed by movements of capital, the process of liberalisation can be stopped and reduced even below the existing limit (art. 73). The disturbance must have been caused by movements of capital and not by other circumstances, such as the liberalisation of payments on current account or services across the frontiers; in the latter case, other action may be called for (arts. 108, 109 and, until 1970, under art. 226), but it may be difficult to attribute a single cause to any one disturbance. Such disturbances as are envisaged by the Treaty (art. 73 (1)) may be due to movements inside the Community in consequence of the obligations arising under arts. 67(1) and 71, but they can occur as a result of a flight of capital into third countries (art. 70(2)).

> *Measure:* Commission, after consulting the Monetary
> Committee, authorises protective measures (art.
> 73(1), 1st para.). Council acting by a qualified
> majority may revoke or modify the measures
> (art. 73 (1), 2nd para.).

---

1   The German text speaks of "*sich ins Benehmen setzen*". The French text states more specifically "*après consultation*"; see also the Italian and Dutch versions "*previa consultazione*", "*naar raad-pleging*". Cp. arts. 73(2), 109(1), 115, 2nd para. which permit unilateral action, at least provisionally, and contrast arts. 25(3), 26, 108(3) which require previous consent. As regards the question whether a threat of action envisaged in art. 70(2) suffices to set the procedure in motion see *Mégret*, Vol. III, p. 190.

In case of urgency[1]

> *Measure:* Member state may take unilateral action and
> must inform the Commission and member states
> (art. 73 (2), 1st and 2nd sentence).
> Commission after consulting the Monetary
> Committee decides to require the member state
> to abrogate or to modify the unilateral measure
> (art. 73(2), last sentence).

The details of the liberalisation of movements of capital are laid down by
the directives issued by virtue of art. 69 and art. 63.[2]

The First Directive of 11 May 1960[3] enjoins member states to permit
between residents, by way of general and unlimited exchange authorisation, direct investments and their realisation, investments in real property,
short and medium term commercial credits involving local residents,
surety bonds, guarantees and liens and any transfers arising therefrom,
insurance payments, inheritance taxes, damages respecting capital losses,
repayments arising from the cancellation of contracts, the acquisition of
patents, trademarks, designs and copyrights, transfers of means required
for the attention of services and capital movement of a personal nature.[4]
These transfers are to be made at the current rate of exchange. General
authorisation is also to be granted, with limited exceptions, for dealings in
securities, whether domestic or foreign, by non-residents.[5] Subject to
restrictions relating to the realisation of the objectives of the economic
policy of a member state, the same applies to raising of capital by floating
securities of domestic enterprises on a foreign capital market or of foreign
enterprises on the domestic market and to the acquisition of securities,
both domestic and foreign, not traded on the stock exchange and the
transfer of the proceeds of their sale, shares in domestic or foreign mutual
investment groups (unit trusts, investment trusts?), foreign debentures as
well as their physical transfer and transactions in connection with long
term credits in which a local resident participates or medium and long
term credits in which no local resident participates, loans not connected
with commercial transactions or the rendition of services, surety, bonds
etc. for long term credits relating to commercial transactions or services in
which a resident participates, and medium or long term if no resident
participates, or if the credit is not connected with a commercial transaction.[6] Thus, generally speaking, only short term capital movements
remain subject to restrictions.[7]

---

1 See above, p. 172, n. 1.
2 See above, p. 170 and nn. 2–6.
3 OJ, 1960, 921; *Mégret*, Vol. III, p. 129*.
4 Art. 1 and Annex I, List A; for a detailed classification of the various entries see Annex I.
5 Art. 2 and Annex I, List B. For the difference between the freedom accorded by List A
   and the general authorisation in List B see *Mégret*, Vol. III, 202, 203.
6 Art. 3 and Annex I, List C.
7 See *Mégret*, Vol. III, pp. 206–207 with examples.

The Second Directive of 18 December 1962 modified art. 1 and the Annexes.[1]

The proposed Third Directive of 7 February 1967[2] superseding that of 14 April 1964 requires the abolition of all restrictions on the floating and the sale of securities based on nationality or residence (art. 1) and on their listing on the Stock Exchanges (art. 2), on the purchase of foreign securities by financial institutions,[3] if these securities provide the same safety as to quality and soundness as authorised domestic securities, subject to certain conditions as to their quotation in the country of the purchasing financial institution and to their denomination or *option de change* in the country of the purchasing financial institution (art. 3).

Some difficulty has arisen over the interpretation of the Explanatory Note attached to Annex II of the First Directive which includes in indirect investment (Position I, 2) any participation in enterprises for the purpose of creating or maintaining lasting economic ties. The Explanatory Note states that participation in joint stock companies qualifies as a direct investment, if the shares vested in the holder enable him, according to the domestic law governing the enterprise or otherwise, to participate in the management or the supervision of the company concerned. The domestic law on participation and supervision may vary from country to country, *e.g.*, as regards the admissibility of non-voting shares.

Finally it must be remembered that member states must permit nationals of other member states to participate financially in the companies within the meaning of art. 58(2), subject to any specific provisions elsewhere in the Treaty (art. 221).[4]

---

1 OJ, 1963, 62; *Mégret*, Vol. III, p. 143*.
2 C.C.H., Common Market Reporter, para. 1671 (see above, p. 170, n. 6); *Mégret*, Vol. III, pp. 209–215.
3 They include banks, savings banks which are not merely local, short, medium and long term credit institutions, public and private insurance institutions, building and loan societies and investment companies; see *ibid.*, Annex I.
4 See above, p. 142, n. 1. For the meaning of this proviso see *e.g. Wohlfahrt-Everling-Glaesner-Sprung, ad* art. 221.

9

Transport

(Articles 74–84)[1]

I GENERAL PRINCIPLES

Transport as a means of rationalising production and as a factor determining the cost of the product occupies a place of some importance in the structure of the EEC (art. 3(e)), just as its importance had previously been recognised in the ECSC (art. 70), which is unaffected by the EEC Treaty (art. 232). Thus harmonisation of tariffs and non-discrimination by the tariffs themselves and in the methods by which the tariffs are calculated are an important concern of the Community. The formulation of a clear-cut common transport policy and its translation into provisions of the EEC Treaty proved difficult, seeing that in the Netherlands[2] and also in Germany[3] transport not unlike in the United Kingdom, especially by rail, may be State owned in the last resort, but is free from governmental intervention. It is not employed as a means of social or economic policy and is within limits left open to the general play of competition.[4] In other countries of the EEC, especially in France, transport, particularly by rail, is treated as part of the "service public" and is subject to the rules applicable thereto. This means that transport can be used or directed by the State to reach certain economic or other objectives. Among these figure the following:

(a) to increase the competitive position of producers in remote areas or in areas which are economically weak, and who would normally be charged higher tariffs owing to the remote situation of the area or the small amount of goods to be carried from the centre of production, by the imposition of a uniform tariff for these and the more profitable areas;

(b) to bring about a decentralisation of industry by the imposition of more favourable tariffs for those industries which move to designated areas;

---

1 *Mégret*, Vol. III, pp. 261, 326; 159*–223*; Thiebaut, Juriscl. Dr. Int., Fasc. 164 J (1966); Rodière in *Ganshof van der Meersch*, pp. 773–792, Nos. 1921–1970.
2 Law of 26 May 1937; of 1 November 1951; cp. *Mégret*, Vol. III, p. 278.
3 Law of 13 December 1951, 1955 I BGBl 955 as amended 14 July 1953, 1953 I BGBl 583; 5 August 1955, 1955 I BGBl 489; 1 August 1961, 1961 I BGBl 1161, para. 28; 6 March 1969, 1969 I BGBl 191, para. 28a; 21 December 1970, 1970 I BGBl 1765.
4 Fulda (1963) 12 A.J.C.L. 303, at pp. 307, 313; *von der Groeben-Boeckh*, Introductory Note 3 to arts. 74–84; *Wohlfahrt-Everling-Glaesner-Sprung*, Introductory Note 5 *ad* art. 74.

(c) to support certain types of producers, such as small producers, or certain sections of the population.

Apart from railway tariffs, the various regimes of granting licences or administering quotas for road traffic raise similar problems of policy. The technical requirements for permitting vehicles to participate in road transport and the formalities at the frontier also differ from country to country. On the other hand, it must not be overlooked that some aspects of transport have been regulated by international agreements outside the EEC Treaty.[1]

The ECSC Treaty (art. 70) envisages a system of tariffs which offers the same rates to all consumers in a comparable condition. For this purpose all discrimination in tariffs between transports in or to member countries must be abolished (art. 70, 2nd para.), exceptional tariffs in the nature of a subsidy must be approved by the High Authority (art. 70, 4th para.) and direct tariffs from one member country to another are to be introduced.[2] In order to permit a proper control, all tariffs must be published (art. 70, 3rd para.). Moreover, the tariffs and conditions of transport are to be harmonised in so far as this is required for the efficient functioning of the Common Market.[3] In effect this has led to a fixed tariff system within the ECSC given the wide definition of discrimination.[4]

In view of the close relationship between the EEC and the ECSC and of the fact that all tariffs concerning goods forming the object of the ECSC are regulated and remain regulated by the ECSC Treaty (EEC Treaty, art. 232), the law and practice in the ECSC will have to be kept in mind

---

1   *Railways:*
   (a) Berne Convention on Carriage of Goods by Rail (C.I.M.) 25 February 1961, Cmnd. 2187, T.S. 67/1965, Cmnd. 2810, in force 1 January 1966 (replacing the Convention of 1890, last revised 25 October 1952, Cmd. 9889 T.S. 46/1958, Cmnd. 564. See also Protocol 7 February–30 April 1970, T.S. 57/1972, Cmnd. 4985. And see the amendments made in 1967, T.S. 24/1969, Cmnd. 3900, 1970, T.S. 86/1971, Cmnd. 4830.
   (b) Berne Convention and Statute concerning the Transport of Persons and their Luggage by Railways (C.I.V.) of 25 February 1961, Cmnd. 2186, T.S. 66/1965, Cmnd. 2811, replacing the Convention of 25 October 1952, Cmd. 9852, T.S. 47/1958, Cmnd. 565. See also the Protocol (above (a)) and see the Carriage by Railways Act 1972.
   (c) Geneva Convention on the International Regime of Railways, 9 December 1923, 47 LNTS 70; Hudson, (1931) II Int. Leg. 1130, 1138, 1155 especially art. 18 ff.
   Road Traffic:
   (a) Geneva Convention on Road Traffic, 19 September 1949, 125 UNTS 22 T.S., 49/1958, Cmnd. 578 ratified 8 July 1957, replacing the Convention of 24 April 1926, 97 LNTS 83; Hudson, (1931) III *op. cit.* 1872.
   (b) Convention concerning Customs Facilities for Touring of 4 June 1954, 276 UNTS 192, 230 and on the Temporary Importation of Private Road Vehicles of 4 June 1954, 282 UNTS 249.
   (c) Geneva Convention on the International Carriage by Road, 18 May 1956, 327 UNTS 123; 338 *ibid.* 103; 339 *ibid.* 3. See Carriage of Goods by Road Act 1965.
2   Convention containing Transitional Provisions of 18 April 1951, s. 10, para. 3(2), 261 UNTS 277 (1957). Such direct tariffs of a degressive character have since been established.
3   Convention of 18 April 1951 (above, n. 2) s. 10, para. 3(3).
4   The High Authority has no normative power under art. 70 of the ECSC Treaty; see *Netherlands* v. *High Authority* (1960) 6 **Rec.** 723, at pp. 757, 760; Valentine II, 309.

when it comes to interpreting the corresponding provisions on transport of the EEC Treaty, although it must also be remembered that they differ considerably from each other.

As stated before, the formulation of clear-cut rules on transport proved difficult in the EEC Treaty since no definite policy crystallised during the negotiations, given the different structure of transport undertakings in the member states, the different attitudes towards the function of public transport within a national community and, possibly, owing to geographical differences. As a result, only certain details could be formulated.[1] It was not even possible to state with any certainty at the outset whether the chapter on transport purports to regulate the topic exhaustively to the exclusion of the general principles laid down elsewhere in the Treaty or whether they apply here as well.[2] It is now reasonably clear that, within the framework set for transport, the general principles in arts. 7, 48–51, 52–58, 85–94,[3] 99 and 117 apply here as well. Yet even within this framework the particular rules on transport remain general to the point of being vague and imprecise.

In order to pursue the purposes of the Treaty (art. 2) the member states agree to follow a common transport policy (arts. 3(e), 74). This obligation is not limited to a process of co-ordination (arts. 6(1), 105), but it does not go so far as to require a uniform policy; it leaves sufficient room for the consideration of the needs of particular regions (arts. 75(3), 80(2)). On the other hand, it includes all aspects of transport which may be relevant, whether they may arise nationally or internationally. Thus it concerns the admission of transport undertakings which are to operate between the member states or in transit (art. 75(1)(a)) as well as in one particular member state from a base in another member state (art. 75(1)(b)), subventions (art. 77) and the formation of tariffs (arts. 78–80). The provisions on transport affect only transport carried out by railways, road haulage and inland waterways (art. 84(1)),[4] but in the view of the Commission they extend also to pipelines for the carriage of oil and other fuel.[5] Maritime and air transport may be included in the future (art. 84(2)).[6]

---

1   See Juriscl. Dr. Int., Fasc. 164 J, No. 9; Fulda, (1963) 12 A.J.C.L. 303, at p. 319; *Mégret,* Vol. III, pp. 262(2), 282 and see below, text to n. 2.

2   Juriscl. Dr. Int., Fasc. 164 J, No. 10; Fulda, (1963) 12 A.J.C.L. 303, at pp. 318–319; *Mégret,* Vol. III, pp. 283–285; Rodière in *Ganshof van der Meersch,* pp. 777–778, Nos. 1926–1928 with lit.; Commission Memorandum of April 1961, below, p. 183.

3   See below, pp. 198–252.

4   As regards transport on the Rhine, collaboration with the Central Commission for the navigation of the Rhine is necessary and possible (art. 229). See *Mégret,* Vol. III, pp. 292–293.

5   See the Commission Memorandum of April 1961, below, p. 183; Juriscl. Dr. Int., Fasc. 164 J, no. 92; Fulda, (1963) 12 A.J.C.L. 303, at p. 334; Commission Memorandum and Programme of 10 February 1967, 1967 EEC Bull., Suppl. to No. 3.

6   They are excluded for the present since maritime and air traffic bear features which are much more directed towards the world at large than to the Community alone, but the Commission has initiated studies on air transport within the Community. It has been argued, however, that as regards all aspects of the Treaty, except transport, *e.g.* freedom of competition, the Treaty is applicable; see Rodière, in *Ganshof van der Meersch* p. 779, No. 1929.

> *Measure:* Council, unanimously decides whether, to what
> extend and according to what procedure mari-
> time and air traffic is to be regulated
> (art. 84(2)).[1]

II   THE SCHEME OF THE PROVISIONS ON TRANSPORT

In order to carry out the common transport policy, the Council, by
a qualified majority, upon the proposal of the Commission and after consulting the Economic and Social Committee and the Assembly may take
the following

> *Measures:* (a) Establish common rules concerning
> international transport from or to member
> states or for transit transport affecting one
> or several member states (art. 75(1)(a);[2]
> (b) establish the conditions for the admission of
> transport undertakings resident in one
> member state of the EEC to exercise their
> calling in another country of the EEC
> (art. 75(1)(b));[3]
> (c) to lay down any other provisions which are
> suitable for the purpose of carrying out a
> common transport policy (art. 75(1)(c)).[4]

The term "rules" (*règles, Regeln*) which is employed in art. 75(1)(a),
though not in subsections (b) and (c), has a non-technical meaning and
appears to envisage measures of a general character. As will be seen later
on,[5] the Council has used the form of regulations, decisions and directives
in the course of implementing art. 75. These measures must take into
consideration the special character of transport (art. 75(1), first sentence).
The meaning of this requirement is not entirely clear, unless it expresses
the obvious. As was shown before, the character of the chapter on transport as a separate *lex specialis* was much debated during the early days of
the Treaty and is now rejected, on the whole.[6] Nevertheless the wording
of art. 75(1), first sentence, seems to demand that the ancillary functions
of transport must be taken into account and that the principle of complete
liberalisation is not to be introduced as such into the sphere of transport.
This is clearly expressed elsewhere (art. 61(1)) where the rules on the
liberalisation of services across the frontiers are expressly declared to be

---

1   In the field of transport, the negotiation of international agreements with third states is now
   the exclusive preserve of the Commission. See *EEC Commission v. EEC Council*, (1971),
   17 Rec. 263; [1972] C.M.L.R. 335.
2   Cp. Fulda, (1963) 12 A.J.C.L. 303, at p. 319.
3   Cp. Fulda, *op. cit.* at pp. 319, 322.
4   For the ambit of this broadly formulated provision see *Mégret*, Vol. III, p. 264 (2).
5   See below, p. 184, n. 5.
6   See above, p. 177.

inapplicable in the field of transport.[1] But this covers only a small sector of liberalisation; other sectors extend to transport. Thus the right of establishment (arts. 52–58) is not excluded by the section on transport which restricts only the application of the rules on services across frontiers.[2] The rules on competition have been rendered applicable with suitable adaptations[3] after considerable wavering,[4] and while it seems to be accepted today that the general principles on discrimination (art. 7) and on subvention (art. 92) apply, the relationship between these provisions and the specialised prohibitions against discrimination in calculating freight charges or in imposing conditions (art. 79(1)) and aids to co-ordinate transport or to discharge particular obligations arising from the nature of a public utility (art. 77) remains to be cleared up.[5] At this stage the words of art. 75(1), calling for special regard to the peculiar character of transport, may come into their own.

Since railways operate within their own areas, measures to be taken by the Council in this field are mainly concerned with direct tariffs and the mutual admission of rolling stock and goods.[6] Road haulage attracts the principal attention. Since in most countries of the EEC road haulage is subject to regulations limiting competition by co-ordinating services on the basis of bilateral or multilateral arrangements, the Council is mainly concerned with the admission of foreign transport undertakings, the procedure and conditions of its exercise, as well as with tariffs, the establishment of standards of qualifications, social, security and labour practices. Inland shipping appears to be less subject to restrictions on a national level and the needs of this industry appear to lie in different fields, such as education of boatmen's children.

The rules envisaged by art. 75 may touch also upon transport to and from third countries. In those circumstances the need arises to reconcile the competence of the member states united in the Council in matters of transport affecting the EEC with those of the Commission, subject to the approval of the Council, to put the commercial policy of the Community into practice by negotiating agreements with third countries (arts. 113(3), 116).[7] In this latter area, according to the Community Court, the competence of the Commission is exclusive.[8] On the other hand, the wording of art. 75(1)(c) enabling the Council, in establishing and carrying out a common transport policy, to make "any other appropriate provision",

---

[1] See Fulda, *loc. cit.*, at p. 322; cp. art. 75(1)(b).

[2] Juriscl. Dr. Int., Fasc. 164 F, No. 31; 164 J, No. 4; *Wohlfahrt-Everling-Glaesner-Sprung, ad* art. 74, n. 4.

[3] Council Reg. 1017/68, OJ, 1968, L 175/1; implemented by Commission Regs. 1629/69 and 1630/69, OJ, 1969, L 209/1/11.

[4] Council Reg. 141, OJ, 1962, 2751; 165/65, OJ, 1965, 3141; 1002/67, OJ, 1967, 1.

[5] Cp. Fulda, (1963) 12 A.J.C.L. 303, at pp. 327, 328; *Mégret*, Vol. III, pp. 266–268.

[6] But see Reg. 11, art. 2(3).

[7] Contrast art. 228 which restricts the initiative of the Commission to cases "where this Treaty provides for the conclusion of agreements between the Community and one or more states . . .".

[8] *EEC Commission* v. *EEC Council* (1971), 17 Rec. 263; [1972] C.M.L.R. 335.

represents an omnibus clause which permits the Council to take very broad measures. Thus it may be possible for the Council to regulate transport, even in so far as it is local and does not cross the frontiers of the member states.

At the same time, the powers of the Council to issue rules are hedged around with certain safeguards. In so far as the rules, conditions and provisions (art. 75(1)(a)–(c)) concerning the regulation of transport may (but need not necessarily) affect the standard of living or the employment situations in certain areas or the use of certain means of transport the Treaty allows the following

> *Measure:* Council, unanimously decides (art. 75(3)), having
> regard to the need to adapt transport
> to the economic development of the EEC.

It would seem that the interests of any part of the population, and not of the population as a whole, may be taken into consideration and that detrimental effects upon the standard of living and the level of employment can arise from many causes, such as increases of tariffs, the closing of unremunerative lines, and that the effects may be direct or indirect.

Until the Council has issued the rules in virtue of art. 75, a standstill is declared (art. 76), subject to exemptions to be granted by the Council acting unanimously. The generality and vagueness of the provisions of art. 75 which seem to require extensive and detailed regulations on many topics connected with transport between states raises the question as to whether this standstill must be regarded as perpetual; the more so since the Council has acted only piecemeal in a limited number of transport matters during the last fourteen years. At the same time the standstill purports to affect "the various provisions governing this subject which exist when this Treaty comes into force" (art. 76). This seems to imply that all rules which affect transport in one way or another, including fiscal legislation specifically applicable to transport, may be covered by the standstill. However, the subsequent passage of art. 76 ("in such a way as to make them less favourable in their . . . effect . . . for carriers of other member states . . .") might suggest that this article is a specialised prohibition of discrimination. If this should be correct, every member state could take new restrictive measures, provided that they affect uniformly all transport enterprises which are nationals of member states and carry on business within the EEC. The doubts have been removed by the Decision of the Council of 21 March 1962,[1] which enjoins member states to inform the Commission of all measures by way of legislation, delegated legislation or administration, which are "apt to interfere in a substantial measure with the realisation of the Common Transport Policy."[2] Thus the objects of the Treaty, not non-discrimination alone, set the criteria for the application of art. 76. Until the Commission has given its opinion or

---

1　OJ, 1962, 720; proposed amendment OJ, 1972, C 113/14, 142/15.

2　". . . *susceptibles d'interférer d'une manière substantielle avec la réalisation de la politique commune des transports*".

the time limit for giving it has expired, the state concerned must normally refrain from putting the measure into operation.[1]

A specific prohibition of discrimination concerns the calculation of freight and the insertion of conditions (art. 79(1)), but unlike the ECSC Treaty (art. 70) the EEC Treaty does not require the adoption of a uniform tariff system for all transport enterprises in a comparable position and directs itself only to discrimination by individual transport undertakings.

> *Measure:* Council, by a qualified majority, upon the proposal of the Commission and after consulting the Economic and Social Council—Regulation (art. 79(3)).[2]

However, the concept of discrimination in the formation of tariffs for the carriage of goods is not strictly determined by the Treaty and may be extended (art. 79(2)).

> *Measure:* Council (art. 79(2), art. 75(1)).

In this connection the control of tariffs and conditions of transport is to be facilitated by appropriate measures (art. 79(3), 2nd para.). In practice this means that the tariffs and conditions can be made public.

> *Measure:* Council, by a qualified majority, regulations.

In case of any violation by the provisions of non-discrimination—

> *Measure:* Commission, of its own motion, or on application by a member state, after consulting the

---

1 See *e.g.* the following Commission Opinions issued
   (a) by virtue of the Council Decision of 21 March 1962, OJ, 1962, 720: OJ, 1962, 228, 1921; 1963, 2498; 1964, 742, 36/4; 1965, 45, 861, 2390, 2652, 3052; 1966, 436; 1967, 692, 693, 303, 364, 373, No. 150/11/13, No. 261/22, No. 293/7; 1968, L 18/17/18, L 35/14, L 75/5, L 83/27, L 167/17, L 218/13; 1969, L 110/4/6, L 138/6, L 152/12; 1970, L 13/8, L 189/10; 1971, L 32/19, L 39/19, L 57/25, L 100/12, L 134/2;
   (b) by virtue of Council Reg. 117/66, art. 12(1), OJ, 1966, 2688: OJ, 1970, L 185/14; 1971, L 6/34, L 7/10/12;
   (c) by virtue of Commission Reg. 1018/68, art. 6(1), OJ, 1968, L 175/13: OJ, 1971, L 7/14;
   (d) by virtue of Council Reg. 543/69, art.18(1), OJ, 1969, L 77/49: OJ, 1969, L 220/19, L 253/20; 1970, L 22/16, L 63/16, L 965/9; 1971, L 57/26, L 155/6, L 182/12;
   (e) by virtue of Council Reg. 1191/69, art. 18(1), OJ, 1969, L 156/1: OJ, 1969, L 220/20; 1970, L 63/14, L 126/20/22/24;
   (f) by virtue of Council Reg. 1192/69, art. 14(1), OJ, 1969, L 156/8: OJ, 1970, L 63/17, L 126/20, L 126/24;
   (g) by virtue of Council Reg. 1172/68, OJ, 1968, L 194/1 art. 12(1); Commission Reg. 358/69, OJ, 1969, L 53/1: OJ, 1971, L 7/10–13, L 155/2–5, L 182/10, L 182/14, L 182/17.
2 Reg. 11, art. 4(1), OJ, 1960, 1121, now prohibits all discrimination in tariffs and conditions for the same type of goods in respect of the same routes on the ground of the place of origin or destination of the goods so transported. See also Commission Recommendation 14 June

[*footnote continued on next page*

> interested member states *decides* within the ambit
> of the regulations issued in virtue of art. 75(3)
> for the same type of goods in respect of the same
> routes on the ground of the place of origin or
> destination of the goods so transported
> (art. 79(4)).

Another prohibition affects disguised subvention consisting in the imposition within the Community of tariffs and conditions other than competitive tariffs (art. 80(3))[1] by a member state upon transport undertakings which aid or protect individual enterprises or industries (art. 80 (3)).[2] This provision aims at suppressing governmental interference of a discriminatory character in favour of particular enterprises or industries; it does not touch tariffs and conditions affecting goods to be supplied to all industries, nor any imposed tariffs on social grounds, such as those in favour of workers, of families with many children or disabled persons.

> *Measure:* Commission, of its own motion or on application
> by a member state after consulting interested
> member states, examines the tariffs and
> conditions having regard, *inter alia*, to
> considerations involving regions, underdeveloped
> areas, political purposes and to the effect of these
> tariffs and conditions upon the position of various
> transport undertakings—Decision (art. 80(2)).

The principle of non-discrimination is thus not without exceptions. Moreover, in conformity with the general provisions on subventions, (arts. 92–94)[3] aids, if granted by the state or with means provided by the budget, are compatible with the Treaty in the following circumstances: they are lawful, if they serve to co-ordinate transport, which is the case whenever a better co-operation or the mutual integration of transport is supported;[4] they are also lawful if they represent the counterpart of the supply of services by what has been called a "public service" (art. 77).[5]

1961, OJ, 1961, 975, 1148. For the place of the Decision of 21 March 1962, OJ, 1962, 720 in the general scheme see Rodière in *Ganshof van der Meersch*, p. 781, No. 1939, who stresses its interim character.

1 For the meaning of this term see *Mégret*, Vol. III, p. 272.

2 The wording of art. 80(1) ". . . involving any element of support or protection in the interest of one or more enterprises" leaves it open whether the measure must not only have the effect but also the purpose of supporting or protecting any enterprise or industry.

3 See Council Reg. 1107/70, art. 2, OJ, 1970, L 130/1.

4 Reg. 1107/70, art. 3 (above, n. 3): co-ordination of transport if the aid compensates for additional charges, compared with other transport, arising out of Reg. 1192/69 (above, p. 181, n. 1(e)) or for charges or costs of infrastructure, which other transport does not support, or for the development of research and techniques intended for the more economic use of transport.

5 The French text which mentions *"remboursement de certaines servitudes inhérentes à la notion de service public"* is clearer than the German version which runs *"die der Abgeltung bestimmter*

Such are exceptionally low tariffs or rates required for social, demographic or public reasons or the maintenance of uneconomic lines.[1]

The measures contemplated in arts. 75(1), 79 and 80 must always take into account, in determining tariffs and conditions in the field of transport, the economic position of the transport undertakings involved (art. 78, second sentence). This does not mean that a study must be made of the profit and loss account of every enterprise, but only that a basic average must be ascertained which must also take into account the extent of outstanding liabilities.

A number of collateral provisions serve the purpose of bringing about a stabilisation and gradual reduction of frontier charges (art. 81),

> *Measure:* Commission, recommendation to member
> states (art. 81(3)),

to legalise certain measures of assistance in favour of the economy of some parts of Germany suffering economic disadvantages (art. 82, see also art. 92(2)(c)), and to facilitate the work of the Commission in the field of transport by setting up an Advisory Committee on Transport (art. 83).[2]

III IMPLEMENTATION

The general and vague character of the provisions on transport required a concentrated effort by the Commission to identify and define in some detail the objectives of this part of the Treaty. The Commission achieved this in two stages.

First, it submitted a Memorandum.[3] This analysed the legal and economic foundations of transport in the EEC,[4] suggested a series of

---

dem Begriff des öffentlichen Dienstes zusammenhängender Leistungen entsprechen"; cp. Fulda, (1963) 12 A.J.C.L. 303, at p. 327.

"*Obligations de service public*" are now defined by Council Reg. 1191/69, art. 2. OJ, 1969, L 156/1 as "duties which an enterprise would not assume, or would not assume to the same extent or under the same conditions, if it relied on its own commercial interests (art. 2(1)) . . . the duty to operate a service to transport and to charge tariffs (art. 2(2)) . . . take . . . all measures necessary to ensure a transport service which complies with rigid rules about continuity, regularity and size . . . to ensure the operation of ancillary services . . . to maintain routes and material . . . in excess of the needs of the area as a whole (art. 2(3)) . . . to accept and to carry all transport . . . at rates and conditions . . . which are fixed (art. 2 (4)) . . . to apply fixed rates fixed . . . by superior order contrary to the commercial interests of the enterprise (art. 2(5))".

1 See Council Reg. 1191/69, OJ, 1969, L 156/1. The cases in which aid may be granted are now set out authoritatively in Council Reg. 1107/70, art. 3, OJ, 1970, L 130/1 (co-ordination of transport, reimbursement for obligations inherent in public service).

2 For the constitution of this Committee see Council Decision 15 September 1958, OJ, 1958, 509, amended 22 June 1964, OJ, 1964, 1602.

3 *Memorandum sur l'Orientation à donner à la Politique Commune des Transports* (10 April 1961), Doc. VII Com. (61) 50 final, Brussels 1962.

4 It finds transport to be an industry of imperfect competition, showing a lack of elasticity of offer and demand, and subject to the intervention of public authorities.

approaches and goals,[1] but did not make concrete proposals for their realisation.

Secondly, the Commission submitted a Programme.[2] This singled out seven areas and outlined the action required and proposed in respect of each of them. The areas were—

(a) access to markets in the EEC;
(b) elaboration and control of tariffs;
(c) harmonisation of fiscal, social and technical provisions;
(d) co-ordination of investments;
(e) general organisation of transport;
(f) implementation of arts. 79, 80, 81, 84 (2);
(g) transport costs.

A first reading of the Programme indicates, once again, the disparate and fragmented tasks facing the Council and the Commission. The subsequent developments bear out this analysis, for the Council and the Commission have attacked piecemeal the numerous, mainly technical, problems arising in the various branches of transport. Their basis is to be found in Council Decisions 65/271 of 13 May 1965[3] and 67/790 of 14 December 1967.[4] The solution provided for each individual problem, added to all the others, will probably lead in the end to an integrated system of transport throughout the EEC, but the beginning must be to render transport across the frontiers a branch of commerce which enjoys the benefit of equality of treatment and the challenge of competition. As a result it is only possible to draw attention in respect of each topic selected, and subsequently regulated, by the Council and the Commission, to the measures taken hitherto and to indicate briefly their bearing upon transport in general. The measures were mostly taken by virtue of arts. 75, 79, 99 and 235.[5]

---

1   Co-ordination of the various branches of transport, harmonisation of particular types of transport, equality of treatment (price, conditions, taxes, aids), financial autonomy, freedom of action, free choice for users, co-ordination of investments.

2   *Programme d'Action en Matière Politique Commune des Transports*, Doc. VII. Com. (62) 88 final, Brussels, 23 May 1962.

3   OJ, 1965, 1500; for the earlier Council Decision of 21 March 1962, OJ, 1962, 720, see above, p. 180, n. 1.

4   OJ, 1967, No. 322, p. 4.

5   **(i) Access to markets in the EEC.**

   (a) *Establishment:* occupations serving transport and travel agents, hauliers serving transport and travel agents: Proposed Council Directives of 21 December 1965, OJ, 1966, 1095, 1099 (see also OJ, 1966, 3475, 3477; 1967, 284, 286) submitted finally as proposed Council Directives of 31 March 1970, OJ, 1970, C 72/10–17. Non-wage earning occupations serving transport of persons by road or goods by road. Non-wage earning occupations serving transport of persons and goods by waterways (see above, p. 145, n. *s.v.* Transport Industry).

   (b) *Goods:* Council Directive, 23 July 1962, OJ, 1962, 2005 amended by Council Directive 19 December 1972, OJ, 1972, L 291/155; common acccess without quotas or licenses; frontier transport; casual to and from airports if change of route as well as baggage; mail; damaged vehicles, refuse and manure, animal carcasses, bees and fish for stocking; human remains.

(c) *Waterways*: Commission Proposal, 29 November 1967 on free access of transport of goods by waterways, OJ, 1968, C 95/1, 100/1.

(ii) Elaboration and control of tariffs

Commission proposal for forked tariffs, 10 May 1963, OJ, 1964, 1687, 2652; see also Council, 22 June 1965, Commission, 27 October 1965, OJ, 1966, 361.

Council Reg. 1174/68, 30 July 1968, OJ, 1968, L 194/1, amended by Council Reg. 293/70 16 February 1970, OJ, 1970, L 40/1; 2826/72; OJ, 1972, L 298/12: forked tariffs for road traffic (bracket rate); 16 February 1970, OJ, 1970, L 40; for proposed amendments see OJ, 1972, C 94/25, 113/12; 131/12.

Commission Reg. 358/69, 26 February 1969, OJ, 1969, L 53/1.

Council Reg. 1192/69, 26 June 1969, OJ, 1969, L 156/8: railway accounts.

Council Directive, 8 December 1969, OJ, 1969, L 323/7: statistics.

(iii) Harmonisation of provisions relating to transport

General: Council Decision 21 March 1962, OJ, 1962, 720: consultation concerning new measures; Council Decision 65/271, 13 May 1965, OJ, 1965, 1500: harmonisation of certain rules affecting competition in the field of transport by road, rail and waterways; double taxation of vehicles, uniform system of tax/subsidies for public service routes; approximation of working conditions.

(a) *Fiscal*

Council Directive 68/297 of 19 July 1968, OJ, 1968, L 175/5: uniform rules of admission free of duty of fuel in tanks of utility vehicles (for transport of more than nine persons).

Council Directives 67/227 of 11 April 1967, OJ, 1967, 1301: value added tax, 67/228 of 11 April 1967, OJ, 1967, 1303.

(b) *Social*: Proposed Council Reg.—access to profession of road haulage undertakers of

    (1) goods: 15 June 1967, 67/630, OJ, 1967, No. 254/3;

    (2) persons: 17 July 1967, OJ, 1968, C 95/39;

    (3) waterways: 29 November 1967, OJ, 1968, C 95/1.

Council Reg. 543/69, 25 March 1969, OJ, 1969, L 77/51 modified by Regs. 514/72, 515/72, of 28 February 1972, OJ, 1972, L 67/1/11: harmonisation of social provisions on road traffic (age, team, periods of work, rest). For the relationship of Reg. 543/69 to the European Road Transport Agreement and of the competence of the Commission or the member states to conclude the necessary agreements see *EEC Commission* v. *EEC Council* (1971), 17 Rec. 263.

Council Reg. 1463/70, 20 July 1970, OJ, 1970, L 164/1: control device, implementing Reg. 543/69.

Commission Dec. 70/325 of 18 June 1970 implementing Council Reg. 543/69, art. 17(1) & (2), OJ, 1970, L 140/20.

Proposed Council Decision 11 February 1971, OJ, 1971, C 37/5 amending Council Reg. 543/69, art. 14.

Council Reg. 1191/69, 26 June 1969, OJ, 1969, L 156/1: obligations inherent in notion of public service.

Commission Decision 65/362, 5 July 1965, OJ, 1965, 2184: Consultative Committee for Social Problems of Road Transport.

Commission Decision 67/745, 28 November 1967, OJ, 1967, No. 297/13: same, inland waterways, amended by Commission Decision 70/326, OJ, 1970, L 140/24.

Council Directive 72/166, 24 April 1972, OJ, 1972, L 103/1: third party motor car insurance; amended Council Directive 72/430, OJ, 1972, L 291/162.

Council Reg. 1107/70, OJ, 1970, L 130/1 (implementing Council Reg. 1191/69).

Commission Decision 72/366, 16 October 1972, OJ, 1972, L 250/16, modifying model of account, Reg. 543/69.

(c) *Technical*: See Council Resolution, 28 May 1969, OJ, 1969, C 76/1. Commission proposal of a Directive concerning the harmonisation of the weight and dimensions of utility vehicles. 1965 Bull EEC No. 2, p. 40, No. 3, p. 42, No. 5, p. 31, No. 6, p. 56; 1970, No. 3, p. 71, No. 7, p. 60; 1972, No. 7, p. 67.

Council Directive 70/156 of 6 February 1970, OJ, 1970, L 42/1: approximation of laws on acceptance of motor vehicles on application of manufacturer.

Council Directive 70/157 of 6 February 1970, OJ, 1970, L 42/16: approximation of laws on noise level and silencers of motor vehicles.   *[footnote continued on next page*

Council Directive 70/220, 20 March 1970, OJ, 1970, L 76/1: approximation of laws on pollution by exhausts of internal combustion engines in motor vehicles.

Council Directive 70/221 of 30 March 1970, OJ, 1970, L 76/23: approximation of laws concerning fuel tanks and rear protection in motor vehicles.

Council Directive 70/222 of 20 March 1970, OJ, 1970, L 76/25: placement and attachment of number plates at the rear of motor vehicles and trailers.

Council Directive 70/311 of 8 June 1970, OJ, 1970, L 133/10: approximation of laws on the steering mechanism of motor vehicles and trailers, amended OJ, 1970, L 196/14.

Council Directive 70/387 of 27 July 1970, OJ, 1970, L 176/5: approximation of laws on doors of motor vehicles and trailers.

Council Directive 70/388 of 27 July 1970, OJ, 1970, L 176/12: approximation of laws on acoustic warning instruments.

Council Directive 71/127, 1 March 1971, OJ, 1971, L 68/1: approximation of laws on motor vehicles' rear mirrors.

Council Directive 71/320, 26 July 1971, OJ, 1971, L 202/37: approximation of laws—brakes on motor vehicles, made in virtue of art. 100.

Council Directive 72/245, 20 June 1972, OJ, 1972, L 152/15: radio-electric interference with electrical equipment of motor cars.

Council Directive 72/306, 2 August 1972, OJ. 1972, L 190/1: pollution by Diesel engines in motor vehicles.

Proposed Directive concerning approximation of laws on motor vehicles for lighting and signalling of trailer, OJ,, 1968, C123/28.

Proposed Directive 65/424 concerning approximation of laws on motor vehicles—indicators, 26 July 1965, OJ, 1965, 2565 made in virtue of art. 100 EEC.

(iv) Co-ordination of investment

Council Decision 66/161, 28 February 1966, OJ, 1966, 583.

(v) General organization of transport

Council Directive 65/269, 13 May 1965, OJ, 1965, 1469: authorization of transport by road—national jurisdiction—EEC model.

Council Reg. 117/66, 28 July 1966, OJ, 1966, 2688, following OJ, 1965, 905: international transport of persons by bus (more than nine persons including driver, regular, shuttle, occasional; own workers = free).

Commission Reg. 1016/68, OJ, 1968, L 173/8 (documents of control, Reg. 117/66).

Commission Reg. 212/66, 16 December 1966, OJ, 1966, 3949: transport of own workers; documents of control.

Proposed Decision, 23 July 1968, OJ 1968, C 123: adaptation of bilateral contingents.

Council Reg. 1018/68, 19 July 1968, OJ, 1968, L 175/13: community quota for carriage of goods by road (not interior traffic) supplemented by Council Reg. 2829/72, OJ. 1972, L 298/16.

Commission Reg. 1224/68, 9 August 1968, OJ, 1968, L 204 (implementing arts. 4, 5 of Reg. 1018/68).

Council Reg. 542/69, 18 March 1969, OJ, 1969, L 77/1: transit within EEC (art. 235).

Commission Reg. 1617/69, 31 July 1969, OJ, 1969, L 212: form of transit declaration.

Proposed Reg., 27 January 1970, OJ, 1970, C 33: shuttle services, autocars.

Commission Decision 70/41, 19 December 1969, OJ 1970, L 13/13.

Commission Reg. 1279/71, 17 June 1971, OJ, 1971, L 132/33, implementing Council Reg. 542/69, art. 58 (transit documents).

Council Reg. 516/72, 28 February 1972, OJ, 1972, L67/13: shuttle services—buses—inter-state.

Commission Reg. 304/71, OJ, 1971, L 35/31 transit procedure—merchandise carried by railway.

Commission Reg. 1226/71, OJ, 1971, L 129/1—transit procedure—merchandise.

Council Reg. 517/72, 28 February 1972, OJ, 1972, L 67/19: (line buses, inter-state services).

(vi) Implementation of arts 79, 80, 81(2)

(a) Art. 79. Council Reg. 11, 27 June 1960, OJ, 1960, 1121: abolition of discrimination in transport charges and conditions. Commission Proposal 29 October 1965, OJ, 1966, 964—same.

(b) Art. 80. See e.g. Commission Decisions: Italy, 16 February 1962, OJ, 1962, 1229, 1232, 1234, 1237, 1239 (Italian railways special tariff); extended by a Commission Decision 31 March

1965 (France) 1965 EEC Bull., No. 6, p. 29; 29 June 1965 (France), 1965 EEC Bull., No. 8, p. 56; 15 December 1965, 1966, EEC Bull., No. 2, p. 36. *Germany*, OJ, 1962, 2371, 2719; Decision 63/117, OJ, 1963, 365; Decision 71/87 CECA OJ, 1971, L 36. *France*, OJ, 1964, 710, 885, 728; 1965, 1100, 2205; 1966, 433; 1970, L 129/21, L 189/15.

(*c*) *Art.* 81. See *e.g.* Commission reply OJ, 1964, 2453.

(*d*) *Art.* 84(2). See European Parliament, 14 May 1965, OJ, 1965, 1702 (air); 25 March 1963, OJ, 1963 1287 (pipe lines).

(vii) Transport costs

Council Decision 65/270, 13 May 1965, OJ, 1965, 1473: enquiry on costs of infrastructure for road etc. transport—see also Council Decision 64/389, 22 June 1964, OJ, 1964, 1598; Commission Decision 65/258, 27 April 1965, OJ, 1965, 1405: survey on utilisation of infrastructure of transport. For the completion of this work see 1969 EEC Bull., p. 62. Council Reg. 1108/70, 4 June 1970, OJ, 1970, L 130/4: accounts concerning costs of infrastructure for rail, road, etc.

10

Cartels and Monopolies—
The Law of the Member States

(Articles 85–94)

The liberalisation of trade set in motion by the states, members of the EEC, would remain ineffective if the freedom guaranteed to producers and traders could be exploited by groups through monopolies, restrictive practices and dumping, and by member states themselves by setting up public enterprises or by providing privileges or subsidies. Consequently the Treaty prohibits such activities (arts. 3(f), 85–94).

The movement against cartels and monopolies on the *international* plane is not entirely new. The Havana Charter of 24 March 1948, Ch. V (arts. 46–54) embodies a first attack on this problem, but the GATT did not include the relevant sections. The efforts of the Economic and Social Council of the United Nations (1951–1955) were not successful,[1] and the Draft of a European Convention on Restrictive Practices (1951) never came into fruition.[2] Only the Treaty setting up the ECSC[3] prohibits every discrimination between producers, purchasers and consumers, and forbids under pain of nullity any arrangements of a restrictive character;[4] monopolistic concentrations require the consent of the High Authority (now the Commission)[5] which can also intervene where previously established monopolies are found to exist.[6]

I Germany

Among the member states, Germany possesses the most elaborate legislation against monopolies and restrictive practices.[7] In principle

---

1 Resolution 375 (XIII) of 13 September 1951; see Solomon, Hearings before the Sub-committee on Anti-trust and Monopoly . . . 89 Congress. Second Session, April 20–August 30 1966, at pp. 456, 457; Focsaneanu, 1966 Rev. M.C., 862, at p. 868.
2 Hearings (above, n. 1), p. 456, prepared by the Council of Europe. For efforts made by OECD, see *ibid.*, p. 457; Edwards, *ibid.*, p. 314; Fikentscher, *ibid.*, p. 425; Zimmerman, *ibid.*, p. 494; Focsaneanu, 1966 Rev. M.C. 862, at p. 868.
3 Arts. 4(b), 60(1), 63(1).
4 Arts. 65(1), (4), (5).
5 Art. 66.
6 Art. 66(7).
7 Gesetz gegen Wettbewerbsbeschränkungen (GWB) of 27 July 1957, 1957 I BGBl 1081, amended by a Law of 15 September 1965, 1965 I BGBl 1963, republished 1966 I BGBl 37, and as further amended by Law of 20 May 1968 art. 85(1), 1968 I BGBl 444; Law of 24

restrictive practices are prohibited, subject to exemptions in virtue of special permission[1] and to general exemptions in virtue of the particular character of the cartel agreement (conditions, rebate, standards, rationalisation or export cartel)[2] which are only illegal if they constitute an abuse of economic power. Both horizontal and vertical agreements are affected, but certain vertical agreements (concerning branded goods, publishers) are exempted;[3] agreements which force the purchaser to dispose of the goods in a certain manner, not to deal with third parties or to buy other goods unconnected with the purchase may be prohibited[4] and licensing agreements, if unreasonable, are void.[5] Abusive operations of market-controlling enterprises[6] can be declared void,[7] and the creation, through agreements, of a merger of a group of enterprises must be registered, if one or all of the enterprises together control 20 per cent of the market,[8] or are predominant as to their labour force (10,000 plus) or turnover (500 millions) or capital (1,000 millions) during the year before the merger.[9] Discriminatory action for the purpose of achieving results prohibited by the Act or by an order of the Cartel Office is illegal.[10]

II FRANCE[11]

The French Penal Code,[12] which prohibits certain obnoxious combinations, has largely remained a dead letter. However, the basic Decree 45–1483 of 30 June 1945 amended by the Decree 53–704 of 9 August 1953,[13] supplemented and amended by Decree 58–545 of 24 June 1958 and Decree 59–1004 of 17 August 1959,[14] the Law 63–628 of 2 July 1963 and the Ordinance 67–835 of 28 September 1967 laid the foundations.

Unlike in German law, the French regulations form part of the law on the control of prices, and any contraventions are punished as criminal offences. On the other hand, being built around the element of price

---

May 1968, art. 62, 1968 I BGBl 503; Law of 22 July 1969 art. 1, 1969 I BGBl 901; see Schapiro (1962) 62 Col. L.R. 1, 201 and, for a shorter account, Fikentscher, Hearings (above, n. 2), at pp. 429–438.

1 Paras. 1, 4, 7, 8.
2 Paras. 2, 3, 5, 5a, 6.
3 Para. 16.
4 Para. 18.
5 Para. 20.
6 For the definition see para. 22(1)(2).
7 Para. 22(4).
8 Para. 23.
9 Para. 23(1).
10 Paras. 25–27.
11 Goldstein, (1958) 12 SW.L.J. 405; (1958) 37 Texas L.R. 188; (1963) 11 A.J.C.L. 515; Riesenfeld, (1960) 48 Calif. L.R. 574; Bergsten, (1960) 49 Ia.L.R. 42; Reboul, (1966) 19 Vanderbilt L.R. 303; Starr, (1965) 14 A.J.C.L. 98.
12 Arts. 419, 420.
13 JO, 10 August 1953.
14 For the procedure see Decree 45–1483 of 30 June 1945; 54–97 of 27 January 1954 as amended by 59–1004 of 17 August 1959.

formation and control, they lay less stress on the fact that an agreement or any concerted action exists, except in one instance.[1]

Producers, traders, persons engaged in industry or craftsmen[2] must not

    (a) refuse to sell to prospective buyers or withhold their services from prospective customers, if the request is normal and made in good faith, upon the customary trade terms and to their best ability, provided that the transaction is not illegal;[3]

    (b) impose habitually discriminatory or increased prices unless justified by economic reasons;[4]

    (c) require the buyer to purchase at the same time other goods or a minimum quantity or to order a supply of unconnected services;[5]

    (d) individually or by concerted action fix, maintain or impose minimum resale prices or trading margins by means of lists or scales of charges, unless an exemption is granted by the minister responsible for economic affairs.[6] Such exemptions may only be given for a limited time and on grounds which are indicated by way of illustration, such as novelty of goods or services, the exercise of rights under a patent, licence or registered design, or if the specification requires a warranty of quality or condition or an initial publicity campaign;[7]

    (e) enter into cartel agreements of the kind envisaged by art. 59bis. This prohibits all concerted action, express or implied, which *either* has the object *or* may have the effect of interfering with full competition by hindering the reduction of production costs or by encouraging the artificial increase of prices.[8]

French law is thus concerned with price fixing and with agreements having this purpose only. Exceptions are provided for statutory cartels and for those which are shown to improve or to extend the market for the products concerned by, or for the purpose of, rationalisation and specialisation.[9] It may be necessary for the authorities concerned to balance the harmful and the beneficial effects of the combines concerned.

---

1   Decree 45–1483 as amended, arts. 37(3), 59bis.
2   *I.e.* a person who by reason of his calling is able to sell the product; see Circular of 31 March 1960, Tit. II, s. I, para. 1.
3   Decree 45–1483 as amended, art. 37(1)(a) as amended by the decrees mentioned above. For a commentary see the Circular of 31 March 1960 (above, n. 2). The Circular is not a regulation. Conseil d'Etat 5 May 1961, *Soc. A. Quillet et al.*, [1961] Rec. Lebon 297, D. 1961, J., 407; 1961 Gaz. Pal. 411; 1961 II J.C.P. No. 12, 135bis.
4   Decree 45–1483 as amended, art. 37(1)(a).
5   Decree 45–1483 as amended, art. 37(1)(c).
6   Decree 45–1483 as amended, art. 37(4); Decree 58–545. This provision affects primarily vertical price maintenance, but it touches also horizontal agreements. For loss leaders see the Act 63–628 of 2 July 1963, below, p. 191.
7   Decree 45–1482 as amended, art. 37(4). This provision is less generous than that of German law exempting price maintenance for branded goods.
8   Decree 45–1483 as amended, art. 37(3), 59bis.
9   Decree 45–1483 as amended, art. 59ter.

While the other prohibitions against price fixing are visited by criminal proceedings following an investigation, warning, persuasion or agreed penalty administered by the Economic Investigation Branch of the Price and Economic Investigation Directorate and of the Director General of Prices and Economic Investigations, combines are subject to the Technical Commission on Combines[1] to whom the Minister of Economic Affairs may refer any matter, after an enquiry by the authorities generally charged with the investigation of prices. The advice of the Commission is not binding on the Minister, who can either decide to start criminal proceedings[2] or may invite the interested parties to take certain recommended action.[3]

The Act 63–628 of 2 July 1963 adds a prohibition against loss leader selling, except for seasonal products, goods no longer in demand because they have fallen out of fashion or which can be obtained at a lower price on restocking or reduced in price in order to equal the lower price charged for the same product by another trader.[4]

III BELGIUM

The law of 27 May 1960,[5] otherwise than the German and French legislation which prohibits, or requires the licensing of, certain agreements embodying restrictive practices or which, respectively, influences the free movement of prices and (in Germany) controls the formation of monopolies, aims, quite generally, at the abuse of economic power.

This power is affected, whether it is exercised by a natural person, a corporation or by a combination of either of these, through industrial, commercial, agricultural or financial activities, if it occupies a dominant influence over supplies of merchandise, capital markets or over the price or quality of specific merchandise or services.[6] The Act aims, thus, in one article, at controlling both monopolies and restrictive practices.

The power is abused if the public interest is prejudiced by practices which distort or restrict the normal play of competition or which interfere either with the economic freedom of producers and distributors or with the development of production or trade.[7] Here the notion of "abuse" is defined by a number of objective tests which, once again, fit the operation of monopolies, horizontal and vertical price agreements, area agreements and the carving up of supplies of raw materials and the like, but prejudice must always be proved. The operation of these provisions is controlled by the Council for Economic Disputes[8] which, after an investigation,[9] must

---

1 Decree 68–1027 of 23 November 1968.
2 Decree 45–1483 as amended, art. 59*quater.*
3 Decree 45–1483 as amended, art. 59*quater*; Decree 68–1027, art. 21.
4 JO, 3 July 1963, 5915, 11 July 1963, 6243; D. 1963 Legisl. 196.
5 Mon. Belge. 22 June 1960, p. 4674; del Marmol and Fontaine, (1960–61) 109 U. Pa. L. Rev. 922.
6 Art. 1.
7 Art. 2.
8 Art. 3.
9 Arts. 4–8.

hear argument[1] and submit a reasoned opinion to the Minister of Economic Affairs.[2] He summons the parties who may either accept or refuse to follow the recommendations of the Minister.[3] In case of refusal a royal decree may embody the recommendations as administrative measures;[4] failure to comply with the decree is a punishable offence.[5]

IV NETHERLANDS

Dutch cartel legislation[6] is based on the assumption that a cartel, though potentially dangerous, is not *malum per se* and that unlimited competition is not necessarily identical with *bonum publicum*.[7] In this approach it comes near to the tacit assumption expressed in the Belgian legislation. Given this pragmatic approach, the control of cartel agreements and monopolies is not entrusted to the courts but to the authorities concerned with economic affairs.[8] Today the legal basis is to be found in the Economic Competition Act of 28 June 1956 as amended on 16 July 1958.[9] As distinct from the French and Belgian rules, Dutch law establishes a general duty to register any agreement or decision subject to private law to regulate economic competition between owners of enterprises[10] and thus appears to except concerted action;[11] exemption from notification must be granted to export cartels.[12] Certain agreements[13] may be declared void by royal decree, unless notified.[14] Conversely, if the number or the joint turnover of the enterprises, parties to the cartel agreement, is considerably larger than that of the outsiders, the cartel agreement may be extended by governmental decision to the non-participating sector, if the general interest of the Dutch community as a whole coincides with the interest expressed in the cartel agreement,[15] provided always that an application is made to this effect[16] and subject always to the power of the Minister concerned to exempt individual enterprises from the binding force of the extended cartelisation.[17]

On the other hand, certain types of clauses in cartel agreements may be

---

1   Arts. 9–12.
2   Art. 13.
3   Art. 14.
4   Art. 14.
5   Art. 18 ff.
6   Ter Kuile, 1962 I.C.L.Q. Suppl. 4, at p. 40; Smit (Hearings, above, p. 188, n. 1), at pp. 390–394; 401–402.
7   Law of 28 June 1956 s. 16; the public interest matters: arts. 10, 16.
8   The Cartel Decree of 1941 had a limited effect in respect of exclusive dealings and prices; it did not operate so as to suspend a cartel but only by declaring it to be ineffective.
9   Stb. 1956, p. 1061; 1958, p. 412, further amended in 1971.
10 Art. 2.
11 Art. 1(4), unless in writing.
12 Art. 4(1).
13 *Quaere* whether they must be in writing.
14 Art. 5(1).
15 Art. 6(1).
16 Art. 7(1).
17 Art. 8.

declared void by royal decree,[1] with power to exempt,[2] and any attempt to embody such clauses in agreements or to enforce them is ineffective.[3] Moreover, cartel agreements which in the opinion of the Minister are contrary, wholly or in part, to the general interest, or are being applied in a manner contrary to that interest, may be declared non-binding, as a whole or in part, either conditionally or unconditionally,[4] and thereupon the agreement must not be observed or enforced[5] and may, in urgent cases, be suspended.[6]

Monopolies are regulated if they conflict with the general interest.[7] They may be enjoined to refrain from any practices to be determined, to supply goods or services according to market prices and conditions, to omit exclusive dealings or to abstain from requiring purchasers to buy other goods at the same time.[8] Thus vertical agreements are caught by the provisions against monopolies. Sanctions are provided.[9] In coming to a decision the Minister is assisted by a committee.[10] An appeal lies to the ordinary courts.[11] Foreign cartel and monopoly decisions or orders must not be deliberately observed in the Netherlands, unless the Dutch Government grants an exemption or dispensation.[12] This provision, which has its counterpart in the English Shipping Contracts and Commercial Documents Act 1964 serves the purpose of offering a solution for the problem raised in *British Nylon Spinners Ltd.* v. *ICI*.[13]

V ITALY[14]

During the Fascist era which favoured the corporate state, compulsory[15] and voluntary[16] associations were encouraged, but since compulsory associations exist by special statute only it is necessary here to consider solely voluntary cartels. These are governed, in principle, by the Civil

---

1 Art. 10.

2 Art 12(1).

3 Art. 15(1).

4 Art. 19.

5 Art. 21.

6 Art. 23(1).

7 Art. 24.

8 Art. 24; cp. Order in Council of 24 July 1962 concerning arbitration clauses contained in such agreements, and of 1 April 1964 (resale price maintenance), amended 31 August 1964).

9 Arts. 26, 27.

10 Economic Competition Committee; art. 28.

11 Art. 33.

12 Art. 39.

13 [1952] 2 All E.R. 780 (C.A.); [1953] Ch. 19; [1954] 3 All E.R. 88 (Ch.D.); [1955] Ch. 37; Shipping Contracts and Commercial Documents Act 1964, and see Mann, (1971 I) 111 Hague Rec. 107, at p. 164.

14 Venturini, (1964) 13 I.C.L.Q., 617; Torre, (1965–66) 14 A.J.C.L. 489.

15 Law No. 834 of 16 June 1932, subject to regulations which were never published. Probably the law is therefore ineffective. See Venturini, above, n. 14, at pp. 650–652 with cases.

16 Supplemented by Legislative Decree No. 1396 of 13 April 1936, perpetuated by Law No. 961 of 22 April 1937. *Quaere* whether this legislation remains effective today.

Code[1] which lays down elaborate machinery for the registration, authorisation and dissolution of such associations and for the creation of compulsory associations. The Civil Code[2] also prohibits to a certain extent the creation of interrelated companies and seeks to control monopolies by imposing the duty of general dealing without discrimination.[3] In so far as voluntary associations are concerned, the provisions of the Civil Code are self-executing.[4] Restraints of competition must not violate the interests of the national economy,[5] but in the absence of any such harm, cartels are permissible, subject to restrictions concerning the form of the agreement,[6] its duration[7] and the geographical and substantive range. Special rules apply to trade associations for the co-ordination of production and commerce.

VI   LUXEMBURG

After legislation in 1965 on the lines of the French law prohibiting price fixing and refusal to deal, a law against restrictive commercial practices was introduced on 17 June 1970.[8] It aims at agreements, decisions between associations of enterprises and concerted practices having the object or effect of preventing, restricting or distorting competition and the abusive exploitation of a dominant market position by one or more enterprises. It draws on the experience gained by the EEC in administering the relevant provisions of the Treaty.

VII   DENMARK

The Danish Monopolies and Restrictive Practices Control Act No. 102 of 31 March 1955[9] emphasises the need for control rather than for strict legal rules in order to prevent unreasonable prices and business conditions and in order to secure the best possible conditions for the freedom of trade.[10] The Act applies to trades[11] in which competition, either in Denmark as a whole or in certain areas, is restricted with the result that enterprises exercise, or are potentially in a position to exercise, a substantial influence

---

1   Arts. 2596–2620.
2   Arts. 2359–60.
3   Art. 2597.
4   As regards compulsory associations, art. 111 of the Introductory Rules of the Civil Code refers to regulations as yet not made.
5   Art. 2595. See also art. 41 of the Constitution of 1947.
6   In writing.
7   Five years.
8   Memorial 1970, Part A, p. 892.
9   As amended on 25 May 1956, 6 July 1957, 10 June 1960, 4 June 1965 and 2 April 1971; Van Eyben, GRUR, 1964, Ausl. 300.
10   Arts. 1, 3.
11   Wages and labour conditions are excluded, as are price conditions and business activities which by virtue of special statutory provisions are regulated or approved by the authorities having jurisdiction in this sphere; see art. 2 (2).

on prices, production, distribution or on the terms of transport.[1] Thus both restrictive practices and monopolies are covered.

For this purpose, all agreements between enterprises and decisions of associations of enterprises must be registered with the Monopolies Control Authority, if the agreements or decisions exercise, or are potentially in a position to exercise, a substantial influence on prices, production, distribution or on the terms of transport either in Denmark as a whole or in certain areas.[2] Individual enterprises or combinations which exercise a similar influence must register as such, if so requested by the Monopolies Control Authority; they must also, upon request, register any restrictive practices adopted by themselves alone.[3] Thus, once again, monopolies are also covered. The purpose of registration is to ensure publicity and is administrative only,[4] for any such agreements or decisions are valid and enforceable in the courts, if registered within the prescribed time limit,[5] with the exception of resale price maintenance agreements as well as decisions and business practices to this effect, which must not be enforced unless the Monopolies Control Authority has approved the agreements, decisions or practices.[6] It appears that by enjoining the parties not to enforce the agreements the legislature wished to confer upon them the character of recommendations only. All other types of agreements, etc., which in the opinion of the Monopolies Control Authority constitute a restrictive practice in the meaning of art. 2 of the Act and have as their effect unreasonable prices or business conditions or unreasonable restraint of trade or discrimination[7] as envisaged by art. 1 of the Act must be adjusted by way of negotiations.[8] If negotiations cannot serve this purpose, the Monopolies Control Authority may issue an order cancelling wholly or partly the agreement, decisions or practice concerned or prescribe the price, weight, measure or composition of the article be indicated; where freedom of trade is unreasonably restrained the Commission, as a measure of last resort, may order an enterprise to supply goods to particular buyers on its usual terms against cash or adequate security.[9] When all other means are insufficient or other measures are regarded as more efficient, the Monopolies Control Authority must report to the Minister of Commerce.[10]

---

1 Art. 2(1).

2 Arts. 6(1); 2(1); for details concerning registration see arts. 7, 9.

3 Art. 6(2); for the powers of the Authority see arts. 15–16; for its procedure and appeals against its decisions see arts. 17–18.

4 Failure to register is visited by penalties; see arts. 20, 22.

5 Art. 8.

6 Art. 10; approval is only to be given in special circumstances. See also art. 13 concerning compulsory invoicing of goods sold to or by resellers.

7 In determining whether prices are unreasonable, the conditions in enterprises must be taken into account which operate with comparable technical and commercial efficiency; see art. 11(2). For the procedure of enquiry see the Price Supervision Act No. 215 of 2 April 1971.

8 Art. 11(1).

9 Art. 12; for a general order requiring the marking of prices in a particular trade see art. 13.

10 Art. 14.

VIII IRELAND

The Irish Restrictive Trade Practices Act 1953[1] does not render restrictive practices illegal and includes monopolies or oligopolies in its operation. A body known as the Fair Trade Commission[2] watches over the administration of unfair trade practices. These practices are defined[3] as measures, rules, agreements or acts put into effect or intended to be put into effect by a person alone or in combination or agreement, express or implied, with others or through a merger, trust, cartel, monopoly or otherwise which limit unreasonably or restrain free and fair competition or are likely to have this effect; unreasonably restrain trade; unjustly eliminate a trade competitor or are likely to have this effect; unjustly enhance the price of goods or promote unfairly the advantage of suppliers or distributors of goods at the expense of the public; secure a substantial or complete control of the supply or distribution of goods, or of any class of goods, unfairly or contrary to the public interest, or are likely to secure such a control; without just cause prohibit or restrict the supply of goods to any person or class of persons or give preference in providing goods or in placing orders for their supply; restrict unjustly the exercise by a person of his freedom of choice as to what goods he will supply or distribute, or the area in which he will supply or distribute his goods, or are likely to have this effect; impose unjust or unreasonable conditions in connection with the supply or distribution of goods; exclude without good reason new entrants to any trade or industry, or are likely to have this effect; secure unjustly the territorial divisions of markets between particular persons or classes of persons to the exclusion of others, or are likely to have this effect; in any respect operate against the public interest or are not in accordance with the principles of social justice.

The Commission may issue rules concerning fair trading conditions with regard to the supply and distribution of certain goods or to the rendering of services in the course of carrying out a particular trade or business.[4] These rules do not have the force of law. The Commission may also promote enquiries into the conditions which obtain in regard to the supply and distribution of any kind of goods[5] or to services affecting such supply or distribution.[6]

The Commission must report to the minister if in its opinion any fair trading rules so established are not being observed, or if it has engaged in an enquiry. The report must state whether and, if so, how competition is restricted, trade is restrained or resale price mantenance is practised and whether, in the opinion of the Commission, this interference with competition or trade is unfair or operates against the public interest.[7] The

---

1 No. 14 of 1953; amended by the Restrictive Practices Amendment Act 1959 No. 37.
2 Section 2; and see the 1st Sched. for its organization.
3 Section 2 and 2nd Sched.
4 Section 4; for the procedure see s. 5; for the review of the operation of such rules see s. 6.
5 Section 7(1).
6 Section 7(5).
7 Section 8(1).

Commission may recommend that the minister should make an order in terms to be suggested by the Commission,[1] and the minister may make such an order relating to the goods covered by the report. The order may prohibit particular arrangements or agreements; the withholding of supplies of goods or services rendered in connection therewith from any particular class of persons; the giving of specified preferences in connection with the provision of goods or the placing of orders for their supply or the rendering of any such services; the imposition of specified conditions concerning the supply or distribution of goods or the rendering of such services; and may ensure the equitable treatment of all persons concerning the supply or distribution of such goods or the rendering of such services as well as the avoidance of unfair practices or may make such provision in regard to restrictive practices affecting the supply and distribution of goods or the rendering such services as the minister thinks fit.[2] If confirmed by Act of the Oireachtas, the order obtains the force of law.[3] Compliance with an order may be sought by means of an injunction,[4] and any contravention of an order constitutes a criminal offence.[5]

---

1 Section 8(2).
2 Section 9(1).
3 Section 9(3).
4 Section 11.
5 Section 12(1).

11

Cartels and Monopolies— Cartels in the EEC Treaty[1]

I THE SCHEME

While the individual laws on cartels remain in force in the countries of the EEC where trade within any one of the member states or between such a country and third states are concerned, the Treaty itself (arts. 85–91) provides overriding rules which apply within the limits indicated by arts. 85 and 86 to combinations and monopolies operating within the EEC beyond the limits of one state only. Thus the national laws on restrictive practices and monopolies and the Community law on the same subject can overlap;[2] in addition, Community law on cartels and monopolies may fall to be applied concurrently by the authorities of the Community (Commission and Court) and by national courts.[3] These aspects will be discussed after an examination of the relevant provisions of the Treaty and of the regulations made thereunder.

The provisions of the EEC Treaty are influenced by those of the ECSC Treaty, but they are more flexible than the latter (arts. 4(c), 65), especially in so far as subventions are concerned. At times their application may overlap, since the ECSC does not cover finished and semi-finished products. They are restricted in their sphere of application. The general rules of the EEC did not apply automatically to agriculture (art. 42) and to transport (arts. 77, 75(1)), but they have been extended to these areas,[4] and the provisions on competition themselves apply only with some modifications to enterprises which are charged with the execution of

---

1 See de Roux and Voillemot, *Le Droit de la Concurrence des Communautés Européennes* (2nd Edn., 1972); Honig, Brown, Gleiss, Hirsch, *Cartel Law of the EEC* (1963); Braun, Gleiss, Hirsch, *Le Droit des Ententes de la CEE* (1967); Oberdorfer, Gleiss, Hirsch, *Common Market Cartel Law* (1967); Gleiss–Hirsch, *EWG Kartellrecht* (2nd Edn., 1966); Graupner, *The Rules of Competition in the EEC* (1965); Deringer, *The Competition Law of the EEC* (1968); Deringer, *Das Wettbewerbsrecht der EWG* [1962–]; Deringer *et al.*, 1966 Rev. M.C. 39, at pp. 142, 197, 660, 706, 765, 818, 821; 1967 *ibid.* 38, at pp. 95, 261, 317, 415, 520, 579, 647; Plaisant, Franceschelli, Lassier, *Droit Européen de la Concurrence* (1966); Goldman, *Droit Commercial Européen* (1970), No. 218, p. 224—No. 579, p. 541; Stoufflet in Juriscl. Dr. Int., Fasc. 164 G; Cerexhe in *Ganshof van der Meersch* pp. 805–852, nos. 2001–2148; Ebb, (1967) 115 U. Pa. L. Rev. 855; Buxbaum (1961) 61 Col. L.R. 402; Cawthra, *Restrictive Agreements in the EEC* (1972); Jacobs, (1972) 88 L.Q.R. 483; Emmerich, 1971 EuR 295; Mégret, Vol. IV (1972).

2 See below, p. 226.

3 See below, p. 227; *Mailänder Zuständigkeit und Entscheidungsfreiheit nationaler Gerichte* (1965).

4 *Agriculture*: Reg. 26 of 4 April 1962, OJ, 1962, 993, amended by Reg. 49 of 29 June 1962, OJ, 1962, 1571, subject to exceptions (Reg. 26, art. 2)—see below, pp. 228 ff. *Transport*: Reg.

services of a general economic interest or have the character of a fiscal monopoly (art. 90(2)). In addition the rules do not apply where essential interests of security are involved in connection with the production of weapons, ammunition and war materials for specifically military purposes (art. 223(1)(b)).

During the early stages of the EEC two questions arose. The first was whether the provisions of the Treaty were self-executing or directly applicable and created individual rights enforceable in domestic courts. This was answered affirmatively in *De Geus* v. *Bosch*.[1] The second, which is closely related to the first, was whether prior to the enactment of the implementing regulations envisaged in art. 89, these provisions could be applied by domestic courts, as distinct from the organs of the EEC itself. The answer was again provided by the *Bosch* case[1] which held that before the promulgation of the implementing Reg. 17, municipal courts were alone competent (art. 88) to apply art. 85. Now that the relevant Reg. 17[2] has been promulgated, the jurisdiction of domestic courts in this field has been somewhat restricted,[3] except in so far as a violation of art. 85 may form a preliminary question in an action brought in contract or tort.[4]

Given the fact that the provisions against cartels contained in the Treaty (arts. 85–90) give rise primarily to proceedings before the Commission and the Court, it is proposed to discuss the position of these provisions in the domestic law of the member states at a later stage.[5] The Treaty itself covers all agreements between enterprises, all decisions of groups of enterprises[6] and all concerted practices[7] which are apt to affect trade between the member states *and* which have as their object or as their effect the prevention, restriction or distortion of competition within the Common Market (art. 85(1), 1st para.).

For the purposes of the ECSC Treaty (art. 65) an enterprise in the meaning of this article is an "organisation unitaire d'éléments personnels,

---

1017/68, OJ, 1968, L 175/1, replacing Reg. 141, OJ, 1962, 2741 and Reg. 165/65, OJ, 1965, 3141 which had postponed the application of arts. 85–90 to transport.

1 (1962), 8 Rec. 89, at pp. 102, 103; [1962] C.M.L.R. 1.

2 OJ, 1962, 204, supplemented by Commission Reg. 27/62, OJ, 1962, 1118, amended by Commission Reg. 153/62, OJ, 1962, 2918; Commission Reg. 99/63, OJ, 1963, 2268 (hearings), Council Reg. 19/65, OJ, 1965, 533; Commission Reg. 67/67, OJ, 1967, 849; Council Regs. 2822/71, OJ, 1971, L 285/49.

3 Reg. 17 art. 9(3); see below, p. 226; for the relationship between art. 85 and the corresponding provisions of domestic law in a domestic jurisdiction see below, p. 227.

4 See below, p. 205.

5 See below.

6 Such as associations of manufacturers or of wholesalers and retailers organized as unincorporated associations or as legal entities.

7 A concerted practice is a form of co-ordination between undertakings which, without going so far as to amount to an agreement properly so called, knowingly substitutes a practical co-operation between them for the risks of competition; apparent from the behaviour of the participants, to be gauged, *inter alia.*, from parallel behaviour. *ICI* v. *EEC Commission*, [1972] C.M.L.R. 557, at p. 622 (64–68); BASF, paras. 22–23; *Beyer*, paras. 25–26; *Geigy and Sandoz*, paras. 26–27; *Francolor*, paras. 51–55; *Mainkur*, paras. 64–68; *ACNA*, paras. 55–59; De Jong, 1971 Cah. Dr. Eur. 550.

matériels et immatériels, rattachés à un sujet juridiquement autonome, poursuivant d'une façon durable un but économique déterminé."[1] Thus the enterprise must be capable of acting (even if it has no legal personality, *e.g.* the German O.H.G. and other unincorporated associations), and it must be endowed with economic elements and purposes. The activity forming the object of the prohibition consists of express agreements, concurrent but separate determinations having an identical content or independent action geared to that of others. This definition may not apply without qualifications to the EEC Treaty where the mere fact that an entity is legally autonomous may not be sufficient to characterise it as an enterprise for the purpose of art. 85, if it is in fact controlled by another.[2] It is already clear that it does not include similar arrangements reached within a single unit of jurisdiction in which the distribution by the single branches has been integrated.[3]

(a) The agreements, decisions or concerted practices concerned must be apt to affect the trade (*i.e.* economic exchanges) between member states. Thus trade which is purely confined to the territory of a single member state[4] or which is restricted to the exchange of goods with countries other than member states,[5] is not normally[6] touched by the prohibition of art. 85. Nevertheless, if a domestic contract is part of a series of contracts of the same character binding to a small number of national producers an important number of retailers in the same country, this complex of agreements may in certain circumstances affect trade between the member states,[7] but the fact that one of the parties to the agreement is situated or resident outside the EEC does not exclude the operation of art. 85, if the agreement has an effect inside the Community.[8] The range is not purely geographical or jurisdictional, but functional in support of

---

1   *Kloeckner Werke* v. *High Authority* (1962), 8 Rec. 615, at p. 646; *Mannesmann* v. *High Authority* (1962), 8 Rec. 681, at pp. 701–706; *Soc. Nouvelles Usines de Pontlieue (SNUPAT)* v. *High Authority* (1961), 7 Rec. 99, at pp. 151–152; Kovar, 1963 Clunet 832, at pp. 838, 844, 850; see also Commission Decision of 18 June 1969, *Re Christiani and Nielsen*, OJ, 1969, L 165/2; 1969 Rev. Trim. Dr. Eur. 844, at p. 845; Goldman, *Droit Commercial Européen* (1970), No. 243, p. 252; Franceschelli, 1968 Rev. Trim. Dr. Eur. 538; Cerexhe in *Ganshof van der Meersch*, pp. 816–817, nos. 2017–2019; Stoufflet in Juriscl. Dr. Int. no. 9.

2   *Re Christiani and Nielsen* (above, n. 1); and see below, n. 3.

3   *Consten and Grundig* v. *EEC Commission*, (1966), 12 Rec. 429, at p. 493; [1966]; C.M.L.R. 418; *Italy* v. *EEC Council and Commission* (1966), 12 Rev. 563, at p. 592; [1969] C.M.L.R. 39 *Béguelin Import Co.* v. *SAGL Import Export* (1971), 17 Rec. 949, at p. 959 (8); [1972] C.M.L.R. 81.

4   *Bilger Söhne GmbH* v. *H. & M. Jehle* (1970), 16 Rec. 127, at p. 136 (5); *Brasserie de Haecht* v. *Wilkin-Janssen* (1967), 13 Rec. 525, at p. 537; [1968] C.M.L.R. 26.

5   See *Grossfillex*, 11 March 1964, OJ, 1964, 915; [1964] C.M.L.R. 237; DECA, 22 October 1964, OJ, 1964, 2761, and see below, p. 217, n. 1.

6   See below, p. 217, nn. 1, 2, but see the *Thin Paper Agreement*, 26 July 1972, OJ, 1972, L 182/24 II if export quotas to non-member states are attributed.

7   *Bilger* v. *Jehle* (1970), 16 Rec. 127, at p. 136 (5); *Brasserie de Haecht* v. *Wilkin-Janssen* (1967), 13 Rec. 525, at p. 537; [1968] C.M.L.R. 26; *Vereeniging van Cementhandelaaren*, 16 December 1971, OJ, 1972, L 13/34 at p. 41(17); *Dyestuffs*, 4 July 1969, OJ, 1969, L 195/11 at p. 16.

8   See *Béguelin Import Co.* v. *SAGL Import Export* (1971), 17 Rec. 949, at p. 959(11)–(14); [1972] C.M.L.R. 81.

integration.[1] For some time it was a matter of controversy whether trade between member states must be affected adversely, if art. 85(1) is to apply. The German, Italian and Dutch texts support this view,[2] while the French text is neutral.[3] The European Court in the *Consten and Grundig* case has provided guidance when it held that—

> ". . . it matters in particular whether the agreement is capable of endangering either directly or indirectly,[4] actually or potentially, the freedom of trade between member states in a manner which *could harm the realization of the purposes of* a single market between States."[5]

Thus the fact that an agreement favours an increase, be it even a considerable one, in the volume of trade between states is not sufficient to exclude the possibility that this agreement might "affect" trade in the sense set out above.[6] Similarly, the intent to prevent, restrict or distort the free exchange of goods in the Community renders an agreement capable of affecting trade between member states, even if the effect is insignificant.[7]

The Community Court has since added that there must be some degree of probability; it need not be reasonably predictable,[8] yet it must have an objective basis grounded on elements of law and fact.[9] In order to be apt to affect competition between the member states, the agreement need not necessarily limit competition between the parties; it is equally caught by art. 85 if it prevents or distorts competition between one of the parties to the agreement and third parties.[10]

(b) The agreements, decisions or concerted practices concerned must

---

1 *Bilger* v. *Jehle* (1970), 16 Rec. 127, at p. 136(5). The range of the terms of art. 85(1), *i.e.* apt to affect trade between member states, is wider than that of Reg. 17/62 art. 4(2) which touches only on imports and exports. See note in (1967) Harv. L.R. 1594, 1598; Kruithof, (1964) 2 C.M.L.Rev. 91–92.

2 They employ the terms: "*zu beeinträchtigen geeignet, che possono pregiudicare, welche . . . kunnen ongoenstig beeinvloeten*"; cp. Cohn, (1964) 13 I.C.L.Q. 1468.

3 It speaks of "*affecter*". See Adv. Gen. Lagrange in *De Geus* v. *Bosch* (1962), 8 Rec. 89, at pp. 139–140; [1962] C.M.L.R. 1; *Consten and Grundig* v. *EEC Commission* (1966), 12 Rec. 429, at p. 495; [1966] C.M.L.R. 418; Cerexhe in *Ganshof van der Meersch*, pp. 823–824, nos. 2038–2041, with lit.

4 Ca. Adv. Gen. Roemer in *Consten and Grundig* v. *EEC Commission* (above, n. 3) at p. 517; Goldman, *Droit Commercial Européen*, No. 223, p. 233; No. 231, p. 239.

5 *Consten and Grundig* v. *EEC Commission* (1966), 12 Rec. 429, at p. 495; [1966] C.M.L.R. 418. *Italy* v. *EEC Council and Commission* (1966), 12 Rec. 563, at p. 592; [1969] C.M.L.R. 39; *Soc. Technique Minière* v. *Maschinenbau Ulm GmbH* (1966), 12 Rec. 337, at p. 359; [1966] C.M.L.R. 357; *Völk* v. *Vervaecke*, (1969), 15 Rec. 295, at p. 302[5]; [1969] C.M.L.R. 273.

6 *Consten and Grundig* v. *EEC Commission* (1966), 12 Rec. 429, at p. 495; [1966] C.M.L.R. 418.

7 *ACF Chemiefarma* v. *EEC Commission* (1970), 16 Rec. 661, at pp. 698 (129), 702 (160).

8 *Soc. Technique Minière* v. *Maschinenbau Ulm GmbH* (1966), 12 Rec. 337, at p. 359; [1966] C.M.L.R. 357; *Cadillon* v. *Höss* (1971), 17 Rec. 351, at p. 356 (6); [1971] C.M.L.R. 420.

9 *Völk* v. *Vervaecke* (1969), 15 Rec. 295, at p. 302 (5); [1969] C.M.L.R. 273; *Cadillon* v. *Höss* (above, n. 8). See also the Commission Reply of; 2 June 1972 to Question 29/71, OJ, 1972, C 68/10.

10 *Consten and Grundig* v. *EEC Commission* (1966), 12 Rec. 429, at p. 493; [1966] C.M.L.R. 418; *Italy* v. *EEC Council and Commission* (1966), 12 Rec. 563, at p. 592; [1969] C.M.L.R. 39. Commission Decision 16 December 1971, *Vereeniging van Cementhandelaaren*, OJ, 1972, L 13/34, at p. 41(17).

have as their object or as their effect the prevention, restriction or distortion of competition within the Common Market. Thus, alternatively, the object and the effect must be considered, but it must be considered in its economic setting, and having regard to the agreement as a whole or of parts of it.[1] If an agreement has the *purpose* of preventing, restricting or distorting competition in the meaning of art. 85, it is irrelevant whether it has objectively this *effect* in the particular case.[2] If the effect is in issue, the nature and the quantity of the products available which form the object of the agreement, the importance of the parties in the particular field of the Market, the isolated nature of the agreement or its place within a network of agreements, the rigidity or flexibility of the restrictions, must all be taken into account.[3] Consequently, an agreement falls outside the operation of art. 85 if it affects the Market only insignificantly, as a result of the weak position which the interested parties hold in the market of the products in question.[4]

(c) The prohibition of agreements, decisions or concerted practices envisaged by art. 85 is directed equally against horizontal and vertical agreements,[5] including sole distributorship,[6] trademark[7] and patent[8] or copyright[9] licensing agreements if the underlying agreements offend against the prohibition of art. 85(1).[10] They do so when they set up

---

1 *Consten and Grundig* v. *EEC Commission* (1966), 12 Rec. 429, at p. 497; [1966] C.M.L.R. 418; *Brasserie de Haecht* v. *Wilkin-Janssen* (1967), 13 Rec. 525, at p. 537; [1968] C.M.L.R. 26. *Soc. Technique Minière* v. *Maschinenbau Ulm GmbH* (1966), 12 Rec. 337, at p. 359; [1966] C.M.L.R. 357; for criticisms see Goldman, *Droit Commercial Européen*, p. 298, No. 389; Focsaneanu, 1966 Rev. M.C. 862.

2 *Consten and Grundig* v. *EEC Commission* (1966), 12 Rec. 429, at p. 496; [1966] C.M.L.R. 418.

3 *Soc. Technique Minière* v. *Maschinenbau Ulm GmbH* (1966), 12 Rev. 337, at p. 360; [1966] C.M.L.R. 357; *Béguelin Import Co.* v. *SAGL Import Export* (1971), 17 Rec. 949, at p. 960(16)–(18) [1972] C.M.L.R. 81; *SAFCO*, 16 December 1971, OJ, 1971, L 13/44, at p. 45 II; [1972] C.M.L.R. D 83.

4 *Völk* v. *Vervaecke* (1969), 15 Rec. 295, at p. 302 (7); [1969] C.M.L.R. 273; *Cadillon* v. *Höss* (1971), 17 Rec. 351, at p. 356(9); *Burroughs-Delplanque*, 22 December 1971, OJ, 1972, L 13/50 II; *Burroughs-Geha*, *ibid.*, L 13/53 II; [1972] C.M.L.R. D 67, 72.

5 *Consten and Grundig* v. *EEC Commission* (1966), 12 Rec. 429, at p. 493; [1966] C.M.L.R. 418; *Soc. Technique Minière* v. *Maschinenbau Ulm GmbH* (1966), 12 Rec. 337, at p. 359; [1966] C.M.L.R. 357; *Italy* v. *EEC Council and Commission* (1966), 12 Rec. 563, at pp. 591, 593; [1969] C.M.L.R. 39.

6 *Consten and Grundig* v. *EEC Commission* (1966), 12 Rec. 429, at pp. 492–493, 496; [1966] C.M.L.R. 418; *Italy* v. *EEC Council and Commission* (1966), 12 Rec. 563, at p. 593; [1969] C.M.L.R. 39; *Soc. Technique Minière* v. *Maschinenbau Ulm GmbH* (1966), 12 Rec. 337, at p. 358; *Völk* v. *Vervaecke* (1969) 15 Rec. 295, at p. 302 (5), with a note by Van Damme, 1970, Cah. Dr. Eur. 63; Schluep, *Der Alleinvertriebsvertrag* (1966).

7 *Sirena Srl* v. *Eda Srl* (1971), 17 Rec. 69, at p. 81(4), (5), (9)–(11); [1971] C.M.L.R. 260.

8 *Parke Davis & Co.* v. *Probel et al.* (1968), 14 Rev. 81, at p. 110 (2); [1968] C.M.L.R. 47; *Burroughs-Delplanque*, 22 December 1971, OJ, 1972, L 13/50 II. For a restrictive interpretation of art. 85 in the case of patent licensing see Stoufflet, Juriscl. Dr. Int., Nos. 62–65.

9 *Deutsche Grammophom GmbH* v. *Metro-SB-Grossmärkte* (1971), 17 Rec. 487, at pp. 499(6), 500(11); [1971] C.M.L.R. 631.

10 See above, n. 6. And see *Deutsche Grammophon GmbH* v. *Metro-SB-Grossmärkte* (1971), 17 Rec. 487, at p. 499 (7); [1971] C.M.L.R. 631; *Raymond-Nagoya*, 9 June 1972, OJ, 1972, L 143/39 at p. 40 II; *Davidson Rubber Co.*, *ibid.*, p. 34 II. And see generally Gardiner, (1972) 88 L.Q.R. 507; Korah, (1972) 35 M.L.R. 634.

"cloisonnements nationaux" (cocoons),[1] by eliminating the intrusion of other distributors licensed in other EEC countries into the territory of the particular distributor,[2] and interfere with the free movement of goods.[3] It is the restrictive agreement excluding competition by other distributors or licensees which attracts the operation of art. 85(1) and not the exercise of an exclusive right of a proprietary nature by itself, such as a patent[4] or trademark[5]. These proprietary rights are not touched by the Treaty (arts. 36, 222), but their exercise is limited by the Treaty itself (art. 36).[6]

II   INSTANCES OF PROHIBITED CARTEL AGREEMENTS

The prohibition expressed in art. 85(1) to exclude, restrict or distort competition is stated specifically to have been violated (art. 85(1)) if—

(a) the purchase or sale price or any trading conditions are fixed (art. 85(1)(a)—cp. ECSC art. 65(1)(a)). Thus standard conditions in cartel agreements are forbidden, unlike in Germany[7] where uniform trading—though not price-conditions—is valid, if the cartel authority does not intervene;

(b) the production, sale, technical development or investment are restricted or controlled (art. 85(1)(b)—cp. ECSC art. 65(1)(b)).

Again, rationalisation cartels can be permitted in Germany,[8] but it must be noted that under the EEC Treaty, too, exemption may be granted.

(c) Area agreements provide for the sharing of markets or sources of supply (art. 85(1)(c)—cp. ECSC art. 65(1)(c));

(d) discriminatory conditions for the supply of goods or services of equal kind are imposed upon contracting parties whereby the latter are *adversely* affected in their ability to compete (art. 85(1)(d)—cp. ECSC art. 60(1)).

---

1 *Consten and Grundig* v. *EEC Commission* (1966), 12 Rec. 429, at p. 494; [1966] C.M.L.R. 418; *Soc. Technique Minière* v. *Maschinenbau Ulm GmbH* (1966), 12 Rec. 337, at p. 359; [1966] C.M.L.R. 357; *Italy* v. *EEC Commission* (1966), 12 Rec. 563, at p. 593; *Völk* v. *Vervaecke* (1969), 15 Rec. 295, at p. 302 (3); *Deutsche Grammophon GmbH* v. *Metro-SB-Grossmärkte* (1971), 17 Rec. 487, at p. 500 (12); [1971] C.M.L.R. 631; a clause forbidding export, coupled with another requiring the purchaser to sell only to consumers is not necessarily covered by this prohibition; *Parfums Rochas* v. *Bitsch* (1970), 16 Rec. 515, at p. 524(7); [1971] C.M.L.R. 104; and see generally Stoufflet, Juriscl. Dr. Int., No. 174 as to whether in vertical agreements "cocooning" is of the essence of illegality.

2 *Consten and Grundig* v. *EEC Commission* (1966), 12 Rec. 429, at p. 497; [1966] C.M.L.R. 418.

3 *Deutsche Grammophon GmbH* v. *Metro-SB-Grossmärkte* (1971), 17 Rec. 487, at p. 499 (7); [1971] C.M.L.R. 631.

4 *Parke, Davis & Co.* v. *Probel et al.* (1968), 14 Rev. 81, at p. 110(6), (7); [1968] C.M.L.R. 47.

5 *Sirena Srl* v. *Eda Srl* (1971), 17 Rec. 69, at p. 81(4), (5), (9)–(11); [1971] C.M.L.R. 260.

6 *Deutsche Grammophon GmbH* v. *Metro SB-Grossmärkte* (1971), 17 Rec. 487, at p. 499 (6)–500(13); [1971] C.M.L.R. 631.

7 GWB para. 2.

8 GWB para. 5.

For the purposes of this paragraph it is not sufficient if the activity concerned is intended to affect or in fact affects competition. It must in fact have a deleterious effect.

> (e) Conditions are attached to the main contract which force the other contracting party to accept additional obligations which are not by their nature or according to commercial usage connected with the subject matter of the contract (art. 85(1)(e)).[1]

The prohibition extends thus not only to goods but also to services.

III EFFECT OF VIOLATION OF ART. 85(1)

Agreements in contravention of art. 85(1) are void (art. 85(2))[2] subject to the blue pencil rule, unless the offending part cannot be separated from the agreement as a whole.[3] It will be noted that the sanction in art. 85(2) does not purport to affect concerted action for the simple reason that action, as distinct from any agreements or decisions, is neither valid nor invalid. It is prohibited (art. 85(1)).

The question remains to be examined whether the invalidity expressed in art. 85(1) operates automatically or only upon a pronouncement by the Commission or Court. It is now clear in respect of proceedings in domestic courts that "old" agreements, i.e. which existed before Reg. 17/62 came into force,[4] remain valid, at least provisionally,[5] to use the language employed by the Community Court,[6] since the operation of art. 85(2) depends upon the consideration of legal and economic elements which cannot be reached except through an explicit statement that the particular case combines all the elements set out in art. 85(1) and none of art. 85(3). In technical terms, the nullity by operation of law[7] operates only from the time when the Commission has decided that art. 85(1) applies and that no ground exists for granting an exemption under art. 85(3).[8] In the words of the Court—

> "It would be contrary to the general principle of legal security to conclude from the uncertain character of the validity of the agreements which have

---

1 Contrast ECSC Treaty art. 65(1).
2 For this concept in the domestic law of the countries of the EEC see Deringer, *The Competition Law of the EEC*, paras. 209 ff.
3 *Consten and Grundig* v. *EEC Commission* (1966), 12 Rec. 429, at p. 498; [1966] C.M.L.R. 418; *Soc. Technique Minière* v. *Maschinenbau Ulm GmbH* (1966), 12 Rec. 337, at p. 360; [1966] C.M.L.R. 357; and see Van der Heuvel, (1963) 12 A.J.C.L. 173, at p. 175; Deringer, *The Competition Law of the EEC*, paras. 287 ff.
4 *Brasserie Haecht* v. *Wilkin* (*No. 2*), [1973] C.M.L.R. 287, at p. 302(8), (9).
5 *SA Portelange* v. *SA Smith Corona Marchant International*, (1969), 15 Rec. 309, at p. 316 (9–17); *Bilger Söhne* v. *H. & M. Jehle* (1970), 16 Rec. 127, at p. 136(11).
6 *De Geus* v. *Bosch* (1962), 8 Rec. 89, at p. 105; [1962] C.M.L.R. 1; *SA Portelange* v. *SA Smith Corona*, (1969), 15 Rec. 309, at p. 316 (10)–(14).
7 *Nullité de plein droit: SA Portelange* v. *S.A. Smith Corona* (1969), 15 Rec. 309, at p. 316 (10).
8 See below; and see *SA Portelange* v. *S.A. Smith Corona* (1969), 15 Rec. 309, at p. 316 (14).

been notified[1] that, until the Commission has decided whether art. 85(3) applies,[2] such agreements are less than completely valid. It might be inconvenient if it turns out later on that they are invalid, but it is still more inconvenient if they were to remain in a state of provisional invalidity."[3]

If the agreement is a "new" one, no provisional validity can be asserted. The same may hold good if the agreement is covered by a group exemption from notification. It is another question whether such agreements are invalid *ex nunc* or *ex tunc* once the competent authority has made a pronouncement,[4] and what is the position in domestic law during the interval of agreements which are valid "provisionally".[5]

The domestic law of the member state concerned must determine, on the other hand, whether a violation of art. 85(1) justifies an action in tort[6] by third parties, excludes an action for breach of contract,[7] or supports an action for unjustifiable enrichment,[8] and whether art. 85(2) can be pleaded as a defence by a party to a cartel agreement.

IV EXEMPTIONS FROM ART. 85(1) AND (2)—ART. 85(3)

The rigidity of the prohibitions set out in art. 85(1) is mitigated by the general power to waive their application if the agreements concerned contribute (1) to improve production or distribution,[9] or (2) to promote technological or economic progress while offering the consumer an

---

1 The same applies if the agreement has not been notified, whether it could have been notified or not: *Soc. Technique Minière* v. *Maschinenbau Ulm GmbH* (1966), 12 Rec. 377, at p. 358; [1966] C.M.L.R. 357; or is subject to a group exemption: *Cadillon* v. *Höss* (1971) 17 Rec. 351, p. 357(15); [1971] C.M.L.R. 420; as to agreements which were not notified and were not subject to notification: see *Bilger* v. *Jehle*, (1970), 16 Rec. 127, at p. 137(9).

2 Or has issued a notice by virtue of Reg. 17/62, art. 17(6): *SA Portelange* v. *SA Smith Corona* (1969), 15 Rec. 309, at p. 316(19); at that moment the parties are at risk if they continue to perform the contract.

3 *SA Portelange* v. *SA Smith Corona* (above, p. 204) (1969), 15 Rec. 309, at p. 316(14)–(16); *Bilger* v. *Jehle* (1970), 16 Rec. 127, at p. 137 (11).

4 See below, p. 222; Reg. 17/62 art. 6(1), (2); *Brasserie de Haecht* v. *Wilkin* (*No. 2*), [1973] C.M.L.R. 287, at p. 304(27): *ex tunc*.

5 See Stoufflet, Juriscl. Dr. Int. Nos. 282, 283; Cass. belg. 8 June 1967, *Chaufourniers*, 1968 Cah. Dr. Eur. 436 with a note by Simont and Foriers; and see the practice in other EEC countries, *ibid.* p. 465: staying, or provisional measures are envisaged; Vandersanden, 1969 Rev. M.C. 473; Deringer, *The Competition Law of the EEC*, paras. 246–257; Franceschelli, Plaisant and Lassier, *Droit Européen de la Concurrence*, Nos. 841 ff. But see the divergent opinion of Daig, (1971) 35 Rabels Z. 1, at pp. 46, 47, 53 (summary) according to whom the provisional validity applies only to agreements dating from the time before Reg. 17/62 was introduced; accord: Franceschelli *et al.* (*supra*) No. 857 who regard new agreements as being subject to a suspensive condition, but see the exceptions admitted No. 858 which would leave the agreement provisionally valid *inter partes*, but not in regard to third parties, *ibid.*, No. 859.

6 It must depend upon the local law and the interpretation of art. 85 whether the duty is imposed for the benefit of the public in general or of individuals. See Van der Heuvel, (1963) 12 A.J.C.L. 173, at pp. 183, 186 with cases.

7 Mailänder, *Zuständigkeit und Entscheidungsfreiheit nationaler Gerichte* (1965), pp. 20–21.

8 Van der Heuvel, (1963) 12 A.J.C.L. 190.

9 Art. 85(3); for some criteria see *Consten and Grundig* v. *EEC Commission* (1966), 12 Rec. 429, at p. 502; [1966] C.M.L.R. 418.

adequate share of the profits, either directly or indirectly.[1] In addition, (3) the restrictions must be essential for the purposes mentioned above (art. 85(3)(a)) and, (4) must not make it possible to exclude competition in respect of a substantial portion of the goods concerned (art. 85(3)(b)). The conditions for granting exemption are thus partly positive, partly negative, partly technical and partly economic. Since art. 85 envisages trade within the EEC, export cartels directed to third countries are not affected,[2] although this principle may perhaps be restricted to cartel agreements made between enterprises in one single country of the EEC.

Measures: Regulation 17/62, arts. 6, 7, 8, 9 issued in virtue of EEC art. 87.[3]

In carrying out its task under art. 87 and Reg. 17, the Commission is not restricted to the evidence produced by the parties, but may engage in investigations *proprio motu.*[4]

In determining whether an agreement contributes to an "improvement of production" it is not possible to rely on broad criteria such as that of the "true economic balance sheet", having regard to the economy as a whole,[5] or to the rule of reason.[6] Instead the four conditions set out in art. 85(3) must be examined separately with strict regard to their wording.[7]

(1) There must be an improvement in *production* or *distribution*. Clearly the improvements must relate to the objects with which the agreement is concerned and not to the improvement of the production or distribution of extraneous goods. This is important if the agreement concerns unfinished goods. Yet the improvement need not consist in an *increase* in production.[8]

(2) Alternatively, the agreement must promote technological or economic progress. These requirements coincide with those of art. 59 *ter* of the French Decree.[9]

It must be noted that in either case art. 85(3) requires only that the agreement should *contribute* to these goals. It suffices, perhaps, if it has objectively an incidental potential to assist in an improvement or advance and is prospective only. This argument is supported by the consideration that specific proof of such an effect is excluded, *ex hypothesi*, since the agreement must be notified to the Commission upon its conclusion.[10]

---

1 Cp. ECSC Treaty, art. 65(2) (a)–(c), 1st para.

2 See above, p. 200, n. 5; below, p. 217, n. 1.

3 OJ, 1962, 204; *De Geus* v. *Bosch* (1962), 8 Rec. 89; [1962] C.M.L.R. 1.

4 *Consten and Grundig* v. *EEC Commission* (1966), 12 Rec. 429, at p. 501; Van der Heuvel, (1963) 12 A.J.C.L. 172. For examples see below, pp. 218 ff.

5 Cp. art. 59*ter* of the French Decree 53–704 as interpreted by the Commission des Ententes.

6 *Standard Oil Co. of New Jersey* v. *US* (1918), 221 US 1, at p. 62; 55 L.Ed. 619 at p. 646; *Chicago Board of Trade* v. *US* (1918), 246 US 231, at p. 238; 62 L.Ed. 683, at p. 687; *White Motor Co.* v. *US* (1963), 372 US 253, at p. 261; 9 L.Ed. (2d) 738, at p. 745.

7 For an example see *Davidson Rubber Co.*, 9 June 1972, OJ, 1972, L 143/31; [1972] C.M.L.R. D 52.

8 Deringer, *EWG Wettbewerbsrecht* (1962–73), *ad* art. 85(3), para. 24, with lit.

9 Plaisant and Lassier, 1962 B.B.A.W.D. 185, at p. 187.

10 Reg. 17/62 art. 4—see below, p. 220; and see Deringer, *loc. cit.*, para. 27.

The agreement must offer the consumers an adequate share of profits.[1] It would seem that these need not accrue to the ultimate consumers directly; it suffices if the direct profit accrues at an earlier stage of production. A profit or advantage consists, according to the prevailing view, not only in a reduction of the price, but in any advantage, such as better quality or service, earlier delivery dates, increased choice or improved means of obtaining the goods.[2]

The third and fourth conditions are negative. They figure disjunctively in the French, Italian and Dutch texts and in the English translation, but the German text links them by the word "oder" (or). Nevertheless, it is believed by writers that the two negative conditions operate conjunctively and not alternatively.[3] The first relates to the internal, the second to the external, effects. Both are limited to the effects of the agreement upon the parties to it. The effect upon third parties is only relevant indirectly inasmuch as it may indicate a restriction upon the parties to the agreement.[4]

(3) According to condition (3) the restrictions must be essential for attaining the effects set out in conditions (1) and (2), or, in the form of a double negative set out in art. 85(3), they must not be such as to be not indispensable for this purpose. The restrictions envisaged here are naturally those prohibited by art. 85(1) and no others. Possibly they include implied restrictions or restrictions which ensue as a result of the absence of certain clauses to the contrary.

If the purpose of conditions (1) and (2) can be reached by other means, no exemption can be granted, but the particular situation of the enterprises concerned rather than considerations of a general character may determine whether the restrictions serve the purposes indicated in art. 85(3).

A restriction appears to be justified according to the wording of condition (3) even if its extent is not proportionate to the effects which it may lawfully bring about according to art. 85(3), condition (3), but it has been argued that a balance must be struck between the permitted purposes and the permissible means.[5]

(4) Condition (4) concentrates on the external effect of the restriction by stressing two criteria. The first is whether the restriction affects a substantial part of the market in the goods concerned. The second is whether it eliminates competition in this sphere. Naturally, only the market in the products concerned,[6] limited to the area of the EEC, is involved. The products concerned are represented by certain types of goods and, possibly, by the quantity involved.[7] Further, the type of goods involved may re-

---

1 The wording of the Treaty is ambiguous. "*Verbraucher, gebruikers*" are broader notions than "*utilisateurs, utilizzatori*" which could be understood to exclude the ultimate consumer. Cp. ECSC Treaty art. 3(b).

2 Deringer, *loc. cit.* para. 33; and see below, pp. 218 ff.

3 Deringer, *ad* art. 85(3), para. 38.

4 Deringer, *ad* art. 85(3), para. 39.

5 Deringer, *ad* art. 85(3), para. 45.

6 French text: "*produits en cause*".

7 Deringer, *ad* art. 85(3), para. 48 and n. 47.

quire definition by reference not only to the same, but to a comparable, range made of similar materials and serving the same purpose.[1] It is doubtful, however, whether the existence of substitute materials and the products thereof can be taken into account in defining the effect on the market. It is also not clear what is to be understood by a *substantial* part of the market. Probably it is less than a market controlling share,[2] but the Notice of the Commission dealing with Exclusive Dealership Agreements dated 9 November 1962[3] seems to imply that a substantial part is equal to a dominant part. On the other hand, the Community Court, applying the ECSC Treaty, relies on the criterion whether the effects are not merely minor or ancillary.[4] Following the Commission Notice on Agreements of Minor Importance it would seem that the structure of the relevant branch of the economy and the number and size of the competition, as well as the size of the share in the market, counts.[5]

V   GROUP EXEMPTIONS

The wording of art. 85(3) by referring to "any agreements or group of agreements",[6] makes it clear that exemptions may be granted to individual agreements and to groups of agreements generally, thus facilitating the work of the Commission which was threatened with a flood of applications for exemptions or negative clearance[7] without jettisoning the principle contained in art. 85(3) itself.

Council Reg. 17/62,[8] art. 4(2) initiated the process of general exemption (without sacrificing the principle itself) by freeing from the duty of notification not only purely domestic agreements[9] which do not involve exports and imports between member states, but also vertical resale price maintenance, patent, trademark, design or know-how, licensing agreements and standardisation or joint research agreements (the latter if open to both parties) between two parties only. After the Commission had employed the device of an official notice to inform the public of its policy under art. 85(1) on Exclusive Dealer(Distributor)ship Agreements (of

---

1   Deringer, *loc. cit.*, n. 48; ca. Gleiss–Hirsch *ad* art. 85, no. 108.
2   Deringer, *loc. cit.*, para. 49; it may be as low as 20–45 per cent, since not the share by way of percentage, but the size of the enterprise and the size and the number of the competitors count; cp. *Geitling* v. *High Authority* (1962), 8 Rec. 165, at pp. 216–219; [1962] C.M.L.R. 113.
3   OJ, 1962, 2627; Deringer, *ad* art. 85(3), para. 49, n. 49.
4   *Geitling* v. *High Authority* (1962), 8 Rec. 165, at p. 216; [1962] C.M.L.R. 113.
5   See below, p. 214, and n. 1. For some criteria, restricted to specialisation cartels see the Commission Reg. 2779/72, art. 3, OJ, 1972, L 292/23, below, p. 209. And see Reg. 2822/71, OJ, 1971, L 285/49 modifying Reg. 17/62 art. 4(2). Below, p. 215.
6   *Categorie, Gruppen, categoria, groep.*
7   For these procedures see below, p. 215.
8   OJ, 1962, 204.
9   But see *Bilger* v. *Jehle* (1970), 16 Rec. 127, at p. 136(5) for such agreements which may affect trade between member states; *Omega*, Commission Decision 18 October 1970, OJ, 1970, L 242/22 at p. 26 II (6); 1970 Rev. Trim. Dr. Eur. 812, at p. 818; [1972] C.M.L.R. D49.

9 November 1962),[1] Exclusive Representation concluded with Commercial Agents,[2] and concerning Patent Licensing[3] Agreements (both of
24 December 1962), the Council stepped in and by virtue of art. 87 issued
Reg. 19/65[4] designed to implement arts. 85(3) and 87 of the Treaty. It
enables the Commission in clearly defined circumstances (below (1)) to
exercise its powers under art. 85(3) by regulation rather than by individual
determination and similarly to implement its delegated powers under
Reg. 17/62.[5] As a result the Commission issued Reg. 67/67[6] on Groups of
Exclusive Dealership Agreements (superseding its previous Notice of
9 November 1962).[7] In addition, the Commission has set out its views on
agreements etc., concerning Co-operation between Enterprises and concerning Practices of Minor Importance not falling within the ambit of
art. 85(1).[8]

On 20 December 1971 the Council, acting once again under art. 87 of
the Treaty, issued Reg. 2821/71[9] enabling the Commission to declare by
way of regulation in the exercise of its powers under art. 85(3) that a
further batch of agreements, decisions and concerted practices is exempt
from the operation of art. 85(1). These agreements must involve co-
operation between enterprises in order to rationalise their operation and to
adapt their productivity and competitiveness to the enlarged market. By
way of enumeration Reg. 2821/71 mentions agreements etc. concerning
the application of standards and types, research and development up to
the stage of industrial development, the utilisation of the results including
the exploitation of industrial property rights and know-how and specialisation, including agreements to obtain the latter goal.[10] This power, like
that under Reg. 19/65 is limited in time.[11] The Commission has exercised
this power in 1972, and has published a Regulation limited in time
until 31 December 1977[12] which embodies Council Reg. 2821/71 and

1 OJ, 1962, 2627, 2628, amended 2687, now superseded by Council Reg. 19/65, OJ, 1965,
   533 after the introduction of a special form of notification for exclusive dealing agreements
   in which two enterprises take part *and* which concern either a specified area in the EEC or
   certain goods for resale, or a combination of the two; Commission Reg. 27/62, art. 4(2)(a)
   amended by Commission Reg. 153/62, art. 1, OJ, 1962, 2918, rescinded and replaced by
   Reg. 67/67 art. 7(1), now in the wording of Reg. 1133/68, OJ, 1968, L 189/1; see below,
   n. 2.
2 OJ, 1962, 2921; for the form of notification see Commission Reg. 27/62, OJ, 1962, 1118,
   amended by Commission Reg. 153/62, OJ, 1962, 118, replaced by Commission Reg. 67/67,
   art. 7, OJ, 1967, 849, now in the wording of Reg. 1133/68, OJ, 1968, L 189/1, art. 4(2)*bis*.
3 OJ, 1962, 2922.
4 OJ, 1965, 533, upheld in *Italy* v. *EEC Council and Commission* (1966), 12 Rec. 563; [1969]
   C.M.L.R. 39.
5 OJ, 1962, 204, arts. 6, 7.
6 OJ, 1967, 849.
7 Above, n. 1.
8 OJ, 1968, C 75/3, to be implemented by decisions or by general notices; OJ, 1970, C 64/1.
9 OJ, 1971, L 285/46, amended by Council Reg. 2743/72, OJ, 1972, L 291/144.
10 Reg. 2821/71, art. 1(1).
11 Reg. 19/65, art. 2(1); Reg. 67/67, art. 1(1); Reg. 2821/71, art. 2(1).
12 Commission Reg. 2279/72, OJ, 1973, L 292/23; see also the Commission Notice of 29 July
   1968, OJ, 1968, C 75, below, p. 213, n. 12.

applies to restrictive agreements between enterprises of a certain type.[1]
At the same time, by a further Draft Regulation, it extended the operation
in time of Commission Reg. 67/67, art. 1.[2]

1   Exclusive Dealership Agreements

(A) Council Reg. 19/65[3] empowered the Commission to exempt by
regulation from the operation of art. 85(3) groups of agreements or concerted practices[4] between *two* enterprises only involving exclusive dealings—

   (i) (a) for the purpose of delivery for resale in a defined area of the
             Common Market by one enterprise; *or*
        (b) for the purpose of purchase with a view to resale by one
             enterprise; *or*
        (c) for the purpose of delivery and purchase with a view to resale
             mutually by both enterprises and which
  (ii) contain restrictions which are imposed in connection with the
        acquisition or use of rights such as patents, utility models,
        designs or trademarks by one enterprise or mutually by both or
        in connection with rights under contracts assigning or licensing
        manufacturing processes or know-how for the use or application
        of industrial techniques.[5]

The Commission was enjoined to define the group of agreements and in
particular the restrictions which must be included or excluded.[6] The
Commission regulation was to be limited in time[7] and was to have the
same retroactive effect as was attributed to individual exemptions by Reg.
17/62.[8]

In addition the Commission was given the power to exempt by regulation, for a limited period of time, agreements and concerted practices
existing before Reg. 17/62 came into operation[9] which violate art. 85(1), if
the agreements are modified in accordance with the future Commission
regulation and are notified to the Commission.[10] The power of the Commission to grant exemptions in situations which are generally exempt under
the Commission regulation to be issued but violate art. 85(3) in the parti-

---

1   Reg. 2822/71, OJ, 1971, L 285/49.
2   Draft Reg. OJ, 1972, C 79/3: in force until 31 December 1982.
3   OJ, 1965, 443.
4   Reg. 19/65, art. 1(2).
5   Reg. 19/65, art. 1(1); for the criteria whether any such agreement violates art. 85(1) see
    above, p. 201.
6   Reg. 19/65, art. 1(2).
7   Reg. 17/62, art. 24;; Reg. 19/65, art. 2(1); Commission Reg. 67/67, art. 1(1) (above,
    n. 2): 31 December 1972; proposed Commission Reg. extends it to 31 December 1982,
    OJ, 1972, C 79/3.
8   Reg. 17/62, art. 6; see also Reg. 19/65, art. 3; Commission Reg. 67/67, arts. 4, 5.
9   *I.e.* 13 March 1962; see Reg. 19/65, art. 4(1).
10 The agreement must have been notified originally in accordance with Reg. 17/62, art. 5.
    See Reg. 19/65, art. 4(2).

cular case was maintained.[1] The fact that the agreement had not been notified in reliance on the general exemption to be granted under the forthcoming Commission regulation was to be no obstacle.[2]

The Commission, while reserving the right of enterprises to apply for individual exemption,[3] thought it unnecessary to deal with groups of agreements entered into within one member state only[4] and concentrated on exclusive dealings agreements, the beneficial effects of which are set out in detail[5] provided that parallel imports are safeguarded[6] and that patents and similar rights are not abused.[7] Accordingly, Commission Reg. 67/67 exempted from the operation of art. 85(1) for a period of time expiring on 31 December 1972 but extended to 31 December 1982[8] agreements between *no more than two* enterprises involving exclusive dealings—

(i) (a) for the delivery for resale within a defined area of the Common Market by one enterprise; *or*

   (b) for the purpose of purchase with a view to resale by one enterprise; *or*

   (c) for the purpose of delivery and purchase with a view to resale mutually by both enterprises[9]

     and which contain any of the following restrictions—

(ii) (a) not to manufacture or distribute during the duration of the agreement or until one year after its termination any products which compete with those forming the object of the contract, *or*

   (b) not to advertise, or to maintain a sales branch for, or a stock of, the goods which form the object of the agreement, outside the agreed territory of the exclusive dealer,[10]

     including the obligation

   (c) to purchase complete ranges of products or minimum quantities;

   (d) to sell the products under trademarks and in a form of presentation specified by the manufacturer;

   (e) to promote sales by advertising, maintain a sales network or a stock of goods; as well as an after-sale and warranty

---

1 Reg. 19/65, art. 7; see *Omega*, Commission Decision 18 October 1970, OJ, 1970, L 242/22 at p. 2 III, (7); 1970 Rev. Trim. Dr. Eur. 812, at p. 818.

2 Reg. 19/65, art. 7; see Reg. 17/62, arts. 4, 5, 6, 8.

3 Commission Reg. 67/67, OJ, 1967, 849, Preamble para. 7 and art. 6.

4 *Ibid.*, Preamble, para. 8 and art. 1(2); for the effect see 1968 Rev. Trim. Dr. Eur. 803: 31550 agreements notified, 14500 covered by Reg. 67/67; 11870 abandoned or adapted; another 12000 accepted.

5 *Ibid.*, Preamble, paras. 10, 11.

6 *Ibid.*, Preamble, paras. 13, 14.

7 *Ibid.*, Preamble, para. 13.

8 *Ibid.*, art. 1(1). For the extension see above, p. 210, n. 2.

9 *Ibid.*, art. 1(1)(a)–(c).

10 *Ibid.*, art. 2(1)(a), (b); see the *Omega* case, above, n. 1499.

service or to employ specialised or technically qualified staff.[1]

On the other hand the exemptions do not apply where manufacturers of competing products enter into mutually exclusive distribution agreements[2] or where the parties try to prevent other dealers from obtaining the goods from distributors elsewhere in the Common Market.[3] In particular the attempt to use patents or trademarks and similar rights in order to prevent other distributors or consumers from obtaining products lawfully produced and marketed elsewhere, or to restrict distributors elsewhere from marketing the product in the area covered by the agreement under review is illegal.[4]

(B) Over the course of years, the Commission has indicated that certain types of agreements do not, in its opinion, constitute a violation of art. 85(1) in any circumstances and should not, therefore, give rise to any doubts which might justify an application for negative clearance or for exemption under art. 85(3). The Commission indicated, however, that any such expression of opinion or indication of a course of action by that body does not bind other competent authorities, including courts.[5] These include the following.

2   Agreements for Exclusive Representation[6]

These do not violate art. 85(1) if a broker acts on behalf of an enterprise or as an agent in the name and/or behalf of an enterprise or acts in his own name on behalf of an enterprise as an undisclosed principal. However, if the agent shows the characteristics of an independent trader by assuming the financial risk other than *del credere*, by binding himself to maintain, as owner, a considerable stock of the products which form the subject matter of the contract, or to set up (or in fact sets up) and to maintain an important and gratuitous service for the customers at his own expense, or if he may fix or fixes himself prices or trading conditions, the agreement falls outside the scope of the Commission Notice.

3   Patent Licensing Agreements[7]

These do not violate art. 85(1) if they contain restrictions, imposed upon the licensee, on methods of exploitation which are determined by patent law,[8] of the manufacture of the patented goods[9] or the use of the patented process for certain technical applications,[10] of the quantity to be manu-

---

1   Commission Reg. art. 2(2)(a)–(c).
2   *Ibid.*, art. 3(a).
3   *Ibid.*, art. 3(b); *Béguelin Import Co.* v. *SAGL Import Export* (1971), 17 Rec. 949, at pp. 960(19)–961(24); [1972] C.M.L.R. 81.
4   *Ibid.*, art. 3(b), (1) and (2).
5   OJ, 1962, 2922 end of the notice, 2923 III, 2nd para.
6   OJ, 1962, 2921.
7   OJ, 1962, 2922; Reinhart, 1972 B.B.A.W.D. 498.
8   *Ibid.*, I A (1), see also IV.
9   *Ibid.*, I A (2)(a).
10 *Ibid.*, I A (2)(b).

factured or the number of acts of exploitation,[1] of the exploitation in time,[2] space,[3] or of the form of disposition[4] of the patent itself, which define the duty to affix patent marks,[5] to observe standards of quality including the duty to purchase certain ingredients,[6] to communicate experiences acquired in the course of exploitation and to grant licences of inventions for improvement or use provided that the obligation is not exclusive and is mutual.[7]

Similarly restrictive obligations assumed by the licensor do not violate art. 85(1) if they bind the licensor not to grant to another the right to exploit the invention[8] or not to exploit the invention himself.[9]

The notice expressly refrains from any general pronouncement where agreements set up a patent pool or reciprocal licences or multiple parallel licences[10] and does not extend to agreements which cover a period of time beyond that during which the patent is valid.[11]

4 Agreements etc. concerning Co-operation between Enterprises[12]

In order to encourage co-operation between small and medium enterprises, the Commission has indicated that in its view certain types of agreements do not normally[13] offend against art. 85(1) and need not be notified for negative clearance.[14] Of course, the parties are free to do so, or to apply for exemption under art. 85(3).

The types of agreements envisaged by the Commission are those which have as their sole object, without imposing restrictions[15]—

(a) the search for information, namely, an exchange of opinions or experience, joint marketing research, joint comparative studies of enterprises or industries or joint preparation of statistics and calculating models;

(b) matters other than the supply of goods and services, namely, co-operation in accounting matters; joint furnishing of credit guarantees; joint debt-collecting associations, joint business or tax consultant agencies;

---

1 *Ibid.*, I A (3).
2 *Ibid.*, I A (4)(a).
3 *Ibid.*, I A (4)(b).
4 *Ibid.*, I A (4)(c).
5 *Ibid.*, I B.
6 *Ibid.*, I C.
7 *Ibid.*, I D.
8 *Ibid.*, I E (1).
9 *Ibid.*, I E (2).
10 *Ibid.*, II (1)–(3), reserved for a subsequent decision; see *ibid.* III, last para.
11 *Ibid.*, II, last para.
12 OJ, 1968, C 75/3 of 29 July 1968; it affects also ECSC art. 65. See Joliet, 1969 Cah. Dr. Eur. 127.
13 OJ, 1968, C 75/3, I, para. 6; II, paras. 2, 3; see below, n. 15, rectified OJ, 1968, C 84/14.
14 *Ibid.*, I para. 8; Reg. 17/62, art. 2.
15 *Ibid.*, II (1), paras. 1, 2, 4; (2), para. 4; (3), paras. 4, 5, 6; (4), para. 1; (5), para. 1; (7), para. 1.

(c) the pooling of research, namely, joint implementation of research and development projects; joint placing of research and development contracts; dividing-up of sectors of research and development projects among the participating enterprises;

(d) the joint use of production facilities and of storage and transport equipment;

(e) the creation of partnerships for the common execution of orders, if the participating enterprises do not compete with each other in the work to be done or where each alone is unable to execute the orders;

(f) joint selling arrangements and joint after-sale and repair services, even if the enterprises compete with each other;

(g) joint advertising;

(h) the use of a common label indicating a certain quality provided that the label is available to all competitors under the same conditions.

5   Agreements etc. of Minor Importance[1]

With the object of its previous Notice on Agreements concerning Co-operation between Enterprises in mind the Commission issued a further notice in order to encourage co-operation between small and medium sized enterprises. The Commission now indicates a tendency to treat only those restrictive agreements as falling within the ambit of art. 85(1) which have *appreciable* effects on market conditions; these are defined as "agreements through which the market position of foreign enterprises and consumers, that is their sales potential and sources of supply, is *appreciably* altered."[2] The test is quantitative, and in this Notice the Commission attempts to give it a concrete meaning while admitting that in individual cases even agreements which exceed the clear limits set by the Notice may not be caught by art. 85(1). Once again, such agreements need not be notified for negative clearance, and no decision whether the agreement violates art. 85(1) or is exempt is required. Once again, the parties are free to do so or to apply for exemption under art. 85(3).

An agreement does not have an *appreciable* effect on market conditions if—

(a) the products subject to an area agreement constitute not more than five per cent of the turnover of the same products or products considered similar by consumers having regard to their properties, utility or price;

(b) the total annual turnover of the enterprises, parties to the agreement, does not exceed 15 million units of account, or 20 million units of account in the case of trading enterprises.

If the share of the market or the size of the turnover rises up to 10 per cent for two consecutive fiscal years, the character of the agreement as one

---

1   OJ, 1970, C 64/1, of 2 June 1970; 1970 Rev. Trim. Dr. Eur. 578.

2   OJ, 1970, C 64/1, I, para. 4; Reg. 17/62, art. 2.

which does not offend against art. 85(1) is not changed thereby. The methods for determining the turnover are laid down in some detail.[1]

VI PROCEDURE

In order to give effect to the provisions of arts. 85 and 86 (monopolies), and in particular in order to establish the machinery for investigating infringements, enforcing sanctions and granting exemptions under art. 85(3) and to co-ordinate the relevant rules and competences established by the Treaty with those existing in the domestic laws of the member states, art. 87 confers the power upon the Council to issue regulations on the substance and procedure appropriate to this subject matter. In addition, art. 89 invests the Commission with the powers necessary to carry out the supervision of cartels and monopolies in so far as they affect trade between the member states and determines the duties of the authorities of the latter towards the Commission in carrying out these tasks.

It may investigate possible infringements and make recommendations (art. 89(1)); if these prove abortive it may decide that an infringement has occurred and may authorise specific enforcement measures (art. 89(2)). After an interim period (1958–1961) during which the duties of the Commission were discharged by the authorities of the member states pending the promulgation of the regulations envisaged by art. 87 (art. 88), the procedure of the Commission was established by Reg. 17/62.[2] Its framework is provided by art. 87; Reg. 17 fills in the details and makes it clear that it merely serves to enforce arts. 85 and 86, not to modify or to supplement them.[3]

The Regulation distinguishes between three different types of procedure:[4]

Firstly, it introduces a preliminary examination, called *negative clearance*, which enables the parties to an agreement to consult the Commission as to whether or not the latter sees any grounds for objecting to the agreement, decision or practice.[5] The application is not followed by an investigation. Instead, the Commission reaches its decision on the strength of the facts adduced by the parties and without engaging in an investigation of its own,

---

1 OJ, 1970, C 64/1, II, paras. 5 ff.; now supported by the amended version of Reg. 17/62, art. 4(2) in the wording of Council Reg. 2822/71, art. 1, OJ, 1971, L 285/49.

2 OJ, 1962, 204, in force 13 March 1962, supplemented by Commission Regs. 27/62, OJ, 1962, 1118 (applications and notifications), amended by 153/62, OJ, 1962, 2918, amended by 67/67 art. 7(1), OJ, 1967, 849, 1133/68, OJ, 1968, L 189/1 (modifying 27/62), 2822/71, OJ, 1971, L 285/49 (modifying Reg. 17/62, art. 4(2)); see also Council Reg. 99/62, OJ, 1963, 2268 (hearings).

3 Reg. 17/62, art. 1; cp. Alexander, 1965 Rev. Trim. Dr. Eur. 323.

4 Reg. 17/62, arts. 2, 3, 6. For the form or application or notification see Commission Reg. 1133/68, OJ, 1968, L 189, replacing Reg. 27/62, OJ, 1962, 1118 as amended by Reg. 153/62, OJ. 1962, 2918; *Parfums Rochas* v. *Bitsch* (1970), 16 Rec. 515, at pp. 522 (3), 523(4); [1971] C.M.L.R. 104.

5 Reg. 17/62, art. 2. For the form of notification see Reg. 27/62, art. 4 and Annex, Form A/B as substituted by Commission Reg. 1133/68, OJ, 1968, L 189; the amendments in Reg. 153/62, OJ, 1962, 2918 replaced by Reg. 67/67 art. 7, OJ, 1967, 849 are abrogated.

as it does otherwise.[1] Its finding is declaratory only and does not prevent the Commission or domestic courts from holding subsequently that art. 85(1) has been violated, even if the agreement has been given negative clearance previously, because the facts as stated by the parties did not give rise to any objections. Such a declaration will prevent any penalties[2] for an infringement of art. 85(1) running in respect of the facts stated by the parties. Thus negative clearance is advantageous for parties who may entertain doubts as to whether their agreement may infringe art. 85(1) and who neither intend to enter into a prohibited restrictive agreement nor to admit an infringement of art. 85(1) and to claim a special justification leading to an exemption under art. 85(3)[3] and do not wish, as an alternative, to refrain from registering their agreement, with the result that they may lay themselves open to heavy penalties, if the agreement should be prohibited. A request for negative clearance under art. 85(1) does not include an application for exemptions under art. 85(3) and does not rank as a notification in the meaning of Reg. 17, art. 15(5). The two measures are alternatives.

The procedure of negative clearance has been resorted to frequently,[4] and a rich practice has grown up which seeks to determine the boundaries between agreements which are, and those which are not, contrary to art. 85(1).[5]

In general Commission terms Regs. 67/67 and 2871/71 and the Commission notices examined above[6] have released certain groups of agreements from the area where negative clearance may be required. Specifically, in individual cases, the following principles have been established.

Exclusive dealership agreements escape the effect of art. 85(1) if they do not cocoon the dealer by granting him protection against competition with the same products traded by others, allow parallel imports and do not profit the dealer alone by raising the price.[7] In addition, in order to exclude negative clearance, the restriction of trade must be perceptible by affecting an important sector of the market[8] and must have effects inside the EEC, thus leaving such agreements with dealers outside the EEC un-

---

1   Reg. 17/62, arts. 10–14.
2   Reg. 17/62, art. 16(1); negative clearance will also prevent the parties from relying on the nullity of their agreement; but see Reg. 17/62, art. 15(1)(a) as regards fines for false or misleading statements.
3   Reg. 17/62, arts. 4, 5.
4   It has been argued that in failing to take action under art. 2, the Commission may fail to discharge a duty and may be liable, see Steindorff, 1963 B.B.A.W.D. 353.
5   See for the earlier practice Fulda, (1965) 65 Col. L.R. 947.
6   Above, pp. 208 ff.
7   *DRU-Blondel*, 8 July 1965, OJ, 1965, 2194; 1966 Rev. Trim. Dr. Eur. 120; [1965] C.M.L.R. 180; see also *Hummel Isbeque*, 17 September 1965, OJ, 1965, 2581; [1965] C.M.L.R. 242; *Mertens and Straet*, 1 June 1964, OJ, 1964, 1426, 1966 Rev. Trim. Dr. Eur. 119; [1964] C.M.L.R. 416; see below, n. 1567.
8   *Mertens and Straet*, above, n. 7; *Nicolas Frères*, OJ, 1964, 2287, 1966 Rev. Trim. Dr. Eur. 119, at p. 179, para. 15; [1964] C.M.L.R. 505; *Rieckermann, AEG-Elotherm*, OJ, 1968, L 276/25, 1968 Rev. Trim. Dr. Eur. 952; [1968] C.M.L.R. D78; *Re SOCEMAS*, 17 July 1968, OJ, 1968, L 201/ 4, 1968 Rev. Trim Dr. Eur. 929, [1968] C.M.L.R. D28.

affected[1] as well as those between parties inside one member state which affect only that country of the EEC,[2] or must concern assignments of assets and goodwill, including customers, coupled with an undertaking by the assigner not to compete for five years or to use the assigned trademark in the EEC.[3]

Also, negative clearance was accorded to agreements to establish a joint sales organisation outside the EEC, where the partners indicate the quantities which they will make available and where the profits are distributed by calculating one single price,[4] joint purchasing agreements,[5] agreements to protect the common interests of the manufacturers;[6] agreements to promote certain products by the maintenance of certain standards of production and of quality, coupled with the use of a common trademark,[7] or with a certain degree of price maintenance;[8] joint sales organisations by small and medium type manufacturers, all being individual specialists not competing with each other and contracting in their own name;[9] agreements between mother and daughter companies in different member states of the EEC, totally owned by the mother company with the result that restrictions are identical with techniques of internal organisation;[10] where one side to the agreement has ceased to be a serious competitor;[11] where the scope of the agreement is restricted to research avail-

---

1 *Grossfillex*, 11 March 1964, OJ, 1964, 915 [1964] C.M.L.R. 237; *DECA*, 21 October 1964, OJ, 1964, 2761; 1965 Rev. Trim. Dr. Eur., 149; [1965] C.M.L.R. 50; distinguish the situation where the producer is outside the EEC and the dealer within it: see *Mertens and Straet*, above, p. 216, n. 7; *SupExie*, 23 December 1970, OJ, 1971, L 10/12; 1971 Rev. Trim. Dr. Eur. 285; [1971] C.M.L.R. D1; *Kodak*, 30 June 1970, OJ, 1970, L 147/24; 1970 Rev. Trim. Dr. Eur. 582; [1970] C.M.L.R. D19; *SEIFA*, 30 June 1969, OJ, 1969, L 173/6, II(6), 1969 Rev. Trim. Dr. Eur. 851, at p. 854; *Vereeniging van Vernis- en Verffabrikanten*, 25 June 1969, OJ, 1969, L 168/22, 1969 Rev. Trim. Dr. Eur. 847; [1970] C.M.L.R. D1; *Rieckermann, AEG-Elotherm* (above, p. 216, n. 8; *Cobelaz*, 6 November 1968, OJ, 1968, L 276/13; 1968 Rev. Trim. Dr. Eur. 938; [1968] C.M.L.R. D45.

2 *SEIFA* (above, n. 1) *Comptoir Français de l'Azote (CFA)*, 6 November 1968, OJ, 1968, L 276/29, 1968 Rev. Trim. Dr. Eur. 957; [1968] C.M.L.R. D57; *Cobelaz-Cokeries*, 6 November 1968, OJ, 1968, L 276/19, 1968 Riv. Trim. Dr. Eur. 946; [1968] C.M.L.R. D68; *Thin Paper Agreement*, 26 July 1972, OJ, 1972, L 182/24.

3 *Nicolas Frères* (above, p. 216, n. 8).

4 *SupExie* (above, n. 1); *CFA* (above, n. 2); *Cobelaz-Cokeries* (above, n. 2).

5 *SOCEMAS*, 17 July 1968, OJ, 1968, L 201/4; 1968 Rev. Trim. Dr. Eur. 929; [1968] C.M.L.R, D28.

6 *ASPA*, 30 June 1970, OJ, 1970, L 148/9; 1970 Rev. Trim. Dr. Eur. 586; [1970] C.M.L.R. D25; see generally Joliet, 1969, Cah. Dr. Eur. 127.

7 *ASBL*, 29 June 1970, OJ, 1970, L 153/14, 1970 Rev. Trim. Dr. Eur. 579; [1970] C.M.L.R. D31.

8 *Vereeniging van Vernis- en Verffabrikanten (VVVF)* 25 June 1969, OJ, 1969, L 168/22; 1969 Rev. Trim. Dr. Eur. 847; [1970] C.M.L.R. D1.

9 *Alliance de Constructeurs Français de Machines-Outils*, 17 July 1968, OJ, 1968, L 201/1, 1968 Rev. Trim. Dr. Eur. 926; [1968] C.M.L.R. D23; see also *Wild-Leitz*, 23 February 1972, OJ, 1972, L 61/27; [1972] C.M.L.R. D36.

10 *Re Christiani and Nielsen*, 18 June 1969, OJ, 1969, L 165/2, 1969 Rev. Trim. Dr. Eur. 844; [1969] C.M.L.R. D36; cp. *Kodak*, 30 June 1970, OJ, 1970, L 147/24; 1970 Rev. Trim. Dr. Eur. 582, at p. 584(14); [1970] C.M.L.R. D19.

11 *Chaufourniers* (Limeburners) 5 May 1969, OJ, 1969, L 122/8; 1969 Rev. Trim. Dr. Eur. 408; [1969] C.M.L.R. D15.

able to all who join as members,[1] joint purchasing agencies which transmit offers to members who are free to accept or to decline them[2] and to mutual manufacturing and sales agreements where different regions have different technical requirements which cannot be satisfied easily by foreign producers, who remain free to compete, especially if statistics show a rise in imports,[3] if necessary, after suitable modification.[4]

Secondly, Reg. 17 enables the Commission to investigate on request by member states, natural and legal persons and associations of interested persons or *ex officio*, any infringements of art. 85(1) and to render a decision requiring the parties to put an end to the infringement[5] after having made the necessary recommendations.[6] The Commission can act even if the time limit for notification has not expired.[7]

Thirdly, Reg. 17 provides for the grant of exemptions under art. 85(3).[8] Exemption was granted in the following circumstances: exclusive dealership agreements without any undertakings to prohibit parallel imports, where similar articles made by others are available, though the distributor is precluded from selling the latter, on the ground that distribution is rendered easier and that the users profit. According to the Commission exclusive dealership offers quicker information and technical aid by distributors who have a better knowledge of the market and easier access to it by the elimination of linguistic and legal barriers while the obligation not to sell products of other manufacturers is indispensable.[9]

A sales organisation of paint manufacturers which assures a uniform standard of production and sale under its own trademark, leaving the members free to sell inferior and superior products under their own trademarks, to fix their own prices, to sell themselves products conforming to the uniform standard, produced either by themselves or by other members with the latter's consent, but binding them to pay a commission, subject to the condition not to belong to a similar association or to subcontract to an outsider, because the agreement furthered distribution and rationalisation, was advantageous to users and only contained indispensable restrictions.[10]

---

1 *Eurogypsum* 26 February 1968, OJ, 1968, L 57/9; 1968 Rev. Trim. Dr. Eur. 460; [1968] C.M.L.R. D1.
2 *SOCEMAS*, 17 July 1968, OJ, 1968, L. 201/4; 1968 Rev. Trim. Dr. Eur. 929; [1968] C.M.L.R. D28.
3 *Pirelli-Dunlop*, 5 December 1969, OJ, 1969, L 323/21;
4 *Vereeniging van Vernis- en Verffabrikanten (VVVF)*, 25 June 1969, OJ, 1969, L 168/22; 1969 Rev. Trim. Dr. Eur. 847; [1970] C.M.L.R. D1.
5 Reg. 17/62, art. 3(1), (2).
6 Reg. 17/62, art. 3(3).
7 Reg. 17/62, art. 9(2).
8 Reg. 17/62, art. 6; for the forms of notification see above, p. 215, n. 5.
9 See above, p. 216, n. 1; *Jalatte*, 17 December 1965, OJ, 1966, 37; 1966 Rev. Trim. Dr. Eur. 575, also 531; [1966] C.M.L.R. D1. For other exclusive dealership agreements see *Omega, Brandt et al.*, 28 October 1970, OJ, 1970, L 242/22, 1970 Rev. Trim. Dr. Eur. 812; [1970] C.M.L.R. D 49.
10 *Transocean Marine Paint Ass.* 27 June 1967, OJ, 1967, No. 163/10; 1967 Rev. Trim Dr. Eur. 735; [1967] C.M.L.R. D9.

An unincorporated association of manufacturers of textile machinery controlling trade fairs to be held every four years, and consisting of most European producers who had to bind themselves not to exhibit elsewhere during that year but were free to exhibit anywhere in the intervening years, and were at liberty to resign at any time, though this step would deprive them of the right of exhibiting at the periodic fairs organised by the association, because the arrangement assisted distribution and economic progress by reducing the number of fairs, rendered them cheaper and thus reduced costs without eliminating competition.[1]

Others include: specialisation cartels serving better distribution and technical progress, leading to an increase in trade and to the absorption of price increases of raw materials in the world markets without eliminating competition;[2] pooling of research facilities;[3] an agreement for the mutual exploitation of a patent, whereby the patent holder in Belgium undertook to supply only the other party in France and only one manufacturer each in every other country of the EEC, the other contracting party undertaking to purchase the machinery in question only from the first party; the restrictions affecting third parties were offset by an increase in production, a division of labour in research and production while the *probability* existed that consumers would profit.[4]

On the other hand, exemption was refused to a rebates cartel of the German ceramic tiles industry affecting German purchasers only which operated a scheme whereby the rebate increased with the number of purchases from anyone of the members, thus discriminating against producers in the other member states. The fact that the rebate was calculated on the basis of purchases from any one German producer, and not from one individual producer, excluded an exemption.[5] The same applied to an area agreement within the EEC.[6]

If exemption is sought, the agreements and concerted practices which have come into being after Reg. 17 had been promulgated must be

---

1 *CEMATEX*, 24 September 1971, OJ, 1971, L 221/26, 1971 Rev. Trim. Dr. Eur. 896; see also *CECIMO*, 13 March 1969, OJ, 1969, L 69/13, 1969 Rev. Trim. Dr. Eur. 399, [1969] C.M.L.R. D1. Distinguish *Nederlandse Cement-Handelmaatschappij N.V.*, 23 December 1971; OJ, 1972, L 22/16; [1972] C.M.L.R. D94.

2 *FN-CF*, 28 May 1971, OJ, 1971, L 134/6, 1971 Rev. Trim. Dr. Eur 717; see also *Jaz-Peter*, 22 July 1969, OJ, 1969, L 195/5; 1969 Rev. Trim. Dr. Eur. 885; [1970] C.M.L.R. 129; *Clima Chappée and Buderus*, 22 July 1969, OJ, 1969, L 195/1; 1969 Rev. Trim. Dr. Eur. 880; [1970] C.M.L.R. D7; D7; *Sopelem-Langen*, 20 December, 1971, OJ, 1972, L 13/47, at p. 49; [1972] C.M.L.R. D77; *Man-Saviem*, 17 January 1972, OJ, 1972, L 31/29; [1972] C.M.L.R. D94; *Thin Paper Agreement*, 26 July 1972, OJ, 1972, L 182/26, III (3).

3 *Henkel-Colgate*, 23 December 1971; OJ, 1972, L 14/14, II and III; [1972] C.M.L.R. D94.

4 *ACEC-Berliet*, 17 July 1968, OJ, 1968, L 201/7; 1968 Rev. Trim. Dr. Eur. 933; [1968] C.M.L.R. D35; see also *Davidson Rubber Co.*, 9 June 1972, OJ, 1972, L 143/31, at p. 36(13), (14); [1972] C.M.L.R. D52.

5 *German Ceramic Tiles Rebates*, 29 December 1970, OJ, 1971, L 10/13; 1971 Rev. Trim. Dr. Eur. 289; [1971] C.M.L.R. D6; Commission Recommendation, *Faience Agreement*, May 1964 Bull. EEC 46, at p. 49.

6 *Van Katwij and Julien*, 28 October 1970, OJ, 1970, L 242/18; 1970 Rev. Trim. Dr. Eur. 808; [1970] C.M.L.R. D43.

notified.[1] This duty is restricted to requests for exemption; notification is not required of all those agreements, decisions and concerted practices which the parties know, or suspect to be unlawful, but for which they do not claim exemption under art. 85(3). Such parties can apply for negative clearance, or they can modify their agreements[2] or desist, or they can continue with their arrangements subject to the threat of proceedings brought by the Commission or by the authorities in the member states.[3] The purpose of Reg. 17/62, art. 4(1) is to enable the Commission to proceed to an investigation whether an exemption can be granted. Therefore the Commission is precluded from so proceeding to an exemption in the absence of notification. If notification is made, a finding that the agreement violates art. 85(1) and is not exempt under art. 85(3) excludes the imposition of fines,[4] unless the Commission as previously informed the parties after a *preliminary examination* that art. 85(1) does apply in the circumstances and art. 85(3) does not.[5] Thus the interim period between notification and decision—which may be prolonged—may be cut down.

As was shown above, this duty of notification does not apply to a variety of types of agreements, unless special circumstances suggest that a violation of art. 85(3) may be involved.[6] The duty of notification does not apply either if these particular types of agreements were entered into before Reg. 17/62 came into force.[7] In all other circumstances, agreements, decisions and concerted practices entered into before that date which fall under art. 85(1) and for which exemption is claimed under art. 85(3) had also to be registered at certain dates between 1 November 1962 and 1 February 1963.[8]

VII   EFFECT OF NULLITY UNDER ART. 85(2)

Although art. 85(2) of the Treaty states that agreements or decisions prohibited by art. 85(1) shall be void, and Reg. 17/62, art. 1 states that such agreements, decisions and concerted practices shall be prohibited

---

1   Reg. 17/62, art. 4(1): for agreements existing before 13 March 1962, when Reg. 17/62 came into force, see below, text to n. 7.
2   *CEMATEX*, 24 September 1971, OJ, 1971, L 227/26; 1971 Rev. Trim. Dr. Eur. 896; *Omega, Brandt et al.*, 28 October 1970, OJ, 1970, L 242/22; 1970 Rev. Trim. Dr. Eur 812; [1970] C.M.L.R. D49.
3   *SA Portelange* v. *SA Smith Corona* (1969), 15 Rec. 309, at p. 317(17)–(19), see Reg. 17/62, art. 15(6).
4   Reg. 17/62, art. 15(5).
5   *Ibid.*, art. 15(6). The Commission must accompany the decision with a reasoned argument of sufficient clarity. See *SA Cimenteries CBR . . . et al.* v. *EEC Commission* (1967), 13 Rec. 93, at p. 119; [1967] C.M.L.R. 77. As regards a decision under Reg. 17/62, arts. 3, 6, see *ACF Chemiefarma* v. *EEC Commission* (1970), 16 Rec. 661, at pp. 692(76)–693(88) allowing an exception in respect of *obiter dicta*, at p. 693(86). For cases see Franceschelli, Plaisant and Lassier, *Droit Européen de la Concurrence*, para. 210 and nn. 139–141. The Community Court has permitted considerable laxity in the use by the Commission of facts not pleaded: *ICI* v. *EEC Commission*, [1972] C.M.L.R. 557, at p. 619 (21–22); *BASF* paras. (7)–(8), (13)–(14); *Bayer*, paras. (7), (8); *Francolor*, paras. (20)–(27); *Mainkur*, para. (22); *ACNA*, paras (21)–(27).
6   *Ibid.*, art. 4(2) and above, pp. 208–215.
7   *Ibid.*, art. 5(2) as amended by Reg. 59/62, art. 2.   8   *Ibid.*, art. 5(1)

ipso jure and without requiring any decision to this effect, the problem remains whether the prohibition is absolute and any decision is declaratory and not constitutive,[1] or whether the agreement remains valid, at least provisionally.[2] The need for a decision, either that the agreement offends against art. 85(1) or that, while it so violates art. 85(1), is nevertheless exempt under art. 85(3), remains paramount;[3] and Reg. 17/62 provides the means. The Commission must render a decision on the compatibility of the agreement etc. with art. 85(1), *either*

(a) *proprio motu* (art. 3), *or*

(b) upon request by a member state or a person having a legitimate interest (art. 3(2))[4], *or*

(c) upon a notification coupled with an application for exemption (art. 6(1)).

Where the agreements etc. existed before Reg. 17/62 came into force on 13 March 1962, were notified within the time limits set by art. 5(1) with a request for exemption[5] and were subsequently modified so as not to offend against art. 85(1) or to satisfy the requirements of art. 85(3), a decision is required, if only in order to determine the period during which the prohibition of art. 85(1) is to be treated as having been applicable to the agreement. However, this decision is restricted to the parties and does not bind enterprises, parties to the agreement, which had not given their express assent to the notification.

The indication of the *date* from which the *exemption* under art. 85(3)—or the compliance with art. 85(1)—is to operate has important consequences not only in the special circumstances of art. 7(1), but also in the general framework of art. 6 (1). The Commission must state the exact time from which the decision, *i.e.* the declaration that the agreement violates art. 85(1) but is exempt under art. 85(3), is to take effect.[6] The only exceptions to this rule concern groups of agreements which are exempted from notification by Reg. 17/62,[7] if future or which existed before 13 March 1962[8] or those exempted under Commission Reg. 67/67.[9] Of course, if

---

1 See above, p. 204; *Parfums Rochas* v. *Bitsch* (1970), 16 Rec. 515, at p. 524(7); [1971] C.M.L.R. 104.

2 See the cases cited above, p. 204, n. 6, and see Vandersanden, 1969 Rev. M.C. 473.

3 For the form of the decision by the Commission see *S.A. Cimenteries CBR . . . et al.* v. *EEC Commission* (1967), 13 Rec. 93, at p. 119; [1967] C.M.L.R. 77.

4 Thus the right to require the Commission to act is restricted where individual persons or legal entities are concerned. Moreover, such a report does not oblige the Commission to give a decision on the merits. It may refuse to proceed. See Reg. 99/63, OJ, 1963, 2268, art. 6.

5 If the agreement etc. belonged to the group which did not require notification according to art. 5(2) of Reg. 17/62 in conjunction with Reg. 17/62 art. 4(2), the time limit was 1 January 1967; see *ibid.*, art. 7(2) as amended by Council Reg. 118/63, OJ, 1963, 2696.

6 Reg. 17/62, arts. 6(7), 7(1).

7 Reg. 17/62, art. 4(2) in the wording of Council Reg. 2822/71, art. 1, OJ, 1971, L 285/49.

8 Reg. 17/62 art. 5(2). For the problem whether a series of identical contracts made with a number of enterprises is covered by Reg. 17/62 art. 5(2) see *Parfums Rochas* v. *Bitsch* (1970), 16 Rec. 515, at pp. 524(8)–525(12); [1971] C.M.L.R. 104; *Brasserie de Haecht* v. *Wilkin* (*No. 2*), [1973] C.M.L.R. 287, at p. 303(21).

9 Reg. 67/67, art. 4.

an agreement requiring notification because it offends against art. 85(1) and requires an exemption is not notified, the declaratory effect of the decision refers to the time when the agreement was concluded or when Reg. 17/62 came into force, whichever is later.[1]

An exemption is valid for a certain time and may be accompanied by conditions and stipulations.[2] It can be renewed.[3] It can also be revoked or modified[4] or a certain course of action may be prohibited in consequence of a change of circumstances and with or without retroactive effect, if a stipulation attached to the exemption has been contravened, if the exemption was based on false facts or was obtained fraudulently or if the exemption is abused.[5]

The discussion on the effect of the procedure of notification on the validity of the agreements etc.[6] leads to the following conclusions.

(a) Agreements in force at the time when Reg. 17/62 came into effect which have been notified under Reg. 17/62, art. 5(1) are valid until they have been declared void.

(b) The same applies to agreements etc. which existed at the time when Reg. 17/62 entered into force which have not been notified.

(c) Agreements exempt from notification under Reg. 17/62, art. 5(2) may be equally valid until a decision has been issued declaring art. 85(1) to be applicable, but the exemption from fines (Reg. 17/62, art. 15(5)) does not apply.

(d) Agreements exempt from the operation of art. 85(1) by virtue of Reg. 67/67 are valid with variable retroactive effect if the agreements were entered into before Reg. 17/62 came into force and were notified in accordance with Reg. 17/62 art. 5(1). All other agreements within the groups enumerated in Reg. 67/67 are valid with retroactive effect from the time of notification, prior to the date when Reg. 67/67 came into effect[7] or when the conditions for applying Reg. 67/67 were fulfilled.

All other agreements which have not been notified and do not qualify under a group exemption are void *ab initio*;[8] if they qualify, the absence of notification is innocuous.[9]

---

1   *Béguelin Import* v. *SALG Import Export* (1971) 117 Rec. 949, at pp. 961(25)–962(29); [1972] C.M.L.R. 81.
2   Reg. 17/62, art. 8(1).
3   Reg. 17/62, art. 8(2).
4   Reg. 17/62, art. 8(3)(a).
5   Reg. 17/62, art. 8(3)(b)–(d).
6   See above, pp. 204–205.
7   *I.e.* 1 May 1967.
8   *Béguelin Import* v. *SALG Import Export* (1971), 17 Rec. 949, at pp. 961(25)–962(29); [1972] C.M.L.R. 81.
9   *Cadillon* v. *Höss*, (1971), 17 Rec. 351, at p. 357(15); [1971] C.M.L.R. 420.

VIII   ANCILLARY MEASURES

In order to carry out its investigations for the purpose of determining whether art. 85(1) applies or an exemption is justified under art. 85(3), the Commission acts in close co-operation with the member states. The latter must be informed of all applications, requests and modifications involving art. 85.[1] A Consultative Committee composed of officials of the member states who are experts in this subject must be called in for a joint meeting before the Commission takes a decision.[2] The Commission may ask for information from the governments and competent authorities of the member states and from enterprises.[3] If the information is not given or is incomplete, the Commission may make a decision embodying the request under the threat of penalties for non-compliance.[4] An appeal against such a decision lies to the Community Court.[5] More generally, the Commission may investigate any sector of the economy if indications exist that competition within the Community in this field is being restricted and may ask for information.[6] The Consultative Committee must be called in.[7] In carrying out its investigations, the Commission, acting through its agents, may examine the books and other business documents, copy them and ask for verbal explanations.[8] It must be given access to premises, land and vehicles of the enterprises concerned.[9] The investigation must be ordered by a decision of the Commission against which an appeal lies to the Community Court.[10] The member states, upon request, must lend their assistance.[11] especially if the investigation is resisted by the enterprise.[12] Alternatively, the competent authorities of the member state must carry out the investigation,[13] if necessary with the assistance of the agents of the Commission.[14]

---

1 Reg. 17/62, art. 10(1), (2). The same applies to proceedings under art. 86 of the Treaty. See also art. 11(1), (6).

2 Reg. 17/62, art. 10(3)–(6). For some aspects of the procedure of consultation see *Boehringer* v. *EEC Commission* (1970), 16 Rec. 769, at p. 801(19), (20).

3 Reg. 17/62, art. 11(1)–(4).

4 Reg. 17/62, art. 11(5); arts. 15(1)(b), 16(1)(c); see CICG-ZVEI/ZPU, Commission Decision 1 February 1971, OJ, 1971, L 34/13; 1971 Rev. Trim. Dr. Eur. 892; [1971] C.M.L.R. D23; *Re Soc. Italiana degli Autori ed Editori*, 9 November 1971, OJ, 1971, L 254/15; [1972] C.M.L.R. D112.

5 Reg. 17/62, art. 11(5).

6 Reg. 17/62, art. 12; it applies also to art. 86 of the Treaty. Such investigations were undertaken for beer (6 November 1969), cables and insulated power lines (3 March 1969), margarine (26 June 1970).

7 Reg. 17/62, art. 12(4).

8 Reg. 17/62, art. 14(1)(a)–(c); see the *Dyestuffs Agreement*, Decision of 24 July 1969, OJ, 1969, L 195/11; 1969 Rev. Trim. Dr. Eur. 892; [1969] C.M.L.R. D23.

9 Reg. 17/62, art. 14(1)(d); for the procedure see *Quinine Agreement*, Decision 16 July 1969, OJ, 1969, L 192/5, 1969, Rev. Trim. Dr. Eur. 856, at p. 866; [1969] C.M.L.R. D41.

10 Reg. 17/62, art. 14(2).

11 Reg. 17/62, art. 14(5).

12 Reg. 1762, art. 14(6).

13 Reg. 17/62, art. 13(1).

14 Reg. 17/62, art. 13(2).

By a decision the Commission may impose fines[1] for supplying wilfully or negligently false or misleading information in applications for negative clearance or in notifications for exemption,[2] in response to requests for information connected with a general or with specific investigations, including failure to supply information[3] or for submitting in incomplete form or for refusing to submit the books and documents required for an investigation.[4] Fines may also be imposed by a decision in respect of infringements of art. 85(1)[5] or for a violation of a stipulation attached to an exemption[6] after hearing the Consultative Committee.[7] Such fines are not to be regarded as penal in character;[8] their amount is fixed, within a flexible range, and includes a percentage of the turnover.[9] Nevertheless, the duration and the gravity[10] of the violation will have to be considered in fixing the fine, as well as the subjective element. The gravity of the violation is determined by the nature of the restrictions, the number and size of the parties to the agreement, the share of the market controlled by each, and the market situation at the time of the violation,[11] as well as by the wilful or negligent nature of the conduct.[12] It would seem that in keeping with the statutory terminology, fines established by Reg. 17/62 have the characteristics of penalties as they are generally accepted.[13] In particular, their economic effect is irrelevant[14] and a global sum may be fixed to be apportioned among the defendants.[15] No period of limitation runs.[16]

---

1   The French text speaks of *"amendes"*, the German text of *"Geldbussen"*. Both are current in the criminal law of these countries and denote pecuniary penalties.

2   Reg. 17/62, art. 15(1)(a); see arts. 2, 4, 5.

3   Reg. 17/62, art. 15(1)(b); see arts. 11(3), (5), 12.

4   Reg. 17/62, art. 15(1)(c); see arts. 13, 14.

5   Reg. 17/62, art. 15(2)(a); also for violations of art. 86 of the Treaty, see *Quinine Agreement*, Decision 16 July 1969, OJ, 1969, L 192/5; 1969 Rev. Trim. Dr. Eur. 856, at p. 875(35); [1969] C.M.L.R. D.41.

6   Reg. 17/62, art. 15(2) (b).

7   Reg. 17/62, art. 15(3).

8   Reg. 17/62, art. 15(4); they can be enforced in the member states by virtue of art. 192 of the Treaty, possibly in addition to penalties under domestic law: Franceschelli, Plaisant and Lassier, *Droit Européen de la Concurrence*, No. 804.

9   Reg. 17/62, art. 15(1) (2).

10   *Dyestuffs Agreement*, Decision 24 July 1969, OJ, 1969, L 295/11; 1969 Rev. Trim. Dr. Eur. 892; *Quinine Agreement* (above, n. 5); 1969 Rev. Trim. Dr. Eur. 856, at p. 876(38).

11   *ACF Chemiefarma* v. *EEC Commission* (1970), 16 Rec. 661, at p. 704(176), on appeal from *Quinine Agreement* (above, n. 5); *Buchler* v. *EEC Commission* (1970), 16 Rec. 733, at p. 765(49); *Boehringer* v. *EEC Commission* (1970), 16 Rec. 769, at p. 811(53). Lyklema, 1971 Cah. Dr. Eur. 522.

12   *Boehringer* v. *EEC Commission* (1970), 16 Rec. 769 at p. 812(55), (58); *ICI* v. *EEC Commission*, [1972] C.M.L.R. 557 at p. 630(147); *Bayer, ibid.* para. 42; *Francolor*, para. (107); *Geigy*, para. (53); *Mainkur*, paras. (42)–(44).

13   *ACF Chemiefarma* v. *EEC Commission* (1970), 16 Rec. 661, at pp. 703(172)–704(176); *Buchler* v. *EEC Commission* (1970), 16 Rec. 1733, at p. 765(49); *Boehringer* v. *EEC Commission* (1970), 16 Rec. 769, at p. 811(53).

14   *Buchler* v. *EEC Commission* (1970), 16 Rec. 733, at p. 765(5), (51).

15   *Boehringer GmbH* v. *EEC Commission* (1970), 16 Rec. 769, at p. 812(55). Fines imposed in a non-member state for the same conduct cannot be taken into account: *Boehringer*, 25 November 1971, OJ, 1971, 282/46, paras. 10, 11; [1972] C.M.L.R. D121.

16   *ACF Chemiefarma* v. *EEC Commission* (1970), 16 Rec. 661, at p. 685(18)–686(20); *Buchler*

Penalties, in the meaning of the Treaty,[1] on the other hand, are variable sums fixed on a daily basis and calculated from the date fixed by a decision which enjoins the termination of an infringement of art. 85,[2] the discontinuance of any action prohibited by the Commission by virtue of Reg. 17/62, art. 8(3),[3] the supply of information requested by the Commission by virtue of Reg. 17/62, art. 11(5)[4] or the submission to an investigation ordered by virtue of Reg. 17/62, art. 14(3).[5] The Consultative Committee must be called in.[6] To a certain extent the variable character of the penalty, which is open to a subsequent adjustment, recalls an affinity with the *astreinte* of French law but no more.[7]

In the proceedings before the Commission leading to a decision[8] the enterprises concerned[9] and, if necessary, other natural persons or associations of persons or legal entities[10] are to be heard.[11] The Community Court has jurisdiction to review decisions of the Commission imposing a fine or penalty.[12] In addition it may review the legality of interim measures of

(1970), 16 Rec. 733, at p. 752(6)–753(7); *Boehringer* v. *EEC Commission* (1970), 16 Rec. 769 at p. 798(6). See also Commission Decision 16 July 1969, OJ, 1969, L 192/5 (36); [1969] C.M.L.R. D41. *ICI* v. *EEC Commission*, [1972] C.M.L.R. 557, at p. 621(46)–(49); *Bayer, ibid.*, paras. (19)–(21); *ACNA, ibid.*, paras. (32)–(37).

1 The French text speaks of "*astreintes*"; the German text of "*Zwangsgelder*". Both measures serve to ensure the observance of a duty, the former by way of specific performance in contract, the latter by way of physical act in administrative law. See de Roux and Voillemot, *op. cit.* pp. 157.

2 Reg. 17/62, art. 16(1)(a); also art. 86 of the Treaty. The question of periods of limitation has not yet been solved; see the cases cited above, p. 224, n. 10. But note the Draft Regulation of 30 December 1971 concerning the limitation of proceedings for fines and penalties under arts. 75, 79 and 87, OJ, 1972, C 43/1, 89/21, 129/10.

3 Reg. 17/62, art. 16(1)(b).

4 Reg. 17/62, art. 16(1)(c).

5 Reg. 17/62, art. 16(1)(d).

6 Reg. 17/62, art. 16(3).

7 Stoufflet, Juriscl. Dr. Int. Nos. 310, 311; but see Franceschelli, Plaisant and Lassier, *Droit Européen de le Concurrence*, No. 282; for *astreintes* in French law see N. Catala, (1959) Jurid. Rev. (N.S. 4) 163; (1961) *ibid.* (N.S. 6) 53.

8 *I.e.* Reg. 17/62, arts. 2 (negative clearance); 3 (infringements of art. 85(1)); 6 (exemption); 7 (modification of notified agreements); 8 (renewal, revocation, alteration of exemptions, prohibition of certain action); 15 (fines); 16 (penalties). For the requirements in form and substance of a decision by the Commission see *ACF Chemiefarma* v. *EEC Commission* (1970), 16 Rec. 661, at pp. 686(24)–687(29), 692(76)–(81), 693(90)–(93). And see above, p. 220, n. 5.

9 Reg. 17/62, art. 19(1); Reg. 99/63, OJ, 1963, 2268; for the legality of these measures see *ACF Chemiefarma* v. *EEC Commission* (1970), 16 Rec. 661, at pp. 690(60)–691(67).

10 Reg. 17/62, art. 19(2), (3); Reg. 99/63, art. 5; if interested, on demand; if affected in their rights: *ex officio*.

11 The procedure for hearings by the Commission may be determined by the Commission as a measure implementing Reg. 17/62 and delegated to it by art. 24 of Reg. 17/62. See *ACF Chemiefarma* v. *EEC Commission* (1970), 16 Rec. 661, at pp. 690(60)–691(67); and see generally *Consten and Grundig* v. *EEC Commission*, (1966), 12 Rec. 429, at pp. 491–492; [1966] C.M.L.R. 418. The Commission cannot sub-delegate these powers: *ICI* v. *EEC Commission*, [1972] C.M.L.R. 557, at p. 618(12).

12 Reg. 17/62, art. 17 implementing EEC Treaty art. 172; Franceschelli, Plaisant and Lassier, *Droit Européen de la Concurrence*, Nos. 876–897.

investigation and of decisions made by virtue of Reg. 17/62, arts. 2, 3 or 6 (art. 173).[1]

IX JURISDICTION OF COMMUNITY AND OF NATIONAL AUTHORITIES

The broad provisions of the Treaty (arts, 89, 88) confer jurisdiction upon the Commission and upon the courts of the member states concurrently. The relationship between the domestic law of the member states dealing with restrictive practices and monopolies, on the one hand, and the relevant provisions of the Treaty and of the regulations issued thereunder on the other hand, was to be determined by subsequent legislation (art. 87(2)(2)). In so far as the relationship between the substantive rules of the Treaty and of the law of the member states is concerned, such a determination has not been forthcoming[2] and is probably both unnecessary and difficult.[3] In the sphere of jurisdiction, Reg. 17/62 ensures the primacy of the Commission and of the Community Court to determine whether any agreements violate art. 85(1) and whether an exemption can be granted under art. 85(3).[4]

Before Reg. 17/62 was issued on the strength of art. 87, the authorities of the member states were alone competent to control the admissibility of cartel agreements and monopolies. According to art. 85 they had to apply their own domestic law and the provisions (arts. 85, 86) of the Treaty. They were also entrusted with the granting of exemptions (art. 85(3)). Now that Reg. 17/62 has established the procedure before the Commission[5] several overlaps remain. In particular Reg. 17/62 acknowledged[6] that the authorities of the member states retain a concurrent jurisdiction to declare that art. 85(1)[7] has been infringed, provided that no proceedings have been initiated by the Commission for negative clearance, for terminating an infringement of art. 85(1) or for an exemption under art. 85(3).[8] To that extent the jurisdiction of the Commission is exclusive, and domestic courts have lost the power to grant exemptions under art. 85(3). The question remains as to the exercise of the concurrent jurisdiction; it is determined by a priority in time or in functions? Does it make any difference whether the domestic court purports to apply art, 85(1) or the corresponding rules of its own domestic law? In either case.

---

1 Goldman, *Droit Commercial Européen*, No. 388, p. 386; Nos. 415–418, pp. 405–406; Franceschelli, Plaisant and Lassier, *Droit Européen de la Concurrence*, now pp. 906–971.

2 *Wilhelm (Walt)* v. *Bundeskartellamt* (1969), 15 Rec. 1, at p. 14(4); [1969] C.M.L.R. 100.

3 See below, p. 227; Goldman, *Droit Commercial Européen*, No. 336, p. 346; *Consten and Grundig* v. *EEC Commission* (1966), 12 Rec. 429, at p. 500; [1966] C.M.L.R. 418.

4 Reg. 17/62, art. 9(1).

5 OJ, 1962, 204; Reg. 27/62, OJ, 1962, 1118; Reg. 99/63, OJ, 1963, 2268.

6 Art. 9(3).

7 Also regarding art. 86.

8 Reg. 17/62, art. 9(3). For the question as to the moment when proceedings have been initiated by the Commission see de Roux and Voillemot, *Le Droit de la Concurrence des Communautés Européens*, pp. 84, 148–150. The practice of the Commission relies on the date of the notice sent to the interested parties and to member states.

must an authority of a member state which has been seized with a case before proceedings were initiated by the Commission stay proceedings?[1]

While it was disputed at one time whether the reference to the "authorities of the Member States" in Reg. 17/62 art. 9(3) includes the courts of the member states,[2] it is now clear that it does.[3] In practice an overlap can be avoided if the pleadings in the court of the member state do not disclose any reliance on a justification based on art. 85(3) and if no application for exemption has been submitted to the Commission,[4] provided that the Commission does not act under Reg. 17/62, art. 3. The courts of the member states appear to retain jurisdiction to take interim measures.[5]

It remains, therefore, to examine the exercise of concurrent jurisdiction by the courts of the member states. In principle the Treaty, and thus the jurisdiction of the Commission and of the Community Court, must take precedence over that of domestic law and of the jurisdiction of domestic courts.[6] The Treaty itself envisages the concurrent application of Community and domestic law in this field (art. 87(2)(e)), but the application of domestic law by the courts of the member states must not prejudice the uniform application of community law[7] which cannot vary from member state to member state.[8] The consequences are the following.

1 Application of Community Law by Domestic Courts

The courts of the member states have jurisdiction to entertain actions involving art. 85(1) and to make findings under art. 85(2), as long as the Commission has not begun proceedings.[9] It would seem, therefore, that proceedings must be stayed, if the Commission embarks upon some action.

2 Application of Domestic Law by Domestic Courts

The courts of the member states have jurisdiction to entertain actions based on their domestic law relating to restrictive practices, provided that

---

1 Notification to the national authorities which have not raised any objections does not oust the jurisdiction of the Commission: *ACF Chemiefarma* v. *EEC Commission* (1970), 16 Rec. 661, at pp. 684(10)–685(12), *obiter*, Daig, (1971) 35 Rabels Z. 1, at pp. 29–35.

2 Mailänder, *Zuständigkeit und Entscheidungsfreiheit nationaler Gerichte* (1965), pp. 25, 26, n. 13 with lit.; Robert, (1963) 1 C.M.L.Rev. 228; van der Heuvel, (1963) 12 A.J.C.L. 172, at p. 179; Goldman, *Droit Commercial Européen*, Nos. 339–341, pp. 349–354.

3 *Wilhelm (Walt)* v. *Bundeskartellamt* (1969), 15 Rec. 1, at p. 13; [1969] C.M.L.R. 100; in conjunction with *Bilger* v. *Jehle* (1970), 16 Rec. 127, at p. 137(9). The question whether arbitral tribunals are included is therefore now obsolete but see: Goldman, *Droit Commercial Européen* No. 341, p. 352; cp. Cohn, 1965 B.B.A.W.D. 267; Franceschelli, Plaisant and Lassier, *Droit Européen de la Concurrence*, No. 716; Stoufflet, Juriscl. Dr. Int. Nos. 290–297.

4 Mailänder, *Zuständigkeit und Entscheidungsfreiheit nationaler Gerichte*, pp. 48–49.

5 Mailänder, above, *op. cit.*, p. 58 with references and lit.

6 *Wilhelm (Walt)* v. *Bundeskartellamt* (1969), 15 Rec. 1, at p. 13 (4)–(8).

7 *Ibid.*, p. 13(4), (5), (7), (8).

8 *Ibid.*, p. 13(6).

9 *Bilger* v. *Jehle* (1970), 16 Rec. 127, at p. 136(9). Note the use of this criterion which relies on a step by the Commission and not on requests by outsiders (Reg. 17/62, art. 3) or on notification by the parties (*ibid.*, arts. 2, 4, 5). For the practice of French courts see Goldman, *Droit Commercial Européen*, Nos. 337–338, pp. 346–348. And see *Brasserie de Haecht* v. *Wilkin (No. 2)*, [1973] C.M.L.R. 287, at p. 303(16).

the application of the latter does not prejudice the uniform application of Community Law.[1] In the absence of a regulation solving the conflict between the relevant rules of Community law and domestic law[2] Reg. 17/62, art. 9(3) does not prohibit the exercise of domestic jurisdiction even after the Commission has begun proceedings, as long as the uniform application of Community law is not disturbed.[3] In exercising its separate jurisdiction the Commission must take any prior sanctions into account which were imposed by a court in a member state.[4]

It may be argued, therefore, that the two jurisdictions are not alternative but cumulative and that domestic courts may apply domestic law either if the latter is more stringent than art. 85(1) or if in their opinion a purely domestic situation is involved. It remains an open question whether domestic courts remain free to impose penalties or to declare an agreement void according to a more stringent domestic law after the Commission has granted an exemption under art. 85(3).[5] On the one hand, the application of a more stringent domestic rule in excess of Community law may be said to differ from a disregard of an exemption by Community authorities. The former follows, but enlarges, the policy against restrictions enshrined in the Treaty. The latter sets aside a specific Community measure. On the other hand it can be argued that in both cases the uniform application of Community law is affected.

The domestic courts of the member states must also determine according to their own law whether a violation of art. 85(1) justifies an action in tort[6] or in damages for a breach of contract.[7] On the other hand, since art. 85 is directly applicable, it can be relied upon on a defence by a party to a cartel agreement which is not purely domestic.[8]

X   PARTICULAR AREAS—SPECIAL PROVISIONS—AGRICULTURE, TRANSPORT

In accordance with the provisions of the Treaty on agriculture (arts. 42, 43) a special regulation applies to restrictive practices and monopolies in this field.[9] Similarly the Treaty provisions on transport (art. 75) called

---

1   See above, p. 227 n. 7.

2   See above, p. 227; EEC Treaty art 87(2)(e).

3   *Wilhelm (Walt)* v. *Bundeskartellamt* (1969), 15 Rec. 1, at p. 13(9); [1969] C.M.L.R. 100.

4   *Ibid.*, p. 13(11)

5   Mailänder, (*op. cit.*, above, p. 227, n. 4) at p. 22, but see Stoufflet, Juriscl. Dr. Int. No. 298; Deringer, *The Competition Law*, paras. 280 ff. Doubtful: Franceschelli, Plaisant and Lassier, *Droit Européen de la Concurrence*, No. 229 and, in the negative, No. 804. Cp. the European Communities Act 1972, s. 10(1).

6   See Van der Heuvel, (1963) 12 A.J.C.L. 173, at pp. 183, 186 with cases; de Roux and Voillemot, *op. cit.*, pp. 160–162; Cerexhe, in *Ganshof van der Meersch*, Nos. 2111–2112, p. 843.

7   *E.g. SA Portelange* v. *SA Smith Corona* (1969), 15 Rec. 309; *Parfums Rochas* v. *Bitsch* (1970), 16 Rec. 515; [1971] C.M.L.R. 104; *Cadillon* v. *Höss*, (1971), 17 Rec. 351; [1971] C.M.L.R. 420; *Béguelin Import* v. *SALG Import Export* (1971), 17 Rec. 949; [1972] C.M.L.R. 81.

8   For some criteria see *Consten and Grundig* v. *EEC Commission* (1966), 12 Rec. 429, at p. 502; [1966] C.M.L.R. 418.

9   Reg. 26/62, art. 1, OJ, 1962, 993, amended by Reg. 49/62, OJ, 1962, 1571; Gleiss and Wolff, (1971) 21 WuW 310.

for special measures to control restrictions of competition concerning transport by road, rail and inland waterways, resulting in the adoption of a special Regulation.[1]

In the realm of *agriculture*, the rules on restrictive practices do not apply to agreements, decisions and practices of domestic organisations of the agricultural markets, *i.e.* which are composed of farmers, farmers' associations or unions of farmers' associations under the jurisdiction of one member state only to the extent that, without imposing the obligation to charge a certain price, they are limited to the production or sale of agricultural products, or the use of common installations for storage, treatment or processing of agricultural products.[2] Thus art. 85(1) applies to price fixing only, but the rules prohibiting dumping (art. 91(1)) and state aids are rendered applicable to the production of, or trade in, agricultural products (art. 93(1) and (3), first sentence).[3]

In the *transport* sector, the particular needs of this industry have influenced first the suspension,[4] and now the introduction of rules on competition.[5] The Regulation is much more detailed than that on agriculture both in respect of the provisions dealing with the substance of the agreements, decisions and concerted practices and abuse of a dominant position, and with the procedure. The latter is fashioned upon that provided by Reg. 17/62 generally, but is adapted to the special needs of transport.

In substance, the Regulation covers agreements etc. which have the purpose or the effect of (a) fixing terms and conditions of transport, (b) limiting or regulating the supply of transport services, (c) sharing transport markets, (d) applying technical improvements or technical co-operation and (e) jointly financing or acquiring transport material or equipment directly linked with the provision of transport, in so far as may be required, for the joint operation of a group of transport undertakings by road or inland waterway.[6] In addition it covers the exercise of dominant positions in the transport market. For both purposes transport includes any activities ancillary to transport.[7]

Any agreements between undertakings on these topics, any decisions by associations of enterprises and all concerted practices likely to affect trade between member states are prohibited, if their purpose or effect is to restrict or to distort competition in the EEC. By way of illustration only, it applies to agreements, decisions and concerted practices of the

---

1 Reg. 1017/68, OJ, 1968, L 175/1 superseding Regs. 141/62, OJ, 1962, 1792; 1002/67, OJ, 1967.

2 Reg. 26/62, art. 2(1). See Commission Dec. 73/109, OJ, 1973, L 140/17, at p. 42 (III).

3 Reg. 26/62, arts. 3, 4.

4 Reg. 141/62, OJ, 1962, 2751; Reg. 1002/67, OJ, 1967, L 306/1; Wagenbauer, 1970 Cah. Dr. Eur., 645.

5 Reg. 1017/68, OJ, 1968, L 175/1 closely following art. 85 of the Treaty in view of the problem discussed above, p. 177, whether or not the general provisions of the Treaty apply to transport as well in so far as Reg. 1017/68 does not apply. See Wagenbauer, 1970 Cah. Dr. Eur., 649. For the procedure see Commission Reg. 1629/69, OJ, 1969, L 209/1.

6 The reference in Reg. 1017/68, art. 1 to art. 4 does not add anything to the definition set out in art. 1.

7 Reg. 1017/68, art. 1.

kind set out above which are concerned with any one of the objects enumerated in art. 1, *i.e.*—

(a) fixing terms and conditions of transport or other business conditions;

(b) limiting or regulating the supply of transport markets, technical development or investments (see also above (d)–(e));

(c) sharing transport markets;

(d) applying unequal conditions of equivalent services in relation to commercial associations with the result that they are placed at a commercial disadvantage;

(e) making the conclusion of contracts subject to the acceptance, by associates, of supplementary obligations unconnected with transport services.[1]

It will be noted that, as in art. 85 (1) of the Treaty, where the agreements, decisions and concerted practices affected are all concerned with the same general practices, Reg. 1017/68, art. 2 enumerates, once again by way of illustration, the activities which restrict competition, but this enumeration is adapted to the peculiar character of the transport industry.

As in the case of art. 85(1), certain groups of agreements are exempt from the general prohibition. These include agreements etc. concerning the creation and operation of transport undertakings, the joint financing or acquisition of transport material or equipment which is directly concerned with, and necessary for, the operation of the transport group, provided that, in the latter case, the total load capacity of the group does not exceed a certain tonnage so as to characterize the group as being of small or medium size.[2] Equally, as in the case of art. 85, any individual agreement etc. of the type falling within the exempted group may constitute an unlawful restriction unless it satisfies the conditions for a specific exemption.[3] On the other hand, agreements concerning technical improvements and technical co-operation are exempt *per se*.[4]

Exemption, as in the case of art. 85(3), may be granted, even with retroactive effect, for any agreement, decision or concerted practice, or any category of any of these measures which contribute towards—

(a) the improvement of the quality of transport services;

(b) the promotion of greater continuity and stability in the supply of transport, if the supply and demand fluctuates considerably in time;

(c) the growth of productivity;

(d) the promotion of technical or economic progress.

Again, as in the case of art. 85(3) the interests of the consumers—here the users of transport—must be taken into consideration, and the restrictions

---

1 Reg. 1017/68, art. 2.
2 Reg. 1017/68, art. 4(1), 2nd para.
3 Reg. 1017/68, art. 4(2).
4 Reg. 1017/68, art. 3(1); contrast art. 85(3) of the EEC Treaty.

(a) must be essential in order to achieve the aims set out above;
(b) must not be such as to enable the undertaking to eliminate competition in respect of a substantial part of the transport market concerned.[1]

In addition, an innovatory rule provides for the exemption of agreements, decisions and concerted practices which are likely to reduce disturbance in a particular transport market, pending the enactment or appropriate stabilising measures by the Council.[2] This exemption, too, is only to be granted subject to the same safeguarding conditions (a) and (b) under which a general exemption can be granted according to art. 5.[3] A much improved article,[4] reproducing in substance art. 85(2) of the Treaty, makes it clear that agreements and decisions which offend against the prohibition of restraint of competition are null and void, once they have been annulled.[5] Special provisions deal with monopolies and with public undertakings entrusted with managing services of general economic interest.[6]

The Commission is enjoined, in general terms, to establish a procedure, upon the complaint of member states or of persons or legal entities having a legitimate interest,[7] for putting an end to prohibited measures or restraint of competition, abuse of dominant positions and abuse of the exemption accorded to undertakings of a small or medium size.[8] The Regulation follows closely Reg. 17/62 when it provides for recommendations and decisions to be made by the Commission for putting an end to any infringement of the rules on restriction of competition or to grant exemptions.[9] The procedure for granting exemptions reflects the experience gained in administering art. 85(3) of the Treaty,[10] subject to some relaxations.[11] The provisions on the period of operation of exemptions and their revocation[12] follow closely those in Reg. 17/62.[13] The same applies to the division of competence between the Commission and the member states.[14] The Commission has exclusive jurisdiction to grant general (art. 5) and specific (art. 6) exemptions and to impose the obligation to modify or stop activities arising under a group exemption of small and medium sized undertakings (art. 4(2)).[15] The authorities of the member states have

---

1   Reg. 1017/68, art. 5; cp. art. 85(3) of the EEC Treaty, especially the Proviso (a) and (b).
2   Reg. 1017/68, art. 6(1); for the procedure of exemption in accordance with art. 6(1) see arts. 6(2) end and 14.
3   Reg. 1017/68, art. 6(3).
4   Reg. 1017/68, art. 7.
5   See above, pp. 204–205.
6   Reg. 1017/68, arts. 8, 9.
7   Reg. 1017/68, art. 10; cp. Reg. 17/62, art. 3(2).
8   Reg. 1017/68, art. 10.
9   Reg. 1017/68, art. 11; cp. Reg. 17/62, art. 3(1), (2).
10 Reg. 1017/68, art. 12; cp. Reg. 17/62, art. 6; Wagenbauer, 1970 Cah. Dr. Eur. 654.
11 Reg. 1017/68, art. 12(3).
12 Reg. 1017/68, art. 13.
13 Reg. 17/62, art. 8.
14 Reg. 1017/68, art. 15.
15 Reg. 1017/68, art. 15, 1st para.; cp. Reg. 17/62, art. 9.

concurrent jurisdiction to annul agreements (art. 2), unless the Commission has pre-empted the jurisdiction by instituting proceedings or has notified the parties that grave doubts exist whether an exemption can be granted.[1] In pursuing its task under Reg. 1017/68, the Commission must co-operate with the authorities in the member states and with the Consultative Committee on Agreements and Dominant Positions.[2] As in Reg. 17/62,[3] enquiries in an economic sector are foreseen,[4] the Commission may issue requests for information[5] or ask the competent authorities of member states to carry out an inspection[6] or carry out inspections itself.[7] Similarly, fines and financial penalties are foreseen in accordance with previous practice[8] and the *compétence de pleine juridiction* in the meaning of art. 172 of the Treaty is preserved.[9] The remaining provisions on units of account, hearings, trade secrets, publication of decisions and implementing provisions[10] follow closely the corresponding provisions in Reg. 17/62.[11]

---

1   Reg. 1017/68, art. 15, 2nd para.
2   Reg. 1017/68, arts. 16, 17; cp. Reg. 17/62, art. 10.
3   Reg. 17/62, art. 12.
4   Reg. 1017/68, art. 18.
5   Reg. 1017/68, art. 19; cp. Reg. 17/62, art. 11.
6   Reg. 1017/68, art. 20; cp. Reg. 17/62, art. 13.
7   Reg. 1017/68, art. 21; cp. Reg. 17/62, art. 14.
8   Reg. 1017/68, arts. 22, 23; cp. Reg. 1762, arts. 15, 16.
9   Reg. 1017/68, art. 24; cp. Reg. 17/62, art. 17.
10 Reg. 1017/68, arts. 25–29.
11 Reg. 17/62, arts. 18–21, 24.

12

Abuse of Dominant Position

(Article 86)[1]

In addition to restrictive trade practices and cartels, the Treaty prohibits (art. 86) the abusive exploitation by one or more enterprises of a dominant position within the Common Market or within a substantial part of it in so far as trade between member states could be affected thereby. By way of enumeration the Treaty refers with suitable modifications to the practices which attract the operation of art. 85, *i.e.*,

(a) the direct or indirect imposition of any purchase or selling price or of any other trading conditions *which are inequitable*;[2]

(b) the limitation of production, markets or technological development *to the prejudice of consumers*;[3]

(c) the application of unequal conditions to parties undertaking equivalent engagements in commercial transactions, thereby placing them at a competitive disadvantage;[4]

(d) making the conclusion of a contract subject to the acceptance by the other party to the contract of additional obligations which, by their nature or according to commercial usage, have no connection with the subject of such contract.[5]

---

1 Deringer, *The Competition Law of the EEC*, pp. 153–176, paras. 501–559; Braun, Gleiss and Hirsch, *Le Droit des Ententes de la CEE*, pp. 179–195; Franceschelli, Plaisant and Lassier, *Droit Européen de la Concurrence*, Nos. 161–199, pp. 59–81; de Roux and Voillemot, *Le Droit de la Concurrence des Communautés Européennes*, Nos. 41–55, pp. 67–81; Willemetz, 1966 Cah. Dr. Eur. 583; Joliet, "Monopolisation et Abus de Position Dominante", 1969 Rev. Trim. Dr. Eur. 645; Cerexhe in *Ganshof van der Meersch*, Nos. 2087–2099, pp. 837–840; Stoufflet in Juriscl. Dr. Int. Fasc. 164 G, Nos. 151–161; Scheufele, 1971 A.W.D. 457; Bienaymé, 1972 Rev. Trim. Dr. Eur. 65; Cerexhe, 1972 Cah. Dr. Eur. 272; Dubois, *La Position Dominante et son Abus dans l'Art. 86 du Traité CEE* (1968).

2 This condition distinguishes art. 86(a) from art. 85(1)(a); for a comment see Joliet (above, n. 1), at pp. 682–685.

3 The emphasis on the prejudice inflicted upon the consumer distinguishes art. 86(b) from art. 85(1)(b). The elements of control of production and limitation of investment, which figure in art. 85(1)(b) are omitted, having regard to the acceptance of dominant positions; for a discussion see Stoufflet, Juriscl. Dr. Int. Fasc. 164 G, No. 154.

4 Art. 86(c) is identical with art. 85(1)(d); naturally art. 85(1)(c) dealing with market-sharing has no equivalent in art. 86; for comment see Joliet, above, n. 1, at pp. 685–687.

5 Art. 86(d) which is identical with art. 85(1)(e); for comment see Joliet, (above, n. 1), at p. 687.

I   DOMINANT POSITION

Article 86 fastens on the dominant position[1] of one or more enterprises within the Common Market only if their exploitation is abusive and capable of affecting trade between member states.   The insistence that the exploitation of the dominant position must be abusive, before the prohibition can operate distinguishes art. 86 of the EEC Treaty to some extent from its counterpart in the ECSC Treaty (but see art. 66(7)).   The latter (art. 66(1)) enables the Executive to control the creation of concentrations.   The EEC Treaty prohibits the use, for purposes contrary to those of the EEC Treaty, of a dominant position which protects the enterprises concerned from effective competition in a substantial part of the Common Market.   Thus the ECSC Treaty (art. 66(1), (3), (7)) seems to be aimed against monopolies, oligopolies and concentrations as such.

The potential threat of the dominant position for purposes contrary to the ECSC Treaty justifies intervention by the authorities, but unlike in art. 86 of the EEC Treaty it is not an integral part of the prohibited conduct.   Article 86 of the EEC Treaty, on the other hand, does not appear to outlaw monopolies and oligopolies as long as their power is not abused with potential effects upon trade between member states.[2]

The question has been debated as to the effect of art. 85 upon concentrations of enterprises, thus linking it to art. 86 so as to close possible gaps.[3] It would appear, however, from what little practice exists at present, that the respective functions of these articles are separate.[4]   The former concentrates on agreements, the latter on behaviour.[5]

According to the Commission,[6] enterprises occupy a dominant position if for a certain range of production[7] they have the possibility of independent action which enables them to operate without taking account, in particular, of competitors, buyers or suppliers.   This is the case when, by reason of their share of the market, or of their share of the market in conjunction, particularly, with the distribution of technical know-how, raw materials or capital, they can determine prices or control production

---

1   Deringer, *The Competition Law of the EEC*, para. 520 points out that the divergence of the Dutch text which speaks of "*Machtpositie*" does not indicate the absence of a uniform notion; for the absence of a definition see Franceschelli, Plaisant and Lassier, *Droit Européen de la Concurrence*, No. 167; Braun, Gleiss, Hirsch, *Le Droit des Ententes de la CEE*, No. 204.

2   Buxbaum, (1961) 61 Col. L.R. 402 at p. 415 and see below, p. 238, n. 1.

3   For literature see Joliet (above, p. 233, n. 1), at p. 691, n. 3.

4   Deringer, *The Competition Law of the EEC*, para. 504; Franceschelli, Plaisant and Lassier, *Droit Européen de la Concurrence*, No. 163; Bienaymé 1972 Rev. Trim. Dr. Eur. 65, at p. 72.

5   See *e.g.* Bienaymé (above, n. 2), at p. 283. *Quaere* whether it includes legal acts (*actes juridiques*); see Cerexhe, 1972 Cah. Dr. Eur. 272, at p. 293.

6   *Continental Can*, 9 December 1971, OJ, 1972, L 7/25 at p. 35 II 3, see also pp. 35(4)–37(19); [1972] C.M.L.R. D11; cp. ECSC Treaty art. 66(7): "which protects them from competition in a substantial part of the Common Market"; *Wohlfahrt-Everling-Glaesner-Sprung, ad* art. 86, n. 1; Willemetz, 1966 Cah. Dr. Eur. 583, at p. 590. For other criteria and formulations see Deringer, *The Competition Law of the EEC*, paras. 525–529.

7   Deringer, *The Competition Law of the EEC*, para. 515.

or distribution in respect of a significant part of the products concerned. This possibility does not necessarily depend upon the absolute domination which enables enterprises in such a position to eliminate all freedom of action of their economic partners, but it suffices if it is strong enough, as a whole, to ensure for such enterprises a complete independence of behaviour, even if there are differences of intensity in their influence upon the different sectional markets.[1] In addition, the dominant position as a trader, not as a producer, must be held within the Common Market or within a substantial part of it. Consequently the holder of such a dominant position must be able to impede the continuation of effective competition within an important part of the Market concerned, having regard in particular to the potential existence and strength of producers and distributors of similar products or of products serving as substitutes.[2] For this purpose, a dominant position in Germany, a member state, may be sufficient to satisfy the test of art. 86,[3] and it is irrelevant that the German enterprise is owned and controlled by an American company.[4]

II   Abusive Exploitation

No authoritative definition of the abuse of a dominant position has been forthcoming hitherto, but the formulation of the examples in art. 86, as compared with their counterparts in art. 85(1) shows an insistence upon the *inequitable nature* of the prices and conditions which are imposed or upon the *prejudice to the consumer* resulting from any limitation of production, markets or technological development.[5] The criteria are thus objective[6] centred on the purchasers or users rather than on the competitors.[7]

The Commission in its limited practice has given some support for this interpretation when it found an abusive exploitation of a dominant position in a discrimination by a trade association against nationals of

---

1   The Commission included in this category a "*Wirtschaftlicher Verein*" established in accordance with para. 22 of the German Civil Code with the necessary governmental authorisation and exercising a statutory function (German Copyright Act 1965, para. 53(5); Law of 9 September 1965, (1965) I BGBl 1294; see *GEMA*, below, p. 236 n. 1).

2   *Sirena Srl* v. *Eda Srl* (1971), 17 Rec. 69, at p. 84(16); [1971] C.M.L.R. 260 (trademark); *Deutsche Grammophon GmbH* v. *Metro-SB-Grossmärkte GmbH* (1971), 17 Rec. 487, at p. 501(17); [1971] C.M.L.R. 631. For a practical example see *Continental Can* (below, n. 2), at p. 37(15)–(19).

3   *GEMA*, 2 June 1971, OJ, 1971, L 134/15, at p. 21C; [1971] C.M.L.R. D35; *Continental Can*, OJ, 1972, L 7/25, at p. 35(3)–(8); but see the additional considerations concerning the predominance of Continental Can through its control of machine construction and know-how exercised through licensing in the Netherlands and France within and, in Great Britain, Denmark, Switzerland and Austria, outside the EEC: OJ, 1972, L7/25, at p. 36(9)–(14).

4   *Continental Can* case, OJ, 1972, L 7/25, at p. 35(4), but see p. 36(9)–(10), (12).

5   For a commentary see Braun, Gleiss, Hirsch, above, p. 232, n. 1, nos. 208–220; see also Cerexhe, 1972 Cah, Dr. Eur. 272, at p. 291.

6   Joliet in 1969 Rev. Trim. Dr. Eur. 645, at p. 680.

7   Joliet, *loc. cit.*, at pp. 688–689.

other member states,[1] in the imposition of obligations which are not objectively essential for the purpose of the relationship and which complicate *inequitably* the transition from one category of membership in the association to another, thus impeding stronger participation in the management of the association and in the distribution of profits;[2] in the creation of obstacles against the establishment of one single market in respect of services (*in casu* music publishing) by a process of national cocooning;[3] in extending, by means of contractual obligations, the sphere of copyright to works unprotected by it[4] and in charging importers a full licence fee for records, without taking into account previous payments under the same head.[5]

The decision of the Commission in the *GEMA* case in holding upon a recital of a certain set of facts, that a commercial practice was discriminatory, impeded the establishment of a single market or was excessively onerous by disregarding previous payments in respect of the same products, that the obligations imposed were unnecessarily onerous because not objectively essential, relies on the two criteria, as alternatives, that the practice is discriminatory or objectively inequitable or impedes as such the purpose of the Treaty to create a single market.[6] By including a contractual extension of copyrights to areas in which the right could not be asserted on a proprietary basis, the Commission followed the pointers given by the Community Court in respect of the manner of the exercise (as distinct from the existence)[7] of copyrights,[8] trademarks[9] and similar rights,[10] which must not constitute a means of arbitrary discrimination or a disguised restriction of trade between member states (art. 36).[11] However, the level of pricing does not necessarily disclose an abusive exploitation.[12]

---

1   *GEMA*, 2 June 1971, OJ, 1971, L 134/15, at p. 21 C1; 1971 Rev. Trim. Dr. Eur. 526, [1971] C.M.L.R. D35, notwithstanding the statutory provision to this effect in the German Law of 9 September 1965 (above, p. 235, n. 1) para. 6; see also p. 26, C6.

2   *Ibid.*, p. 22, C2.

3   *Ibid.*, p. 24, C3; see also *Deutsche Grammophon GmbH* v. *Metro-SB-Grossmärkte* (1971), 17 Rec. 487, at p. 500(12), (13).

4   *Ibid.*, p. 25, C4.

5   *Ibid.*, p. 25, C5.

6   See EEC Treaty art. 36; Deringer, *The Competition Law of the EEC*, para. 532; Commission Memorandum, below, p. 238, n. 5, at p. 1207(25), but see Bienaymé, 1972 Rev. Trim. Dr. Eur. 65, at p. 74; according to *Wohlfahrt-Everling-Glaesner-Sprung, ad* art. 86, n. 4 the discrepancy between the advantages sought in the market and the actual value of the performance is determining. See also to the same effect the Memorandum of the Commission (below, n. 1748) at p. 1201(4), 2nd para.

7   *Parke, Davis & Co.* v. *Probel et al.* (1968), 14 Rec. 81, at pp. 110, 1st para., 111; [1968] C.M.L.R. 47; *Sirena Srl* v. *Eda Srl* (1971), 17 Rec. 69, at p. 84(16); [1971] C.M.L.R. 260.

8   *Parke, Davis & Co.* v. *Probel et al.* (1968), 14 Rec. 81, at p. 111; [1968] C.M.L.R. 47.

9   *Sirena Srl* v. *Eda Srl* (1971), 17 Rec. 69, at p. 84(14)–(17); [1971] C.M.L.R. 260.

10   *Deutsche Grammophon GmbH* v. *Metro-SB-Grossmärkte* (1971), 17 Rec. 487, at p. 499(11)–500(13), 500(14)–501(16); [1971] C.M.L.R. 631.

11   *Parke, Davis & Co.* v. *Probel et al.* (1968), 14 Rec. 81, at p. 109 [1968] C.M.L.R. 47; *Sirena Srl* v. *Eda Srl* (1971), 17 Rec. 69 at p. 82(9)–83(13); *Deutsche Grammophon GmbH* v. *Metro-SB-Grossmärkte* (1971), 17 Rec. 487, at p. 499(7)–(10); [1971] C.M.L.R. 631.

12   *Sirena Srl* v. *Eda Srl* (1971), 17 Rec. 69, at p. 84(17); *Deutsche Grammophon GmbH* v. *Metro-SB-Grossmärkte* (1971), 17 Rec. 487, at p. 501(19); [1971] C.M.L.R. 631.

In the *Continental Can* case[1] the Commission went further and found a violation of art. 86 in the acquisition by a New Jersey company through its Delaware and Belgian subsidiaries, all producers of packing containers, of a Netherlands company, the biggest producer of similar goods in the Benelux countries, seeing that the intending purchasers already controlled the largest specialist producer in the Common Market, situated in Germany. According to the Commission[2] the purchase of a majority participation in a competing enterprise by an enterprise or a group of enterprises holding a dominant position can in certain circumstances constitute an abusive exploitation of this position.[3] Thus, according to the Commission, it is an abusive exploitation if a dominant enterprise reinforces its dominant position by means of a *concentration* with another, as a result of which the competition which would have existed *effectively* or *potentially* despite the existence of the initial dominant position is practically eliminated for the products in question,[4] the more so if the eliminated competitor holds a strong position in part of the Common Market and if its acquisition changes the structure of the competition in the market irreversibly.[5]

III   CRITIQUE

The conclusion reached by the Commission has not found widespread approval[6] and has led to an appeal to the Community Court.

Firstly, the notion of a dominant enterprise[7] as being one which can operate without taking into account competitors, buyers and suppliers and which determines prices or controls production or distribution in respect of a significant part of the products concerned, makes the absence of an effective competition the outstanding element of a dominant position.

Secondly, the Commission has now made the elimination of a competing enterprise by an enterprise holding a dominant position an element of abusive exploitation of a dominant position.

Thus while the status of a dominant position is not outlawed but accepted by art. 86, the acquisition of an extensive dominant position is treated as an abusive exploitation of the dominant position although the

---

1   Above, p. 234, n. 6.
2   *Ibid.*, p. 37, C. (22)–p. 39(33).
3   *Ibid.*, p. 37, C. (22).
4   *Ibid.*, p. 37, C. (23).
5   *Ibid.*, p. 37, C. (24); the element of irreversibility forms the dividing line between arrangements caught by art. 85 and structural changes affected by art. 86; see the Commission Memorandum (below, p. 238, n. 5) at p. 1204(14); but see the critique by Franceschelli, Plaisant and Lassier, *Droit Européen de la Concurrence, op. cit.* Nos. 197, 198.
6   Favourable: Bienaymé, 1972 Rev. Trim. Dr. Eur. 65. Contra: Cerexhe, 1972 Cah. Dr. Eur. 272, at pp. 294 ff.; (1972) I J.C.P. 2452; see also 1971 Rev. M.C., 476, at p. 485(54): note to *GEMA* (above, p. 236, n. 1). And see generally Joliet, "Monopolisation et Abus de Position Dominante, "1969", Rev. Trim. Dr. Eur. 645, at p. 689: no dismantling of economic power as such.
7   See above, p. 234.

methods of acquisition by a commercial purchase were not, in the particular circumstances, chastised as sharp practices. The conclusion suggests
itself inevitably that the acquisition of a monopolistic dominant position
is regarded by the Commission as an abusive exploitation of an oligo-
polistic dominant position.

Such an attitude could only be justified if the EEC Treaty prohibited
monopolies, but it does not do so.[1] While art. 85 is directed against market
restricting agreements both horizontal and vertical, art. 86 seeks to
exclude market restricting behaviour born out of a dominant position of
one or several enterprises.[2] The Commission and now the Community
Court has accepted that a relationship between mother and daughter
enterprises does not fall under art. 85.[3] Such relationships, including
those of sister companies, should not fall under art. 86 unless the actual
market behaviour is abusive, and disclosure of a monopoly concentration
through the removal of the corporate veil should not suffice to attract
the operation of art. 86.[4]

The Commission, from 1966 onwards, and the majority of writers have
taken a different view[5] where monopolistic concentrations are concerned,
unless special circumstances exist, and its practical application in the
Continental Can case should not cause any surprise. It must remain an
open question whether the Commission practice correctly represents
Community law, since it transposes the act of abusive exploitation of the
market into an earlier phase where it figures as an abusive intention,
which is that of forming the concentration which will then present a
threat of abusive exploitation.[6]

---

1   Heffermehl in *Festschrift für Nipperdey* II (1965), p. 771; Franceschelli, Plaisant and Lassier,
   Droit Européen de la Concurrence, No. 163; Cerexhe, 1972 Cah. Dr. Eur. 272, at p. 295; Joliet,
   1969 Rev. Trim. Dr. Eur. 645, at p. 682. For attempts to define this term see Franceschelli,
   1968 Rev. M.C. 855, at p. 858.

2   *Italy* v. *EEC Council and Commission* (1966), 12 Rec. 563, at pp. 591–592; [1969] C.M.L.R. 39;
   Focsaneanu, 1971 Rev. M.C., 476, at p. 485(54) and n. 5 with lit.; Joliet, 1969 Rev. Trim.
   Dr. Eur. 645, at p. 693 with lit.

3   *Christiani-Nielsen*, OJ, 1969, L 165/12; *Kodak*, OJ, 1970, L 147/24; *Dyestuffs*, OJ, 1969,
   L 195/11; *ICI* v. *EEC Commission*, [1972] C.M.L.R. 557, at p. 629(132)–(134).

4   Focsaneanu, 1971 Rev. M.C. 476, at p. 485 (54) and n. 5; see also the analysis by Cerexhe,
   1972 Cah. Dr. Eur. 272, at p. 284.

5   Le Problème de la Concentration dans le Marché Commun 1966, EEC *Etudes* Série Concurrence No. 3, Doc. 81–82/VII/1966/5; especially para. 26; 1966 Riv. Soc. 1182, at pp.
   1201(4), 1205(16)–1208(27); Ninth General Report on the Activities of the Communities
   (1966), p. 83(77); see the comment by De Jong (1966–67) 4 C.M.L.Rev. 166. And see
   generally: Mestmäcker in *Festschrift für Hallstein* (1966), p. 322; Steindorff, 1968 Rev. M.C.
   186, and p. 288 with lit. at pp. 212–214; Schlieder, *ibid.* 215; Lassier, *ibid.* 243; Markert, *ibid.*
   254; Franceschelli, Plaisant and Lassier, *Droit de la Concurrence*, No. 195 and n. 125 with further
   lit.; de Roux and Voillemot, *Le Droit de la Concurrence des Communautés Européennes*, No. 53;
   von der Groeben, 1965 Rev. Trim. Dr. Eur. 399, at p. 410; *Contra:* Joliet 1969 Rev. Trim.
   Dr. Eur. 645, at pp. 693, 694. For contractual co-operation agreements between minor
   enterprises see the Commission Notice of 29 July 1968, OJ, 1968, C 75/3. And see above,
   p. 213, n. 12.

6   See also Cerexhe, 1972 Cah. Dr. Eur. 272, at p. 297; Joliet, 1969 Rev. Trim. Dr. Eur. 645,
   at pp. 694, 695.

IV PROCEDURE

Generally speaking, the procedure laid down in Reg. 17/62 applies, subject however to the necessary modifications. Thus negative clearance is possible, but the procedure of modifications and exemptions is not available here where conduct, and not agreements, is in issue.[1] The Commission may find that an infringement of art. 86 exists and may by means of a decision oblige the enterprise or enterprises concerned to put an end to such an infringement.[2] For this purpose it can impose fines and penalties.[3]

V PUBLIC ENTERPRISES[4] (art. 90)

As shown above,[5] the abolition of quantitative restrictions also affects state trading monopolies in their practices of buying and selling, although the duty imposed upon the latter to "adjust themselves" gradually (art. 37(1)) is a less than perfect obligation to eliminate discrimination and to refrain from measures which restrict the scope of the undertaking to abolish quantitative restrictions. In addition, as regards the particular sphere of competition, the Treaty requires the member states neither to enact nor to maintain any measures to the contrary which apply to public enterprises and to enterprises which have been granted special or exclusive rights by the member states (art. 90(1)).[6] These enterprises are therefore included, in general, in the scheme which outlaws restrictive practices and monopolies, but the Treaty acknowledges that the play of free competition meets here the member states face to face as legislative or administrative agencies, and as participants in transactions affecting commerce.[7] The duties imposed by art. 90(1) far exceed those imposed by art. 37, which are gradually to adjust state trading monopolies (art. 37(1)) and to maintain a standstill (art. 37(2)). Article 90(1) may be directly applicable[8] inasmuch as it subjects the enterprises mentioned there to the operation of arts. 85 and 86 although the wording of art. 90(3) provides

---

1 Deringer, *The Competition Law of the EEC*, para. 503.
2 Reg. 17/62, art. 3.
3 Reg. 17/62, arts. 15, 16.
4 Colliard in *Ganshof van der Meersch*, Nos. 2149–2170, pp. 853–860; 1965 Rev. Trim. Dr. Eur. 1; Schindler, (1970) 7 C.M.L.Rev. 57 with further lit. p. 58, nn. 5, 6; Van Hecke, (1966) 3 C.M.L.Rev. 450, at pp. 452–454; Deringer, (1964–65) 2 C.M.L.Rev. 129; Catalano in *Festschrift für Riese* (1964), p. 133.
5 P. 58; art. 37.
6 Schindler, (1970) 7 C.M.L.Rev. 57, at p. 58 states that art. 90(1) wrongly appears in the section dealing with competition, since it is exclusively addressed to member states. It is true that this section originally featured elsewhere (see Franceschelli, 1968 Rev. M.C. 855, at pp. 856, 873); but it may yet be directly applicable owing to the absolute obligation imposed upon them, thus protecting individual customers and restraining enterprises in the meaning of this section, even if they bear a public character or fulfil public functions.
7 Catalano in *Festschrift für Riese* (1964), pp. 136, 139.
8 See above, p. 30 and n. 4; Catalano in *Festschrift für Riese* (1964), p. 147.

an argument to the contrary inasmuch as it empowers the Commission to ensure the application of this article (and not only of art. 90(2)) by directives and decisions.[1]

The purpose of art. 90(1) is to ensure that, since the general rules of the Treaty on competition apply, member states must not enact new legislation and must abrogate existing legislation or other measures which would frustrate the provisions of the Treaty.[2]

The notion of public enterprises and of enterprises to which member states have granted exclusive rights is not a technical one.[3] It appears to exclude any service of a governmental character or forming part of local government.[4] In accordance with the notion of enterprise as developed elsewhere[5] it embraces any single organisation which combines personal and intangible elements connected with a legally autonomous entity which pursues in a constant manner a specific economic purpose. Given the place of art. 90, such enterprises are covered if they are engaged in production, distribution or services other than services governed by administrative law.[6] Since they must be public enterprises, a close relationship with the public authorities in some form or another, possibly in the management and control, must exist.[7] Such is the case if an enterprise enjoys certain privileges for the purpose of carrying out the task with which it is entrusted by law,[8] but the principle is not absolute.[9] It is necessary to consider both the intrinsic need for carrying out the particular task entrusted to the enterprise and that to safeguard the interests of the Community.[10] This function is exercised by the Commission (art. 90(3)).[11]

It is still more difficult to offer a clear description of enterprises to which member states grant special or exclusive rights.[12] They would seem to include all those to which governmental functions have been delegated or upon which special privileges have been conferred which are not connected with governmental functions.

The principle expressed in art. 90(1) is overshadowed by the exception set out in art. 90(2). Enterprises in the meaning of art. 90(1) which are entrusted with the management of services of general economic interest or having the character of a fiscal monopoly are only subject to the provisions of the Treaty to the extent that their application does not

---

1 But see Colliard, in *Ganshof van der Meersch*, nos. 2159 ff.
2 For a survey of Italian law see Minervini, (1967) 3 Riv. Dir. Priv. Proc. 759.
3 Schindler, (1970) 7 C.M.L.Rev. 57; cp. *GEMA*, 2 June 1971, OJ, 1971, L 134/15, at p. 27 III.
4 Colliard, *Ganshof van der Meersch*, No. 2164.
5 Above, p. 199.
6 Colliard, *loc. cit.*, no. 2164(2).
7 *Ministère Public of Luxemburg* v. *Müller* (1971), 17 Rec. 723, at p. 730(11); Colliard, *loc. cit.*, no. 2164(3); Schindler, (1970) 7 C.M.L.Rev. 57, at p. 61, goes much further.
8 *Ministère Public of Luxemburg* v. *Müller* (above, n. 7).
9 *Ibid.*, p. 730(13).
10 *Ibid.*, p. 730(14).
11 *Ibid.*, p. 730(15).
12 Cp. GATT art. XVII (I)(a); for the test of exclusiveness as determining see *GEMA*, 2 June 1971, OJ, 1971, L 134/15, at p. 27 III 1 (above, p. 236, n. 1).

obstruct the fulfilment *de jure* or *de facto* of the tasks entrusted to such an enterprise. Yet this exception is tempered by another, namely that the disregard of rules of the Treaty in favour of the specific tasks entrusted to the enterprise concerned must not, in turn, affect the development of trade to an extent contrary to the interests of the Community.

The enterprises concerned must be entrusted[1] with the management of services of general economic interest or have the character of a fiscal monopoly. As regards the former, it is clear that they do not necessarily coincide with public enterprises and enterprises to which member states grant special or exclusive rights. They may be of a public or of a private character, but they must be charged with the management of services of a general economic interest[2] in the sense that a general burden of duty is cast upon them by the authorities. The burden of these duties, as distinct from the authoritative or privileged status of the enterprises mentioned in art. 90(1), justifies the relaxation of the rules of competition. Again, the notion of services of general economic interest is not a technical one. The services must be for the public as a whole and individually, as distinct from public services as such.[3]

A fiscal monopoly in the meaning of art. 90(2) is a monopoly which has as its purpose to provide direct income for public authorities. The only difficulty is that in practice such monopolies frequently combine their fiscal with a commercial character,[4] thus attracting the combined operation of arts. 37 and 90(2). Since art. 37 envisages the gradual withering away of commercial trading monopolies while art. 90(2), as distinct from art. 90(1), does not contemplate the disappearance of enterprises charged with the management of services of general economic interest and of fiscal monopolies, a difficult problem of precedence arises.[5]

Even treated in isolation, art. 90(2) leaves a wide margin to the discretion of member states which may conflict with the duty not to affect the development of trade contrary to the interests of the Community. In the absence of any procedure comparable to that for negative clearance the conflict must be resolved, in advance or *ex post* by the following.

---

1 The French text says: "*chargées de la gestion de services . . .*"; the German text says: "*die mit Dienstleistungen . . . betraut sind*"; the Italian text says: "*incaricati della gestione*", and the Dutch text, like the French, says: "*belast met het beheer van diensten*". For these terms see Franceschelli, 1968 Rev. M.C. 855, at p. 867. For the problem whether this term is one of Community law open to interpretation by the Commission and the Court see Catalano, *Festschrift für Riese* (1964), p. 142, who answers it in the negative; ca. Minervini, (1967) 3 Riv. Dir. Int. Priv. Proc. 759.

2 See Colliard, *Ganshof van der Meersch*, No. 2168, p. 859, first col.

3 As an example the services entrusted to the Bank of England come to mind. Not services as such but the performance of services as a function of the enterprise is involved: see Schindler, (1970) 7 C.M.L.Rev. 57, at p. 70; for some functions which fail to satisfy art. 90(2) see *GEMA*, 2 June 1971, OJ, 1971, L 134/15, at p. 27 III 2.

4 See above, p. 58, n. 2; Colliard, *Ganshof van der Meersch*, no. 2169; Franceschelli, 1968 Rev. M.C., 855, at pp. 861–862.

5 Franceschelli, 1968 Rev.M.C. 855, at p. 875; in case of conflict art. 37 must prevail since art. 90 is permissive; but see p. 861: art. 90(2), being more liberal prevails in particular with regard to fiscal monopolies; ca. Deringer cited by Franceschelli.

Measure: Commission—Directives or decisions to member
states (art. 90(3)).

Clearly art. 90(2) is not directly applicable.[1]

---

1   See above, p. 30, n. 10: *Ministère Public of Luxemburg* v. *Müller* (1971), 17 Rec. 723, at pp.
730(12)–(16).

13

Dumping

(Article 91)[1]

The free exchange of goods within the EEC subject to prices and conditions which are determined alone by the level of offer and demand is distorted not only by agreements, decisions and concerted practices between groups of individuals and by Governments operating enterprises on a commercial or fiscal basis or as a public service. It can also be distorted by individuals who engage in dumping.

Dumping has been authoritatively defined by a Council Regulation[2] as having occurred

(a) when the export price . . . is lower than the comparable prevailing price in the normal course of trade for the like product . . . in the country of origin from which the product was exported;

(b) when a product is not imported direct from the country of origin but is exported . . . from an intermediate country, the comparison of prices . . . shall as a general rule be made between the export price of that product . . . and the comparable price of the like product on the domestic market of the exporting country. However, the comparison may be made with the . . . price in the country of origin if . . . the product is the subject of transit trade in the exporting country, or if there is no producing industry of that product or no comparable price in the exporting country.[3]

Special criteria are laid down for the cases where no like product is sold in the normal course of trade on the domestic market of the exporting country or where such sales do not allow of a valid comparison[4] and where there is no export price or where it appears that the export price may not be taken as a basis on account of the existence of an association or compensation arrangement between the exporter and the importer or a third party.[5] Imports from countries where trade is subject to a total or almost total monopoly and where domestic prices are fixed by the

---

1 Colliard in *Ganshof van der Meersch*, No. 2171, pp. 861–862; de Roux and Voillemot, *Le Droit de la Concurrence des Communautés Européennes* Nos. 140–145, pp. 171–176.

2 459/68, OJ, 1968, L 93/1; cp. GATT art. VI (1), and see the Geneva Agreement of 30 June 1967 by the parties to GATT, Annex D containing an Anti-Dumping code, OJ, 1968, L 305/12.

3 Reg. 459/68, art. 3(1)(a), (b).

4 Reg. 459/68, art. 3(2).

5 Reg. 459/68, art. 3(3).

state are to be judged on a broader basis,[1] but a product is not to be considered as dumped for the reason only that it is exempted from duties or taxes which are imposed upon the like product when the latter is intended for consumption in the country of origin or export or because such duties or taxes are reimbursed.[2]

The prohibition of dumping laid down by the EEC Treaty (art. 91(1)) and the obligation to re-admit dumped exports free of all customs duties and the like (art. 91(2)) are directed against such practices within the Common Market. Consequently they only envisage situations between member states as long as exports differ from domestic markets because customs barriers exist between those states (art. 91).[3] These have ceased to have any effect with the final abolition of customs barriers and the creation of a common customs tariff.[4]

Nevertheless, the prohibition of dumping has a place in Community law. In the first place, it affects dumping practices by exporters outside the Common Market whose exports reach the Common Market through direct or indirect imports. While art. 91 cannot serve to inhibit this practice, the provisions of the Treaty dealing with commercial policy (art. 113, until 1 January 1969, art. 111) offer the necessary basis for action and the Council has made use of it by promulgating Reg. 459/68.[5] An anti-dumping duty may be imposed if a dumped product causes or threatens to cause substantial injury[6] to an established Community producing industry or causes considerable delay in setting up a Community producing industry which is envisaged for the near future.[7]

In the second place, art. 91(1) itself may still be applicable in certain circumstances. The agricultural section of the Treaty is not exempted from the operation of this provision, and Reg. 26/62[8] made by virtue of arts. 42 and 43 of the Treaty states that notwithstanding art. 46, art. 91(1) applies to the products enumerated in Annex II of the Treaty.[9] The exemption created by art. 46 must be noted. In so far as domestic market organisations are concerned, countervailing duties are levied subject to the

---

1   Reg. 459/68, art. 3(6).

2   Reg. 459/68, art. 3(5).

3   While art. 91 was operative, its application was further defined by Commission Reg. 8/60, OJ, 1960, 597 amended by Commission Reg. 13/61, OJ, 1961, 585.

4   Colliard, *Ganshof van der Meersch*, p. 862; de Roux and Voillemot, *Le Droit de la Concurrence des Communautés Européennes*, p. 172, no. 141, p. 173, no. 144; for an account of the work of the Commission during this period in allowing member states to take protective measures see the *Tenth General Report of the EEC* (1966–67), p. 100(63); *Eighth General Report* (1964–65), p. 79(72).

5   OJ, 1968, L 93/1; see above, p. 243, n. 2.

6   According to Reg. 459/68, art. 2(2) injury is identical with the practice of dumping, premiums or subsidies by a non-member state (art. 1(1)).

7   Reg. 459/68, art. 2(1).

8   OJ, 1962, 993—see above, p. 228, n. 9.

9   Reg. 26/62 art. 3(1); Braun, Gleiss and Hirsch, *Le Droit des Ententes de la CEE*, no. 622, p. 367; Deringer, *The Competition Law*, p. 383, paras 2651–2652. For processed agricultural products see Council Decision 4 April 1962, OJ, 1962, 999; Council Regs. 160/66, arts. 3, 10, OJ, 1966, 3361; 189/66, art. 3, OJ, 1966, 3713.

control of the Commission, and art. 91(1) does not apply. It operates, therefore, only in relation to private enterprises which are not part of a domestic market organisation. Given that most agricultural products are covered today either by a common market or a domestic market organisation, the sphere of operation of art. 91(1) is very limited.

Measures: Commission—authorises member state to take protective measures—determines conditions and details (art. 91(1)).

14

Aids

(Articles 92–94)[1]

A distortion of the free exchange of goods can also occur indirectly if a member state concedes to its producers subventions and premiums of various kinds which aid these producers to compete more effectively in the markets of the Community in disregard of the ordinary forces of competition. In order to counter this danger, aid granted by a member state or through state resources, in whatever form, is prohibited, provided always

    (a) that such aid distorts or threatens to distort competition by favouring certain enterprises or the production of certain goods;
    (b) that it affects trade between member states (art. 92(1)).

I THE PRINCIPLE

Aids, for the purpose of this article, have been defined by the Commission (subject to control by the Community Court) as any subventions, exemptions from duties and taxes, reduction of interest, guarantees of loans at particularly favourable rates, the gratuitous grant of premises or land or on particularly favourable conditions; the supply of goods or services on preferential terms, the promise to make good any losses arising from running an enterprise and any measure having an equivalent effect.[2] The Commission has since added the following:[3] reimbursement of costs in case of success, direct or indirect state guarantees of grants of credits; preferential application of discount rates; preferential settlement of public accounts; deferred collection of fiscal or social contributions,[4] and has indicated that a waiver of interest upon capital put at the disposal

---

1 Colliard in *Ganshof van der Meersch*, nos. 2172–2183, pp. 863–867; de Roux and Voillemot, *Le Droit de la Concurrence des Communautés Européennes*, nos. 132–139, pp. 163–170; Servidio, 1970 Riv. Dir. Eur. 173 ff; 249 ff.

2 Commission Reply No. 48 of 30 July 1963, OJ, 1963, 2235(1); cp. Commission Reply No. 88 of 15 October 1963, OJ, 1963, 2867.

3 Doc. 20 502/IV/68, cited by Venceslai, 1969 Riv. Dir Eur. 257 at p. 272 and n. 26.

4 Colliard, in *Ganshof van der Meersch*, nos. 2172–2183, pp. 863–867, notes the absence in the catalogue of the following measures: payments by the state to an enterprise which holds the concession for a public service (see below), the reimbursement to such an enterprise of losses due to a statutory fixing of unremunerative charges; the provision of capital for nationalised industries. For some aspects of these aids, which touch upon art. 90, as well see the Commission Reply No. 48 of 30 July 1963, OJ, 1963, 2235, above, n. 2.

of a public enterprise can bear the same character if in comparable circumstances a private creditor, acting upon economic considerations only, would not have waived his rights, or at least not to the same extent.[1] The Court has added preferential discount by a state, limited to export of national products.[2]

The aid must emanate from a member state or through state resources in any form whatsoever. Thus it does not matter that the grantor of the favours is not the government itself; regional or local authorities, or possibly entities of a non-territorial character are included, provided that the benefits concerned are fed by state resources or can be traced to those resources which, without providing payments, confer pecuniary advantages by preferential treatment and exemptions.[3] The aid must distort or threaten to distort competition by favouring certain enterprises or the production of certain goods. By requiring that competition must thereby be distorted or that a threat of distortion must have arisen, art. 92(1) appears to lay down stricter conditions than art. 85, where it suffices if the agreements etc. have as their object *or* effect the distortion of competition.

Moreover, the aid is illegal only to the extent that it affects trade between member states. In 1963, the Commission stated that the latter notion could not be defined in abstract terms, but that every case had to be considered on its merits and that in view of the great variety of aids and of their economic effects general principles could only be developed on the basis of an extensive practice over a considerable number of years.[4]

II   EXCEPTIONS

A series of aids are declared to be compatible with the Common Market (art. 92(2)) and are therefore lawful. They concern: aid of a social character granted to individual consumers without discrimination based on the origins of the products concerned (art. 92(2)(a)), aid intended to remedy damage caused by natural calamities or other extraordinary events (art. 92(2)(b)) and aid to the economy of certain regions of the Federal Republic of Germany, subject to certain qualifications (art. 92(2)(c)).[5]

Other types of aids may be regarded as compatible with the Common Market (art. 92(3)) but are not necessarily exempt. These include: aid to regions in general where the standard of living is too low or which suffer from serious unemployment (art. 92(3)(a),[6] aid for important projects of common European interest or to remedy a serious disturbance

---

1   Commission Reply 48 of 30 July 1963, OJ, 1963, 2235(3).
2   *EEC Commission* v. *France* (1969), 15 Rec. 523, at pp. 540(18)–541(23).
3   Cp. Veneslai, 1969 Riv. Dir. Eur. 257, at p. 265.
4   OJ, 1963, 2867–2868.
5   According to Venceslai, 1969 Riv. Dir. Eur. 257, at p. 260 and n. 7 member states notify the Commission of these aids nevertheless.
6   Any such aid necessarily involves considerations of economic policy (art. 103).

in the economy of a member state (art. 92(3)(b)); aid for the development
of certain activities or of certain economic sectors,[1] if it does not change
trading conditions contrary to the common interest (art. 92(3)(c)). A
special provision concerns aids to shipbuilding (art. 92(3)(c), last sentence). If such aid was established on 1 January 1957, and only served
to balance the absence of customs duties, it was to be reduced between
member states according to the same principles as customs duties. In
relation to imports from third countries, the rules on common commercial
policy are applicable (arts. 92(3)(c), last sentence, and arts. 110–116).
Finally the Council may specify other types of permissible aids.

> *Measure:* Council—by a qualified majority—on a proposal
> of the Commission—decision (art. 92(3)(d)).

III SUPERVISION AND PROCEDURE

The range of aids which benefit from the qualified privilege laid down
in art. 92(2), (3) is sufficiently broad to require constant supervision by the
Commission. Consequently, the Commission and the member states are
enjoined to examine constantly the systems of aids. In this connection the
Commission may propose measures (art. 93(1)), but such proposals are
persuasive only.[2] Furthermore, plans to grant or to modify any aid must
be placed before the Commission in advance, so as to enable the latter to
examine them and to take action (art. 93(3)).[3]

For this purpose the Commission has the power to make decisions to
the effect that a particular aid of the kind is incompatible with art. 92 or
that, while so compatible, is applied in an abusive manner. In this case
the member states may be asked to abolish or to modify the aid within a
certain time limit.

> *Measure:* Commission—after notice to the parties to sub-
> mit comments—Decision (art. 93(2), 1st para.).[4]

Until such a final decision has been pronounced, a member state must
not put the aid into effect (art. 93(3), last sentence). Upon a failure to

---

1 This term reproduces the German version of art. 92(3)(c): *Wirtschaftsgebiete* which is not
   territorial but functional; but contrast the corresponding French, Italian and Dutch versions:
   régions économiques, regioni economiche, regionale economieën, which take up a notion treated before
   (art. 92(3)(a)).
   But see the First Resolution of 20 October 1971 of the Representatives of Governments
   meeting within the Council, OJ, 1971, C 111/1, C 116/11.
2 For a recent case see Commission Reply 357/72, 14 November 1972, OJ, 1972, C 128/8:
   France, fiscal advantages.
3 On the problems raised by art. 93(3) see Venceslai, 1969 Riv. Dir. Eur. 257 especially as to
   the stage in the preparation of the aid when the project should be submitted, *ibid.,* pp. 261–
   264, 274 ff. For a change in the practice of notification see *Third General Report* (1969), p. 73,
   s. 43; *Fourth General Report* (1970), p. 31, s. 35.
4 See *e.g.* Commission Decision 72/261 of 28 June 1972, OJ, 1972, L 166/12.

comply with the decision of the Commission the normal remedies for failure to observe the Treaty are available here as well.

Measure: Commission or interested member state refers the matter to the Court (art. 93(2), 2nd para.).

The same procedure applies to new plans for aid. While it is pending, a member state can by-pass or forestall any proposals by the Commission under art. 93(1), second sentence, if it applies to the Council for approval of the aid concerned. The Council may declare that any such aid may be treated as compatible with the Common Market, even if it is contrary to art. 92, or to any regulations passed under art. 94.[1]

Measure: Council—by a unanimous vote—Decision (art. 93(2), 3rd para.).

In these circumstances, the Commission must suspend its investigation in which it may be engaged and cannot make any proposals, until the Council has made a pronouncement (art. 93(2), 3rd para., second sentence), but the Commission regains its freedom of action, if the Council has not made a pronouncement within three months after having received a request by the member state concerned (art. 93(3), 4th para.). Article 93 is not directly applicable.[2]

IV   IMPLEMENTING LEGISLATION

Provision is made for measures to carry arts. 92 and 93 into effect, especially concerning the procedure to be followed before the Commission (art. 93(3)) and for exempting certain types of aids from this procedure.

Measure: Council, by a qualified majority—on proposal of the Commission—Regulations (art. 94).

Few such measures have been promulgated as yet.[3]

On the other hand, in the course of organising competition in the agricultural market Reg. 26/62[4] in addition to letting in the rules on dumping[5] within the restricted framework set out above,[6] has provided

---

1 Few such regulations have been promulgated hitherto. The Commission submitted a proposal on 30 March 1966, COM(66)95 and 10 November 1966, COM(66)457; Venceslai, 1969 Riv. Dir. Eur. 257, at p. 258, n. 2; for the preparatory work done by the Commission see Venceslai, *ibid.*

2 See above, p. 30, n. 11; *Costa* v. *ENEL* (1964), 10 Rec. 1141, at p. 1162; [1964] C.M.L.R. 425.

3 See above, n. 1; Council Reg 1107/70, 4 June 1970, OJ, 1970, L 130/1, art. 3; see above, p. 182, n. 3.

4 OJ, 1962, 993.

5 Reg. 26/62, art. 3.

6 Above, pp. 244–245.

also that, within the same sphere, art. 93(1) and (3), first sentence apply.[1] In omitting to refer to the general prohibition of aids and the absolute and qualified exemptions set out in art. 92, as well as to the power of a member state to obtain exemption from the Council, Reg. 26/62 shows that in the realm of agriculture aids are not prohibited as such and are not subject to a procedure of exemption, but only to a process of notification and adjustment;[2] and special aid figures as a legitimate device in a number of agricultural regimes set up by the Community.[3] Thus, once again, the sphere of operation of Reg. 26/62 art. 4 is limited.[4]

V   PRACTICE

In the course of years the Commission has considered aids of a general character in a limited number of circumstances[5] and special aids frequently.[6] Difficulties can arise if the aid in question involves the consideration not only of art. 92, but also of other provisions of the Treaty which affect the issue directly or indirectly. In the first place, the advantage accorded by a state or through an infusion of its resources may concern a public enterprise or any other enterprise covered by art. 90.[7] In the opinion of the Commission any aid given to enterprises entrusted with the management of services of a general economic interest, if it does not exceed the broad limits set by art. 90(2), is permitted, since the more liberal special provision of art. 90(2) must prevail over the general rule represented by art. 92.[8]

In the second place, it has been suggested by the Commission and confirmed by the Court that an aid which would otherwise qualify as being compatible with the Treaty is yet illegal to the extent that the manner in

---

1   Reg. 26/62, art. 4.
2   Deringer, *The Competition Law of the EEC*, para. 2661.
3   See above, p. 76.
4   *E.g.* to potatoes; see Commission Reply No. 99/72 of 20 November 1972, OJ, 1972, C128/1–2. For a suspected disguised aid see OJ, 1972, C 134/2, Question 236/72.
5   Reorganisation of coalmining areas (Belgium: *e.g.* Commission Decision 72/173, OJ, 1972, L105/13), industrial development (France), less developed regions and for small and medium industries (Italy), structurally weak regions, regions near the border with the DDR and secondary development centres (Germany), generally (Luxemburg); see EEC, *Tenth Report* (1966–67), p. 100, s. 64; *Eleventh Report* (1968), p. 59, s.46. For a scheme concerning the application of regional aid see the resolution of the governments meeting within the Council of 20 October 1971, OJ, 1971, C 111/1 and the Commission Report, OJ, 1971, C 111/9.
6   The following industries have been primarily involved: film, shipbuilding and repairs (see Council Directive 28 July 1969, OJ, 1969, L206/25; Commission Directive 20 July 1972, OJ, 1972, L169/28), agricultural processed products; lead and zinc; mining; fuel and power; aircraft and gliders; brewing; textile; road, rail and inland transport, computer, pulp and laminated board; recently apple and pear growers in the Netherlands affected by hail (Commission Decision 72/251, OJ, 1972, L163/19); and the following types of aid have come under review: export aid, credit guarantees, loans, reduction of interest rates, special equipment bounties.
7   Above, p. 239.
8   Commission Reply No. 48 of 30 July 1963, OJ, 1963, 2235(2).

which it is financed contravenes the Treaty.[1] The apodictic statement by the Court that in order to determine its compatibility with the Treaty it is not possible to consider aid properly speaking in isolation independently of the manner in which it is being financed[2] because the source of the aid is linked to the aid itself, lacks conviction if it purports to express an abstract rule. It does not become more persuasive in the light of the Court's reasoning that in determining the compatibility of aid with the Treaty

> "it is necessary to consider the factual and legal elements which make up the aid and in particular where an imbalance exists between the charges which must be borne by the interested industries and productions on the one hand and the benefits resulting from the aid in question on the other hand."

In the particular circumstances of the case, the aid was destined for the French textile industry in order to support the re-structuring of the industry and to finance research and was financed specifically by a levy on all textile goods sold in France, whether locally produced or imported. Such a tax, being applied equally to local and imported products, complied with the fiscal provisions of the Treaty (art. 95(1)). If the aid to the particular industry as such was compatible with the Treaty (art. 92), as the Commission appears to have thought, at least in the alternative, the illegality resulting from the particular method of financing it must be found in the imposition of a tax on the products of that industry, whether imported or home produced. The reason (which does not appear clearly from the decision)[3] is thus that the efficient competitors, inside France or elsewhere in the Community, who increase their sales at the expense of inefficient producers in the same field are penalised for having been efficient, and that competition is thereby discouraged.[4] Thus the Court was concerned with the relationship between aid, its temporary or permanent character and its curtailment of competition through a specialised form of financing. In so far as the Court denied the payments the character of aid in the proper sense of the word,[5] it confused a permanent source earmarked for aid with aid itself in the meaning of the Treaty. Seen in isolation, the Court, following the Commission, did not deny that aid to the textile industry was compatible with the Treaty and that the levy did not contravene art. 95 and was lawful. The problem is therefore why the combination of a lawful aid with a lawful method of obtaining finance produced a result which was unlawful under the Treaty.

The answer appears to be that the nature of the levy may change the character of the aid. Normally aid is intended to render an industry more competitive or a particular sector of it or even some particular enterprises

---

1 *France* v. *EEC Commission* (1970), 16 Rec. 487, at pp. 494(4), (8), 495(13)–496(17), (19); [1970] C.M.L.R. 351.
2 See above, n. 1.
3 See *e.g. ibid.*, p. 496(18)–(19): permanent aid; p. 496(20): protectionism.
4 See *ibid*, p. 496(21).
5 *Ibid.*, p. 496(19), (20).

in a special situation. The finance is raised out of revenue which burdens the community as a whole. If the subsidy is obtained directly through a charge on the products of the same industry, the aid to the needy part of the industry is obtained at the expense of the more efficient competitors. Thus the aid discourages competition, especially if the levy feeding the subsidy is statutory and permanent.

Aid is intended to render an industry more competitive and should not be a means of rendering it less so. The fallacy in the case before the Court was that the products of the industry to be subsidised were themselves subjected to the levy and that the competition gap was not lessened in practice. The real reason which moved the Court appears to have been either that all German producers were rendered less competitive on the French market or that, although the measure was in a form compatible with the Treaty, competitors in other member states engaging in export to France were called upon to contribute to the rationalisation of their French competitors, possibly in perpetuity. Thus the motive and the effect of the levy and not the nature of the aid proved objectionable, but arts. 92 and 93 are not really suited to provide a remedy for this situation, despite the holding of the Community Court.

15

Fiscal Provisions

(Articles 95–99)[1]

Indirectly but very effectively trade and competition can be affected by governmental handling of taxation.[2] Thus the entire field of raising revenue is potentially within the ambit of the economic and commercial policy of the EEC as a whole and subject to regulation by the Community as a body. Nevertheless, the Treaty confines itself to controlling a sector of taxation only. Moreover, the simultaneous introduction of a uniform system (though not a uniform rate) of turnover tax, coupled with the abolition of national customs barriers, has reduced the possibilities of discrimination through taxation and has removed the particular threat of discrimination which the Treaty sought to counter. Consequently the relevant provisions of the Treaty have lost their practical interest, although as examples of directly applicable rules purporting to override existing domestic legislation which has not yet been adapted to the requirements of the Treaty they continue to attract attention.[3] It is, therefore, only necessary to outline these provisions and the practice of the Community Court interpreting them, before proceeding to set out the Community regulations which have superseded the various types of domestic legislation which the Treaty sought to control.

The provisions of the Treaty under review form the counterpart of those which prohibit the levy of customs duties and of equivalent charges. Member states must not impose directly or indirectly[4] on products imported from other member states any internal charges[5] of whatever kind

---

1   Van Houtte in *Ganshof van der Meersch*, nos. 2184–2205, pp. 869–879; Hostert, (1968–69) 43 B.Y.I.L. 147; Ehle, 1967 N.J.W. 1689.

2   For a full discussion of the very complex problems of the effect on trade of uniform and separate distinct systems of taxation see the Report of the Fiscal and Financial Committee on Tax Harmonisation in the Common Market (Neumark Report) 1962, C.C.H., paras. 2301–3284, especially as regards the problems raised here, para. 3224; EEC Commission *Tenth Report* (1967), s. 85, p. 113 (Approximation of Provisions on Direct Taxes); see also, *e.g.* Debatin, 1969 B.B.A.W.D. 125.

3   See above, p. 30 and n. 12, especially *Molkerei-Zentrale Westfalen-Lippe GmbH* v. *Hauptzollamt Paderborn* (1968), 14 Rec. 211, at p. 228; [1968] C.M.L.R. 187; *Lück* v. *Hauptzollamt Köln-Rheinau* (1968), 14 Rec. 359, at p. 370.

4   This term must be interpreted broadly: *Molkerei-Zentrale Westfalen-Lippe GmbH* v. *Hauptzollamt Paderborn* (1968), 14 Rec. 211, at pp. 226, 229; [1968] C.M.L.R. 187; see also below, p. 254, n. 9.

5   An internal charge is one which is applied equally to imports and to local products: *Milch-, Fett- und Eierkontor GmbH* v. *Hauptzollamt Saarbrücken* (1968), 14 Rec. 305, at p. 324; [1968] C.M.L.R. 225; *Fink Frucht GmbH* v. *Hauptzollamt München-Landsbergerstrasse* (1968), 14 Rec.

[*footnote continued on next page*

in excess of those applied directly or indirectly to similar domestic products[1] (art. 95(1)). Discrimination is forbidden.[2] In addition, member states must not, on products imported from other member states, impose any fiscal charges[3] of a kind which protect other productions[4] indirectly (art. 95(2)). These prohibitions apply even if no identical or similar national products are available,[5] but they do not apply to imports from third countries.[6] A fiscal charge is allowed, but disguised protectionism is not to be countenanced.[7] A time limit, which expired on 1 January 1962, put an end to any previous legislation to the extent that it contravened these requirements.[8]

The same prohibitions operate in reverse, inasmuch as upon export a member state may not allow drawbacks which are greater than the internal charges levied upon the national product concerned either directly or indirectly (art. 96).[9]

In all other circumstances, compensatory charges on imports and exemptions and drawbacks on exports are prohibited (art. 98). The scheme is thus clear. Unlike customs duties and charges equivalent to customs duties (art. 12), fiscal charges are not prohibited, provided that the charge is the same for imported goods and national products. At this stage practical difficulties faced the drafters of the Treaty. The current charge on products in the member states of the EEC was a turnover tax, but it existed in two forms: in France (*taxe à valeur ajoutée*) the tax at each stage took into account any charges suffered at earlier stages, and the final charge was one final sum which could be easily ascertained. In Germany, each stage attracted its own charge (the so-called "cascade" system), and

327, at p. 340; [1968] C.M.L.R. 228; *Stier v. Hauptzollamt Hamburg-Ericus* (1968), 14 Rec. 347, at p. 357; [1968] C.M.L.R. 222; *Lück v. Hauptzollamt Köln-Rheinau* (1968), 14 Rec. 359, at p. 369.

1   Similar products are those covered by the same fiscal classification: *Fink Frucht v. Hauptzollamt München-Landsbergerstrasse* [1968], 14 Rec. 327, at p. 342; [1968] C.M.L.R. 228; For an example see *EEC Commission v. Belgium* (1970), 16 Rec. 237, at p. 243(7)–(10).

2   *Stier v. Hauptzollamt Hamburg-Ericus* (1968), 14 Rec. 347, at p. 356; [1968] C.M.L.R. 222.

3   See above, p. 253, n. 5, and see Hostert, (1968–69) 43 B.Y.I.L. 147, at p. 158. This term is identical with an internal charge. See *e.g.*, *Fink Frucht v. Hauptzollamt München-Landsbergerstrasse* (1968), 14 Rec. 327, at pp. 342, 343; [1968] C.M.L.R. 228.

4   Other productions are *competing* products; their function, not their fiscal classification, matters here or that, without competing directly with national products, they are burdened with a special charge owing to their nature, distribution or other circumstances: *Fink Frucht v. Hauptzollamt München-Landsbergerstrasse* (1968), 14 Rec. 327, at pp. 342–343; [1968] C.M.L.R. 228.

5   *Fink Frucht v. Hauptzollamt München-Landsbergerstrasse* (1968), 14 Rec. 327, at p. 341; [1968] C.M.L.R. 228. *Stier v. Hauptzollamt Hamburg-Ericus* (1968), 14 Rec. 347, at p. 356; [1968] C.M.L.R. 222.

6   *Kunstmühle Tivoli v. Hauptzollamt Würzburg* (1968), 14 Rec. 293, at p. 302; [1968] C.M.L.R. 235.

7   *Stier v. Hauptzollamt Hamburg-Ericus* (1968), 14 Rec. 347, at p. 356; [1968] C.M.L.R. 222.

8   See above, p. 30, and n. 12; p. 253, and n. 3; *Lütticke v. Hauptzollamt Sarrelouis* (1966), 12 Rec. 293, at p. 320; [1971] C.M.L.R. 674.

9   See *EEC Commission v. Italy* (1965), 11 Rec. 1057, at p. 1069; [1966] C.M.L.R. 97; direct charges are those burdening the finished product; indirect charges affect raw materials and intermediate stages of production, *EEC Commission v. Italy* (1969), 15 Rec. 433, at p. 438.

the final charge did not disclose the amounts which had been charged and paid during earlier stages.[1] Thus the calculation of equal charges to be imposed upon imports from other member states created difficulties, if Germany was to avoid the practical necessity of violating the precept of art. 95(1) to the effect that charges imposed upon imported goods must not exceed the local charge.

As a result the Treaty enables member states which levy a turnover tax on the German model, calculated by a cumulative multi-stage system, to establish average rates[2] for specific products or groups of products, if they impose internal charges[3] upon imported goods or grant drawbacks on exported products provided always that they do not exceed the charges levied at home or are not of a protectionist nature (art. 97). In practice the maintenance of such a system in Germany has led to two problems.

The first was whether any such average rates represented a compensatory tax in lieu of the local turnover tax or a customs duty;[4] the second was whether art. 97(1) was directly applicable so as to enable individuals to challenge the application of such rates to themselves. Given the discretionary nature of the enabling provision (art. 97(1)) and the power of the Commission to take the necessary

Measures: Commission—Directives or decisions (art. 97(2))

if the average rates established by a member state were not in accordance with the requirements of the Treaty, it is clear that art. 97 constitutes a special rule distinct from art. 95[5] and is not directly applicable.[6]

In a carefully worded article (99(1)) the Commission is enjoined to consider how the laws of the member states concerning turnover taxes, excise duties and other forms of indirect taxation, including compensatory measures, can be harmonised.[7]

---

1   See van Hecke, No. 2189, p. 874.

2   They depend upon the previous existence of a cumulative multi-stage system and the actual exercise of the power to establish such rates: *Molkerei-Zentrale Westfalen-Lippe GmbH* v. *Hauptzollamt Paderborn* (1968), 14 Rec. 211, at p. 231; [1968] C.M.L.R. 187; *Kurt Becher* v. *Hauptzollamt München-Landsbergerstrasse* (1968), 14 Rec. 275, at p. 287; [1968] C.M.L.R. 232; *Milch-, Fett- und Eierkontor* v. *Hauptzollamt Saarbrücken* (1968), 14 Rec. 305, at p. 322; [1968] C.M.L.R. 225.

3   For the notion of internal charges see above, p. 253, n. 5, and cp. *Molkerei-Zentrale Westfalen-Lippe GmbH* v. *Hauptzollamt Paderborn* (1968), 14 Rec. 211, at p. 229; [1468] C.M.L.R. 187.

4   *H. Wöhrmann* v. *Hauptzollamt Reichenhall* (1968), 14 Rec. 261, at pp. 271, 272; [1968] C.M.L.R. 234; *Kunstmühle Tivoli* v. *Hauptzollamt Würzburg* (1968), 14 Rec. 293, at p. 302; [1968] C.M.L.R. 235; *Stier* v. *Hauptzollamt Hamburg-Ericus* (1968), 14 Rec. 347, at p. 356; [1968] C.M.L.R. 222. See also *Lütticke* v. *EEC Commission* (1971), 17 Rec. 325, at p. 339(16)–(17).

5   *Lütticke* v. *Hauptzollamt Sarrelouis* (1966), 12 Rec. 293, at p. 303; [1971] C.M.L.R. 674.

6   *Molkerei-Zentrale Westfalen-Lippe GmbH* v. *Hauptzollamt Paderborn* (1968), 14 Rec. 211, at pp. 226, 229; [1968] C.M.L.R. 187; *Kurt Becher* v. *Hauptzollamt München-Landsbergerstrasse* (1968), 14 Rec. 275, at p. 287; [1968] C.M.L.R. 232; *Milch- Fett- und Eierkontor GmbH* v. *Hauptzollamt Saarbrücken* (1968), 14 Rec. 305, at p. 321; [1968] C.M.L.R. 225; *Lück* v. *Hauptzollamt Köln-Rheinau* (1968), 14 Rec. 359, at p. 369.

7   For harmonisation in general see above, p. 18.

> *Measures:* Council, unanimously[1]—upon Commission pro-
> posal (art. 99(2))—acting by virtue of arts. 99
> and 100.[2]

As a result, the Council issued a Directive[3] in order to eliminate the difficulties arising from setting average rates while cumulative multi-stage
systems of turnover tax were still in force. The limited functions of the
Directive will lapse in so far as the adoption in all member states of harmonised added value tax proposed by the First Council Directive on the
Harmonisation of Member State Laws on Turnover Taxes of 11 April
1967[4] as extended by the Third Council Directive of 9 December 1969[5]
until 1 January 1972 has taken place.[6] The details are set out in the
Second Directive.[7]

I   VALUE ADDED TAX[8]

The new tax, known as "value added tax"[9] was to be promulgated in
each member state as soon as possible and not later than 1 January 1972
(originally 1 January 1970),[10] and from that date flat rate turnover
equalisation taxes were prohibited in trade between member states.[11]
The new value added tax must be a general consumption tax proportional to the price of goods and services, regardless of the number of
transactions in the course of production and distribution preceding the
stage at which the tax is applied.[12] At each stage the tax is levied after
deducting the amount of value added tax which has been levied on the
various cost factors.[13] It is applied at all stages including the retail stage,
subject, in respect of the latter, to a temporary potential exemption
coupled, in the member state's discretion, with an autonomous supple-
mental retail tax.[14]

The tax is exacted on all deliveries of goods and the performance of

---

1   The reference in art. 99(2) to art. 101 opens the way to a vote by a qualified majority.
2   See Teucci, 1969 Riv. Dir. Eur. 285; Ballarino, 1965 Dir. Int. 115 with lit., n. 2.
3   OJ, 1968, L 115/14.
4   67/227, OJ, 1967, 1301; for the original Commission proposal see OJ, 1963, 2631. For
    literature see: Teucci, 1969 Riv. Dir. Eur. 285, at p. 297; Tamchina, 1970 B.B.A.W.D. 37.
5   69/463, OJ, 1969, L 320/34.
6   For an exception concerning Italy, where the last time limit lapsed on 1 January 1973, see
    the Fourth Council Directive 71/401 of 20 December 1971, OJ, 1971, L 283/41 and the Fifth
    Council Directive 72/250 of 4 July 1972, OJ, 1972, L 162/19.
7   67/228, OJ, 1967, 1303.
8   See *e.g.* Teucci, above, n. 4; Prouzet, 1971 Rev. M.C. 294.
9   First Directive, art. 1, 1st para.; Second Directive, art. 1.
10 *Ibid.*, art. 1, 2nd para.
11 *Ibid.*, art. 1, 3rd para.
12 *Ibid.*, art. 2, 1st para.; Second Directive, art. 2(a).
13 *Ibid.*, art. 2, 2nd para.
14 *Ibid.*, art. 2, paras. 3 and 4, the latter reproducing in attenuated form a suggestion made by
    the Neumark Committee; and see *ibid.*, art. 2, referring to the procedure of art. 102.

services for valuable consideration[1] by a taxpayer within the country[2] *and* upon imported goods.[3] A taxpayer for this purpose is a person who independently and regularly effects operations connected with the activities of a producer or merchant or one who performs services, whether for gain or not.[4] These activities are to be understood broadly and embrace all economic activities including mining, farming and the liberal professions.[5] The freedom accorded to member states in applying the Directive is to be exercised, as regards the definition of taxable activities, by means of exemptions[6] and not by excluding certain economic activities as such from the range of activities subject to the First and Second Directives.[7] At the same time member states are free to include persons who engage in the relevant activities occasionally only,[8] but the wording of the Directive which envisages as subject to the tax all those who independently and regularly carry out operations arising out of the activities of a producer or merchant seeks to exclude from liability to taxation all those wage earners and salaried employees whose relations with their employer are governed by a labour contract.[9] According to the comment expressed in the Annex,[10] this wording also enables member states to exclude all those who, while working independently, are tied to each other by economic, financial or organisational relationships. It is difficult to enlarge on this notion, which may perhaps include co-operatives. As the comment in the Annex underlines, the definition of a taxpayer excludes public authorities and organisations governed by public law, operating in the exercise of their duties. However, if they engage in the activities of a producer, merchant or purveyor of services, member states may treat them on the same footing as other persons liable to value added tax.[11]

Since the tax falls due upon delivery of goods, the performance of services and import of goods,[12] these terms are defined in detail.[13]

1 Delivery

Delivery of an *object* is the transfer of the power to dispose of a *corporeal* object as an owner.[14] At the same time it is made clear that the term "corporeal object" includes both movable and immovable corporeal goods.[15] Thus only incorporeal goods are excluded, but an exception is

---

1   The French text runs: "*à titre onéreux*".
2   For the definition of this term see Second Directive, art. 3 and Annex A(1).
3   Second Directive, art. 2.
4   Second Directive, art. 4.
5   Second Directive: Annex A(2), 1st para.
6   See below, p. 262; Second Directive, art. 10.
7   Second Directive, Annex A(2), 2nd para.
8   Second Directive, Annex A(2), 3rd para.
9   Second Directive, Annex A(2), 4th para.
10 Second Directive, Annex A(2), 4th para., 2nd line.
11 Second Directive, Annex A(2), 5th and 6th paras.
12 Above, p. 256, and p. 257, nn. 1–3.
13 Second Directive, arts. 5, 6 and 7.
14 Second Directive, art. 5(1).
15 Second Directive, Annex A(3), 1st para.

made for electric current, gas, heat, cooling elements and similar products.[1] Since this effect may be reached in various ways and at different times, difficult questions of choice of law might be thought to arise, where movables are concerned.   However, the catalogue (discussed below) alleviates this difficulty to a certain extent by equating a series of situations with delivery in the sense used here, and the adoption of a statutory place of delivery (art. 5(4)) removes most problems of choice of laws. Member states retain the liberty to treat a company which acquires all or part of the assets of another person as a contribution in kind as if it had stepped into the shoes of the contributor as a taxpayer.[2]   A long catalogue enumerates what are deliveries in the meaning of the Directive, what transactions are deemed to be deliveries for valuable consideration and where delivery takes place.   Deliveries include: surrender of possession of an object[3] under a contract of lease for a specified time, instalment sales of objects with a proviso that title is acquired not later than upon payment of the last instalment;[4] the transfer of goods against payment of compensation following a compulsory purchase order made by a public authority or in its name;[5] the transfer of title to goods by virtue of a contract to buy or to sell for an undisclosed principal,[6] the delivery of a product made up with the customer's own material, irrespective of whether the craftsman has supplied a part of the materials used in the process;[7] the delivery of work involving immovables, including work which incorporates a movable into an immovable.[8]   Since in some countries of the EEC, contracts of the latter two types must be characterised not as contracts involving a transfer of title but as contracts of services, member states are given the opportunity to include such contracts under the heading of services, dealt with separately in the Directive (art. 6).[9] Deliveries for valuable consideration are deemed to include: the setting apart by the taxpayer within the framework of his enterprise of an object for his private use or handed over as a gift;[10] the use by the taxpayer for

---

1   Second Directive, Annex A(3), 2nd para.

2   Second Directive, Annex A(3), 3rd para.

3   The term *"bien"* is used in Second Directive, art. 2(a), in the sense described above, p. 257, nn. 14 and 15.

4   Second Directive, art. 5(2)(a). The contract in question must not split up partly as a lease and partly as a sale, but must be considered from the outset as contract involving a taxable delivery; see Second Directive, Annex A(4).

5   Second Directive, art. 5(2)(b).

6   Second Directive, art. 5(2)(c).

7   Second Directive, art. 5(2)(d).

8   Second Directive, art. 5(2)(e); this includes the construction of buildings, bridges, roads, harbours and the like under a contract of work; earthworks and landscaping, installation work, *e.g.* of central heating, repairs to immovables other than current maintenance; see Annex A(5), 2nd para.

9   Annex A(5), 1st para.

10   Second Directive, art. 5(3)(a); if the object had been purchased by the taxpayer himself, the value added tax may be waived by a member state, but the price originally paid cannot, in these circumstances, be set-off or, if already set-off, the allowance must be adjusted; see Annex A(6). Objects of little value are to be disregarded for the purpose of VAT; see Annex A(6), last para.

the purpose of his own enterprise of an object produced or extracted by himself or by another on his behalf.[1]

The place of delivery is the place where the object is situated at the moment when the dispatch or transport to the purchaser begins, if the object is dispatched either by the supplier, or by the purchaser or by a third person;[2] it is the place where the object is situated at the time of delivery, if the object is not dispatched or transported.[3]

In all these cases the tax arises at the moment when delivery occurs. However, it may be provided that in respect of payments on account, to be made before delivery, the tax arises at the time when the invoice is delivered or, at the latest, at the time when the payment on account is received, to an extent equal to the amount set out in the invoice or received.[4]

2   Services

Services are defined negatively as any operations which do not constitute delivery in the meaning of art. 5,[5] but the imposition of value added tax is only mandatorily required in respect of services set out in Annex B of the Second Directive.[6] These are: assignments of patents, trademarks, designs and similar rights and grants of licences concerning such rights, and all work carried out for a taxpayer in respect of corporeal movable property other than that referred to in art. 5(2); services for the purpose of preparing or of co-ordinating the execution of work affecting immovables, *e.g.* the services of architects and of offices supervising such work; advertising, transport and storage of goods including ancillary services; letting movable goods to a taxpayer;[7] supplying staff to a taxpayer;[8] services rendered by consultants, engineers, planning offices and the like in the technical, economic or scientific field; the performance of an undertaking not to exercise, altogether or in part, any professional activity or right set out in Annex B and, finally, services of forwarders, brokers, commercial agents and other independent intermediaries, in so far as they concern the delivery or import of goods or the performance of services set out in Annex B.

This list is supplemented in Annex A[9] which extends the notion of services to assignments or transfers of any intangible object, the performance of an undertaking not to engage in some activity, the performance of a service rendered in consequence of a requisition made by a public

---

1   Second Directive, art. 5(3)(b); this provision aims only at achieving equality of taxation between purchases intended for the enterprise, which do not benefit from any immediate or full deduction, and those produced or obtained by the taxpayer or by another on his behalf which are used for the same purpose; see Annex A(7).
2   Second Directive, art. 5(4)(a).
3   Second Directive, art. 5(4)(b).
4   Second Directive, art. 5(5); Annex A(8).
5   *Ibid.*, art. 6(1).
6   Art. 6(2), and Annex B.
7   The restriction *ratione personae* of the beneficiary should be noted: cp. art. 4.
8   Above, n. 7.
9   Annex A(9).

authority or on its behalf, the performance of work concerning an object, unless such work must be considered to be a delivery in the meaning of art. 5(2)(d) or (e), such as current maintenance, laundry service etc. In addition member states remain at liberty to impose VAT on certain operations by a taxpayer which may be treated as "services to himself", if such a measure should become necessary in order to prevent distortions.[1]

However, while only the services enumerated in Annex B are subject to the rules of the Second Directive,[2] member states are exhorted at the same time not to grant exemption from taxation, as far as possible, to any of the services in that Annex.[3]

The place of the service is, generally speaking, to be regarded as that where the service is rendered, the right is assigned or granted or where the leased object is used or put to work,[4] but the power to allow special derogations concerning particular services was reserved.

Measure: Council, unanimously—on proposal by the Commission—before 1 January 1970.[5]

Pending the enactment of such a measure, member states retain the power to derogate from the general principle in order to simplify the enforcement of the tax while avoiding cumulations or liability for or exemption from the tax.[6]

The tax arises when the service is performed. However, as in the case of delivery an exception is provided.[7] If the services are for an indefinite duration or exceed a specified period or if payments on account are to be made, it may be provided that the tax arises at the time when the invoice is delivered or, at the latest, at the time when the payment on account is received, to an extent equal to the amount set out in the invoice or received.[8]

As regards imported goods, the tax arises upon entry into the country,[9] but member states are free to link it to the accrual of liability for customs and other duties, taxes and import levies. The same applies to the fixing of the time when the tax payment falls due.[10]

3   Basis of Assessment

For deliveries and services, the assessment is based on the value of the consideration given respectively in return for the delivery or the services,

---

1   Second Directive, Annex A(9).
2   Second Directive, art. 6(2).
3   Second Directive, Annex A(10).
4   Second Directive, art. 6(3).
5   No such measure was promulgated.
6   Second Directive, Annex A(11).
7   Second Directive, art. 6(4).
8   Second Directive, art. 6(6).
9   Second Directive, art. 7; for the meaning of "country" see Second Directive, art. 3 and Annex A(1). As regards imports by travellers see Council Directive 69/169 of 28 May 1969, OJ, 1969, L 133/6; Second Directive 72/230, OJ, 1972, L 139/28; cp. above, p. 63, n. 11.
10 Second Directive, art. 7.

including all expenses and taxes other than value added tax.[1] In so far as the act of a taxpayer in setting apart for his private use an object within the framework of his enterprise attracts the incidence of taxation[2] the purchase price of the goods or of similar goods or, failing these, the cost price forms the basis of assessment.[3] For imported goods the customs value is the basis, increased by all duties and levies, except the value added tax itself. The same applies if the goods are exempt from customs duties or not subject to the *ad valorem* duties.[4] Special provision is made for the temporary device discussed above[5] that a member state charges Value Added Tax up to the wholesale stage and supplements it by a retail sales tax.[6]

4 Rate of Taxation

In accordance with the tenor of the Neumark Report, the EEC does not set the rates of taxation, which remain a matter reserved for the member states, but must be the same for the delivery of goods and the performance of services[7] as well as for local transactions and imported goods.[8] Member states retain the liberty to set increased or reduced rates for certain types of deliveries and services.[9]

5 Zero or Nil-Rating

Zero or nil-rating of value added tax is admitted; in some cases it is mandatory, in some discretionary. Deliveries to places outside the state concerned and all services connected therewith or with goods in transit are zero-rated, but the Directive leaves it to the member states to determine the conditions.[10]

---

1 Second Directive, art. 8(a); see also Annex A(13): the value of the consideration includes reimbursements for all ancillary costs such as for packing, transport, insurance, not only in money, but also in goods, as well as compensation for compulsory purchases or requisitions by public authorities (Annex A(13), 1st para.), but member states are free to exclude such items from the calculation of the costs for delivery and to treat them separately as the consideration for services if they are incurred after delivery as defined in the Directive (Annex A(13), 2nd para.). Any expenses paid in the name and for the account of the buyer and entered in the supplier's books as a temporary account (*compte de passage*) are not to be taken into account in assessing VAT for their services (Annex A(13), 3rd para.). The same applies to customs duties and the like paid at the time of import by customs agents etc. in their own name (Annex A(13) 4th para.).

2 Second Directive, art. 5(3)(a).

3 Second Directive, art. 8(b).

4 Second Directive, art. 8(c); Annex A(14) deals with the assessment in trade between member states; such assessments are to be made as far as possible on the same basis as that employed for local deliveries; a temporary provision concerns the assessment of imports from third countries.

5 P. 256, and n. 14.

6 Second Directive, Annex A(12); First Directive, art. 2, 4th para.

7 Second Directive, art. 9(1).

8 Second Directive, art. 9(3).

9 Second Directive, art. 9(2); Annex A(15).

10 The French text speaks of goods and services which were "*exonérées*" as distinct from "*non-imposables*" (exempt). See art. 11(2). The Second Directive, art. 10(1)(a) & (b); Annex

[*footnote continued on next page*

Services in connection with the import of goods may be exempted, subject to consultation of the Commission[1] which must consider art. 102 of the Treaty.[2] In addition member states, after having consulted the Commission, may establish any other nil-ratings which appear necessary.[3]

6   Deductions

In calculating his liability to value added tax, a taxpayer may deduct any value added tax paid or due by him for deliveries, services, imports and for the use by his enterprise of an object produced or extracted by himself or by another on his behalf.[4] However, any value added tax which has been borne by goods or services which were employed in order to effect a zero-rated or exempt operation cannot be deducted,[5] subject to an exception[6] and one modification.[7] Details are provided as to the manner and the timing of deductions[8] and the methods of accounting.[9]

Pending the abolition of import taxes and export drawbacks[10] the member states have the power, in exceptional circumstances, to introduce special measures in order to simplify the collection of the tax and in order to prevent certain tax evasions.[11] Other member states and the Commission must be informed, and if either a member state or the Commission objects,

> *Measure:* Council—upon proposal of the Commission—
> decides within three months—with a qualified
> majority if the measure is of the kind described
> above—unanimously if the measure is capable
> of contravening the system of taxation estab-
> lished by the Second Directive and the prin-
> ciple of non-interference in competition.[12]

A(16) enables member states to extend zero-rating to a stage prior to that executed by the exporter or to allow deductions in respect of the prior states (Annex A(17) first sentence). It also enables states to curtail the zero-rating accorded to these services (Annex A(17), second sentence.).

1   Second Directive, art. 10(2); and see Annex A(18), (19).
2   Second Directive, art. 16.
3   Second Directive, art. 10(3); subject to the proviso in Annex A(19).
4   Second Directive, art. 11(1); for the cases where payment is received upon submission of an invoice (arts. 5(5), 6(4)), see Annex A(2).
5   Second Directive, art. 11(2), final para.; and see art. 11(4) for the faculty to exclude from deduction those goods or services capable of being used wholly or in part for the private needs of the taxpayer or his employees.
6   Second Directive, art. 11(2), 2nd para., Annex A(21).
7   Second Directive, art. 11(2), 3rd para.; Annex A(22).
8   Second Directive, art. 11(3); and see Annex A(23), (24) for possible variations.
9   Second Directive, art. 12; Annex A(25), (26).
10 Second Directive, art. 13, last para.
11 Second Directive, art. 13, first para.
12 Second Directive, art. 13, paras 2–4; the effect of an objection is suspensive: *ibid.*, art 13, para. 6.

Finally, member states retain the power to devise, subject to the usual consultation, special rules for small enterprises[1] as well as for agricultural products, limited however in the latter case until the Council has issued a directive for this purpose.[2]

With the introduction of a value added tax in Italy on 1 January 1972,[3] the same type of turnover tax is now in force throughout the Community.[4]

II OTHER FISCAL MEASURES—COMPANIES RAISING CAPITAL

Acting in the exercise of its task under the Treaty to consider the harmonisation not only of turnover taxes and excise duties, but also of other forms of indirect taxation (art. 99), the Commission submitted a proposal to the Council on the harmonisation of Taxes on Contributions of Capital[5] in 1965, and the Council issued Directive 69/335 to this effect in 1969.[6]

The Directive enjoins the member states to harmonise duties to be levied on the occasion of the provision of capital for joint stock companies[7] (French term: *droit d'apport*). The duties involved are those arising in connection with the creation of a joint stock company either *de novo* or by way of transformation of another type of enterprise,[8] the transfer of such a company from one country to another[9] or the increase of its capital.[10] Member states are empowered to include among the incidents attracting the tax any increase in the capital of a company resulting from the capitalisation of profits, general reserves or contingency reserves;[11] an increase in the assets of a company contributed by a member which does not

---

1 Second Directive, art. 14; Annex A(27).

2 Second Directive, art. 15; cp. the Commission proposal of 26 February 1968, OJ, 1968, C C 48/2.

3 Above, p. 256, n. 6.

4 Belgium: Law of 3 July 1969 (*Taxe sur la Valeur Ajoutée, Belasting over de Toegevoegde Waarde*); France: Law 54–404 of 10 April 1954; Law 66–10 of 6 January 1966; Decree 67–1164 of 16 December 1967; Decree 68–372 of 24 April 1968 (*Taxe sur la Valeur Ajoutée*); Germany: Law of 29 May 1967, 1967 I BGB1 545 as amended (*Umsatzsteurgesetz (Mehrwertsteuer)*); Italy: Law of 17 October 1972, (*Tassa sul valore aggiunto*); Luxemburg: Law of 1970; Netherlands: Law of 28 June 1968, Stb 1968, 329 (*Belasting over de Toegevoegde Waarde*).

5 OJ, 1965, 2227.

6 OJ, 1969, L 249/25 amended OJ, 1973, L 103/13; to be carried out by 1 January 1972 (*ibid.*, art. 13); Campbell, *Common Market Law*, Suppl. 2(1971), Ch. 11, 144.

7 Council Directive 69/335, art. 1; the range of joint stock companies (*sociétés de capitaux*) is defined in art. 3.

8 *Ibid.*, art. 4(1)(a), (b).

9 *Ibid.*, art. 4(1)(e)–(h). A transfer includes either that of the seat of the administration or that of the registered office whether from a third state to a member state, or from one member state to another, provided always that the enterprise is regarded as a joint stock company in the latter State.

10 *Ibid.*, art. 4(1)(c).

11 *Ibid.*, art. 4(2)(a).

increase the capital but which is balanced by a modification of membership rights or is capable of raising the value of shares;[1] a loan raised by a joint stock company, if the loan agreement entitles the lender to a share of the company's profits,[2] or a loan granted to a joint stock company by a member, his spouse or child, or by a third party, if the loan is guaranteed by a member, provided that the loan serves the same purpose as an increase in the capital.[3]

In order to eliminate double impositions which would distort the uniform incidence of duty, only the authorities of the member state where the company has its real seat, or failing such a real seat within the EEC, where it has its statutory seat, may levy the duty.[4]

The basis of valuation for the purpose of this tax on contributions to the capital of a joint stock company is spelt out in detail.[5] Pending a Council Regulation which was to be promulgated before 1 January 1971[6] establishing common rates for the tax on contributions to capital, maximum (two per cent) and minimum (one per cent) rates were provided,[7] subject to a reduction of 50 per cent in case of mergers.[8]

Member states are free to exempt from all or part of the tax any contributions to any public utility companies if the state or some other territorial entity owns at least half of the company's capital[9] or if the companies concerned are engaged in law and in fact in cultural or charitable activities.[10] Member states also have the possibility of exempting, reducing or increasing in whole or in part certain types of operations or companies for reasons of fiscal equity, social policy or in order to meet a special situation.[11]

Outside the ambit described above, charges of any kind in respect of the transactions set out here are prohibited altogether.[12] The same applies to charges in respect of the creation of securities,[13] their issue, admission to the stock exchange, placing on the market or negotiation[14] and in respect of loans, including fixed interest obligations, raised by means of bonds or any negotiable instruments, no matter by whom they are issued, the incidental formalities connected therewith and, as in the case of shares,

---

1   Council Directive 69/335, art. 4(2)(b).
2   *Ibid.*, art. 4(2)(c).
3   *Ibid.*, art. 4(2)(d).
4   *Ibid.*, art. 2.
5   *Ibid.*, arts. 5, 6.
6   *Ibid.*, art. 7(2); a proposal was submitted by the Commission on 1 February 1971, OJ, 1971, C 34/1 and is now embodied in Council Directives 73/79/80, OJ, 1973, L 103/13/15. For its operation in the United Kingdom see Treaty of Accession, Pt. II, Annex VII, V(2), p. 149, Cmnd. 4862.
7   *Ibid.*, art. 7(1)(a); now one per cent; Council Directive 73/80, art. 1.
8   *Ibid.*, art. 7(1)(b); now between nil and 0·50 per cent; *ibid.*, art. 2.
9   *Ibid.*, art. 8, para. 1.
10 *Ibid.*, art. 8, para. 2; the term charitable is used here in the sense employed in English law.
11 *Ibid.*, art. 9 in conjunction with art. 102 of the Treaty.
12 *Ibid.*, art. 10.
13 Or any warrant or scrip certificate.
14 *Ibid.*, art. 11(a).

their creation, issue, admission to the stock exchange, placing on the market or negotiation.[1]

On the other hand, the following are not excluded by the Directive: taxes and duties upon a transfer of shares or bonds,[2] and of immovables or of a business to a company association or legal entity engaged in profit making activities[3] or upon the transfer of assets of any kind to any such enterprise[4] provided that, in the last case, the transfer is remunerated otherwise than by the allocation of shares,[5] upon the creation or discharge of a mortgage,[6] charges in the nature of fees and value added tax.[7] However, this freedom is restricted in one respect inasmuch as any such tax, other than that levied on the transfer of securities (Directive, art. 11(a)) must be levied and assessed on the same basis irrespective of whether the real or the statutory seat of the company, association or legal entity engaged in profit-making activities is situated within the member state or not.[8]

III Proposed Fiscal Measures

The Neumark Report[9] envisaged as a first measure the harmonisation of turnover taxes, but it also envisaged a regulation concerning withholding taxes for dividends and other interest payments,[10] and an overhaul of double taxation conventions, the initiation of a company tax reform and of work on direct taxes[11] (income, company, land), followed by consideration of a net tax on net wealth, a re-appraisal of death duties, the abolition or harmonisation of excise duties,[12] in particular on tobacco, and the abrogation of taxes on capital transfers.

The Commission has been active in some of these fields[13] and proposals of directives have been submitted in respect of the common tax treatment of mergers between companies in different member states,[14] of parent and

---

1 *Ibid.*, art. 11(b).
2 *Ibid.*, art. 12(1)(a).
3 *Ibid.*, art. 12(1)(b).
4 *Ibid.*, art. 12(1)(c).
5 *Ibid.*, art. 12(1)(c).
6 *Ibid.*, art. 12(1)(d).
7 *Ibid.*, art 12(1)(e), (f).
8 *Ibid.*, art. 12(2).
9 Part VII.
10 See Schulze-Brachmann, 1970 B.B.A.W.D. 289.
11 Gosset, 1970 Rev. M.C. 349.
12 Vandamme, 1967 Rev. M.C. 624; Commission Memorandum of 8 February 1967 (below, n. 13).
13 Memorandum of 8 February 1967, 1967 EEC Bull., Suppl. to Bull No. 8 as regards excise duties and direct taxes. See *Tenth Report* (1966–67), s. 77, pp. 106 ff., at s. 80, 85 (General Programme of 7 February 1967 especially concerning direct taxation); *First General Report* (1967), s. 71, pp. 74 ff.; *Second General Report* (1968), s. 48 pp. 61 ff.; *Third General Report* (1969), s. 47, pp. 76 ff., especially s. 53, p. 83 (withholding tax on dividends); *Fourth General Report* (1970), s. 39, pp. 35 ff.; *Fifth General Report* (1971), s. 148, pp. 104 ff. And see Vogelaar, 1970 B.B.A.W.D. 198; Fischer, 1968 N.J.W. 321.
14 16 January 1969, OJ, 1969, C 39/1; 1969, C 100/4; Sasse, 1970 B.B.A.W.D. 533.

daughter companies in the same circumstances[1] and of excise duties on fuel oil and alcoholic beverages.[2] The Council adopted on 19 December 1972 a directive envisaging the harmonisation of excise duties on tobacco products.[3]

---

1   16 January 1969, OJ, 1969, C 39/7; 1969, C 100/7; Sasse, 1970 B.B.A.W.D. 533.
2   28 December 1970, OJ, 1971, C 14/15.
3   OJ, 1972, L 303/1. Chiniard and Giuffrida, 1970 Rev. M.C. 340.

16

Implementation of the Treaty by Indirect Means[1]

Generally speaking, the Treaty and the implementing measures taken under the powers provided therein constitute an independent legal system which functions side by side with the laws of the member states and operates directly upon the member states and at times upon individuals.[2] The member states determine, each for itself, how to adjust their domestic legal systems to Community law.[3]

In addition, the Community organs can rely, when necessary, on implied powers to achieve directly the objectives of the Treaty, if the latter has not provided the requisite means (art. 235: Council; art. 155: Commission). Furthermore, although the Treaty refrains from interfering with the domestic law of the member states directly, it enables the Community organs to achieve the same effect indirectly in substance, if not in form, by means of directives instructing the member states to approximate,[4] to co-ordinate[5] or to harmonise[6] a particular branch or rule of their domestic law or administrative rules if they directly affect the functioning of the Common Market.[7] For this purpose three distinctive methods are provided. Either the power is limited to directives bearing upon domestic law which touches upon a specific object of the Treaty,[8] or the power is general so as to promote any one object of the Treaty by touching upon any one branch of domestic law,[9] or it is incumbent upon the member states, encouraged by Community organs, to conclude a convention which brings their laws into line.[10]

---

1 Goldman in *Ganshof van der Meersch*, nos. 2206–2254, pp. 881–899 with lit.; Van Ommeslaghe, 1969 Cah. Dr. Eur. 495 at pp. 513–516.

2 See above, pp. 21–31.

3 See above, pp. 39–44.

4 Arts. 3(h); 27; 100(1); 117, 2nd para.; the equivalent terms in the other languages of the Treaty are: *rapprochement, Angleichung, ravvicinamento, nader tot elkaar brengen*.

5 Arts. 6(1), 40(2)(b)(1), 54(3)(g), 56(2), 57(2), (3), 66, 70(1), 105(1), 111(1). The equivalent terms in the other languages of the Treaty are: *koordinieren, coordonnent, coordinano, coördineren*.

6 Arts. 99, 112(1), 117, 1st and 2nd paras. The equivalent terms in the other languages of the Treaty are: *harmonisiert werden, être harmonisées, armonizzare, worden geharmoniseerd*, but see art. 112(1): *vereinheitlicht, harmonisés, armonizzati, met elkaar in overeenstemming gebracht*; art. 117: *Angleichung, égalisation, parificazione, onderlinge aanpassing, Abstimmung, harmonisation, ravvicinamento, harmonisatie*.

7 For a discussion of this condition see Goldman, *Ganshof van der Meersch*, nos. 2219–2222.

8 See above, nn. 4–6.

9 Art. 100 in conjunction with arts. 235, 115.

10 Art. 220.

It must not be overlooked that in very restricted circumstances a member state must even undertake a specific change of domestic law (arts. 101, 102).

Many attempts have been made to attribute a specific and distinct meaning to each of these three terms[1] and none of them has succeeded completely,[2] given that the terms are used interchangeably.[3] Nevertheless a preponderant pattern seems to emerge; laws are approximated;[4] activities and policies are co-ordinated,[5] and pecuniary contributions or aids are harmonised.[6]

I   AREAS OF APPROXIMATION, CO-ORDINATION AND HARMONISATION

In order to achieve the approximation, co-ordination or harmonisation required in order to make the market function, the Treaty provides the following

Measure: Council—upon proposal of the Commission— unanimously—Directives (art. 100).

Acting by virtue, at times, of the specific and, at times, of the general powers conferred upon them the Commission has proposed,[7] and the Council has adopted from among these for the time being directives for the approximation, co-ordination and harmonisation of the domestic law of the member states in the following areas covered by the Treaty: customs legislation,[8] quantitative restrictions,[9] agriculture,[10] free move-

---

1   See van Ommeslaghe (above, p. 267, n. 1) at pp. 513–516.

2   *Ibid.*, 516, nn. 39 and 40 with lit.; Goldman in *Ganshof van der Meersch*, nos. 2208, 2209.

3   See above, p. 267, nn. 4–6.

4   Arts. 3(h); 27; 100(1); 117, 2nd para., last two lines.

6   Arts. 6(1), 40(2)(b), 70(1), 105(1), 111(1) and cp. arts. 54(3)(g), 56(2).

6   Arts. 99; 112(1); 117, 1st and 2nd paras.

7   See the comprehensive list in 1967 EEC Bull., Suppl. No. 12, covering the period from 1 January 1958 until 31 March 1967; 1972, Suppl. 9; see also *EEC General Report* (1967), s. 85; 1968, s. 75; 1969, s. 62; 1970, s. 64; 1971, s. 166.

8   Council Directive 68/321, 30 July 1968, OJ, 1968, L 194/13; 69/73, 4 March 1969, OJ, 1969, L 58/1; 69/74, 4 March 1969, OJ., 1969, L 58/7; 69/75, 4 March 1969 OJ 1969, L 58/11; 69/76, 4 March 1969, OJ, 1969, L 58/14; 70/538, 15 December 1970, OJ, 1970, L 143/28; Commission Directive, 30 June 1971, OJ, 1971, L 161/17; Council Directive 72/242, 27 June 1972, OJ, 1972, L 151/16 (all art. 100).

9   See above, p. 56, n. 2 (art. 33(7)).

10 *Food-Colouring Material in Foodstuffs:* Council Directive 23 October 1965, OJ, 1962, 2645, am. 25 October 1965, OJ, 1965, 2793; 24 October 1967, OJ, 1967, No. 263/4; 20 December 1968, OJ, 1968, L 309/24; 13 July 1970, OJ, 1970, L 157/36.

Preservatives in food: Council Directive 5 November 1963, OJ, 1964, 161, am. 23 December 1965, OJ, 1965, 3263; 14 December 1966, OJ, 1966, 3947; 27 June 1967, OJ, 1967, No. 148/1 (citrus fruit); 20 December 1968, OJ, 1968, L 309/25; 13 July 1970, OJ, 1970, L 157/38; 30 March 1971, OJ, 1971, L 87/12; 20 December 1971, OJ, 1972, L 2/22; 26 December 1972, OJ, 1972, L 298/48 (art. 100).

ment of goods,[1] free movement of workers,[2] establishment[3] and services,[4] free movement of capital,[5] the regulation of transport,[6] dumping,[7] and aids[8] as well as fiscal measures[9] or of a general technical character.[10]

II   Uniform Rules through Conventions

At the same time the member states have gone a step further and, acting in accordance with the invitation extended by the Treaty (art. 220), have concluded two Conventions, one dated 29 February 1968 for the

---

Preservatives, purity: Council Directive 26 January 1965, OJ, 1965, 373; 27 June 1967, OJ, 1967, No. 148/10 (art. 100).

Anti-oxidants in foodstuffs: 13 July 1970, OJ, 1970, L 157/31 (art. 100).

Livestock, Fresh Meat: Council Directive 64/432, 26 June 1964, OJ, 1964, 1977, am. 25 October 1966, OJ, 1966, 3294; 64/433, 26 June 1964, OJ, 1964, 2012 am. 25 October 1966, 3302; 6 October 1969, OJ, 1969, L 256/5; 13 July 1970, OJ, 1970, L 157/40; 27 October 1970, OJ, 1970, L 239/42; 19 July 1971, OJ, 1971, L 179/1; 7 February 1972 OJ, 1972, L 38/95; 28 December 1972, OJ, 1972, L 298/49, 12 December 1972, OJ, 1972, L 302/24/28.

Fresh Poultry: Council Directive 71/118, 15 February 1971, OJ, 1971, L 55/23.

Control of Animal Foodstuffs: 20 July 1970, OJ, 1970, L 170/2; Commission Directives 15 June 1971, OJ, 1971, L 155/13; 18 November 1971, OJ, 1971, L 279/7; Council Directive 20 July 1972, OJ, 1972, L 171/39. And see generally, Schaub and Beuve-Méry (1971) 5 EuR. 135.

Plants and Seeds—Marketing: beet: 14 June 1966, OJ, 1966, 2290; OJ, 1972, L 287/22; *forage plants:* 14 June 1966, OJ, 1966, 2298; *cereal:* 14 June 1966, OJ, 1966, 2309; *seed potatoes:* 14 June 1966, OJ, 1966, 2320, all as amended 18 February 1969, OJ, 1969, L 48/1–8; *oleaginous and fibrous plant seed:* 30 June 1969, OJ, 1969, L 169/3; *vegetable seed:* 29 September 1970, OJ, 1970, L 255/7.

Catalogue of Varieties of Types of Agricultural Plants: 29 September 1970, OJ, 1970, L 225/1; Commission Directive 14 April 1972, OJ, 1972, L 108/8, all amended 20 July 1972, OJ, 1972, L 171/37; 6 December 1972, OJ, 1972, L 287/22.

Vine Propagation Material: 9 April 1968, OJ, 1968, L 93/15.

Forestry Reproductive Material: 14 June 1966, OJ, 1966, 2326, am. 18 February 1969, OJ, 1969, L 48/12; 30 March 1971, OJ, 1971, L 87/14.

Timber in the Rough: 23 January 1968, OJ, 1968, L 32/12.

Campaign against Potato Wart, Potato Root Eelworm, San José Louse: 8 December 1969, OJ, 1969, L 323/1/3/5 (all arts. 43, 100).

1   *Free Movement of Goods*

Drugs—Proprietary drugs: 26 January 1965, OJ, 1965, 369, am. 28 June 1966, OJ, 1966, 2658; *hazardous substances, classification, labelling, packing:* 27 July 1967, OJ, 1967, No. 196/1–98, am. 13 March 1969, OJ, 1969, L 68/1; 6 March 1970, OJ, 1970, L 59/33; 22 March 1971, OJ, 1971, L 74/15.

Crystal glass: 15 December 1969, OJ, 1969, L 326/36.

Textiles, designation, composition, labelling: 26 July 1971, OJ, 1971, L 185/16; L 244/80 (all art. 100).

2   *Free Movement of Workers:* see above, p. 87, n. 2.

3   *Freedom of Establishment:* see above, p. 130, n. 4, p. 133, n. 4, p. 134, n. 13, p. 135, n. 1, p. 143, n. 13, p. 144, n. 1, p. 146, n. 1 (arts. 54(2), 54(3)(g), 57, 63(2), 66).

4   *Services:* see above, p. 165, n. 4, p. 167, n. 10.

5   *Capital:* see above, p. 170, nn. 2–6 (arts. 67, 69).

6   *Transport:* see above, p. 184, n. 5 (arts. 75, 99, 100).

7   *Dumping:* see above, p. 244, n. 5.

8   *Aids:* see above, p. 248, nn. 3, 4.

9   *Fiscal Measures:* see above, p. 256, nn. 3–7, p. 263, n. 6 (arts. 99, 100); Vogelaar, (1970) 7 C.M.L. Rev. 323.

10 *Technical—Measuring Instruments:* 26 July 1971, OJ, 1971, L 202/1 (metric measures);

[footnote continued on next page

Mutual Recognition of Companies,[1] the other of 27 September 1968, relating to the Jurisdiction and the Implementation of decisions on Civil and Commercial Matters.[2] A Draft Convention on Jurisdiction and the Enforcement of Decisions in matters of Bankruptcy, Arrangements and like Procedures in the version of 16 February 1970[3] is now available for discussion.

A CONVENTION ON THE JURISDICTION AND THE ENFORCEMENT OF DECISIONS IN CIVIL AND COMMERCIAL MATTERS[4]

The Convention of 27 September 1968,[5] based on a number of surveys of the law of the member states,[6] differs from almost all[7] previous conventions on the recognition and enforcement of foreign judgments inasmuch as it concentrates on establishing common rules of jurisdiction for the member states. In all previous conventions and in the domestic law of member states, the recognising or enforcing court determined by reference to the conventions or its own notion of jurisdiction whether the foreign court, the judgment of which was sought to be enforced, was a competent court for the purposes of recognition and enforcement. The foreign court remained at liberty to exercise jurisdiction according to its own rules, irrespective of whether its decision was likely to be enforced abroad. Thus the bases of jurisdiction on which the trial courts in the respective countries proceeded differed from each other, and the recognition and enforcement in other countries were ensured in a limited number of situations only in so far as a convention or the domestic law of the

---

amended Council Directive 19 December 1972, OJ, 1972, L 291/156; OJ, 1971, L 202/21 (gas); OJ, 1971, L 202/32; OJ, 1971, L 239/9 (liquids other than water); OJ, 1971, L 202/14 (weights); 12 October 1971, OJ, 1971, L 239/1 (for cereals); OJ, 1971, L 239/15, (gauging ships' tanks); 18 October 1971, OJ, 1971, L 243/29 (units of measurement).

1 See above, p. 148, n. 3, with lit.

2 OJ, 1972, L 299/32; 1969 EEC Bull., Suppl.

3 Nadelmann, 1970 Riv. Dir. Int. Proc. 501 and the text, *ibid.*, p. 692; Nadelmann, *Conflict of Laws: International and Interstate* (1972), p. 340, is based on a document dated 4 July 1969.

4 See generally Droz, *Compétence Judiciaire et Effets des Jugements dans le Marché Commun* (1972), with a comprehensive survey of lit. at pp. 11, n. 1, 16–17, which includes some of the following: K. Newman in *Legal Aspects of an Enlarged EEC* (1972), pp. 58 ff.; Nadelmann, (1967–68) 5 C.M.L.Rev. 409; (1967) 67 Col. L.R. 995; (1969) 82 Harv. L.R. 1282; *Conflict of Laws, International and Interstate* (1972), pp. 222–270; Hay, (1968) 16 A.J.C.L. 149; Zaphiriou, 1969 J. Bus. L. 74; Goldman, 1971 Rev. Trim. Dr. Eur. 1; Weser, (1969) *Travaux du Comité Français de Droit International Privé* 353 and in *Ganshof van der Meersch*, no. 2541, p. 1009, no. 2546, p. 1016; Arnold, 1969 B.B.A.W.D. 89; 1972, 389; Jeantet, 1972, Cah. Dr. Eur. 375.

5 OJ, 1972, L 299/32 in force 1 February 1973; 1969 EEC Bull., Suppl.; Campbell, *Common Market Law*, Suppl., Ch. 9.

6 See Droz, *Compétence Judiciaire et Effets des Jugements dans le Marché Commun*, p. 3, n. 1; for the preparatory work see Bellet, 1965 Clunet 833; Bülow, (1965) 29 Rabels Z. 473 ff. and 549 (text of the Draft Convention); Dubbink, *Sociaal-Economische Wetgeving* (1965), p. 301.

7 But see the Franco–Belgian Treaty of 8 July 1899, the Dutch–Belgian Treaty of 28 March 1925 and the Benelux Treaty of 24 November 1961. See Bülow, (1965) 29 Rabels Z. 473, at p. 478, n. 17.

requested court acknowledged the jurisdiction of the original court. If these bases did not coincide the foreign judgment, though validly rendered by a foreign court which had jurisdiction according to its own law, was possibly without effect in the requested country.[1]

The EEC Convention starts from the jurisdiction of the trial court, seeks to lay down uniform rules for the exercise of jurisdiction by the original court and, subject to limited exceptions, treats the ensuing recognition and enforcement as automatic consequences of the exercise of jurisdiction by the original court on the strength of a uniform rule of jurisdiction. By these means any disparity is avoided between the rules of jurisdiction which enable the original court to determine a dispute and those of the requested court which prevent that court from giving effect to the foreign judgment.

It must be admitted that another method would have been to unify the rules of jurisdiction on the basis of which recognition and enforcement was to be accorded. As in all previous bilateral conventions this would have left outside the ambit of recognition and enforcement all those decisions of the original court in another member state which had been rendered on a broader basis than that accorded by the Convention for the purposes of recognition and enforcement. Given the aim of the EEC Treaty to approximate, co-ordinate and to harmonise the laws of the member states which directly affect the establishment and functioning of the Common Market (art. 100), the way was clear for the more radical solution by way of a Convention (art. 220).

1 Sphere of Application

a Ratione materiae and ratione personae

Ratione materiae the Convention applies to decisions in civil and commercial matters with the exception of those concerning the status and capacity of individuals, matrimonial property regimes, wills and successions, bankruptcy,[2] social security[3] and arbitration.[4] *Ratione personae* it applies primarily to all persons, irrespective of their nationality, who are *domiciliés*, "*die ihren Wohnsitz . . . haben*"[5] within a member state, on an equal footing with nationals of that member state.[6] While the Treaty clearly opts for residence rather than nationality, the precise meaning of

---

1 If the jurisdictional requirements of a convention are not satisfied, it may still be possible to rely on the ordinary rules of private international law of the requested country which permit recognition and enforcement according to different jurisdictional criteria.

2 This term includes winding-up proceedings and arrangements with creditors.

3 Social security was expressly excluded on account of its position in Belgian law; see Bülow, (1965) 29 Rabels Z. 473, at pp. 477–478.

4 Art. 1. For the reasons for omitting arbitration, notwithstanding that art. 220 of the Treaty includes awards in the catalogue of topics to be settled by conventions, see Bülow, (1965) 29 Rabels Z. 473, at p. 476. Cp. Foreign Judgments (Reciprocal Enforcement) Act 1933, s. 11(2).

5 See below, p. 271, nn. 3, 4.

6 Art. 2.

this term may require clarification in so far as English lawyers are concerned. Clearly the Treaty does not require a domicile in the meaning of English private international law,[1] but the Treaty does not attach a uniform technical meaning to this term, and leaves it to the member states to characterise this connecting factor.[2] According to German law a "*Wohnsitz*" is the place or one of several places where a person resides permanently, and which is lost through intentional abandonment.[3] According to French law it is the place, and only the place, where a person has his principal establishment,[4] but certain persons are attributed a domicile by operation of law or as a domicile of dependence. In these circumstances, English courts will rely on a test which is less exacting than domicile and more permanent than presence or perhaps even than residence as such. Permanent or ordinary residence and, if English or Scottish law applies, perhaps, in the case of dependents or of persons whose residence is fixed by operation of law, that attributed to them by law, will serve the purposes of the Convention.

The Convention introduces two novel exceptions: in ascertaining the [ordinary] residence of a party, the court, whether acting as an original court or a requested court, can only rely on its own notion of [ordinary] residence, where [ordinary] residence in the country of that court is in issue.[5] However, if it is alleged that a party is [ordinarily] resident in another member state the court must rely on the notions of [ordinary] residence in that country.[6] Secondly, a domicile of dependence is to be determined by reference to the national law of the person or authority on which it is alleged to depend.[7] Companies, associations and other legal entities are to be treated as [ordinarily] resident at the place of their seat which is determined by the rules of private international law of the *forum*.[8]

b   Ratione loci

Ratione loci the jurisdiction of the courts of the country where the defendant is ordinarily resident is comprehensive,[9] except where the Convention provides a concurrent jurisdiction[10] or ousts the general jurisdiction provided in art. 2 and replaces it by an exclusive jurisdiction[11] or

---

1   See above, p. 271, n. 5.

2   Art. 52; Bellet, 1965 Clunet 833, at p. 866.

3   German Civil Code, para. 7; for the *Wohnsitz* of dependent persons see *ibid.*, paras. 8, 9, 11; Kegel in Soergel-Siebert, *Kommentar zum Bürgerlichen Gesetzbuch*, (10th Edn., 1970), Vol. 7, n. 26 before art. 7.

4   *Code Civil*, art. 102; Mazeaud & Mazeaud, *Leçons de Droit Civil*, (4th Edn., 1968) Vol. I, nos. 572–584.

5   Art. 52, 1st para.

6   Art. 52, 2nd para.

7   Art. 52, 3rd para.

8   Art. 53.

9   Art. 3.

10   Arts. 5–15.

11   Art. 16.

within limits[1] allows the parties to select a jurisdiction themselves[2] or accepts submission.[3] For good measure the Treaty states expressly that a number of grounds for assuming jurisdiction, which are sanctioned by the laws of the member states and have acquired a certain notoriety, are to be suppressed.[4] However, this suppression, and thus the elimination of the previously existing rules of jurisdiction in so far as they are incompatible with the Convention is partial only. If the defendant is not ordinarily resident in one of the member states, member states are free to disregard the Convention and to apply other jurisdictional criteria.[5] Thus the jurisdiction based on nationality or the *forum arresti* reappears, despite the opposition raised against them,[6] but now with a vengeance. Henceforth such decisions rendered, *e.g.* in Germany, against a Swedish national ordinarily resident in Sweden, will have to be enforced in England, where such a jurisdiction has never been accepted (unlike in Scotland). It is true that the requested country is enabled to fend off attempts to enforce decisions given on such exorbitant jurisdictional grounds, but the conditions laid down by the Convention for achieving this result make its realisation impracticable.[7] The requested state must have concluded a Convention on the Recognition and Enforcement of Judgments with the home country of the national of a non-member state whereby it undertakes not to enforce such judgments given by the courts in other member states.[8] Thus it is impossible to deny generally any effect to judgments given against nationals of third countries by virtue, not of the jurisdictional provisions of the Convention itself but of the exorbitant provisions of French, German or Dutch law in so far as they were left untouched by the Convention; only nationals of particular non-member states with whom a special type of Treaty has been made, excluding *inter alia* the effect of such judgments towards nationals of that state, can hope to escape the net of art. 4 of the Convention. Yet it is doubtful whether the proper functioning of the Common Market requires such a provision. It aims at re-enforcing the exorbitant jurisdiction of member states in others where previously enforcement may have been excluded by making assets in other member states available for levy of execution, when this result cannot be achieved directly by an action in the member state where the assets are situated. This is not a process of harmonisation but of subordination.[9]

---

1 Arts. 12, 15, 16.
2 Art. 17.
3 Art. 18.
4 Art. 3, 2nd para. These are principally the nationality of the plaintiff or of the defendant and the existence of assets within the jurisdiction.
5 Art. 4, which refers expressly to the more extensive jurisdiction accorded by domestic law.
6 See Nadelmann above, p. 270, n. 4.
7 Art. 59.
8 Art. 59.
9 See Nadelmann, (1967) 67 Col. L.R. 995; *Conflict of Laws: International and Interstate* (1972), p. 238 and the Postscript at pp. 268–270.

2   Concurrent Jurisdiction

While the courts of the country where the defendant is [ordinarily ?] resident can exercise general jurisdiction, which is only excluded where the Treaty establishes an exclusive jurisdiction elsewhere,[1] a concurrent jurisdiction can be invoked in certain circumstances by the plaintiff,[2] whereby the general jurisdiction of the courts of the defendant's [ordinary] residence is ousted.[3] In certain cases the general nature of the claim,[4] in others the need to strengthen the weaker position of the plaintiff having regard to the underlying relationship[5] determines the available choice of jurisdictions.

a   General Nature of the Claim

Jurisdiction can be exercised by the courts of the place of performance, if the claim is contractual;[6] by the courts of the country where the plaintiff has his habitual residence, if the claim is for maintenance;[7] by the courts of the country where the damage was suffered, if the claim arises out of a tort or of an act equivalent to a tort;[8] by the courts of the country where a public prosecution is brought, if the claim is for damages or restitution arising out of a criminal offence, provided that the courts concerned can entertain claims of a private law nature;[9] by the courts of the country where the branch, agency or any establishment is situated, if the claim arises out of its management.[10]

As the *forum connexitatis* the court of the country where one of several defendants [ordinarily] resides has jurisdiction over any co-defendants,[11] over persons against whom a third party notice has been issued[12] or in interpleader proceedings[13] provided that such a claim has not been made for the sole purpose of ousting the jurisdiction of the courts which exercise

---

1   Arts. 16, 17.

2   Arts. 5, 6, 7–15.

3   Art. 17.

4   See arts. 5, 6.

5   Arts. 7, 8, 9, 10, 11, 12, 13, 14, 15.

6   Art. 5(1); an exception exempts persons [ordinarily] resident in Luxemburg from this jurisdiction; see Protocol art. I; and see Bülow, (1965) 29 Rabels Z. 473, at p. 484, n. 30.

7   Art. 5(2).

8   Art. 5(3).

9   Art. 5(4).

10   Art. 5(5).

11   Art. 6(1).

12   Art. 6(2); a third party notice under Ord. 16, r. 1 comes nearest to the *demande en garantie* referred to in the Convention which is a remedy known in France (C. Proc. civ., arts. 59, 181–185); Belgium (Law of 25 March 1876, arts. 50, 52); Luxemburg (C. Proc. civ., arts. 59, 181–185); the Netherlands (Regtsvordering, art. 126, no. 14) and Italy (C. proc. civ., art. 32), but not in this form in Germany (ZPO, para. 72 ff). See Bülow, (1965) 29 Rabels Z. 473, at p. 485, n. 36. Consequently the Protocol (art. V) provides that the equivalent provisions of German law apply according to which no judgment can be rendered against the third party. Having regard to Ord. 16, r. 7, the English procedure comes near to that envisaged in the Convention.

13   Art. 6(2).

general jurisdiction over them,[1] and in respect of counterclaims arising from the same contract or situation on which the original claim before the court is based.[2]

b Specific Nature of the Claim

In order to strengthen the position of certain types of plaintiffs, mainly parties to adhesion contracts, additional jurisdictions are provided for any beneficiaries parties to a contract of insurance or buyers, parties to a sale by instalments.

(i) *Insurance Contracts*—Claims against an insurer can be brought not only in the courts of a country having general or concurrent jurisdiction,[3] but also in the country where the insurer is [ordinarily] resident[4] or, if there are several insurers, in the courts of the country where any one of them has his [ordinary] residence as well as in the courts of the country where the other party to the contract [ordinarily] resides.[5]

If the law of a member state so provides, jurisdiction may also be exercised against an insurer who is [ordinarily] resident elsewhere if an intermediary (broker, agent), who took part in the conclusion of the contract, is ordinarily resident there, provided that this latter residence is mentioned in the policy or the proposal for insurance.[6] Additional *fora* are provided for the case of insurance of immovables and liability insurance. In both cases the courts of the country where the damage occurred have jurisdiction.[7] In the case of liability insurance, if the local law so permits, the insurer is also subject to the jurisdiction of the courts of the country where an injured party is suing the assured.[8] If the injured party wishes to sue the insurer directly (as the law of some of the member states permits), the provisions concerning jurisdiction in disputes between the assured party and the insurer apply.[9] In the latter case the assured, whether a party to the contract of insurance or not, is also subject to the jurisdiction, provided that the law governing the direct action by the injured party against the insurer allows third party notice.[10]

The insurer, on the other hand, can only sue the assured, whether he be a party to the contract of insurance or not, by proceeding in the courts of the country where the latter is [ordinarily] resident,[11] subject to two exceptions.

In the first place, if the injured party brings a direct action in accordance with art. 10 in any one of the jurisdictions made available in arts. 7,

---

1 Art. 6(2).
2 Art. 6(3).
3 Art. 7.
4 A branch office or agency is sufficient for this purpose: see art. 8, para. 3.
5 Art. 8, 1st para.
6 Art. 8, 2nd para.
7 Art. 9; the same rule applies if the insurance covers both immovables and movables.
8 Art. 10, 1st para.
9 Art. 10, 2nd para.
10 For this notion in the Convention see above, p. 274, n. 12. See art. 10, 3rd para.
11 Art. 11, 1st para.

8 or 9, the insurer may bring an action against the assured in that jurisdiction as well. In the second place, the insurer may bring a counterclaim in any one jurisdiction which has been seized under arts. 7–10.

In view of the power given to the parties to select a *forum* by agreement,[1] the Convention provides by way of an exception that the parties to a contract of insurance can make such a choice only if *either*

(a) the agreement is made after the dispute has arisen;[2] *or*

(b) the assured, whether a party to the contract or not, or a beneficiary, is enabled thereby to seize a jurisdiction which is additional to those provided by the Convention;[3] *or*

(c) if both parties to the contract are ordinarily resident in the same member state and agree to submit to the jurisdiction of the courts of that country, even if the act giving rise to damage should have occurred abroad.[4]

(ii) *Instalment Sales and Hire-Purchase Contracts*—In a contract of sale by instalments or of hire-purchase directly connected with financing a sale involving corporeal movables[5] the seller or lessor is subject to the jurisdiction of the courts both of the country where the seller or lessor and where the buyer or hirer has his [ordinary] residence.[6] In addition two of the grounds for assuming concurrent jurisdiction apply here as well but no others.[7] On the other hand, only the courts of the country where the buyer or hirer is [ordinarily] resident have jurisdiction in an action by the seller or lessor against the buyer or hirer,[8] subject to the right to being a counterclaim, if sued elsewhere.[9] Any derogation from these provisions by an agreement for the submission to the jurisdiction of courts elsewhere is only permitted under the same conditions as those which apply in the case of contracts of insurance.[10]

3   Exclusive Jurisdiction

In a limited number of circumstances, which are enumerated by the Convention,[11] exclusive jurisdiction is vested in the courts of one country only. Actions involving proprietary rights in immovables, including leaseholds, must be brought in the country of the *situs*;[12] concerning the validity, nullity or dissolution of companies and legal entities and the validity or nullity of acts of their organs in the country where the company

---

1   Art. 17; see below, p. 277.
2   Art. 12(1).
3   Art. 12(2).
4   Art. 12(3). Provided that the *lex fori* permits it.
5   Art. 13.
6   Art. 14(1).
7   Art. 13; see arts. 4 and 5(5); above, pp. 273, 274.
8   Art. 14(2).
9   Art. 14(3).
10   Art. 15; see art. 12; above, text to nn. 2–4.
11   Art. 16.
12   Art. 16(1).

or legal entity has its seat;[1] concerning the validity of entries in public registers in the country where the register is kept;[2] concerning the registration or the validity of patents, trademarks, designs and similar rights requiring a deposit or registration, in the country where the deposit or registration is requested, has been effected or is deemed to have been effected in accordance with an international Convention;[3] concerning the execution of judgments, in the country of the member states where the judgment is to be executed.[4]

4   Contractual Submission *prorogatio fori*

The parties are free to agree in writing or orally, if subsequently confirmed in writing,[5] that any present or future dispute arising out of a specific relationship is to be submitted to the courts of a particular country.[6] For this purpose the Convention requires that one of the parties at least must be [ordinarily] resident within the EEC.[7] This freedom is only restricted by the specific provisions attached to the rules dealing with concurrent and exclusive jurisdiction.[8] In addition the right to apply to a particular jurisdiction, which has been accorded in favour of one party only by a contractual agreement to submit, may be waived by that party.[9]

5   Submission by Appearance

If a defendant appears otherwise than in order to contest the jurisdiction, the court may assume jurisdiction even if the Convention does not provide for it, except where the subject matter of the dispute is reserved for an exclusive jurisdiction.[10]

6   Scrutiny of the Basis of Jurisdiction

The structure of the Convention, which regulates the jurisdiction of the original court in order to ensure the unimpeded recognition and enforcement of its decisions in the other member states, requires a strict control of the basis of jurisdiction in the individual case by the court seized of the dispute. Consequently the Convention provides in the first place that,

---

1   Art. 16(2); it is not immediately clear how this provision is to be reconciled with those of the Convention on the Mutual Recognition of Companies and Legal Entities of 29 February 1968. See above, p. 148, n. 3.
2   Art. 16(3).
3   Art. 16(4).
4   Art. 16(5).
5   The wording raises the question whether the requirement of writing is a matter of form or of evidence. See Bülow, (1965) 29 Rabels Z. 473, at p. 493 referring to the Hague Convention of 25 November 1965 on the Choice of Court, art. 4, 1st para.
6   Art. 17, 1st para.
7   The reason is that if both parties are [ordinarily] resident outside the EEC the general scheme of the Convention, which is based on the primary jurisdiction of the country of the defendant's ordinary residence (art. 3), is inoperative.
8   Art. 17, 2nd para; see arts. 12, 15, 16, above, pp. 276–277.
9   Art. 17, 3rd para.
10 Art. 18.

where the Convention provides an exclusive jurisdiction,[1] courts elsewhere must decline jurisdiction *ex officio*.[2] In the second place a court in a member state other than that where the defendant has his [ordinary] residence[3] must decline jurisdiction if the defendant does not appear,[4] unless the Convention confers concurrent or exclusive jurisdiction upon the former.[5] Even if jurisdiction is established, the court must suspend the proceedings in the absence of the defendant until it has been established that notice has been given to the defendant in reasonable time so as to enable him to appear or that all necessary steps have been taken in order to give him notice.[6]

7 *Lis pendens*

Given the possibility that under the Convention several jurisdictions may be available it is provided that, if several actions are begun between the same parties on the same cause of action before the courts of more than one country, the proceedings which were brought first in time oust any subsequent jurisdiction elsewhere.[7] All other courts must decline jurisdiction, unless jurisdiction is disputed in the first court, when proceedings elsewhere need only be stayed.[8] Where connected claims[9] are the object of actions brought in the courts of several member states, the court in which the second action is brought may stay proceedings.[10] Alternatively the second court may refuse to assume jurisdiction upon application by one of the parties, provided that the *lex fori* permits the joinder of actions and that the court first seized of the matter may entertain both actions.[11]

If two exclusive jurisdictions are involved, that which has been seized first ousts all others.[12] On the other hand, provisional or protective measures allowed by the law of one country can be set in motion there even if a court in another member state has jurisdiction under the Convention to try the case.[13]

---

1 It does so only in the case of art. 16; see above, p. 276.

2 Art. 19.

3 See art. 3.

4 See above, p. 277, n. 10.

5 Art. 20, 1st para.

6 Art. 20; with the coming into force of the Hague Convention of 15 November 1965 on the Service Abroad of Judicial and Extrajudicial Documents in Civil or Commercial Matters, the procedure provided therein (art. 15) must be observed. See also Protocol, art. IV.

7 Art. 21, 1st para.

8 Art. 21, 2nd para.

9 Art. 22(3) defines connected claims in a sense which recalls the notion of a necessary or proper party in Ord. 11, r. 1(j).

10 Art. 22(1).

11 Art. 22(2); the reference to the law of procedure of the two countries concerned is an admission that the law of some member states does not admit joinder of actions. See Bülow, (1965) 29 Rabels Z. 473, at p. 502.

12 Art. 23.

13 Art. 24. The French version speaks of *connaître du fond*, the German *in der Hauptsache*. Both distinguish thus between procedural or interlocutory matters and the principal or main questions; cp. *In Re Henderson, Nouvion v. Freeman* (1888), 37 Ch.D. 244, at p. 251.

8   Recognition and Enforcement—Recognition

Following an established technique in continental law the Convention deals first with the recognition and then with the execution of foreign judgments,[1] but the provisions are to a certain extent interchangeable. For the purposes of recognition and enforcement, but subject to an additional characteristic where enforcement is sought, any decision whatever given by a judicial body qualifies, irrespective of the denomination appearing on its face.[2] It includes expressly two types of orders peculiar to German law, the *"Vollstreckungsbefehl"*[3] and the *"Kostenfestsetzungsbeschluss"*,[4] the latter of which emanates from a subordinate official.

A comparison of the general provision on recognition[5] and that on enforcement[6] shows that for the purposes of recognition the fact that a decision has been rendered abroad, and no more, is required. The decision need not be final and conclusive in the sense of English law[7] and still less have the force of *res judicata* in the sense that the time for lodging an appeal must have lapsed.[8] Thus decisions given by German courts which are provisionally enforceable there must be recognised, subject to the power of the court to stay recognition pending an appeal.[9] Recognition must be granted automatically, and no procedure of recognition is required.[10] It can only be refused either, it would appear, *ex officio* or at the request of the judgment debtor:[11] if the jurisdictional provisions of the Convention establishing the special jurisdiction in matters of insurance and instalment[12] sales and the exclusive jurisdiction in matters of rights in immovables, companies, public registers, patents and similar rights as well as for the execution of judgments[13] have not been observed[14] or in the exceptional circumstances discussed above[15] when the original court assumed jurisdiction on the basis of the exorbitant provision of domestic law not embodied in the Convention but admitted in suits against defendants permanently or habitually resident in a third country, provided that

---

1   Contrast the Foreign Judgments (Reciprocal Enforcement) Act 1933, s. 8 (recognition); ss. 1–7 (enforcement) where the position is reversed. Accordingly the procedural details (arts. 46–49) will be discussed below in connection with the enforcement of judgments.

2   Art. 25.

3   ZPO paras. 699, 794(4); the French version is *mandat d'execution*. For this institution and that discussed below (n. 4) see Bülow, (1965) 29 Rabels Z. 473, at p. 503.

4   ZPO, paras. 104, 794(2); the French version is *fixation par le greffier du montant des frais du procès*; cp. Foreign Judgments (Reciprocal Enforcement) Act 1933, s. 2(6).

5   Art. 26, 1st para.

6   Art. 31.

7   *Nouvion* v. *Freeman* (1889), 15 App. Cas. 1 to the effect that it cannot be re-opened in that instance.

8   Bülow, (1965) 29 Rabels Z. 473, at p. 503.

9   Art. 30.

10   Art. 26, 1st para.

11   See Droz, *Compétence Judiciaire et Effets des Jugements dans le Marché Commun*, p. 307, no. 482 relying on the mandatory wording of art. 27.

12   Arts. 7–12, 13–15.

13   Art. 16.

14   Art. 28, 1st para.

15   Pp. 272–273; see art. 59.

such recognition in the requested state is excluded by a convention between the latter and the state of the defendant's residence.[1] However, the finding of fact on which the original court based its assumption of jurisdiction under the Convention cannot be challenged;[2] nor can recognition or enforcement be refused for failure to observe the rules of procedure of the country having jurisdiction with the result that, while the court rightly exercised international jurisdiction under the Convention, it was incompetent according to the domestic distribution of judicial functions.[3]

In addition to these jurisdictional grounds, recognition can only be refused for the following reasons of substance: firstly, if recognition would be contrary to local public policy,[4] but the fact that jurisdiction has been exercised by a court in a country having jurisdiction in disregard of the local rules on the distribution of competences is no reason for refusing recognition on the ground of public policy;[5] secondly, if the defendant has failed to appear in the original proceedings and process was not duly served on him and in sufficient time in order to enable him to defend the proceedings;[6] thirdly, if the foreign judgment is incompatible with a decision between the same parties rendered in the requested country:[7] it must be noted that the Convention does not require the two decisions to have concerned a dispute about the same subject matter between the parties;[8] and it is an open question whether a decision rendered in the requested country includes a decision rendered in a third country which must be recognised in the requested state;[9] fourthly, if, in reaching its decision, the original court determined a question concerning the status or the capacity of individuals, matrimonial property rights, wills or successions, in disregard of the rules of private international law of the requested state, provided that the result would not have been the same, if the private international law of the latter state had been applied.[10]

In no circumstances may the court in the requested state re-open or review the case.[11]

A somewhat obscure provision[12] envisages a dispute involving the

---

1   Art. 28, 1st para.
2   Art. 28, 2nd para.
3   Art. 28, 3rd para.
4   Art. 27(1).
5   Art. 28(3).
6   Art. 27(2); the use of the terms *"signifié ou notifié"* in the French version is based on the distinction between personal and substituted notice; see Poission in Dalloz, *Répertoire de Droit International* (1969), Vol. II, p. 476 *s.v. Notification et Signification des Actes*. Art. II of the Protocol contains a general exception from recognition and enforcement if the defendant did not appear in criminal proceedings to which *partie civile* proceedings were attached.
7   Art. 27(3).
8   Bülow, (1965) 29 Rabels Z. 473, at p. 504, n. 105; for other aspects of this question see Droz, *Compétence Judiciaire et Effets des Jugements dans le Marché Commun*, p. 324, no. 514.
9   Droz, *loc. cit.*, p. 333, no. 524.
10   Art. 27(4); Droz, *loc. cit.*, p. 334, no. 525, p. 340, no. 533.
11   Art. 29: *révision au fond.*
12   See Droz, *loc. cit.*, p. 285, no 453–p. 289, no. 457.

recognition of a foreign judgment. According to the most informed commentators it appears to be agreed that such a dispute is not identical with an objection based on any one of the jurisdictional or substantive grounds set out above,[1] but envisages situations in which the plaintiff's right embodied in the judgment is the basis of a claim against a third person, who may even be confronted with evidence of other rights to the contrary.[2] In these circumstances the Convention, adopting hesitant attempts in the practice of French and Belgian courts, and following a similar practice in Italy and Germany,[3] allows an action by any interested party on the lines of an action provided by the Convention for the execution of judgments.[4] It is still disputed whether the provision is facultative, or whether those member states which have so far shown little inclination to support its existence must now introduce it, but the better view is probably that it must be made available everywhere.[5] If the dispute concerning the recognition arises as an incidental question in the courts of a third member state (i.e. which is neither the original court nor the court where execution is sought), the latter has jurisdiction to determine any question of recognition.[6]

9 Enforcement

If recognition can be accorded, execution must also be granted, provided that the foreign decision is one which would support levy of execution in the country of the original court.[7] For this purpose (as distinct from recognition) certain official documents embodying an undertaking to pay a certain sum of money and which can form the basis of an immediate levy of execution in the original country[8] and settlements which have been made an order of the court[9] are treated as if they were judgments.[10] The Convention states expressly that, upon application by any interested party, the foreign judgment must be certified as one on which execution can be issued[11] and that the form and the details of the application are determined by the domestic law of the requested court.[12] The production is required of a copy of the decision which is sufficient to prove

---

1 *I.e.* arts. 27, 28.
2 Droz, p. 286, no 453.
3 See Droz, *loc. cit.*
4 Art. 26, 2nd para.; arts. 31–49.
5 Droz, *loc. cit.*
6 Art. 26, 3rd para.
7 Art. 31.
8 *Vollstreckbare Urkunden* (ZPO paras. 794(5), 797); *actes authentiques reçus et exécutoires;* cp. Droz, *Compétence Judiciaire et Effets des Jugements dans le Marché Commun,* p. 389, no. 606–p. 393 no. 615, especially p. 392, n. 1.
9 *Transactions conclues devant le juge au cours d'un procès et exécutoires dans l'Etat d'origine; Gerichtlicher Vollstreckbarer Vergleich* (ZPO, para. 794(1)).
10 Arts. 50, 51.
11 Art. 31.
12 Art. 33; the procedure in England is therefore comparable to that available for the registration of judgments under the Foreign Judgments (Reciprocal Enforcement) Act 1933; see the European Communities (Enforcement of Community Judgments) Order 1972, No. 1590.

its authenticity[1] and, if the judgment is one by default, the original or a certified copy of the document establishing that notice of the proceedings has been served on the defendant who did not appear.[2] Simple as this provision may appear it may create difficulties since continental lawyers assume that a judgment is accompanied by a written statement of reasons while English judgments are not.[3]

In addition the judgment creditor must submit documentary proof that execution may be levied on the judgment and that the decision has been served on the judgment debtor; if necessary documentary evidence must also be supplied that the claimant has been granted legal aid in the original country.[4]

If the evidence required in the case of a judgment by default or concerning legal aid is not produced, the requested court may set a time limit for submitting documents of equivalent value or dispense with them, if satisfied.[5] If the requested court so requires a certified translation must be furnished.[6]

The Convention specifies the types of courts to which application must be made,[7] leaving it to the local law which court within the country is competent.[8] It also requires the applicant to appoint a local representative unless, to use the words of the Convention, he "elects a domicile" in the latter country.[9] This notion is alien to German law, as it is to English law, but the alternative of appointing a representative serves the same purpose.

Enforcement is granted *ex parte*, and can only be rejected by the requested court on one of the grounds which also justify a refusal to recognise the foreign judgment.[10] An exception, restricting refusal to enforce, seems to apply to foreign official documents embodying an undertaking to pay a certain sum of money which can form the basis of an immediate levy of execution in the original court.[11] In this case only a violation of the public policy of the requested court can justify a refusal to grant enforcement.[12]

The decision of the requested court granting or refusing recognition is

---

1 Art. 46(1).
2 Art. 46(2) and compare art. 27(2) according to which recognition or enforcement must be refused if the notice of the action was not served regularly or in sufficient time.
3 Cp. Droz, *Compétence Judiciaire et Effets des Jugements dans le Marché Commun*, p. 380, no. 594, n. 1; as regards the enforcement of English judgments in France, French courts have been satisfied with less. See Lipstein and Sialelli, Juriscl. Dr. Int. Fasc. 593, No. 190 with cases.
4 Art. 47. This entitles him to an automatic grant of legal aid in the requested state: art. 44.
5 Art. 48(1).
6 Art. 48(2).
7 Art. 32, 1st para.
8 Art. 32, 2nd para.
9 Art. 33, 2nd para.
10 Art. 34, 1st para; see arts. 27, 28, above, pp. 279–280.
11 Art. 50; see above, p. 281.
12 See art. 50, 1st para, second sentence; but see Droz, *Compétence Judiciaire et Effets des Jugements dans le Marché Commun*, p. 394, no. 619 who believes that the nullity of the instrument is also a defence.

open to an objection[1] by the respondent or by the applicant respectively.[2] The Convention sets out which courts in each member state are competent to hear such objections[3] and regulates also what further appeals are possible according to the domestic law of the member states.[4] While the time limit fixed by the Convention for lodging an objection is still running[5] and until the objection lodged either by the respondent or by the applicant[6] has been disposed of, only protective measures may be taken.[7] When an objection has been lodged, the requested court may stay the proceedings if an appeal has been lodged in the ordinary course of events in the country of the original court or if the time limit for appealing has not yet expired.[8]

If the foreign judgment determines several claims and levy of execution cannot be accorded to all of them, partial enforcement may be allowed.[9] Foreign judgments condemning the defendant to pay a sum of money if he fails to carry out an order of the court are also included.[10] No security can be demanded other than any which may be required of local residents or nationals.[11]

By a Protocol of 3 June 1971 signed in Luxemburg the member states agreed that when the provisions of the Convention or of the Protocol come up for interpretation in their courts the highest courts, other courts when hearing appeals and the courts which must hear objections against an order granting enforcement to a judgment of a court in another member state,[12] shall have the power to submit the question to the Community Court for a preliminary ruling.[13]

If the question arises in proceedings before the highest court of the member state, the latter must submit it to the Community Court if it is of the opinion that a decision on this point is necessary.[14] All other courts envisaged by the Protocol[15] may, if they see fit, formulate a question for the Community Court.[16] These provisions are thus modelled on those of the EEC Treaty (art. 177), with the important exception that the highest court, while bound to submit a question of interpretation of the Con-

---

1   The French text says *recours*; the German text *Widerspruch*.
2   Arts. 36, 40.
3   Arts. 37, 40. The courts are the same for both types of objections except in Belgium and the Netherlands.
4   Art. 37, last para., art. 41.
5   Art. 36.
6   See Droz, *Compétence Judiciaire et Effets des Judgements dans le Marché Commun*, p. 364, no. 569.
7   Art. 39.
8   Art. 38.
9   Art. 42.
10 Art. 43. This provision is intended to deal with the *astreinte* of French law and *Zwangsgelder* of German law (ZPO, para. 888) (see above, p. 255, n. 1).
11 Art. 45.
12 Protocol on Interpretation, art. 2(3); see Convention of 27 September 1968, art. 37.
13 Protocol on Interpretation, art. 2(1)–(3); Mok, (1971) 8 C.M.L.Rev. 485.
14 Protocol on Interpretation, art. 3(1).
15 *I.e.* art. 2(2), (3).
16 Protocol on Interpretation, art. 3(2).

vention to the Community Court, need do so only "if it holds that a decision on this point is necessary".[1] The effect of a preliminary ruling is the same as that provided in the EEC Treaty.[2]

In addition the competent authority of a member state[3] may ask the Community Court for a preliminary ruling if any decision rendered in that member state on the basis of the Convention or the Protocol thereto conflicts with an interpretation given by the Community Court or by any of the courts in another member state[4] which are enabled to ask the Community Court for a preliminary ruling.[5] This procedure is fashioned to a certain extent on one known in Belgium, France and the Netherlands.[6] As in the case of an application for a preliminary ruling under the EEC Treaty (art. 177), an interpretation supplied by the Community Court in the course of an application under art. 4 of the Protocol on Interpretation does not have any effect upon the decision in the particular case by the court of the member state which asked for the preliminary ruling.[7]

B THE CONVENTION ON THE MUTUAL RECOGNITION OF COMPANIES AND LEGAL ENTITIES OF 29 FEBRUARY 1968

This was examined above in the chapter on Establishment.[8]

C DRAFT CONVENTION TO REGULATE JURISDICTION AND THE ENFORCEMENT OF DECISIONS IN MATTERS OF BANKRUPTCY, ARRANGEMENTS AND LIKE PROCEDURES OF 4 JULY 1969[9]

The Draft Convention on Jurisdiction and the Enforcement of Decisions in matters of Bankruptcy consists partly of rules of the conflict of laws and jurisdiction and partly of uniform rules of substantive law.[10] In accordance

---

1 Protocol on Interpretation art. 3(1); Droz, *Compétence Judiciaire et Effets des Jugements dans le Marché Commun*, p. 461, no. 705.
2 *Ibid.*, art. 5.
3 The domestic law of the member state must designate the competent authority, but the *procureurs généraux* attached to the highest courts are given this power by the Protocol itself; see *ibid.*, art. 4(3).
4 Other than those entitled to do so in the course of proceedings on an objection against enforcement: see the Protocol on Interpretation, arts. 4(1), 2(3).
5 Protocol on Interpretation, art. 4(1).
6 See Droz, *Compétence Judiciaire et Effets des Jugements dans le Marché Commun*, p. 464, no. 712 and n. 1.
7 Protocol on Interpretation, art. 4(2); for the problems arising from this provision see Droz, *loc. cit.*, p. 468, no. 717.
8 Above, pp. 148–151, and p. 148, n. 3.
9 Muir Hunter, (1972) 21 I.C.L.Q. 682; Nadelmann, *Conflict of Laws: International and Interstate* (1972), p. 340; 1970 Riv. Dir. Int. Priv. e Proc. 501; Colesanti, *ibid.* 522; Farrar, 1972 J. Bus. L. 256; Noel and Lemontey, 1968 Rev. Trim. Dr. Eur. 703; Hirsch, 1970 Cah. Dr. Eur. 50; Ganshof, 1971 Cah. Dr. Eur. 146; Lanza, (1970) 15 Riv. Soc. 667; Bleutge, 1971 B.B.A.W.D. 451; Jahr (1972) 36 Rabels Z. 620; see also Houin in *Ganshof van der Meersch*, p. 1017, no. 2565–p. 1022, no. 2581. For the text see Doc. 3327/XIV/1/70 of 16 February 1970; 1970 Riv. Dir. Int. Priv. e Proc. 693; (1970) I Dir. Fal. 146; (1972) 36 Rabels Z. 734.
10 See in particular, art. 76(1), Annex I, art. 39(1).

with continental legal tradition bankruptcy includes compulsory winding-up of companies by the courts. The unity[1] and the universality[2] of bankruptcy proceedings are its guiding principles.

1 *Ratione loci*

Ratione loci the courts of the country, if within the EEC, have exclusive jurisdiction in which the debtor's centre of affairs is situated.[3] This is the place in which he normally attends to his interests; in the case of companies and other legal entities it is the real or statutory seat in the absence of evidence to the contrary.[4] If the centre of affairs is situated outside the EEC, jurisdiction in bankruptcy may be exercised by the courts of the country where the debtor has a branch.[5] If the debtor has neither his centre of affairs nor a branch in the EEC the courts of any one country in the EEC may assume jurisdiction if its own law so permits.[6] If the debtor has transferred his centre of affairs or, failing such a centre, his branch to another member state within the last six months before proceedings were begun, *potentially concurrent* jurisdiction is vested in the courts of either state.[7] If, however, at the time of the transfer, proceedings comparable to those involving a composition or scheme of arrangement under English law[8] were pending, the courts of that member state retain their exclusive jurisdiction, if these proceedings are replaced by bankruptcy proceedings proper.[9] Before any such proceedings have been converted into bankruptcy proceedings, the courts of the second state may open bankruptcy proceedings in the course of enforcing a scheme of arrangement or may initiate new proceedings in respect of debts which arose after the scheme of arrangement had been formally approved. The commencement of either type of proceedings in the second state *ousts* the jurisdiction of the courts in the first state.[10] If the debtor has moved into a non-member state, the courts in the member state where he has his centre of affairs or a branch retain their jurisdiction for a period of six months from the time of the transfer.[11]

Truly concurrent jurisdiction may be exercised by the courts of any member state where the debtor has a branch or, if the *lex fori* confers jurisdiction, on other grounds, if the courts of the member state which have

---

1 Art. 2.
2 Art. 33, subject to two exceptions (arts. 9(2) and 60) arising from the technique of the Convention, which seeks to exclude a total absence of jurisdiction within the EEC, if the domestic law of the member state which has primary jurisdiction refuses to exercise it, and introduces, for this purpose, non-exclusive subsidiary jurisdictions. See also art. 20.
3 Art. 3(1).
4 Art. 3(2).
5 Art. 4.
6 Art. 5.
7 Arts. 6(1), 8.
8 See the types of proceedings of this character in the various member states enumerated in the Protocol, art. I(b).
9 Art. 6(2), 1st para.; art. 8.
10 Art. 6(2), 2nd para.; art. 8.
11 Art. 8.

exclusive jurisdiction based on the debtor's centre of affairs cannot open bankruptcy proceedings because he is not a merchant or is a small trader only.[1]

2   *Ratione personae*

Ratione personae the Convention applies irrespective of the nationality of the debtor or of any interested person,[2] but it does not extend to enterprises of any kind engaged in any branch of insurance other than those which are exclusively engaged in re-insurance.[3] In addition it does not apply to various types of enterprises in the member states which are set out in a catalogue.[4] If the court assumes jurisdiction in respect of an association or legal entity, some members of which are jointly and severally liable without limitation for the debts of the former, the latter may be joined in the proceedings. In a number of situations which are set out in an Appendix, a director or manager who is alleged to have concluded the business of the enterprise for his own benefit may also be joined.[5]

In addition the courts of the member state having primary jurisdiction in bankruptcy over the association or entity are also acknowledged to be competent to entertain actions and subsequent bankruptcy proceedings against the persons enumerated in the Appendix who have managed the enterprise.[6] If, however, the law of the member state having primary jurisdiction does not permit bankruptcy proceedings against the persons envisaged in the last three cases,[7] the courts in any other member state having jurisdiction over those persons under the Convention may open bankruptcy proceedings against them.[8] At the same time a previous assumption of bankruptcy jurisdiction over such persons by a court having personal jurisdiction over them ousts any subsequent assumption of jurisdiction over them by the courts of the country exercising jurisdiction over the enterprise or legal entity.[9] Although the Convention seeks to establish as far as possible a single jurisdiction in bankruptcy and to solve possible conflicts for each type of situation individually,[10] general provision is made for the cases where jurisdiction is either asserted by the courts in several member states[11] or is denied by all.[12]

In the former case the court of the country which has predominant jurisdiction according to the Convention ousts all others in the Com-

---

1   Art. 9. Thus a negative conflict of jurisdictions is avoided. See also arts. 13, 16.
2   Art. 1(1).
3   Art. 1(3), 2nd para.
4   Art. 1(3) and Protocol art. II.
5   Art. 11 and Appendix I art. 1.
6   Art. 12 and Appendix I, art. 2. The Convention contemplates actions brought by the trustee but not derivative actions brought by shareholders or members. See art. 14.
7   Arts. 10, 11, 12.
8   Art. 13(1).
9   Art. 13(2).
10   See above, p. 285 and above, n. 1.
11   Art. 15.
12   Art. 16.

munity.[1] If the Convention attributes concurrent jurisdiction to courts in several member states the rule *prior tempore* applies and the courts elsewhere must stay proceedings pending a determination by the first court.[2]

On the other hand, if a court in one member state finds that predominant jurisdiction is vested in the courts of another member state, it may stay proceedings on application or *proprio motu* or decline to assume jurisdiction.[3] If this situation has arisen, courts in other member states must not decline jurisdiction on the ground that the first court has jurisdiction.[4]

3 *Ratione materiae*

Ratione materiae the Convention covers various types of proceedings in the member states which are enumerated in the Protocol either as constituting bankruptcy proceedings strictly speaking,[5] or as proceedings equivalent in character,[6] particularly proceedings in connection with compositions and schemes of arrangement.[7] In the course of such proceedings, the court vested by the Convention with jurisdiction in bankruptcy has also jurisdiction, which is exclusive, to entertain proceedings involving the avoidance of acts by the debtor and claims of the estate arising therefrom, claims to assets of the estate, the validity of dispositions made by the trustee and actions involving his liability, as well as a number of other claims.[8]

4 Choice of Law

The courts of the country exercising jurisdiction in bankruptcy on the strength of the Convention apply the *lex fori* both to questions of substance[9] and of procedure.[10] With certain exceptions, the *lex fori* also determines the effects of the bankruptcy even in regard to third parties.[11]

In the first place, these effects are to be recognised in all member states.[12] This principle is developed by a series of rules of a substantive character: in other member states all actions by creditors based on claims which arose before the bankruptcy order was made or on a claim of title must be disallowed, unless secured on assets of the debtor,[13] and must be

---

1 Art. 15(1).
2 Art. 15(2).
3 Art. 16(1).
4 Art. 16(2).
5 Art. 1(1) and Protocol, art. I(a).
6 Art. 1(1) and Protocol, art. I(b).
7 Art. 1(2).
8 Art. 17.
9 Art. 18.
10 Art. 19(1); but see art. 24 which lays down time limits for objections by a person whose centre of affairs, domicile or residence is in a member state other than that where the bankruptcy was declared.
11 Art. 19(2).
12 Art. 20; see also art. 33.
13 Art. 21(1).

stayed, if pending,[1] unless contested and already covered by a decision other than in matters of jurisdiction.[2] All claims may be continued against the trustee in accordance with the law of the court seized with the matter.[3] Fiscal claims may, however, be prosecuted by any special procedure, if existing.[4] Any levy of execution in process must be stayed in accordance with the rules of the *lex fori* on the effect of a local bankruptcy.[5]

In the second place the Convention provides its own rules not only in respect of time limits to be observed in the courts where the bankruptcy was declared[6] and on the effect upon any limitation of actions in proceedings which had to be disallowed or stayed.[7] It lays down its own rules concerning the publicity to be given to the bankruptcy order,[8] the registration in the commercial register of other member states,[9] the period from the date of publication after which the order has effects in other member states,[10] but it leaves the effects upon registered property of the bankrupt to be determined by the *lex situs*.[11]

On the other hand, the Convention provides that the powers of the trustee in other member states are those granted by the law of the state where the bankruptcy order was made[12] and regulates how his appointment is to be proved[13] as well as the position in other member states of a trustee if more than one were appointed.[14] The court which made the bankruptcy order may require that the bankrupt's correspondence is to be forwarded to the trustee, and that the postal authorities in other member states must assist.[15] The submission of claims to the trustee is regulated in some detail[16] as well as any objections by others against the submission to such claims.[17] At the same time the law of the country where the bankruptcy order was made determines whether the trustee may continue the bankrupt's business[18] and his powers to take protective measures or to dispose of assets.[19]

---

1 Art. 21(2), first sentence. Nevertheless they prevent the period of limitation from running: see art. 23.
2 Art. 21(2), second sentence; 21(3).
3 Art. 21(5).
4 Art. 21(4).
5 Art. 20.
6 See art. 24, above, p. 287, n. 10.
7 See art. 23; above, n. 1.
8 Art. 25(1), (3)–(5).
9 Art. 25(2).
10 Art. 26.
11 Art. 27.
12 Art. 28(1).
13 Art. 28(2).
14 Art. 28(3).
15 Art. 29 and Protocol, art. VIII.
16 Art. 30(1) and Protocol, art. IX.
17 Art. 30(2).
18 Art. 31.
19 Art. 32(1)–(3).

While the Convention subscribes to the principle of universality,[1] it exempts from the universal effect of a bankruptcy order not only such orders as are given in other member states when the courts of the state having exclusive jurisdiction cannot do so under their own law[2] or when the latter's order cannot be recognised elsewhere,[3] but also after-acquired property in other member states, if the *lex situs* exempts it.[4] Presumptions that the property of a spouse has been acquired with moneys supplied by the bankrupt spouse may be rebutted[5] but the law of the court where the bankruptcy order was made determines to what extent matrimonial property rights of, and gifts to, a spouse can be asserted against the estate so as to diminish the assets available to the creditors.[6]

On the other hand, the Convention itself regulates the question as to what acts of the bankrupt are void as against the creditors and when a set-off can be claimed.[7] Only the trustee's powers to act on behalf of the estate and, in particular, to avoid transactions entered into fraudulently by the bankrupt are determined by the law of the member state where the bankruptcy order was made.[8] The Convention also establishes rules of the conflict of laws in order to determine the effect of the bankruptcy order upon contracts of employment,[9] hire and leases,[10] sale,[11] including contracts combining a sale with the supply of services[12] and conditional sales with reservation of title,[13] but in the last case the reference to the law of a member state is coupled with provisions of substance.[14]

The *lex situs* determines whether any civil or commercial claims rank as general preferences,[15] but a limited effect is also allowed to unsatisfied claims by public authorities elsewhere which are fiscal or represent social security contributions.[16] The *lex situs* at the time of the order of bankruptcy determines further the existence, extent and rank of any security, such as a pledge or mortgage,[17] but if a ship, aircraft or motorcar provides the security, the law of the flag or of the place of registration applies.[18]

---

1   Art. 33(1); see also art. 20, above, p. 285, n. 2.
2   Art. 9(2).
3   Art. 60.
4   Art. 33(2), (3).
5   Art. 34(1) and Appendix I, art. 3.
6   Art. 34(2).
7   Art. 35(1) and Appendix I, arts. 4 and 5.
8   Art. 35(2).
9   Art. 36.
10 Art. 37; cf. art. 45; characterisation of an object as movable or immovable is left to the *lex situs*.
11 Art. 38(1).
12 Art. 38(2).
13 Art. 39 and Appendix I, art. 6.
14 Art. 39(1).
15 Arts. 40, 41. Described by the Convention as general statutory privileges they include preferred claims by wives and children in respect of the estate of the husband or parent.
16 Art. 42.
17 Art. 43(1), the Convention speaks of guarantees and special privileges.
18 Art. 43(2); cp. art. 37(2).

Liens are governed by the *lex situs*.[1] The order in which general and special privileges rank is determined by the *lex situs*,[2] except where registered rights in movables are concerned, when the law of the place of registration applies.[3] Any release or remission of debts accorded in proceedings in connection with composition or a scheme of arrangement does not affect secured creditors in other member states.[4] The effect of the bankruptcy order upon the capacity of the bankrupt himself is determined by each member state according to its own law.[5]

5   Recognition and Execution of Judgments and Orders in Bankruptcy Proceedings

Subject to the exceptions set out above[6] all decisions (in the broadest sense)[7] of a court having jurisdiction under the Convention are to be recognised without further proceedings[8] and are effective there.[9] If bankruptcy orders have been made in several member states and the Convention attributes overriding jurisdiction to the courts in one member state, the decisions and orders made by the latter must prevail over all others.[10] If concurrent jurisdiction exists under the Convention on an equal footing, the decision which is first in time must prevail.[11] In either case the Convention states expressly that the acts of the trustee carried out before it appeared that the jurisdiction had been ousted by that in another member state retain their validity.[12]

The recognition and enforcement in one member state of a decision or order in bankruptcy made in another member state in accordance with the Convention may be opposed[13] on a limited number of grounds, namely that without any fault on his part the debtor did not have sufficient time to appear or[14] that the judgment is contrary to public policy.[15] It is stated expressly that the plea of public policy cannot be based on any one of the following grounds: that such proceedings, if enumerated in art. I of the

---

1   Art. 43(3).

2   Art. 44.

3   Art. 45; in the case of proceedings in connection with a deed of arrangement abandoned for bankruptcy proceedings the *lex situs*, for the purposes of arts. 41–43, is that at the time when the last proceedings were begun.

4   Art. 48.

5   Art. 47.

6   Above, p. 285, n. 2.

7   Art. 50(2). This applies to deeds of arrangement and settlements in court as well as a number of other instruments which entitle the holder to levy execution.

8   Art. 50(1).

9   Art. 54.

10   Art. 51.

11   Art. 52(1); the Convention makes somewhat artificial provision for the case that two bankruptcy orders were made on the same day in different member states: see art. 52(2).

12   Art. 53.

13   For the name of the court in each member state where an objection must be lodged see art. 57 and the Protocol, art. X.

14   Art. 56(1).

15   Art. 56(2).

Protocol, are unknown locally; that the original court lacked jurisdiction; that under the law of the requested state no such order could have been made in the circumstances; that the debtor could not have been the object of bankruptcy proceedings in the requested state or that the judgment was rendered *ex officio* or on the application of one party.[1] If it is sought to enforce a bankruptcy order[2] made in another member state in accordance with the Convention, an enforcement order must be obtained.[3] An objection may be lodged against such an order on the same grounds as those which can support an objection against recognition.[4]

D DRAFT EUROPEAN PATENT LAW CONVENTION[5]

During the early stages of the European Common Market a strong movement in favour of a uniform protection of patents led to the early formulation of a Draft Convention in 1962,[6] revised in 1965.[7] Subsequently little progress was made until a second Intergovernmental Conference in 1970 devoted its attention to two separate tasks.[8] Taking up the links with the Council of Europe, which had engaged in similar activities, it elaborated a Draft Convention on a European System of Patent Registration in which not only the member states of the EEC but also other European states participate[9] and another Draft Convention on an Independent Autonomous Patent for the EEC[10] side by side with domestic patents.[11] Since the Draft Convention will be considered finally by a Conference of States, it must suffice to draw attention to it here.

---

1 Art. 56(2)(a)–(e). For the procedure and effects of an objection see arts 58–60; if successful, the foreign bankruptcy order becomes ineffective and local jurisdiction in bankruptcy revives; see art. 60. The same applies if a successful objection is lodged against an enforcement order. See art. 65.

2 Or a document having equivalent effects; art. 61(2), art. 54. See above, p. 290, n. 7.

3 Art. 61(1). For an enumeration of the courts in the various member states where application for an enforcement order may be made see the Protocol, art. XI; for the procedure see art. 62; for the provisional effects of such an order see art. 67.

4 Arts. 63, 56; see above, p. 290; for the procedure see arts. 63, 64 and, as regards the competent court, see the Protocol art. XII. For further remedies see art. 66.

5 For surveys see Demaret, 1970 Rev. Trim. Dr. Eur. 215; Marchetti, 1970 Riv. Dir. Int. Priv. e Proc. 557; 1972 *ibid.*, 82; Dasesse in *Ganshof van der Meersch*, p. 1030, no. 2594; Thompson, (1973) 22 I.C.L.Q. 50; van Empel (1972), 9 C.M.L.Rev. 456.

6 8065/1–2/X/1962/5; Demaret, 1970 Rev. Trim. Dr. Eur. 215, at p. 216, n. 1.

7 Marchetti, 1972 Riv. Dir. Int. Priv. e Proc. 557, n. 1. with lit. p. 558, n. 2. See Froschmaier, (1962) 11 I.C.L.Q. Suppl. No. 4, p. 50; (1963) 12 I.C.L.Q. 886; Johnston, (1963–64) 1 C.M.L.Rev. 17; Tookey, (1965) 14 I.C.L.Q. 281.

8 *Conférence Intergouvernementale pour l'Institution d'un Système Européen de Délivrance de Brevets*, 2 vols., (Luxemburg, 1971).

9 See Demaret, 1970 Rev. Trim. Dr. Eur. 215, at pp. 241–258. For the text see (1970), I.I.C. 80 (International Review of Industrial Property and Copyright Law).

10 See Demaret, 1970 Rev. Trim. Dr. Eur. 215, at pp. 258–270. For the text see (1970), I.I.C. 340.

11 See the lit. above, nn. 5 and 7; Guttman, 1970 J. of Bus. L. 333.

III   APPROXIMATION, CO-ORDINATION AND HARMONISATION AFFECTING THE LAWS OF ONE PARTICULAR MEMBER STATE ONLY

It may happen that a legislative or administrative provision of one member state impedes the free exchange of goods in the broad sense envisaged by the Treaty. In these circumstances the law or administrative practice of one member state must be brought into line with the purposes of the Treaty (art. 101).

> *Measures:* Commission—enters into consultation with the member state (art. 101(1)); if these fail:
> Council—upon Commission proposal—by a qualified majority—Directive (art. 101(2)).
> Commission and Council—take measures provided elsewhere in the Treaty (art. 101(2), last sentence).

In the course of the first ten years the Commission examined twenty-five cases of potential legislative or administrative infractions of the principle of free competition.[1] In most cases it either found that the suspected provisions did not interfere with trade or that, as a result of consultations, the member state had modified the offending rule. Since 1967 approximately twenty more cases have come up for examination.[2]

Furthermore, in compliance with the requirements of art. 102 of the Treaty the Commission, in turn, has been consulted by the member states which were concerned whether any proposed legislation or new administrative provision introducing or amending the existing law or administrative practices might have the effect of distorting the free flow of goods.[3] Such consultations were encouraged by the Commission with special reference to legislation affecting the quality, composition, preparation, conservation and control of industrial and agricultural products.[4]

> *Measure:* Commission—Recommendations (art. 102(1)).

Three such recommendations have been issued. The first, addressed to the Federal Republic of Germany concerning the Seventeenth Law amending the Turnover Tax Act, failed initially to receive a response, but a proposal for a Council Directive dated 13 June 1967 never reached the final stage.[5] Two further recommendations were addressed to Italy[6]

---

1   See 1967, EEC Bull., Suppl. 12, p. 13, heading 8(a).
2   See *General Report* 1967, pp. 99, s. 91 and Table, p. 89(8)(a); 1968, p. 88, s. 91; 1969, p. 104, s. 74; 1970, p. 62, s. 73 and Table 5, p. 64; 1971 p. 128, and Table 2.
3   See *General Report* 1967, p. 99, s. 91 and Table, p. 90(8)(b); 1968, p. 89, para. 3, s. 91; 1969, p. 104, s. 74 and Table 13, p. 95(8)(a); 1970, p. 63, s. 73 and Table 5, p. 64, last case; 1971, p. 128, No. 178 and Table 2, two cases.
4   65/428 of 20 September 1965, OJ, 1965, 2611.
5   20 December 1966; see *General Report* 1967, p. 99, s. 91 and Table, p. 89(8)(a).
6   67/563 of 31 July 1967, OJ, 1967, no. 198/10.

and the Federal Republic of Germany[1] respectively. The possibility of a failure of a member state to comply with a Commission recommendation made by virtue of art. 102(1) is considered in a strangely conceived negative provision to the effect that other member states must not be requested by virtue of art. 101 to amend their laws in such a way as to eliminate the distortion (art. 102(2), 1st para.).[2] At the same time the defaulting member state is not subject to any sanctions, if the distortion of trade as a result of its domestic law or administrative practices operates to its own detriment alone (art. 102(2), 2nd para.).

---

1 69/14, of 11 December 1968, OJ, 1969, L 18/3.
2 Such a measure savours of retaliation according to international law. See, however, *EEC Commission* v. *Belgium and Luxemburg* (above, p. 44, n. 3) to the effect that the rules of public international law concerning the rights of parties to an agreement which has been broken by another do not apply here.

17

Economic Policy

(Articles 103–116)[1]

Under this heading the Treaty deals with three topics: policy relating to business cycles[2] (art. 103), balance of payments (arts. 104–109) and commercial policy (arts. 110–116).

Of these, policy relating to business cycles embraces, first of all, short term problems concerning prices and salaries, employment and the balance of payments, and thus indirectly budgetary matters including both expenditure and revenue (art. 104). Given the economic criteria to be observed, which may not be easily translatable into legal duties, it is not surprising that the relevant sections of the Treaty rely primarily on consultation[3] and co-ordination,[4] collaboration between administrative departments,[5] consideration of the common interest[6] and unilateral action.[7] However, the member states are enjoined to treat their policy towards business cycles as a matter of common interest (art. 103(1)). The Council can employ for this purpose the following

> *Measures:* Council—on Commission proposal— unanimously—Appropriate measures (art. 103(2);[8]
> Council—on Commission proposal—by a qualified majority—in order to carry out measures taken under art. 103(2)—Directives (art. 103(3).

The wording of art. 103(2) which states that it is to be applied "without prejudice to any other procedure provided for in this Treaty" has given

---

1 Waelbroeck in *Ganshof van der Meersch*, p. 901, no. 2255–p. 916, no. 2286 with further lit.
2 The French text of Tit. II, Chap. I is: *"La politique de conjoncture"*; the German: *"Die Konjunkturpolitik"*; these and the equivalent texts in Italian and Dutch have been translated into English as "Policy relating to Economic Trends" or "Policy relating to Current Trends", but the term adopted in the text seems to come nearer to the original texts.
3 Arts. 103(1).
4 Art. 105(1)(2); see also art. 145.
5 Art. 105(1), second sentence.
6 Arts. 103(1), 107(1), 110(1).
7 Arts. 108(1), 109(1).
8 These measures are probably restricted to decisions, since art. 103(2) envisages directives for their execution. This would not be appropriate for carrying out regulations. Cp. Waelbroeck in *Ganshof van der Meersch*, no. 2270(b).

rise to some doubts as to whether those other procedures are treated as additional or are expressly reserved,[1] but the latter interpretation seems to be more apposite. Certain it is from the nature of the subject matter and from the combined reading of art. 103(2) and (3) that the measures at the disposal of the Council are unlikely to be directly binding upon the member state and that legal enforcement is remote.[2]

The Council has encouraged the technique of consultation and collaboration by setting up a number of committees[3] and has itself engaged in periodic surveys[4] and recommendations[5] concerning economic trends and the policies to be pursued by the member states.

By way of decisions the Council has dealt with such diverse matters as the co-ordination of short term economic policy,[6] medium term financial assistance mechanism;[7] by way of regulations it has sought to counter the effects of the French devaluation in 1968[8] and any fluctuations in the currency margins in agriculture;[9] and by way of a directive it has sought to control the assembling of crude oil stocks.[10]

In pursuing their concerted but generally uncontrolled action relating to business cycles by maintaining a high level of employment and stable prices, the member states are bound to maintain policies which keep the overall balance of payment in equilibrium and, generally, to maintain confidence in their currency (art. 104). While in general co-ordination of policies and collaboration between administrative departments are the technical means for achieving these results, it is possible to rely on the following

Measure: Council—on recommendation of Commission—
appropriate measures (art. 105(1)).[11]

---

1 Waelbroeck in *Ganshof van der Meersch*, no. 2270(a).

2 Cp. Waelbroeck, *loc. cit.*, nos. 2262, 2265.

3 9 March 1960, OJ, 1960, 764: Economic Trends; 15 April 1964, 64/247, OJ, 1964, 1031: Medium Term Economic Policy; 8 May 1964, 64/299, OJ, 1964, 1205: Budgetary; 64/300, OJ, 1964, 1206: Central Bank Collaboration.

4 See Waelbroeck in *Ganshof van der Meersch*, no. 2258.

5 See Waelbroeck, *loc. cit.*, nos. 2260, 2268, 2269 with references, OJ, 1964, 1029; 1965, 985; 1966, 4059; 1967, No. 159/6; 1968, L 63/5; Second Programme of Medium Term Economic Policy 30 May 1969, OJ, 1969, L 129/7 (Short Term Economic Policy).

6 17 July 1969, OJ, 1969, L 183/41; 22 March 1971, OJ, 1971, L 73/12 (arts. 103(2), 145(1)); 8 May 1964, OJ, 1964, 1207: international monetary co-operation (art. 105(1)); 22 March 1971, OJ, 1971, L 73/14: strengthening Central Bank Collaboration (art. 105(1)); see also OJ, 1971, C 28/1; 22 March 1971, OJ, 1971, L 73/15: mechanism of medium term financial assistance (arts. 105, 108).

7 22 March 1971, OJ, 1971, L 73/15.

8 Reg. 1586/69, OJ, 1969, L 202/1; 1505/70, OJ, 1970, L 166/33; for the power to make regulations in this area see Pescatore in *Ganshof van der Meersch*, p. 926, no. 2306.

9 Reg. 974/71, OJ, 1971, L 106/1; see also Commission Regs. 1013/71, 1014/71, OJ, 1971, L 110/8/10) as amended; below, p. 296, n. 4.

10 19 December 1972, OJ, 1972, L 291/154; see also 20 December 1968, OJ, 1968, L 308/14.

11 Art. 105(1) like art. 103(2) does not specify what form of measures the Council can take; in practice the Council has acted by way of decisions and regulations. See the lists of measures above, nn. 6–10.

In particular, a Monetary Committee with consultative status is provided for (art. 105(2)) in addition to the committees mentioned above.[1]

The liberalisation of payments in connection with the exchange of goods, services and capital, the limits allowed by the Treaty (art. 106) and its implementation by directives were discussed above in connection with the abolition of restrictions on the movement of capital.[2]

Since the Treaty does not enable the Community organs to control the fixing and the alteration of the rates of exchange by the member states, but exhorts the member states to treat exchange rates as a matter of common interest (art. 107(1)), the representatives of the Governments meeting within the Council have agreed on prior consultation before any one member alters the parity of its currency.[3] Only indirectly the intra-Community rate for agricultural interventions relies on a common rate of exchange, for this rate merely reflects the ratio of the respective rates of exchange at a given moment and is disturbed by any one unilateral change in this rate.[4]

Indirectly the Community can control fluctuations in the currencies of the member states by five means. Firstly, if a member state alters its exchange rate in such a manner as to contravene the general economic policy inspiring the Treaty (art. 104) and to distort competition

> *Measure:* Commission—after consulting the Monetary
> Committee—authorises member states to take
> temporarily the necessary remedial action
> (art. 107(2)).

Secondly, if a member state experiences, or is seriously threatened with, difficulties in its balance of payments which are apt to affect the functioning of the Common Market[5]

> *Measure:* Commission—recommendations (art. 108(1), 1st
> para.).

Thirdly, if the measures taken by the member states and those recommended by the Commission are insufficient:

> *Measures:* Commission—after consulting the Monetary
> Committee recommends mutual assistance and
> appropriate methods to Council (art. 108(1),
> 2nd para.);

---

1 See above, p. 295, n. 3, Council Decision 18 March 1958, OJ, 1958, 390.
2 P. 170 and nn. 2–6; First Directive of 11 May 1960, OJ, 1960, 921; Second Directive of 18 December 1962, OJ, 1963, 62; Council Directives 31 May 1963, OJ, 1963, 1609; 30 July 1963, OJ, 1963, 2240.
3 8 May 1964, OJ, 1964, 1226; Waelbroeck in *Ganshof van der Meersch*, no. 2281.
4 See above, p. 295, n. 9 and a series of Commission regulations made under Council Reg. 974/71; see OJ, 1972, L 5/1; 19/1; 80/1; 113/1; 175/21; 248/5.
5 See von Horn, 1969 EuR 37.

> Council—by a qualified majority—grants
> mutual assistance—issues directives or decisions
> on conditions and details (art. 108(2), 1st
> para.).[1]

Fourthly, if no mutual assistance, as recommended by the Commission, is granted, or if the assistance so granted is insufficient,

> *Measures:* Commission—shall authorise protective
> measures by the member state in difficulties—
> lay down conditions and details (art. 108(3),
> 1st para.);[2]
> Council—by a qualified majority—may revoke
> the authorisation by the Commission—amend
> conditions and details of the authorisation
> (art. 108(3), 2nd para.).

Fifthly, if a member state experiences a sudden crisis in the balance of payments and no mutual assistance in accordance with art. 108(2) is immediately forthcoming,

> *Measures:* Member state—may provisionally take necessary
> minimum of protective measures (art. 109(1)—
> must inform Commission and other member
> states (art. 109(2);
> Commission—recommendation—mutual
> assistance (art. 109(2), 108(1));
> Council—by a qualified majority—on the
> basis of a Commission opinion—after consulting
> Monetary Committee—decides—on amendment,
> suspension, abolition of protective measures
> (art. 109(3)).[3]

It may be noted that despite the great variety of competences and measures, one contingency does not appear to have been regulated. The Treaty fails to state expressly what the position is if the Commission, faced with a member state in balance of payments difficulties, does not make any positive recommendation for mutual assistance in the exercise of its powers under art. 108(1) with the result that the Council cannot grant assistance under art. 108(2) and the Commission cannot authorise the

---

1   The assistance may take the form of concerted action in taking recourse to an international organisation; in avoiding diversions of trade as a result of quantitative restrictions by the member state in relation to third countries; in arranging limited credits by other member states (art. 108(2)(a)–(c)).

2   For the possibility of further alternatives see von Horn, 1969 EuR 37, at p. 39.

3   For the relationship between art. 109(3) and 108(3) see von Horn, 1969 EuR 37, at pp. 40–41. And see generally *EEC Commission* v. *France*, (1969), 15 Rec. 523, at p. 540(14)–(17).

member state to take protective measures under art. 108(3). It is believed that in these circumstances the member state concerned must fall back on the power to take crisis measures (art. 109(1)).[1]

Commercial policy[2] as understood within the framework of the EEC Treaty involves trade with third states and, thus, primarily all aspects of imports, in particular tariffs, quotas and safeguarding measures (arts. 113(1), 115), and of exports, and in particular aids to export (art. 112), restrictions of exports and sales promotion. It involves also commercial agreements with foreign states (arts. 111, 113), especially with countries having a state trading system, and with international organisations (art. 116).[3] Incidentally it touches upon the internal operation of the Common Market itself inasmuch as goods *en libre pratique* after having been imported into one member state from a country outside the EEC may yet cause a diversion of trade in another member state.[4] Although in substance economic, all these measures have a bearing in form or in content upon the rights and duties of the member states and possibly upon their inhabitants directly. The provisions of the Treaty are directed, in part, towards the transitional period and, to this extent, they will be touched upon only briefly.

The Treaty required that during the transitional period member states should co-ordinate their commercial relations in order to be able to implement at the end of it the common policy on external trade (arts. 111(1), 112). During this period the Council issued a Programme on 25 September 1962[5] with the aim of rendering uniform, as regards imports, the lists of liberalised goods, quotas and safeguarding measures[6] and, as regards exports, the types of aids to exports to third states, the gradual abolition of restrictions on international trade by limitations of exports and the promotion of export drives,[7] but excluding agricultural products.[8] In particular areas the Council, by way of decision, initiated preliminary work; it created a Co-ordinating Group relating to Policies in matters of of Credit and Guarantee Insurance,[9] established a procedure of consultation pending the conclusion of commercial agreements by member states with third countries[10] and imposed upon member states the duty to include in any commercial agreement to be concluded by a member state with a third country a time limit which was determined by the end of the

---

1   See von Horn, 1969 EuR 37 at p. 42.
2   Pescatore in *Ganshof van der Meersch*, p. 917, no. 2287–p. 942, No. 2348; Cae-One Kim, (1971), 7 C.M.L.Rev. 148; Bianconi, 1971 Riv. Dir. Eur. 115, at p. 235; Le Tallec, (1971) 17 B.B.A.W.D. 105; (1971) I.C.L.Q. 732; Maas, (1972) 8 C.M.L.Rev. 2; Schapira, 1972 Clunet 99; Everling, (1966–67) 4 C.M.L.Rev. 141.
3   See Pescatore in *Ganshof van der Meersch*, nos. 2294–2296.
4   Pescatore in *Ganshof van der Meersch*, no. 2289.
5   OJ, 1962, 2353.
6   OJ, 1962, 2353, at pp. 2354–2356.
7   OJ, 1962, 2353, at pp. 2356–2357.
8   OJ, 1962, 2353, at p. 2357 D.
9   27 September 1960, OJ, 1960, 1339.
10 9 October 1961, OJ, 1961, 1273.

transitional period,[1] and was to last for one year only, unless it was accompanied by the right to terminate it from year to year or contained the so-called EEC clause.[2] In addition, all commercial agreements, including all Treaties of Commerce and Navigation, were to be reviewed by the Commission[3] and a uniform time limit for reviewing all bilateral treaties was to be introduced.[4]

The EEC clause, which was approved by the Council on 20 July 1960, provided: "When the obligations derived from the Treaty creating the European Economic Community concerning the progressive introduction of a common commercial policy so require, negotiations will be opened within the shortest time possible in order to add to the present agreement all necessary modifications."[5] After the end of the transitional period, much of the necessary legal framework came into being. This will be set out in accordance with the principal subdivision of topics which together make up commercial policy within the EEC,[6] (arts. 113, 115), keeping in mind that within the framework of international organisations of an economic character the member states must act together in all matters of particular concern to the EEC (art. 116).

I IMPORTS

On 25 May 1970 a common regime was established for imports from third states.[7] It sets out the products which are to be imported freely[8]

---

1 9 October 1961, OJ, 1961, 1274, art. 1; and see Council Decision 74/455 of 19 December 1972, OJ, 1972, L 299/46.

2 *Ibid.*, art. 2.

3 *Ibid.*, art. 3; the original date, *i.e.* 1 January 1966 was prolonged until 31 December 1967, Council Decision 29 December 1965, OJ, 1965, 3275. For further extensions see *General Report* 1968, s. 531, p. 383; 1969, s. 445, p. 381; Council Decisions 16 December 1969, OJ, 1969, L 326/39; 28 January 1969, OJ, 1969, L 43/15; 26 June 1969, OJ, 1969, L 169/2; 30 June 1969, OJ, 1969, L 169/2; 15 September 1969, OJ, 1969, L 238/9; 8 December 1969, OJ, 1969, L 323/10; 20 December 1969, OJ, 1970, L 6/1; 8 June 1970, OJ, 1970, L 133/14; 13 July 1970, OJ, 1970, L 157/29; 29 September 1970, OJ, 1970, L 225/22/24; 13 October 1970, OJ, 1970, L 231/7; 23 November, OJ, 1970, L 262/18; 1 February 1971, OJ, 1971, L 31/18; 1 March 1971, OJ, 1971, L 56/8; 25 May 1971, OJ, 1971, L 122/24; 25 October 1971, OJ, 1971, L 248/7; 28 February 1972, OJ, 1972, L 56/10; 25 April 1972, OJ, 1972, L 112/10; 6 June 1972, OJ, 1972 L 133/61; 18 October 1972, OJ, 1972, L 250/1/5.

    Exemptions: France–USSR, Council Decision 1 August 1969, OJ, 1969, L 206/33; Benelux–Roumania etc., Council Decision 16 December 1969, OJ, 1969, L 326/43/44/45; 19 January 1970, OJ, 1970, L 18/23/24; 12 February 1970, OJ, 1970, L 38/7; and see generally, Council Decision 72/455 of 19 December 1972, OJ, 1972, L 299/46.

4 *Ibid.*, art. 4.

5 OJ, 1960, 1965, n. 1.

6 Above, p. 298.

7 Reg. 1025/70, OJ, 1970, L 124/6 as amended by subsequent regulations enumerated in Reg. 1415/72, 27 June 1972, OJ, 1972, L 151/4; consolidated by Commission Decision 72/309, 10 August 1972, OJ, 1972, L 197/9; rectified OJ, 1972, L 215/12; applicable also to French Overseas Territories: Reg. 1026/70, OJ, 1972, L 124/48, amended by Council Reg. 2747/72, OJ, 1972, L 291/150; see also Council Decision 19 December 1972, OJ, 1972, L 299/46.

8 Art. 1 and Annex I: superseding earlier lists; other products may be included in the future: art. 2.

from non-member states.[1] If member states envisage the need for taking safeguarding measures, a Community procedure of consultation[2] and a statistical control mechanism are provided.[3] As a last resort, the Commission, at the request of a member state or of its own motion, can take limited safeguarding measures[4] and the Council[5] as well as any member state provisionally[6] can take more drastic measures. A similar common regime applies to imports from third states acting through state trading agencies.[7]

Together with a common regime for imports from third states, a common regime on quantitative restrictions was created on 25 May 1970.[8] It governs both imports[9] and[10] exports[11] other than agricultural products.[12] The Council, upon a proposal of the Commission, acting upon a qualified majority, must establish a Community quota and its distribution among the member states.[13] A detailed procedure regulates the administration of Community quotas by the member states;[14] it is controlled in part by a management committee.[15] The same procedure applies if a trade agreement between the Community and a third state enables that state unilaterally to restrict its exports, and if the Community proposes or accepts an increase in such exports.[16] In order to determine or to control the origin of imported goods for the purpose of applying the common customs tariff, quantitative restrictions or any other rules governing commercial exchanges, common provisions defining the origin of merchandise have been introduced[17] and a uniform regime of Community transit was created.[18]

---

1   Art. I and Annex II; other states may be included in the future: art. 2.

2   Arts. 3–6.   3   Arts. 7–9.

4   Art. 10.

5   Art. 11.

6   Art. 12.

7   Reg. 109/70 of 19 December 1969, OJ, 1970, L 19/1 as amended by subsequent regulations enumerated in Reg. 1414/72 of 27 June 1972, OJ, 1972, L 151/1; Reg. 1751/72 of 2 August 1972, OJ, 1972, L 184/1, consolidated by Commission Decision 72/322, 31 August 1972, OJ, 1972, L 208/1, rectified OJ, 1972, L 215/13; applied to French Overseas Territories, Reg. 110/70, OJ, 1970, L 19/43, amended by Council Reg. 2747/72, OJ, 1972, L 291/150.

8   Reg. 1023/70, OJ, 1970, L 124/1 extended to French Overseas Territories by Reg. 1024/70, OJ, 1970, L 124/5, amended by Council Reg. 2747/72, OJ, 1972, L 291/150.

9   Reg. 1570/70, OJ, 1970, L 172/1 (hand-made products), amended Reg. 2262/70, OJ, 1970, L 245/1; 1742/71, OJ, 1971, L 180/1; Reg. 2825/71, OJ, 1971, L 285/54 (processed and raw tin); 2826/71, OJ, 1971, L 285/57 (raw tin); 2827/71, OJ, 1971, L 285/60; 2162/72, OJ, 1972, L 232/1 (raw magnesium); Reg. 2828/71, OJ, 1971, L 285/63 (colophanes) and the other materials covered by Regs. 2772/71–2800/71, OJ, 1971, L 287/1–162.

10   For examples see Reg. 2824/71, OJ, 1971, L 285/52 (copper, aluminium, tin).

11   Reg. 1023/70, art. 1.

12   Ibid., art. 13.

13   Ibid., art. 2(1); including its redistribution and augmentation: art. 2(2), (3).

14   Ibid., arts. 3–10.

15   Ibid., arts. 10–12.

16   Reg. 1471/70 of 20 July 1970, OJ, 1970, L 164/41.

17   Reg. 802/68 of 27 June 1968, OJ, 1968, L 148/1; Commission Regs. 582/69, 26 March 1969, OJ, 1969, L 79/1; 518/72, 8 March 1972, OJ, 1972, L 67/25.

18   Reg. 542/69, 18 March 1969, OJ, 1969, L 77/1.

Among the safeguarding measures, those directed against dumping are of paramount importance, and Reg. 459/68[1] offers the necessary means.[2] In addition the Commission, acting within the powers conferred by art. 115(1) of the Treaty, may authorise a member state to exclude from admitting as part of the free exchange of goods within the Community goods which have been admitted regularly to free circulation (*en libre pratique*) by another member state on the ground that the differences in the measures of commercial policy adopted by the applicant member state towards the third state, as distinct from the other member states, encourage a deflection of trade and impede the measures of commercial policy set in train by the applicant member state in relation to the third state.[3]

II EXPORTS

Shortly before a common regime on imports was created, an equivalent regime on exports was promulgated by Reg. 2603/71 on 20 December 1969.[4] It acknowledges that, except for goods enumerated in the Annex to the Regulation, exports from Community states are free, subject only to safeguarding measures based on Reg. 2603/71 itself.[5] If such measures are being contemplated a procedure of information and consultation must be followed[6] and a statistical enquiry may be ordered. Safeguarding measures may be applied, in the first place, by the Commission acting on its own or at the request of a member state, if a critical shortage is threatening and the interests of the Community so demand.[7] It can subordinate exports to an authorisation subject to certain conditions, pending a decision by the Council.[8] In the second place, the Council, on the proposal of the Commission, acting upon a qualified majority, may take

---

1 5 April 1968, OJ, 1968, L 93/1.
2 See above, p. 243, and p. 244, n. 2.
3 See the annual lists of individual safeguarding measures allowed by the Commission on the strength of art. 115, OJ, 1968, C 15/1; OJ, 1970, C 83/1; OJ, 1971, C 57/16 and the following Commission Decisions 72/9, 72/12, 72/13, 72/17, OJ, 1972, L 3/22/25/27/31; 72/195, 72/196, 72/197, 72/202, 72/204, OJ, 1972 L 123/1/3/4/27/39; 72/264, 72/265, 72/266, 72/267, OJ, 1972, L 166/18/19/20/21; 72/326, 72/327, OJ, 1972, L 220/23/24. A general measure was authorised by the Commission Decision 70/60, 22 December 1969, OJ, 1970, L 14/12 concerning certain sources of energy with a petroleum basis; renewed to a limited extent by Commission Decision 72/43, 15 December 1971, OJ, 1972, L 16/14.

  Such an authorisation may derogate from the guiding principles on a uniform customs area and the prohibition of quantitative restrictions (arts. 9, 30), but since art. 115 constitutes an exception, it must be interpreted restrictively: *Bock (Werner A.)* v. *EEC Commission*, (1971), 17 Rec. 897, at p. 910(14), (15); [1972] C.M.L.R. 160.
4 Reg. 2603/69, OJ, 1969, L 324/25; amended Reg. 234/71, OJ, 1971, L 28/2; 1078/71, OJ, 1971, L 116/5; 2182/71, OJ, 1971, L 231/4, amended by Council Reg. 2747/72, OJ, 1972, L 291/150.
5 *Ibid.*, art. 1.
6 The consultations are held within the setting of a Committee of representatives of the member states presided over by a member of the Commission; see *ibid.*, arts. 4, 9(1).
7 *Ibid.*, art. 6(1).
8 *Ibid.*, arts. 6(1), 7.

appropriate measures to counter a critical shortage of essential products or in order to permit the performance of international obligations entered into by the Community or by all its member states, especially in respect of raw materials.[1] In addition, a member state, in whose territory a shortage has arisen, may take protective measures, pending a decision of the Commission[2] which cease to operate when the Commission acts.[3] If the Commission refuses to act, the same rule applies, unless the member state refers the request to the Council.[4] While the measures are in force, the Committee keeps them under review.[5] According as the measures were ordered by the Council or the Committee, the former or the latter is competent to abrogate them.[6]

Among *aids* (art. 112) credit insurance ranks high. Upon a proposal by the Commission the Council began to work on this problem in 1960.[7] On 15 June 1965 it issued a Decision[8] on the terms of the automatic incorporation of sub-contractors in other member states or elsewhere in a scheme of credit insurance. Two Directives of 27 October 1970 and 1 February 1971 respectively sought the adoption of a common policy of credit insurance, firstly in respect of long and medium term transactions by public[9] and private[10] buyers and secondly concerning the essential provisions of such credit insurance policies for short term (political) risks by public and private buyers.[11]

Tariff modifications, and the conclusion of tariff and trade agreements with third countries (art. 113(1)(3)) also fall within the original competence of the Commission, which must submit proposals (art. 113(2)) and make recommendations to the Council.[12] The negotiations themselves are conducted by the Commission in consultation with a special committee of the Council and are concluded by the Council (art. 114).[13] In the exercise of these powers treaties were concluded with individual countries, namely, Israel,[14] Spain,[15] Iran,[16] Lebanon,[17] Yugoslavia,[18] Argentina,[19]

---

1 Art. 7(1).
2 Art. 8(1)–(3).
3 Art. 8(3), 1st para., art. 6(1)–(4).
4 Art. 6(3), 2nd para.
5 Art. 9(1).
6 Art. 9(2).
7 27 September 1960, OJ, 1960, 1339.
8 OJ, 1965, 1867.
9 70/509, OJ, 1970, L 254/1.
10 70/510, OJ, 1970, L 254/26.
11 71/86, OJ, 1971, L 36/14.
12 The latter acts by a qualified majority: arts. 113(4), 114.
13 See generally, Bianconi, 1971 Riv. Dir. Eur. 115. For the powers of the Commission to enter into international agreements outside the ambit of arts. 113, 114, 238 see *EEC Commission* v. *EEC Council* (1971), 17 Rec. 263, at p. 274(16); for transport: p. 275(2), 281(76); [1971] C.M.L.R. 335.
14 26 June 1970; Reg. 1526/70, 20 July 1970, OJ, 1970, L 183/1; safeguard measures, Reg. 1527/70, 20 July 1970, OJ, 1970, L 183/218; Council Decision 70/450, 29 September 1970, OJ, 1970, L 218/30 replacing 4 June 1964, Council Decision 8 May 1964, OJ, 1964, 1517–1524; Reg. 2394/71, 8 November 1971, OJ, 1971, L 249/47.

Austria,[1] Switzerland,[2] Sweden,[3] Iceland,[4] and Portugal[5] with other parties to multilateral agreements, *i.e.*, within the framework of GATT,[6] with international organisations[7] or as parties to international commodity agreements.[8] Many bilateral agreements on aid to other states were also concluded over the years[9] and a series of Council regulations and decisions made by virtue of art. 113 have supplemented association agreements.[10]

---

15 29 June 1970, Reg. 1524/70, 20 July 1970, OJ, 1970, L 182/1; safeguard measures, Reg. 1525/70, 20 July 1970, OJ, 1970, L 182/175, Council Decision 70/498, 27 October 1970, OJ, 1970, L 245/21; Reg. 2393/71, 8 November 1971, OJ, 1971, L 249/42.

16 14 October 1963, Council Decision 63/574, OJ, 1963, 2554; renewed Council Decision 27 October 1966, OJ, 1966, 3742; 3 October 1967, OJ, 1967, No. 309/6; 5 November 1968, OJ, 1968, L 284/10; L 287/20; Reg. 1874/68, 26 November 1968, OJ, 1968, L 287/2; 10 November 1969, OJ, 1969, L 302/15; 10 November 1970, OJ, 1970, L 250/13.

17 21 May 1965, Council Decision 18 June 1968, OJ, 1968, L 146/1 renewed 22 July 1971, Council Decision 12 July 1971, OJ, 1971, L 181/11, 26 July 1972, Council Decision 13 July 1972, OJ, 1972, L 201/12.

18 6 February 1970, Council Decision 6 March 1970, OJ, 1970, L 58/1–13.

19 Reg. 2387/71, 8 November 1971, OJ, 1971, L 249/18.

1   Reg. 1196/70, 15 June 1970, OJ, 1970, L 140/1; 2813/72, 21 November 1972, OJ, 1972, L 294/86 (transit); Interim Agreement 25 September 1972, OJ, 1972, L 233/1; Convention 22 July 1972, OJ 1972, L 300/1; safeguarding measures, OJ, 1972, L 300/94.

2   Reg. 2812/72, 21 November 1971, OJ, 1972, L 294/1 (transit); Convention 22 July 1972, OJ, 1972, L 300/188; for Liechtenstein see OJ, 1972, L 300/281; safeguarding measures, OJ, 1972, L 300/284.

3   Convention 22 July 1972, OJ, 1972, L 300/96; safeguarding measures, OJ, 1972, L 300/186.

4   Convention 22 July 1972, OJ, 1972, L 301/1; safeguarding measures, OJ, 1972, 301/162.

5   Convention 22 July 1972, OJ, 1972, L 301/164; safeguarding measures, OJ, 1972, L 301/368.

6   With Canada, Uruguay and the United States Council Decision 27 November 1967, OJ, 1967, No. 292/44; with the USA 30 May 1968, OJ, 1968, L 131/18; with South Africa, Council Decision 28 July 1969, OJ, 1969, L 206/26: with Canada, Council Decision 22 April 1969, OJ, 1969, L 97/15; 3 March 1970, OJ, 1970, L 54/4/16; Australia *ibid.*, L 54/1, 15 October 1968, OJ, 1968, L 258/9; Chile, OJ, 1970, L 54/6; with Spain, Council Decision 27 October 1970, OJ, 1970, L 245/21; with New Zealand, Council Decision 23 November 1970, OJ, 1970, L 257/5 (all GATT art. XXVIII). With the USA and the United Kingdom Council Decision 30 May 1968, OJ, 1968, L 131/14 (GATT art. XXIV(6)). With the other members of GATT as a whole: Council Decision 27 November 1967, OJ, 1968, L 305/1 concerning multilateral agreements signed as a result of the conference on commercial negotiations 1964–67; Council Decision 14 January 1970, OJ, 1970, L 124/49.

7   With the World Health Organisation: Council Decision 6 March 1970, OJ, 1970, L 59/34/39 (aid to underdeveloped countries); General Food Aid Convention: Council Decision 17 March 1970, OJ, 1970, L 66/25.

8   International Wheat Agreement: Council Decision 17 March 1970, OJ, 1970, L 66/1; Cotton: Council Decision 29 September 1970, OJ, 1970, L 225/28; 25 May 1971, OJ, 1971, L 122/26; Tin: Council Decision 22 March 1972, OJ, 1972, L 90/1.

9   See *e.g.* with Mali, OJ, 1969, L 206/30; Morocco, OJ, 1971, L 53/1; Sudan, OJ, 1970, L 236/43; Yemen, OJ, 1970, L 236/36; Afghanistan, Bangladesh, OJ, 1972, L 299/19/24; Red Cross, *ibid.*, L 299/29.

10 See *e.g.* Council Decision 20 December 1968, OJ, 1968, L 311/26; 1584/70, OJ, 1970, L 173/1; Council Reg. 1885/71, 1 September 1971, OJ, 1971, L 197/1; 2830/71, 2831/72; 2832/71; 2833/71; 28 December 1972, OJ, 1972, L 298/26/31/35/40.

18

Social Provisions and the European Social Fund

(Articles 117–122)[1]

The Treaty states on several occasions that it seeks to raise the standard of living and working conditions and to improve the possibilities of employment for workers[2] so as to equalise these conditions in the course of their improvement.[3] In general, harmonisation of social systems and approximation of legislative and administrative provisions[4] are the means of pursuing these aims.[5] Technically this goal is to be achieved by a close collaboration between the Commission and the member states.[6]

> *Measures:* Commission—in consultation with the Economic and Social Committee—studies and opinions (art. 118).[7]

The range of activities is wide and is set out by way of illustration but not of exhaustive enumeration (art. 118). Firstly, it embraces employment. Here the Commission has initiated studies only.[8] Secondly it includes labour law and working conditions. Here the Commission has issued a Recommendation on 23 July 1962 encouraging the creation of social services to aid migrant workers before their departure, during their journey and on arrival abroad, a special training scheme and co-operation between the services.[9] The protection of young workers was the object of a Recommendation of 31 January 1967[10] which sets out in considerable detail the conditions in which such persons are to be employed.

Thirdly it covers elementary and advanced training. In a somewhat broadly phrased Decision of 2 April 1963,[11] the Council has formulated its

---

1 Troclet in *Ganshof van der Meersch*, p. 943 no. 2439–p. 966, No. 2424; Brown, (1965–66) 3 C.M.L.Rev. 184; Collins, 1966 J.C.M.S. 26.
2 Arts. 2, 3(h)(i), 117, 1st para.
3 Art. 117, 1st para.
4 For the meaning of these terms see above, p. 268.
5 Art. 117, 2nd para. *Quaere* whether art. 117, 1st para. imposes binding obligations upon the member states. See Troclet in *Ganshof van der Meersch*, no. 2351.
6 Note the word "particularly" in art. 118, 1st para.
7 The Commission, here as elsewhere, can act in reliance upon implied powers (art. 155).
8 Troclet (above), No. 2357.
9 Commission Recommendation 23 July 1962, OJ, 1962, 2118, rectified OJ, 1964, 2270.
10 Commission Recommendation 67/125, 31 January 1967, OJ, 1967, 405.
11 Council Decision 63/266, 2 April 1963, OJ, 1963, 1338 (art. 128) taken up by the Council

policy in ten principles. Training is to be available for all; the quantitative and qualitative needs of the Community are to be taken into consideration; collaboration, distribution of information and exchange of experiences among the member states are encouraged; the supply of teachers, the maintenance of an approximately equal level of instruction, the elaboration of programmes covering all member states and the reservation of a place for special cases are urged upon the member states.

In the fourth place social security is included.[1]

In the fifth place protection against occupational accidents and diseases is to be strengthened. A Commission Recommendation of 23 July 1962[2] stresses the need for a European list of professional illnesses as a basis for claims for compensation and urges member states to make these diseases notifiable. This Recommendation was supplemented by another, dated 20 June 1966[3] which takes up the request for a European list of professional illnesses, advocates the introduction of legislation to provide compensation for such illnesses, and the circulation of descriptions of symptoms of noxious agents, and advises that all presumptions of liability of employers arising from and limited to such illnesses should be abolished in favour of an independent judicial appreciation which includes other illnesses not included in the list.

In the sixth place industrial hygiene is to be expanded. A Commission Recommendation of 20 July 1962[4] underlines the need for specialised medical supervision in factories, for the training of medical practitioners in this particular field, their employment and for guarantees which ensure their professional independence.

In addition the Commission has begun a series of studies and enquiries on related topics.[5]

On 31 December 1961 the member states became obliged to ensure and to maintain the principle of equal remuneration for the same work as between men and women (art. 119),[6] but this delay was extended until 31 December 1964 by the member states acting upon a joint agreement. For this purpose remuneration means the basic wage or salary, in cash or in kind, payable directly or indirectly,[7] calculated on the basis of the same unit of measurement, if at a price rate, or at a time rate (art. 119, end).

---

on 26 July 1971, OJ, 1971, C 81/5 in a statement entitled "General Indications for the Elaboration of a Programme of Activities on a Community Level in matters of Vocational Training". More specifically see Council Recommendation 70/449, 29 September 1970, OJ, 1970, L 219/1 concerning the use of the European Vocational Monograph on the training of qualified machine-tool operators.

1 See above, pp. 93–128.
2 Commission Recommendation 23 July 1962, OJ, 1962, 2188.
3 Commission Recommendation 66/462, 20 June 1966, OJ, 1966, 2696.
4 Commission Recommendation 20 July 1962, OJ, 1962, 2181.
5 See Troclet in *Ganshof van der Meersch*, nos. 2357–2385 and see *e.g.*, Council Reg. 151/62, OJ, 1962, 2841; Reg. 2395/71, OJ, 1971, L 249/52.
6 Following Convention No. 100 (1951) of the ILO. Unlike arts. 117 and 118, art. 119 creates a binding obligation upon the member states. See *Defrenne* v. *Belgium* (1971), 17 Rec. 445, at p. 457 *per* Adv. Gen. Dutheillet de Lamothe *arguendo*.
7 The reference to wages or salaries payable indirectly seems to aim at perquisites.

This definition includes expatriation allowances which are intended to provide some compensation for the additional expenses and specific disadvantages resulting from entering the service of the Communities in cases where officials have to change their place of residence.[1] It is granted not only in consideration of the personal situation of the beneficiary but also of the family ties resulting from the marriage.[2] Consequently the new family situation acquired by an official counts when he or she marries a person who does not meet the conditions required to be granted an expatriation allowance.[3] If this change in the family situation brings to an end the state of expatriation, the expatriation allowance may be withdrawn,[4] but the criterion must not be whether the expatriated official or his spouse who does not fulfil the conditions for an expatriation allowance is the "head of the family".[5]

On the other hand, the principle of equality of remuneration as defined in art. 119[6] does not extend to social, general and special security benefits, such as retirement pensions including those for particular categories of workers, which are directly determined by law, fed by contributions from employers, workers and public revenues, and are payable irrespective of whether the employer's contribution has materialised or not.[7]

The European Social Fund was created in order to improve the possibilities of employment of workers by promoting new openings for employment and by supporting the geographical and occupational mobility of workers.[8]

Its function was to contribute at the request of a member state 50 per cent of the expenses incurred by that member state or an organisation of a public law character in that state in carrying out *either*

(a) a process of re-employment through, (i) occupational training *or* (ii) resettlement;[9] *or*

(b) the supplementation of wages of workers whose work is temporarily reduced or wholly or partly suspended as a result of the conversion of the enterprise in which they are employed, so as to maintain the same wage-level before they can be again employed fully.[10]

If a grant is sought for re-training, it can only be paid if it is proved that the workers were unemployed, could not be found employment unless

---

1   *Sabbatini* v. *European Parliament* (1973), 18 Rec. 344; [1972] C.M.L.R. 945, at p. 958(8).
2   *Ibid.*, 958(9).
3   *Ibid.*, 958(10).
4   *Ibid.*, 958(11).
5   *Ibid.*, 958(12)–(13).
6   For other criteria see Adv. Gen. Dutheillet de Lamothe in *Defrenne* v. *Belgium* (1971), 17 Rec. 445, at p. 457(II).
7   *Defrenne* v. *Belgium* (1971), 17 Rec. 445, at p. 452(7)–(13). The provision enjoining member states to maintain the existing equivalence of paid holidays is directory only (art. 120).
8   Art. 124.
9   Art. 125(1)(a).
10   Art. 125(1)(b).

re-trained for another occupation and that they have been so employed in that new occupation for at least six months.[1]

If the grant is sought for resettlement, it can only be paid if it is proved that the workers were unemployed, were obliged to change their residence within the Community and that they have been productively employed in their new place of residence for at least six months.[2]

If the grant is sought for supplementary wages pending the conversion of an enterprise, it can only be paid if it is proved that the workers in question have been fully employed in that enterprise for at least six months, that the Government concerned has previously submitted a plan, drawn up by that enterprise, for its conversion and financing and that the Commission had approved of this plan.[3]

The Fund was administered by the Commission, assisted by a Committee.[4] Provisions implementing arts. 124–126 were to be formulated.

> *Measure:* Council—upon a proposal of the Commission—
> after consulting the Economic and Social
> Committee and the Assembly—by a qualified
> majority—lays down provisions (art. 127).

The future of the Fund was to be reviewed at the end of the transitional period.

> *Measure:* Council—upon an opinion of the Commission—
> after consulting the Economic and Social
> Committee and the Assembly—
> by a qualified vote—terminates all or part of the
> assistance envisaged in art. 125 (art. 126(1)(a))
> unanimously—determines new tasks for the
> Fund—within the framework of art. 123 (art.
> 126(1)(b)).

Acting by virtue of art. 127, the Council passed Reg. 9/60[5] which governed the operation of the Fund until 1 January 1972, when it was abrogated.[6] The Council, in the exercise of the powers given by art. 126 of the Treaty, passed a Decision on 1 February 1971 on the reform of the European Social Fund,[7] which departed completely from the scheme adopted by the treaty. This was implemented by a Council Regulation of 8 November

---

1 Art. 125(2), 1st para.
2 Art. 125(2), 2nd para.
3 Art. 125(2), 3rd para.
4 Art. 124; for its Statute of 25 August 1960 see OJ, 1960, 1201; see also Reg. 2396/71, OJ, 1971, L 249/54 arts. 9, 10.
5 OJ, 1960, 1189, modified by Reg. 47/63, OJ, 1963, 1605; Reg. 12/64, OJ, 1964, 537; Reg. 37/67, OJ, 1967, 526.
6 Council Reg. 2396/71, art. 12, OJ, 1971, L 249/54; for the transitional period see *ibid.*, art. 12.
7 71/66, OJ, 1971, L 28/15.

1971 concerning the reform of the European Social Fund.[1] Its resources are now available *ratione personae* for the benefit of any persons who belong to the working population and who are called to exercise an occupation for a wage or salary, after having enjoyed the benefit of a measure which falls within the competence of the Fund.[2] However, in special cases, to be determined by the Council, the Fund may also assist self-employed persons,[3] and it was so extended to handicapped persons and persons who are directly engaged in self-employed occupations in agriculture.[4]

Ratione materiae the Fund may intervene if the employment situation

(a) is adversely affected or threatened by particular measures taken by the Council within the framework of the common economic policy or through actions taken by common agreement for the purpose of enhancing the realisation of the objectives of the Community, *or*

(b) discloses the need for specific common action in order better to match demand and supply of labour within the Community,[5] *or*

(c) is affected, in certain regions, in certain branches of the economy or in certain groups of enterprises, by difficulties which do not follow directly from an individual measure taken by the Council within the framework of a Community policy, but which follow indirectly from the operation of the Common Market or which hamper the harmonious development of the Community.[6] In these circumstances aid may be granted in order to eliminate unemployment and long-term under-employment due to structural reasons in order to create a highly qualified workforce or, *inter alia*, in order to support actions which aim at fitting into, or reinstating in, economic life handicapped persons, aged workers, women and young workers.[7]

> *Measure:* Council—in accordance with the procedure laid down in art. 127 of the Treaty—issues implementing regulations—defining types of aids and criteria to be followed in applications for aid.[8]

In compliance with this provision the Council issued three Regulations.[9]

---

1 2396/71, OJ, 1971, L 249/54, supplemented, as regards types of aids, by Reg. 2397/71, OJ, 1971, L 249/58 and as regards non-salaried persons by Reg. 2398/71, OJ, 1971, L 249/61.
2 Council Decision 71/66, 1 February 1971, art. 3(1), OJ, 1971, L 28/15.
3 Council Decision 71/66, art. 3(2).
4 Reg. 2398/71, 8 November 1971, OJ, 1971, L 249/61.
5 Decision 71/66, art. 4(1).
6 Decision 71/66, art. 5(1) 1st para.
7 Decision 71/66, art. 5(1) 2nd para.
8 Decision 71/66, art. 5(2).
9 2396/71, OJ, 1971, L 249/54; 2397/71, OJ, 1971, L 249/58 and 2398/71 (above, n. 4), all of 8 November 1971.

The first enlarged on the circumstances in which, on the basis of the third alternative discussed above (art. 5(1) of Council Decision 71/66), aid may be granted to certain types of measures. These are that a serious and prolonged under-employment exists in a region where growth has been retarded or the prevailing activities are declining[1] or that certain branches of economic activities are to be adapted to the requirements of technical progress which necessitate important changes in the manpower and of vocational proficiencies[2] or that important modifications of the conditions of production and marketing among groups of enterprises engaging in the same or connected activities forces them to discontinue, to reduce or to transform their activities irrevocably.[3] The measures qualifying for support by the fund are, once more, those enumerated in Council Decision 71/66.[4] Normally they must form part of a specific programme designed to remedy the imbalance of employment in the particular region, economic sector, groups of enterprises or categories of persons.[5] The types of aid which can be granted are generally those likely to remedy the situations deserving support described above and are enumerated in outline in Reg. 2396/71.[6] They are set out in detail in Reg. 2397/71.[7]

Applications for aid must originate from the member state or states and be submitted to the Commission.[8] The latter forwards the projects and demands for aid to the Committee of the European Social Fund for examination.[9] If supported by the latter and found to comply with the requirements of the relevant regulations and decisions,[10] the Commission makes a proposal to the Council if the aid is solicited on one of the two grounds enumerated in Council Decision 71/66, art. 4(1),[11] but in these two situations the Commission may act *proprio motu* or upon an initiative by the Council.[12]

> *Measure:* Council—by a qualified majority—upon con-
> sidering the conditions laid down in Decision
> 71/66 art. 4(2)—specifies the areas susceptible
> to aid—the type of aid—if necessary the range of
> self-employed beneficiaries.[13]

If aid is sought on the third general ground enumerated in Council

---

1 Reg. 2396/71, art. 1(a).
2 *Ibid.,* art. 1(b).
3 *Ibid.,* art. 1(c).
4 Art. 5(2). See above, p. 308, text to n. 7; Reg. 2396/71, art. 1(2)(a)–(c), (3).
5 Decision 71/66, art. 6; Reg. 2396/71, art. 1(4).
6 Reg. 2396/71, art. 3.
7 Reg. 2397/71 art. 1, OJ, 1971, L 249/58.
8 Decision 71/66, art. 6; Reg. 2396/71, art. 5.
9 Decision 71/66, art. 7; for the Committee see above, p. 307 and n. 4.
10 Decision 71/66, art. 7; Reg. 2396/71, art. 6.
11 See above, p. 308.
12 Decision 71/66 art. 4(1), last para.
13 Decision 71/66, art. 4(2)(a)–(c).

Decision 71/66[1] it is considered only by the Commission and by the Committee.[2]

The Fund continues to support 50 per cent of the admissible expenses[3] incurred by public administrations, by organisations of a public character and by social organisms established on a basis of parity for the discharge of functions of public interest[4] as well as organs or entities of a private law character, if the public authorities of the state or states concerned certify that the measures will be properly applied.[5] No aid can be given in order to finance the first training of school-leavers immediately upon the termination of compulsory attendance. However, such aid can be accorded if they are available for employment, but cannot find it because they lack any qualification or have the wrong qualification.[6]

The Council will review the present arrangements based on its Decision of 1 February 1971 at the latest when five years have passed since the implementing legislation came into force, *i.e.* on 1 January 1977.[7]

---

1 Decision 71/66, art. 5(1).
2 Decision 71/66, art. 5(2), last para.
3 The real amount of the expenses counts: Reg. 2396/71, art. 3(3).
4 Decision 71/66, art. 8(1).
5 Decision 71/66, art. 8(2); a list of the organs qualified to certify this fact must be submitted by member states to the Commission; see Reg. 2396/71, art. 4.
6 Reg. 2396/71, art. 3(2), last para.
7 Decision 71/66, arts. 11, 10(1); Reg. 2396/71, art. 15.

PART III

Remedies and Procedure

19

Remedies[1]

I General Survey

The Community Court fulfils a great variety of functions. It watches over the observance not only of the EEC Treaty (art. 164) but also of the ECSC and Euratom treaties. Although, in practice, the remedies enshrined in these treaties are either identical or invite constructive comparison, it is sufficient here to set out the remedies under the EEC Treaty only.

Even within the framework of the EEC Treaty the Court discharges a number of duties; some concern matters involving the member states and the organs of the Community only;[2] others involve individuals as well[3] or alone;[4] sometimes it is advisory only[5] and once it is appellate;[6] normally the jurisdiction is exclusive, but in certain circumstances it is concurrent with that of national courts.[7]

For the present purposes, which are not directly concerned with the duties of member states towards the Community and the other member states, it is only necessary to touch upon these aspects in so far as they may affect private interests or rights.

II By and against Member States (arts. 169, 170, 171)[8]

In supervising the observance of the Treaty by member states at the request of the Community organs or of other member states, the Court functions not unlike an international tribunal, to the exclusion of any other international jurisdiction, such as the I.C.J., which may otherwise be competent (art. 219). Conversely, the Community Court may entertain any dispute between member states not covered by the jurisdictional

---

1 Jeantet and Kovar, Juriscl. Dr. Int., Fasc. 161 C; Gand, Bebr, Goffin, Dumon, Marchesini, in *Ganshof van der Meersch*, pp. 295–389, nos. 827–1088; Ipsen, pp. 752–770; Ule in *Judicial Protection against the Executive* (Köln and Dobbs Ferry N.Y.), (1970) Vol. II, pp. 1179–1216; Bebr, *Judicial Control of the European Communities* (1962); Steindorff, *Rechtsschutz und Verfahren im Recht der europäischen Gemeinschaften* (1964).
2 Arts. 93(2), 169, 170, 171; 180, 182, 225.
3 Arts. 173, 175.
4 Arts. 172, 177, 178, 179, 184.
5 Art. 228.
6 Euratom Treaty art. 18.
7 Arts. 181, 183.
8 See above, n. 2; Marchesini in *Ganshof van der Meersch*, p. 367, no. 1016–p. 378, no. 1041; Cahier, 1967 Cah. Dr. Eur. 123.

provisions of the Treaty but bearing upon its objects, if the member states, partners to the agreement, submit to the jurisdiction by special agreement (art. 182).

The procedure differs somewhat according as the Commission or a member state initiates proceedings on the ground that another member state has failed to fulfil its obligations under the Treaty.[1] In the former case the Commission must prepare a reasoned opinion, invite the member state concerned to submit its comments, and if the member state does not comply with the terms of the opinion within a certain time limit, the Commission may refer the matter to the Community Court (art. 169).[2]

If a member state wishes to raise a similar complaint, it must refer the matter to the Commission. At this stage two possibilities exist. Either the Commission invites the member states concerned to present their case and to comment on that presented by the other member state and terminates these proceedings by giving a reasoned opinion (art. 170(2), (3)).[3] If the Commission has not given an opinion within three months after the matter had been referred to it, the member state which has lodged the complaint may seize the Court with the matter (art. 170(1), (4)). If the Court finds that the complaint is well founded, the member state concerned must take the necessary measures in order to fulfil the obligations incumbent upon it (art. 171).[4] No sanctions are provided,[5] and it remains for the Com-

---

1   Arts. 169, 170. These obligations are determined not only by the Treaty as such, but also by regulations and any other acts to the extent that they are binding upon member states. An abstention, as well as a positive act, can constitute a failure by a state to carry out its obligations. See *EEC Commission* v. *Italy* (1970), 16 Rec. 25, at p. 33(9); [1970] C.M.L.R. 175. It is irrelevant which organ of the member state has broken a duty: *EEC Commission* v. *Belgium* (1970), 16 Rec. 237, at p. 244(15).

2   The need for speedy action explains the curtailment of this procedure in arts. 92, 225; see Jeantet and Kovar, Juriscl. Dr. Int., Fasc. 161 C, Pt. III, No. 58.

3   Given the alternative envisaged in art. 170(4), it would seem that the Commission can exercise its discretion. See Jeantet and Kovar (above) Fasc. 161 C, Pt. III, Nos. 50, 57. For the extent to which reasons must be supplied see *EEC Commission* v. *Italian Government* (1961), 7 Rec. 633, at p. 642; [1962] C.M.L.R. 39: a coherent statement of the grounds.

4   It is irrelevant whether the member state has complied with the Treaty after the proceedings against it have been begun; see *EEC Commission* v. *Italian Government* (1961), 7 Rec. 633, at pp. 653–654 (above); *EEC Commission* v. *Italian Government* (1965), 11 Rec. 1057, at p. 1068; [1966] C.M.L.R. 97; *EEC Commission* v. *Italian Government* (1968), 14 Rec. 617; [1969] C.M.L.R. 1; see also *EEC Commission* v. *Luxemburg and Belgium* (1962), 8 Rec. 813, at p. 825; [1963] C.M.L.R. 199; *EEC Commission* v. *France* (1970), 16 Rec. 565, at p. 577(10); [1970] C.M.L.R. 444. Events subsequent to the time when the complaint was lodged cannot be taken into account as a defence; nor can they support a complaint brought on other grounds; see *EEC Commission* v. *Italy* (1970), 16 Rec. 25, at p. 34(12); see also *EEC Commission* v. *Italy* (1970), 16 Rec. 111, at p. 118(5); [1970] C.M.L.R. 97; *EEC Commission* v. *Italy* (1970), 16 Rec. 961, at p. 967(10). However, the question arises as to whether a sufficient interest exists for determining the cause of action if the member state concerned has more or less made good the default: see *EEC Commission* v. *France* (above); *EEC Commission* v. *Italy* (below, p. 315, n. 1).

   In the absence of any time limit in art. 169 the Commission must determine the choice of the moment when to start proceedings in the Court: *EEC Commission* v. *Italian Government* (1968), 14 Rec. 617, at p. 625; [1969] C.M.L.R. 1; *EEC Commission* v. *France* (1971), 17 Rec. 1003, at p. 1017(5)(6); [1972] C.M.L.R. 453.

5   *Humblet* v. *Belgium* (1960), 6 Rec. 1125, at pp. 1145–1146; Valentine II, p. 817. For this

munity Court to give a declaratory judgment containing a finding that the member state has failed to carry out its obligations under art. 171.[1] It is irrelevant that according to the constitutional law of the member state the failure to act is due to an organ over which the state has no control.[2]

III AGAINST COMMUNITY ORGANS BY MEMBER STATES, OTHER COMMUNITY ORGANS OR PRIVATE PERSONS

1 Jurisdiction to Annul (arts. 173, 174)[3]

The Court exercises jurisdiction not unlike an administrative or constitutional tribunal in determining the legal validity of the acts, other than recommendations and opinions, emanating from the Council and the Commission (art. 173(1); *recours en annulation*).[4] Here the parties are not confined to the member states and the community organs. While an organ of the Community appears as the defendant, another organ of the Community,[5] of a member state or, in certain circumstances, an enterprise or an individual may appear as the plaintiff.[6] However, legal entities and individuals only have a *locus standi*[7] if the act complained of is a decision addressed to the complainant or while purporting to be a regulation or a decision addressed to another, concerns the plaintiff directly and individually.[8]

(a) While the nature of the act of the Community organ is only defined

---

reason, directly applicable rules of the Treaty or made thereunder supplement the *lacuna* left by art. 169; see *EEC Commission v. Italy* (1970), 16 Rec. 25, at p. 33(9); *Molkerei-Zentrale Westfalen-Lippe v. Hauptzollamt Paderborn* (1968), 14 Rec. 211, at pp. 236–237; [1968] C.M.L.R. 187 *per* Adv. Gen. Gand *arguendo* citing *Van Gend en Loos v. Nederlandse Administratie der Belastingen* (1963), 9 Rec. 1, at p. 25; [1963] C.M.L.R. 105.

1 *EEC Commission v. Italy*, 13 July 1972, No. 48/71, 1972 Rev. Trim. Dr. Eur. 670 with a note by Ruzié, [1972] C.M.L.R. 699.
2 *EEC Commission v. Italy* (1970), 16 Rec. 961, at p. 967; (1972), 18 Rec. 529, at pp. 534–535.
3 Bebr (above, p. 313, n. 1) 37–127 and in *Ganshof van der Meersch*, p. 309, no. 868–p. 331, no. 919; Fromont, 1966 Rev. Trim. Dr. Eur. 47 (on the influence of French and German administrative law); 1969 EuR 202.
4 *Contentieux de l'excès de pouvoir.*
5 *EEC Commission v. EEC Council* (1971), 17 Rec. 263; [1971] C.M.L.R. 335; see also OJ, 1973, C 3/11, Case 81/72.
6 Art. 173, paras. 1 and 2.
7 In the terminology of the Court the claim must be "receivable" or "admissible". This reflects continental law, which envisages three stages in the examination of a claim. They concern respectively jurisdiction, admissibility and the merits. Admissibility involves such matters as the capacity to be a party to the proceedings and to act, whether the claim has been lodged properly, whether the plaintiff's statement of claim discloses a legal interest in the subject matter of the proceedings and whether the matter is *res judicata*. The Rules of the Court have made this concept their own (r. 91) under the heading of "Preliminary Objection". In keeping with the practice of continental courts, this aspect may be joined to the merits. See r. 91(4); *Plaumann v. EEC Commission* (1963), 9 Rec. 197, at p. 221; [1964] C.M.L.R. 29. It can be raised by the Court of its own motion: *Fives Lille Cail v. High Authority* (1961), 7 Rec. 559, at p. 588.
8 Art. 173, 2nd para.

negatively, the terminology employed to exclude some acts from judicial review (namely recommendations and opinions) is drawn from art. 189. Although the enumeration of Community acts in art. 189 is exhaustive, all acts issued by Community institutions other than those which are in substance recommendations or opinions, and not only Regulations and Decisions, can form the object of a recourse under art. 173, 1st para.[1] Nevertheless, difficulties can arise if either the Community organ couches an act in a form which cannot easily be characterised as a regulation or as a decision, or if a regulation authorises measures which do not lend themselves easily to such a characterisation.[2] In these circumstances, the nature of the act counts and not its outward appearance. If the act purports to apply generally or to an individual in such a manner as to affect a legal situation, it falls within the ambit of a regulation or decision in the meaning of art. 189, and therefore of art. 173, 1st para.

(b) If a legal entity wishes to sue it must have capacity according to the law which governs its creation and existence. Such are entities which enjoy the right of establishment (art. 58) and which must be recognised by virtue of the Convention on the Mutual Recognition of Companies and Legal Entities of 29 February 1968.[3]

(c) Unless the decision is addressed to the plaintiff such a legal entity or natural person only has a *locus standi* if a decision in the guise of a regulation or a decision addressed[4] to another person[5] concerns the plaintiff directly and individually.[6] Notwithstanding the order of these two adverbs, the Court has consistently examined first whether the plaintiff was individually concerned,[7] and only if the answer was in the affirmative did the Court embark upon the second question whether the plaintiff was

---

1   *EEC Commission* v. *EEC Council* (1971), 17 Rec. 263, at p. 277(42); [1971] C.M.L.R. 335.

2   *E.g.* Reg. 17/62, art. 15(6): information given by the Commission to enterprises; *SA Cimenteries CBR Cementsbedrijven NV* v. *EEC Commission* (1967), 13 Rec. 93, at p. 118; [1967] C.M.L.R. 77; *Confédération Nationale des Producteurs de Fruits et Légumes* (1962), 8 Rec. 901, at p. 918; [1963] C.M.L.R. 160; see also *Plaumann* v. *EEC Commission* (1963), 9 Rec. 197, at pp. 222–223; [1969] C.M.L.R. 180.

3   Above, p. 148. For an earlier example under the ECSC Treaty see *Nold* v. *High Authority* (1959), 5 Rec. 89, at p. 110; Valentine II, p. 215.

4   The term "addressed to another", *"adressée"*, *"gerichtet"* does not correspond literally to that used in art. 189, para. 4, *i.e.* *"destinataire"*, *"die sie bezeichnet"*, but the meaning is the same.

5   "Another person" in the meaning of art. 173, para. 2 includes a member state; see *Plaumann* v. *EEC Commission* (1963), 9 Rec. 197, at p. 222; [1969] C.M.L.R. 180.

6   Cp. ECSC, art. 33, para. 2.

7   *Confédération Nationale des Producteurs de Fruits et Légumes* v. *EEC Council* (1962), 8 Rec. 901, at p. 918; [1963] C.M.L.R. 160; *Fédération Nationale de la Boucherie en Gros* v. *EEC Council* (1962), 8 Rec. 943, at p. 959; [1963] C.M.L.R. 160; *Plaumann* v. *EEC Commission* (above, n. 1); *SA Glucoseries Réunies* v. *EEC Commission* (1964), 10 Rec. 811, at p. 823; [1964] C.M.L.R. 596; *Getreide-Import Ges.* v. *EEC Commission* (1965), 11 Rec. 263, at p. 270; [1965] C.M.L.R. 276; *Sgarlata* v. *EEC Commission* (1965), 11 Rec. 279, at p. 295; [1966] C.M.L.R. 314; *Zuckerfabrik Watenstedt GmbH* v. *EEC Council* (1968), 14 Rec. 595, at p. 604; [1969] C.M.L.R. 26; *Industria Molitoria Imolese* v. *EEC Council* (1968), 14 Rec. 171, at pp. 179, 180; *Eridania* v. *EEC Commission* (1969), 15 Rec. 459, at p. 480(5), (7); *Nordgetreide GmbH* v. *EEC Commission* (1972), 18 Rec. 105.

directly concerned.[1] The reason is that a regulation proper, being a rule of general application, concerns a person directly, but it does not concern him individually. A decision concerns specific persons, burdening them alone and individually, if it affects these persons by reason of certain qualities peculiar to themselves or having regard to a special factual situation which singles them out in relation to all others and thus individualises them analogously to the addressee.[2] Thus the test is whether the act concerns specific parties in their individual capacity or whether it has immediate legal effects in all the member states with respect to categories of persons designated in a general objective and abstract manner.[3] A producer or dealer in certain types of produce, a trade open to all, past, present and future, is thus not in the same position as a member state allowed[4] or refused[5] free import quotas or permitted to impose import restrictions.[6] Even if the possibility exists to determine with greater or lesser certainty the number or even the identity of the subjects to which it applies at a particular moment, a regulation does not concern a person individually as long as it is clear that the determination takes place on the strength of an objective legal and factual situation defined by the measure in connection with the purpose of the latter. The fact that the same legal provision can have different concrete effects for different legal subjects to which it applies does not deny its character as a regulation, if the situation is objectively determined.[7]

On the other hand, a group of importers, holders of import licences granted to them alone on specific terms prevailing on a particular day, is individually concerned by subsequent safeguarding measures against imports;[8] and the same applies to specific measures sought and taken against pending applications for import licences which would otherwise have to be granted.[9]

Once it has been found that the plaintiff is individually concerned, the

---

1   *Toepfer* v. *EEC Commission* (1965), 11 Rec. 525, at p. 533, see also p. 540; [1966] C.M.L.R. 111; *International Fruit Co.* v. *EEC Commission* (1971), 17 Rec. 411, at pp. 421(9), (13), 422(17), (20), (22), 423(28); *Bock (Werner A.)* v. *EEC Commission* (1971), 17 Rec. 897; [1972] C.M.L.R. 160: application by member state for authorisation of safeguard measure in order to refuse applications for import licences already submitted; concerns the plaintiff directly (p. 908(8)) and individually (p. 908(9)(10)). For a case where the direct concern was the prime question see *SA Alcan* v. *EEC Commission* (1970), 16 Rec. 385, at pp. 393(3), 394(8), (9); [1970] C.M.L.R. 337.

2   *Plaumann* v. *EEC Commission* (1963), 9 Rec. 197, at pp. 222–223; [1969] C.M.L.R. 180.

3   *Confédération Nationale des Producteurs des Fruits et Légumes* v. *EEC Council* (1962), 8 Rec. 901, at p. 918; [1963] C.M.L.R. 160; *Industria Molitoria Imolese* v. *EEC Council* (1968), 14 Rec. 171, at pp. 179, 180; *Zuckerfabrik Watenstedt GmbH* v. *EEC Council* (1968), 14 Rec. 595, at pp. 604–606; [1969] C.M.L.R. 26; *Nordgetreide GmbH* v. *EEC Commission* (1972), 18 Rec. 105; *International Fruit Co.* v. *EEC Commission* (1971), 17 Rec. 411, at p. 422(21).

4   *Alcan* v. *EEC Commission* (1970), 16 Rec. 385, at pp. 393(3), 394(8), (9); [1970] C.M.L.R. 337.

5   See the cases above, p. 316, n. 7.

6   *International Fruit Co.* v. *EEC Commission* (above, n. 3).

7   *Zuckerfabrik Watenstedt GmbH* v. *EEC Council* (1968), 14 Rec. 595, at pp. 605–606; [1969] C.M.L.R. 26.

8   *Toepfer* v. *EEC Commission* (1965), 11 Rec. 525, at p. 533; [1966] C.M.L.R. 111.

9   *International Fruit Co.* v. *EEC Commission* (above, n. 3).

causal link must be established which makes him directly concerned. It would seem that for this purpose it suffices that the measure is immediately operative.[1] Such is a measure which authorises, refuses or confirms an Act by a member state which affects private persons, but a measure which merely confers a power or imposes a duty upon a member state and leaves the latter little margin of discretion may have the same effect.[2]

(d) The complaint can only be based, and the annulment jurisdiction can only be exercised, on any one of four grounds which in one form or another appear in the administrative law of the original member states, namely the following.

(i) *Absence of Jurisdiction*[3]—Lack of competence to take a certain measure is generally acknowledged to be a ground for annulling it, and the EEC Treaty acknowledges it too, as do the ECSC and the Euratom Treaties. However, the Community has had little occasion to consider the principle in practice. Since the competence to act must be found in the Treaty itself, an overlap between the complaint of absence of jurisdiction and that of violation of the Treaty (which forms another ground of annulment) cannot be easily avoided.

(ii) *Infringement of Basic Procedural Rules*[4]—A remedy of this character figures in the laws of the original member states and in the three Community treaties. Although the latter do not offer express guidance as to what procedural rules to be employed in arriving at a Community measure must be regarded as basic, it seems to be agreed that rules requiring a qualified majority, the co-operation or consultation of particular organs or bodies, and the rule that regulations, directives and decisions of the Council and of the Commission must be supported by reasons and by references to the proposals or opinions which are required by the Treaty, constitute basic procedural rules.

In administering the EEC Treaty, the Community Court has had little occasion to consider this remedy.[5] The requirement of reasons applies to regulations and decisions alike, without regard to any differences in their functions. Reasons enable the parties, the Court and the member states to assess their legal position in contemplation of any challenge of their validity.[6] For this purpose it is necessary only to indicate broadly the

---

1   See above, p. 317, n. 8.
2   *Sgarlata* v. *EEC Commission* (1965), 11 Rec. 279; [1966] C.M.L.R. 314.
3   Art. 173, 1st para.: *incompétence, Unzuständigkeit.*
4   *Violation des formes substantielles, Verletzung wesentlicher Formvorschriften.*
5   *German Federal Republic* v. *EEC Commission* (1963), 9 Rec. 129, at p. 143; [1963] C.M.L.R. 347; *Schwarze* v. *Einfuhr- und Vorratsstelle für Getreide* (1965), 11 Rec. 1081, at p. 1096; [1966] C.M.L.R. 172; *Beus GmbH* v. *Hauptzollamt München* (1968), 14 Rec. 125, at p. 143; [1968] C.M.L.R. 131; see also *German Federal Republic* v. *EEC Commission*, (1963), 9 Rec. 269, at p. 294; [1963] C.M.L.R. 369.
6   *German Federal Republic* v. *EEC Commission* (1963), 9 Rec. 129, at p. 143 (above). But the extent to which the details of the reasons underlying the decision must be set out may depend upon the material possibilities and the technical conditions and time limits within which the decision is rendered: *Schwarze* v. *Einfuhr- und Vorratsstelle für Getreide* (1965), 11 Rec. 1081, at p. 1096 (above).

background and the general purposes of the measures[1] if it is a regulation, but to set out succinctly, in clear and pertinent terms, the principal points of law and fact which support a decision and which are necessary to explain the grounds on which it is based.[2]

(iii) *Infringement of the Treaty*[3]—This remedy is fundamental to every review of administrative acts. The Treaty and implementing measures form together the basis and the limits of Community action. While it may be possible to change regulations, to modify directives and to revoke decisions, they must be observed by the Community organs while they are in force. The Treaty itself, including the protocols and annexes, provides not only the point of departure for every measure; it also circumscribes its ambit, either inflexibly, if no discretion is conceded to the Community organs, or elastically, if the organ concerned enjoys a power of discretionary appreciation.[4] In all cases the written rule must be supplemented, if necessary, by the rules of interpretation[5] by the fundamental principles of the EEC Treaty[6] and by the implied powers (arts. 235, 155).

(iv) *Abuse of Power (détournement de pouvoir)*[7]—This also figures in one form or another in the domestic law of the original member states, but its features vary according as the notion itself has a predominantly objective or subjective content. It occurs if an administrative authority takes a measure within its regular powers but arbitrarily and for a purpose other than that for which the powers were intended.[8] In the absence of a single notion of *détournement de pouvoir*, both the subjective French approach, which fastens on the extraneous purpose[9] and the German, which is objective and comes near to equating it to an infringement of the law (*i.e.* the Treaty)[10] have been considered by the Court, though inconclusively. It would appear that in the hands of the Community Court its function as

---

1 *Beus GmbH* v. *Hauptzollamt München* (above, p. 318, n. 5).

2 *German Federal Republic* v. *EEC Commission* (1963), 9 Rec. 129, at p. 143; [1963] C.M.L.R. 347.

3 Bebr, *Judicial Control of the European Communities* (1962), pp. 89–98.

4 *German Federal Republic* v. *EEC Commission* (1963), 9 Rec. 129, at p. 142; [1963] C.M.L.R. 347; *Same*, (1963), 9 Rec. 269, at p. 296; [1963] C.M.L.R. 369.

5 See above, p. 14.

6 *German Federal Republic* v. *EEC Commission* (1963), 9 Rec. 269, at p. 296.

7 The texts other than the French use the following expressions: *Ermessensmissbrauch, sviamento di potere, misbruik van bevoegdheid.* See generally Bebr, *op. cit.* (above, n. 3), at pp. 98–108, especially pp. 101 ff.

8 See above, p. 16, n. 1(b). Jeantet and Kovar, Juriscl. Dr. Int., Fasc. 161 C, Pt. II(2), No. 46. The fact that a decision is based on reasons which were not put forward by the parties is irrelevant. See *German Federal Republic* v. *EEC Commission* (1963), 9 Rec. 269, at p. 302; [1963] C.M.L.R. 369.

9 *Netherlands* v. *High Authority* (1955), 1 Rec. 201, at pp. 226, 227; Valentine II, 203; *Groupement des Hauts Fourneaux et Aciéries Belges* v. *High Authority* (1958), 4 Rec. 223, at p. 256; Valentine II, 511; *Chambre Syndicale de la Sidérurgie Française* v. *High Authority* (1965), 11 Rec. 567; see also *Cie. des Hauts Fourneaux de Chasse* v. *High Authority* (1958), 4 Rec. 129, at p. 147; Valentine II, 502; *ibid.* (1958), 4 Rec. 155, at p. 195; Valentine II, 485; *Eva von Lachmüller* v. *EEC Commission* (1960), 6 Rec. 933, at p. 956; Valentine II, 777. The corresponding approach in English law is expressed in *Schmidt* v. *Secretary of State for Home Affairs*, [1969] 2 Ch. D. 149, at pp. 166, 168; *R.* v. *Brixton Prison (Governor), Ex p. Soblen*, [1963] 2 Q.B. 243, at p. 302.

10 *Fédéchar* v. *High Authority* (1956), 2 Rec. 291, at p. 309; Valentine II, 103; Bebr, *op. cit.* above, n. 3, at p. 106.

a remedy is limited by the consideration that incidental or subsidiary motives of an extraneous character are disregarded.[1]

The time for applying to the Community Court for the review and annulment of a measure by the Council or the Commission is two months either from the date when the measure was published or when the applicant was notified of the measure or when he came to know of it (art. 173, 3rd para.)[2] If the application for annulment is successful, the Court must declare the measure to be null and void (art. 174, 1st para.),[3] subject to the blue pencil rule, if a regulation is involved (art. 174, 2nd para.). In stating that the measure is void, the Treaty has emphasised the effect *inter partes* of an annulling decision by imposing upon the Community organ involved the duty to take the necessary measures for implementing this decision (art. 176). This provision has been held to imply that the prior position must be restored.[4] The measure must be abrogated and must not be confirmed or re-introduced.[5]

2 Jurisdiction to Declare a Failure to Act (art. 175)[6]

The rules on the appeal for annulment are balanced by those which deal with complaints against the failure of the Council or the Commission to act, contrary to the Treaty[7] (art. 175; *recours en carence*). Here again the parties are not restricted to the member states and the Community organs. While an organ of the Community appears as the defendant, another organ of the Community or a member state or, in certain circumstances, a legal entity or an individual may appear as the plaintiff.[8]

The complaint can only be brought, if the Community organ has been requested to act, and has not stated its attitude within two months after the request has been made; it must be lodged within another two months. The failure of the Community organ to rule or to take a position is the object of the charge, which cannot be levelled if, following the request to act, the Community organ has taken a measure, though not in terms which the complainant wanted to see adopted or thought necessary.[9] However, a legal entity or an individual only has a *locus standi*[10] if the Community organ has failed to address to him or it an act other than a recommendation or an opinion.[11]

---

1 Jeantet and Kovar, Juriscl. Dr. Int., Fasc. 161 C, Pt. II(2), Nos. 53, 57.
2 For examples see *Milchwerke Heinz Wöhrmann* v. *EEC Commission* (1962), 8 Rec. 965, at p. 981; [1963] C.M.L.R. 152; *Germany* v. *EEC Commission* (1971), 17 Rec. 669; [1972] C.M.L.R. 431.
3 For the problem of "inexistent" public measures see Empel, 1971 Cah. Dr. Eur. 251, at p. 269. For the revocation of such measures see Däubler, 1965 N.J.W. 1646.
4 *EEC Commission* v. *EEC Council* (1971), 17 Rec. 263, at p. 279(59)–(60); [1971] C.M.L.R. 335.
5 *Bode* v. *EEC Commission* (1971), 17 Rec. 465, at p. 476(12).
6 Bebr, *Judicial Control of the European Communities*, pp. 111–129; in *Ganshof van der Meersch,* p. 320, no. 893–p. 330, no. 920; Reuter, 1972 Cah. Dr. Eur. 159.
7 Or to any regulations made thereunder; see below, n. 9, p. 321, n. 5.
8 Art. 175, 1st and 3rd paras.
9 *Deutscher Komponistenverband* v. *EEC Commission* (1971), 17 Rec. 705, at p. 710(2).
10 See above, p. 315, n. 7.
11 Art. 175, 3rd para.

The insistence, at least where complaints by individuals or legal entities are concerned, that the act should have been addressed to them, but has not, and must not be in the nature of a recommendation or opinion, indicates positively that the action which has been requested must have been for a decision.[1] Negatively it has been held to exclude a request for a measure of a general character, such as a regulation,[2] or in respect of the omission by the Commission, upon a request by an individual, to take action against a member state for having failed to carry out its obligations under the Treaty,[3] if this omission occurred in pre-contentious proceedings and did not involve a binding act of the Commission.[4] At the same time the refusal of the Commission to revoke a previous decision is not a failure to act which attracts the *recours en carence*.[5] The Community Court has indicated generally that the notion of a "measure" as envisaged by art. 175 is identical with that employed in art. 173.[6] In the latter connection, it will be remembered, the nature of the act and not its outward appearance counts.[7]

Thus a request for what in substance was advice by the Commission as to the duty of the complainant to comply with a draft statute of a member state was held to fall outside the ambit of the *recours en carence* as circumscribed by art. 175 since it could not culminate in a decision.[8]

As in the case of a successful complaint for annulment, a judgment declaring a Community organ to have defaulted on its obligations under the Treaty obliges the organ to make good the defect (art. 176, para. (1)).[9]

IV BY PRIVATE PERSONS IN PROCEEDINGS BY OR AGAINST THE COMMUNITY (arts. 172, 178, 181)

While the jurisdiction of the Court in the circumstances considered hitherto, and in most circumstances still to be examined, is restricted to the control of the legality of the acts of the Community organs or of member states in proceedings which are not unlike those in England involving *certiorari*, the Court, in certain cases, has also jurisdiction to determine a claim on the merits by considering the facts and then by applying the applicable Community law, not unlike a domestic court dealing with matters of private law.

---

1 *Chevalley* v. *Italy* (1970), 16 Rec. 975, at p. 980(10)–(11).
2 *Mackprang* v. *EEC Commission* (1970), 17 Rec. 797, at p. 804(4); [1972] C.M.L.R. 52.
3 Art. 169.
4 *Lütticke GmbH* v. *EEC Commission* (1966), 12 Rec. 27, at p. 39; [1966] C.M.L.R. 378.
5 *Eridania* v. *EEC Commission* (1969), 15 Rec. 459, at pp. 482(16), 483(17); the proper remedy is a complaint in accordance with art. 173 subject to the conditions laid down in that article. Arts. 173 and 175 embody one and the same remedy: see *Chevalley* v. *Italy* (below) and are not concurrent.
6 *Chevalley* v. *Italy* (1970), 16 Rec. 975, at p. 979(6).
7 See above, p. 316, n. 2.
8 *Chevalley* v. *Italy* (above); *Borromeo* v. *EEC Commission* (1970), 16 Rec. 815, at p. 819(6)–(9); [1970] C.M.L.R. 436.
9 See above, p. 320, n. 4.

(a) Such is the case, in the first place, where a Council regulation made on the strength of an enabling provision of the Treaty confers on the Court jurisdiction to try a case on the merits (art. 172). The extent of this potential jurisdiction is not quite clear. The French texts speak of *"compétence de pleine juridiction en ce qui concerne les sanctions . . ."* which is a term well known in French administrative law.[1] In the words of Neville Brown and Garner "The 'fullness' of the jurisdiction lies in the fact that the court goes beyond merely annulling what the administration has done; it seeks in addition to amend what has been done by awarding damages against the administration in favour of the victim . . . it exercises the full and complete powers of a judge, just as the civil courts habitually do in compensating for torts or breaches of contract . . . the judge may go beyond the quashing of the administrative act in order to revise the decision itself.[2] The German text, which is framed in terms alien to German law, appears to paraphrase the French version when it refers to ". . . *Zuständigkeit . . . welche die Befugnis zur unbeschränkten Ermessensnachprüfung und zur Änderung oder Verhängung solcher Massnahmen umfasst"*.[3]

Based on an enabling provision of the Treaty (art. 87) the Council has provided in Reg. 17/62[4] that the Court has full jurisdiction within the meaning of art. 172 of the Treaty to adjudicate by way of judicial review on proceedings instituted against decisions by which the Commission has imposed a fine[5] or penalty upon an individual or upon a legal entity[6] for a violation of arts. 85 or 86 of the Treaty and may cancel, reduce or increase them. So far the Court has been called upon to exercise this power in three cases only.[7]

Acting by virtue of another provision of the Treaty (art. 79) the Council promulgated Reg. 11/60 dealing with discriminatory action by carriers in inter-Community transport.[8] In so far as it empowers the Commission to impose penalties for failure to submit information required under the Regulation, for supplying false information or for maintaining discriminatory practices,[9] the Community Court has jurisdiction to try the case on the merits by virtue of the power granted in art. 172 and exercised by Reg. 11/60.[10]

(b) While arts. 87 and 79 of the Treaty and Council Regs. 17/62 and 11/60 deal with complaints by individuals and legal entities against fines

---

1 Neville Brown and Garner, *French Administrative Law* (2nd Edn. 1973), p. 94.

2 *Ibid.*

3 *Competenza giurisdizionale anche di merito per quanto riguarda le sanzione previste; volledige rechtsmacht . . . wat betreft de sancties . . .*

4 OJ, 1962, 204, art. 17; see above, p. 215.

5 Reg. 17/62, art. 15.

6 Reg. 17/62, art. 16.

7 *ACF Chemiefarma* v. *EEC Commission* (1970), 16 Rec. 661; *ICI* v. *EEC Commission*, [1972] C.M.L.R. 557; *Continental Can* v. *EEC Commission*, [1973] C.M.L.R. 199. It must not be overlooked, however, that any Commission decision made by virtue of Reg. 17/62 is also subject to the Court's annulment jurisdiction under art. 173.

8 OJ, 1960, 1121.

9 Reg. 11/60, arts. 17, 18.

10 Art. 25(2).

and penalties imposed upon them, art. 178 envisages the exercise by the Court of its full jurisdiction on the merits in actions in tort brought by individuals and legal entities against the Community for damages caused by its institutions or by its employees in the performance of their duties (art. 215, 2nd para.).

In determining the liability of the Community in tort the Court is to follow the general principles common to the laws of member states (art. 215, 2nd para.).[1] Given the dichotomy in continental law which distinguishes between the liability in tort of individuals determined by private law and that of the state for its own acts and for those of its employees in the exercise of their duties determined by special rules of administrative law in some countries and by the general law of civil liability in others, the question has been put whether the general principles common to the laws of member states which are to be observed in the present context are confined to those enshrined in administrative law.[2] The answer must be found in the broad notion of state responsibility for torts, and not in the procedural and jurisdictional niceties of the domestic law of the member states.[3]

There must be damage, an illegal act for which the Community is to be blamed and a causal link between the damage and the act of the Community.[4] A claim for unliquidated damages is insufficient[5] and if the liability of a member state is also engaged, the local remedies must have been exhausted first.[6] The requirement that the act must be illicit raises the problem, much disputed in continental law, whether it suffices if the act complained of violates a public duty in general, or whether it must adversely affect a protected interest of the plaintiff.[7] The practice of the Court, which was concerned with the infringement of agricultural marketing regulations, shows that the violation of the Treaty or of any implementing legislation alone coupled with damage supports a claim, even if the rule which has been infringed is not individually or directly for

---

1   See above, p. 14, n. 1; Jeantet and Kovar, Juriscl. Dr. Int., Fasc. 161 C, Pt, III, Nos. 23, 28; Goffin in *Ganshof van der Meersch*, p. 333, no. 922–p. 339 no. 947. Much in *Haftung des Staates für rechtswidriges Verhalten seiner Organe* (1967), pp. 723–752; Lagrange, (1965–66) 3 C.M.L.Rev. 32.

2   Jeantet and Kovar, Juriscl. Dr. Int., Fasc. 161 C, Pt. III, No. 23 citing *Plaumann* v. *EEC Commission* (1963), 9 Rec. 197, *per* Adv. Gen. Roemer at p. 241; *Kampffmeyer* v. *EEC Commission* (1967), 13 Rec. 317, at pp. 339 and 352 *per* Adv. Gen. Gand and see the note by Goffin, 1968 Cah. Dr. Eur. 83.

3   See *Kampffmeyer* v. *EEC Commission* (above) at p. 352, *per* Adv. Gen. Gand.

4   *Lütticke* v. *EEC Commission* (1971), 17 Rec. 325, at pp. 337–338(1); *Richez-Parise* v. *EEC Commission* (1970), 16 Rec. 325, at p. 339(31), (36); *Zuckerfabrik Schöppenstedt* v. *EEC Council* (1971), 17 Rec. 975, at p. 985(11); *Kampffmeyer* v. *EEC Commission* (1967), 13 Rec. 317, at pp. 339, 340.

5   *Zuckerfabrik Schöppenstedt* v. *EEC Council* (above) at p. 984(9); nor is an estimated sum sufficient: *Luhleich* v. *EEC Commission* (1965), 11 Rec. 727, at p. 753.

6   See *Kampffmeyer* v. *EEC Commission* (1967), 13 Rec. 317, at p. 341; André, 1968 N.J.W. 331.

7   See Goffin, 1968 Cah. Dr. Eur. 83, at pp. 87–89. For protected interests in the law of tort see Lipstein, 1963 C.L.J. 85. In terms of English law the question is whether the duty must be to the plaintiff; see *Phillips* v. *Britannia Hygienic Laundry Co., Ltd.*, [1923] 1 K.B. 539.

the plaintiff's benefit.[1] The act violating the Treaty or its implementing legislation must be one for which the Community is to be blamed.[2] In the words of the Commission a *"faute de service"* must be proved.[3] This consists in the malfunctioning of the public service, although no specific fault can be imputed to any one officer of that service.[4] Thus the Community has been held responsible for the misinterpretation of a regulation after a request for a detailed examination of its provisions and implications.[5] It has likewise been held responsible for what had turned out to be a wrong application of an agricultural regulation,[6] not because the defendant Commission had misinterpreted the implications of certain facts when it exercised its regulating powers, but because it misinterpreted the range and purpose of the regulations within its own setting.[7] At the same time the suggestion that it was necessary to prove *faute lourde* or gross negligence was rejected without further argument.[8] The fact that a recourse may lie under arts. 173 or 175 for a violation of the Treaty or of implementing legislation is no bar to an action for damages under arts. 178, 215(2) as an alternative. The claim against the Community for damages in respect of liability in tort for its own acts or that of its employees is an autonomous remedy.[9] While the former leads to the suppression of the measure, the latter facilitates the recovery of damages caused by an institution in the exercise of its functions.[10] However, if the alternative complaint arises under art. 173(2), the question remains as to whether a claim for damages can be brought by an individual unless and until the underlying decision has been annulled first.[11]

Actions in tort against the Community are barred after the lapse of five years from the time when the facts occurred which gave rise to the claim,[12] subject to the usual exceptions which prevent the period of limitation from

---

1 *Kampffmeyer* v. *EEC Commission* (1967), 13 Rec. 317, at p. 340. It must be noted that the term directly and individually is employed here in relation to a regulation and not, as in arts. 173 and 175, to a decision; but see *Zuckerfabrik Schöppenstedt* v. *EEC Council* (1971), 17 Rec. 975, at p. 985(11).

2 *Richez-Parise* v. *EEC Commission* (1970), 16 Rec. 325, at p. 339(31); *Fiehn* v. *EEC Commission* (1970), 16 Rec. 547, at p. 549(18); but see Goffin, 1968 Cah. Dr. Eur. 83, at p. 86 and n. 7.

3 *Richez-Parise* v. *EEC Commission* (above); *Kampffmeyer* v. *EEC Commission* (1967), 13 Rec. 317, at p. 339, 6th para.

4 Neville Brown and Garner, *French Administrative Law* (2nd Edn. 1973), at p. 100.

5 See above, n. 2.

6 *Toepfer* v. *EEC Commission* (1965), 11 Rec. 525.

7 *Kampffmeyer* v. *EEC Commission* (1967), 13 Rec. 317. The particular act of misinterpretation is described successively (p. 339) as *fautive, erronnée* and *abusive.*

8 *Kampffmeyer* v. *EEC Commission* (above) at p. 340, 1st para., but see Goffin, 1968 Cah. Dr. Eur. 83, at p. 87 and n. 11.

9 *Lütticke* v. *EEC Commission* (1971), 17 Rec. 325, at p. 337(6); *Zuckerfabrik Schöppenstedt* v. *EEC Council* (1971), 17 Rec. 975, at p. 984(3).

10 *Zuckerfabrik Schöppenstedt* v. *EEC Council* (as above). For the same practice under the ECSC Treaty see *Vloeberghs* v. *High Authority* (1961), 7 Rec. 391, at p. 424.

11 *Plaumann* v. *EEC Commission* (1963), 9 Rec. 197, at p. 225; Goffin in *Ganshof van der Meersch*, p. 338, no. 944.

12 Protocol on the Statute of the Court of Justice, art. 43. It is debated whether this is the time of acting or the time when the damage occurred.

running. The *compétence de pleine juridiction* of the Community Court is restricted to claims against the Community for damages sounding in tort (arts. 178, 215, 2nd para.). It does not extend to contractual claims arising out of a contract entered into by or on behalf of the Community unless the parties have included in the contract a clause submitting to the jurisdiction of the Community Court (art. 181).[1] Adopting the technique and the terminology of French administrative law, which distinguishes between "contrats administratifs" and "contrats privés",[2] the Treaty states that a contractual submission to the jurisdiction is valid in both cases (art. 181).

Such contracts are governed by the law applicable to the contract concerned (art. 215, 1st para.) but this seemingly straightforward rule assumes that uniform choice of law rules in matters of contract exist within the Community which determine, above all, the validity and the extent of free choice of law and indicate the law applicable when no express choice of law has been made. To complicate matters the choice of law governing "administrative contracts" must raise new problems if the law of the only member state which may be involved ignores this distinction, and is not easily solved even if it does.[3]

(c) The Community also has *compétence de pleine juridiction*, within the limits laid down by the Statute of Service[4] and the terms of employment, in disputes between the Community and its employees (art. 179). In view of its special character affecting functionaries of the Community only, the considerable practice of the Court in this field need not be considered here.

V By any Party in Proceedings in the Community Court— Exception d'Illégalité (art. 184)[5]

While the legality of any Community measures other than recommendations and opinions can be challenged within a short time-limit in order to have the measure annulled (art. 173),[6] a regulation of the Council or of the Commission which is the subject of legal proceedings in the

---

1 In the absence of such a clause, the jurisdiction of the domestic courts of the member states remains untouched, even if the Community is the defendant (art. 183). However the Community enjoys immunity from levy of execution: see the Protocol on the Privileges and Immunities of the European Economic Community, art. 1.

2 Neville Brown and Garner, *French Administrative Law* (2nd Edn. 1973), at pp. 70–73, 110–114.

3 Batiffol, *Droit International Privé* (1967, 4 Edn.) p. 631, no. 577, n. 30; same in Dalloz, *Répertoire de Droit International* (1968), Vol. I, p. 564, no. 14; Toubiana, *ibid.*, p. 576, no. 9; Conseil d'Etat 11 January 1952, S. 1952.3.67, [1952] Rec. Lebon 30; *Habib Bechara.*

4 Reg. 31/62, OJ, 1962, 1385, as amended by Reg. 259/68, OJ, 1968, L 56/1; 1473/72, OJ, 1972, L 170/1; Reg. 2647/72, OJ, 1972, L 283/1; 558/73, OJ, 1973, L 55/1; see also OJ, 1972, C 122/52.

5 Bebr, *Judicial Control of the European Communities*, at pp. 138–148; same, (1966–67) 4 C.M.L.Rev. 7; Jeantet and Kovar, Juriscl. Dr. Int., Fasc. 161 C, Pt. II(1), No. 82; Goffin in *Ganshof van der Meersch*, p. 334, no. 928–p. 339, no. 947.

6 See above, p. 315.

Community Court[1] may be challenged in these proceedings[2] without any restriction in time with a view to obtaining a declaration that the regulation concerned or a measure based on it,[3] if it concerns a complainant directly or indirectly,[4] is inapplicable (art. 184). The principle formulated here expresses the rule enshrined in art. 184 as developed by the practice of the Community Court.

A regulation of the Council or of the Commission must be the subject of legal proceedings (art. 184, beginning). Although the text of art. 184 does not restrict the exception of illegality to proceedings in the Community Court and does not exclude in so many words the consideration of exceptions of illegality on a reference from domestic courts where legal proceedings are pending, the parallel remedy provided by art. 177 which enables domestic courts but not the parties to request a preliminary ruling by the Community Court, *inter alia* on the validity of acts of the institutions of the Community, appears to rule out a second remedy for the control of Community acts in domestic courts. The Community Court has pointed out that any other conclusion would enable the parties, as distinct from the Court, as art. 177 provides, to force a suspension of the proceedings in a domestic court and, moreover, to avail themselves of a remedy which is equivalent in substance to that provided by art. 173, even after the time limit set in art. 173(3) has expired.[5] Thus the proceedings must be pending in the Community Court.

The regulation of the Council or of the Commission must be in issue, directly or indirectly, in the proceedings pending before the Community Court.[6]

The parties concerned, as the reference to art. 173, 3rd para. indicates (art. 184), are those which can raise a complaint of annulment, namely member states,[7] possibly the Council or the Commission as an intervener or by an invitation of the Court[8] and individual parties. The latter, as the express reference in art. 184 to art. 173, 1st para., and the omission of a reference to art. 173, 2nd para. shows, are placed on an equal footing with member states and are not restricted to situations involving decisions addressed to them or to decisions in the form of regulations or of decisions addressed to other persons which are of direct and individual concern to

---

1   *Milchwerke Heinz Wöhrmann* v. *EEC Commission* (1962), 8 Rec. 965, at p. 979; [1963] C.M.L.R. 152.

2   The particular regulation or measure based on it must be in issue in these proceedings on the ground that it is directly or indirectly applicable; the remedy of the *exception d'illégalité* does not extend to the application of any regulation in any proceedings whatsoever. See *Italy* v. *EEC Council and Commission* (1966), 12 Rec. 563, at p. 594; [1969] C.M.L.R. 39.

3   Bebr, *op. cit.* above, p. 325, n. 5, at p. 146; but see Bebr, (1966–67) 4 C.M.L.Rev. at p. 13.

4   *Italy* v. *EEC Council and Commission* (1966), 12 Rec. 563, at p. 594 (above).

5   *Milchwerke Heinz Wöhrmann* v. *EEC Commission* (1962) 8 Rec. 965, at pp. 979–980; see also *Hessische Knappschaft* v. *Singer* (1965), 11 Rec. 1191, at p. 1199, [1965] C.M.L.R. 257.

6   *Italy* v. *EEC Council and Commission* (1966), 12 Rec. 563, at p. 594.

7   Or in proceedings under arts. 169, 170; Bebr, *Judicial Control of the European Communities*, at pp. 144–145.

8   Bebr, (1966–67) 4 C.M.L.Rev. 7, at pp. 16–17.

them. This is natural, since art. 184 envisages an exception of illegality against regulations only.

The grounds on which the exception of illegality may be raised are the same as those enumerated in art. 173 for a complaint of annulment.[1]

In pleading the exception of illegality a party alleges that the regulation in issue is inapplicable (art. 184). If the plea succeeds the Court must make a declaration to this effect, which operates *inter partes* only and from the time of the judgment only. The Community Court cannot and does not, thereby annul the regulation concerned, which remains in force nominally, but is likely to be amended or revoked in response to the decision of the Community Court.

VI On a Reference by Domestic Courts administering Community Law (art. 177)[2]

While the exception of illegality cannot be pleaded in proceedings before a court in a member state where the Treaty or a regulation made thereunder falls to be applied, another device enables the court, though not the parties, to test the validity of Community measures[3] by the same procedure which serves principally to safeguard the uniform interpretation of the Treaty and of regulations promulgated by the Community (art. 177).[4]

The Community Court has jurisdiction to make a preliminary ruling[5] concerning the interpretation of the EEC Treaty, the validity and interpretation of acts of the institutions of the Community and (what is less important) the interpretation of the statutes of any bodies set up by an act of the Council, if these statutes so provide (art. 177(a)–(c)).

The jurisdiction to make a preliminary ruling can only be invoked by the courts of the member states. If a question involving the interpretation (as distinct from the application) of Community law or the validity of acts of institutions of the Community is raised in such a court, the latter, if not a court of last resort, may refer the question to the Community Court, if it considers that the determination of this question is necessary for the determination of the litigation pending before it. If the domestic court is a court of last resort from which no appeal lies according to domestic law,

---

1 See above, pp. 315–320.

2 Jeantet and Kovar, Juriscl. Dr. Int., Fasc. 161 C, Pt. IV, Nos. 1–160; Dumon in *Ganshof van der Meersch*, p. 341, no. 948–p. 366, no. 1015; Bebr, *op. cit.* above, p. 326, n. 7, at pp. 180–202; Hay, 1971 Cah. Dr. Eur. 503; Mashaw, (1970) 6 C.M.L.Rev. 258, 423; Buxbaum, (1969) 21 Stanford L.R. 1041; Daig, 1968 EuR 259, at p. 371; Juillard, 1968 Rev. Trim. Dr. Eur. 293; Constantinesco, 1967, B.B.A.W.D. 125; Gaudet in *Festschrift für Hallstein* (1966), p. 202; Ferrari-Bravo, in *Communicazioni e Studi* XII (1966), p. 415; Pepy, 1966 Cah. Dr. Eur. 459.

3 *Grad* v. *Finanzamt Traunstein* (1970), 16 Rec. 825, at p. 839(6); [1971] C.M.L.R. 1; *Transports Lesage* v. *Hauptzollamt Freiburg* (1970), 16 Rec. 861, at p. 875(6); [1971] C.M.L.R. 1; *Haselhorst* v. *Finanzamt Düsseldorf* (1970), 16 Rec. 881, at p. 894(6); [1971] C.M.L.R. 1.

4 *Molkerei-Zentrale Westfalen-Lippe* v. *Hauptzollamt Paderborn* (1968), 14 Rec. 211, at p. 228, [1968] C.M.L.R. 187, at p. 219; *Klomp* v. *Inspektie der Belastingen* (1969), 15 Rec. 43, at p. 50(12).

5 "*A titre préjudiciel*", "*Vorabscheidung*", "*in via pregiudiziale*", "*prejudiciële beslissing*".

it must refer the question to the Community Court (art. 177, 2nd and 3rd paras.).[1]

1 Problems arising out of Domestic Law

The request for a preliminary ruling must be presented by a Court. According to the Community Court a decision-making body has this characteristic if it is regularly established in accordance with the domestic law of the member state where it functions, is a permanent organ charged generally with the determination of certain types of disputes, is bound by rules of contentious procedure similar to those applicable in the ordinary courts, if its members are appointed by the authorities of the state concerned, if it exercises compulsory jurisdiction over the parties and applies rules of law.[2] The problems have been much debated whether courts exercising jurisdiction to take urgent measures[3] and arbitral tribunals[4] are called upon to submit requests for a preliminary ruling. It is now clear that it applies to *ex parte* proceedings.[5] As regards arbitral tribunals, the wording, at least in the French version, which speaks of a "jurisdiction" of a member state, does not provide clear guidance.[6] However, the purpose of art. 177, which is to guarantee a uniform application of Community law, does not require an extension to arbitral tribunals, the territorial situation of which is determined by the parties who can also select the law to be applied. Moreover, in English law the faculty to have a case stated opens the way to the Community Court through the corridors of the High Court in London.

If a reference to the Community Court by a lower court in a member state coincides with an appeal to a higher court within the member state, the local appeal does not oust the jurisdiction of the Community Court to give a preliminary ruling.[7] At the same time it is no bar to a request for a preliminary ruling that the request is raised for the first time on appeal.[8]

---

1 Within the framework of the question submitted for a Preliminary Ruling, legal arguments by a party attacking a measure under review on grounds other than those raised in the court of the member state are admitted; see *Beus GmbH* v. *Hauptzollamt München* (1968), 14 Rec. 128, at p. 144; [1968] C.M.L.R. 131.

2 *Vaassen-Göbbels* v. *Beambtenfonds voor het Mijnbedrijf* (1966), 12 Rec. 377, at pp. 394–395; [1966] C.M.L.R. 508; Storm, 1967 Cah. Dr. Eur. 311, at pp. 313 ff. attributes little general importance to this decision on the ground that it only describes the judicial nature of the particular Dutch tribunal under review and omits the characteristic that it must give binding decisions (at p. 314). However, the enumeration of its characteristics indicates the tests on which the Community Court relies, and the criterion of compulsory jurisdiction seems to imply a compulsory termination of disputes. It is true that the Community Court has not stated that these criteria constitute the minimum requirements if a body is to qualify as a court for the purposes of art. 177.

3 Jeantet and Kovar, Juriscl. Dr. Int., Fasc. 161 C, Pt. IV, Nos. 29, 31.

4 Mok and Johannes, 1965 B.B.A.W.D. 181; Cohn, 1965 *ibid.* 267 with lit., n. 1; Storm, 1967 Cah. Dr. Eur. 311, at pp. 315 ff with lit., p. 316, n. 3; Mok, (1967–68) 5 C.M.L.Rev. 458.

5 *Politi* v. *Italy* (1971), 17 Rec. 1039, at p. 1048(4).

6 The German and the Dutch texts referring to a *"Gericht"* or *"een rechterlijke instantie"* support a negative answer.

7 *De Geus* v. *Bosch GmbH* (1962), 8 Rec. 89, at pp. 101–103; [1962] C.M.L.R. 1.

8 *Parke, Davis & Co.* v. *Probel* (1968), 14 Rec. 81, at p. 84; [1968] C.M.L.R. 47.

According to the Treaty (art. 177, last para.) a court of last resort in a member state from whose decisions no appeal lies under municipal law is bound to ask for a preliminary ruling, if a question arises which involves the interpretation of Community law or the validity of Community law. Here the question is whether the possibility of an appeal, by leave of the court *a quo* or *ad quem*, renders the court *a quo* a court of last resort retrospectively, if leave to appeal to the highest court is refused. In practice the answer is likely to be that leave will be given if a pertinent question of Community law is raised in the appeal.

The fact that the domestic court, whether acting *proprio motu* or at the invitation of the parties, must formulate and submit the question which is to be the object of a preliminary ruling, ensures the objective evaluation of the pertinence of the question placed before the Community Court. Consequently it suffices that in contentious proceedings in a court of a member state a question has been formulated which clearly concerns the interpretation or validity of Community law or acts[1] to be determined by the Community Court in non-contentious proceedings; the form of the question and its pertinence in the proceedings before the court of the member state are no concern of the Community Court.[2] The court, unless it is a court of last resort, remains free not to refer to the Community Court a question of Community law which it is willing to answer itself in the exercise of a concurrent jurisdiction.[3] The wording of art. 177, last para., appears to impose an absolute restriction on the exercise of such a concurrent jurisdiction upon courts of last instance in the member states, but in practice the prohibition is less than complete. In the first place, a question of interpretation can, but need not, be referred, if the Community Court has already pronounced on it elsewhere.[4] In the second place, the practice of the *Conseil d'Etat* in France (*acte clair*)[5] and of some

---

1 The parties to the underlying dispute are not strictly speaking parties to the proceedings for a Preliminary Ruling, which are non-contentious; see *Da Costa en Schaake* v. *Nederlandse Administratie der Belastingen* (1963), 9 Rec. 59, at p. 76; [1963] C.M.L.R. 224; *Hessische Knappschaft* v. *Singer* (1965), 11 Rec. 1191, at pp. 1198–1199, [1965] C.M.L.R. 257; *Rheinmühlen Düsseldorf* v. *Einfuhr- und Vorratsstelle für Getreide* (1971), 17 Rec. 719, at p. 720(1), (2).

2 *Milchwerke Heinz Wöhrmann* v. *EEC Commission* (1962), 8 Rec. 965, at p. 980; [1963] C.M.L.R. 152; *Van Gend en Loos* v. *Nederlandse Administratie der Belastingen* (1963), 9 Rec. 1, at p. 22. [1963] C.M.L.R. 105; *Hessische Knappschaft* v. *Singer* (as above); *LTM* v. *Maschinenbau Ulm GmbH* (1966), 12 Rec. 337, at p. 357; [1966] C.M.L.R. 357.

3 Thus the lower courts of a member state would appear to be able to refuse to apply Community acts on the ground that they are invalid. See Jeantet and Kovar, Jur.scl. Dr. Int., Fasc. 161 C, Pt. IV, No. 77.

4 *NV Internationale Crediet- en Handelsvereniging "Rotterdam"* v. *Minister of Agriculture etc.* (1964), 10 Rec. 1, at p. 25; [1969] C.M.L.R. 198; *Milch-, Fett- und Eierkontor GmbH* v. *Hauptzollamt Saarbrücken* (1964), 15 Rec. 165, at p. 180(3); [1969] C.M.L.R. 390: the Community Court's interpretation binds national courts, but leaves it to the latter to decide whether further instruction is needed; see above, p. 33, n. 7.

5 *Soc. des Pétroles Shell-Berre*, 19 June 1964, [1964] Rec, Lebon 344, at p. 347; see also *Syndicat Nationale des Importateurs des produits laitiers*, 25 January 1967, [1967] Rec. Lebon 41, at p. 42; *Soc. des Et. Petitjean*, 10 February 1967, [1967] Rec. Lebon 63, at p. 65; *Comité Nationale de la Meunerie d'Exportation*, 15 February 1967, [1967] Rec. Lebon 73; Colliard,
[footnote continued on next page

other courts of last resort[1] shows that a question of interpretation in the meaning of art. 177, last para., is not identical with the need to apply Community law and poses a problem only if it is of such complexity[2] as to give rise to serious doubts in the minds of the members of the court of last resort; that it gives rise to a controversy between the parties is insufficient.

2   Problems arising out of Community Law

The wording of art. 177 and the function of the Community Court, as the Court itself sees it, as the guardian of a uniform interpretation of the Treaty,[3] have induced the Court, from an early time onwards, to offer only an abstract interpretation of the Treaty provision or implementing measure to which it is referred.[4] The Court cannot consider the facts of the case[5] or any aspects or characteristics of domestic law[6] and cannot render a decision on the merits by applying the Treaty or any implementing measures.[7] Nor can it determine whether the question submitted for a preliminary ruling is pertinent in the circumstances of the particular case which led to the reference by the national court,[8] except, perhaps, if the reliance by the domestic court on the text of the Treaty or an implementing measure is manifestly erroneous.[9] It is difficult to see how such a conclusion can be reached, divorced from the facts, even if the criterion put forward tentatively by the Community Court is adopted, whether the Community rule is directly applicable or the Community act directly affects the private party to the dispute.[10] Since proceedings for a prelimin-

---

D. 1964, Chr. 263; Lesguillons, 1968 Cah. Dr. Eur. 253; Lassalle, (1971) 11 Riv. Dir. Eur. 193.

1   See above, p. 42, n. 1, Jeantet and Kovar, Juriscl. Dr. Int., Fasc. 161 C, Pt. IV, No. 77; Gaudet in *Festschrift für Hallstein* (1966), pp. 202, 216.

2   *Albatros* v. *SOPECO* (1965), 11–3 Rec. 1, at p. 10; [1965] C.M.L.R. 159.

3   See above, p. 326, n. 7, *Hagen* v. *Einfuhr- und Vorratsstelle für Getreide* (1972), 18 Rec. 23, at pp. 35(5), 36(9).

4   See above, p. 32, n. 4.

5   *Salgoil* v. *Foreign Trade Ministry of the Italian Republic* (1968), 14 Rec. 661, at p. 672; [1969] C.M.L.R. 181.

6   *Costa* v. *ENEL* (1964), 10 Rec. 1141, at p. 1158; [1964] C.M.L.R. 425; *Witt* v. *Hauptzollamt Lüneburg* (1970), 16 Rec. 1021, at p. 1026(2); [1971] C.M.L.R. 163; *Grad* v. *Finanzamt Traunstein* (1970), 16 Rec. 825, at p. 842(17); *Lesage* v. *Hauptzollamt Freiburg* (1970), 16 Rec. 861, at p. 878(18); *Haselhorst* v. *Finanzamt Düsseldorf* (1970), 16 Rec. 881, at p. 897(18); [1971] C.M.L.R. 1.

7   *Costa* v. *ENEL, Witt* v. *Hauptzollamt Lüneburg* (above, n. 6) and the cases cited above, p. 33, n. 2; *Caisse Régionale de Sécurité Sociale du Nord* v. *Torrekens* (1969), 15 Rec. 125, at p. 135(8); [1969] C.M.L.R. 377; *SA Portelange* v. *Smith Corona* (1969), 15 Rec. 309, at p. 315(5), (6); *Henck* v. *Hauptzollamt Emmerich* (1971), 17 Rec. 743, at p. 750(3).

8   See above, p. 33, n. 3; *SA Portelange* v. *Smith Corona* (1969), 15 Rec. 309, at p. 315(5)–(7); *Politi* v. *Italy* (1971), 17 Rec. 1039, at p. 1048(3).

9   *Salgoil* v. *Italy* (above, n. 5). The Community Court is very liberal in its practice which attributes the correct form and substance to the question as formulated by the domestic law, even if it is manifestly defective in its original form. See *Schwarze* v. *Einfuhr- und Vorratsstelle für Getreide* (1965), 11 Rec. 1081, at p. 1094; [1966] C.M.L.R. 172; *Beus* v. *Hauptzollamt München* (1968), 14 Rec. 125, at p. 139; [1968] C.M.L.R. 131.

10   *Grad* v. *Finanzamt Traunstein* (1970), 16 Rec. 825, at p. 839(6); [1971] C.M.L.R. 1.

ary ruling on a matter of interpretation are often specifically concerned with this very question, and always by implication, while the answer is sometimes positive and sometimes negative, it will be difficult for the Community Court to reject a request for a preliminary ruling on a point of interpretation as manifestly erroneous on this ground.[1] The criterion, which recalls the restriction of complaints for annulment (art. 173, 2nd para.), may, however, be of some use where the validity of Community acts is in issue. However, the Community Court can consider the facts as presented by the national court in order to elucidate the purport of the abstract question presented to it and in order to extract those aspects of the Treaty which require interpretation.[2] Furthermore, the Community Court will have regard to the complex of domestic law in the setting of which the request is made for a preliminary ruling on a question of Community law.[3] Thus the facts of the case, including domestic law as a separate legal order, are taken into account to a limited extent. Apparently it is impossible to interpret law in the abstract since interpretation assumes a dispute allowing for at least two possible answers.[4] The facts which give rise to the dispute must be considered for two purposes. They must be considered, firstly, in order to understand why a particular rule of Community law requires interpretation. This requires a knowledge of alternatives. Secondly they must be considered if the question formulated by a domestic court is not sufficiently clear and needs to be made more precise. However, the Community Court may only consider the facts to this limited extent, which defines the question in issue.[5] The decision itself is not concerned with the application of Community law to the facts and with any final determination on the merits.

The same conclusion applies to the consideration of the complex of domestic law in the setting of which the request for a preliminary ruling was made. The Community Court cannot interpret national law,[6] cannot determine its compatibility with Community law[7] or annul it.[8]

---

1 The conclusions to the contrary in *Grad* v. *Finanzamt Traunstein* (as above); *Lesage* v. *Hauptzollamt Freiburg* (1970), 16 Rec. 861. at p. 875(6); *Haselhorst* v. *Finanzamt Düsseldorf* (1970), 16 Rec. 881, at p. 894(6); [1971] C.M.L.R. 1 confuse questions of admissibility with those concerning the merits.

2 See *e.g. LMT* v. *Maschinenbau Ulm GmbH* (1966), 12 Rec. 337, at p. 357; [1966] C.M.L.R. 357; *Völk* v. *Vervaecke* (1969), 15 Rec. 295, at p. 302(2); [1969] C.M.L.R. 273; *Witt* v. *Hauptzollamt Lüneburg* (1970), 16 Rec. 1021, at p. 1026(2); *Deutsche Grammophon GmbH* v. *Metro-SB-Grossmärkte GmbH* (1971), 17 Rec. 487, at p. 498(3); [1971] C.M.L.R. 631; *Ministère Public of Italy* v. *Società Agricola Industria Latte*, [1972] C.M.L.R. 723, at p. 740(3); *Merluzzi* v. *Caisse d'Assurance Maladie de la Région Parisienne* (1972), 18 Rec. 175, at p. 179(4).

3 *Henck* v. *Hauptzollamt Emmerich* (1971), 17 Rec. 743, at pp. 750(3), 767, 774(3), 786(3).

4 See also Hay, 1971 Cah. Dr. Eur. 503, at pp. 512 ff.

5 In the result, this distinction may be blurred; see *e.g. Deutschmann* v. *Germany* (1965), 11 Rec. 601, at p. 608; Mashaw, (1970) 6 C.M.L.Rev. 258, pp. 266 ff, 424 ff.

6 See above, p. 33, n. 6.

7 See above, p. 33, n. 4.

8 See above, p. 33, n. 5.

VII ANCILLARY PROVISIONS

The fact that a Community measure has been made the object of proceedings in the Community Court does not automatically stay the operation of the measure, but the Court may order that its execution be suspended (art. 185) or may allow interim measures (art. 186). It will do so only if the need is urgent and is *prima facie* justified because grave and irreparable damage may occur.[1] Moreover, the measure in question must form the object of an appeal to the Community Court.[2] No stay can be granted to the effect that a statutory provision is inapplicable.[3] The Court may also order interim measures (art. 186).[4]

Decisions of the Council or of the Commission which impose a duty to pay a sum of money upon an individual or a legal entity must be enforced by member states in accordance with their rules of civil procedure as if they were judgments of a court (arts. 187, 192, 1st and 2nd paras). No control of the decisions is permitted other than that the document embodying it is authentic (art. 192, 2nd para.). The courts of the member state where execution is sought are alone competent to supervise the regularity of the measure of execution (art. 192, 4th para.), but the Community Court retains jurisdiction to suspend the levy of execution (art. 192, fourth para.).

---

1 *Europemballage and Continental Can* (1972), 18 Rec. 157, at p. 159(2); cp. *Germany* v. *EEC Commission* (1969), 15 Rec. 449, at p. 457(4) *per* Adv. Gen. Gand; *Acciaierie Stefana* v. *High Authority* (1967), 13 Rec. 365, at p. 367; *Plaumann & Co.* v. *EEC Commission* (1963), 9 Rec. 197, at pp. 261, 267(3); [1964] C.M.L.R. 29; *Lassalle* v. *European Parliament* (1964), 10 Rec. 57, at pp. 117, 118; [1964] C.M.L.R. 259; *Ley* v. *EEC Commission* (1965), 11 Rec. 175, at p. 176; *Gutmann* v. *Atomic Energy Commission* (1966), 12 Rec. 195, at pp. 197–198.
2 Rules of Procedure 83(1); *Leroy* v. *High Authority* (1963), 9 Rec. 433; [1964] C.M.L.R. 562.
3 *Leroy* v. *High Authority* (above).
4 See generally Ehle, 1964 B.B.A.W.D. 39.

20

Procedure[1]

I IN THE COMMUNITY COURT

While the Community Court must administer in differing circumstances the substantive provisions of the ECSC, the EEC and the Euratom Treaties, its procedure in applying them in contentious and non-contentious litigation is fairly uniform. Each of the Treaties is accompanied by a Protocol on the Statute of the Court of Justice (henceforth cited as "Statute"). Of these the protocols attached to the EEC and Euratom Treaties are practically identical;[2] that attached to the ECSC shows differences, but since the present discussion is concentrated on the EEC, the divergences in the protocol to the ECSC Treaty can be disregarded here. The protocols supply the basic structure for the Court and its daily operation.[3] They are supplemented by a single set of Rules of Procedure (henceforth called "Rules")[4] and by the instructions to the Registrar.[5]

The procedure is fashioned in accordance with the traditions of European courts which are based on practices which grew up in the 16th century and after. The initiative lies with the parties and to this extent the proceedings are adversary, but the conduct of the proceedings, especially the selection, production and taking of evidence, lies firmly in the hands of the Court, and to that extent the proceedings are inquisitorial. Unlike in the common law, the preparation of the case does not culminate in the day in court when the trial takes place. Instead, written pleadings, supplemented by the production of evidence, which is taken in separate sessions of the Community Court or upon request by a court in a member state,[6] precede the hearing which is formal in character.

---

1 Wall, *The Court of Justice of the European Communities* (1966), pp. 180–310; Cohn, *The Solicitor* (1962), p. 309; (1962) 223 L.T.Jo. 342; Jeantet and Kovar, Juriscl. Dr. Int., Fasc. 161 C, Pt. V; Chevalier in *Ganshof van der Meersch*, p. 391, no. 1090–p. 405, no. 1133; Ipsen, pp. 756–759; Valentine, *The Court of Justice of the European Communities I* (1965), pp. 43–108; Ule in *Gerichtsschutz gegen die Executive* (1970), pp. 1179–1215 *passim*.
2 A distinguishing feature of the Euratom Treaty is the appeal to the Community Court from the Arbitration Committee (art. 18).
3 EEC Treaty art. 188. For the organisation of the Community Court see Mathijsen, *A Guide to European Community Law* (1972), pp. 150–152, paras. 3.42–3.43; pp. 170–172; nos. 3.71–3.72; Lasok and Bridge, *Introduction to the Law and Institutions of the European Communities* (1972), pp. 146–153.
4 OJ, 1960, 17, amended by the Supplementary Rules, OJ, 1962, 1113 (Judicial Assistance) replacing the previous Rules, OJ, 1959, 349.
5 OJ, 1960, 1417, amended OJ, 1962, 1115; OJ, 1965, 2413.
6 Statute, arts. 24–28; Rules, arts. 47–53; Suppl. Rules, arts. 1–3.

1   The Complaint

The proceedings are begun by a complaint (*requête*)[1] which must be addressed to the Registrar.[2] It must contain the name and address of the petitioner,[3] a description of the respondent,[4] the subject matter of the action coupled with a summary of the main arguments,[5] the relief sought by the plaintiff[6] and an outline of the evidence, if any.[7] While the member states and the institutions of the Community are represented by an agent, who may be assisted by a legal adviser or counsel who is a member of the Bar of one of the member states, other parties must be represented by counsel who is a member of a Bar of one of the member states.[8] The complaint lodged with the Registrar must indicate the status of the person who signed it.[9] If he is not an agent but counsel, he must submit a certificate that he is a member of the Bar of a member state.[10] If the petitioner is a legal entity established according to private law, the memorandum and articles of association must be attached, together with evidence that counsel is acting under a valid authority.[11]

If the complaint is one for annulment in accordance with art. 173 or for a declaration establishing a failure to act according to art. 175 of the Treaty[12] the act complained of or (as the case may be) a document establishing the date of the request must be annexed to the complaint or produced within a reasonable time, which may exceed the time limit for appealing.[13]

If the jurisdiction of the Court is based on a submission clause in a contract (art. 181 of the Treaty) or an agreement concluded by member states (art. 182 of the Treaty)[14] a copy of the submission agreement must be attached.[15] On the other hand, if the request is for a preliminary ruling in accordance with art. 177[16] of the Treaty, the domestic court making the request must itself submit its request to the Community Court, which must notify the parties to the case, the member states and the Commission and

---

1   Statute, art. 19; Rules, art. 38.
2   Statute, art. 19.
3   Statute, art. 19; Rules, art. 38(1)(a).
4   Statute, art. 19; Rules, art. 38(1)(b).
5   Statute, art. 19; Rules, art. 38(1)(c).
6   Statute, art. 19; Rules, art. 38(1)(d).
7   Rules, art. 38(1)(e).
8   Statute, art. 17. For the rights, duties, privileges and immunities of Counsel see Rules, arts. 32–36.
9   Statute, art. 19; Rules, art. 37(1).
10   Rules, art. 38(3); no evidence is required to show that counsel has been lawfully instructed, unless his entitlement to represent the party is contested; see *Barge* v. *High Authority* (1965), 11 Rec. 4, at p. 10. For the legal status of counsel during the proceedings see Rules, arts. 32–36.
11   Rules, art. 38(5).
12   Above, pp. 315, 320.
13   Statute, art. 19; Rules 38(4).
14   See above, pp. 325, 313–314.
15   Rules, art. 38(6).
16   See above, p. 325.

in addition the Council, if the interpretation or validity of an act of the Council is in dispute,[1] but no others.[2] The complaint must contain the entire subject matter in dispute coupled with a complete statement of the relief sought, since no new matter can be submitted and no fresh relief can be sought during the later stages of the proceedings[3] except by leave of the Court for good reason.[4] Only a summary exposition of the nature of the complaint and of the arguments in support is required at this stage.[5] Further details, enlarging upon previous statements but not containing substantial modifications, are not excluded by this rule and can be put forward in the reply and in the oral proceedings.[6] In presenting the arguments in support of the claim it is sufficient if their substance is set out, even if they are not framed in the legal terminology of the rules on which the party relies, provided that it is clear which rules of the Treaty or of any implementing legislation are involved. Mere abstract references to any such rules, standing by themselves, do not fulfil the requirements of the Rules of Procedure (art. 38(1)(c), (d)), and the facts as alleged must support the grounds of the statement of claim.[7]

The Community Court has explained[8] the purpose of this practice which is to guide the Court in reaching its decision and to enlighten the respondent. The Court has not the power to adjudicate according to its own views as to what the claim or the defence should be. Its power of adjudication is determined by the statement of claim, and its insistence on a clear presentation of the subject matter in dispute, of the main arguments and the relief sought, is due to its concern not to go *ultra petita* and not to overlook any claims put forward. Moreover, the respondent must be enabled to formulate his defence.[9] Thus the danger exposed by Cohn (above, p. 333, note 1) is met by the Court itself.

The statement of claim must naturally appear in the complaint and cannot be put forward for the first time when the proceedings are no longer in the hands of the parties, but are directed by the Court (*instruction*).[10] However the Court has indicated that the complaint may contain

---

1 Statute, art. 20.

2 *De Cicco* v. *Landesversicherungsanstalt Schwaben* (1968), 14 Rec. 689, at p. 699; [1969] C.M.L.R. 67.

3 *Reinarz* v. *EEC Commission* (1969), 15 Rec. 61, at p. 73(47); but see Rules, art. 42(2); additional information enlarging on the original claim for damages is admissible; see *Plaumann.* v. *EEC Commission* (1963), 9 Rec. 197, at p. 224; [1964] C.M.L.R. 29.

4 Rules, art. 42(2); see below (3); *Cie. des Hauts Fourneaux de Chasse* v. *High Authority* (1962), 8 Rec. 719, at p. 736; *Krawczynski* v. *EEC Commission* (1965), 11 Rec. 773, at p. 785.

5 *Lemmerz Werke* v. *High Authority* (1965), 11 Rec. 835, at p. 858; [1968] C.M.L.R. 280.

6 *Müller* v. *EEC Commission* (1965), 11 Rec. 307, at pp. 322–323; *Plaumann* v. *EEC Commission* (1963), 9 Rec. 197, at p. 224; [1964] C.M.L.R. 29; see below, p. 337(3) for further details.

7 *Meroni* v. *High Authority* (1962), 8 Rec. 783, at p. 801.

8 *Fives Lille Cail* v. *High Authority* (1961), 7 Rec. 559, at pp. 588–589. However, a mistake in indicating the correct legal provision relied upon by the party is innocuous; see *X* v. *Commission of Control* (1969), 15 Rec. 109, at p. 115(7).

9 *Meroni* v. *High Authority* (above, n. 7).

10 *Fiddelaar* v. *EEC Commission* (1960), 6 Rec. 1077, at p. 1093; see Statute, arts. 21–27; Rules, arts. 45–54.

such a statement of claim implicitly.[1] The complaint must specify an address in Luxemburg for the purpose of accepting service and the name of the person authorised and willing to accept service there.[2]

If the complaint does not comply with the conditions enumerated in art. 38(2)–(6) of the Rules of Procedure[3] the Registrar must invite the petitioner to supplement the complaint or to produce the necessary documents within a reasonable time. If the petitioner fails to do so, the Court may refuse to entertain the complaint on the ground that it is deficient in form.[4] It will be noted that only the requirements of art. 38 (2)–(6) of the Rules of Procedure can be supplemented at the request of the registrar. It follows that the registrar has no such power in respect of the basic requirements of the complaint contained in art. 38(1) of the Rules,[5] and that, therefore, any such complaint must be refused on the ground that it is affected by a fundamental deficiency which denies it the character of a complaint according to the Rules of Procedure.

2   The Defence

The complaint must be served on the defendant either upon its receipt by the registry or after it has been supplemented in accordance with the requirements set out by the Registrar in accordance with art. 38(7) of the Rules or after the Court has accepted it nevertheless.[6] Like all service, it is effected by the registrar.[7] Within a month after service,[8] the respondent must submit his defence. This must contain the name and address of the defendant,[9] the arguments of fact and law on which he intends to rely,[10] his submissions or the relief sought by him[11] and an outline of his evidence.[12] The same rules which determine some of the ancillary matters

---

1 *Fiddelaar* v. *EEC Commission* (above); see also *SIMET* v. *High Authority* (1967), 13 Rec. 39, at p. 53.
2 Rules, art. 38(2); in terms of French law, the party "elects a domicile" for procedural purposes; for the costs incurred in retaining counsel in Luxemburg for this purpose see *Maudet* v. *EEC Commission* (1964), 10 Rec. 1209, at p. 1215.
3 *I.e.* election of domicile (art. 38(2)); counsel's credentials (art. 38(3)); the documents establishing the date of the request for an annulment (art. 173 of the Treaty) or for a declaration of failure to act (art. 175 of the Treaty) (art. 38(4)); the memorandum and articles of association and evidence that counsel acting for the legal entity is acting under a valid authority (art. 38(5)); the contractual submission clause or agreement to submit (art. 38(6)).
4 Rules, art. 38(7); Instructions to the Registrar, art. 5(1).
5 See above, p. 334, nn. 3–7; *Fournier* v. *EEC Commission* (1970), 16 Rec. 249, at p. 255(9).
6 Rules, art. 39.
7 Rules, art. 79; Instructions to the Registrar, art. 3(2), (3).
8 The time limit is calculated by reference to the deposit of the defence at the Registry and delay is excused if due to an inevitable accident (*cas fortuit*); see *SIMET* v. *High Authority* (1967), 13 Rec. 39, at p. 52; the time limit may be extended by the President at the defendant's request if good reasons exist: Rules, art. 40(2).
9 Rules, art. 40(1)(a).
10 Rules, art. 40(1)(b).
11 Rules, art. 40(1)(c).
12 Rules, art. 40(1)(d).

to be set out in the complaint (Rules, art. 38(2)–(5)) apply here as well.[1]

3 Reply and Rejoinder

Within certain time limits to be set by the President of the Court[2] the parties may submit respectively a Reply and a Rejoinder.[3] These may contain the submission of further evidence, but the delay in presenting it must be justified.[4] It must be noted, however, that even later the submission of further evidence is not impossible, if the Court is prepared to make an order to admit it.[5] As was shown above,[6] no new grounds are to be pleaded, unless they are based on points of law or fact which came to light during the written proceedings.[7] If they are pleaded the other party may be allowed to reply to them.[8] The question whether such new grounds can be admitted is not dealt with as a preliminary issue, but is joined to the judgment on the merits.[9]

4 Form of Documents—Languages

The original of every document must be signed by the agent or counsel of the party concerned.[10] Two copies must be submitted for the Court, coupled with as many additional copies as there are parties; they must all be certified by the submitting party.[11] Every document representing a procedural act must be dated, but for the purpose of calculating time limits the date of submission to the Registry counts.[12] Any supporting exhibits and documents must be presented in an annex, together with a schedule enumerating them.[13]

Of the official languages of the Court,[14] only one can be employed in any particular proceedings.[15] In principle the choice lies with the petitioner[16] but in practice it applies only if the respondent is a Community institution. If the defendant is a member state or an individual or a legal entity having

---

1 Rules, art. 40(1), last para.
2 Rules, art. 41(2).
3 Rules, art. 41(1). They need not do so and can waive this right expressly; see Rules, art. 44(1)(a), (b).
4 Rules, art. 42(1).
5 Rules, art. 60; *X* v. *Commission of Control* (1969), 15 Rec. 109, at p. 118(41).
6 See above, p. 335 and n. 6.
7 Rules, art 42(2), 1st para.; see also *Krawczynski* v. *Euratom Commission* (1965), 11 Rec. 773, at p. 792(3).
8 Rules, art. 42(2), 2nd para.
9 Rules, art. 42(2), 3rd para.
10 Rules, art. 37(1), 1st para.
11 Rules, art. 37(1), 2nd para.
12 Rules, art. 37(3); delays due to unforeseeable circumstances or Act of God (*force majeure*) are disregarded; see Statute 42, 2nd para.; *SIMET* v. *High Authority* (1967), 13 Rec. 39, at p. 52.
13 Rules, art. 37(4); for bulky or lengthy documents see Rules, art. 37(5).
14 These are the languages of the member states.
15 Rules, art. 29(1).
16 Rules, art. 29(2).

the nationality of a member state, the language of that state applies;[1] moreover the parties to the dispute may agree upon another language,[2] and upon a unilateral application by one party the Court may give permission to the same effect.[3] In non-contentious proceedings for a preliminary ruling submitted by a court of a member state the language of that court applies.[4] Until he has been admitted as an intervener, an intervening party[5] can employ any language of the Court, but once he has been admitted he must use the language employed in the principal proceedings.[6]

5 Legal Aid

Either before proceedings are begun[7] or in the course of the proceedings, a party who is partly or wholly unable to defray the costs of the proceedings, may apply for free legal aid.[8] The application must be accompanied by supporting evidence[9] and, if made before the proceedings are begun, it must briefly indicate the object of the proceedings but need not, in this case, be signed by counsel.[10] The application is not considered by the full Court but by the chamber to which the judge in charge of the case (*juge rapporteur*) belongs[11] and to which the case has been assigned after the complaint had been filed.[12] If aid is granted, the pay office of the court makes the disbursements.[13] The order granting aid must also contain the appointment of Counsel for the indigent party. If the party has not expressed his choice, or if the Court disapproves of it, the order must be sent for action to the competent authority in the member state of which the petitioner is a national.[14]

6 Discontinuance

At any stage of the proceedings before judgment has been given, the petitioner may discontinue his complaint,[15] and the parties are free to settle the dispute,[16] except (as regards the EEC Treaty) if the complaint involves the application of arts. 173 or 175.[17]

---

1 Rules, art. 29(2)(a); if there are several official languages, the petitioner is given a choice.
2 Rules, art. 29(2)(b).
3 Rules, art. 29(2)(c).
4 Rules, art. 29(2), last sentence.
5 See below, p. 342.
6 *Gezamlijke Steenkolenmijnen, Limburg* v. *High Authority* (1961), 7 Rec. 91, at pp. 93–94.
7 Rules, art. 76(2).
8 Rules, art. 76(1).
9 Rules, art. 76(1), 2nd para.; for failure to discharge the burden of proof see below, p. 339, n. 13.
10 Rules, art. 76(2).
11 Rules, art. 76(3), (4).
12 Rules, art. 24.
13 Rules, art. 76(5); Supplementary Rules, art. 5. These sums must be recovered from the party ordered to pay them: Rules, art. 76(5); *X* v. *Commission of Control* (1970), 16 Rec. 291, at p. 295(21).
14 Supplementary Rules, art. 4, and Annex 1 for the list of these authorities.
15 Rules, art. 78.
16 Rules, art. 77, 1st para.
17 Rules art. 77, 2nd para.; see above, pp. 315, 320.

7 Determination and Taking of the Evidence (Instruction)[1]

Upon the completion of the pleadings the initiative passes from the parties to the Court, which now assumes the direction of the proceedings in preparing the collection of the evidence and in taking the evidence itself (the *instruction.*)[2]

(i) *Determination of Evidence*—The Court does not necessarily undertake this task. After the rejoinder has been submitted, or after the time for submitting a rejoinder has lapsed, or if the parties have waived, respectively, their right to submit a reply or rejoinder, the Court, having heard the report of the judge in charge of the case (*juge rapporteur*), decides whether the official stage of preparation (*instruction*) is required.[3] If an *instruction* takes place, it may be carried out either by the full Court or by a chamber of the Court.[4] The Court (or the chamber) acting *proprio motu*, without the assistance of the parties, formulates the issues of fact to be proved and determines the means by which the evidence is to be produced.[5] The order of the Court to this effect must be served on the parties.[6] In order to obtain the evidence required by it, the Court may request the parties to appear personally,[7] or to produce documents and to supply any information which may be wanted,[8] may invite the evidence of witnesses and summon them,[9] commission a report by an expert[10] or arrange for an inspection.[11] In addition, the parties adducing reasons for their request[12] may ask the Court to hear a witness for the purpose of proving certain specified facts.[13] Finally, the Court may request member states and institutions which are not parties to the case to supply any information which is necessary in its opinion.[14]

(ii) *Taking Evidence*—The testimony of the witnesses is circumscribed by the practice current in continental legal systems, which is reproduced by the Rules of Procedure of the European Court,[15] that the order of the Court must set out the facts which are to be established.[16] The witnesses

---

1 Statute, arts. 21–27; Rules, arts. 45–54.
2 Although the parties should indicate their evidence in the regular course of the proceedings, the Court may admit evidence which is offered subsequently: *X* v. *Commission of Control*(1969), 15 Rec. 109, at pp. 115(14), 118(41).
3 Rules, art. 44(1).
4 Rules, art. 44(2); see also art. 46.
5 Rules, art. 45(1); for the execution see art 45(3).
6 *Ibid.*, last sentence.
7 Rules, art. 45(2)(a).
8 Statute, art. 21, 1st para.; Rules, art. 45(2)(b).
9 Statute, arts. 23–24; Rules, arts. 45(2)(c), 47(1)–(3).
10 Statute, art. 22; Rules, arts. 45(2)(d), 49.
11 Rules, art. 45(2)(e); see *e.g. SNUPAT* v. *High Authority* (1961), 7 Rec. 101, at p. 141.
12 Rules, art. 47(1), 3rd para.
13 Rules, art. 47(1)–(3). If the party does not back up the request with an offer of proof, the request can be rejected; see *ILFO* v. *High Authority* (1966), 12 Rec. 125, at p. 139; [1966] C.M.L.R. 220.
14 Statute, art. 21(2).   15 Statute, arts. 23, 29; Rules, art. 47.
16 Rules, art. 47(1); if a party requests that the evidence of a certain witness is to be taken, the request must be accompanied by a precise indication of the facts on which he is to be heard; see Rules, art. 47(1), last para.

are heard by the Court, after the parties have been invited to be present.[1]
When a witness has testified about the facts put to him, the President of
the Court may examine him. He does so either *proprio motu* or at the request of the parties.[2] Questions may also be put by the other judges or by
the Advocate General.

It will be noted that this procedure does not come near to a cross-
examination, since the parties are limited to putting formal questions
relating directly to the facts to be proved, as formulated by the Court,
and must put them indirectly through the President of the Court.

In administering the oath, the Court may permit a form provided by
the national law of the witness concerned.[3] The depositions of each witness
are set out in a record which is read over to the witness and signed by
him, the President or judge in charge of the case and the registrar.[4]
Alternatively, the evidence of a witness may be taken on commission by a
court at his place of residence.[5]

Detailed provisions deal with the summoning of witnesses,[6] the failure
of a witness to appear,[7] objections to witnesses[8] and violations of oaths.[9]

Expert evidence is rendered by a single expert who is appointed by the
Court[10] which fixes the terms of reference[11] to which he must adhere strictly.[12]
The expert must work in close contact with the judge in charge of the
case.[13] His evidence is presented in the form of a written report to the
Court, but the Court may decide to hear him at a session of which notice
must be given to the parties who may attend.[14]

The rules concerning taking evidence of witnesses, on commission,[15]
on oaths[16] and their violation[17] and on objections to a witness[18] apply
mutatis mutandis.

8 Preliminary Objections

The parties can apply in the course of the proceedings for a preliminary
ruling for one of two reasons. They may raise an *exception* or an incidental
question of fact (*incident*).[19] It is not possible to define these objections

---

1 Rules, art. 47(4), para. 2.
2 Statute, art. 29; Rules, art. 47(4), para. 2.
3 Statute, art. 25; Rules, art. 47(5).
4 Rules, art. 47(6).
5 Statute, art. 26, Rules, arts. 52, 109; Suppl. Rules, arts. 1–3.
6 Rules, art. 47(2), (3).
7 Statute, art. 24, Rules, art. 48.
8 Rules, art. 50.
9 Statute, art. 27.
10 Statute, art. 22; Rules, art. 49.
11 Rules, art. 49(1).
12 Rules, art. 49(4); he may ask the Court to hear witnesses; see Rules, art. 49(3).
13 Rules, art. 49(2).
14 Rules, art. 49(5).
15 Statute, art. 26; Rules, art. 52; Suppl. Rules, arts. 1–3.
16 Statute, art. 25; Rules, art. 49(6).
17 Statute, art. 27; Suppl. Rules, arts. 6, 7.
18 Rules, art. 50.
19 Rules, art. 91(1).

exhaustively, since the Rules of the Court assume that they represent common notions which serve to arrest the proceedings before they reach points of substance culminating in a judgment on the merits (*au fond*). If it is correct that these objections are technical devices strongly influenced by, though not identical, with French law, *exceptions* include defences based on lack of jurisdiction, the type of complaint, the party's *locus standi*, nullity of procedural acts, failure to serve notices, requests for staying or for security for costs.[1] *Incidents*, on the other hand, understood in a narrow sense, are issues of fact, such as the death of a party, satisfaction, set-off, settlement, *res judicata* and the expiry of time-limits or the submission of additional claims.[2] The application must be in a form similar to that of a complaint itself.[3] Within a time limit set by the President, the other party may state its position and make submissions.[4] This concludes the written proceedings, which are oral thereafter.[5] At their conclusion the Court either accepts the preliminary objection or rejects it or joins it to the merits.[6] In addition, the Court acting at any time of its own motion may refuse to hear a case on grounds of public policy, which is that of the Court itself and not that obtaining in a member state.[7]

9   Oral Proceedings

After the evidence has been taken (if an *instruction* had been ordered) or after the exchange of pleadings (if no *instruction* has taken place), the President of the Court must fix the date for the oral proceedings,[8] but he may allow the parties to submit further written observations.[9] According to the Statute of the Court the hearing is made up of the report by the judge in charge, of addresses by counsel of the parties, and of the submissions of the Advocate General, as well as of the hearing of witnesses and experts, if necessary,[10] but in practice the report of the judge in charge is circulated and taken as read,[11] and the evidence has been taken during the *instruction* and is available in the depositions.[12] However, the Court

---

1   Morel, *Traité élémentaire de Procédure Civile* (2nd Edn. 1949), nos. 46–51*bis*; Solus, *Droit judiciaire privé* (1961), Vol. I, no. 306; Smit (ed.), *Civil Procedure in France* (1967), p. 268. For a brief comparative study see Abi-Saab, *Les Exceptions dans la Procédure de la Cour Internationale* (1967), pp. 19 ff; Ule., *Gerichtsschutz gegen die Executive*, pp. 1203–1204; see also for German law ZPO para. 274.

2   Morel, (above), no. 460.

3   Rules, art. 91(1), 2nd para.

4   Rules, art. 91(2).

5   Rules, art. 91(3).

6   Rules, art. 91(4).

7   Jeantet and Kovar, Juriscl. Dr. Int., No. 61; it includes the question whether the complaint can be entertained at all (*fins de non-recevoir*; *recevabilité*; *Sachurteilsvoraussetzungen*); see *Groupement des Industries Sidérurgiques Luxembourgeoises* v. *High Authority* (1956), 2 Rec. 53, at p. 86; Valentine II, 131; *Milchwerke Heinz Wöhrmann* v. *EEC Commission* (1962), 8 Rec. 965, at pp. 974, 991, 992; [1963] C.M.L.R. 152.

8   The date may be postponed at the joint request of both parties, and by a decision of the Court, if only one party so demands: Rules, art. 55(2).

9   Rules, art. 54.   10   Statute, art. 18.

11   Jeantet and Kovar, Juriscl. Dr. Int., Fasc. 161 C, Pt. V, para. 45.

12   Rules, arts. 47(6), 53.

is free to order at any time that further evidence be taken.[1] Thus the proceedings are in fact confined to formal addresses by the representatives of the parties, followed by the submissions of the Advocate General. The President may put questions to the representatives of the parties; the same right is accorded to the other judges and to the Advocate General.[2] On the other hand, counsel for the parties may only address themselves to the Court.[3]

10 Joinder of Parties—Intervention

The Court has the power at any time, after hearing the parties and the Advocate General, to order the joinder or the subsequent separation of several pending actions if they relate to the same subject and are interconnected.[4]

While the joinder of actions lies primarily in the hands of the Court, a unilateral request to be joined to pending proceedings in order to support one of the parties to the litigation is left to the initiative of the applicant. This request, known in Community law as a request for intervention[5] must not be regarded as a substitute for a third party notice, which does not feature in the procedure of the Community Court.[6] It is a right accorded to the third party, not to the parties to the dispute.

Member states and the institutions of the Community may intervene in any circumstances,[7] but other persons[8] who show an interest[9] in the result of a case before the Court enjoy the same right, except where the principal litigation is between member states, between Community institutions or between member states and Community institutions.[10] The purpose of

---

1 Rules, art. 60.

2 Rules, art. 57.

3 Rules, art. 58.

4 Rules, art. 43.

5 Statute, art. 37; Rules, art. 93. See Vandersanden, 1969 Cah. Dr. Eur. 1; Telchini, 1961 Riv. Dir. Eur. 389; Tommasi di Vignano, 1966 *ibid.* 25; Abate, 1962 Riv. Trim. Dir. e Proc. Civ. 1699; Berri, 1964 *ibid.* 682 = Studi Segni; *ibid.* (1971) 8 C.M.L.Rev. 5–15; Behr, *Judicial Control of the European Communities*, p. 169.

6 The joinder of actions provided by Rules, art. 43, comes nearest to it; see Vandersanden, 1969 Cah. Dr. Eur. 1, at p. 2. In so far as the wording of Statute, art. 39, concerning third party proceedings to set aside a judgment of the Court suggests the contrary (*sans qu'ils aient été appelés*), it is not taken up anywhere else and is recognised to be a *lapsus calami.* See Vandersanden, pp. 6–7.

7 Statute, art. 37, 1st para. For the rejection of an intervention by an individual in such circumstances see *Netherlands* v. *High Authority* (1960), 6 Rec. 787, at p. 791; Valentine II, 313; for the admission of German Länder see *Barbara Erzbau* v. *High Authority* (1960), 6 Rec. 367, at p. 398; Valentine II, 325.

8 Other persons include—Individuals: see *e.g. SNUPAT* v. *High Authority* (1961), 7 Rec. 101, at p. 141; *Netherlands* v. *High Authority* (1962), 8 Rec. 413, at p. 447; [1962] C.M.L.R. 59; see also (1960), 6 Rec. 723, 734; *Ned. Hoogovens en Staalfabriek* v. *High Authority* (1962), 8 Rec. 485, at p. 513; *Mannesmann* v. *High Authority* (1962), 8 Rec. 675, at p. 703; Legal Entities: see *Confédération des Fruits et Légumes* v. *EEC Council* (1962), 8 Rec. 937, at p. 940 and distinguish *Lassalle* v. *European Parliament* (1964), 10 Rec. 97, at pp. 105–106.

9 The criterion of an interest is difficult to establish and the following examples must suffice: *Gezamlijke Steenkolenmijnen in Limburg* (below, p. 343, n. 4) and the cases, above, nn. 7, 8.

10 Statute, art. 37, 2nd para.

the intervention expressed in the intervener's submissions must be to support the submissions of one of the parties.[1] The combined effect of the three requirements, *i.e.* an interest in the result of the case by supporting the submissions of one of the parties, is clearly to restrict the intervener's freedom of action which must concentrate on the conservation of rights of his own which may be affected by the dispute by assisting the cause of one party. He cannot assert independently any rights of his own[2] or seek to establish abstract legal propositions without having an interest related to the claims of one of the parties to the suit.[3] On the other hand, the purpose of allowing an active intervention would be defeated, if the intervener were precluded from adducing arguments other than those marshalled by the principal party to the suit, provided that they support the principal party's or oppose the adversary's submissions.[4] The contentious character of an intervention excludes its use in non-contentious proceedings.[5]

The request for intervention must be submitted before the oral proceedings begin[6] and must contain the information enumerated in the Rules of Procedure.[7] It is served upon the parties to the dispute who must be given the opportunity of submitting written or oral observations as to whether the request is to be admitted.[8] If the request is granted, the intervener must receive all the procedural documents served on the parties;[9] in all other respects the intervener must accept the developments of the case as he finds them.[10] It has not been determined as yet whether an intervention is possible in proceedings where the defendant, the principal party, does not appear or does not plead. The dominant

---

1   Statute, art. 37, 3rd para.; and see generally *Breedband NV* v. *Soc. des Aciéries du Temple* (1962), 8 Rec. 272, at p. 303; [1963] C.M.L.R. 60.
2   See also Vandersanden, 1969 Cah. Dr. Eur. 1, at p. 2; *Lemmerz Werke* v. *High Authority* (1965), 11 Rec. 883, at p. 884. Thus the participation known in German law as *Hauptintervention* (ZPO, para. 64) is excluded, and only that known as *Nebenintervention* (ZPO, para. 66) is admitted; for the solutions in the laws of the Six see Telechini, 1961 Riv. Dir. Eur. 389, at p. 388.
3   *Grundig* v. *EEC Commission* (1966), 12 Rec. 556, at p. 558; *Grundig* v. *EEC Commission* (1966), 12 Rec. 559, at p. 560.
4   *Lemmerz Werke* v. *High Authority* (1965), 11 Rec. 883; *Gezamlijke Steenkolenmijnen in Limburg* v. *High Authority* (1961), 7 Rec. 1, at p. 37, see also (1961), 7 Rec. 91, 93; *SNUPAT* v. *High Authority* (1961), 7 Rec. 101, at p. 145: new *exception d'illegalité*.
5   *Costa* v. *ENEL* (1964), 10 Rec. 1141, at pp. 1197, 1198; [1964] C.M.L.R. 425.
6   Rules, art. 93(1); for the *terminus a quo* see *SIMET* v. *High Authority* (1959), 5 Rec. 331, at p. 350; Valentine II, 590.
7   Rules, art. 93(2); these embrace particulars of the case and the parties, name and address of the intervener, an outline of the grounds establishing an interest in the outcome of the case, submissions supporting one party or opposing the other party to the dispute, an outline of the evidence accompanied by documents and the address in Luxembourg for the purpose of accepting service coupled with the name of the person authorised and willing to accept service. It would seem that several interveners may apply by one request to be admitted; see *Netherlands* v. *High Authority* (1960), 6 Rec. 723, at p. 734; Valentine II, 309.
8   Rules, art. 93(3); at the stage of admissibility no reply or rejoinder is allowed; see *Netherlands* v. *High Authority* (1960), 6 Rec. 787, at p. 790; Valentine II, 313.
9   Rules, art. 93(4).
10 Rules, art. 93(5).

opinion appears to be that such an intervention is possible, limited at most to the rejection of the complaint.[1]

11 The Judgment

The decision of the Court, which must comply with certain formal requirements[2] is delivered in open Court.[3] The parties are invited to attend.[4] The decision has the force of *res judicata* between the parties, even if it concerns the annulment of an act of a Community organ.[5] Clerical and arithmetical errors or obvious inaccuracies can be corrected by the Court itself or upon the application of one of the parties[6] within a certain time,[7] and if a particular point in the submissions or on costs has been overlooked by the Court, a request for a further decision may be lodged within one month of the notification of the decision by the party intending to rely on it.[8] After an exchange of submissions the Court must determine at the same time whether the request is admissible and justified.[9]

12 Judgment by Default—Opposition

If a respondent upon whom the complaint has been properly served does not enter an appearance in proper form and in proper time, the petitioner may apply for a judgment in default.[10] This may be granted subject to certain safeguards, if the allegations of the petitioner appear to the Court to be well founded, but the Court may order evidence to be taken (*instruction*).[11] The judgment is immediately enforceable, but the Court may stay execution, if an application is lodged to set aside the judgment in default, or it can require security to be given, which is returned if no application is lodged in time to set aside the judgment.[12]

Such an application to set aside a judgment by default must be made within one month from the date when the judgment was served on the party[13] and must be lodged in the form prescribed for a complaint.[14] The procedure is the same as that for the hearing of the complaint itself.[15]

---

1 Telchini, 1961 Riv. Dir. Eur. 389, at p. 395; Vandersanden, 1969 Cah. Dr. Eur. 1, at p. 22; Tommasi di Vignano, 1966 Riv. Dir. Eur. 25, at p. 31. The suggestion that the intervener may only be able to intervene in this case on the side of the petitioner assumes that the intervener must support a party. However, he may also oppose a party—see Rules, art. 93(2). See Tommasi di Vignano, at p. 31.

2 Rules, art. 63; see also art. 64(2), (3).

3 Rules, art. 64(1).

4 Rules, art. 64(1).

5 *Barge* v. *High Authority* (1965), 11 Rec. 4, at p. 10; [1965] C.M.L.R. 215.

6 It must concern a *lapsus calami* and must not seek to modify or to review a previous decision; see *Fives Lille Cail* v. *High Authority* (1961), 7 Rec. 629, at p. 630.

7 Rules, art. 66(1); for the procedure see art. 66(2), (3).

8 Rules, art. 67, 1st para.

9 Rules, art. 67, 2nd and 3rd paras.

10 Statute, art. 38; Rules, art. 94(1).

11 Rules, art. 94(2).

12 Statute, art. 38; Rules, art. 94(3).

13 Statute, art. 38; Rules, art. 94(4); see also Rules, art. 64(2).

14 Rules, arts. 94(4), 37, 38.

15 Rules, arts. 94(5), 44–62.

13 Costs

In accordance with a practice to be found in all legal systems, provision is made for an order on costs as part of a judgment of the Court.[1] While no charges or fees are payable to the Court,[2] the losing party must be ordered to pay the costs of the case, including the costs due to the Court[3] if the other party makes application to this effect.[4] The parties may be ordered to pay their own costs, if each is only successful in part, or if exceptional reasons exist.[5] Furthermore the Court may order any party, even if it is entirely successful, to pay the costs of the other party which the former has caused the latter to incur, if in the opinion of the Court they were obstructive or vexatious.[6] Upon a discontinuance of proceedings the parties pay their own costs in the absence of an application to the contrary, which must succeed unless the discontinuing party was justified in so acting by the conduct of the other party.[7] When the Court finds that no adjudication on the merits is required, costs are in the discretion of the Court.[8] Whenever a complaint is brought against the Community by one of its officials or servants, the costs of the institution must be borne by the latter unless the complainant caused them to occur and if in the opinion of the Court they were thrown away or vexatious.[9]

Costs include, in addition to the parties' own disbursements and expenses[10] for the purpose of the proceedings, counsel's, agent's or legal adviser's fees[11] and the costs incurred by the Court,[12] travel expenses and subsistence allowances of witnesses and experts[13] and the costs incurred by a party in enforcing the decision in a member state.[14] Disputes as to

---

1 Rules, arts. 69–75.
2 Rules, art. 72.
3 Rules, art. 72(a) and (b).
4 Rules, art. 69(1), (2); between several losing parties the Court divides the costs.
5 Rules, 69(3), 1st para.
6 Rules, art. 69(3), 2nd para. See *e.g. Rittweger* v. *EEC Commission* (1969), 15 Rec. 393, at p. 398(11), (12); *Danvin* v. *EEC Commission* (1969), 15 Rec. 463, at p. 474; *E. Henricot* v. *High Authority* (1963), 9 Rec. 439, at p. 456; *Alvis* v. *EEC Commission* (1963), 9 Rec. 99, at p. 117; *Leroy* v. *High Authority* (1963), 9 Rec. 399, at p. 421; *Ned. Hoogovens en Staalfabriek* v. *High Authority* (1963), 9 Rec. 457, at p. 481; *Same* (1967), 13 Rec. 149, at p. 166; *Barge* v. *High Authority* (1963), 9 Rec. 529, at p. 570; *Forges de Claberg* v. *High Authority* (1963), 9 Rec. 719, at p. 751; *Meroni* v. *High Authority* (1962), 8 Rec. 783, at p. 807; *Bauer* v. *EEC Commission* (1967), 13 Rec. 511, at p. 519; *Stippinger* v. *High Authority* (1965), 11 Rec. 661, at p. 668; *Soc. Métallurgique de Knutange* v. *High Authority* (1960), 6 Rec. 9, at p. 28.
7 Rules, art. 69(4).
8 Rules, art. 69(5); an agreement by the parties as to costs is accepted by the Court; see *Geitling* v. *High Authority* (1960), 6 Rec. 45, at p. 66.
9 Rules, art. 70; *X* v. *Commission of Control* (1970), 16 Rec. 291, at p. 295(8), (21); *Rittweger* v. *EEC Commission* (1969), 15 Rec. 393, at p. 398(10), (12).
10 Rules, art. 73(b); they must arise strictly in connection with the proceedings in Court; see *Hacke* v. *EEC Commission* (1970), 16 Rec. 901, at p. 902(1).
11 Only the fees of counsel who appeared are allowed, but not those of the advocate in Luxembourg at whose address a party has accepted service, except in so far as they arose from this activity; see *Maudet* v. *EEC Commission* (1964), 10 Rec. 1213, at p. 1215.
12 Rules, art. 72(a), (b)—above, n. 3.
13 Rules, arts. 73(a), 51.
14 Rules, art. 71; the scale is that applicable in the member state.

what costs are recoverable are decided, upon application, by the chamber to which the case is assigned.[1]

14 Summary Proceedings—Staying—Interim Measures

Since the Treaty provides that the Community Court may stay measures of Community institutions which are the object of a complaint,[2] may prescribe interim measures[3] and may stay the enforcement in domestic courts of decisions of the Council or the Commission involving pecuniary obligations,[4] the Statute of the Court[5] and the Rules of Procedure[6] establish a summary procedure for ordering staying of enforcement and interim measures.[7]

The stay of a Community measure must be sought by the petitioner who has challenged the measure in the Community Court;[8] interim measures must be applied for by a party to the litigation in the Community Court.[9] The application, which must be lodged in the same form as a complaint,[10] must specify the subject of the dispute, explain the need for urgency and must make a *prima facie* case for granting the particular interim measure.[11] In speedy proceedings, which follow in outline the procedure governing the ordinary litigation in the Community Court,[12] the President of the Court must determine whether a stay or an interim measure is to be allowed.[13] No appeal lies,[14] but the order may require security before enforcement can take place[15] and fix a time limit after which the measure ceases to have effect.[16] The life of an interim measure is naturally determined by the fate of the principal action.[17]

---

1 Rules, art. 74; see *Hacke* v. *EEC Commission* (1970), 16 Rec. 901; *Reinarz* v. *EEC Commission* (1970), 16 Rec. 1; *Acciaierie San Michele* v. *High Authority* (1969), 15 Rec. 383, at p. 385.

2 Art. 185; the Community measure itself must be the object of the summary proceedings and not another measure connected with it; see *Leroy* v. *High Authority* (1963), 9 Rec. 435, at p. 437.

3 Art. 186.

4 Art. 192; see also art. 187, and Rules, art. 89 for the decisions of the Community Court itself.

5 Statute, art. 36.

6 Rules, arts. 83–90.

7 For the substantive conditions in which such interim measures may be ordered see above, p. 332(VII).

8 Rules, art. 83(1), 1st para.

9 Rules, art. 83(1), 2nd para.

10 Rules, arts. 83(3), 37, 38.

11 Rules, art. 83(2); for the absence of potential danger to the interests of the petitioner see *Erba* v. *EEC Commission* (1964), 10 Rec. 553, at pp. 555, 556; for the absence of an urgent need see *Plaumann* v. *EEC Commission*, (1963), 9 Rec. 255, at 258; if unsuccessful it may be repeated; see Rules, art. 88.

12 Rules, art. 84.

13 Rules, art. 85.

14 Rules, art. 86(1).

15 Rules, art. 86(2).

16 Rules, art. 86(3).

17 Rules, art. 86(4); for its amendment or revocation prior to the determination of the principal question see Rules. art. 87.

15 Enforcement

While the Treaty rightly fails to contemplate enforcement measures against the Community without the consent of the Community Court[1] or against member states,[2] judgments of the Court which impose a duty upon an individual or a legal entity to pay a sum of money must be enforced by member states in accordance with their rules of civil procedure[3] (arts. 187, 192, 2nd para.). Domestic courts may only contest the authenticity of the document embodying the decision (art. 192, 2nd para.).

16 Applications for the Interpretation of Judgments

If any difficulty is experienced in determining the meaning or scope of a judgment of the Community Court, a party or an institution showing an interest therein may apply to the Court for an interpretation.[4] Although nothing more than an application in the normal form of a complaint is required, which specifies the judgment in question and the provision of which interpretation is sought,[5] the application must be rejected if the petitioner cannot make a case that a difficulty[6] exists or a need for an interpretation.[7]

17 Reconsideration of a Judgment—Revision[8]

If after the Court has given judgment new facts are discovered which are likely to exercise a decisive influence in renewed proceedings and which, at the time when judgment was rendered, were unknown both to the Court and to a party to the case,[9] the latter may apply to the Court for a reconsideration of the judgment (*révision*).[10] Naturally only facts which could have affected the parties at the relevant time are capable of exercising a decisive influence in renewed proceedings.[11] If the party concerned could have asked the Court to order the production of a particular document during the stage of determining and taking the evidence (*instruction*) no new facts are involved.[12] The circumstance alone that a relevant document was lodged before the oral proceedings in a language other than that applicable in the proceedings is equally insufficient.[13]

---

1 See the Protocol on the Privileges and Immunities of the European Community, annexed to the Treaty, especially art. 1. Ordinance, (1971), 17 Rec. 363.
2 Cp. EEC Treaty arts. 171, 176.
3 See also Rules, arts. 71, 74(2), 89.
4 Statute, art. 40.
5 Rules, arts. 102(1), 37, 38; for the procedure see Rules, art. 102(2).
6 *Williame* v. *European Atomic Energy Commission* (1966), 12 Rec. 411, at p. 417.
7 *Reinarz* v. *EEC Commission* (1970), 16 Rec. 1.
8 Plouvier, 1971 Cah. Dr. Eur. 428.
9 Including an intervening party; see Plouvier, (above), at p. 433.
10 Statute, art. 41; Rules, arts. 98–100. Only final judgments (*arrêts*) can be reconsidered, but not interlocutory decisions (*référé*, Ordinances). It is an open question whether default judgments can be subject to *revision*, but the answer is probably in the affirmative. See Plouvier, (1971) Cah. Dr. Eur. 428, at p. 435.
11 *Müller* v. *Council of EEC and ECSC* (1967), 13 Rec. 183, at p. 188.
12 *Fonderie Acciaierie G. Mandelli* v. *EEC Commission* (1971), 17 Rec. 1, at pp. 3, 4(6)–(11).
13 *Acciaieria Ferriera di Roma* v. *High Authority* (1960), 6 Rec. 351, at p. 363; apparently the fact

[*footnote continued on next page*

The application for reconsideration must be lodged within three months from the day when the applicant obtained knowledge of the fact on which the application is based[1] and cannot be made when ten years have expired since the judgment was rendered.[2] The application must be made in the same form, *mutatis mutandis*, in which a complaint is made which initiates contentious proceedings[3] and must be directed against all parties to the judgment which is to be reconsidered.[4] The Court must first decide in chambers whether a *prima facie* case has been made out for allowing the application.[5] If the application is held to be admissible, the proceedings are continued in accordance with the Rules of Procedure as they apply to contentious proceedings,[6] culminating, if successful, in a revision of the original judgment.[7]

18   Reconsideration of a Judgment—*Tierce Opposition*[8]

Where a judgment affects adversely the rights of third parties, whether member states, Community institutions or any individual or legal entity, such parties may bring third party proceedings (*tierce opposition*) to set aside or to modify the judgment, if the proceedings had not been brought to their notice.[9] The application, which must follow the form and procedure of a complaint,[10] must therefore allege damage to the petitioner[11] and not only an interest, as is required of an intervener.[12] It must also indicate the reasons why the applicant was not able to take part in the proceedings leading to the judgment sought to be modified or set aside.[13] By imposing the latter requirement upon the applicant the Rules of Procedure[14] solve the difficulty created by the wording of the principal provision in the

---

alone that an available document is expressed in one of the languages of the Court, though not in that applicable in the particular proceedings, cannot be regarded as likely to influence the Court decisively after it has been translated.

1   Rules, art. 98.
2   Statute, art. 41, 3rd para.
3   Rules, art. 99(1).
4   Rules, art. 99(2).
5   Statute, art. 41, 2nd para.; Rules, art. 100(1).
6   This is the most plausible conclusion to be drawn from the wording of Rules, art. 100(2); see also Plouvier, 1971 Cah. Dr. Eur. 428, at p. 439.
7   Rules, art. 100(3).
8   Vandersanden 1969 Cah. Dr. Eur. 666; Gleiss and Kleinmann, 1966 N.J.W. 278; Däubler, B.B.A.W.D. 172; Tomassi di Vignano, 1967 Riv. Dir. Eur. 141.
9   Statute, art. 39; the French version says "... *contre les arrêts sans qu'ils aient été appelés*".
10 Rules, art. 97(1), first sentence.
11 Rules, art. 97(1)(b); *Breedband NV* v. *Soc. Aciéries du Temple* (1962), 8 Rec. 273, at p. 303; [1963] C.M.L.R. 60; *Belgium* v. *Vloeberghs and High Authority* (1962), 8 Rec. 331, at p. 356; [1963] C.M.L.R. 44.
12 See above, p. 342, nn. 7–9; Vandersanden, 1969 Cah. Dr. Eur. 666, at p. 674. Consequently it cannot be directed against Preliminary Rulings under art. 177 of the Treaty, which are abstract. See Vandersanden, at p. 678. It is a disputed question whether the need to prove damage excludes *tierce opposition* by an individual or a legal entity against a judgment involving the legality of a regulation or a directive. See Vandersanden, at pp. 676–677 with lit.
13 Rules, art. 97(1)(c).
14 Rules, art. 97(1)(c).

Statute of the Court[1] which suggests that the applicant making *tierce opposition* must allege that he should have received a third party notice and that none was addressed to him. However, third party notices do not figure in the procedure of the Community Court, and it is now clear that the applicant must only show that he could not intervene in the proceedings leading to the judgment because he did not have, and could not have had, notice of them or because he was unable to appear.[2]

The application must be addressed to all the parties to the dispute[3] and may include a request for a stay of execution.[4] If the judgment[5] was published in the Official Journal of the European Communities, the application must be submitted within two months of the date of that publication.[6] If the applicant succeeds, the original judgment must be amended in so far as the *tierce opposition* was allowed.[7] The effect would seem to be that in a judgment *inter partes* the tenor is varied only in so far as the applicant is concerned; if, however, the judgment is *erga omnes* (if this should be possible in the circumstances) it is difficult to restrict the modification or cancellation to the effects upon the applicant alone.[8]

19 Time-Limits

Provision is made generally for the calculation of time limits set up by the Treaty, the Statute of the Court and the Rules of Procedure and for their extension.[9] Whenever the introduction of proceedings against an act of a Community institution is made to depend upon the observation of a time-limit running from notification, the day counts after the person concerned received notice of the act in the Official Journal of the European Communities.[10] Special rules apply to proceedings against the Community for extra-contractual liability.[11]

II BEFORE THE COMMISSION[12]

In carrying out its duties under art. 89 of the EEC Treaty to ensure the observation of arts. 85 and 86 the Commission acting by virtue of Reg.

---

1 Statutes, art. 39; see above, p. 348, n. 9.
2 *Breedband NV* v. *Soc. Aciéries du Temple* (1962), 8 Rec. 273; [1963] C.M.L.R. 60; *Belgium* v. *Vloeberghs and High Authority* (1962), 8 Rec. 331.
3 Rules, art. 97(1), last para.
4 Rules, art. 97(2).
5 As in the case of *révision* only final judgments (*arrêts*) and not interlocutory decisions (*Référé*, Ordinances) can be reconsidered.
6 Rules, art. 97(1), last para.
7 Rules, art. 97(3).
8 See Vandersanden, 1969 Cah. Dr. Eur. 666, at p. 680.
9 Rules, arts. 80, 81, 82.
10 Rules, art. 81(1).
11 Statutes, art. 43; *Kampffmeyer* v. *EEC Commission* (1967), 13 Rec. 317, at p. 337; the period of limitation is calculated either from the date when the request is brought before the Court or when the preliminary demand is sent to the appropriate institutions.
12 See Deringer, *The Competition Law of the EEC* (1968), s. 2342 ff.; Franceschelli, Plaisant and Lassier, *Droit Européen de la Concurrence* (1966), nos. 721 ff., especially 756–795, pp. 259–

[footnote continued on next page

17/62 engages in investigations and takes a variety of measures which affect individuals and legal entities in the member states.[1] In order to safeguard the latter, Reg. 17/62 provides that the enterprises concerned are to be given an opportunity to express their views on points[2] which the Commission has taken into consideration and to which it objects.[3] Other individuals or legal entities must also be heard, if they so request and show that they have a sufficient interest.[4]

Acting within the powers granted by Reg. 17/62[5] the Commission issued an implementing regulation which establishes the procedure to be followed by the Commission.[6]

Before approaching the Consultative Committee[7] the Commission must conduct a hearing.[8] For this purpose the Commission must inform in writing the enterprises concerned or the representatives appointed by them[9] of the charges brought against them.[10] It must invite them to comment in writing on these charged within a time limit.[11] The enterprises must submit their views in writing within the period indicated to them.[12]

282; Gide, Loyrette and Noel, *Le Droit de la Concurrence des Communautés Européennes* (2nd Edn 1972) pp. 141–156; Gleiss-Hirsch, *EWG Kartellrecht* (2nd Edn. 1966), p. 363–392.

1   Reg. 17/62, arts. 2, 3, 6, 7, 8, 15, 16; see above, pp. 215–220.

2   "Points" in the meaning of this article (*griefs*) are facts. See Deringer, *op. cit.*, s. 2346.

3   Reg. 17/62, art. 19(1).

4   Reg. 17/62, art. 19(2). They may be heard, even if they have no sufficient interest, if the Commission so determines; see Reg. 17/62, art. 19(2), first sentence.

5   Reg. 17/62, art. 24.

6   Reg. 99/63, OJ, 1963, 2268. For its validity see *ACF Chemiefarma* v. *EEC Commission* (1970), 16 Rec. 661, at pp. 690(59)–691(70).

7   See above, p. 223; Reg. 17/62, art. 10(3).

8   Reg. 99/63, art. 1; it would seem that no hearing is required if the Commission is prepared to decide in favour of the enterprises concerned; see Deringer, *loc. cit.*, s. 2346. For the form of the notice see Reg. 99/63, art. 10. It may be, however, that representations made after the expiry of the time limit will have to be taken into account; see Deringer, *op. cit.*, para. 2348.

9   Substituted service by publication in the *Official Journal of the Community* is permitted, especially if many enterprises are involved and no common representative has been appointed; see Reg. 99/63, art. 2(2). However no fine or penalty may be imposed in proceedings initiated by these means; see Reg. 99/63, art. 2(3). The Commission has been held to have discharged this duty if in the course of the administrative proceedings it furnished the elements necessary for the defence. See *ACF Chemiefarma* v. *EEC Commission* (1970), 16 Rec. 661, at p. 686(27); *Buchler* v. *EEC Commission* (1970), 16 Rec. 733, at p. 753(9); *Boehringer* v. *EEC Commission* (1970), 16 Rec. 769, at pp. 798(9)–799(10). It must be noted that the Court did not require that the elements necessary for the defence must be necessarily identical with the elements making up the totality of the charges or who is to determine what information is necessary for the defence. For a refusal of the Commission to disclose documents see *ACF Chemiefarma* v. *EEC Commission* (above), at pp. 687(31)–(42); *Buchler* v. *Same* (above), at pp. 755(16)–(18); *Boehringer* v. *Same* (above), at pp. 799(12)–800(15). But see *BASF AG* v. *EEC Commission*, [1972] C.M.L.R. 557, at pp. 630, 631[7]–[8]; *Francolor* v. *EEC Commission*, [1972] C.M.L.R. 557, at pp. 641, 642[22]–[27].

10   Reg. 99/63, art. 2(1).

11   Reg. 99/63, arts. 2(4), 11. The practice of the Commission in setting these time limits has been criticised as being always set too short, but the Court has not found fault with them so far. See *ACF Chemiefarma* v. *EEC Commission* (1970), 16 Rec. 661, at pp. 688(45)–689(46); *Farbenfabriken Bayer AG* v. *EEC Commission*, [1972] C.M.L.R. 557, at pp. 634, 635[13]–[15].

12   Reg. 99/63, art. 3(1). They are not obliged to do so; see art. 2(4): *ont la faculté*.

Oral hearings must be requested specifically in the written observations submitted by the enterprises concerned,[1] and will only be granted if the enterprises can prove a sufficient interest in support of such a hearing or if the Commission proposes to inflict fines or penalties.[2] If an oral hearing is arranged, the Commission summons the parties to be heard[3] and invites the competent authorities of the member states to send a representative.[4]

Other individuals or legal entities with a sufficient interest may also, upon request, be given an opportunity to express their views in writing within a time limit set by the Commission[5] and may be heard orally.[6] The same applies to member states, and to individuals and legal entities with a sufficient interest, who have submitted to the Commission a complaint against an enterprise or enterprises on the ground that arts. 85 or 86 are being infringed, if the Commission is unwilling to act.[7]

The hearing is conducted by a person appointed by the Commission.[8] Those summoned can either appear in person or by their legal or statutory representatives or by a member of their permanent staff who has been properly appointed for this purpose.[9] These persons may be assisted by counsel who have the right to appear before the Community Court[10] or by other qualified persons.[11] The hearing is in private and those attending are heard separately or in the presence of each other, but in the latter case care is taken that the legitimate interests of the enterprises to protect the secrecy of their affairs are safeguarded.[12] The essential[13] statements of each person who attends are taken down as part of the record, and are read over and signed by that person.[14]

The decision of the Commission addressed to the enterprises must be confined to the charges upon which the enterprises were given the opportunity to comment.[15]

---

1 Reg. 99/63, art. 7(1).
2 Reg. 99/63, art. 7(1); according to Deringer, *op. cit.*, s. 2352 this power is discretionary.
3 Reg. 99/63, art. 8(1).
4 Reg. 99/63, art. 8(2).
5 Reg. 99/63, art. 5.
6 Reg. 99/63, art. 7(2).
7 Reg. 99/63, art. 6.
8 Reg. 99/63, art. 9(1); see *Buchler* v. *EEC Commission* (1970), 16 Rec. 733, at pp. 756(19)–(20); *Boehringer* v. *EEC Commission* (1970), 16 Rec. 769, at p. 802(23).
9 Reg. 99/63, art. 9(2), 1st para.; *BASF AG* v. *EEC Commission*, [1972] C·M.L.R. 557, at pp. 630, 631[10]–[11].
10 Reg. 99/63, art. 9(2), 2nd para.; Protocol on the Statute of the Court, art. 17.
11 *Ibid.*; it is not clear who these persons are.
12 Reg. 99/63, art. 9(3).
13 The determination of what is essential lies in fact with the chairman or with the clerk.
14 Reg. 99/63, art. 9(4).
15 Reg. 99/63, art. 4. It is sufficient if the essential facts are set out summarily and clearly on which the Commission bases its decision; but the decision need not deal with all the charges and may modify or complete the grounds of those which were brought originally; see *ACF Chemiefarma* v. *EEC Commission* (1970), 16 Rec. 661, at pp. 686(25)–687(30), 692(76)–(81), 693(88), (92); *Mainkur* v. *EEC Commission*, [1972] C.M.L.R. 644, at p. 645[17]; *ACNA* v. *EEC Commission, ibid.*, at p. 648[27].
It would seem, however, that this minimum standard laid down by the Community

[footnote continued on next page

The decisions of the Commission are subject to review by the Community Court.[1]

Court may be wanting in effectiveness if the charges, too, need be set out in their elements only, and not in detail, restricted moreover to a cluster of elements which the Commission regarded as necessary and sufficient for the defence.   These considerations are reinforced by the attitude of the Court which treats certain findings of fact by the Commission as *obiter* only and therefore not in need of supporting evidence; see *ACF Chemiefarma* v. *EEC Commission* (above), at pp. 693(86)–(88); and which permits the Commission to rely on facts not mentioned in the statement of objections on the ground that the latter contained the essential facts; see *ICI* v. *EEC Commission*, [1972] C.M.L.R. 557, at p. 619[21]–[26]. Similarly the laxity of the Court must be noted in allowing a Commission decision against a number of defendants, if based on grounds which are not specifically connected with a particular defendant; see *BASF AG* v. *EEC Commission*, [1972] C.M.L.R. 557, at pp. 630, 631[13]–632[14] and see *Mainkur* v. *EEC Commission*, [1972] C.M.L.R. 644, at p. 646[22].

1   EEC Treaty arts. 172, 87; Reg. 17/62, art. 17; see also Reg. 17/62, art. 9(1).

Index

COMMUNITY COURT,—*contd*
further decision of, request for, 344
incidents, 340–341
instruction, 339, 341, 344
interim measures by, 332, 346
interpretation by, 15*n.*–16*n.*
intervention, request for, 342–343
joinder of parties, 342–344
judgment of, 344
  default, by, 344
  interpretation of, application for, 347
  reconsideration of—
    révision, 347–348
    tierce opposition, 348–349
jurisdiction of—
  annul, to, 315–320, 334
  claim on the merits, to determine, 321–322
  contractual claims, over, 325
  declaration of failure to act, 320–321, 334
  levy of execution, to suspend, 332
  member states, complaints against, 314–315
  submission to, by agreement, 313–314, 325, 334
languages in, 337–338, 347, 348*n.*
legal aid, 338
legal represen ation, 334, 338
oral proceedings, 341–342
preliminary objections, 340–341
preliminary ruling by—
  arbitral tribunals, 328
  Community law, problems arising out of, 330–331
  court, nature of, 327–329
  domestic law—
    consideration of, 13*n*, 331
    problems arising out of, 328–330
  interpretation of Convention and Protocol, 283–284
  questions referred for, 327–328
procedure in—
  nature of proceedings, 333
  Protocol on the Statute, 333
  Rules of, 333
regulation inapplicable, declaration that, 325–327
reply and rejoinder, 337
review by, of Commission decisions, 352
stay of Community measures by, 332, 346
summary proceedings in, 346
time limits for proceedings, 349
tort, actions in, against the Community, 323–325
witnesses, 339–341, 345

COMMUNITY LAW,
concurrent jurisdiction with domestic law, 39, 226–228
contravention of constitution of member state by Treaty, 22–26
directly applicable to individuals—
  definition, 27–29
  whether provisions are, practice of Community Court, 29–31
domestic law, relationship with, 21, 44–45
  Community Court, practice of, 31–39
  domestic courts, practice of, 39–44
  member states, as part of law of, 31–44
effect of—
  previous domestic law, on, 39–40
  subsequent domestic law, on, 40–45

COMMUNITY LAW,—*contd*
incorporation of Treaty and implementing measures into domestic law, 22–27
preliminary ruling on interpretation of, reference for, 21, 32–33, 327–331
primacy of, over domestic law, 34–36, 39, 44
social security, to determine claimants for, 103
special legal system, as, 24, 34

COMMUNITY ORGAN,
acts of, validity of, 315–320
annulment of act of, 315–320
failure to act, judgment declaring a, 320–321

COMPANY,
agency, branch or subsidiary, establishment of, 130, 137–139, 141
"association", as, 135
capital of, contributions to, 263–265
central management or principal place of business, 136–139, 149
daughter, 160, 265
delegation of powers by, 147
effective link with Community, requirement of, 138, 142
European. *See* EUROPEAN COMPANY
formation of, 147, 151, 263
incorporation of, in accordance with law of member state, 136–139, 148–150
information as to, publication of, 146
investment in, in another member state, 130, 174
joint stock, 263–264
jurisdiction—
  exclusive, on validity, nullity and dissolution, 276, 279
  residence as basis of, 272
law, co-ordination of, 129, 141–142
  directives on, 142*n.*
liability of, 147
loans, 264
management of, in another member state, 130
merger of, across frontiers, 140, 152–153, 265
nationality of, 19, 136
non-profit making, 136, 149*n.*
publication of information concerning, 146
public utility, contributions to, 264
real seat of, 136–139, 149–150, 264
recognition of, mutual, 148–151, 165
  Convention on, 148–151, 269–270
  criteria for, 149–150
  disabilities, public law, 150
  refusal of, on ground of public policy, 151
  statutory seat not coincident with real seat, 149–150
services across frontiers, provision of, by, 165–166
shareholders and creditors, protection of, 142, 146
statutory seat of, 136–139, 149–150, 264
tax reform, 265
transfer of seat of, 139–140, 148
ultra vires doctrine, 147, 155
validity of, law governing, 136–139, 148
winding-up of, 146, 285

COMPETENCES,
transfer of, to EEC organs, 13